THE PRACTICE OF
POLICY EVALUATION

The Practice of Policy Evaluation

Edited by
DAVID NACHMIAS

St. Martin's Press
New York

Acknowledgments

David N. Kershaw, "A Negative-Income-Tax Experiment." Reprinted with permission. Copyright © 1972 by Scientific American, Inc. All rights reserved.

Albert Rees, "An Overview of the Labor-Supply Results." Reprinted from *The Journal of Human Resources*, IX, 2 (1974), pp. 155–180, by permission of the University of Wisconsin Press.

Gerald Somers and Ernest Stromsdorfer, "A Cost-Effectiveness Analysis of In-School and Summer Neighborhood Youth Corps." Reprinted from *The Journal of Human Resources*, VII, 4 (1972), pp. 446–459, by permission of the University of Wisconsin Press.

Harrison McKay et al., "Improving Cognitive Ability in Chronically Deprived Children." Reprinted with permission from *Science*, vol. 200, pp. 270–278, 21 April 1978. Copyright © 1978 by the American Association for the Advancement of Science.

Micheal W. Giles, "White Enrollment Stability and School Desegregation: A Two-Level Analysis." Reprinted from *American Sociological Review*, vol. 43, December 1978, pp. 848–864, by permission of the American Sociological Association.

Donald McCrone and Richard J. Hardy, "Civil Rights Policies and the Achievement of Racial Economic Equality 1948–1975." Reprinted with permission from the *American Journal of Political Science*, vol. 22, no. 1, February 1978, pp. 1–17. Copyright © 1978 by the University of Texas Press, 2100 Comal, Austin, Texas 78722.

Anthony Downs, "The Successes and Failures of Federal Housing Policy." Reprinted with permission of the author from: *The Public Interest*, No. 34 (Winter 1974) pp. 124–145. © 1974 by National Affairs, Inc.

Yong Myo Cho, "A Multiple Regression Model for the Measurement of the Public Policy Impact on Big City Crime." Reprinted from *Policy Sciences*, 3 (1972), 435–455, by permission of Elsevier Scientific Publishing Company.

Acknowledgments and copyrights continue at the back of the book on page 478, which constitutes an extension of the copyright page.

TO MY DAUGHTER, ANAT

PREFACE

The last decade has seen an enormous increase of interest in policy evaluation. Every discipline within the social and behavioral sciences that studies public policy (and that includes economics, sociology, and psychology, as well as political science) now conducts systematic policy evaluations. Funded by public and private agencies, these investigations examine the consequences of public policies on major aspects of our lives. In the present political climate—one of little trust in government, with demands from citizens for increased accountability—we can expect ever greater interest in policy evaluations.

The purpose of this book is to introduce students and professionals to research that has been done in policy evaluation. It contains twenty-one policy evaluation studies of domestic topics that are currently major concerns of policymakers and the attentive publics. These topics include such vital issues as equality of opportunity, human resources development, income maintenance, health care, education, housing, energy, transportation, and criminal justice. In choosing the studies, I have attempted to demonstrate the breadth of concern and the variety of concepts and methods of investigation that characterize the field of policy evaluation, as well as to represent the major policy areas. Seven of the studies appear in print for the first time here.

One obvious advantage of an anthology over an integrated text is that it can more readily illustrate similarities and differences in the ways in which evaluation research is conducted within and across policy areas. But readings alone may disappoint those who seek a comprehensive, integrated view of the field. To meet the latter expectation, the Introduction to the book provides an overview of the state of the craft. In addition, the introductory notes to the chapters point out the broad context in which the evaluated policies and programs have developed. By way of summary, the last chapter offers a discussion of problems related to the use of evaluation research and of the prospects for improving the making of public policy. Users of this anthology may also be interested in my brief textbook, *Public Policy Evaluation: Approaches and Methods* (St. Martin's, 1979).

I would like to express my thanks to professors Guy C. Colarulli of the University of Hartford, Stuart S. Nagel of the University of Illinois at Urbana-Champaign, David S. Sorenson of Denison University, and Khi V. Thai of the University of Maine at Orono for reviewing the manuscript and offering thoughtful and useful suggestions. Bertrand Lummus, my editor at St. Martin's Press, and Michael Weber, the project editor, were helpful throughout the process of transforming an idea into a book.

DAVID NACHMIAS

CONTENTS

THE PRACTICE OF
POLICY EVALUATION

Introduction
PUBLIC POLICY
EVALUATION:
AN OVERVIEW

David Nachmias

Although the United States government has, in recent years, devoted a growing share of the nation's resources to policies and programs for meeting societal needs, dissatisfaction with many of these programs has never been more widespread. Manifestation of this discontent can be seen in complaints about inefficiency, ineffectiveness, and waste; by the fact that voters are rejecting the proposals of their elected officials with increasing frequency; and by the tax revolt movement. Trust in the government has been steadily declining. Dissatisfaction with the consequences of public policies is widespread, not only among the citizenry, but also among public officials. One government official defined the situation by saying that "the federal government has developed two defects that are central to its existence: (a) it does not know how to tell whether many of the things it does are worth doing at all, and (b) whenever it does decide something is worth doing, it does not know how to create and carry out a program capable of achieving the results it seeks."[1]

Documentation of this state of ignorance was provided in a study funded by the Department of Housing and Urban Development and conducted in close cooperation with the Executive Office of the President. The authors of the study concluded:

> The most impressive finding about the evaluation of social programs in the federal government is that substantial work in this field has been almost non-existent. Few significant studies have been undertaken. Most of those carried out have been poorly conceived. Many small studies around the country have been carried out with such lack of uniformity of design and objective that the

1

results rarely are comparable or responsive to the questions facing policy makers. There is nothing akin to a comprehensive federal evaluation system. Even within agencies, orderly and integrated evaluation operations have not been established.[2]

Today many legislators, policymakers, government officials, and members of the academic community are committed to researching the implementation and consequences of public policies and programs. This commitment is reflected in the rapid growth of policy evaluation as a scientific field and, concomitantly, in the requirement by many federal, state, and local agencies that systematic evaluation become a routine organizational function. In the early 1970s about two hundred new evaluation studies were begun each year with direct federal support and with average budgets of about $100,000 each. By now the number of policy- and program-evaluation studies started each year has doubled, and the costs have risen markedly.[3] Other indicators of the growing interest in policy evaluation are the relatively large number of professional journals and magazines now being published; the multiplicity of conferences and workshops being held; and the large number of academic courses and professional training programs now offered by universities and research institutions.

EVALUATION AND EVALUATION RESEARCH

Notwithstanding its relatively recent emergence as a scientific undertaking, evaluation as a human activity is not new. Evaluation itself is hardly a new concern even of the social sciences. Questions of ethics, what constitutes a "good society," and the actions of public officials and their consequences and implications for people have been a subject of great concern throughout human history. Eduard Suchman wrote: "Man's need to know is closely coupled with the wish to judge. The natural curiosity which leads man to ask the question 'Why?' also underlies his drive to discover 'Cui bono?' or 'What good is it?' "[4] The judgment of worth and quality is a fundamental activity of individuals, groups, and organizations. The very processes of learning and socialization involve either maintenance or a change in patterns of behavior according to what could be termed "evaluation feedback."

Current policy evaluation departs from earlier evaluation attempts in the social sciences in several important aspects. Its primary concern is with explanation and prediction; it relies on empirical evidence and analysis; it emphasizes middle-range theory building and testing, and it is concerned with being useful to policymakers. The chief concern is with evaluation as a scientific research activity. The major emphasis is upon research, that is, on "those procedures for collecting and analyzing data which increase the possibility for 'proving' rather than 'asserting' the worth of some social activity."[5]

FOCUS AND OBJECTIVES OF EVALUATION RESEARCH

Evaluation as a research activity is concerned with the consequences of public policies.* Government is viewed as an institution that makes decisions about what it should do; these decisions result in policy outputs. For example, the amount of money spent, the kinds of services provided, the number of cases handled, the number of staff employed by service-delivery agencies are policy outputs. These outputs, however, do not indicate whether, to what extent, and with what costs the desired policy objectives have been achieved. The complexities of the real world, coupled with the imperfections of the policy process (e.g., incomplete information, disagreements with policy objectives, and vested interests), challenge, as Dye points out, the naïve assumption that "once we pass a law, establish a bureaucracy, and spend money, ... the purpose of these acts will be achieved, and the results will be what we expected them to be."[6]

Policy evaluation research is concerned with the study of the impacts of policy outputs. The importance of drawing an analytic distinction between outputs and impacts or outcomes is clearly articulated by Ronald Pennock:

> We are no longer discussing only outputs, in the sense of finding policies and decisions; rather, we are considering *outcomes*. We are talking about the consequences of outputs—consequences for the people, for the society as a whole, or for some subset other than the polity, as, for instance, the economy or the family. We are indeed still dealing with the attainment of political goals, but the focus of attention is upon those goals that satisfy "needs"—not just needs of the state as such, [which] will enable it to persist, but also human needs, whose fulfillment makes the polity valuable to man and gives it justification.[7]

By investigating the immediate and the distant impacts of policy outputs, evaluation research can generate new knowledge that could be incorporated into the public decision-making process. Although it is too early to assess systematically the contributions of evaluation research to knowledge, a few examples are worth mentioning. First, from evaluations of

---

*The terms "policy," "program," and "project" will be used interchangeably because the same research principles apply to them all. Analytically, however, the terms can be distinguished along a continuum of specificity with projects being the more specific set of actions designed to attain an objective.

school integration, it has become clear that in its conventional form, the "racial contact" theory is incorrect, and that prolonged contact among several races does not automatically reduce prejudice. Second, evaluation research in the field of criminology suggests that theories of deterrence must include propositions pertaining to the perceived impact of deterrence and law enforcement procedures against offenders. Finally, evaluations of preschool educational programs for disadvantaged children resulted in the knowledge that in order to maintain the children's cognitive gains, reinforcement is necessary when the children enter primary grades.

The other objective of evaluation research is the improvement of the public policymaking process. Policy evaluation research could help policymakers make better choices than they might otherwise make without systematic information. With systematic, empirical information about the impact of policies, better decisions can be reached: Ineffective programs can be abandoned or radically modified; effective programs can be expanded; and more responsible budget allocations can be made. Although the potential of evaluation research to contribute to public policymaking is great, so far its actual impact has been less than substantial. Underutilization is one of the major research problems in evaluation research. At present the issue is not the search for a grand theory of utilization, but rather, for the identification of key variables and the construction of plausible models that account for patterns of utilization.

TYPES OF EVALUATION RESEARCH

With the growth of policy evaluation research activities, three distinct but interrelated types of evaluation research have emerged: process evaluation, impact evaluation, and cost-effectiveness evaluation.

Process Evaluation

Process evaluation is primarily concerned with the extent to which a particular policy or program is implemented according to its stated guidelines or intent. It involves the periodic assessments of program functioning to detect deviations from goals, plans, and procedures. Often it involves auditing the integrity of the program's financial transactions, accounting system, and the accuracy of records.

The significance of process evaluation stems from the fact that program goals may be drastically revised and even negated during implementation. For example in 1967 President Lyndon Johnson proclaimed a new program known as New Towns In-Town to create model communities on surplus federal land in metropolitan areas. The objectives of the program were to demonstrate the government's commitment to helping troubled cities, to building new housing for the poor, and to showing that much can be accomplished by combining zeal with the resourcefulness and imaginativeness of urban planners. After four years no new towns had been started.[8] Such action, or nonaction, points to the fact that policymakers at all levels of government cannot merely assume that their decisions will be carried out. This is true for domestic as well as foreign policy. As former Secretary of State Henry Kissinger once remarked, "The outsider believes a presidential order is consistently followed. Nonsense. I have to spend considerable time seeing that it is carried out in the spirit the president intended . . ."[9]

One major reason for problems in implementation is that "the implementation of policies of one level of government often constitutes the decision making of the level below."[10] For example although the federal government sets certain operational procedures and requirements that states must meet in using grant-in-aid funds, state officials implement these in light of what they perceive to be their constituencies' needs. Implementation usually involves numerous participants and a multiplicity of decisions. Participants may include legislators, judges, interest groups, private citizens, and always, bureaucrats. Participants may be supportive of the program, opposed to it, or indifferent. Such dispositions are inevitably manifested in the implementation stage. And even if all the participants are supportive of a program, they may have differing perspectives on how to implement it.[11] Bureaucrats often implement programs according to organizational needs rather than program objectives. A study of the implementation of Title V of the 1965 Elementary and Secondary School Act found great variations in implementation. Each state education agency developed its own standard operating procedures, which were designed to accommodate the existing bureaucratic structure and operations rather than to adapt the bureaucracy to the program objectives and the legislative intent.[12] Indeed, the vaguer and more ambiguous a policy is, the more discretion policy implementers have.

Impact Evaluation

Impact evaluation is concerned with assessing the effects of policies and, more specifically, with the extent to which a policy has achieved its stipulated objectives. To study the impact of a policy is essentially to ask how the conditions of the environment or the lives of individuals are changed by specific policies or programs.

At the heart of impact evaluation research is the idea of causality, the notion that a policy is expected to produce a change in the target population in the direction and of the magnitude intended by policymakers. Causality can never be directly observed; it can only be inferred. For example an empirical observation that when program A is implemented, goal B will be accomplished does not necessarily mean that any cause-and-effect relationship exists. As Hubert M. Blalock pointed out: "If X is a cause of Y, we have in mind that a change in X produces a change in Y and not merely that a change in X is followed by or associated with a change in Y."[13]

Causality is a theoretical construct, and, consequently, cause-and-effect relationships cannot be empirically observed: "One thinks in terms of a theoretical language that contains notions such as causes, forces, systems, and properties. But one's tests are made in terms of covariation, operations, and pointer readings."[14] Recent methodological developments in the social sciences have been directed toward bridging the gap between theory and empirical observations. An early influential contributor to these developments was Herbert Simon, who suggested restricting the notion of causality to simplified models that are subject to few limitations and that would apply to the real world.[15] After testing, if the model proves inadequate, it can be modified by introducing additional variables and/or by respecifying the expected relations between the variables. Underlying this model-building process must be the understanding that "there is nothing absolute about any particular model, nor is it true that if two models make use of different variables, either one or the other must in some sense be 'wrong.' "[16] Having constructed a causal model, one proceeds in two directions. Employing the causal assumptions, empirical predictions that can be translated into testable hypotheses are deduced. At the same time operational procedures that can be applied to test the hypotheses are formulated.

The principles of making causal inferences in the social sciences are applied in impact evaluation research through impact models and systematic methods for measuring and testing such models. An impact model translates theoretical ideas about the change of behavior and/or societal conditions into a set of variables relevant to the policy under evaluation, as well as into a number of concrete predictions pertaining to the relationships among these variables. An impact model characteristically consists of policy or program variable(s), target variable(s), intervening variable(s), and one or more predictions concerning the changes that the program variable(s) are expected to produce in the target variable(s). Ideally both action and research can be based upon such models. Further elaborations of impact models consist of attempts to delineate the unintended consequences of a policy; to outline the boundaries within which the variables included in the model operate; to specify the time lag between implementation and manifestations of program effects, and to specify the predicted causal relations—direct versus indirect causal variables, and recursive relations (a relationship in which a change in one variable produces a change in another variable, but not vice versa) versus nonrecursive relations (a relation representing two-way causation). To construct and empirically test impact models, three fundamental methodological issues have to be dealt with effectively: goal identification, research design, and measurement.

IDENTIFICATION OF GOALS

In basic social science research, the investigator usually starts with a research problem of his or her choice. Next, based on a theory or theories, one or more dependent variables are selected to be explained. Then hypotheses about independent variables that are expected to explain or predict the dependent variables are generated. In evaluation research the process is often reversed: "One begins with an independent variable—the program—and is asked to assess how it affects a set of only vaguely identified goals."[17]

When the goals of a program are ambiguous and diffuse, assessment of the extent to which they have been achieved becomes a formidable task. For example much of the controversy over Head Start has been related to its objectives. The program's proclaimed goals were to compensate alleged educational disadvantages suffered by poor children that hindered their educational achievement when they entered regular school programs. One evaluation, the Westinghouse study, showed that Head Start children were not appreciably helped in developing cognitive skills.[18] In turn, critics of the evaluation findings charged that such a finding was beside the point because there were other important goals, such as improving the children's physical conditions, that the program was to achieve.

Not all public programs are subject to a great degree of ambiguity in their goals. The goal of manpower-retraining programs, for instance, is to impart marketable occupational skills, and their effectiveness can be assessed by the extent to which they manage to do so. In general, though, the problems of public policy are likely to be "squishy" problems,[19] that is, they may have no definite formulation and no rule of thumb to tell the researcher when he or she has found a solution. Furthermore the style of public decision making, in which negotiation and compromise are common steps before reaching mutually acceptable policy outputs, contributes to the emergence of ambiguous, often conflicting, and difficult-to-operationalize policy objectives. Moreover, goals may not be static, but may change in accordance with changes in the policymakers' perceptions of the societal problems or with the political climate.

Several procedures and considerations are helpful when attempting to identify a program's goals. First, it is useful to distinguish between immediate and distant goals. Immediate objectives are the anticipated results of the specific project with which policymakers are momentarily concerned, such as school integration. Distant goals refer to the effect of the immediate goals on long-term activity or policy. In the case of school integration, these may be educational achievement and racial integration. Distant goals are the final anticipated consequences of public policies. The distinction between immediate and distant goals is especially important in cases where the program cannot be expected to cause instantaneous changes in the target population. Indeed, it frequently takes time to detect changes in certain dispositions, attitudes, and behaviors as a result of program intervention.

A second helpful procedure for determining goals is to consult the program personnel. Sometimes, the personnel do not reach a consensus regarding the program's goal. In such cases one can "read everything about the program . . . talk to practitioners at length, observe the program in operation, and then sit down and frame the statement of goals himself."[20] With such an indirect procedure, however, a bias may be introduced. The researcher "may read his own professional preconceptions into the program and subtly shift the goals (and the ensuing study) in the direction of his own interest."[21]

Perhaps the most useful procedure for delineating goals is for the researcher to collaborate with the program initiators and personnel in the very early stages of the program. The researcher can make suggestions regarding the goals, which the program staff can modify or accept. Discussion can continue until agreement is reached.[22]

EVALUATION DESIGNS

The search for cause-and-effect relations inevitably leads to the problem of designing an evaluation study. The simplest and most credible way to infer causality is to compare what actually happened to what would have happened if everything had been exactly the same as it was except that the policy had not been implemented. However, in the real world it is almost never possible to empirically assess what "would have happened if. . . ." Consequently, alternative methodological and statistical procedures have been developed to infer causality. Three general types of research designs are concerned with inferring cause-and-effects relations between program variables and their target variables: experimental, quasi-experimental, and structural equation models. The evaluations included in this book show applications of these types of designs. The following section briefly describes each type.

EXPERIMENTAL EVALUATIONS

Experimental research designs provide the most credible evidence concerning the causal effects of program variables. As Gilbert, Light, and Mosteller concluded after reviewing some forty programs: "Randomization, together with control and implementation, gives an evaluation a strength and persuasiveness that cannot ordinarily be obtained by other means."[23]

An experiment can be viewed as an investigation in which a researcher interferes with an ongoing process, so that the random units processed are differentially treated and measurements are collected in such a way that the variability among units treated similarly (experimental group) can be estimated. The ideas of intervention and randomization and their effective application distinguish experiments from other types of evaluations. Public programs are governmental attempts to change the environment and/or individuals' behavior, and in this sense they fulfill the requirement of intervention called for in experimental designs. Randomization is difficult to attain, however, since it involves the assignment of individuals, or other units, of a target population to experimental and comparison groups in such a way that for any given assignment to a group, every member of the target population has an equal, nonzero probability of being selected for that assignment.

The underlying rationale of randomization is the notion that every member of a target population has an equal, nonzero chance of being selected, and that members with certain distinct attributes, e.g., those in the lower or upper social classes and those in urban or rural areas, will, if selected, be counterbalanced by the selection of other members of the target population with the opposite quality or quantity of the attribute. Effective randomization makes a study unbiased, since it can have no a priori tendency to favor one group over another.

QUASI-EXPERIMENTAL DESIGNS

Public programs are not always amenable to the straightforward application of experimental designs. Political, ethical, financial, and implementational considerations frequently prevent the application of randomization and, consequently, the use of experimental designs. In recent years considerable attention has focused on developing research designs for situations in which experimentation is either impossible or impractical. Quasi-experimental designs involve approximating some, but not all, of the control mechanisms embodied in the experimental model. Although the use of such designs allows some bias into the investigation, it is usually known beforehand where the contamination might occur.

Among the various quasi-experimental designs, three are more persuasive than others, and have proved useful in evaluation research: time-series design, multiple time-series design, and nonequivalent, control-group design. The time-series design provides for sequential assessment of a program before, during, and after implementation. In this way changes over time that are presumably related to the program can be measured. One major weakness of this design is that changes resulting from outside events, e.g., increased rates of inflation, elections, and severe weather conditions, might mistakenly be attributed to the program.

The multiple time-series design is an extension of the time-series. It involves staged longitudinal measurement of program variables of equivalent programs. By staging the implementation of programs over an extended time, a comparison group is established for each program. In this way one can more effectively control for contamination of findings due to outside events.

The nonequivalent, control-group design closely approximates the experimental model, but it uses a comparison group that has not been randomly selected. For example program dropouts are used as a comparison group for those who remain in the program. To control for bias that might result from self-selection, e.g., dropouts may share certain important attributes not shared by those who continue to participate, units can be matched on important and relevant variables.

STRUCTURAL EQUATION MODELS

Structural equation models rely on multivariate, statistical data-analysis procedures in attempting to infer cause-and-effect relations. To a certain extent statistical manipulation and control compensate for the inability to manipulate program variables physically and randomize. Theoretical causal models are typically constructed, and statistical techniques such as multivariate regression or path analysis are used to assess the extent of congruence between a model and the data. After testing, if the model proves inadequate, additional variables can be introduced, or the entire model can be modified. In addition to an overall estimation of the model's adequacy, structural equations allow the estimation of the direct and indirect effects that one variable exerts upon another. For example, in Figure 1, it is observed that X_1 has a direct effect on X_4 (the target variable); X_1 has also indirect effects on X_4 via its effects on X_2 and X_3. Thus one can calculate the magnitude of the direct and indirect effects that help in understanding the operative causal mechanisms of a program.[24]

Figure 1. A four-variable causal model.

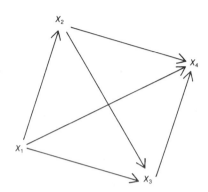

MEASUREMENT

The objectives in most programs are not clearly measurable. Congressional bills and acts are general and allow a great amount of flexibility in interpreting them. A researcher cannot expect program goals and criteria of success to be defined operationally in a program mandate, yet the process of specifying valid ways of measuring the effectiveness of a program and of program variables and target variables is a fundamental and integral part of the evaluation process.

Perhaps the major measurement problem in evaluation research is that even when one is able to identify a single, clear-cut, agreed-upon goal, often indirect measures that only approximate what one would like to measure are used. For example to measure the success of school integration, the percentage of minority students is taken; to measure the effectiveness of a law enforcement program, the number of crimes reported is taken; and to measure the quality of medical care in a community, the infant mortality rate is used. Such measures, referred to as proxy measures, are used because they are considered to be positively correlated with and more readily measurable than other aspects of a program's goal. Still, proxy measures are indirect and incomplete. For instance measuring the effectiveness of a law enforcement program by the number of the crimes reported is far from being a complete and an accurate measure of effectiveness for several reasons. First, the number of crimes reported is always fewer than the number of crimes committed; second, certain types of crime are not reported; third, crimes vary in their seriousness; fourth, official crime statistics tend to be inaccurate; and finally, reported crimes do not always lead to arrest, and arrests do not always lead to conviction. Thus proxy measures, although necessary, can introduce ambiguity, and at times can miss the intent of a program.

The incompleteness of measurement can also result from the character and frequency of missing data. Some observations are always missing; these include lost records, incomplete questionnaires, program dropouts that cannot be reached, or refusals to cooperate with researchers. The higher the rate of missing data, and the more systematic the character of the missing data, the lower the credibility of the study findings.

Strategies for assuring the quality of measurement in evaluation research in principle are no different from those used in social science research. These include empirical evidence indicating the extent to which measurement is valid and reliable. Certain measurement problems are more common in evaluation research than in social science research. With respect to validity, the most obvious source of bias in measuring the effectiveness of a program occurs when the results of an evaluation are believed by program participants to have implications for them, or when program personnel have a vested interest in the decisions on which the findings are based. In such cases the observations can have a systematic bias congruent with the beliefs of program personnel and participants. Furthermore, unintentional distortion may occur in instruments designed to elicit subjective information about behavior that ranges along a continuum of "social desirability." Participants are likely to report that they benefited from a program, if they perceive the program goal to be socially desirable. The Hawthorne effects, i.e., when the knowledge that one is researched may lead to behavior that is consonant with the study objectives, are also likely to be operative in many programs.

Reliability is especially significant in programs that are expected to have weak effects, but such effects must be detected. The more sensitive the measures, the greater the likelihood that weak effects will be detected. Gilbert, Light, and Mosteller found only few studies that reported marked positive effects. Even programs "that turned out to be especially valuable often had relatively small effects—gains of a few percent, for example, or larger gains for a small subgroup of the population treated. Because even small gains accumulated over time can add up to a considerable total, they may have valuable consequences for society."[25] The detection of such effects calls for the construction of highly sensitive and reliable measures.

The timing of measurement is often another serious problem in evaluation research. In many cases there is difficulty in telling how soon program effects can be expected, and how stable and durable any changes brought about by a program will prove to be. In theory such a problem can be tackled by repeated measurement of target variables. In practice, however, one may have only one opportunity for measurement. The timing of such a measurement may be crucial for the evaluation findings. For example after reviewing longitudinal evaluations of preschool educational programs targeted at disadvantaged children, Bronfenbrenner concluded:

> Almost without exception, children showed substantial gains in IQ and in other cognitive measures during the first year of the program, attaining or even exceeding the average for their age. . . . By the first or second year of completion of the program, sometimes while it was still in operation, the children began to show a progressive decline, and by the third or fourth year of follow-up, they had fallen back into the problem range of the lower 90s and below.[26]

Obviously, without such repeated measurement of the target variable, the extent to which changes due to the program are stable and durable cannot be assessed. Furthermore, if a single measurement were to be taken, say, two years after the children completed the program, no significant changes in the target variable would be measured.

COST-EFFECTIVENESS EVALUATION

Associated with any policy is not only its expected impact, but also its cost. The concern of cost-effectiveness analysis in evaluation research is with determining a program or a combination of program variables that maximize the desired objective for any particular resource or budget constraint.

In many ways cost-effectiveness analysis is not a new form of evaluation research so much as it is one that attempts to integrate cost considerations into evaluation-research designs. Because a major portion of the cost-effectiveness analysis is based upon the comparative effectiveness of various programs and program variables, the method presumes that such information will be provided by experimental, quasi-experimental, and structural-equation models. The information on the probable differences in impact of particular programs is then combined with data on the costs of implementing them in order to make cost-effectiveness comparisons. Based on these comparisons, recommendations as to which programs and which program variables will maximize the desired objectives for any particular level of resource use can be made.

Although the concepts of cost and effectiveness provide a useful framework for evaluation research, various conceptual and measurement problems are associated with them. With regard to costs, some of the questions to be addressed include: What tangible costs are associated with actions regarding personnel, material, and capital expenditures? What kinds of costs are involved, including spillover costs, community disruption, and other undesirable external effects? In what time periods will these costs fall? How certain are they? Who will pay for them? What are the foregone opportunity costs, that is, what costs are associated with adopting one program over another?

With respect to effectiveness, validity is a major problem. For example what should be viewed as the impact of a program to reduce automobile air pollution: the reduction in grams per mile of certain pollutants per car, the reduction in total weight of emissions of these pollutants into the atmosphere from all of the autos in a given area, the concentration of various pollutants in the atmosphere over certain areas or regions, or various measures of the effects of the pollutants on various elements such as health or the clarity of the air? Another problem involved in the measurement of effectiveness within a cost-effectiveness framework is related to the many cases in which benefits are not reflected in the marketplace. Educational programs, for instance, may increase individuals' cognitive skills without increasing their earning power. Similarly, if a program is designed to improve the environment, how does one obtain a market price for the reduction of hydrocarbons and visible particles in the air, or for the reduction of pollution in water? In general, measures of program effectiveness cannot always be expressed in monetary terms, and complementary measures such as rating or judgment scales have to be developed in order to assess effectiveness.[27]

The other important problem in cost-effectiveness evaluation is the specification of the relationship between costs and effectiveness, which defines the alternative courses of action available to decision makers. In principle the rule of choice is rather simple: The optimal system is the one that yields the greatest excess of positive impacts over costs. An optimal allocation of resources occurs when the marginal benefits associated with a small increase in costs are the same for all programs. For example, in Figure 2 the relation between costs and effectiveness for a hypothetical program, P, is portrayed. It is assumed that the program is currently operating at a level represented by cost, C, and effectiveness, E. The average cost-effectiveness ratio is given by the slope of the line segment OA_1 or OE_1/OC_1.

If the decision is whether or not to add resources equal to C_1C_2, the relevant cost-effectiveness ratio is that represented by the slope of A_1A_2 which is equal to E_1E_2/C_1C_2.

In practice there are difficulties in applying such an optional decision rule. Usually, one has to specify either required effectiveness measures, which means that the cost is minimized for that effectiveness, or a required cost, which means that the effectiveness is maximized. There is no agreed upon method for subtracting costs spent from cognitive skills obtained, for example, in an educational program. Notwithstanding these problems and given the reality of scarce resources, the cost-effectiveness approach is a useful type of evaluation, as some of the contributions included in this volume demonstrate. Its limitations, however, should be recognized.

Figure 2. A cost-effectiveness curve for Program P.

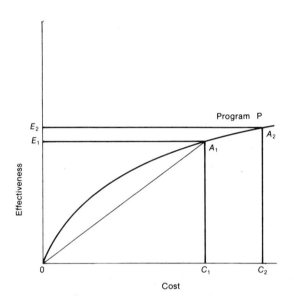

ADMINISTRATION OF EVALUATION RESEARCH

Although evaluation research may be undertaken without any formal sponsorship, because of problems of cost and access to information, it is often a sponsored activity. This, in turn, creates problems that are less common in basic social science research, one of which is that evaluators, policymakers, and administrators tend to have conflicting interests and expectations. Policymakers, program implementors, and researchers often have dissonant notions regarding the purposes of evaluation. For example, in a study of ten research grants, Weiss found that:

> Some program administrators and staff saw evaluation as a ritual to secure funding; others viewed it as a potential guide to adaptations that would strengthen the program during its course; still others expected evaluation to provide program vindication . . . to help obtain further funding. Evaluators . . . tended to see their role as assessing the effectiveness of the program . . . so that NIMH [the National Institute of Mental Health] . . . could decide whether to continue, adopt, or advocate it elsewhere. A few evaluators also expected to make contributions to basic knowledge.[28]

These conflicting interests were especially intense during the drafting of the final reports: "Administrators wanted to put the rosiest interpretation on evaluation findings; evaluators fought for the integrity of the data."[29]

Some authors take the position that conflicts of interest can be mitigated if the researcher and the program manager agree before the study begins on "specific and detailed answers to a list of questions not unlike those that newspaper reporters are taught to ask: who, what, when, where, how, and how much. What are the program objectives, both immediate and ultimate? For what target population is the research being done? What changes are anticipated as indications that the objectives have been met? When and how will the changes be manifested? What kinds of activities are supposed to produce these changes? How much change will be necessary? How are the program activities intended to produce change to be conducted? Where and for what length of time will research be carried out? What kind and how many resource inputs will be employed?"[30] In other words agreement on the impact model and definitions of variables, the research design, and the measurement procedures will tend to mitigate conflicts of interest, and at the same time will increase the potential for eventual utilization of research findings.

Conflicts also tend to emerge in situations where the target population believes that the research findings will have policy consequences. Evaluations may take place in a variety of institutional settings, such as school systems, courts, rehabilitation centers, and residential communities. Evaluation studies may generate pressure from the community to alter the character of the program variables, to take part in the sampling procedures, to hire local people for jobs on the research staff, or even to prevent the execution of the study completely if community leaders feel the study may have deleterious effects. For example the New Jersey Negative Income Tax Experiment discussed in chapter 1 required substantial negotiations with the communities and considerable effort to preserve the integrity of the research design. In one community an entire public housing project refused to cooperate with the researchers until the latter got the approval of the "community leader."[31] The research team, therefore, must be attentive to the ways in which a study is viewed by the community and must establish collaborative relationships with community members and leaders. Such relationships facilitate the execution of the study, and at the same time, preserve the integrity of the research design.

EVALUATION AND POLICYMAKING

Like all other social science research, policy-evaluation research is neither all powerful nor all weak. Since one of its major goals is to contribute to public policymaking, however, the issue of determining the extent to which, and the conditions under which, evaluation findings are incorporated into the policy process is an important research task. Some observers take the position that political realities inevitably dominate the extent to which evaluation evidence influences public policymaking: "Evaluations can influence fine-grain program decisions, and that's about it. For any of the big policy decisions, research is marginal. These yea/nay decisions are made on the basis of political tea leaves."[32] Whereas political factors constitute an important component in the utilization of evaluation research (see chapter 9), there are other significant components that also must be taken into account.

In general the role of evaluation research in a decision process depends on the structure of that process and the incentives that guide decision makers in it. In an ideal decision-making process, policy decisions are affected by systematic analysis of the extent to which programs are meeting their objectives, their costs, and the distribution of program effects among various target populations. Evaluation research constitutes an integral part of the decision-making process, and policymakers demand and rely upon systematic evidence to guide their decisions. Such policy decisions serve the public better than decisions made in the absence of, or in disregard to, systematic information. Aaron Wildavsky wrote:

> The ideal organization would be self-evaluating. It would continuously monitor its own activities so as to determine whether it was meeting its goals or even whether these goals should continue to prevail. When evaluation suggested that a change in goals or programs to achieve them was desirable, these proposals would be taken seriously by top decision makers. They would institute the necessary changes; they would have no vested interest in continuation of current activities. Instead they would steadily pursue new alternatives to better serve the latest desired outcomes.[33]

Compared with these ideal characteristics, actual decision-making processes are inadequate. Program objectives are not known with certainty, nor are they unanimously accepted by the policymakers. Even the cost and effectiveness of programs are sometimes controversial. Policymakers are vulnerable to numerous pressures that induce behavior inconsistent with either the stated objectives or the evaluation findings. Policymakers seek systematic information, but they are also motivated by the search for power and influence. Votes are traded; coalitions based on special interests are formed; and success is often associated with organizational survival rather than with the attainment of goals. Such factors seriously constrain the utilization of evaluation research in policymaking.

At the same time policy-evaluation research is receiving increasing amounts of political and funding support, and evaluation activities are becoming increasingly institutionalized. In fact, in a few agencies, a specified percentage of program funds are allotted for evaluation purposes; Congress is growing more aware of the need to evaluate policies and programs; and bureaus with the word "evaluation" in the title are rapidly being established at all levels of government. Although these indicators of institutionalization reflect to a certain extent the potential for evaluation research in future policymaking, only time will tell whether evaluation research will be more effectively incorporated in public policymaking.

PURPOSE AND STRUCTURE OF THIS BOOK

The purpose of this book is to introduce students and practitioners of public policy to the central issues involved in evaluation research. It brings together case studies about evaluation research drawn from a variety of policy areas, including equal educational opportunity, equal employment opportunity, income maintenance, human resources development, health care, housing and community development, energy and transportation, and criminal justice. These policy areas, although not inclusive of the scope of public policy, represent major current concerns of policymakers and the attentive publics. Policy decisions with respect to these areas have preoccupied politicians, civil servants, and the public for some time now, and recently, they have done so with increasing intensity.

Rather than emphasize the general principles of evaluation research, this book brings together examples of actual applications of these principles. Although some of these principles are briefly discussed in the present chapter, this book cannot serve as a substitute for a basic text.[34]

Several criteria served as guides for the selection of this material: the political saliency of an issue, the extent of controversy over an issue, the extent to which a case study contributes to systematic knowledge, the rigorousness of its methodology, and its potential for utilization in the public-policy process. These criteria are what evaluation research is all about.

The first four chapters include evaluations of programs that originated as part of the War on Poverty. The War on Poverty policy was based on the idea that poverty and inequality are cyclical. Persons born into poverty encounter barriers that weaken their motivation and self-esteem, limit their opportunities to obtain quality educational and occupational training, and restrict their economic and social mobility. Their limited opportunities lead to inequality. An individual's chances of breaking out of a poverty cycle are slim unless his or her educational, occupational, and economic opportunity structures are opened up. More accessible opportunity structures help to bring about attitudinal and motivational changes in individuals, which, in turn, enable them to become self-supporting.

Accompanying this concept, and spurred on by the civil-rights movement, a greater policy emphasis has been placed on equalizing opportunities in terms of achieving equality of condition. President Lyndon B. Johnson said:

> You do not take a person who for years has been hoveled by chains and liberate him, bring him to the starting line of a race, and say, "you are free to compete with all the others," and still justly believe that you have been completely fair.
>
> Thus it is not enough to open the gates to opportunity. All our citizens must have the ability to walk through these gates.[35]

The Economic Opportunity Act of 1964 was designed to combat the causes of poverty and inequality and to equalize conditions. The act is the federal government's most ambitious and direct policy attempt to tackle the complex problems of poverty, discrimination, and inequality in American society.

The evaluations included in chapters 1, 2, 3, and 4 analyze income-maintenance programs, educational programs, human resources development programs, and the overall effects of occupational and economic opportunity policies on minorities. Chapter 5 focuses on the evaluation of housing and community development policies in general, and those aimed at the housing consumption of lower income groups in particular. Indeed, adequate housing is an important component of the opportunity structure of Americans, and it is closely related to education, occupation, and economic well-being. Chapter 6 brings together evaluations of law enforcement and criminal justice programs. The components of the criminal justice system—police, courts, and corrections—cannot be divorced from the environment within which they operate, and they are related to many of the problems discussed in the previous chapters. Chapters 7 and 8 include evaluations of health, transportation, and energy policies. These areas have topped the nation's priority list and are likely to remain salient and critical in years to come. Finally, the papers in chapter 9 are devoted to the problems involved in making evaluation research an integral component of public policy.

NOTES

1. Jack W. Carlson, "Can We Do Anything Right?" *Washington Monthly*, 1 (November 1969), 75.
2. Joseph S. Wholey et al., *Federal Evaluation Policy* (Washington, D.C.: Urban Institute, 1975), p. 15.

3. Howard E. Freeman, "The Present Status of Evaluation Research," in *Evaluation Studies: Review Annual*, II, ed. Marcia Guttentag (Beverly Hills, Calif.: Sage, 1977), p. 19.
4. Eduard A. Suchman, *Evaluative Research: Principles and Practice in Public Service and Social Action Programs* (New York: Sage, 1967), p. 11.
5. Ibid., p. 8.
6. Thomas R. Dye, *Policy Analysis: What Governments Do, Why They Do It, and What Difference It Makes* (University, Ala.: University of Alabama Press, 1976), p. 95.
7. J. Roland Pennock, "Political Development, Political Systems, and Political Goods," *World Politics*, 18 (April 1968), 420.
8. See Martha Derthick, *New Towns In-Town* (Washington, D.C.: Urban Institute, 1972).
9. Quoted in Morton H. Halperin, *Bureaucratic Politics and Foreign Policy* (Washington, D.C.: Brookings Institution, 1974), p. 245.
10. George C. Edwards, III, and Ira Sharkansky, *The Policy Predicament: Making and Implementing Public Policy* (San Francisco: Freeman, 1978), p. 295.
11. Jeffrey L. Pressman and Aaron Wildavsky, *Implementation: How Great Expectations in Washington Are Dashed in Oakland, or, Why It's Amazing That Federal Programs Work at All* (Berkeley: University of California Press, 1973). *See also* Eugene Bardach, *The Implementation Game: What Happens After a Bill Becomes a Law* (Cambridge, Mass.: M.I.T. Press, 1977).
12. Jerome T. Murphy, *State Education Agencies and Discretionary Funds* (Lexington, Mass.: Heath, 1971). *See also* Walter Williams, *Social Policy Research and Analysis* (New York: Elsevier, 1971), chap. 8.
13. Hubert M. Blalock, Jr., *Causal Inferences in Nonexperimental Research* (Chapel Hill: University of North Carolina Press, 1964), p. 9.
14. Ibid., p. 5.
15. Herbert Simon, *Models of Man* (New York: Wiley, 1957).
16. Blalock, *Causal Inferences*, p. 15.
17. Ilene N. Bernstein, "Validity Issues in Evaluative Research: An Overview," in *Validity Issues in Evaluative Research*, ed. Ilene N. Bernstein, Sage Contemporary Social Science Issues, XXIII (Beverly Hills, Calif.: Sage, 1976), p. 8.
18. Robert L. Granger et al., *The Impact of Head Start: An Evaluation of the Effects of Head Start on Children's Cognitive and Affective Development*, I (Westinghouse Learning Corporation and Ohio University, June 1969), p. 8.
19. This term was introduced by Ralph E. Strauch in "A Critical Assessment of Quantitative Methodology as a Policy Analysis Tool," P-5282 (Santa Monica, Calif.: Rand Corporation, 1974).
20. Carol H. Weiss, *Evaluation Research* (Englewood Cliffs, N.J.: Prentice-Hall, 1972), p. 28.
21. Ibid.
22. The Delphi method is one systematic way to make this process operational. *See*, for example, Norman C. Dalkey et al., *Studies in the Quality of Life: Delphi and Decision Making* (Lexington, Mass.: Lexington Books, 1972).
23. John P. Gilbert, Richard J. Light, and Frederick Mosteller, "Assessing Social

Innovations: An Empirical Base for Policy," in *Evaluation and Experiment: Some Critical Issues in Assessing Social Programs*, eds. Carl A. Bennett and Arthur A. Lumsdaine (New York: Academic, 1975), p. 44.

24. For a detailed discussion of these and other types of research designs, see David Nachmias, *Public Policy Evaluation* (New York: St. Martin's, 1979), chaps. 2, 3, and 6.

25. Gilbert, Light, and Mosteller, "Assessing Social Innovations," pp. 39–40.

26. Sally Ryan, ed., U.S. Department of Health, Education, and Welfare, Office of Human Development, *Longitudinal Evaluations: A Report on Longitudinal Evaluations of Preschool Programs*, vol. L (OHD) 74–24 (Washington, D.C.: Department of Health, Education, and Welfare, 1974).

27. For the various methods of constructing such measures, see Nachmias, *Public Policy Evaluation*, chap. 4.

28. Carol H. Weiss, "Where Politics and Evaluation Research Meet," *Evaluation*, 1: 2(1973): 22.

29. Ibid.

30. Lee Gurel, "The Human Side of Evaluating Human Service Programs: Problems and Prospects," in *Handbook of Evaluation Research*, eds., Marcia Guttentag and Elmer L. Struening, vol. 2 (Beverly Hills, Calif.: Sage, 1975), p. 22.

31. David N. Kershaw, "Issues in Income Maintenance Experimentation," in *Evaluating Social Programs*, eds., Peter H. Rossi and Walter Williams (New York: Seminar Press, 1972), pp. 11–49.

32. Quoted in Lois-ellin Datta, "The Impact of the Westinghouse/Ohio Evaluation on the Development of Project Head Start," in *The Evaluation of Social Programs*, ed. Clark C. Abt (Beverly Hills, Calif.: Sage, 1976), p. 174.

33. Aaron Wildavsky, "The Self-Evaluating Organization," in chapter 9 of this book.

34. *See*, for example, Nachmias, *Public Policy Evaluation*; Weiss, *Evaluation Research*; Wholey et al., *Federal Evaluation Policy*, and Suchman, *Evaluative Research*.

35. Lyndon B. Johnson, address to graduating class, Howard University, June 4, 1965. Quoted in Thomas R. Dye, *Understanding Public Policy* (Englewood Cliffs, N.J.: Prentice-Hall, 1972), p. 64.

Chapter 1

INCOME MAINTENANCE

Income maintenance is the largest single item of government spending. In the mid-1970s general income maintenance, which includes social security, unemployment insurance, and medical assistance, accounted for slightly more than 32 percent of federal spending. Public assistance, the more specific income-maintenance policy that distributes cash and in-kind assistance (such as food stamps and housing, medical, and educational subsidies) accounted for another 11 percent of federal funds.

The present role of government in income-maintenance programs has evolved from a lengthy, complex process involving problems, conflicting ideologies, political compromises, and bureaucratic pressures. Prior to the 1930s the public believed that federal government should play no role in income maintenance. The idea of receiving something without contributing in return ran counter to the American belief of individual responsibility and the work ethic. The Great Depression led to significant changes in attitudes toward public welfare and income-maintenance policies. One out of four Americans was unemployed, and one out of six received some sort of welfare aid.

The Social Security Act of 1935 was an important turning point. In this act the federal government committed itself to the establishment of a comprehensive framework for income-maintenance programs at all levels of government, thus formulating a new approach to the problem of poverty—social insurance. Social insurance is designed to prevent poverty resulting from unemployment, old age, death of a family wage earner, or physical disability by requiring individuals to purchase insurance to cover such events. Social insurance is a preventive approach to poverty, and, indeed, it has been interpreted in the present

Social Security Administration as being within the tradition of individual self-help. The Social Security Act also induced the individual states to enact unemployment-compensation programs through the imposition of a payroll tax on all employers.

In the Social Security Act of 1935, the federal government also committed itself to aid the states in providing public assistance payments to certain needy persons to alleviate the conditions of poverty. The intent was to provide a minimum level of subsistence to certain categories of needy adults—mothers with children, the physically disabled, the blind, and the aged. This subsistence was implemented by providing small amounts of cash in monthly payments through state-administered welfare programs. At the time it was believed that the federal role in public assistance would decline and that social insurance would take the major responsibility of helping the needy.

Expectations for a diminishing role of the federal government in public assistance have not materialized. The dependence upon public assistance has increased at a rapid rate, most notably in the Aid to Families with Dependent Children (AFDC) program. Furthermore, although dependence upon public assistance has increased, many of the nation's poor do not receive any public assistance. In fact there are "working poor" who are ineligible for welfare assistance because they hold jobs, even though these are low-paid jobs.

Since the launching of the War on Poverty in 1964, various approaches have been advocated and tried to reduce poverty and lower the cost of alleviating its impact. Some programs have emphasized income supplements; others, in-kind aid, and still others, educational and vocational training. Generally, the objective has been to assist the poor and the unemployed become self-supporting and capable of earning adequate incomes by changing their attitudes, behavior, and the immediate environment. Significantly, most programs have been targeted, either explicitly or implicitly, at curing the roots of poverty rather than at alleviating its symptoms. In this sense such programs continue to reflect the American belief in the work ethic and the public's attitude toward poverty. In the words of the Council of Economic Advisers:

> Conquest of poverty is well within our power. The majority of the Nation could simply tax themselves enough to provide the necessary income supplements to their less fortunate citizens. . . . But this "solution" would leave untouched most of the roots of poverty. Americans want to *earn* [a] standard of living by their own efforts and contributions.[1]

This philosophy is manifested in the general policy and the specific programs that the government has either proposed or activated. Evaluation research has focused on a number of central operational questions that derive from this philosophy. These include:

1. How will proposed programs affect the incentive to work? More specifically, if incomes are raised to a point where some persons on welfare are as well off as persons in unattractive, low-paying jobs, will this encourage individuals to leave the labor force and go on public assistance?
2. How will proposed programs affect mobility and migration patterns?
3. Will family stability be affected by changes in income-maintenance policies and, if so, what types of public programs will lead to what consequences?
4. Will demand for social services be affected?
5. Will consumption patterns change among low-income families?
6. How will the program affect the well-being of the community?

Obviously, no one single evaluation study can provide all the answers to these questions. Instead, studies have been limited to a few carefully designed and well-controlled experiments, each of which would furnish some answers to some critical questions. The following four major income-maintenance projects were experimented with:

The New Jersey Income Maintenance Experiment. This OEO-sponsored experiment was designed to assess the effects of a negative income taxation (NIT) on the work incentives of male-headed households. Essentially, with negative income taxes, or tax credits, the government makes up the difference in cash when income is below the minimum-subsistence level. The cash grant is reduced proportionally as earnings go beyond a break-even point. The experiment, which concentrated on the urban poor in five communities in New Jersey and Pennsylvania, lasted for a period of five years, involved 1,350 families, and cost $8 million.

The Rural Income-Maintenance Experiment. The Institute of Research on Poverty at the University of Wisconsin, under the sponsorship of OEO, has examined the work-incentive effects of a negative income tax scheme on the rural populations in Iowa and North Carolina.

The Gary (Indiana) Experiment. This project was designed to test a negative-income-tax scheme, combined with day care and other social services, on black one- and two-parent families.

The Seattle/Denver Income-Maintenance Experiment. This evaluation was aimed at urban white, black, and Mexican-American families having either one or two parents present. The study was designed to assess the combined effect of a negative-income-tax scheme with manpower programs in areas of low and high unemployment.

Papers in this chapter focus on the New Jersey Income Maintenance Experiment, which was among the first attempts to apply a controlled experiment to the controversial policy issue: Do governmental cash payments reduce the incentive to work? David N. Kershaw discusses the theoretical and political rationale of the experiment, describes its structure and operation, and points out some of the difficulties inherent in policy experimentation—the choice of research sites, the selection of the target population, and the unforeseen problems emerging in the field. Notwithstanding these difficulties, the evaluation reports that as a result of the introduction of payments, weekly earnings did *not* significantly decline. The data collected in the course of the experiment enabled the testing of additional and more refined hypotheses concerning the labor-supply behavior of the 1,300 families who participated in the study. The article by Albert Rees reports on the differential impact of the program on four components—husbands, wives, young adults, and families—and also compares behaviors among various ethnic groups. Rees shows the importance of formulating theoretical expectations prior to designing the evaluation, and he notes the problems involved in constructing valid measures of the target variable. Indeed, the experimental families were more sensitive to the program treatment, which, in turn, could have caused spurious differences between their behavior and that of the control group. Variations in impact are estimated with regression equations. These enable the introduction of control variables and the reduction of bias that might occur from the nonrandom assignment of families to the experimental groups.

NOTE

1. *Economic Report to the President* 1964, (Washington D.C.: Government Printing Office, 1964/) p. 77.

A NEGATIVE-INCOME-TAX EXPERIMENT

David N. Kershaw

The welfare-reform proposals of both President Nixon and Senator Mc-Govern embody the concept of the negative income tax: a downward extension of the income-tax system that would pay out cash (negative taxes) to families at the low end of the income scale. An essential feature of the concept is that as a family's income rises above the poverty level the tax payments are reduced by an amount less than the earnings, so that the family is always better off the higher its own earnings are. The concept was first presented to a broad public in 1962 by Milton Friedman of the University of Chicago, who argued that the negative income tax would strengthen the market economy and individual initiative by enabling poor people to make their own decisions on spending and saving and would cut back on the large and growing apparatus of social-welfare programs.

It is difficult to predict what the impact of a negative-income-tax plan would be on the people covered and on the economy. The word "experiment" is often applied to new social programs, but it is not used in the normal scientific sense. For the past four years, however, my colleagues and I at Mathematica Incorporated, working with a group at the Institute for Research on Poverty of the University of Wisconsin, have been conducting a more rigorous kind of social experiment to test the effects of a negative income tax. Money for the experiment was provided by the U.S. Office of Economic Opportunity. The main objective of the work has been to explore the key question about the negative tax, namely the extent to which it would reduce the incentive of the recipients to work. The extent of such a work reduction will determine both the actual cost of a new program and whether or not it is acceptable to the taxpayers. Our preliminary findings indicate that a negative income tax does not significantly reduce the earnings of the recipients. We think the findings also point to the value of social experimentation as a tool for policymakers.

The need for some such technique arises from the large sums that the government regularly commits to the eradication of one social ill or another: additional housing for the poor, health facilities for the elderly, medical care for the indigent, school lunches for poor children and so on. Since the supply of skills and money for these activities is limited, the legislative process becomes essentially a system of bargaining or of trading off one set of programs for another. On what basis do government officials recommend one set of programs rather than another? What criteria do legislators employ to measure the probable effectiveness of one idea as opposed to another? The fact is that there have been few effective ways for determining the effectiveness of a social program before it is started; indeed, in most cases it is impossible even to forecast the cost of a new social program until it has been in operation for some time.

Clearly this situation is not conducive to sound and effective decision making. Moreover, it results in such unforeseen disasters as the Medicaid scandals, empty public-housing projects and relentlessly increasing costs for welfare programs. Social experimentation of the kind I am discussing is a tool that has been developed and tested in the past five years for avoiding unanticipated developments in new social programs and for measuring in advance what the programs will cost.

What is usually unforeseen in a new program is how the people affected by it will behave. What they do, of course, is likely to have a profound effect on the program. For example, in the Medicaid program unexpectedly high fees charged by physicians and hospitals and unexpectedly high use of the services took policymakers by surprise. Various behavioral changes induced in the recipients similarly determine the cost and effectiveness of new income-transfer programs. Since most major social programs will induce changes in behavior, which, in turn, will affect the program, it is clearly vital for policymakers to understand the magnitude and direction of such changes in behavior in advance in order to make the most rational choices among new programs.

A social experiment as we view it has the same general design as an experiment in the natural sciences. One undertakes to identify the experimental population, then to change one of the variables affecting its behavior and finally to compare its subsequent behavior with that of a control population in which the variable has not been changed. If the experiment is well designed, the investigator can attribute any difference in the behavior of the experimental population to the stimulus. The question we faced was whether or not this approach would work when the population consisted of human beings, when the laboratory was the community, and when the stimulus was a complex new social program.

Our experiment was the first attempt to answer the question. The experiment has been conducted as the New Jersey Negative Income Tax Experiment because its first operations were in Trenton, although it was later extended to Scranton, Pa., as well as to three other cities in New Jersey:

Paterson, Passaic, and Jersey City. Negative-income-tax payments were begun in Trenton in August, 1968, and were ended in Scranton last month [September, 1972]. The only part of the experiment now in progress is the analysis of the data.

The welfare-reform proposals of the two presidential candidates [Nixon and McGovern] are among a number of negative-tax plans that have been advanced in recent years. Although the various plans differ in many ways, all of them are defined by two common variables: the guarantee level and the rate of reduction (sometimes called the tax rate) applied to the guarantee.

The guarantee is the amount paid to a family or an individual with no other income. In a negative-income-tax system the guarantee would be in effect a floor under incomes, providing a basic level of income for everyone. Various guarantee levels have been proposed, ranging from $2,400 annually for a family of four (the amount in H.R. 1, a House of Representatives bill incorporating the Administration's proposals for welfare reform) to $6,600 per year (advocated by the National Welfare Rights Organization).

The rate of reduction is the rate at which the negative-tax payments are reduced as the family's other income rises. The reduction is always less than the amount of the rise in other income. That is to say, for each dollar of other income the family receives, the negative-tax payment is reduced somewhat, but not dollar for dollar. A dollar-for-dollar reduction formerly applied in welfare programs, and the rate in such programs remains high today.

The guarantee and the rate of reduction can be combined in many ways. Suppose the guarantee is $3,000 and the rate of reduction is 50 percent (*see* Figure 1.1). A family with no earned income receives the full $3,000, and the reduction is not applied. If in the next year the family's earned income is $1,000, the rate of reduction of 50 percent means that the negative-tax payment to the family is reduced by $500. The family now receives $2,500 in negative-tax payments and $1,000 of its own income for a total of $3,500. The reduction works just as the positive income tax works; in this example the family is effectively in a 50 percent marginal tax bracket.

The key point is that the family's total income continues to rise as its earned income rises, notwithstanding the reduction in negative-tax payments. Just as in the positive-tax program, the family is always better off with a higher earned income. The point is important because it shows that the negative-income-tax system is designed to minimize the disincentive to work that has often been associated with welfare programs. People who are able to work keep a portion of their earnings just as people in the positive-tax system do.

In the example I have given, the family would continue to receive nega-

Figure 1.1. Relation between the guarantee (shaded) and the earned income (white) is charted for a guarantee of $3,000 and a rate of reduction of 50 percent. The guarantee is the amount paid under a negative-income-tax plan to a family with no other income; the rate of reduction is the rate at which negative-tax payments are reduced as other income rises. The reduction is always lower than the amount of the rise in other income, so that the recipient is always better off by having earnings than by relying solely on the negative tax.

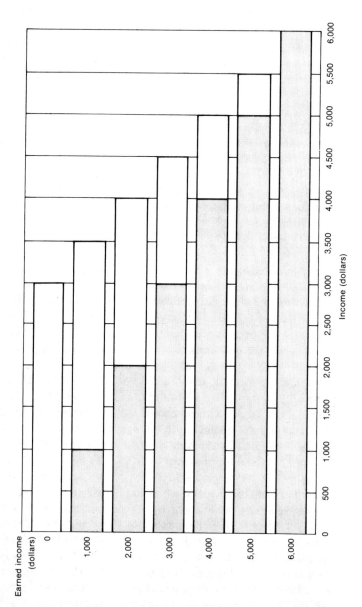

tive-tax payments until its own income reached $6,000. At that level the family would become a taxpayer rather than a tax recipient. As long as the level remained above $6,000 the family would receive no payments. If the income dropped below $6,000, the payments would be resumed.

Choosing the "best" combination of guarantee level and rate of reduction is a difficult problem. The two things one is most concerned with in a welfare system are (1) how much it will cost and (2) whether or not it will have a strong tendency to make the recipients disinclined to work. Unfortunately, the objectives of low cost and minimum work disincentive are in direct conflict (*see* Figure 1.2 on page 32).

The problem is evident if one envisions plans applying rates of reduction of 30, 50, and 70 percent respectively to a guarantee of $3,000. At 30 percent a family would continue to receive payments until its earned income reached $10,000, which is close to the median income in the U.S. for a family of four. Under this plan half of the families in the nation would be recipients of negative-tax payments. Although the low rate of reduction would presumably keep the work disincentive low, the cost would be very high. On the other hand, a rate of reduction of 70 percent would keep the cost of the system down but could severely limit the incentive to work.

The problem of establishing an appropriate guarantee level and rate of reduction, of ascertaining the effect of various combinations on work behavior, and of estimating the cost of a national program led to a decision by the Office of Economic Opportunity that a field experiment should be undertaken as a way of obtaining evidence. In 1967 the office gave money for the experiment to the Institute for Research on Poverty and to Mathematica, which has its headquarters in Princeton, N.J. These organizations shared the responsibility of designing the experiment and of analyzing the data, and Mathematica set up the administrative system.

The design of the experiment was focused on the work-response issue. Given a guaranteed annual income, how much, if any, would recipients reduce their work effort? The designers of the experiment decided that the population of most interest consisted of intact families among the working poor. The work response of single-parent families and of the aged and disabled were of less interest. Data on the work response of single-parent families were partly available through the program of aid to families with dependent children, and it appeared that the cost of a guaranteed income for the aged and the disabled could be estimated without a field test since the variability of their response to negative-tax payments was limited. For these reasons the designers decided that the sample for the experiment should consist of intact families with able-bodied males between the ages of 18 and 58 who were either in the labor force or physically capable of entering it.

Figure 1.2

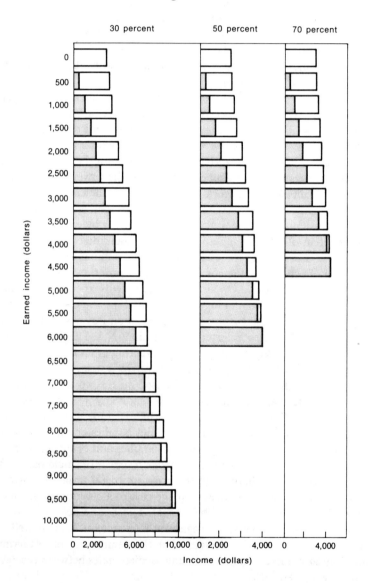

A second major decision concerned the method of choosing the participants. The designers considered a national sample, which would consist of families chosen on a random basis from places in every region of the country; a "saturation" experiment, consisting of all the eligible families in a given area, and a "test-boring" approach involving a limited number of families from several geographic areas. It appeared that a national sample would cost too much and would be risky administratively in view of how little was known about conducting a social experiment of this kind. The saturation approach was rejected both for its cost and because it was difficult to see how data from a single area would be helpful in making generalizations about a national negative-tax program. We decided on the test-boring approach.

Choosing the site involved several considerations. The first decision was to concentrate on an urban area, since most of the working poor live in cities. Second, we focused on the Northeast because it is densely populated and is close to Washington, so that the Office of Economic Opportunity could more easily participate in the decision making. In the end we settled on New Jersey because it is densely populated and has a substantial number of poor people. Moreover, the state government was interested in the experiment. Trenton was chosen as the pilot site because it is close to Princeton (and so to Mathematica) and because as the capital of New Jersey, it facilitated liaison with state officials. Paterson, Passaic, and Jersey City were added later because they are fairly large cities, and Scranton was added because its preponderance of white residents would bring an ethnic balance to a sample that was otherwise largely black or Puerto Rican.

The selection of families was based on two preliminary interviews: a 44-question screening survey administered to about 30,000 families in the five cities and a 340-question "pre-enrollment" interview administered to 2,300 families. Both interviews obtained information on the composition of the family and on income. In addition the pre-enrollment interview provided baseline measurements of certain other sociological and economic variables.

The designers decided to test three rates of reduction: 30, 50, and 70 percent. The reasoning was that this group of rates covered the relevant policy range, inasmuch as a national program would never be designed with a reduction rate lower than 30 percent (on cost grounds) or higher than 70 percent (on work-disincentive grounds). Four guarantee levels were established, ranging from $1,650 (half of the official poverty level for a family of four in 1967) to $4,125 (125 percent of the poverty level). Eight combinations of reduction rate and guarantee level were established, and each one was designated as a "plan" (*see* Figure 1.3 on page 34).

More than 1,300 families have been involved in the program, although some have dropped out and are not reflected in our data. Somewhat more

Figure 1.3. Eight combinations of guarantee and rate of reduction employed in the negative-tax experiment (indicated by the shaded squares). The "poverty line" was established in 1967, when the negative-tax experiment was designed, as $3,300 per year for a family of four.

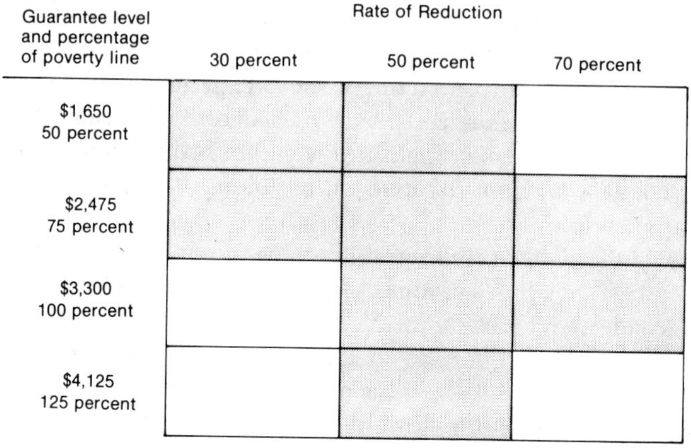

Guarantee level and percentage of poverty line	Rate of Reduction		
	30 percent	50 percent	70 percent
$1,650 50 percent	░	░	
$2,475 75 percent	░	░	░
$3,300 100 percent		░	░
$4,125 125 percent		░	

than half of the 1,300 families were assigned to one or another of the eight negative-tax plans. The other families constituted a control group that received no negative-tax payments, although they were interviewed periodically just as the experimental families were. A control group is necessary in order to be able to compare the families receiving payments with families of similar situation who are not. In this way the experimenter can be sure that random events in the cities are not responsible for the results he is measuring. *Guarantees and reductions* are shown in Figures 1.4, 1.5, and 1.6 in various combinations. For each level of earned income the negative-tax payment (shaded) and the earned income (white) are indicated for three rates of reduction. The problem in arriving at an optimum combination is that a low rate of reduction results in a costly negative-income-tax plan and a high rate tends to make the recipients less inclined to work to increase income.

In order to participate in the experiment, the families in the group receiving payments were required only to report their correct income and any changes in family composition. The reports, which we verified through various auditing procedures, were made every four weeks to the Council for Grants to Families, a corporate body set up by Mathematica and the Institute for Research on Poverty to process and disburse payments. On the basis of income reported to the council, families were paid every two weeks by check sent by mail from Princeton. The council also had an of-

Figure 1.4 Comparison of weekly earnings of the families that received negative tax payments and control families at the beginning of the experiment. The control families (white) received no payments, but were treated otherwise in the same way as the families receiving negative tax payments (shaded). The numeral at the end of each bar shows the number of families in the group.

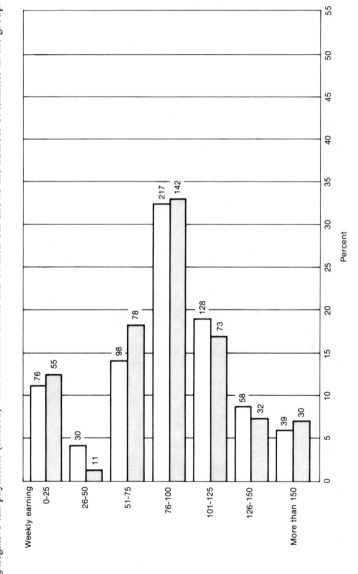

Figure 1.5. Ethnic distribution of families in the experiment. The shaded bars represent families that received negative tax payments, and the white bars are the control families.

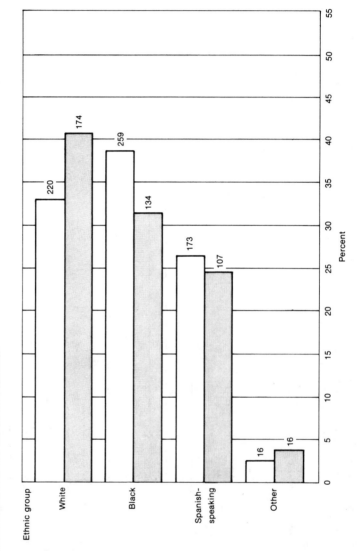

Figure 1.6. Family size of participating families. Again the shaded bars represent families that received payments, and the white bars represent control families. The numerals at the end of the bars give the number of families in each group.

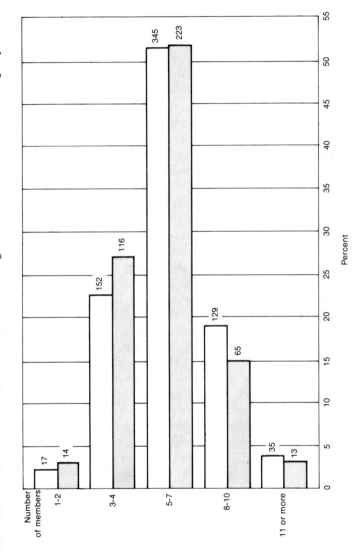

fice in each of the experimental cities to answer questions from the families and from Princeton.

Families were free to do whatever they wished with the payments. They also could move anywhere in the U.S. If a member left the original family unit, he or she still received a share of the family grant. Payments were excluded from taxable income under a ruling obtained from the Internal Revenue Service.

In addition to the income data on the forms mailed in by the experimental families every four weeks, information on the work response and other characteristics of the sample was obtained from interviews administered every three months by the Urban Opinion Surveys Division of Mathematica to both the experimental and the control families. The questionnaires sought information on such matters as participation in the labor force, financial status, medical and educational histories, family structure, and political and social integration. Twelve such interviews were made, and a thirteenth quarterly interview was undertaken to ascertain what understanding the families had of the experiment.

We have now obtained a great deal of information about the 1,300 families. We shall be analyzing the results for another year. Unanalyzed portions of the data will be made available, under controlled conditions, to investigators over the next few years. Even though the analysis is not complete, we have reached a stage where it is possible to describe the principal results in a preliminary way.

The most important results, of course, are those that bear on the work response. The question to be asked here is: How did the work behavior of the families in the experimental group compare with the work behavior of the families in the control group? The preliminary results give no evidence indicating a significant decline in weekly earnings as a result of the introduction of the payments (*see* Figure 1.7). About 31 percent of the families in the experimental group showed earning increases of more than $25 per week, compared with about 33 percent of the controls. About 25 percent of the experimental families showed earning declines of more than $25 per week, compared with 23 percent of the controls. These differences are too small to be regarded as statistically significant. That is a most encouraging finding.

A second finding in terms of work response was identified when improvements in the computer system enabled us to analyze indicators other than earnings. One such indicator was the number of hours worked. An analysis primarily made by Harold Watts of the University of Wisconsin, who is the principal investigator in the experiment, showed that the hours worked by families in the experimental group are about 12 percent lower than the hours worked by families in the control group. The difference is statistically significant.

Figure 1.7. Change of earnings of families that received negative-tax payments (shaded) and of control families (white) is charted for the first two years of the experiment. "Increase" means a rise of more than $25 per week; "slight change," a rise or fall of less than $25 and "decrease," a decline of more than $25. Since the comparisons are so close, there is no statistically valid evidence that the payments curbed the recipients' incentive to work.

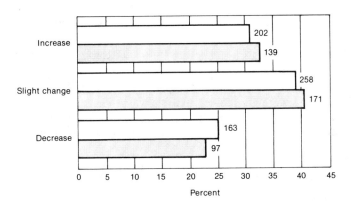

Close examination reveals that about 40 percent of the difference is attributable to primary earners in the experimental group who worked less than primary earners in the control group. The reasons appear to be small differences in overtime pay, in periods of unemployment, and in time spent on a second job. The remaining 60 percent is attributable to spouses and other adult workers in the family. Interestingly enough, it does not appear that these people are leaving the labor force in comparison to the control group; instead it seems that they are entering the labor force less rapidly. This observation suggests that the reason for the lower number of hours worked in the experimental group may be that people in those families take longer to look for better jobs. The availability of the negative-income-tax payment enables the worker to do that instead of having to accept the first job he finds.

The possibility that recipients spend more time looking for better jobs is a hypothesis; it may not be the actual reason for the reduction in hours worked. Attributing precise causes is a complicated process. Further analysis may provide answers. In any case a reduction of only 12 percent suggests that the introduction of a national negative-income-tax program will not give rise to a tidal wave of voluntary idleness. It certainly would be encouraging if people are reducing their work hours in order to look for better jobs.

We have also obtained information on the attitudes of the people in our experimental and control populations toward work. There would appear to be little reason for low-income workers to adhere to the "Protestant ethic." Why should they consider work a good thing? In the labor market they have met discrimination, low wages, poor working conditions, and arbitrary layoffs. For some reason, however, the people we interviewed generally supported the idea of work. This attitude could prove significant if the nation undertakes to develop an income-maintenance system that provides a smooth transition from poverty to reasonable affluence.

It is conceivable that the most important and lasting result of the New Jersey experiment will be the support it provides for the idea of social experimentation. Although the experiment encountered a number of serious unforeseen problems, in general it worked: families were chosen and assigned to experimental or control groups, money was paid, interviews were conducted, data were assembled, analysis was done and results were sent to Washington, where policymakers used them. A more rigorous question is whether social experimentation is a cost-effective way of obtaining answers to policy questions.

The weaknesses of the method are fairly clear: it is an expensive way of gathering information (the cost of the New Jersey experiment will be almost $10 million in the end); it takes a long time to get results, since measuring human behavior with confidence requires at least several years, and it is difficult to control the environment of the experiment. The strengths of social experimentation as a policy tool are also rather clear: It is the only way to obtain information on some kinds of behavioral change before a new program is introduced; it is the best way to collect precise information on specific issues because it is carefully structured and controlled, and it can help to focus the attention of able and imaginative scholars and professionals on new issues. On balance, social experimentation has thus far proved to be an effective new tool.

The New Jersey experiment has given rise to, or at least encouraged, a number of other social experiments. The rural negative-income-tax experiment, sponsored by the Office of Economic Opportunity and conducted by the Institute for Research on Poverty, covers 800 rural families in Iowa and North Carolina. The Department of Health, Education, and Welfare has provided money for income-maintenance experiments in Seattle; Gary, Ind.; and Denver, and also for the Vermont family-assistance-planning study, which was designed to explore the more important administrative issues in the Family Assistance Plan. The experiments in housing allowance, sponsored by the Department of Housing and Urban Development, give housing vouchers to poor families in several cities with the aim of studying the response of families and landlords, the demand and supply of housing and how a national housing-allowance program might be administered. The Office of Economic Opportunity is sponsoring an education-voucher demonstration and a health-insurance experiment. The education-voucher program seeks to measure the effect on communities and students of giving all parents in a particular area vouchers good for education at a school of their choice. In the health-insurance experiment, about 2,000 families will be placed on various health-insurance plans to measure how the utilization of medical services changes in response to differences in the cost of medical care.

Other social experiments are under consideration. They involve such issues as child care, problems of income measurement, and administrative techniques in cash-assistance programs. One can anticipate that an increasing number of policy decisions on major social programs will be made with the assistance of information obtained through social experiments undertaken to explore these issues and others yet unforeseen.

AN OVERVIEW OF THE LABOR-SUPPLY RESULTS

Albert Rees

The purpose of this article is to provide a summary of findings of the Graduated Work Incentive Experiment on labor supply, and to do so in a way that makes them accessible to readers who are not concerned with the finer points of methodology and technique. As a necessary preface to the summary of findings, we begin with a discussion of what we expected to find, and why.

WHAT WE EXPECTED TO FIND

The sponsors of the experiment and the researchers all expected, from the outset, that the payment of substantial amounts of unearned income to poor families would reduce the amount of labor they supplied, though not by very large amounts. These expectations were based in part on theory and in part on the results of nonexperimental empirical research. We begin by reviewing what will be called here the static theory of labor-leisure choice.

Static Theory

Figure 1.8 shows the labor-leisure choices of a hypothetical worker who is capable of earning $2 an hour. We assume that he is able to vary his weekly hours by such devices as voluntary overtime, part-time work, and multiple job holding; we also assume, for simplicity, that all hours worked are paid at the straight-time rate. In the initial situation, the worker is in equilibrium at point X on indifference curve I_0, where he works 40 hours a week and receives a weekly income of $80. He is then offered a negative income tax plan that guarantees him $60 a week if he has no earned income and "taxes" earned income at 50 percent by reducing the guaranteed payment as earned income rises. This plan has a "breakeven" at point C at an earned income of $120; to the left of this point, he receives no payments. The opportunity set facing the worker is now BCA rather than OA, and he chooses point Z on indifference curve I_1. His hours and earned income have decreased and his total income has increased.

The reduction in hours from X to Z can be divided into an income effect and a substitution effect by drawing line DE parallel to AO, which is tangent to I_1 at Y. The distance DO shows the amount of payments that would yield as much satisfaction as the original negative tax plan if the tax rate

Figure 1.8. Response to a negative income tax.

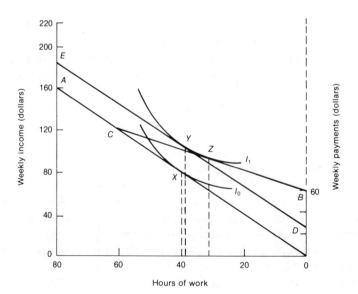

were zero. The horizontal distance from X to Y is the pure income effect on hours, since the wage rate, or the price of leisure, is the same at both points. The horizontal distance from Y to Z is the pure substitution effect of the tax rate, since the level of satisfaction is the same at both points. It should be noted that the income effect refers to the combined effect on welfare or satisfaction of the guarantee and the tax, and not that of the guarantee alone. A guarantee of $60 a week with no tax would enable the worker to reach an indifference curve lying above I_1.

As Figure 1.8 is drawn, both the income effect and the substitution effect of the negative income tax reduce hours of work. The negative substitution effect follows from the usual constraints of neoclassical utility theory on the shapes of indifference curves. If the curves are convex from the Southwest and BC is flatter than OA, then Z must lie to the right of Y. There is no such necessary relation between X and Y. The expectation that Y will lie to the right of X rests on empirical evidence. This is the evidence that as real income has risen through time, hours of work have tended to fall and that, in cross-section, hours of work tend to be shorter in high-paid than in low-paid jobs. In other words, the empirical evidence all indicates that "leisure" (the term used, for convenience, to include all non-work activity) is a normal good. That leisure is not an inferior good might be expected from the fact that most inferior goods have preferred close substitutes, and there is no close substitute for leisure.

In the case of wage increases, not only is the income effect negative, but it is sufficiently large to outweigh the positive substitution effect of a wage increase, which of course makes leisure more expensive. In the case of a negative income tax, both the income effect and the substitution effect will tend to reduce the amount of work supplied. The experiment enables us to observe points X and Z as the behavior of the control and experimental subjects, respectively. (It should be noted that point Y is not observable.)

The preceding discussion has been cast in terms of the choice of hours of work by a single worker. If we think of the family as a single decision-making unit having a collective indifference map, the same analysis would apply to the family. Moreover, it would apply to decisions about labor-force participation as well as to decisions about hours. Thus, a negative income tax might be expected to induce some members of the household to withdraw from the workforce, particularly those whose wage rate was low and who had good nonmarket uses for their time. Teenagers might withdraw to devote their full time to schooling, or wives to devote full time to keeping house.

Our expectations about labor-force participation rest more heavily on substitution effects than do those about hours of work. As real wages have risen through time, male labor-force participation rates have fallen, sug-

TABLE 1.1
Number of Experimental Families by Plan

Guarantee Level[b] (Percent)	Tax Rate[a] (Percent)		
	30	50	70
125	No plan	138	No plan
100	No plan	77	86
75	100	117	85
50	46	76	No plan

[a]The tax rate, sometimes called the "offset rate," is defined as the rate at which the transfer payment is reduced as the family's income increases. All plans are linear and have the algebraic form: $P = G - tY$ for $Y < G/t$, where P is the dollar amount of transfer payment; G is the dollar amount of guarantee for a given family size; t is the tax or offset rate; Y is the family income; and G/t defines the "breakeven" level of income.

[b]Guarantee as a percent of the following basic support levels, referred to here as the poverty levels: 2 persons, $2,000; 3 persons, $2,750; 4 persons, $3,300; 5 persons, $3,700; 6 persons, $4,050; 7 persons, $4,350; 8+ persons, $4,600. These differ slightly from the official poverty levels as of 1968. They were increased annually by the change in the Consumer Price Index.

gesting, as in the case of hours, that negative income effects outweigh the positive substitution effects of real wage increases. For married women, however, the evidence is mixed. In cross-section, holding education constant, the participation rate of wives falls as husbands' incomes rise. However, the participation rate of wives has risen through time as real wages have risen. Either the income effects are smaller than the substitution effects in this context, or they are offset by other changes in the opportunity set confronting wives—such as the availability of work-saving home appliances and prepared foods.

In the presentation above, we have assumed only one specification of the negative income tax plan. In the actual experiment there are eight, with four different guarantee levels and three different tax rates. (The eight plans are defined in Table 1.1.) The general expectation from the theory is that the plans with higher tax rates will have larger substitution effects and hence will produce greater reductions in labor supply, though, strictly speaking, this is true only as among plans that permit the family to achieve the same level of satisfaction. Similarly, one would expect from the empirical evidence on hours of work that, at the same tax rate, the plans with the most generous payments would cause the largest reduction in labor supply, whether generosity is measured in guarantee levels or in the average payments that would be made at the family's normal (preenrollment) income.

Dynamic Considerations

The theory sketched above is too simple in at least three respects. (1) It assumes that the wage rate confronting each worker is exogenously given and that he can do nothing to affect it. (2) It implicitly assumes that the negative income tax is a permanent change in the opportunity set facing the worker. (3) It assumes that the negative income tax plan is introduced into a world without existing welfare plans. Relaxation of these assumptions gives rise to what can loosely be called dynamic modifications of the standard theory. Each will be discussed in turn.

Endogenous Wage Change

The worker could change his market wage in at least three different ways. First, he might withdraw from the labor force or reduce his hours in order to undertake training that would raise his wage at some future time. A permanent negative income tax would make it easier to do this by providing some income during the period of training. A temporary experiment provides an even stronger incentive in the short run, since in this case the training would have to be completed before the end of the experiment. These considerations suggest that there might be a greater reduction in labor supply early in the experiment than the static theory suggests, but that toward the end of the experiment, this might no longer be true. If labor supply is measured in earnings rather than in man-hours, the effect toward the end of the experiment could even be to have a larger labor supply from the experimental group than from the control group. However, few of us gave sufficient weight to this line of argument at the beginning of the experiment to expect this result.

A second set of arguments suggests that earnings might fall more than hours throughout the experiment. The jobs open to a person of given skill and experience usually differ in the extent to which they are pleasant or unpleasant. Some involve heavy physical labor, disagreeable working conditions, inconvenient working hours, or inaccessible places of work. Others are lighter, more pleasant, and more convenient. Under conditions of sustained full employment, the less desirable jobs can be filled only at higher wages; the wage differentials thus called forth are known as compensating differentials.

The payment of a negative income tax could lead workers to shift toward pleasant jobs, sacrificing compensating differentials previously earned. Instead of substituting leisure for labor, they would substitute more agreeable work for disagreeable work. Such behavior would cause earnings to fall more than hours.

To the extent that average hours are reduced, there is another source of reduction in hourly earnings. By choosing not to work voluntary overtime, workers would reduce the hours paid at premium rates. In shifting from full-time to part-time jobs, workers might have to accept lower straight-time rates. It is not uncommon for part-time workers to receive less than full-time workers receive for similar work; for example, such differentials are often found in collective bargaining agreements for clerks in retail food stores.

Another possible influence of experimental payments on wages is through their effects on job search. One of the standard arguments in favor of unemployment insurance is that it permits the unemployed worker to search for a suitable job, rather than being forced by lack of income to accept one of the first job offers he receives, even if the wage offered is very low. More generally, any payments that are increased when a worker is not working will lower the cost of search and increase the expected wage of the job offer finally accepted. Negative income tax payments fall into this category, as supplements to unemployment insurance and even more strongly for those workers who are not eligible for unemployment insurance payments. Low-income workers are more likely than others not to receive unemployment insurance benefits. Some are in uncovered industries such as local government, domestic service, and agriculture. Some are new entrants to the labor force, or new residents in the state. Finally, some will have quit their last jobs or have been discharged for cause. Any difference between experimental and control families in the incidence and duration of unemployment should be considered as a change in labor supply, rather than as a result of deficient demand, because experimentals and controls were selected from the same population and face the same demand conditions.

Limited Duration of Experiment

We turn next to consideration of the effects on labor supply of the limited duration of the experiment. These, too, do not all work in the same direction. Consider first the male household head with a steady job involving hard work and long hours. If he knew that the negative tax payments were permanent, he might decide to take a job with lighter work and more normal hours. Yet, for a period of three years, such a shift might seem too risky. At the end of the experiment, he would need the higher earned income, but might be unable to get his old job back. For the steadily employed male head, the probability is that an experiment of limited duration will have smaller effects on labor supply than would a permanent program.

For other members of the household, whose attachment to the labor force is less secure, the effects of limited duration may be quite the opposite. Wives, teenagers, and other adults in the household are likely to be in and out of the labor force as family circumstances change. To the extent that periods of withdrawal from the labor force are planned in advance, a temporary experiment encourages the concentration of such periods during the experimental years, when the costs of not working are lower than normal. This may be particularly true toward the end of the experiment.

Presence of Welfare

The final consideration is the presence of preexisting welfare plans. At the beginning of the experiment, New Jersey did not give welfare to households with a male head—that is, it did not have a program known as Aid to Families of Dependent Children with Unemployed Parents (AFDC-U). This, indeed, was one of the important reasons for choosing New Jersey as the experimental site. Moreover, at the outset, we did not plan to include a site in Pennsylvania, but it became necessary to do so in order to enroll enough non-Spanish-speaking whites. In January 1969 (three months after the Trenton enrollment but before enrollment in the other sites), New Jersey introduced a welfare program for intact families. Until they were cut back in July 1971, benefits under this plan were more generous than those of most welfare programs in the country.

The presence of welfare complicates the comparison between control and experimental families. In the ninth experimental quarter, 25 percent of control families and 13 percent of experimental families were on welfare (these figures are the highest percentages for any quarter). Among experimental families, the percentage varied by plan, decreasing with plan generosity; ninth quarter figures show 23 percent on the 50-50 and 75-70 plans choosing welfare, compared with only 7 percent on the 125-50 plan. (These abbreviations for the plans are defined in Table 1.1.) It also varied by site, from 6 percent in Jersey City to 21 percent in Paterson-Passaic in the ninth quarter.

The general effect of welfare is to make the observed differences between experimental and control groups smaller than they would be in the absence of welfare. The underestimate occurs essentially because welfare may induce some withdrawal of work effort in the control group. On the other hand, the estimates derived from an experiment in the presence of welfare are perhaps more accurate estimates of the effect of a new national income maintenance program that is superimposed on existing programs.

A very careful analysis of the effects of welfare on the experiment is given in the full report.[1] This analysis suggests that the presence of welfare did not have a major effect on the estimated labor-supply differentials.

Taken as a group, these three arguments lead us to look for certain patterns in the experimental results. However, they do not modify substantially the overall expectations generated by the static theory because, for the household as a whole, they tend to be offsetting.

The Nonexperimental Literature

In the postwar period, there has been a substantial empirical literature on labor supply, and this literature was important in forming our initial expectations. The studies fall into three general groups—studies of hours of work, studies of labor-force participation, and studies concentrating on the effects of nonlabor income.

Hours of Work

The studies of hours of work have already been mentioned. It is these studies that lead us to expect some reduction in labor supply for the experimental group, because they suggest that the income effect as well as the substitution effect of a negative income tax will be to diminish the amount of work supplied.

It should be noted, however, that the studies of hours of work have not been confined to low-income workers. They suggest that at or near the mean wage, increases in wage rates are associated with decreases in hours worked, but this need not be true at wages well below the mean, when the desire for added consumer goods may be stronger and the desire for additional leisure weaker. Low-income workers may have a stronger desire to reach the average level of living of their communities than middle-income workers have to rise above it. Indeed, this is exactly what is shown by the usual textbook diagrams of the backward-bending supply curve of labor, which show a forward-rising curve at very low wages, becoming vertical and then bending back as some higher level of wages is reached. Unfortunately, there is no empirical basis for the forward sloping portion of the curve. Moreover, even if substitution effects are stronger than income effects at low wages, the total effect of a negative income tax will still be to reduce hours, since the tax-induced reduction in net wage rates will not produce an income loss, as would a wage cut with no income transfer. The unique feature of a negative income tax plan is that income is increased at the same time as the net wage rate is reduced.

Labor-Force Participation

The portion of the labor-force participation literature that is relevant deals with the differences in strength of attachment to the labor force by age, sex, and marital status. The studies of such attachment show very high rates of participation by married men with wife present, only weakly affected by differences in education or the strength of demand. For teenagers, the elderly, and married women, average rates of participation are much lower, and such forces as differences in education or in the strength of demand induce much larger differences in participation rates.

Because of the previous studies of participation rates, we never expected any substantial fraction of the male heads of households to withdraw from the labor force when they received payments. It seemed much more likely that the response of male heads would be shorter hours or longer periods of search between jobs. For wives, teenagers, and the elderly, however, reductions in labor-force participation rates seemed a much more likely outcome.

We were aware, of course, of the popular view that large transfer payments can cause widespread idleness. There are experiences that support such a view, such as the experience with unemployment benefits for returning veterans after World War II—payments that were sometimes called "rocking chair money." However, many of the veterans involved were single rather than household heads, and they lacked recent civilian work experience. Popular current views on the effect of welfare on work behavior are similarly based largely on experience other than that of male household heads—in this case, mothers without husbands—and, even here, they tend to be based on anecdotal information rather than on systematic evidence. If there were people who expected our experimental treatment to cause large declines in the participation rates of male heads, they were not in our research group.

Nonlabor Income

The last kind of research that is relevant consists of studies that have emphasized the effects of nonlabor income on labor supply. Several of them were designed explicitly to simulate from nonexperimental data the effects of a negative-income-tax program. Nevertheless, they were not influential in forming our expectations—in part, of course, because most of them have appeared since we began the experiment. The most striking thing about them is the very wide range of values of their results, and this lack of agreement weakens confidence in any of the findings.

First of all, these studies face a problem that may be insurmountable. Much of the nonlabor income reported in income surveys consists of transfer payments such as unemployment compensation; workmen's compensation; old age, survivors, and disability insurance; and temporary disability insurance. All of these payments except survivors insurance are totally or partially work conditioned—that is, they cannot legally be received by those who work, or by those who work or earn more than a stated amount. Work behavior determines whether nonlabor income is received and in what amount. If any of these types of work-conditioned transfers are included in the measure of nonlabor income used to simulate a negative income tax, the size of the negative effects on work effort will be overestimated, perhaps very greatly. There are, of course, types of nonlabor incomes that are not work conditioned—particularly dividends, interest, and certain types of pensions. However, the amount of dividend and interest income of the nonaged poor is negligible, and pensions tend to be received by those past prime working age. The nonlabor income of the working poor that is not work conditioned is hard to find in such existing data bases as the Census or the Survey of Economic Opportunity. Some investigators, searching for this needle in the haystack, seem to have seized in desperation at the handiest pitchfork instead. Even those who are clearly aware of the problem of work-conditioned transfers sometimes report amounts of nonlabor income (supposedly *not* work conditioned) that are so large as to call their definitions or procedures into question.

A second general difficulty with the simulation studies of negative income taxes is that they sometimes truncate their samples by current income, thus tending to include a disproportionate number of households that supply, perhaps temporarily, less than average amounts of labor—a selection which could bias the estimated coefficients toward large supply effects. Truncation on a measure such as hourly wages, which is uncorrelated or less highly correlated with the amount of labor currently supplied, would be far preferable. To be sure, the New Jersey–Pennsylvania sample is also truncated on family income, which may not have been the best variable to choose for this purpose. However, the problem is far less serious in a study that estimates labor-supply effects in a period subsequent to that used to select the sample and derives these estimates from a comparison of experimental and control groups where the experimental group receives an exogenous treatment.

It should also be pointed out that the nonexperimental studies estimate substitution effects from cross-sectional differences in average hourly earnings that may not be entirely independent of the effects of the amount of labor supplied. Those who work over 40 hours per week will receive premium pay for overtime; those who want to work only part time may have to accept lower hourly earnings. In an experiment, differential tax rates create a truly exogenous source of differences in net wages.

Despite these deficiencies, the studies that focus on the effects of nonlabor income reinforce the more general labor-supply studies in one important respect—they consistently find larger supply effects for women than for men; indeed, the estimated effects for men are sometimes very close to zero.

A SUMMARY OF EXPECTATIONS

The researchers involved in the experiment never agreed on and set down in advance a summary of what they felt was the most likely outcome for labor supply. In retrospect, this is unfortunate. Any attempt to do so now is bound to reflect to some extent our present knowledge of the results and thus to understate the degree to which we have been surprised. Despite this caveat, it still seems useful to attempt a summary in retrospect.

We never expected able-bodied male heads of households to withdraw from the labor force in response to temporary payments too small to support large families. We did expect some of them to reduce their hours of work, or to spend more time searching for new jobs when they lost or quit a job. We expected some teenagers to return to school or to stay in school longer as a result of the payments. We expected some working wives to leave the labor force to spend all their time in household work.

On the whole, the reduction in labor supply we expected to find in the experimental group was of the order of 10–15 percent. We did not expect to find any differential effects by ethnic group. However, we did expect to find that higher tax rates would produce greater reductions in labor supply, and so would higher guarantees.

HOW WE ANALYZE THE DATA

The results presented in the following pages are more complex and somewhat more ambiguous than we anticipated they would be, and they are not easy to summarize. In attempting to do so, we must explain why we regard some of the results as more salient than others. This, in turn, requires some brief discussion of our methods of analysis, which will deal with dependent variables, the control variables, the treatment variables, and the time period.

The Dependent Variables

There are at least four possible measures of the amount of labor supplied by the household: labor-force participation rates, employment rates, total hours of work, and total earnings. The total hours of work measure includes those not at work as supplying zero hours, and therefore the average level of this variable will be below the average weekly hours of those who are at work. With hours defined this way, the measures listed above are in order of increasing comprehensiveness. Employment includes changes in labor-force participation and in unemployment, which (as pointed out earlier) must be considered as a supply phenomenon in the context of differences between experimentals and controls. Hours includes variations in the two preceding variables and, in addition, variations in hours per week of those at work. Earnings reflects variations in all three preceding variables and, in addition, variation in earnings per hour worked.

It would therefore seem that earnings furnishes the best summary measure of the effects on labor supply. Unfortunately, however, there is a possible bias in the use of the earnings variable not present in the other measures. Experimental families filled out an income reporting form every four weeks; control families did not. The experimental families, therefore, may have learned more quickly than did the control families that what was to be furnished was gross rather than net earnings (that is, earnings before taxes and other deductions, *not* take-home pay). This differential learning process could have caused a spurious differential in earnings in favor of the experimental group, especially during the early part of the experiment.

The analysis of differences in hourly earnings between experimentals and controls supports the idea of this learning effect. For all three ethnic groups, reported average hourly earnings of male experimentals rise relative to those of controls early in the experimental period. For white and Spanish-speaking males, this differential is later reversed or disappears. For black males, it grows even larger toward the end of the experiment, a phenomenon that seems to result from an unusually small rise in hourly earnings in the black control group.

Because of the possible bias in the earnings measure, we shall emphasize the hours measure in summarizing the results. An exception is made in discussing the labor supply of the household as a *whole*, where the earnings measure, despite its defects, serves as an appropriate way of weighting the hours of different members of the household by the value of the labor they supply. It should also be recalled that family earnings are the basis on which payments were determined.

Control Variables

In measuring supply effects, a large set of control variables was typically entered on the right-hand side of the regression equations. In part these were necessary to control for differences between the experimental and control groups resulting from the fact that families were not assigned to these groups by simple random assignment, but by a more complex stratified design. In part their inclusion was in response to the fact that even in a simple random design, it is important to control for systematic differences that may survive the randomization process.

The control variables are used in two different ways. First, they are entered into the labor-supply equations as variables in their own right. Second, they are often interacted with the variables representing experimental treatments to see whether the treatment has differential effects in different subgroups of the treated population. A control variable that is highly significant in the first of these contexts may not be significant in the second.

One of the most important control variables is the preenrollment value of the dependent variable. Thus, if the dependent variable is hours, hours at preenrollment are usually entered on the right-hand side. This procedure captures the effect of many taste variables that cannot be specified individually, but will also reduce the significance of the control variables that are separately specified. It is worth noting that this kind of control variable cannot be used in a nonexperimental study based on a single body of cross-sectional data.

Some of these control variables, although they could have been expected to be very significant, in fact were not. Thus, after control for ethnicity, there was little systematic difference among experimental sites. On the other hand, health status and ethnicity turned out to be very important variables even when many other control variables were present. For this reason, most of the analyses that follow run separate regressions for the three ethnic groups (white, black, and Spanish-speaking) and control for health status.

It is also important to control for potential earned income, since average income levels are not the same in experimental and control groups as a result of the complexities of the design model, and since there may be differential responses at different income levels. The income variable used for this purpose should be free of any influence from the experimental treatment. For this purpose we have used estimates of normal hourly earnings, either based entirely on observations from the control group or derived by methods that isolate and abstract from treatment effects. Full descriptions of these normal wage variables follow.

Treatment Variables

In one sense, the experimental treatment in this experiment is very simple—it consists of giving families cash payments. These payments can be specified much more precisely than can the more amorphous treatments involved in experimental evaluation of counseling, training, or psychotherapy programs. In another sense, however, the treatment is complex. There were eight different payment plans, and within each plan there was variation in payments by family size. Table 1.1 shows the number of experimental families by payments plan.

In the design stages of the experiment, we all confidently expected significant overall effects of the treatment on labor supply, and attention was focused on measuring differential effects of the treatment plans. In retrospect, this emphasis may have been somewhat misplaced, since the overall treatment effect is not always unambiguous.

In general, two different methods of introducing treatment effects are used. The first is to include a dummy variable for any experimental treatment and two additional sets of variables that specify tax rates and guaran-

TABLE 1.2
Average Payments per Four-Week Period,
Continuous Husband-Wife Families by Site

	All Sites	Trenton	Paterson-Passaic	Jersey City	Scranton
First year	$91.03	$69.93	$79.43	$107.80	$91.46
Second year	93.25	71.91	80.67	109.86	94.72
Third year	96.84	58.67	84.92	120.35	98.26
Percentage change, first to third year	6.4%	−16.1%	6.9%	11.6%	5.2%
Percentage increase in guarantee amount due to CPI		11.7	16.6	16.6	10.5

tee levels.* The second method uses the experimental dummy and a variable measuring average payments levels. The payments reflect the guarantee level, the tax rate, family size, and earned income. To avoid introducing experimental response into the treatment variable, the preenrollment level of income is used in calculating payments. The payments calculation is useful in identifying families who are initially above the breakeven point of their plans, since, although they will be in the experimental group, they all will appear with zero payments.

In practice, two of our plans were dominated by New Jersey welfare during most of the period of the experiment, and attrition from these plans was very high. These were, of course, the two least generous plans—the 50 percent of poverty guarantee with a 50 percent tax rate (50–50 plan) and the 75 percent guarantee with a 70 percent tax rate (75–70 plan). In much of the analysis, these plans are omitted from the treatment group.

Before we discuss effects, it will be useful for the reader to have some idea of the size of the payments and their variation by plan. Table 1.2 gives, by experimental site, the average size of payments to continuous husband-wife families who received payments in a given four-week period for each of the three years of the experiment. The average payments per period can, of course, be converted to annual averages by multiplying by 13. Thus, the first-year annual average for all such families is $1,183. The average payments are slightly lower for all families than for continuous husband-wife families. We show the data for the latter here, since most of the labor-supply analysis is based on these families.

---

*Editor's note: In regression analysis and analysis of variance, dummy variables are constructed for nominal data. Usually scores 1 and 0 are arbitrarily assigned to each value. See, for example, Hubert M. Blalock, *Social Statistics*, 2nd ed., (New York: McGraw-Hill, 1972), pp. 498–502.

The data in Table 1.2 show a mildly rising trend through time, except in Trenton. This trend arises from two sources. First, guarantee levels were escalated annually during the course of the experiment according to the Consumer Price Index. The increase was based on July-to-July changes in the CPI and was implemented in all sites where payments were then being made in September 1969 (5.5 percent), October 1970 (5.9 percent), and September or October 1971 (4.4 percent). Because of differences in the timing of the experimental period in different cities, Trenton received the first two cost-of-living adjustments, cumulating to 11.7 percent; Paterson-Passaic and Jersey City received all three, cumulating to 16.6 percent; and Scranton received the last two, cumulating to 10.5 percent. In Paterson-Passaic and Jersey City, the third increase in guarantees was in effect for less than a full year before the end of payments; in Scranton it was in effect less than two months, and in Jersey City about seven months. The average increase in guarantee levels for the final experimental year in the two sites that received all three increments thus lies between 11.7 and 16.6 percent, closer to the former figure in Paterson-Passaic, and slightly closer to the latter in Jersey City. When these increases are compared with the increases in average payments shown in Table 1.2, it can be seen that in every case the increase in payments is less than the increase in guarantees—and by substantial amounts in all sites but Jersey City.

The second factor tending to produce increasing average payments over time is rising unemployment rates. A weighted average unemployment rate for the four sites rose from 4.4 percent in 1969 to 7.1 percent in 1971, a factor that would also tend to produce rising payments as members of the experimental families who lost jobs experienced greater difficulty finding new ones.

In light of the increases in guarantees and the rise in unemployment, the smallness of the rise in average payments over the life of the experiment suggests that there was not an increasing withdrawal of labor supply or any growing falsification of income reports as experimental subjects

TABLE 1.3
Average Payments per Four-Week Period,
Continuous Husband-Wife Families by Ethnic Group

	All	White	Black	Spanish-speaking
First year	$91.03	$87.65	$ 97.65	$ 86.96
Second year	93.25	91.03	96.59	92.23
Third year	96.84	90.11	102.83	100.32
Percentage increase, first to third year	6.4%	2.8%	5.3%	15.4%

TABLE 1.4
Average Payments in Dollars per Four-Week Period,
Continuous Husband-Wife Families by Plan
(Second Experiment Year)

Guarantee Level (Percent)	Tax Rate (Percent)		
	30	50	70
125	No plan	187.28	No plan
100	No plan	123.72	66.07
75	103.54	44.17	34.91
50	46.23	21.66	No plan

learned to "beat the system." Either of these kinds of behavior would have produced more rapidly rising payments.

Table 1.3 on page 55 gives, by ethnic group, the same kind of data as Table 1.2. The average payments rise most rapidly for Spanish-speaking families. Since these payments rise more than those for all ethnic groups in any one site, something more than the distribution of ethnic groups by site must be at work.

Table 1.4 shows the average payments to continuous husband-wife families by experimental plan for the second experimental year. These payments vary from $187 per four-week period in the most generous plan to $22 in the least generous. In addition, of course, there is substantial variation within plans because of differences in family size and earned income.

Changes in payments from the first to the third year also vary by plan, as shown in Table 1.5. In the three plans with a guarantee equal to or above the poverty line, payments increase between 9 and 14 percent. The low guarantee plans vary more, but three of the five show decreases in payments. The decreases include both the plans with the lowest (30 percent) tax rate.

TABLE 1.5
Percentage Change in Average Payments per Period by Plan,
First to Third Year, Continuous Husband-Wife Families

Guarantee Level (Percent)	Tax Rate (Percent)		
	30	50	70
125	No plan	8.9	No plan
100	No plan	9.1	13.9
75	−4.5	−10.3	15.1
50	−2.6	3.2	No plan

Experimental Time

We had expected, before the experiment began, that the best results from the experiment would be obtained during the middle part of the experimental period. At the outset, participants might still be learning how to report income and how their payments would vary with changes in income. Toward the end of the experiment, anticipation of the termination of payments might also affect labor supply, producing unknown kinds of "end game" effects. When results are presented separately by years, results for the middle year generally should be the most reliable. Often we use the central two years—that is, quarters 3 through 10; for some purposes we average observations over the entire period.

It also should be recalled that experimental time does not have the same meaning in each site in terms of calendar time, because each site entered and left the experiment at a different date. To control for trends in the economy, calendar time is sometimes entered into the analysis in addition to experimental time.

WHAT WE FOUND

A succinct sumary of the findings is presented in Tables 1.6 to 1.8, which show a regression-estimated mean difference in several measures of labor supply for a selected subset of the sample observations—namely, 693 husband-wife families who met criteria for continuous reporting. This subset of families is selected because they are a relatively homogeneous group representing the model family type among the working poor, for whom the analysis is not complicated by the problems of changes in family composition and missing data. Negative differentials, both absolute and percentage, indicate smaller labor supply on the part of the experimental families compared with control families. Within each table, results are reported separately for each ethnic group. It should be noted that these groups showed important differences in responses.

Male Heads

As brought out in Table 1.6, the differences in work behavior between experimentals and controls for male heads of continuous husband-wife families were, as we expected, very small. Contrary to our expectations, all do not show a clear and significant pattern; indeed, they show a discernible pattern only after a great deal of refined analysis. Experimentals show a slightly higher participation rate than controls, a lower employment rate,

TABLE 1.6

**Husband Totals: Regression Estimates of Differentials in
Labor-Force Participation, Employment, Hours, and Earnings
for Quarters 3–10[a]**

	Labor-Force Participation Rate	Employment Rate	Hours Worked Per Week	Earnings Per Week
White				
Control group mean	94.3	87.8	34.8	100.4
Absolute differential	−.3	−2.3	−1.9	.1
Treatment group mean	94.0	85.5	32.9	100.5
Percent differential	−.3	−2.6	−5.6	.1
Black				
Control group mean	95.6	85.6	31.9	93.4
Absolute differential	0	.8	.7	8.7
Treatment group mean	95.6	86.4	32.6	102.1
Percent differential	0	.9	2.3	9.3
Spanish-speaking				
Control group mean	95.2	89.5	34.3	92.2
Absolute differential	1.6	−2.4	−.2	5.9
Treatment group mean	96.8	87.1	34.1	98.1
Percent differential	1.6	−2.7	−.7	6.4

[a]The data for these tables consist of 693 husband-wife families who reported for at least 8 of the 13 quarters when interviews were obtained. The reported differentials in each measure of labor supply are the experimental treatment group mean minus the control group mean, as measured in a regression equation in which the following variables were controlled: age of husband, education of husband, number of adults, number of children, sites, preexperiment labor-supply variables of the husband. These means and the associated control-treatment differentials may therefore be interpreted as applicable to control and treatment groups with identical composition in terms of these variables. Percent differentials are computed using the mean of the control as base.

Official government labor-force concepts, used in the experiment, define someone as in the labor force if he is employed or unemployed. Someone is unemployed if he is actively seeking employment, waiting recall from layoff, or waiting to report to a new wage or salary job.

This and the following two tables appear as Tables 1, 2, and 3 in U.S. Department of Health, Education, and Welfare, *Summary Report: The New Jersey Graduated Work Incentive Experiment,* a Social Experiment in Negative Taxation sponsored by the Office of Economic Opportunity (December 1973), pp. 22–27.

and a correspondingly higher unemployment rate. The unemployment rate difference carries over into hours worked per week. However, on the two measures of earnings, experimentals do better than controls—a result that may reflect greater misreporting of earnings by controls. As a generalization, these differences are all quantitatively small and not statistically significant.

By far the most surprising result of the analysis for male heads is the complete failure to find any significant effect for black male heads in any of the analyses, despite the fact that black husband-wife families received larger average payments than did similar families in the other two ethnic groups. Indeed, the estimated supply response for blacks is not only insignificant, but preponderantly positive. This kind of finding for blacks is not limited to male heads; it recurs in the analysis of other components of the household.

We certainly did not anticipate this outcome; moreover, we have no plausible explanation for it after the fact. There is some indication in the earnings data that something peculiar happened to the black control group, but we don't know why. While there is always some possibility that the result arises from sampling variability, we should note that black continuous husband-wife families comprise more than a third of the total and are a larger group than the Spanish-speaking, for whom consistent and negative supply effects were found.

Married Women, Husband Present

One of the first things to note about the labor supply of wives is that the participation rates are very low—around 16 percent, which is less than half the 1971 rates of all married women in the U.S. population as a whole. This rate is low in part because the average family size in the experiment is very large, and we overrepresent families with small children. In part it is an unfortunate consequence of the decision to truncate the sample by family income, a decision that leads to an underrepresentation of working wives even among large families. In retrospect it might have been preferable to truncate on the basis of husband's income or, better still, husband's wage rate. The same decision probably accounts in part for the rather sharp rise in participation rates of control wives over time, since at the outset we overrepresent families where the wife is temporarily out of the labor force.

The effect of the treatment is shown in Table 1.7 for the three ethnic groups separately. The measured work disincentives are seen to arise mainly from the behavior of white wives; the effects of the treatment on the labor-supply variables of black wives are close to zero and sometimes positive, and the effects on Spanish-speaking wives are negative in Table 1.7 but statistically insignificant.

The results thus indicate that a temporary negative-income-tax program would cause a substantial percentage reduction in the proportion of working wives in large low-income families, at least among white wives. How such a result is evaluated in terms of social priorities will depend on one's

TABLE 1.7
Wife Totals: Regression Estimates of Differentials in
Labor-Force Participation, Employment, Hours, and Earnings
for Quarters 3–10[a]

	Labor-Force Participation Rate	Employment Rate	Hours Worked Per Week	Earnings Per Week
White				
Control group mean	20.1	17.1	4.5	9.3
Absolute differential	−6.7*	−5.9*	−1.4	−3.1
Treatment group mean	13.4	11.2	3.1	6.2
Percent differential	−33.2	−34.7	−30.6	−33.2
Black				
Control group mean	21.1	16.8	5.0	10.6
Absolute differential	−.8	−.3	−.1	.8
Treatment group mean	20.3	16.5	4.9	11.4
Percent differential	−3.6	−1.5	−2.2	7.8
Spanish-speaking				
Control group mean	11.8	10.7	3.4	7.4
Absolute differential	−3.8	−5.2	−1.9	−4.1
Treatment group mean	8.0	5.5	1.5	3.3
Percent differential	−31.8	−48.3	−55.4	−54.7

*Significant at the .95 level (two-tailed test).
[a]The data for these tables consist of 693 husband-wife families who reported for at least 8 of the 13 quarters when interviews were obtained. The reported differentials in each measure of labor supply are the experimental group mean minus the control group mean, as measured in a regression equation in which the following variables were controlled: age of wife, number of adults, number and ages of children, sites, preexperiment family earnings (other than wife's), and preexperiment labor-supply variables of the wife. These means and the associated control-treatment differentials may therefore be interpreted as applicable to control and treatment groups with identical composition in terms of these variables. Percent differentials are computed using the mean of the control as base.

See footnote a of Table 1.6 for the definition of labor-force participation.

views about the value of having mothers care for their own children. It should be remembered that these estimated effects are probably larger than those to be expected in an otherwise similar permanent income-maintenance program. For the control families, no more than 19 percent of wives were in the labor force in any one quarter, but 41 percent were in the labor force in at least one of the 13 quarters (counting preenrollment). In other words this is a group that enters and leaves the labor force frequently. The experimental treatment creates a strong incentive to concentrate periods out of the labor force during the life of the experiment. A permanent program, therefore, could be expected to have a somewhat smaller impact.

A summary of the results is shown in Table 1.8, which applies to the family as a whole, including male heads, wives, and all other members of

TABLE 1.8
Family Totals: Regression Estimates of Differentials in Labor-Force Participation, Employment, Hours, and Earnings for Quarters 3–10[a]

	Number in Labor Force Per Family	Number Employed Per Family	Hours Worked Per Week	Earnings Per Week	Percent of Adults in the Labor Force Per Family	Percent of Adults Employed Per Family
White						
Control group mean	1.49	1.30	46.2	124.0	57.6	51.1
Absolute differential	-.15*	-.18*	-6.2*	-10.1	-5.3*	-6.1*
Treatment group mean	1.34	1.12	40.0	113.9	52.3	45.0
Percent differential	-9.8	-13.9	-13.4	-8.1	-9.1	-12.0
Black						
Control group mean	1.38	1.17	41.7	114.0	54.3	46.9
Absolute differential	-.07	-.07	-2.2	4.1	-1.6	-1.6
Treatment group mean	1.31	1.10	39.5	118.1	52.7	45.3
Percent differential	-5.4	-6.1	-5.2	3.6	-2.9	-3.3
Spanish-speaking						
Control group mean	1.15	1.04	39.0	102.4	48.9	44.7
Absolute differential	.08	-.02	-.4	5.0	2.4	-1.0
Treatment group mean	1.23	1.02	38.6	107.4	51.3	43.7
Percent differential	6.7	-1.5	-.9	4.9	5.0	-2.2

[a]The data for these tables consist of 693 husband-wife families who reported for at least 8 of the 13 quarters when interviews were obtained. The reported differentials in each measure of labor supply are the experimental treatment group mean minus the control group mean, as measured in a regression equation in which the following variables were controlled: age of husband, education of husband, education of wife, number of adults, number and ages of children, sites, and preexperiment labor-supply variables for the husband and wife. These means and associated control-experimental differentials may therefore be interpreted as applicable to control and experimental groups with identical composition in terms of these variables. Percent differentials are computed using the mean of the control as base.

See footnote a of Table 1.6 for the definition of labor-force participation.
*Significant at the .99 level (two-tailed test).

the household sixteen years of age and over. The sample is still restricted to continuous husband-wife families. The hours and earnings effects for whites are consistently negative and range from 8 to 16 percent. For blacks, the earnings effects of the experimental treatment are large and positive. The hours effects are small and differ in sign. For Spanish-speaking families, all estimates are negative.

The results for the family as a whole for whites are thus consistent with those from the separate analyses of male heads and wives in showing appreciable and significant negative effects on labor supply. For blacks, the results again show predominantly anomalous positive responses, though not consistently so for hours. For Spanish-speaking families, the effects are negative, though they are generally smaller and less significant than those for whites.

CONCLUSIONS

In general, the estimated effects of the experimental treatment on labor supply are in accord with our expectations. The major surprise is the absence of any negative effect on the labor supply of black households. For white and Spanish-speaking families, and for the group as a whole, the effects are negative, usually significant, but not very large. They consist of a reduction in hours of white male heads, an increase in the unemployment rate of Spanish-speaking male heads, and a large relative reduction in the labor-force participation rate of white wives.

If one calculates the cost of a negative income tax program on the assumption of no supply response, then these results strongly suggest that the estimated cost will be too low. However, the added cost produced by the supply response is a rather small portion of the total cost—not over 10 percent and probably closer to 5 percent. The estimates suggest that a substantial part of this will, in effect, represent added benefits for mothers whose withdrawal from paid employment is likely to be offset by increased "employment" at home. There is a further suggestion that tax rates higher than 50 percent may lead to a more pronounced supply response and, consequently, a larger increment to total cost. Whatever the percentage change in income, a higher tax rate requires that more of that change will be made up in benefits.

If the results we found by ethnic group were applied to the national low-income urban population using national ethnic weights, then the importance of our results for whites would rise and the importance of the results for the Spanish-speaking would fall. It is not at all clear that results for Puerto Ricans in New Jersey say anything at all about Mexican-Americans in the Southwest.

We place less weight on our results for blacks for a different reason. They are strange results that appear to arise from the unusual behavior of the black control group, whose labor supply and especially earnings fell relative to other control groups for reasons we do not understand. That the experimental treatment effects for blacks are often statistically significant is no assurance that they are not biased.

The patterns of labor-supply response that we have found are not as clear as we had expected. Yet, in many ways they are clearer and more sensible than the results of much of the nonexperimental literature. Certainly, they call into serious question the very large effects estimated in some of the nonexperimental studies. The burden of proof would now appear to be on those who assert that income-maintenance programs for intact families will have very large effects on labor supply. Considering how little had been done in the experimental testing of economic policies when we began, we do not find our results disappointing.

NOTE

1. Irwin Garfinkel, "The Effects of Welfare on Experimental Response," in *Final Report of the Graduated Work Incentive Experiment in New Jersey and Pennsylvania*, Ch. C-II (Madison: Institute for Research on Poverty, University of Wisconsin, 1973).

Chapter 2

HUMAN RESOURCES DEVELOPMENT

The nation's unemployment rate is one of the more significant single indicators of its economic and social well-being. As President John F. Kennedy observed:

> These [labor] statistics are of vital importance as measures of the economic health and well-being of the nation. They serve as guides to public policy in the development of measures designed to strengthen the economy, to improve programs to reemploy the unemployed, and to provide assistance to those who remained unemployed.[1]

Although there was no general tendency for structural unemployment to worsen after World War II, several sectors of the work force have experienced sharply higher unemployment rates. These include teenagers; the inexperienced unemployed; and, during the 1950s, blacks. In the late 1960s and the early 1970s, the rates of unemployment rose markedly, reaching 8.9 percent in September 1974. Because of the current performance of the economy, the prospects for relatively high unemployment in the 1980s are far from unrealistic. Furthermore, the risk of accelerating inflation if the unemployment rate falls too low presents a new, complicating consideration in economic policymaking. In fact given the present federal deficit, the Carter Administration is not only less willing to spend large sums for job-creating programs, but it has reduced its commitment to previously established programs.

Before the 1960s the federal government hardly had an explicit manpower policy. Only limited funds were spent to remove imperfections in the labor market and to provide remedial services for poor persons and disadvantaged ethnic and racial minorities. The Department of Health, Education, and Welfare provided limited training for the physically handicapped and some occupational training in public schools. The Department of Labor funded the U.S. Employment Service, which provided job-placement services at the state and local levels, and the Bureau of Apprenticeship and Training, which offered services to aid entry into skilled-craft occupations.

During the 1960s federal manpower programs underwent enormous expansion. Many new programs and projects were initiated to provide training for the technologically displaced; public employment for youth, the aged, and those on welfare; subsidies to private employers to hire, train, and employ disadvantaged persons; residential vocational education for teenagers, and basic education for adults. Two major pieces of legislation sought to define the role of the federal government in human-resources development. As was pointed out in the *1969 Manpower Report to the President,* the "passage of the Manpower Development and Training Act in 1962 (MDTA) was the chief legislative step toward formulation of a national manpower policy."[2] Initially, MDTA concentrated on retraining within an institutional or classroom setting those individuals whose skills had become nonmarketable as a result of automation. In 1966 a redirection of the MDTA program shifted the focus to the hard-core unemployed; about 65 percent of the entire training efforts were directed toward this group.

The Economic Opportunity Act of 1964 was the second piece of legislation that moved the federal government toward an active manpower policy. This omnibus act included a significant amount of manpower activity targeted at reaching the poor and the ethnic and racial minority groups. The Job Corps and Neighborhood Youth Corps (NYC) were created as part of the act in order to prepare youths, aged sixteen through twenty-one,

> for the responsibility of citizenship and to increase [their] employability by providing them in rural and urban residential centers with education, vocational education, useful work directed toward conservation of natural resources, and other appropriate activities.[3]

In response to the economic recession, the concept of Public Service Employment (PSE) was adopted in 1971 when Congress passed the Emergency Employment Act. This involved federal grant-in-aid funds to localities for the purpose of adding workers to the public payrolls. By the end of the 1960s, there were some seventeen programs, each with its own legislative and organizational base, funding source, and regulations. Out of these flowed more than 10,000 specific man-power projects, many of which competed with each other for clientele and resources.

The Comprehensive Employment and Training Act of 1973 (CETA) emerged from the perceived need for assimilation of the numerous and diverse manpower programs. The legislative intent of CETA was to make local authorities more effective in developing programs to meet local needs. The act transferred control of Department of Labor manpower programs to state and local officials. Thus, under Title I, cities and counties with a population of 10,000 or more receive federal funds to develop and implement the types of programs that they find most appropriate for their needs. Title II provides funds to hire unem-ployed persons in public-service jobs in areas of substantial unemploy-ment. Title III provides for direct federal supervision of manpower pro-grams for minority, older workers, and other disadvantaged groups. Title IV continues the Job Corps, and Title V establishes a National Manpower Commission.

The first article in this chapter is a nationwide evaluation of the func-tion of the NYC projects. NYC, like many other public programs, has more than one objective. In this case it is not only a job-creation pro-gram but also a dropout-prevention effort as well. It has enrolled more than 4 million youths, ages sixteen to twenty-one, in its various proj-ects. The evaluation design is quasi-experimental, and the data analy-sis is performed by the use of structural equations. The authors also estimate the costs and benefits of the program and compare them to the participants' perceptions. Especially noteworthy is the fact that un-like many other evaluations, this study makes use of three distinct types of data—government records, a field questionnaire, and school records. In this way the validity of the results and their generalizability are enhanced.

The second article is among the first attempts to provide a system-atic evaluation of the CETA-Title VI that was implemented in 1977 in Wisconsin. Ronald Hedlund and Chava Nachmias examine the imple-mentation process, as well as the impact of the program on its partici-pants. The evaluation has two objectives: to assess the extent to which program participants were those in greatest need of manpower services and to analyze the impact of Title VI on work orientations. Employing a panel design, the authors selected a random sample of CETA participants, who were interviewed as soon as they entered the program and upon completion. Data provided by the Wisconsin Job Service and the project directors were used to supplement the infor-mation obtained during the interviews. The findings indicate that participants traditionally defined as "disadvantaged" experience positive benefits from their CETA experience, while those who are affected by cyclical unemployment of more temporary nature experience negative or no benefits.

NOTES

1. President's Committee to Appraise Employment and Unemployment Statistics, *Measuring Employment and Unemployment* (Washington, D.C.: Government Printing Office, 1962) p. 1.
2. *Manpower Report of the President, 1969*, Department of Labor (Washington, D.C.: U.S. Government Printing Office, 1969) p. 3.
3. Economic Opportunity Act of 1964, 78 Stat. 508, Title II, Sec. 201(a).

A COST-EFFECTIVENESS ANALYSIS OF IN-SCHOOL AND SUMMER NEIGHBORHOOD YOUTH CORPS: A NATIONWIDE EVALUATION

Gerald G. Somers
Ernst W. Stromsdorfer

INTRODUCTION

The in-school and summer Neighborhood Youth Corps is designed to further the educational attainment and improve the performance of new entrants to the labor force. Its primary operational objective is to increase the high school graduation rate of students who are potential dropouts because of economic reasons. The program attempts to achieve this objective by providing paid work experience to high school students in their schools or in governmental or private employment. The premise underlying this activity is that increased earnings and family income will lead to increased school attendance by covering the opportunity costs of staying in high school. The work experience is also intended to impart labor-market discipline and other skills associated with successful job performance once the student leaves high school and, thereby, to enhance the primary benefit of increased schooling.

This article seeks to evaluate the extent to which the in-school and summer NYC has succeeded in achieving the objectives legislated for it by Congress. This evaluation is conducted by the use of multiple-regression techniques and cost-effectiveness analysis to investigate the costs and benefits of the program. Costs and benefits are estimated in private terms, for society, and for the federal government. The data for measurement of costs and benefits are gained from government records, a field questionnaire, and a school-record data sheet.[1]

STUDY DESIGN

The analysis is based on a sample of 60 in-school and summer NYC projects randomly chosen from the nationwide population of 1,120 projects which operated in fiscal years 1965–66 and 1966–67 inclusively. These were selected equally among three geographic strata—20 each from the North, South, and West.[2] The projects were chosen with probability of selection proportional to size of project. However, the unit of analysis is the NYC participant and not the NYC project; the focus is on the experience of the 334,000 young persons who were enrolled in the NYC one day or longer during this time. The intent of the sampling procedure was to randomly select 10 NYC participants and 10 comparison persons from each of the 60 projects. Thus, the total sample size would be 1,200 observations. In fact, due to nonresponse as well as incomplete field interviews, the analysis of schooling benefits is based on 780 observations (442 NYCs and 338 comparison persons), while the analysis of labor-market benefits is based on 676 observations (338 NYCs and 288 comparison persons).

The comparison group was randomly selected from the same high school as the NYC group and conformed to the age and family-income restrictions established for entry into the program. The NYC group and the comparison group conform closely on a number of sociodemographic characteristics, as shown in Table 2.1. However, as in most retrospective evaluations which do not use a pure experimental-control group design, program effects are measured relative to a "comparison" group rather than a "control" group as this term is understood in a strict experimental model.

In an effort to increase the comparability between the NYC and the comparison groups, a discriminant function was estimated and incorporat-

TABLE 2.1
Characteristics of NYC and Comparison Samples, Unweighted
High School Sample of Graduates and Dropouts

Variable	NYC $n = 436$	Comparison $n = 344$	Total $n = 780$
Probability of graduation	86.47%	82.30%	84.62%
Total school grades completed	11.8	11.7	11.7
	(6.0)	(6.9)	(6.4)
Age in years	19.94	19.99	19.96
	(0.98)	(1.23)	(1.09)
Income per capita per family	659	661	660
	(355)	(249)	(312)
Farm residence	6.65%	9.59%	7.95%
Father's education	8.63	9.01	8.80
	(3.44)	(5.06)	(4.24)
Number of times respondent	0.165	0.212	0.186
dropped out of high school	(0.372)	(0.409)	(0.389)
Sex			
Male	43.35%	44.77%	43.97%
Female	56.65%	55.23%	56.03%
Ethnic origin			
White	56.42%	59.01%	57.56%
Negro	24.77%	25.87%	25.26%
American Indian	8.03%	4.94%	6.67%
Mexican American	9.40%	9.59%	9.49%
Puerto Rican	0.688%	0.0	0.385%

Note: Values in parentheses are the standard deviations of the respective means.

ed in the regression equations used to measure program benefits. The discriminant function is a probability function which estimates the likelihood that a person would be in the NYC, based on sociodemographic, psychological, and motivational characteristics. While it does not completely control for self-selection bias into the program, it is a partial adjustment for such possible bias.[3]

RESULTS OF ANALYSIS

Costs

Private, social, and governmental costs to the program were measured. Both average and marginal costs were estimated.

Cost data from government records break total financial costs into a local sponsor share and a federal share. Due to problems of price imputation

TABLE 2.2
Cost Analysis of the In-School
and Summer Neighborhood Youth Corps

Cost Concept[a]	Average Cost	Marginal Cost[d]
Social:[b]	(in dollars)	
In-school and summer enrollment combined	402	475
In-school enrollment only	492	495
Summer enrollment only	184	189
Federal government:		
In-school and summer enrollment combined	313	409
In-school enrollment only	368	422
Summer enrollment only	102	184
Private:[c]		
In-school and summer enrollment combined	834	
In-school enrollment only	741	
Summer enrollment only	701	

[a]These are marginal and average costs per participant for those participants who stayed in the program one day or longer.

[b]Social costs are here defined as sponsor share plus federal share. As indicated in the text, however, federal share alone is undoubtedly a more accurate measure of the commitment of social resources to the program. The direct transportation and mean costs incurred as a result of program participation are omitted in the social and federal government estimates.

[c]These costs include forgone earnings and the direct costs of holding the NYC job. The forgone earnings are expressed in terms of after-tax earnings. Direct costs of holding the NYC job are estimated from Leonard H. Goodman and Thelma D. Myint, *The Economic Needs of Neighborhood Youth Corps Enrollees* (Washington: Bureau of Social Science Research, Inc., August 1969). Private marginal costs were assumed to equal average costs in the study. Private costs are higher than social costs because those NYC participants which were interviewed stayed in the program a longer average period of time than the population of participants as a whole.

[d]Marginal costs are estimated from a cubic total cost function which has the following general form:

$$Y_{1i}X_{1i}^{1/2} = a_1 X_{1i}^{1/2} + a_2 X_{2i}X_{1i}^{1/2} + a_3 X_{3i}X_{1i}^{1/2} + a_4 X_{3i}^2 X_{1i}^{1/2} + a_5 X_{3i}^3 X_{1i}^{1/2}$$
$$+ a_6 X_{4i}X_{1i}^{1/2} + a_7 X_{4i}^2 X_{1i}^{1/2} + U_{1i}$$

where Y_{1i} = total costs for the time period in the project, in hundreds of dollars, by project; X_{1i} = weight factor, the normalized value of the inverse of the probability of project selection, by project; X_{2i} = length of project, in months; X_{3i} = total in-school and/or summer enrollment, by project; X_{4i} = total out-of-school enrollment, by project; and U_{1i} = a random disturbance.

and the existence of excess capacity and joint cost problems at the sponsor site, the federal financial share, taken alone, was considered to be a better measure of social economic costs (actual resources devoted to the program by society) than the sum of the sponsor share and the federal share. However, federal costs overestimate social economic costs due to the element of subsidy paid to the participants. It should be noted that from a private-cost standpoint, wages to the NYC participant represent both a benefit and an opportunity cost of foregone leisure, study time, and home production. Table 2.2 displays the estimates of cost. The data in this table are largely self-explanatory. Marginal costs are generally higher than average costs, though the difference is sometimes very small and not statistically significant. Private average costs are about twice as high as social average costs due to the fact that the typical NYC participant who was interviewed stayed in the program for a longer period of time than the average NYC participant in the population as a whole. Since private benefits are based on the same sample as that from which private costs are estimated, there is no necessary bias *within* this cost-benefit comparison. But if greater benefits are associated with a longer stay in the program, which appears to be the case, then there is likely to be an upward bias in the estimate of social benefits.

Labor-Market Benefits

As with costs, private, social, and governmental labor-market benefits are estimated by means of multivariate-regression analysis. Marginal and average benefits are estimated. In addition to measuring the influence of participation in the NYC program, the benefit equations adjust for the intervening influence of age, year and quarter when a respondent ultimately left high school, employment experience during high school, marital status, father's education, labor-market area, sex, ethnic origin, and the discriminant function.

The indexes of benefit are average monthly earnings, months of unemployment, and months of voluntary labor-force withdrawal. Before-tax earnings are an explicit measure of social monetary benefits. After-tax earnings are private monetary benefits. Months unemployed are a measure of the employment effect of the program. The labor force participation variable, in this case the months of voluntary labor force withdrawal, is a measure of the degree to which NYC participation encouraged entry into the labor force. Finally, the increase in federal income taxes and social security taxes is considered a benefit to the federal government. Table 2.3 displays the estimated labor-market benefits.

The average NYC participant earned a total of $831 more than his comparison-group counterpart in the year and a half average period after the NYC participant left the program. This amounts to about $46 more per month over the 18.56 month period.

Total private after-tax earnings were $702 for the total sample in this 18.56 month period. There was no net increase in federal government tax benefits due to the NYC program. There was no net difference in the num-

TABLE 2.3

**Analysis of Labor Market Benefits of NYC Participants
Compared with Nonparticipants in the Period
since Final Departure from High School[c]**

Sample Groups	Average Months Available to be in Civ. Labor Force	Total Before-Tax Earnings in Dollars	Total After-Tax Earnings in Dollars	Total Federal Income & Soc. Sec. Taxes in Dollars	Months Unemployed	Months Voluntarily Out of Labor Force
Total	18.56	831*[a]	702*	109	.42	−2.30
n = 676	(21.04)	(346)	(283)	(71)	(.61)	(.98)
Male	14.51	1,171*	876	−129	.79+	−1.02
n = 311	(15.02)	(633)	(509)	(104)	(.44)	(1.21)
Female	22.01	466	423	53	3.11**	−5.12**
n = 365	(24.55)	(368)	(313)	(91)	(1.04)	(1.37)
White	20.36	1,013*	794*	124	−.10	−3.06
n = 398	(19.93)	(477)	(387)	(100)	(.58)	(1.20)
Negro	13.22	1,579**	1,186**	286**	−3.09**	−2.23
n = 166	(13.73)	(542)	(477)	(102)	(.72)	(1.50)
White male	16.28	1,078	445	231	−.44	−1.12
n = 202	(14.79)	(805)	(190)	(152)	(.50)	(1.44)
Negro male	11.39	1,182+	1,094+	271[b]	−6.89**	−.18
n = 57	(12.84)	(686)	(630)	(165)	(1.47)	(2.58)
White female	24.56	382	422	59	1.29	−4.56*
n = 196	(23.41)	(517)	(438)	(141)	(1.08)	(1.78)
Negro female	14.17	1,217+	760	255*	−2.00*	−3.11
n = 109	(14.13)	(681)	(557)	(127)	(.81)	(1.93)

Note: + = significant at the .10 level; * = significant at the .05 level; ** = significant at the
.01 level. All significance tests are two-tailed tests.

[a]These statistics are the partial regression coefficient and the standard error of the partial regression coefficient. They are interpreted as follows: For the total sample, the NYC participants earned $831 more in the 18.56 months after they left the NYC than did their coun-
terparts in the comparison group. The difference is significant at the .05 level. That is, the
chances are only 1 in 20 that the actual difference between the two groups is zero. The
NYC group paid $109 more in federal income and social security taxes in the 18.56
months after they left the NYC than did their comparison group counterparts, but the difference is actually not statistically significant from zero due to the large relative size
(109/71) of the standard deviation.

[b]Significant at the .109 level.

[c]The weighted regression model for estimating social benefits has the following form:

$$W_{1i}X_{1i}^{1/2} = a_1 X_{1i}^{1/2} + a_2 X_{2i}X_{1i}^{1/2} + a_3 X_{3i}X_{1i}^{1/2} + a_4 X_{3i}^2 X_{1i}^{1/2} + a_5 X_{4i}X_{1i}^{1/2}$$
$$+ a_6 X_{5i}X_{1i}^{1/2} + a_7 X_{6i}X_{1i}^{1/2} + a_8 X_{7i}X_{1i}^{1/2} + a_9 X_{8i}X_{1i}^{1/2} + a_{10} X_{9i}X_{1i}^{1/2}$$
$$+ a_{11} X_{10i}X_{1i}^{1/2} + a_{12} X_{11i}X_{1i}^{1/2} + a_{13} X_{12i}X_{1i}^{1/2} + a_{14} X_{13i}X_{1i}^{1/2} + a_{15} X_{14i}X_{1i}^{1/2}$$
$$+ a_{16} X_{15i}X_{1i}^{1/2} + a_{17} X_{16i}X_{1i}^{1/2} + a_{18} X_{17i}X_{1i}^{1/2} + U_{1i}$$

where W_1 = total post-high school before-tax earnings, in dollars; X_1 = the weight factor; X_2 = respondent status—1 = NYC participant, O otherwise; X_3 = age at time of interview, in years; X_4 = year and quarter when respondent ultimately left high school—01 = first quarter 1962, 02 = second quarter 1960, . . . , 39 = third quarter 1969; X_5 = employment experience during high school (other than NYC experience) or during an interim dropout period, in months; X_6 = marital status—1 = single, 0 otherwise; X_7 = marital status—1 = widowed, separated, or divorced, 0 otherwise; X_8 = father's education, in years of schooling completed; X_9 = labor market area—1 = metropolitan economic area, population of central city at least 50,000 but less than 500,000, 0 otherwise; X_{10} = labor market area—1 = rural functional economic area, independent regional area of less than 50,000 population, 0 otherwise; X_{11} = labor market area—1 = rural population density less than two persons per square mile, 0 otherwise; X_{12} = sex—1 = male, 0 = female; X_{13} = ethnic origin—1 = Negro, 0 otherwise; X_{14} = ethnic origin—1 = American Indian, 0 otherwise; X_{15} = ethnic origin—1 = Mexican American, 0 otherwise; X_{16} = ethnic origin—1 = Puerto Rican, 0 otherwise; X_{17} = discriminant function, in percentage; U_1 = an error term; and $a_1, a_2, . . . , a_n$ = parameters to be estimated, i.e., partial regression coefficients.

In addition, those equations for subgroups simply eliminate the entire set of regressors for those variables, such as sex or ethnic origin, which specify the subgroup in question. Thus, for the male subgroup, X_{12} is omitted, while for the Negro male subgroup, X_{12} and X_8 through X_{11} are omitted from the equation.

ber of months unemployed between the NYC and the comparison group; however, the NYC group had 2.30 months less voluntary labor force withdrawal. Thus, while the NYC program had not reduced the unemployment rate among its participants, it did increase the labor-force participation rate, which, in turn, resulted in a statistically significant increase in total earnings.[4] Table 2.3 shows that males benefited more than females in terms of earnings and Negroes benefited more than whites. Negro females benefited more than Negro males. Negroes were the only group which contributed to federal-government benefits, and, within this group, it was Negro females rather than males who made the contribution. There were insufficient data for an analysis of the American Indian and Mexican-American groups.

Table 2.4 shows the labor-market benefits of the NYC by program component. As can be seen, the participant who enrolled only as an in-school participant gained the largest social and federal government benefits. Those who enrolled in both an in-school and a summer program component gained the largest private benefits. The summer program yielded no direct monetary benefits. Continued support of the summer component may well be justified on other economic, social, and political grounds.

TABLE 2.4

Analysis of Labor-Market Benefits of NYC Participants by Program Component in the Period since Departure from High School

Program Component[a]	Total Before-Tax Earnings, in Dollars	Total After-Tax Earnings, in Dollars	Total Federal Income & Social Security Taxes, in Dollars
In-school only	908*[b]	609 +	164
n = 437	(422)	(348)	(96)
Summer only	547	448	71
n = 308	(492)	(403)	(85)
In-school and summer combined	784 +	650 +	64
n = 354	(475)	(391)	(86)

Note: + = significant at the .10 level; * = significant at the .05 level.

[a]In-school only = those participants who enrolled only as in-school NYC participants; summer only = those participants who enrolled as summer NYC participants; in-school and summer combined = those participants who enrolled both as in-school and summer participants.

[b]These statistics are the partial regression coefficient and its standard error in parentheses. See Table 2.3. See Table 37 in the final report for a more elaborate analysis of the effects of program components.

Educational Benefits

Although the post-high school, labor-market benefits of the program are large for the average NYC participant, educational benefits must also be evaluated since a major purpose of the NYC program is to increase school attendance and cut the dropout rate. Four measures of educational benefits were utilized: (1) the probability of high school graduation, (2) the number of years of high school completed, (3) the probability of college attendance, and (4) the probability of post-secondary education other than college. Multiple-regression models were used to measure the net impact of the NYC program on these indexes of benefit. In addition to NYC participation, the regression models control for the effect of age, income per capita per family, urban-rural place of residence during school, number of times the respondent dropped out of high school, father's education, ethnic origin, sex, and the discriminant function.

As Table 2.5 shows, the NYC program taken as a whole had a zero effect on the probability of high school graduation and years of high school completed. When subgroups were studied separately, only Negroes, Negro females, and American Indians experience a positive effect on their probability of graduation from high school. These results apply to regression models which express NYC participation in dummy-variable form. Use of a dummy-variable formulation means that every NYC participant had the same weight in the analysis regardless of whether he was in the program a long or a short period of time.

When NYC participation was expressed as a continuous variable in terms of number of months in the program, the NYC program was seen to have a small positive effect. Namely, one additional month stay in the NYC tends to add one extra day of school attendance.

However, the NYC program had a positive and relatively large effect on the probability of college attendance or other post-secondary education for those NYC participants who graduate from high school. The evidence suggests that the higher earnings due to participation in the NYC may have been partly responsible for enrollment in further education.

In summary, it appears that the income-educational premise upon which the NYC program is based may be an incorrect one. A gross positive relationship was found between income per capita per family and graduation from high school. However, when income per capita per family was considered in conjunction with other sociodemographic variables, in almost every case the effect of the income variable on high school graduation was zero or negative. Thus, for those persons still in high school, the family income variable may not be the most important variable affecting dropout behavior. Approaches other than raising family income may be needed to change the propensity of students to drop out.

However, once a person has graduated from high school, earnings per NYC participant do appear to be an influence on one's likelihood of acquiring some type of college or other post-secondary education.

Investment Analysis

The cost and labor-market earnings data were combined to evaluate the NYC program as a social and private investment. Based on the federal concept of social cost and a benefit period equal to the average length of time the NYC participant had available to participate in the civilian labor force, the social average rate of return was found to be 69.6 percent and the social marginal rate of return was 22.8 percent. Total social average benefits at a 10 percent discount rate were about $171,700,000 for the operation of the NYC program during fiscal years 1965–66 and 1966–67. Total social marginal benefits were about $35,700,000.[5] These are relatively high estimates. Thus, even if there were upward bias in the estimates of benefits or downward bias in the estimates of costs, the biases would have to be considered before net benefits would be reduced to unacceptably low levels from a social standpoint. It therefore appears that in monetary-economic terms, the in-school and summer NYC, taken as a composite, has been an efficient social investment. However, as noted above, the summer program alone yields no net monetary benefit.

TABLE 2.5
Analysis of Education Benefits of NYC Participation
by Sample Groups[d]

Sample Group[c] (Separate Regression Models)	Probability of High School Graduation	Years of High School Completed	Probability of Attending College	Probability of Attending Post-Secondary Education[b]
Total	−.0046[a]	−.04	.1255**	.0650+
n = 780	(.0152)	(.05)	(.0418)	(.1351)
Male	−.0586*	−.08	.1134+	.1529**
n = 343	(.0245)	(.06)	(.0644)	(.0562)
Female	−.0120	−.07	.0830	−.0143
n = 437	(.0177)	(.07)	(.5471)	(.0445)
White male	−.0064	.01	.0404	.0501*
n = 217	(.0238)	(.07)	(.0736)	(.0669)
Negro male	−.0045	.08	.0348	.1136
n = 63	(.0162)	(.15)	(.1458)	(.0996)
White female	−.0132	.18*	.1057	−.0075
n = 232	(.0245)	(.09)	(.0694)	(.0569)
Negro female	.1251**	.07	.1230	−.0611
n = 134	(.0414)	(.09)	(.1058)	(.0911)
White	−.0120	.10	.1036*	.0699
n = 449	(.0167)	(.06)	(.0504)	(.0431)
Negro	.0820**	.02	.0822	−.0302
n = 197	(.0293)	(.08)	(.0844)	(.685)
American Indian	.1464	−.76**	−.6169	−.2043
n = 52	(.0713)	(.23)	(.8689)	(.8576)
Mexican American	−.2121**	−.11	.4937**	.1469
n = 52	(.0626)	(.17)	(.1732)	(.1330)

Note: + = significant at the .10 level; * = significant at the .05 level; ** = significant at the .01 level.

[a]The statistics are the partial regression coefficient and its standard error. The regression coefficient is interpreted as a probability for the three dependent variables labeled "probability." The coefficient for years of high school completed is interpreted as a decimal fraction of a year. Multiplication of the probability by 100 converts it to a percent. Thus, for the total sample, the probability of high school graduation of the average NYC participant is .0046 less than that of his comparison group counterpart. However, the difference is not statistically significant from zero. The NYC participant attends, on the average, .04 of one school year less than his comparison counterpart. This is about eight days less (200 x .04). However, this difference is not statistically different from zero. Finally, the NYC participant is 12.55 more likely to attend some type of college, given that he graduates from high school, compared to his comparison group counterpart.

[b]These regressions apply to high school graduates only.

[c]The sample sizes in this column apply to the first two columns of estimates only. The numbers are slightly smaller for the last two columns.

[d]The weighted regression model for estimating educational benefits is as follows:

$$Z_{1i}X_{1i}^{\frac{1}{2}} = a_1 X_{1i}^{\frac{1}{2}} + a_2 X_{2i}X_{1i}^{\frac{1}{2}} + a_3 X_{3i}X_{1i}^{\frac{1}{2}} + a_4 X_{4i}X_{1i}^{\frac{1}{2}} + a_5 X_{5i}X_{1i}^{\frac{1}{2}}$$
$$+ a_6 X_{6i}X_{1i}^{\frac{1}{2}} + a_7 X_{7i}X_{1i}^{\frac{1}{2}} + a_8 X_{8i}X_{1i}^{\frac{1}{2}} + a_9 X_{9i}X_{1i} + a_{10}X_{10i}X_{1i}^{\frac{1}{2}}$$
$$+ a_{11}X_{11i}X_{1i}^{\frac{1}{2}} + a_{12}X_{12i}X_{1i}^{\frac{1}{2}} + a_{13}X_{13i}X_{1i}^{\frac{1}{2}} + U_{1i}$$

where Z_1 = probability of high school graduation—1 = graduation, 0 otherwise; X_1 = weight factor; X_2 = respondent status—1 = NYC participant, 0 = comparison group member; X_3 = age of respondent, in years, at time of interview; X_4 = income per capita per family during school attendance, in $10 units; X_5 = place of residence during school—1 = farm residence, 0 otherwise; X_6 = number of times the respondent had dropped out of high school prior to ultimately leaving high school; X_7 = father's education, in years of school completed; X_8 = ethnic origin—1 = Negro, 0 otherwise; X_9 = ethnic origin—1 = American Indian, 0 otherwise; X_{10} = ethnic origin—1 = Mexican American, 0 otherwise; X_{11} = ethnic origin—1 = Puerto Rican, 0 otherwise; X_{12} = sex—1 = male, 0 = female; X_{13} = discriminant function, in percentage points; U_1 = a random disturbance; $a_1, a_2, \ldots,$ a_n = parameters to be estimated.

In addition, those equations for subgroups simply eliminate the entire set of regressors for those variables, such as sex or ethnic origin, which specify the subgroup in question. Thus, for the male subgroup, X_{12} is omitted, while for the Negro male subgroup, X_{12} and X_8 through X_{11} are omitted.

Evaluation by NYC Participants

Regardless of the objective facts of their NYC work and their post-high school employment, the participants in the NYC programs evaluated their experience in the most enthusiastic terms. They were highly satisfied with the kind of work assigned to them in the NYC program, they were satisfied with their hourly wage rates, and they praised their supervisors.

Overwhelming majorities of the participants felt that their NYC participation would result in a better job in the future, and they were convinced that the program had improved their attitude toward education, toward work, and toward themselves.

Although there were interesting differences in some of these responses by region, type of program, sex, and ethnic origin, the similarities in the patterns of response were notable, and they added up to a very enthusiastic endorsement of the NYC program by those who had participated in it. These attitudes represent a form of program benefit, for they imply that the target population experienced an improvement in morale and a greater identification with social goals which might contribute to their own and to society's well-being in positive noneconomic ways.

IMPLICATIONS OF THE FINDINGS

Two basic methodological problems were encountered in this study, and these should be considered in evaluating the findings and conclusions. The first problem deals with possible bias caused by self-selection into the program. The second deals with nonresponse bias.

The discriminant function, a measure of the probability of selection into the NYC program, given certain sociodemographic and psychological characteristics, is used to adjust for self-selection. Ideally, this variable should not be statistically significant in the benefit equations. This would imply that an increase or decrease in the probability of selection as an NYC participant has no effect on labor market performance or educational experience. However, it turns out that the partial regression coefficient is zero in 11 of 27 labor market benefit equations, positive for seven models, and negative for nine. Thus, in 16 cases the probability of selection in NYC did have an effect on the outcome. So while self-selection bias has been reduced for some models, its effect has not been eliminated in this study. Our judgment is that this bias is mixed in effect but may yield slightly higher benefits to the NYC. However, the negative sign in nine of the 27 equations indicates some downward bias as well.

Nonresponse may contribute to an upward bias in the benefit estimations. The NYC participants who were located in the survey stayed in the program a longer period of time on the average than the population of NYC participants as a whole. Since there is a positive relation between benefits and length of stay in the NYC program, an upward bias seems apparent.

However, one must remember that monetary economic benefits were quite large. A considerable reduction could occur before these benefits would become unacceptably low to society. If an accurate measure of bias from these sources were available, benefits would probably remain positive even after an adjustment for bias were made.

In summary, net monetary economic benefits of NYC are considered to be positive and large; but, contrary to the participants' own views, there is no evidence in the regression analysis of a net benefit in high school retention and graduation rates. From a morale and psychological standpoint, the program appears to have been a success.

Policy Conclusions

The composite of in-school and summer NYC programs included in this survey yield significant monetary benefits, due mainly to an effect on increasing labor force participation. On this basis, the program warrants continued and perhaps increased funding as an effective social program. The summer NYC program, alone, does not warrant funding on the basis of economic efficiency, but funding may well be justified on social grounds.

However, zero or negative program effects on the high school graduation rate, together with a zero or negative relation between high school graduation and income per capita per family, suggest that one basic operational assumption of the NYC program may not be correct. Variables other than family income may be more important in reducing the dropout rate in the short run. The legislation deserves reexamination on this basis, therefore.

Negroes, particularly Negro females, generally benefit more than whites. However, continuance of the program for white groups may be justified on equity or income-distribution grounds even if not on efficiency grounds. Finally, it appears that American Indians benefit only indifferently from the NYC program, though small sample sizes make this judgment uncertain. Our field work, though, as well as the comments of project directors suggest limited benefit for American Indians. The program should be redesigned to more appropriately fit the needs of American Indians, or it should be dropped in favor of programs which have proved to be more effective in meeting the needs of this group.

NOTES

1. Adapted from a report prepared under contract with the Manpower Administration, U.S. Department of Labor (research contract No. 43-8-025-53). Since contractors performing research under government sponsorship are encouraged to express their own judgments freely, the report does not necessarily represent the department's official opinion or policy. Moreover, the authors are solely responsible for the factual accuracy and all material developed in the report.
2. The definitions of North, South, and West conform to those in the *Country and City Data Book*, 1967, p. viii.
3. The discriminant function was estimated in the following way: (1) Variables which directly determine eligibility into the NYC program were forced into a model estimating the function, regardless of their level of statistical significance. These were age and income per capita per family. In addition, the following variables were also forced into the model: farm residence; number of times a respondent had dropped out of high school; proportion of subjects the respondent found interesting in high school; sex; and ethnic origin. (2) Fifteen additional psychological, educational, and sociodemographic variables were allowed to enter the model explaining the discriminant function if they had a level of statistical significance of .25 or higher. On this basis, four of the 15 entered the model. These were: (a) "When you were in high school, did you ever hear of the NYC program?" Yes = 1; No = 0; (b) average number of hours worked per week while respondent was in high school, exclusive of any NYC work; (c) father's education, in years of school completed; (d) "Is there any particular line of work that you would really like to get into?" Yes = 1; No = 0.
4. Since there was no statistically significant difference in average hourly wage rates between the two samples, the increase in earnings is due mainly to an increase in the labor force participation rate. There is, therefore, the possibility that

NYC participants had simply displaced other youths in the labor market. The result may be that the observed increase in earnings is due to income redistribution alone and does not represent an increase in national income. However, an inspection of the unemployment rates and numbers of employed persons aged 16 to 19 from the third quarter 1965 to the third quarter 1969 shows, in general, that unemployment rates were dropping steadily while the number of persons in the labor force steadily increased. Thus, no necessary displacement effect need be assumed. See *Employment and Earnings* 16 (April 1970), pp. 128–29, and 13 (January 1967), p. 115.

5. See Tables 2.2 and 2.3 and Somers and Stromsdorfer, *A Cost-Effectiveness Study of the In-School and Summer Neighborhood Youth Corps* (Madison: Center for Studies in Vocational and Technical Education, University of Wisconsin, July 1970). Costs are based on federal share only and include the costs of participating in the NYC program such as extra transportation and meals. On a monthly basis, these amount to approximately $17. These costs are based on Leonard H. Goodman and Thelma D. Myint, *The Economic Needs of Neighborhood Youth Corps Enrollees* (Washington: Bureau of Social Science Research, Inc., August 1969).

THE IMPACT OF CETA
ON WORK ORIENTATIONS

Ronald D. Hedlund
Chava Nachmias

The rediscovery of poverty in the early 1960s—amid an affluent society—created a surge of interest in the antecedents of poverty and unequal opportunities for the poor and the disadvantaged, whose lack of education and adequate training made them less prepared than others for the labor market.* With that came a major effort of manpower programs such as the

*This report was prepared using data collected as part of a contract between the Milwaukee County Executive Office for Economic Resource Development and the University of Wisconsin–Milwaukee Political Science Department for the review and evaluation of the County's CETA Title VI projects. The authors wish to acknowledge the support of several individuals. Primary are Milwaukee County Executive William F. O'Donnell, Mary Ellen Powers, Director and Larry Jankowski, Assistant Director of the Milwaukee County Ex-

Manpower Development and Training Act of 1962 (MDTA) and the Economic Opportunity Act of 1964 (EOA), which were directed toward resocializing the poor into the world of work by providing training, remedial education, and work experience. In contrast manpower policies for the 1970s, beginning with legislation such as the Emergency Employment Act of 1971 (EEA), were a response to rising unemployment, and cyclical programs that were designed to provide jobs for the unemployed but not necessarily the disadvantaged (Mirengoff and Rindler, 1976) were initiated. Despite their slightly different focus, manpower programs during the 1960s and the early 1970s were all designed to fit the prescription of centralized administration at the federal level and were almost exclusively outside the legislative or budgetary processes of state and local governments.

This excessive centralization led to general dissatisfaction with these programs. Snedeker and Snedeker (1978: 62) wrote that "the centralized system undercut the regular processes of state and local government for planning, coordinating, and delivering comprehensive services, tailored to local needs and rationalized with the different political bureaucratic social and economic environments of the states and local areas." Advocates of reform in manpower legislation promoted the view that decision making, program planning, and implementation would be most effective at the local labor-market level, where employment and training needs could be more easily assessed.

By the end of 1973, Congress passed a manpower-reform bill, the Comprehensive Employment and Training Act (CETA). The new legislation transferred control of Department of Labor manpower programs to state and local officials. The basic concept of CETA was to give elected officials at the local level decision-making prerogatives and the discretion to decide whom among the eligible target groups to serve, what services to deliver, and which organizations to use as delivery agents.

The essence of CETA was decentralization and decategorization of manpower programs. It grew, in part, out of President Richard Nixon's New Federalism and the revenue-sharing rhetoric of the 1970s. The decentralization of CETA transferred authority to state and local units of government called "prime sponsors." Decategorization meant a free hand in

ecutive Office for Economic Resource Development, and the staff of the CETA Review Project. In addition the University of Wisconsin–Milwaukee College of Letters and Science, Department of Political Science, Social Science Research Facility, and the Urban Research Center have provided resources. Special acknowledgement goes to Chip Biglow and Chris Heitert, who prepared portions of the data analysis used in the preparation of this report. The authors, however, assume full responsibility for the material presented in this paper.

allocating funds among a variety of generic services. Despite the original intent, the categorization and decentralization mandated by the act was incomplete. In fact 34 percent of the original 1975 CETA appropriation went to titles that authorized categorical programs; together with the special Public Service Employment Program (Title VI–PSE), this proportion increased to 58 percent. The intent to decentralize, however, was considerably more successful; including Title VI and the Summer Youth Program, 89 percent of CETA funds were managed by local authorities in fiscal 1975 (Mirengoff and Rindler, 1976).

The initial legislation, passed by Congress in December 1973, had five titles representing a major consolidation of many of the manpower programs which existed prior to CETA.[1] With sharply rising unemployment in 1974, the number and type of unemployed increased rapidly. As a reaction in December 1974, Congress passed the Emergency Jobs and Unemployment Assistance Act, which created Title VI and which added a large public-service employment component (PSE) to CETA. An amendment to the act, passed in October 1976, extended the Emergency Job Program (Title VI),[2] and provided for the creation of public-service work projects administered by local sponsors such as state and local governments; education agencies; community-based organizations; and nonprofit, private organizations engaged in public service (Burnim, 1978).

Title VI was conceived as a short-term, countercyclical component, based on the belief that the severe unemployment problem was only temporary. This is reflected in the legislation indicating that the duration of new Title VI–PSE projects must be short-term—only up to twelve months (Federal Register, 1977, and Manpower Information, Inc., 1976).

Funds are allocated based on the number of persons in an area and the severity of unemployment. The formula allots 2 percent of all available funds to eligible Indian tribes, bands, and groups. Ten percent of the remainder is reserved to the Secretary of Labor for discretionary use. The rest is allocated as follows: 50 percent to the unemployed in the locale, 25 percent to unemployed over 4.5 percent, and 25 percent to the number of unemployed people living in areas with 6.5 percent or more unemployment (Burnim, 1978).

Since its passage the stated purposes of CETA have been "to provide job training and employment opportunities for economically disadvantaged, unemployed and underemployed persons, and to assure that training and other services lead to maximum employment opportunities and enhance self-sufficiency" (Federal Register, 1977: 201). Likewise, the long-term goals of Title VI–PSE projects are to enable all individuals to move from such subsidized employment programs into unsubsidized full-time jobs in the private or public sector, and to emphasize the development of new careers and career-development opportunities (Federal Register, 1977). While the emphasis in Title VI is on providing jobs, this title makes available to a prime sponsor and to subcontractors funding for basic types of manpower activities, including classroom and on-the-job training conducted in a work environment, both of which are designed to enable an individual to learn a skill and/or to qualify for a particular occupation through demonstration and practice. Additional funded program activities designed to provide supportive services include the following: screening for eligibility, that is, the initial determination as to whether a program can benefit the individual and the determination of the manpower activities and services which would be most appropriate, and manpower services, that is, orientation to the world of work, counseling, job development, and job placement (Federal Register, 1977).

Any assessment of CETA in general, and Title VI in particular, is not an easy task, since not all of the goals are specified in the act. Rather, some of CETA's objectives are implied in the intent of the legislation, and intended objectives inevitably lead to disagreement. Further, more local control has permitted additional interpretations regarding goals to be pursued. Nevertheless, CETA's policy objectives can be classified in three general categories (Snedeker and Snedeker, 1978). First, CETA was intended to shift manpower programs from the federal to the local level and away from categorical modes. Second, CETA decategorization and decentralization were seen as means for improving the process of program planning, administration, and service delivery. Third, CETA was viewed as a vehicle for assisting program participants in improving their employability, thereby reducing their dependence on government subsidies.

Evaluations of the first two sets of objectives have been reported elsewhere (Snedeker and Snedeker, 1978; Mirengoff and Rindler, 1976; Van Horn, 1979; Hedlund and Hedge, 1979), but little attention has been given to the third. Thus, this study looks at the third objective, focusing on the effect of CETA-Title VI employment on work-attitude changes in participants. In pursuing this objective, we shall also elaborate on some other outcomes for CETA-Title VI participants, which are both stated and implied by the legislation. Specifically, we consider the following questions:

1. What kinds of persons are selected as participants for CETA-Title VI projects? (To what extent are these project participants the ones who are in greatest need of manpower services as envisioned by the federal legislation and the ensuing rules and regulations?)
2. To what extent did CETA-Title VI employment have an effect on the participants' orientation to the world of work? (Which participants are most likely to change, and in what direction? What elements of CETA-Title VI projects are most closely associated with these changes?)

In the following sections, these questions are addressed by examining CETA-Title VI projects in Milwaukee County, Wisconsin. Following a description of the locale and the study used to collect the data reported here, this study describes the persons who were selected as project participants and analyzes the individual and structural determinants of any attitude changes they experienced.

THE CETA-TITLE VI PROGRAM
IN MILWAUKEE COUNTY, WISCONSIN

In accordance with pertinent federal rules and regulations, nine prime sponsors in Wisconsin applied for authorization to administer CETA programs and were so certified by the U.S. Department of Labor. The largest of these, in terms of the number of persons served, is Milwaukee County, which contains 24 percent of the state's population, approximately one-third of its nonservice production workers, and about 84 percent of the state's metropolitan labor force. Within the county are nineteen political subdivisions, eighteen municipalities, and the city of Milwaukee, with a combined 1975 population projected at 1,027,711.

During the early 1970s, the top local elected officials in Milwaukee County, the county executive and the mayor, appeared reluctant to become involved in local-level manpower planning and service delivery. By default the responsibility for the Milwaukee Manpower Area Planning Council (MAPC) was assumed by the Milwaukee County Executive in 1972. His office became the secretariat for the MAPC, and it began to develop the staff and expertise for local manpower planning and program administration (Kobrak and Perlman, 1974, Part 3). When CETA funding began to replace federally funded manpower programs, the Office of the County Executive was certified as prime sponsor when the Mayor's Office expressed no interest and a proposed consortium never materialized. At the outset the CETA program was administered by a small staff in the county executive's office, working under the direction of the elected county executive. The mandated advisory council consisted of representatives from the major interested parties—business and industry, organized labor, local government, educational institutions, community organizations, and worker and welfare-rights groups. Affected groups were assured of programmatic input. The initial orientation was one of low involvement of elected officials, who preferred to affirm staff decisions and advisory council recommendations rather than initiate their own proposals and actions; however, the election of a new county executive in 1976 signaled a change in outlook and organizational setting for Milwaukee County CETA. Compared with his predecessor, the new county executive was more interested in manpower problems and more supportive of the county government's involvement. As a consequence, responsibility for CETA administration (together with existing staff and the Advisory Council) was transferred in 1976 to a newly created office within the county executive's jurisdiction, the Milwaukee County Executive Office for Economic Resource Development. It became a separate division with its own director. While operations remained much the same, the staff was enlarged and the structure modified to take into account new elements in the federal rules and regulations regarding CETA.

The new county executive continued the tradition of affirming decisions made by the local staff and the CETA Advisory Council, but he initiated his own input into the planning stages of the program, thus providing an elected official's perspective, which had been lacking. For example, he expressed concern toward the development of appropriate work habits and attitudes by CETA participants. In addition he ordered that significant CETA-Title VI funding be directed toward employing welfare recipients in order to implement "workfare rather than welfare," thus reducing the county's welfare payments. Another change was seen in the extensive effort he made to set priorities for public services to be provided by Title VI projects and to fund those project proposals most likely to provide such services. A final change was the degree to which the staff had knowledge of the projects and the project operators so that the prime sponsor could reallocate unspent funds and detect project difficulties.

While unemployment rates in the Milwaukee Standard Metropolitan Statistical Area (SMSA) have always been slightly below the national average (see Table 2.6), this is not true for Milwaukee, the largest city in the project. Only during 1978 was the unemployment rate in the city below the national average. In addition a continuing problem with underemployment has existed in the city. Unemployment and underemployment are even higher in the central city area, where the percentage of poverty-level persons was estimated at 32.2 in 1975, compared with 13.3 for the entire county (Milwaukee County CETA Proposal, FY 1978).

In response to these unemployment rates and the call by the Department of Labor for CETA proposals, the Milwaukee County prime sponsor (the Milwaukee County Executive Office for Economic Resource Development, CETA Division) prepared a document for fiscal year (FY) 1978, Title VI funding, which specified veterans, welfare recipients, minorities, and handicapped persons as priority groups for employment opportunities. (These priorities closely resembled those that had been specified in previous years.) Special efforts were made by the prime sponsor to fund projects directed toward the hiring and serving of these priority groups. These steps

TABLE 2.6
Unemployment Rates for Milwaukee City, Milwaukee County,
Milwaukee SMSA, and U.S., 1970–1978

Year	Milwaukee City Rate	Milwaukee County Unemployment Rate	Milwaukee SMSA Rate	National Rate
1970	6.2%	5.1%	4.6%	4.9%
1971	6.2%	5.1%	4.6%	5.9%
1972	5.0%	4.1%	3.7%	5.6%
1973	5.0%	4.1%	3.5%	4.9%
1974	6.1%	5.0%	4.5%	5.6%
1975	10.0%	8.1%	7.4%	8.5%
1976	8.7%	7.0%	6.3%	7.7%
1977	7.3%	5.9%	5.3%	7.0%
1978	4.8%	4.3%	4.1%	6.0%

Source: Wisconsin Department of Industry, Labor and Human Relations, Bureau of Research & Statistics.

included giving extra points in the evaluation of proposals to such projects and encouraging project operators to hire participants representing these target groups. For FY 1978, $14.4 million was allocated for all CETA Titles in Milwaukee County, with an additional $24.9 million made available from the FY 1977 Economic Stimulus allocation. Thus, the Milwaukee County prime sponsor had a total of $39.3 million, with $21.0 million dedicated to Title VI and its stated expectation of hiring 3,418 persons.

CETA REVIEW PROJECT

As the prime sponsor, the Milwaukee County Executive Office for Economic Development, CETA Division, determined that some type of systematic review and evaluation by an independent agency should be a part of the overall FY 1978-Title VI program. The University of Wisconsin–Milwaukee was asked to prepare a proposal for a CETA-funded project that would review and evaluate PSE-Title VI projects. The resulting proposal called for establishing a field and support staff of thirty, CETA-eligible persons and a small, non-CETA administrative and research staff, who would be assisted by a cross-disciplinary team of faculty-resource persons and graduate students.

The mission of the CETA Review Project (CRP) was to review and evaluate the newly funded CETA-Title VI projects for FY 1978 in terms of:

1. The benefits which accrued to individual CETA employees who were participants in approximately 190 different projects;
2. The projects' contributions to and impacts on the community; and

3. The degree to which individual Title VI projects were able to accomplish their own goals and objectives.

The data used in this report were collected by the CRP as a part of its review and evaluation of CETA-Title VI projects in Milwaukee County.

Data and Methods

In implementing its review and evaluation, the CRP used a longitudinal research design whereby data pertaining to all three aspects of its mission were collected at various times. Since control groups were not available, comparisons and use of an experimental research design were not possible; however, the amount of data collected and the access provided to program participants and project personnel created a useful data base for developing an understanding of the impacts of CETA-Title VI projects during FY 1978 for this prime sponsor.

The actual data collection utilized an array of techniques, which included personal, in-depth interviews with a sample of 478 participants at the beginning of their employment, toward the middle of their project's projected service period, and at the end of their employment. Also included were ongoing participant observation of the work settings and interaction patterns in the projects; review of project documents regarding participant activities; three countywide telephone surveys; five telephone surveys in three geographical areas within the county designated to receive special types of CETA-sponsored services; two interviews or mail questionnaires with project directors about project history, operations, and goal attainment; and a variety of data-collection efforts related to goal fulfillment.

As individuals were hired by various projects, their names were transmitted to the CRP, where random procedures were used to select a sample of individuals, stratified by job category, for interviewing. Efforts were made to interview individuals as soon as possible after beginning their CETA jobs. These interviews served as a baseline to assess attitudinal change from the time of a person's initial involvement in a CETA project. Included in this ninety-minute interview was an extensive series of attitudinal questions. A follow-up interview, which repeated many of the same questions, was administered from three to six months after the intake interview, the exact date being determined by the anticipated length of the project in which the individual was employed. Upon notice of the pending termination of the participants in the sample, a final exit interview was conducted, again repeating many of the same questions. As a result an extensive and rich data file was developed that documents the attitudes of 478 CETA-Title VI participants shortly after hire (intake), 332 persons toward the middle of their project's operating period (mid-term), and with

310 of the participants at termination (exit). (A comparison of the 310 participants giving exit interviews with the 478 in the original intake interview by sex, race, age, and education showed that none of these differences was sufficient to indicate systematic biasing of results.[3]) Interviewing was done by trained interviewers who were staff members of the CRP.

Measures

Past job income and welfare experiences are individual-level data collected from personal interviews with project participants to indicate the prior history of respondents in the labor market. Three different aspects of these experiences were selected for inclusion—welfare receipt, prior jobs, and past income. In each case the question asked for factual information about the respondents' background. Welfare receipt was indicated through three questions related to whether the respondent has received any welfare assistance, food stamps, or housing subsidies in the last year. Prior jobs data were based on two questions related to the number of different jobs and the number of different types of jobs an individual respondent had held since entering full-time employment. Past income was determined through two questions related to the previous year's income for the respondent and for his or her family. These seven questions were submitted to a factor analysis using an orthogonal, varimax-rotated solution. The results indicate three factors corresponding to the three types of experiences described above with the three factors accounting for 74.2 percent of the variance in items.

CETA employment classifications are based on the type of work done by the participants. Each participant was classified into one of the following categories: (1) administrative and professional, (2) artist, (3) semi-skilled, including unskilled, clerical, and paraprofessional jobs; and (4) work assistance, including a wide variety of jobs intended to provide work experience to hard-core unemployed.

Training refers to the number of hours per week of formal training and on-the-job training information that was obtained from project directors. Every participant in a project was assigned this training score for analysis purposes.

Size of organization is measured by the number of full-time, paid, non-CETA employees working for the organization that serves as a project's sponsor. Each CETA participant was assigned the appropriate size of organization score.

Longevity indicates the number of years an organization has been in existence.

Specialization is the number of separate job titles in the organization.

CETA PARTICIPANTS: AN OVERVIEW

Since manpower programs are generally perceived by public officials and by the public to be redistributional in effect, i.e., those having jobs and paying taxes are taxed in order to provide resources for the training and temporary employment of those unable to find jobs after a period of unemployment, one initial concern must be with the recipients of these services. Such a concern is especially important, given the significant fear expressed in official reports (Mirengoff and Rindler, 1976) and in academic articles (Snedeker and Snedeker, 1976) about "creaming," a process whereby the least disadvantaged and most prepared persons are selected for various manpower training and employment programs. This part of the paper will describe CETA-Title VI participants in Milwaukee County for FY 1978 in order to indicate the types of persons that were employed by the projects funded by the prime sponsor. Three factors will be taken into account: demographic characteristics, past job and welfare experiences, and type of job. Before describing the findings, however, it is important to review pertinent rules and regulations regarding who is eligible for CETA-Title VI employment, to consider the target groups that were selected for service by this prime sponsor, and to outline the hiring considerations used by Milwaukee County project operators.

In order to be eligible for CETA-Title VI employment, an individual must be certified (by the Wisconsin Job Service, an agent designated by the prime sponsor) as meeting two requirements: (1) must be unemployed or receiving unemployment compensation for at least fifteeen of the last twenty weeks, and (2) must be classified as economically disadvantaged, i.e., receive cash-welfare payments, have an income at or below 70 percent of the lower living level, or have a foster child who receives government aid. Thus, being unemployed and economically disadvantaged are the criteria for being certified. Although prime sponsors were supposed to insure that employment opportunities were "equitably allocated among the categories of eligible persons" (Federal Registry, 1977), they were permitted to establish target groups in their own areas to be served by Title VI. That and the decentralized nature of CETA administration, the use of subcontractors to provide many public services to the community, and the practice of hiring the most qualified individuals permit the use of creaming in the hiring of CETA participants.

In the FY 1978 proposal, the Milwaukee County prime sponsor identified four target groups as being most in need of manpower services: veterans, welfare recipients, minorities (primarily blacks, Spanish-Americans, and American Indians, and to a lesser degree, women and youth between 16 and 21), and handicapped persons (physical, emotional and/or mental).

Assurances were given that efforts would be made to remove any barriers for the employment of these target groups by CETA-Title VI projects; however, no specific steps or programmatic considerations were specified.

The actual hiring process for CETA participants involved several steps after the certification process that seemed to provide special opportunities for creaming. (Information regarding hiring by other prime sponsors indicates that similar procedures were used [Mirengoff and Rindler, 1976: 136–138].) Once an individual was certified as CETA-eligible, he or she was referred by Job Service counselors to projects registered as having unfilled positions. (This process involved matching job requirements on job-vacancy forms with certified individuals' qualifications.) As one would expect, every effort was made to refer the best-qualified individuals to project personnel. Once referred to a project, the certified individual had to satisfy whatever additional testing and skill requirements were specified by the project operation. And since project operators had to supply an agreed-upon public service, and since the prime sponsor made known its intentions to assess the degree to which each project had delivered its services, project operators had to be concerned about the quality of persons hired and their abilities to help the project meet its public service goals. As a result persons eligible for CETA-Title VI jobs had to convince project operators to hire them based upon prior training, skills, and potential to perform the needed tasks. (From a project operator's point of view, it was rational to seek the most qualified and promising CETA-certified persons for the available positions rather than to accept any person or the most needy person, regardless of qualifications.) In only one project studied were participants chosen at random from those applying. Furthermore, only a few projects directed their recruitment efforts to any of the target groups. The consequences of this approach became evident during interviews with Title VI project directors, when only 20 percent said that they would prefer (or that it made no difference) in their hiring decision if the applicant was a high school dropout with no skills, while 49 percent had similar views regarding college graduates. The operation and needs of project operators in Milwaukee County probably aided in the selection of the most qualified persons as participants rather than the most needy.

Demographic Characteristics

Table 2.7 includes data on sex, race, age, and education during 1977 for the adult population of Milwaukee County, for those county residents who were unemployed, for those unemployed persons who were certified as eligible for CETA, and for those who were included in the sample of participants in CETA-Title VI projects. The data show that the majority of the unemployed were men; however, since a larger proportion of adult men

TABLE 2.7

Demographic Characteristics for Countywide Adults, CETA Certified, and CETA Participants (Percent by Column)

Demographic Characteristics	Countywide Adults–1977[a]	Countywide Unemployment–1977[b]	CETA Certified[c]	CETA Participants[d]
Sex:				
Male	48	51	63	60
Female	52	49	37	40
Total %	100	100	100	100
n	968,672	23,400	8,310	474
Race:				
Black	13	22	48	42
White	84	72	47	53
Other	3	6	5	5
Total %	100	100	100	100
n	968,672	23,440	8,226	470
Age:				
Under 21	6	NA	21	11
21–30	30	NA	46	59
31–45	21	NA	18	19
Over 45	43	NA	15	11
Total %	100		100	100
n	676		8,301	477
Education:				
Grade school or less	7	NA	9	5
Some high school	13	NA	33	18
High school graduate	37	NA	26	23
Trade school	5	NA	0	4
Some college	23	NA	18	24
College graduate	9	NA	10	14
Postcollege	6	NA	3	13
Total %	100		99	101
n	676		8,286	477

[a]The source for sex and race was population estimates for Milwaukee County, 1977 provided by the Wisconsin Department of Administration. The source for Age and Education was a countywide sample survey conducted by the CETA Review Project in September 1977.

[b]The source for the countywide unemployment figures was a reporting requirement document prepared by the Wisconsin Job Service, Department of Industry Labor and Human Relations, 1979 for 1977.

[c]The source for CETA certified was a computerized data file made available by the Wisconsin Job Service and indicating all persons certified as eligible for CETA participation between August 1, 1977, and April 30, 1978.

[d]The source for CETA participants was a sample survey of 478 CETA participants hired by CETA Title VI funded projects in Milwaukee County Wisconsin, October, 1977–March, 1978.

NA = Data not available.

were in the labor force, the unemployment rate was estimated to be somewhat higher among women—5.3 percent for women compared with 4.1
percent for men. An examination of racial differences shows that while
about one in ten county residents was black, about two out of ten
unemployed persons were black. This difference was reflected in the unemployment rates which were estimated at 3.7 percent for whites and 12.6
percent for blacks. Thus, sex and race differences are apparent in comparing the unemployment rates.

The next question concerns the comparative success rates of individuals
who were certified as CETA-eligible in securing a job as CETA participants. Table 2.7 demonstrates that CETA-certification and CETA-partici-
pation rates do not necessarily reflect the unemployment rates. For example while males constituted 51 percent of the unemployed individuals, they
made up 63 percent of those certified as CETA-eligible and 60 percent of
those obtaining CETA jobs. (Data available nationally for CETA–Title VI
in FY 1976 show that 65 percent of the national participants were men
[Snedeker and Snedeker, 1978:91].) These comparisons suggest that wom-
en are encountering disproportionate difficulty becoming CETA-certified;
however, once they are in the CETA pool, their rate of finding CETA jobs
reflects closely their rate of being certified.

Three factors may account for women's problems in entering the pool:
(1) they may not be as informed about CETA, specifically, about how to
obtain CETA eligibility, since some of the burden in certification reportedly rests with the person; (2) they may be systematically discriminated
against during the certification process; and (3) they may be less likely to
meet the eligibility requirements. (During interviews Milwaukee County
staff cited inquiries from women who were declared ineligible because of
family income as evidence that many unemployed women have other family members working. The income of these families exceeded the maximum
allowed, thus explaining this sex-based difference in certification.)

The higher unemployment rates among blacks translated into an even
higher proportion being CETA-certified. While blacks composed 22 percent of the unemployed, they were 48 percent of the CETA-eligible and 42
percent of CETA participants. (National data indicate that in FY 1976, 23
percent of the participants were black and 68 percent white [Snedeker and
Snedeker, 1978:91].) These rates suggest that the certification and hiring
rates for blacks are significantly higher than one might expect from unemployment rates; however, these higher-than-expected rates probably reflect
the greater difficulties blacks have encountered in obtaining and maintaining employment (Sheppard, 1977).

In determining the relationship of employment to age and education,
this report is limited in that estimates for unemployment among differing
age and educational groupings are not available for comparable age

groups. Past estimates suggest that unemployment rates are at least three times higher for the below-21 age group than for the general population (Milwaukee County, CETA–Title VI Proposal, FY 1978). Table 2.7 indicates that while about 6 percent of the population in Milwaukee County is between 18 and 21, 21 percent of those certified as CETA-eligible were also in this group. Similarly, the proportion of those certified was about 50 percent higher for the 21–30 age group than their rate in the population. These comparisons must be tempered in light of the sizeable number of persons in the general population who are over 65 and retired. Regarding educational level, data also indicate that a much larger proportion of those certified for CETA were not high school graduates while college graduates and those with graduate degrees had only slightly different rates from those found in the adult population of the county. The comparable certification rates for persons with high school diplomas, some type of trade or vocational training, or some college experience were somewhat lower than one might expect given the population rates. These figures indicate that persons certified as CETA-eligible were most likely to be those with low levels of education and least likely to be those with middle levels of education. Comparisons with data from the national level for FY 1976 CETA participants indicate somewhat similar rates for age and education (Snedeker and Snedeker, 1978:91).

As already noted, participant rates for women and men and for differing racial groups seem to approximate fairly closely their certification rates, suggesting few differences in their ability to secure participant status once certified. The data on age and education, however, suggests some creaming in the hiring process. In each case relatively larger proportions of the seemingly more experienced and trained persons, i.e., those between 21 and 45 and those with post–high school training, appear more likely to have been hired for CETA–Title VI projects. Certified persons under 21 and over 45 and those without some type of post–high school educational experience seem less likely to have received CETA–Title VI jobs. Thus while younger persons and those with lower levels of education seem *more* likely to be *certified,* they seem *less* likely to be hired than one would expect once they are in the certified pool. These trends seem to result primarily from the stated preferences of project directors, as implemented in hiring decisions for participants who had a post–high school education and who were between 21 and 45. The difficulty women experienced seems to center on the certification process, which suggests difficulties other than creaming.

Past Job, Income, and Welfare Experiences

A second category of variables important in describing CETA participants is their past job and welfare experiences, more specifically, their pri-

TABLE 2.8
Past Job/Welfare Experiences for CETA Title VI Participants[a]
(Percent by Column)

| Level[b] | Type of Experience | | |
	WELFARE DEPENDENCE	PRIOR JOBS	PAST INCOME
High	26	35	40
Low	74	65	60
Total %	100	100	100
n	305	241	282

[a]Included as participants are those respondents who completed the intake and exit interviews.
[b]To determine "level," the standardized, rotated factor-analysis scores for these three dimensions—welfare dependence, prior jobs, and past income—were divided at the mean into two groups.

or income, past employment, and receipt of welfare. Table 2.8 provides information about these three dimensions generated through a factor analysis of seven forced response interview items described earlier. These data show that about one of four participants who completed the exit interview had a high level of welfare dependence. While this rate might seem somewhat high when compared to a cross-section of the population, it probably is not very high considering the needs of CETA-eligible persons. In fact this rate may be quite modest considering that these persons had to be unemployed or receiving unemployment compensation for fifteen of the last twenty weeks prior to being declared CETA-certified.

The second dimension—prior jobs—is based on the number of full-time jobs and the number of different types of full-time jobs held by CETA participants. One common image of the unemployed is of someone who has held numerous different jobs. The fact that only one of three CETA participants, in a factor analysis of these items, can be classified as having a high number of prior jobs suggests that this image may be faulty. Unfortunately, there are no data for comparing this distribution with the population-at-large.

For the final dimension—past income—Table 2.8 indicates that 60 percent of respondents were classified in the factor analysis as having low incomes. Again, given the requirements for being certified, this finding is to be expected. (Reference to the questions used in forming this dimension indicates that only about one out of five respondents reported income for the previous year at or above $6,000.) Based on past job, income, and welfare experiences, this sample of CETA participants seems to have had low income levels when compared to a sizeable number who received some type of welfare payments in the preceding year. The CETA–Title VI program in Milwaukee County seems to have hired large numbers of low-income persons, along with many who had received welfare payments.

Type of CETA Job

A wide variety of jobs were available to CETA-eligible participants under the Title VI program. The approximately eighty different types of jobs were grouped into four categories for analysis purposes. Table 2.9 indicates that about 13 percent of respondents who were included in exit surveys held professional or administrative positions, 27 percent were artists, 49 percent held semiskilled, paraprofessional, or unskilled jobs, and 11 percent were in a special Work Assistance Project.[4] Since the Work Assistance Project differed dramatically from others in terms of its goals and its participants, some background information is necessary prior to describing participants by type of job. While all other CETA–Title VI projects sought to provide some definable public service to the community through the work of previously unemployed persons, the goal of the Work Assistance Project was to provide work experience for handicapped individuals and for individuals referred from the Milwaukee County Welfare Office who were receiving general assistance (hard-to-employ individuals). Thus, the types of persons recruited differed substantially for this project, and furthermore, the stated goal for the Work Assistance Project was to employ virtually every person referred there, regardless of his or her prior skill level or type of experience. No effort was made to recruit the most qualified individuals.

Table 2.9 also provides data about each of the four types of jobs categorized by sex, race, age, and education. Statistically significant ($\alpha \leq .05$) differences, using a chi-square test, were found for race, age, and education, but not for sex. Black respondents were much more likely to hold semiskilled jobs or to be in Work Assistance Projects while whites were more likely to be artists or to hold administrative and professional positions. Very young and older respondents were more likely to have semiskilled positions or to be in the Work Assistance Project than were those between 21 and 45. Respondents with less than a high school diploma were located predominantly in semiskilled positions and in the Work Assistance Project, while those with post–high school education were much more likely to hold professional and administrative posts or to be artists.

This profile of CETA–Title VI participants suggests that important differences do exist in terms of who is unemployed, who is certified as CETA-eligible, and who obtains CETA positions. The data indicate that creaming in the hiring process probably did take place in the vast majority of projects, and that sizeable differences seem to exist for race and education in terms of the type of CETA job held.

TABLE 2.9

**Type of Job Category for CETA Title VI Participants[a]
by Demographic Characteristics (Percent by Row)**

Demographic Characteristic and Categories	Administrative and Professional	Artists	Semiskilled	Work Assistance	Total %	Total N
Sex:						
Male	11	30	49	10	100	178
Female	16	23	49	12	100	130
Total	13	27	49	11	100	308
$x^2 = 2.9\ df = 3\ P > .05$						
Race:						
Black	6	16	59	19	100	108
White	18	34	42	7	101	183
Other	23	8	69	0	100	13
Total	14	27	49	11	101	304
$x^2 = 36.2\ df = 6\ P < .001$						
Age:						
Under 21	6	26	52	16	100	31
21–30	14	30	55	2	101	185
31–45	18	32	39	11	100	56
Over 45	10	8	34	47	99	38
Total	13	27	49	11	100	310
$x^2 = 73.9\ df = 9\ P < .001$						
Education:						
Some high school	0	5	53	42	100	60
High school diploma	4	15	69	12	100	68
Post–high school	21	39	40	0	100	182
Total	13	27	49	11	100	310
$x^2 = 126.7\ df = 6\ P < .001$						

[a]Included as participants are those respondents who completed the intake and the exit interviews.

WORK ORIENTATION

One of the most neglected issues in manpower training programs has been the worker's attitude toward work. The definition of employability has been limited in the past to characteristics and behaviors of participants that can be directly observed, such as obtaining a skill, the number of placements of trainees on jobs, and increases in earnings. This emphasis stems, in part, from a tradition whereby the effectiveness of a manpower program was assessed primarily in terms of the number of participants who were placed in a given period of time. Naturally, program developers were forced to be concerned with immediate placement of trainees in the private sector when the number of placements was the criteria of success for their efforts. This orientation resulted in neglect of the process of change occurring in participants prior to placement. While placement is obviously imperative for the success of any manpower program, changes in work attitudes brought about by that program are no less important.

The concept of work orientation, or attitudes toward work, has been of great interest to social scientists concerned with the problems of individual adjustment to the work role in industrial society. While research has focused largely on psychological factors, recently, it has been treated more on a macrosociological scale, in an attempt to improve productivity and organizational functioning and to monitor the quality of employment (Seashore and Taber, 1975). There is also a growing interest in its consequences. Work orientation has a significant role in self-initiated job change (Ross and Zander, 1957; Mangione, 1973), turnover, and absenteeism (Herzberg, 1957), productivity (Vroom, 1964), and quality of performance (Quinn et al., 1973). It is also related to general life satisfaction, self-esteem, work-related fatigue, and work-related use of self-narcotizing drugs (Mangione and Quinn, 1973; Andrews and Withey, 1974; Quinn et al., 1973).

In the following analysis, we discuss two types of work orientations: work values and work rewards. Work values refer to the goals, objectives, and work characteristics that individuals hold as desirable with respect to their work activities (Kalleberg, 1977; Kohn, 1969), while work rewards refer to valuations made regarding their jobs (Kalleberg, 1977).

It is assumed that individuals are aware of the goals they seek through their work, and that these goals are reflected in the work values they hold. Morever, individuals tend to regulate their activities in pursuit of these goals in their work. Work values are classified into different dimensions, which reflect the range of gratifications that are available from work. A distinction is drawn between the intrinsic dimension, which reflects the characteristics of a job associated with the job itself, such as interest and stimulation, and the extrinsic dimension, which refers to factors that are external to the job itself, such as wages, security, and working conditions. Other dimensions often included are work relations, which refers to relationships with coworkers, and communication and feedback, which reflect the degree to which workers receive praise and encouragement from their supervisors or feel that they receive enough help and support to do their job well.

Whereas work values refer to dimensions that are differentially valued by workers independent of a work situation, work rewards are evaluative judgments concerning features of the participant's own job (Kalleberg, 1977). The same dimensions of work referred to in the concept of work values are included in this concept, except that workers indicate their degree of satisfaction on a dimension with regard to their own jobs. Work rewards do not represent objective properties of one's job; rather, they are subjective statements reflecting how workers experience the various characteristics of their work. In employing work rewards to measure participant satisfaction in CETA positions, it is assumed that job satisfaction is not a unitary concept, but that a participant could be satisfied or dissatisfied with particular aspects of his/her job. Drawing this distinction among dimensions of CETA positions should shed light on the crucial, policy-related question of what aspects of their CETA work most satisfy participants.

MEASURES OF WORK-ORIENTATION

Work Values

Information regarding the importance of eighteen job characteristics to the worker was obtained from the participants. (These items were used in the 1972–1973 Quality of Employment Survey [Quinn and Shepard, 1974].) The participants were asked to evaluate the degree of importance they attached to each characteristic. The intercorrelations among these items were factor-analyzed, using the principal-component method. The factor matrix was rotated by means of varimax orthogonal rotation. Four dimensions of work that were differentially valued by the participants emerged from the analysis:[5] (1) an intrinsic dimension (2) an extrinsic dimension (3) a work-relations dimension, and (4) a feedback dimension. Scales for each of these dimensions were constructed by summing the items in each dimension after standardization and by weighting based on the factor scores. The factor solutions for the intake and exit data were essentially equivalent except for the feedback dimension, which did not emerge for the exit data; thus, it was omitted from the analysis.

Work Rewards

Participants were asked to indicate their degree of satisfaction for each of the eighteen job characteristics with regard to their job. Data were collected for the intake and exit interviews. The intercorrelations among these items were analyzed by means of a principal factor procedure, and the factor matrix was rotated using a varimax-orthogonal rotation.[6] The four dimensions discussed previously emerged for the intake and exit data. Four scales measuring job rewards were constructed by summing the items in each dimension after standardization and by weighting by the factor scores.

Since the measures of values and rewards utilize the same items, they may not constitute separate dimensions; therefore, to test the independence of work values and work rewards, the intercorrelations among the eight original scales (generated for the intake data) were factor analyzed.[7] The results show that the rewards and values scales load on separate factors, indicating very little instrument effect and supporting the argument that values and rewards do represent independent dimensions.[8]

Attitude Change

Change for each of the seven scales was measured by constructing a ratio of exit and intake scores. A ratio of 1 indicates no change. A ratio larger than 1 indicates a positive change, and a ratio smaller than 1 implies negative change.

RESULTS

Table 2.10 presents the changes in attitudes that occurred during the time participants were employed by CETA. The findings are alarming—a consistent decline in work orientations among CETA participants. Between 36 and 51 percent of the participants experienced a decline in work orientations during their employment by CETA. This decline is generally sharper for the work-rewards dimensions. At best, one out of three respondents experienced an improvement in their work orientations, and the remaining participants showed no change.

To an extent, it could be argued that the observed attitude changes simply reflect the unreliability of the instrument between Time 1 and Time 2. Conceivably, participants who had initial high expectations of their CETA positions may also have had inflated work orientations. Perhaps as experience brought more realistic expectations, the work values and work rewards were considerably lower. If this were true, the discrepancy between

TABLE 2.10
Type of Attitude Change in Work Orientations
(Percent by Row)

Work Orientation	NEGATIVE	NO CHANGE	POSITIVE	%	N
	Type of Change			*Total*	
Intrinsic					
Values	38	42	20	100	(310)
Rewards	45	26	29	100	(301)
Extrinsic					
Values	45	27	28	100	(310)
Rewards	51	27	22	100	(252)
Work Relations					
Values	36	29	35	100	(258)
Rewards	40	25	35	100	(276)
Feedback					
Rewards	45	29	26	100	(248)

Time 1 and Time 2 would show a decline, and the opposite could be true for participants with low expectations at the onset of their CETA experiences. In order to assess the validity of these points, two items measuring pre-CETA expectations were used in an analysis of variance for all change scores to examine significant differences in the amount of change in work orientations between participants with initial high expectations and those with low expectations. The analysis shows significant differences in only a few cases, supporting the hypothesis that the observed changes in attitudes were not due to unreliability of the instruments.[9]

Demographic Correlatives of Attitude Change

In the following section, the relationship of participants' socioeconomic and demographic characteristics to their attitude change is explored. Delineating which personal characteristics predict attitude change is important for understanding the process that attitude changes may have undergone. The surveys used in the analysis contain several sociodemographic variables that are potentially relevant to a change in work orientation; these are sex, race, level of education, income, and welfare history. The relationships between these variables and the attitudes' scales are presented in Table 2.11. Since the subject here is changes in work orientation, the discussion will deal only with the positive and negative change categories.

As Table 2.11 shows, there are variations in the nature and amount of change in work orientations, depending on participants' personal characteristics. There are variations in attitude change by sex and race. Females

TABLE 2.11

Attitude Change by Background Characteristics (Percent by Column[a])

Work Orientation		Sex		Race		Education			Income Factor		Welfare Dependency	
		MALE	FEMALE	BLACK	WHITE	SOME H.S. OR LESS	HIGH SCHOOL GRADUATE	SOME COLLEGE OR MORE	LOW DEPENDENCY	HIGH DEPENDENCY	HIGH	LOW
Intrinsic												
Values	Positive change	22	19	18	22	30	16	19	23	19	23	19
	Negative change	35	42	38	37	27	43	40	33	44	26	42
	Total n	(178)	(130)	(108)	(183)	(60)	(68)	(182)	(170)	(112)	(80)	(225)
Rewards	Positive change	32	27	30	30	32	28	29	34	23	30	29
	Negative change	38	53	46	42	35	53	44	43	46	49	43
	Total n	(174)	(132)	(110)	(181)	(60)	(68)	(182)	(170)	(112)	(80)	(225)
Extrinsic												
Values	Positive change	30	25	19	33	27	21	31	28	29	20	31
	Negative change	45	45	53	39	47	49	43	45	46	148	44
	Total n	(176)	(129)	(111)	(180)	(60)	(68)	(182)	(170)	(112)	(80)	(225)
Rewards	Positive change	24	18	25	20	21	26	20	24	19	25	21
	Negative change	50	53	44	54	46	46	55	45	57	48	52
	Total n	(175)	(130)	(109)	(182)	(48)	(55)	(149)	(139)	(91)	(63)	(185)
Work Relations												
Values	Positive change	36	34	36	36	40	32	34	35	40	41	34
	Negative change	36	37	40	32	33	39	37	37	34	35	36
	Total n	(176)	(128)	(110)	(185)	(52)	(56)	(150)	(141)	(96)	(69)	(184)
Rewards	Positive change	38	29	43	30	50	33	30	40	29	42	32
	Negative change	36	47	41	39	32	45	42	38	44	38	42
	Total n	(175)	(133)	(112)	(182)	(54)	(58)	(164)	(152)	(99)	(71)	(200)
Feedback												
Rewards	Positive change	26	27	22	28	21	26	28	26	29	23	27
	Negative change	45	45	52	40	39	51	45	42	46	44	46
	Total n	(176)	(133)	(111)	(179)	(52)	(55)	(141)	(140)	(86)	(68)	(176)

[a]The "No Change" category is not included in this table. The "Total n," however, refers to all three categories.

101

show a higher percentage of negative change in work orientation. The differences between males and females range between 0–11 percent difference and are predominant in the work-rewards dimension. The differences between blacks and whites are even more significant and range between 0 to 14 percent. Whereas 43 percent of black participants experienced an improvement in their work relations, only 30 percent of the white participants did so. On the other hand, 52 percent of black participants (compared with 40 percent of the whites) had a negative experience with the quality of feedback they received on their CETA job.

The level of education of CETA participants is strongly related to attitude change. Participants with a lower level of education seemed to have a more positive attitude change than did their peers who were more educated. Thus, 30 percent of participants with some high school or less valued the intrinsic aspects of their jobs more than they had when they started their jobs. This compares with less than 20 percent of participants who were at least high school graduates and who had the same experience. Similarly, 50 percent of the participants with some high school or less, compared with approximately 30 percent of those who had more education, reported a positive change in the level of satisfaction from the work-relations aspect of their CETA jobs. On the other hand one out of two participants who were at least high school graduates were less satisfied with the intrinsic aspects of their CETA employment as well as with the extrinsic, work relations, and feedback aspects; only one out of three participants with less schooling shared the same experience.

The next two factors, which reflect the participants' economic backgrounds, display the same differentiating pattern. Participants from low-income background or with a high dependency on welfare experience more positive changes in their work orientation than those with a better previous economic situation. Approximately one out of three participants with low incomes were more satisfied with the intrinsic and work relations aspects of their CETA jobs, compared with less than one out of four among the high-income group. Similar differences are observed between those with low and high dependency on welfare regarding the valuation of the extrinsic and work-relations dimensions of work. Significant differences in the amount of negative changes are also observed, with the tendency for participants with higher incomes and lower welfare dependencies to be overrepresented in the negative-change categories. Between 44 and 57 percent of the high-income group valued the intrinsic or extrinsic aspects of work less, compared with only 33 to 45 percent of the low-income group. Similarly, whereas only 26 percent of the high-welfare-dependency group valued the intrinsic aspects of work less than they did when they began their employment, 42 percent of the low-welfare-dependency group did so.

These findings suggest a definite pattern of relationships between change in work orientations and background characteristics. Participants who traditionally would be defined as disadvantaged and less privileged, due to their economic backgrounds and levels of education, seemed to benefit from CETA, largely in terms of experiencing a positive change in their work orientations. On the other hand, for participants who were relatively more educated and better off economically, the CETA experience had a negative effect on their work values and on their levels of satisfaction with their CETA jobs.

In Tables 2.12 and 2.13, attitude change is explained in terms of factors that are directly related to the CETA experience. Table 2.12 presents a set of variables which reflect participants' work experiences—CETA positions and training—and Table 2.13 sets forth the effects of structural parameters of the organizations employing the participants. As is indicated in Table 2.12, the employment status of respondents has an effect on the amount and quality of change in their work orientations. Of particular interest is the Work Assistance Project for the hard-core unemployed, which had the highest frequency of positive change in four out of seven attitude dimensions. Participants who were employed as artists or in semiskilled positions had the sharpest decline in work orientation. This is especially evident with regard to intrinsic and extrinsic values and rewards and with feedback rewards.

The amount of formal and on-the-job training generally had a positive effect on participants' work values and a negative effect on their work rewards. On the whole those who received the longest training had positive changes in their work values, especially in the intrinsic, extrinsic, and work-relations dimensions of work. For example, 30 percent of participants who had more than fifteen hours a week of formal training as a part of their CETA job valued the extrinsic aspects of their jobs, compared with only 18 percent of participants who received less training. Similar differences are observed in the work-relations dimension. On the other hand, participants who received more training, either formal or on-the-job, were less satisfied with the rewards they received from their jobs. Approximately 60 percent of participants with longer training were less satisfied with the intrinsic rewards they received from their jobs, compared with only about 40 percent of those with less training. Similar patterns are observed in the work-rewards dimension of work relations and feedback. These findings suggest that the effect of training on work values is of special significance, particularly since the training component of manpower programs has a potential for long-term effect on the employability of participants by affecting, in a positive way, their work values.

Turning now to Table 2.13, we examine the relationship between the characteristics of organizations with immediate responsibility for the CETA projects and changes in work orientation. The importance of orga-

TABLE 2.12
Attitude Change by CETA Experience (Percent by Column[a])

Work Orientation			Job Classification				Formal Training		On-the-Job Training	
			ADMINISTRATIVE AND PROFESSIONAL	ARTIST	SEMI-SKILLED	WORK ASSISTANCE	15 HOURS OR LESS	MORE THAN 15 HOURS	15 HOURS OR LESS	MORE THAN 15 HOURS
Intrinsic										
	Values	Positive change	24	16	18	39	8	13	15	15
		Negative change	24	49	40	18	42	38	40	38
		Total n	(41)	(84)	(152)	(33)	(38)	(61)	(76)	(60)
	Rewards	Positive change	29	22	31	39	39	22	37	23
		Negative change	42	54	43	30	44	57	32	61
		Total n	(41)	(84)	(152)	(33)	(52)	(74)	(38)	(61)
Extrinsic										
	Values	Positive change	37	32	22	33	18	30	21	32
		Negative change	34	48	47	42	50	41	49	40
		Total n	(41)	(84)	(152)	(33)	(38)	(61)	(76)	(60)
	Rewards	Positive change	26	22	19	27	18	19	15	26
		Negative change	53	57	52	31	44	62	61	43
		Total n	(34)	(69)	(123)	(26)	(45)	(56)	(66)	(46)
Work Relations										
	Values	Positive change	29	31	37	42	27	37	25	42
		Negative change	31	43	35	32	32	40	45	26
		Total n	(35)	(65)	(127)	(31)	(37)	(63)	(56)	(50)
	Rewards	Positive change	33	26	36	27	28	35	33	35
		Negative change	36	50	39	50	33	50	39	43
		Total n	(36)	(80)	(130)	(30)	(36)	(48)	(70)	(49)
Feedback										
	Rewards	Positive change	29	17	32	17	29	19	32	24
		Negative change	36	54	45	38	36	62	43	67
		Total n	(31)	(69)	(119)	(29)	(31)	(42)	(61)	(45)

[a]The "No Change" category is not included in this table. The "Total n," however, refers to all three categories.

TABLE 2.13
Attitude Change by Organizational Characteristics (Percent by Column[a])

Work Orientation		Size		Longevity		Specialization	
		10 AND UNDER	OVER 10	LESS THAN 10 YEARS	10 YEARS AND OVER	LESS THAN 10 JOBS	10 OR MORE JOBS
Intrinsic							
Values	Positive change	17	19	9	23	16	18
	Negative change	46	32	43	38	43	36
	Total n	(105)	(59)	(76)	(98)	(102)	(66)
Rewards	Positive change	25	27	24	27	24	29
	Negative change	51	39	47	48	53	41
	Total n	(105)	(59)	(76)	(98)	(102)	(66)
Extrinsic							
Values	Positive change	30	19	24	29	32	18
	Negative change	46	51	41	48	39	55
	Total n	(105)	(59)	(76)	(98)	(109)	(66)
Rewards	Positive change	21	17	19	18	24	13
	Negative change	51	57	45	61	51	61
	Total n	(57)	(75)	(58)	(84)	(75)	(61)
Work Relations							
Values	Positive change	30	42	23	41	30	38
	Negative change	41	26	44	30	43	27
	Total n	(78)	(50)	(57)	(81)	(77)	(55)
Rewards	Positive change	26	36	27	33	28	35
	Negative change	46	36	38	44	44	40
	Total n	(96)	(56)	(63)	(91)	(85)	(63)
Feedback							
Rewards	Positive change	25	24	28	22	24	25
	Negative change	43	53	41	52	46	51
	Total n	(85)	(51)	(54)	(83)	(72)	(59)

[a]The "No Change" category is not included in this table. The "Total n," however refers to all three categories.

105

nizational structure and its impact on individuals has been noted before (Hall, 1977). Specifically, the satisfaction of the individual with his work has been related to organizational structure (Ivancevich and Donnelly, 1975). Among the more important determinants of structure is the size of the organization (Blau, Heydebrand and Stauffer, 1966), which has been related to morale and job satisfaction (Meltzer and Salter, 1962). Note in Table 2.13 that organizational size has some effect on changes that took place during the period of CETA employment. Large-sized organizations are associated with a positive change in work-relations values and rewards; four out of ten participants in large organizations experienced a positive change, compared with three out of ten participants in small organizations. Large size is also associated with decrease in satisfaction from the amount of feedback received on the job. On the other hand, participants in small organizations experienced declines in their valuation or satisfaction from the intrinsic and work-relations aspects of work; almost 50 percent had a negative change in these dimensions, compared with approximately 35 percent of participants in larger organizations.

The second structural characteristic of an organization to be examined is the degree of specialization or complexity, as measured by the number of job titles in the organization. The degree of specialization in an organization is related to problems of control, coordination, and communication within the organization. While such problems are sources of conflict within the organization, they may enhance effectiveness if conflicts are resolved in an appropriate manner (Lawrence and Lorsch, 1967).

The degree of specialization of an organization directly in charge of a CETA project has a significant impact on the work orientation. Organizations with minimal specialization are associated with a positive effect on extrinsic values and rewards. Between 24 and 32 percent of participants in less specialized organizations reported increases in values and rewards in the extrinsic aspects of work in general and their jobs in particular. This compares with 13 to 18 percent in highly specialized organizations. Organizations with minimal specialization tend to reduce the rewards and valuations of the intrinsic and work-relations aspects of the job: almost one out of two participants in small organizations experienced a decline in this dimension compared with about 35 percent of participants in more specialized organizations.

Finally, the longevity of the organizations is also differentially related to changes in work orientation. Established organizations, that is, those that have been in existence for ten years or more, are conducive to positive-attitude change related to the intrinsic aspects of work as well as to the work-relations aspect. Twenty-three percent of participants in these organizations, compared with only 9 percent in organizations that are fewer than ten years old, had a positive change in their evaluations of the intrinsic aspects of work. Similarly, 41 percent had a positive increase in work-relations values. These same organizations seemed to have a negative effect on work rewards, in particular, on the extrinsic and feedback dimensions. Sixty-one percent reported that they were less satisfied with the extrinsic aspects of their CETA jobs. Similarly 52 percent were less satisfied with the feedback received on their jobs. This compares with approximately 40 percent reporting the same feelings in organizations that were less established.

Individual and Structural Effects on Work Orientation: Regression Analysis

As a final step in the analysis, each of the seven work-orientation-change scales was regressed stepwise upon the independent variables identified in Tables 2.10 to 2.13. The results are presented in Table 2.14 as regression equations. Also presented are the multiple coefficients of determination (R^2) and the stepwise-variance explanations.

The regression analysis permits assessment of the relative independent effects of the various individual and structural factors associated with changes in work orientation. These factors account for between 15 percent and 68 percent of the variance, with 68 percent of the variance explained in the intrinsic-value dimension.

Among the background variables associated with changes in work orientation, race, sex, and welfare dependency account for an average of 6 percent of the variance in four out of the seven scales. Education is significantly related only to change in intrinsic rewards (13 percent).

Of the factors directly associated with the CETA experience, the single most important factor is the job classification of the participant. The type of CETA position held by the participant has a negative effect on changes in all but the work relations and feedback-reward dimensions. It explains approximately 9 percent of the variance in all dimensions where it is included in the regression equation. Formal training is an important predictor, accounting for 15 percent of the variance in changes in extrinsic valuations of work.

Concerning the structural parameters of the organization directly in charge of the CETA project, specialization, longevity, and size all have some direct effect on changes in work orientation. Specialization has a negative effect on intrinsic ($\beta = -2.125$) and work relations rewards ($\beta = -.685$) and a positive effect ($\beta = .304$) on extrinsic rewards. The size of the organization has a positive effect ($\beta = 1.611$) on intrinsic rewards and a negative one ($\beta = -7.14$) on work-relations rewards. In turn the longevity of the organization positively affects intrinsic and feedback rewards ($\beta = .575$ and $\beta = .289$ respectively).

On balance the variables that have the most significant effects on

TABLE 2.14

Stepwise Regression Equations

for Changes in Work Orientations

1. Intrinsic value $= .813^b - .197x_1* - .436x_2* - .249x_4* - .554x_5*$
   $R^2 = .3582$
   Stepwise variance explained $= 10.32\% + 9.3\% + 5.1\% + 11.1\%$

2. Intrinsic reward $= -.957^b + .308x_1* - .529x_2* + .945x_3* - .631x_5* - .814x_6*$
   $+ 1.289x_7* + 1.611x_8* - 2.123x_9* + .575x_{10}*$
   $R^2 = .684$
   Stepwise variance explained $= 3.34\% + 2.81\% + 13.46\% + 9.79\% + 6.53\%$
   $+ 8.72\% + 12.27\% + 6.29\% + 5.19\%$

3. Extrinsic values $= .204^b - .334x_5* + .496x_6*$
   $R^2 = .2482$
   Stepwise variance explained $= 14.87\% + 9.94\%$

4. Extrinsic reward $= .994^b - .285x_5* + .304x_9*$
   $R^2 = .1462$
   Stepwise variance explained $= 6.67\% + 7.96\%$

5. Work relations values $= .132^b + .308x_2* - .241x_4* - .427x_5*$
   $R^2 = .1743$
   Stepwise variance explained $= 5.61\% + 5.18\% + 6.64\%$

6. Work relations rewards $= .289^b + .590x_1* - .419x_4* - 7.14x_8* - .685x_9*$
   $R^2 = .2378$
   Stepwise variance explained $= 7.29\% + 4.86\% + 7.61\% + 4.0\%$

7. Feedback rewards $= .415^b - .321x_2* - .321x_4* + .289x_{10}* + .272x_{11}$
   $R^2 = .2317$
Stepwise variance explained $= 4.89\% + 7.19\% + 4.71\% + 6.3\%$

^{b}a Intercept	x_1 = sex	x_6 = formal training
	x_2 = race	x_7 = on-the-job training
*p < .05	x_3 = education	x_8 = size of organization
	x_4 = welfare dependency	x_9 = specialization
	x_5 = job classification	x_{10} = longevity
		x_{11} = income

changes in work orientation are related to CETA experience either directly through training and employment status or indirectly through structural aspects of the organization monitoring the CETA project. Demographic and socioeconomic characteristics of the participants are of secondary importance in affecting work orientation.

SUMMARY AND CONCLUSIONS

This paper is an evaluation of some aspects of CETA–Title VI in Milwaukee County, Wisconsin. In particular the study had two major objectives: first, it examined the extent to which CETA participants selected were those in greatest need of manpower services as envisioned by federal legislation, and second, it analyzed the effect of CETA employment on the participants' orientation to the world of work.

It has been demonstrated that women are encountering some type of difficulty in being certified as CETA-eligible, whereas certification and CETA employment rates for blacks suggest few differences based upon race, even though a disproportionately large number of blacks who have CETA positions are in Work Assistance Projects and in semiskilled jobs.

Analysis of the sociodemographic characteristics of CETA participants and comments made by project directors during personal interviews provide some evidence of "creaming" in the selection process. The advantage seems to be given to individuals with higher levels of education and to those between ages of 21 and 45. CETA participants with lower education levels also are found disproportionately in the Work Assistance Projects and in semiskilled positions.

Changes in work values and work rewards were observed for the majority of participants, with approximately half experiencing a decline in work orientation during their CETA employment. The decline was predominant among participants who were relatively better educated with higher-income backgrounds or lower dependencies on welfare.

The kind of CETA experience was related to the amount and direction of change in the participant's work orientations. Of particular importance is the type of position held by a participant. Those in Work Assistance Projects benefited the most, whereas workers in semiskilled positions experienced the sharpest decline in work orientations. Also, the amount of training received had a positive effect on work values, but not on work rewards.

Finally, structural parameters of organizations directly in charge of the CETA projects were also associated with the amount and kind of changes in work orientations. Large and established organizations were shown to be associated with a positive change in work orientation.

The findings of this evaluation study suggest that two groups of participants are served in CETA–Title VI. The first group includes those who were victims of structural unemployment, and the second consists of those participants who were affected by cyclical unemployment of a more temporary nature. Participants in the second group are generally more skilled and educated, whereas the structurally unemployed are those who traditionally would be defined as disadvantaged. The findings provide some evidence of a significant shift away from services to the poor in CETA–Title VI allocations. This is partially a result of the definition of eligibility as well as the process of implementation in the Comprehensive Employment and Training Act. CETA–Title VI defines eligible groups in broad terms such as "economically disadvantaged," "unemployed," and "underemployed," with no specification of the relative priority accorded to any of these groups. In the past manpower programs were designed to combat structural unemployment and to focus on the economically disadvantaged. Title VI was not intended exclusively to serve the disadvantaged, but also unemployed persons who were not necessarily disadvantaged. Even though prime sponsors tried to enforce policies that would give priority to the disadvantaged, the federal emphasis on speedy implementation created pressure to fill immediately available slots with any applicant who met the formal eligibility requirements.

In terms of changes in work orientations, the data suggest that participants traditionally defined as disadvantaged, i.e., victims of structural unemployment, benefited from their CETA experiences, whereas participants whose unemployment was of a more temporary nature, experienced a negative impact or no impact at all. This evaluation deals with long-term goals of the program—changes in work orientation that are likely to improve the employability of the "hard to employ." In these terms the CETA projects evaluated were only partially successful. Title VI however, was also intended to provide short-term benefits of lengthened unemployment compensation simply to maintain purchasing power during a recession, and any long-term impact could be looked upon as "icing on the cake."

Ultimately, any manpower program can be considered successful only if it improves the employment status of the persons it serves. Thus, the final evaluation of CETA will be based on the ability of participants to secure employment upon termination of the program. This will have to await further study. Yet, our study suggests that for CETA–Title VI projects to be more effective in terms of their impact on participants, eligibility criteria for participation will have to be more clearly stated, and a distinction will have to be made between participants who are disadvantaged as structurally unemployed and those who are hit by cyclical unemployment due to a recession. For the disadvantaged, CETA will have to be evaluated in terms of traditional manpower goals such as training, skills, work orientation, and eventual job placement, whereas evaluation of the success of programs geared to the second group will be made only with regard to short-term goals of temporary relief from unemployment. Such a distinction will aid considerably evaluators and policymakers.

NOTES

1. Title I was the basis for the establishment of a federal program of financial assistance to state and local governments, who were to be the prime sponsors, for comprehensive manpower services. Title I specifies that prime sponsors—that is, cities, counties, or consortia of governmental units of 100,000 persons or

more—will prepare and submit "a comprehensive plan acceptable to the Secretary of Labor. The plan must set forth the kinds of programs and services to be offered and give assurance that manpower services will be provided to unemployed, underemployed, and disadvantaged persons most in need of help.... The mix and design of services is to be determined by the sponsor, who may continue to fund programs of demonstrated effectiveness or set up new ones."

Eighty percent of the funds authorized under Title I are apportioned in accordance with a formula based on previous level of funding, unemployment, and low income. The 20 percent not under the formula are to be distributed as follows: 5 percent for special grants for vocational education, 4 percent for state manpower services, and 5 percent to encourage consortia. The remaining amount is available at the secretary's discretion.

State government must establish a State Manpower Services Council to review the plans of prime sponsors and make recommendations for coordination and for the cooperation of state agencies.

Title II provides funds to hire unemployed and underemployed persons in public-service jobs in areas of substantial unemployment. Title III provides for direct federal supervision of manpower programs for Indians, migrants and seasonal farm workers; and special groups, such as youth, offenders, the aged, persons of limited English-speaking ability, and other disadvantaged. This title also gives the Secretary the responsibility for research, evaluation, experimental and demonstration projects, labor market information, and job-bank programs. Title IV continues the Job Corps and Title V establishes a national Manpower Commission.

2. The amendment differs from the original version of Title VI in that its focus is on the creation of public service projects whereas the original Public Service Employment Program was aimed at creating jobs for individuals (Burnim, 1978).

3. The comparisons are as follows:

	Intake Interviews	Exit Interviews
Male	60%	57%
Female	40%	42%
Black	42%	36%
White	53%	60%
Other	5%	4%
Under 21	11%	10%
21–30	59%	60%
31–45	19%	18%
Over 45	11%	12%
Some High School	23%	19%
High School Diploma	23%	22%
Post High School	55%	59%

4. Because of a major shift in CETA–Title VI emphasis by the prime sponsor after the review and evaluation was initiated, the proportions of respondents in

these categories are somewhat deceptive. During winter and spring 1978, more CETA–Title VI positions and funding were directed to the Work Assistance Project so that for FY 1978, substantially more than 11 percent of the persons working in CETA–Title VI were in this project; however, since this shift began some time after the initiation of the CRP participant-interviewing effort, it was not possible to alter the participant sample to take this into account. The only consequence of this is an underrepresentation of Work Assistance Project participants in the sample.

5. The analysis produced five factors accounting for 41.8 percent of the total variance among the items. Only the first four factors, accounting for 39.4 percent of the total variance are interpreted.
6. The analysis produced four factors accounting for 57.6 percent of the total variance. All four factors are interpreted.
7. The following table presents the results of the factor analysis:

Scale/Factor	I	II
Intrinsic–Value	.164	.482
Extrinsic–Value	-.019	.562
Work relations–Value	.089	.757
Intrinsic–Reward	.632	.151
Extrinsic–Reward	.613	.128
Work relations–Reward	.686	.177
Feedback–Reward	.505	-.096

8. Similar results were indicated by Kalleberg (1977).
9. The following table presents the mean attitude change and F values for the seven scales.

CETA Expectations

Work Orientation	CETA Will Help Get Other Jobs			Expect Changes in Work Habits		
	YES	NO	F	YES	NO	F
Intrinsic						
Values	.91	1.14	1.6	1.05	.93	2.18
Rewards	1.16	1.62	3.46	1.23	1.28	.14
Extrinsic						
Values	1.15	.95	.55	1.15	1.08	.50
Rewards	.90	1.19	1.46	.92	1.04	1.3
Work Relations						
Values	1.21	1.16	0.45	1.27	1.12	1.88
Rewards	1.17	1.62	3.73*	1.28	1.39	.70
Feedback						
Rewards	1.02	1.36	4.06*	1.04	1.18	1.98

*$p < .05$

REFERENCES

Andrews, F., and S. Withey. "Developing Measures of Perceived Life Quality: Results from Several National Surveys." Social Indicators Research, 1 (1974).

Blau, Peter M., Wolf W. Heydebrand, and Robert E. Stauffer. "The Structure of Small Bureaucracies," American Sociological Review, 31 (1966): 179–91.

Burnim, Mickey L. "An Evaluation of the Public Service Employment Projects in Florida, Created under Title VI of the Comprehensive Employment and Training Act of 1973." A Research Report. Florida Department of Community Affairs (1978).

Federal Register, vol. 42, no. 201 (October 1977).

Hall, Richard H. Organizations: Structure and Process. Englewood Cliffs, N.J.: Prentice-Hall, 1977.

Hedge, David M., and Ronald D. Hedlund. "Delivering Manpower Services: Macro and Micro Analysis." Paper read at the 1979 Annual Meeting of the Southwestern Social Science Association.

Hedlund, Ronald D., and David M. Hedge. "Policy Linkages to Public Opinion: The Responsiveness of Local Public Policy to Citizen Preferences." Paper read at the 1979 Annual Meeting of the Midwest Political Science Association.

Herzberg, Frederick, Bernard Mausner, Richard O. Peterson, and Dora F. Capwell. Job Attitudes: Review of Research and Opinion. Pittsburgh: Psychological Service of Pittsburgh, 1957.

Ivancevich, John M., and James H. Donnelly. "Relation of Organizational Structure to Job Satisfaction, Anxiety-Stress, and Performance," Administrative Science Quarterly 20 (1975):272–280.

Kalleberg, Arne L. "Work Values and Job Satisfaction." American Sociological Review, 42 (1977): 124–143.

Kobrak, Peter, and Richard Perlman. Toward A Comprehensive Manpower Plan: Milwaukee Needs, Programs and Strategies. Milwaukee, Wis.: Milwaukee Urban Observatory, April 1974.

Kohn, Melvin L. "Class and Conformity: A Study in Values." Homewood, Ill.: Dorsey, 1969.

Lawrence Paul R., and Jay W. Lorsch. Organization and Environment: Managing Differentiation and Integration. Cambridge: Harvard Graduate School of Business, 1967.

Mangione, T. W. "Validity of Job Satisfaction." Ph.D. dissertation. University of Michigan, 1973.

Mangione, T. W., and R. P. Quinn. "Job Satisfaction, Counter Productive Behavior, and Self-Narcotizing Withdrawal from Work." Ann Arbor: Survey Research Center, 1973.

Meltzer Leo, and James Salter. "Organizational Structure and the Performance and Job Satisfaction of Physiologists," American Sociological Review, 27 (1962): 351–362.

Milwaukee County Executive Office for Economic Resource Development, CETA Division. "FY 1978 CETA Titles II and IV Funding Proposal to the U.S. Department of Labor."

Milwaukee County Executive Office for Economic Resource Development, CETA Division. "FY 1977 CETA Titles II and IV Funding Proposal to the U.S. Department of Labor."

Mirengoff, William, and Lester Rindler. *The Comprehensive Employment and Training Act.* Washington, D.C.: National Academy of Sciences, 1976.

Quinn, R. P., C. C. Cammann, N. Gupta, and T. A. Beehv. "Effectiveness in Work Roles." Final Report to the Manpower Administration, U.S. Department of Labor (April 1973) (Unpublished).

Quinn, R. P., and L. J. Shepard. The 1972–73 Quality of Employment Survey. Ann Arbor, Michigan: Survey Research Center, 1973.

Ross, J. T., and A. Zander. "Need Satisfaction and Employee Turnover," *Personnel Psychology* 10 (1957): 327–338.

Seashore, Stanley E., and Thomas N. Taber. "Job Satisfaction Indicators and the Correlates," American Behavioral Scientist, 18 (1975): 333–368.

Sheppard, Nathaniel, Jr. "For Blacks, Milwaukee Proves a Hard Place to Find a Job," *New York Times*, December 31, 1977, p. 5.

Snedeker Bonnie B., and David M. Snedeker. 1978 CETA: Decentralization on Trial. Salt Lake City, Utah: Olympus, 1978.

Vroom, V. H. *Work and Motivation.* New York: John Wiley, 1964.

Van Horn, Carl E. "Implementing CETA: The Federal Role," *Policy Analysis*, 4: 159–183.

CHAPTER 3

EQUALITY OF EDUCATIONAL OPPORTUNITY

The contention that education can effectively solve many of the nation's problems has underlined much of government policy in the past two decades. All branches of the federal government have been involved in the formulation and the implementation of educational policies, a sharp departure from the tradition of placing responsibility for public education on state and local governments. The Supreme Court has played a central role in school desegregation, and Congress has, for the first time in United States history, provided funds and entered into the formulation of policy for public elementary and secondary schools. The U.S. Office of Education and other executive departments have sponsored many new programs aimed at various target populations and focusing at the numerous aspects of education.

Many of the programs initiated and carried out by the federal government were designed to reduce inequality in education. Higher education confers increased chances for income, influence, and prestige on individuals who are fortunate enough to obtain it. Indeed, in our society occupational attainment and the allocation of social position is increasingly dependent on higher education. Increased perception of this fact has motivated policymakers to commit resources and develop programs to equalize access to basic education of high quality. Spurred on by the civil rights movement of the 1950s and 1960s, equal opportunity in education has become a salient and important national issue. Many regard it as a necessary condition to ensure the rights and privileges of all persons, and to ensure that they are able to assume their responsibilities as citizens.

Public policies for equalizing educational opportunity were first directed toward the establishment of public responsibility for the education of children in states where public education did not exist. These policies were followed by other policies aimed at establishing adequate educational facilities and diverse educational programs. The struggle over separate but equal schools was legally resolved in 1954 when the Supreme Court ruled that separate schools were intrinsically unequal. In the 1960s demands were made for education of high quality, where possible, on an ethnically and racially integrated basis. Yet, where school segregation existed, demands were advanced for community control of those schools by groups indigenous to the cultures and the communities in which they live. Community control of schools "is intended to create an environment in which more meaningful educational policies can be developed and a wide variety of alternative solutions and techniques can be tested ... a school system devoted to community needs and serving as an agent of community interests will provide an environment more conducive to learning."[1]

Alongside policies aimed at ending *de facto* segregation by racially balancing the assignment of students to public schools, busing students wherever necessary to achieve that racial balance, and initiatives to increase community control in ghetto schools, the idea of compensatory education as a complementary strategy in the equalization of educational opportunity materialized. Most government educational programs reflect, explicitly or implicitly, the compensatory approach. In essence the underlying assumption behind compensatory educational programs is that environmental problems create learning difficulties for the disadvantaged student. These difficulties, e.g., cognitive skills, educational motivation, self-esteem, can be overcome in part by special education programs starting at the preschool level. The major thrust of the compensatory approach came with Title I of the Elementary and Secondary Education Act of 1965 (ESEA), which was designed to assist poverty-impacted schools. Other major programs aimed at increasing the basic cognitive skills of disadvantaged children include Head Start, Follow-Through, and Bilingual Education. A second category of programs, also deriving from the compensatory approach, was developed with the objective of increasing educational attainments of disadvantaged children. This category of programs includes Upward Bound, Educational Opportunity Grants, Work Study, Talent Search, and dropout-prevention projects. Experts state that the success of these programs could be reflected in additional years of schooling acquired by program participants compared to their nonparticipating counterparts.

The articles in this chapter analyze two controversial issues related to policy attempts to equalize educational opportunities. The MacKay et al. article questions the view that efforts at compensatory education cannot possibly succeed because of the disadvantaged child's inferior genetic intelligence. According to this recently revived view, it is inequality in the native ability of children, rather than inequality in schools or society, that determines the success or failure of students.[2] The longitudinal, experimental evaluation reported here was carried out in Cali, Colombia, over a period of forty-two months. Its findings show that the combined nutritional, health, and educational treatment of a child between the ages of three and seven years can prevent large losses of potential cognitive ability and can help to reduce the large intelligence gap between children from severely deprived environments and those from privileged backgrounds.

The Giles article focuses on the relationship between school desegregation and the stability of white enrollment. In contrast to the argument that one significant, unintended consequence of school desegregation has been massive "white flight"[3] and the counterargument that white flight is less an outcome of desegregation policy than a long-term urban trend,[4] Giles points out the specific conditions under which white enrollments decrease as a result of school desegregation. The analysis focuses on 60 districts and approximately 1,600 schools located in the southern states. The *ex post facto* nature of the research design is somewhat compensated by the use of structural equations. Yet, as Giles points out, the findings are tentative, and their policy implications are constrained by the scope and the design of the study.

NOTES

1. Marilyn Gittell and Alan G. Hevesi, eds., *The Politics of Urban Education*, New York: Praeger, 1969, pp. 365–366.
2. Arthur R. Jensen, "How Much Can We Boost IQ and School Achievement?" *Harvard Educational Review*, vol. 39 (Winter 1969), pp. 1–123. Cf. Martin Carnoy, "Is Compensatory Education Possible?" in Martin Carnoy, ed., *Schooling in a Corporate Society*, New York: McKay, 1972, pp. 174–185.
3. See for example, James S. Coleman, Sara D. Kelley, and John A. Moore, "Recent Trends in School Integration," paper presented at the Annual

Meeting of the American Educational Research Association, Washington, D.C.: April 2, 1975.

4. Thomas F. Pettigrew and Robert L. Green, "School Desegregation in Large Cities: A Critique of the Coleman 'White Flight' Thesis," *Harvard Educational Review*, vol. 46 (February 1976), pp. 1–53.

IMPROVING COGNITIVE ABILITY IN CHRONICALLY DEPRIVED CHILDREN

Harrison McKay
Leonardo Sinisterra
Arlene McKay
Hernando Gomez
Pascuala Lloreda

In recent years, social and economic planning in developing countries has included closer attention than before to the nutrition, health, and education of children of preschool age in low-income families. One basis for this, in addition to mortality and morbidity studies indicating high vulnerability at that age,[1] is information suggesting that obstacles to normal development in the first years of life, found in environments of such poverty that physical growth is retarded through malnutrition, are likely also to retard intellectual development permanently if early remedial action is not taken.[2] The loss of intellectual capability, broadly defined, is viewed as especially serious because the technological character of contemporary civilization makes individual productivity and personal fulfillment increasingly contingent upon such capability. In tropical and subtropical zones of the world between 220 and 250 million children below 6 years of age live in conditions of environmental deprivation extreme enough to produce some degree of malnutrition;[3] failure to act could result in irretrievable loss of future human capacity on a massive scale.

Although this argument finds widespread agreement among scientists and planners, there is uncertainty about the effectiveness of specific remedial actions. Doubts have been growing for the past decade about whether providing food, education, or health care directly to young children in poverty environments can counteract the myriad social, economic, and biological limitations to their intellectual growth. Up to 1970, when the study reported here was formulated, no definitive evidence was available to show that food and health care provided to malnourished or "at risk" infants and young children could produce lasting increases in intellectual functioning. This was so in spite of the ample experience of medical specialists throughout the tropical world that malnourished children typically responded to nutritional recuperation by being more active physically, more able to assimilate environmental events, happier, and more verbal, all of which would be hypothesized to create a more favorable outlook for their capacity to learn.[4]

In conferences and publications emphasis was increasingly placed upon the inextricable relation of malnutrition to other environmental factors inhibiting full mental development of preschool age children in poverty environments.[5] It was becoming clear that, at least after the period of rapid brain growth in the first 2 years of life, when protein-calorie malnutrition could have its maximum deleterious physiological effects,[6] nutritional rehabilitation and health care programs should be accompanied by some form of environmental modification for children at risk. The largest amount of available information about the potential effects of environmental modification among children from poor families pertained to the United States, where poverty was not of such severity as to make malnutrition a health issue of marked proportions. Here a large literature showed that the low intellectual performance found among disadvantaged children was environmentally based and probably was largely fixed during the preschool years.[7] This information gave impetus to the belief that direct treatments, carefully designed and properly delivered to children during early critical periods, could produce large and lasting increases in intellectual ability. As a consequence, during the 1960s a wide variety of individual, research-based preschool programs as well as a national program were developed in the United States for children from low-income families.[8] Several showed positive results but in the aggregate they were not as great or as lasting as had been hoped, and there followed a widespread questioning of the effectiveness of early childhood education as a means of permanently improving intellectual ability among disadvantaged children on a large scale.[9]

From pilot work leading up to the study reported here, we concluded that there was an essential issue that had not received adequate attention and the clarification of which might have tempered the pessimism: the relation of gains in intellectual ability to the intensity and duration of meliorative treatment received during different periods in the preschool years.

In addition to the qualitative question of what kinds of preschool intervention, if any, are effective, attention should have been given to the question of what amount of treatment yields what amount of gain. We hypothesized that the increments in intellectual ability produced in preschool programs for disadvantaged children were subsequently lost at least in part because the programs were too brief. Although there was a consensus that longer and more intensive preschool experience could produce larger and more lasting increases, in only one study was there to be found a direct attempt to test this, and in that one sampling problems caused difficulties in interpretation.[10]

As a consequence, the study reported here was designed to examine the quantitative question, with chronically undernourished children, by systematically increasing the duration of multidisciplinary treatments to levels not previously reported and evaluating results with measures directly comparable across all levels.[11] This was done not only to test the hypothesis that greater amounts of treatment could produce greater and more enduring intellectual gains but also to develop for the first time an appraisal of what results could be expected at different points along a continuum of action. This second objective, in addition to its intrinsic scientific interest, was projected to have another benefit, that of being useful in the practical application of early childhood services. Also unique in the study design was the simultaneous combination of health, nutrition, and educational components in the treatment program. With the exception of our own pilot work,[12] prior studies of preschool nutritional recuperation programs had not included educational activities. Likewise, preschool education studies had not included nutritional recuperation activities, because malnutrition of the degree found in the developing countries was not characteristic of disadvantaged groups studied in the United States,[13] where most of the modern early-education research had been done.

EXPERIMENTAL DESIGN AND SUBJECTS

The study was carried out in Cali, Colombia, a city of nearly a million people with many problems characteristic of rapidly expanding cities in developing countries, including large numbers of families living in marginal economic conditions. Table 3.1 summarizes the experimental design employed. The total time available for the experiment was $3\frac{1}{2}$ years, from February 1971 to August 1974. This was divided into four treatment periods of 9 months each plus interperiod recesses. Our decision to begin the study with children as close as possible to 3 years of age was based upon the 2 years of pilot studies in which treatment and measurement systems

TABLE 3.1
Basic Selection and Treatment Variables
of the Groups of Children in the Study*

Group	N IN 1971	IN 1975	Characteristics
T1(a)	57	49	Low SES, subnormal weight and height. One treatment period, between November 1973 and August 1974 (75 to 84 months of age).
T1(b)	56	47	Low SES, subnormal weight and height. One treatment period, between November 1973 and August 1974 (75 to 84 months of age), with prior nutritional supplementation and health care.
T2	64	51	Low SES, subnormal weight and height. Two treatment periods, between November 1972 and August 1974 (63 to 84 months of age).
T3	62	50	Low SES, subnormal weight and height. Three treatment periods, between December 1971 and August 1974 (52 to 84 months of age).
T4	62	51	Low SES, subnormal weight and height. Four treatment periods, between February 1971 and August 1974 (42 to 84 months of age).
HS	38	30	High SES. Untreated, but measured at the same points as groups T1–T4.
T0	116	72	Low SES, normal weight and height. Untreated.

*SES is family socioeconomic status.

were developed for children starting at that age.[14] The projected 180 to 200 days of possible attendance at treatment made each projected period similar in length to a school year in Colombia, and the end of the fourth period was scheduled to coincide with the beginning of the year in which the children were of eligible age to enter first grade.

With the object of having 60 children initially available for each treatment group (in case many should be lost to the study during the $3\frac{1}{2}$ year period), approximately 7500 families living in two of the city's lowest-income areas were visited to locate and identify all children with birth dates between 1 June and 30 November 1967, birth dates that would satisfy primary school entry requirements in 1974. In a second visit to the 733 families with such children, invitations were extended to have the children medically examined. The families of 518 accepted, and each child received a clinical examination, anthropometric measurement, and screening for serious neurological dysfunctions. During a third visit to these families, interviews and observations were conducted to determine living conditions, economic resources, and age, education, and occupations of family members. At this stage the number of potential subjects was reduced by 69 (to 449), because of errors in birth date, serious neurological or sensory dysfunctions, refusal to participate further, or removal from the area.

Because the subject loss due to emigration during the 4 months of preliminary data gathering was substantial, 333 children were selected to assure the participation of 300 at the beginning of treatment; 301 were still available at that time, 53 percent of them male. Children selected for the experiment from among the 449 candidates were those having, first, the lowest height and weight for age; second, the highest number of clinical signs of malnutrition;[15] and third, the lowest per capita family income. The second and third criteria were employed only in those regions of the frequency distributions where differences among the children in height and weight for age were judged by the medical staff to lack biological significance. Figure 3.1 shows these frequency distributions and includes scales corresponding to percentiles in a normal population.[16]

The 116 children not selected were left untreated and were not measured again until 4 years later, at which point the 72 still living in the area and willing once again to collaborate were reincorporated into the longitudinal study and measured on physical growth and cognitive development at the same time as the selected children, beginning at 7 years of age. At 3 years of age these children did not show abnormally low weight for age or weight for height.

In order to have available a set of local reference standards for "normal" physical and psychological development, and not depend solely upon foreign standards, a group of children (group HS) from families with high socioeconomic status, living in the same city and having the same range of birth dates as the experimental group, was included in the study. Our assumption was that, in regard to available economic resources, housing, food, health care, and educational opportunities, these children had the highest probability of full intellectual and physical development of any group in the society. In relation to the research program they remained untreated, receiving only medical and psychological assessment at the same intervals as the treated children, but the majority were attending the best private preschools during the study. Eventually 63 children were recruited for group HS, but only the 38 noted in Table 3.1 were available at the first psychological testing session in 1971.

Nearly all the 333 children selected for treatment lived in homes distributed throughout an area of approximately 2 square kilometers. This area was subdivided into 20 sectors in such a way that between 13 and 19 children were included in each sector. The sectors were ranked in order of a standardized combination of average height and weight for age and per

Figure 3.1. Frequency distributions of height and weight (as percent of normal for age) of the subject pool of 449 children available in 1970, from among whom 333 were selected for treatment groups. A combination of height and weight was the first criterion; the second and third criteria, applied to children in the overlap regions, were clinical signs of malnutrition and family income. Two classification systems for childhood malnutrition yield the following description of the selected children: 90 percent nutritionally "stunted" at 3 years of age and 35 percent with evidence of "wasting"; 26 percent with "second degree" malnutrition, 54 percent with "first degree," and 16 percent "low normal."[16]

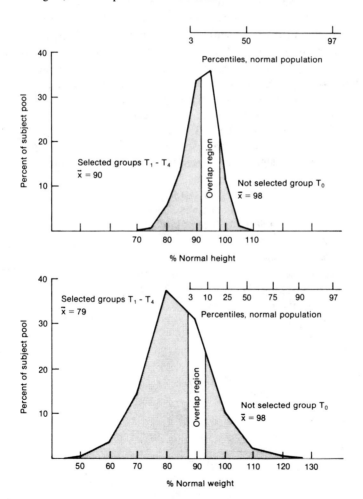

capita family income of the children. Each of the first five sectors in the ranking was assigned randomly to one of five groups. This procedure was followed for the next three sets of five sectors, yielding four sectors for each group, one from each of four strata. At this point the groups remained unnamed; only as each new treatment period was to begin was a group assigned to it and families in the sectors chosen so informed. The children were assigned by sectors instead of individually in order to minimize social interaction between families in different treatment groups and to make daily transportation more efficient.[17] Because this "lottery" system was geographically based, all selected children who were living in a sector immediately prior to its assignment were included in the assignment and remained in the same treatment group regardless of further moves. In view of this process, it must be noted that the 1971 N's reported for the treatment groups in Table 3.1 are retrospective figures, based upon a count of children then living in sectors assigned later to treatment groups. Table 3.1 also shows the subject loss, by group, between 1971 and 1975. The loss of 53 children—18 percent—from the treatment groups over 4 years was considerably less than expected. Two of these children died and 51 emigrated from Cali with their families; on selection variables they did not differ to a statistically significant degree from the 248 remaining.

TABLE 3.2
Selection Variables and Family Characteristics
of Study Groups in 1970 (Means)*

Variable	Group		
	T1–T4	T0	HS
Height as percent of normal for age	90	98	101
Weight as percent of normal for age	79	98	102
Per capita family income as percent of group HS	5	7	100
Per capita food expenditure in family as percent of group HS	15	22	100
Number of family members	7.4	6.4	4.7
Number in family under 15 years of age	4.8	3.8	2.4
Number of play/sleep rooms per child	.3	.5	1.6
Age of father	37	37	37
Age of mother	31	32	31
Years of schooling, father	3.6	3.7	14.5
Years of schooling, mother	3.5	3.3	10.0

*All differences between group HS and groups T1–T4 are statistically significant ($P < .01$) except age of parents. There are no statistically significant differences among groups T1–T4. There are statistically significant differences between group T0 and combined groups T1–T4 in height and weight (as percent of normal), per capita income and food expenditure, number of family members and children, and rooms per child; and between group T0 and group HS on all variables except age of parents and weight.

A longitudinal study was begun, then, with groups representing extreme points on continua of many factors related to intellectual development, and with an experimental plan to measure the degree to which children at the lower extreme could be moved closer to those of the upper extreme as a result of combined treatments of varying durations. Table 3.2 compares selected (T1–T4), not selected (T0), and reference (HS) groups on some of the related factors, including those used for selecting children for participation in treatment.

TREATMENTS

The total number of treatment days per period varied as follows: period 1, 180 days; period 2, 185; period 3, 190; period 4, 172. A fire early in period 4 reduced the time available owing to the necessity of terminating the study before the opening of primary school. The original objective was to have each succeeding period at least as long as the preceding one in order to avoid reduction in intensity of treatment. The programs occupied 6 hours a day 5 days a week, and attendance was above 95 percent for all groups; hence there were approximately 1040, 1060, 1080, and 990 hours of treatment per child per period from period 1 to period 4, respectively. The total number of hours of treatment per group, then, were as follows: T4, 4170 hours; T3, 3130 hours; T2, 2070 hours; T1 (a and b), 990 hours.

In as many respects as possible, treatments were made equivalent between groups within each period. New people, selected and trained as child-care workers to accommodate the periodic increases in numbers of children, were combined with existing personnel and distributed in such a way that experience, skill, and familiarity with children already treated were equalized for all groups, as was the adult-child ratio. Similarly, as new program sites were added, children rotated among them so that all groups occupied all sites equal lengths of time. Except for special care given to the health and nutritional adaptation of each newly entering group during the initial weeks, the same systems in these treatments were applied to all children within periods.

An average treatment day consisted of 6 hours of integrated health, nutritional, and educational activities, in which approximately 4 hours were devoted to education and 2 hours to health, nutrition, and hygiene. In practice, the nutrition and health care provided opportunities to reinforce many aspects of the education curriculum, and time in the education program was used to reinforce recommended hygienic and food consumption practices.

The nutritional supplementation program was designed to provide a minimum of 75 percent of recommended daily protein and calorie allowances, by means of low-cost foods available commercially, supplemented with vitamins and minerals, and offered ad libitum three times a day. In the vitamin and mineral supplementation, special attention was given to vitamin A, thiamin, riboflavin, niacin, and iron, of which at least 100 percent of recommended dietary allowance was provided.[18]

The health care program included daily observation of all children attending the treatment center, with immediate pediatric attention to those with symptoms reported by the parents or noted by the health and education personnel. Children suspected of an infectious condition were not brought into contact with their classmates until the danger of contagion had passed. Severe health problems occurring during weekends or holidays were attended on an emergency basis in the local university hospital.

The educational treatment was designed to develop cognitive processes and language, social abilities, and psychomotor skills, by means of an integrated curriculum model. It was a combination of elements developed in pilot studies and adapted from other programs known to have demonstrated positive effects upon cognitive development.[19] Adapting to developmental changes in the children, its form progressed from a structured day divided among six to eight different directed activities, to one with more time available for individual projects. This latter form, while including activities planned to introduce new concepts, stimulate verbal expression, and develop motor skills, stressed increasing experimentation and decision taking by the children. As with the nutrition and health treatments during the first weeks of each new period, the newly entering children received special care in order to facilitate their adaptation and to teach the basic skills necessary for them to participate in the program. Each new period was conceptually more complex than the preceding one, the last ones incorporating more formal reading, writing, and number work.

MEASURES OF COGNITIVE DEVELOPMENT

There were five measurement points in the course of the study: (i) at the beginning of the first treatment period; (ii) at the end of the first treatment period; (iii) after the end of the second period, carrying over into the beginning of the third; (iv) after the end of the third period, extending into the fourth; and (v) following the fourth treatment period. For the purpose of measuring the impact of treatment upon separate components of cognitive development, several short tests were employed at each measurement point, rather than a single intelligence test. The tests varied from point to point, as those only applicable at younger ages were replaced by others that could be continued into primary school years. At all points the plan was to have tests that theoretically measured adequacy of language usage, immediate memory, manual dexterity and motor control, information and vocabulary, quantitative concepts, spatial relations, and logical thinking, with a balance between verbal and nonverbal production. Table 3.3 is a list of tests applied at each measurement point. More were applied than are listed; only those employed at two or more measurement points and having items that fulfilled the criteria for the analysis described below are included.

Testing was done by laypersons trained and supervised by professional psychologists. Each new test underwent a 4 to 8 month developmental sequence which included an initial practice phase to familiarize the examiners with the format of the test and possible difficulties in application. Thereafter, a series of pilot studies were conducted to permit the modification of items in order to attain acceptable levels of difficulty, reliability, and ease of application. Before each measurement point, all tests were applied to children not in the study until adequate inter-tester reliability and standardization of application were obtained. After definitive application

TABLE 3.3
Tests of Cognitive Ability Applied at Different
Measurement Points (See Text) Between
43 and 87 Months of Age*

Test	Measurement Points
Understanding complex commands	1,2
Figure tracing	1,2,3
Picture vocabulary	1,2,3
Intersensory perception[33]	1,2,3
Colors, numbers, letters	1,2,3
Use of prepositions	1,2,3
Block construction	1,2,3
Cognitive maturity[34]	1,2,3,4
Sentence completion[35]	1,2,3,4
Memory for sentences[34]	1,2,3,4,5
Knox cubes[36]	1,2,3,4,5
Geometric drawings[37]	3,4
Arithmetic[38,38]	3,4,5
Mazes[40]	3,4,5
Information[41]	3,4,5
Vocabulary[39]	3,4,5
Block design[42]	4,5
Digit memory[43]	4,5
Analogies and similarities[44]	4,5
Matrices[45]	4,5
Visual classification	4,5

*Only tests that were applied at two adjacent points and that provided items for the analysis in Table 3.4 are included. The unreferenced tests were constructed locally.

at each measurement point, all tests were repeated on a 10 percent sample
to evaluate test-retest reliability. To protect against examiner biases, the
children were assigned to examiners randomly and no information was
provided regarding treatment group or nutritional or socioeconomic level.
(The identification of group HS children was, however, unavoidable even
in the earliest years, not only because of their dress and speech but also because of the differences in their interpersonal behavior.) Finally, in order
to prevent children from being trained specifically to perform well on test
items, the two functions of intervention and evaluation were separated as
far as possible. We intentionally avoided, in the education programs, the
use of materials or objects from the psychological tests. Also, the intervention personnel had no knowledge of test content or format, and neither
they nor the testing personnel were provided with information about group
performance at any of the measurement points.

DATA ANALYSIS

The data matrix of cognitive measures generated during the 44-month interval between the first and last measurement points entailed evaluation
across several occasions by means of a multivariate vector of observations.
A major problem in the evaluation procedure, as seen in Table 3.3, is that
the tests of cognitive development were not the same at every measurement point. Thus the response vector was not the same along the time dimension. Initially a principal component approach was used, with factor
scores representing the latent variables.[20] Although this was eventually dis-
carded because there was no guarantee of factor invariance across occasions, the results were very similar to those yielded by the analyses finally
adopted for this article. An important consequence of these analyses was
the finding that nearly all of the variation could be explained by the first
component,[21] and under the assumption of unidimensionality cognitive test
items were pooled and calibrated according to the psychometric model
proposed by Rasch[22] and implemented computationally by Wright.[23] The
technique employed to obtain the ability estimates in Table 3.4 guarantees
that the same latent trait is being reflected in these estimates.[24] Consequently, the growth curves in Fig. 3.2 (page 131) are interpreted as representing "general cognitive ability."[25]

Table 3.5 (page 130) shows correlations between pairs of measurement
points of the ability estimates of all children included in the two points.
The correspondence is substantial, and the matrix exhibits the "simplex"
pattern expected in psychometric data of this sort.[26] As the correlations are
not homogeneous, a test for diagonality in the transformed error co-vari-

ance matrix was carried out, and the resulting chi-square value led to rejection of a mixed model assumption. In view of this, Bock's multivariate procedure,[27] which does not require constant correlations, was employed to analyze the differences among groups across measurement points. The results showed a significant groups-by-occasions effect, permitting rejection of the hypothesis of parallel profiles among groups. A single degree-of-freedom decomposition of this effect showed that there were significant differences in every possible Helmert contrast. Stepdown tests indicated that all components were required in describing profile differences.

The data in Table 3.4, plotted in Figure 3.2 with the addition of dates and duration of treatment periods, are based upon the same children at all measurement points. These are children having complete medical, socio-economic, and psychological test records. The discrepancies between the 1975 N's in Table 3.1 and the N's in Table 3.4 are due to the fact that 14 children who were still participating in the study in 1975 were excluded from the analysis because at least one piece of information was missing, a move made to facilitate correlational analyses. Between 2 percent (T4) and 7 percent (HS) were excluded for this reason.

TABLE 3.4

Scaled Scores on General Cognitive Ability, Means and Estimated Standard Errors, of the Four Treatment Groups and Group HS at Five Testing Points

Group	N	Average Age at Testing (Months)				
		43	49	63	77	87
		Mean score				
HS	28	− .11	.39	2.28	4.27	4.89
T4	50	−1.82*	.21	1.80	3.35	3.66
T3	47	−1.72	−1.06	1.64	3.06	3.35
T2	49	−1.94	−1.22	.30†	2.61	3.15
T1	90	−1.83	−1.11	.33	2.07	2.73
		Estimated standard error				
HS	28	.192	.196	.166	.191	.198
T4	50	.225	.148	.138	.164	.152
T3	47	.161	.136	.103	.123	.120
T2	49	.131	.132	.115	.133	.125
T1	90	.110	.097	.098	.124	.108
		Standard deviation				
All groups		1.161	1.153	1.169	1.263	1.164

*Calculated from 42 percent sample tested prior to beginning of treatment.
†Calculated from 50 percent sample tested prior to beginning of treatment.

TABLE 3.5
Correlation of Ability Scores Across
Measurement Points

Measurement Points	1	2	3	4	5
1	–	.78	.68	.54	.48
2		–	.80	.66	.59
3			–	.71	.69
4				–	.76
5					–

For all analyses, groups T1(a) and T1(b) were combined into group T1 because the prior nutritional supplementation and health care provided group T1(b) had not been found to produce any difference between the two groups. Finally, analysis by sex is not included because a statistically significant difference was found at only one of the five measurement points.

RELATION OF GAINS TO TREATMENT

The most important data in Table 3.4 and Figure 3.2 are those pertaining to cognitive ability scores at the fifth testing point. The upward progression of mean scores from T1 to T4 and the nonoverlapping standard errors, except between T2 and T3, generally confirm that the sooner the treatment was begun the higher the level of general cognitive ability reached by age 87 months. Another interpretation of the data could be that the age at which treatment began was a determining factor independent of amount of time in treatment.

It can be argued that the level of cognitive development which the children reached at 7 years of age depended upon the magnitude of gains achieved during the first treatment period in which they participated, perhaps within the first 6 months, although the confounding of age and treatment duration in the experimental design prohibits conclusive testing of the hypothesis. The data supporting this are in the declining magnitude of gain, during the first period of treatment attended, at progressively higher ages of entry into the program. Using group T1 as an untreated baseline until it first entered treatment, and calculating the difference in gains[28] between it and groups T4, T3, and T2 during their respective first periods of treatment, we obtain the following values: group T4, 1.31; group T3, 1.26; and group T2, .57. When calculated as gains per month between testing periods, the data are the following: T4, .22; T3, .09; and T2, .04. This suggests an exponential relationship. Although, because of unequal intervals between testing points and the overlapping of testing durations with treatment periods, this latter relationship must be viewed with caution, it is clear that the older the children were upon entry into the treatment programs the less was their gain in cognitive development in the first 9 months of participation relative to an untreated baseline.

The lack of a randomly assigned, untreated control group prevents similar quantification of the response of group T1 to its one treatment period.

Figure 3.2. Growth of general cognitive ability of the children from age 43 months to 87 months, the age at the beginning of primary school. Ability scores are scaled sums of test items correct among items common to proximate testing points. The solid lines represent periods of participation in a treatment sequence, and brackets to the right of the curves indicate $\pm$ 1 standard error of the corresponding group means at the fifth measurement point. At the fourth measurement point there are no overlapping standard errors; at earlier measurement points there is overlap only among obviously adjacent groups (see Table 3.4). Group T0 was tested at the fifth measurement point but is not represented in this figure, or in Table 3.2, because its observed low level of performance could have been attributed to the fact that this was the first testing experience of the group T0 children since the neurological screening 4 years earlier.

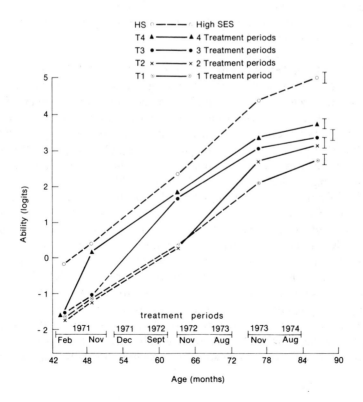

If group HS is taken as the baseline, the observed gain of T1 is very small. The proportion of the gap between group HS and group T1 that was closed during the fourth treatment period was 2 percent, whereas in the initial treatment period of each of the other groups the percentages were group T4, 89; group T3, 55; and group T2, 16. That the progressively declining responsiveness at later ages extends to group T1 can be seen additionally in the percentages of gap closed between group T4 and the other groups during the first treatment period of each of the latter: group T3, 87; group T2, 51; and group T1, 27.

DURABILITY OF GAINS

Analysis of items common to testing points five and beyond has yet to be done, but the data contained in Figure 3.3, Stanford-Binet intelligence quotients at 8 years of age, shows that the relative positions of the groups at age 7 appear to have been maintained to the end of the first year of primary school. Although the treated groups all differ from each other in the expected direction, generally the differences are not statistically significant unless one group has had two treatment periods more than another. A surprising result of the Stanford-Binet testing was that group T0 children, the seemingly more favored among the low-income community (see Table 3.2), showed such low intelligence quotients; the highest score in group T0 (IQ = 100) was below the mean of group HS, and the lowest group HS score (IQ = 84) was above the mean of group T0. This further confirms that the obstacles to normal intellectual growth found in conditions of poverty in which live large segments of the population are very strong. It is possible that this result is due partly to differential testing histories, despite the fact that group T0 had participated in the full testing program at the preceding fifth measurement point, and that this was the first Stanford-Binet testing for the entire group of subject children.

The difference between groups T0 and T1 is in the direction of superiority of group T1 ($t = 1.507$, $P < .10$). What the IQ of group T1 would have been without its one treatment period is not possible to determine except indirectly through regression analyses with other variables, but we would expect it to have been lower than T0's, because T0 was significantly above T1 on socioeconomic and anthropometric correlates of IQ (Table 3.2). Also, T1 was approximately .30 standard deviation below T0 at 38 months of age on a cognitive development factor of a preliminary neurological screening test applied in 1970, prior to selection. Given these data and the fact that at 96 months of age there is a difference favoring group T1 that approaches statistical significance, we conclude not only that group T1

Figure 3.3. Mean scores on the Stanford-Binet Intelligence Test at 8 years of age. Groups T0–T4 had had 1 year of primary school. Group HS children had attended preschool and primary schools for up to five consecutive years prior to this testing point. Mental age minus chronological age is as follows: Group T0 − 18 months; Group T1 − 15 months; Group T2 − 11 months; Group T3 − 9 months; Group T4 − 5 months; Group HS + 10 months.

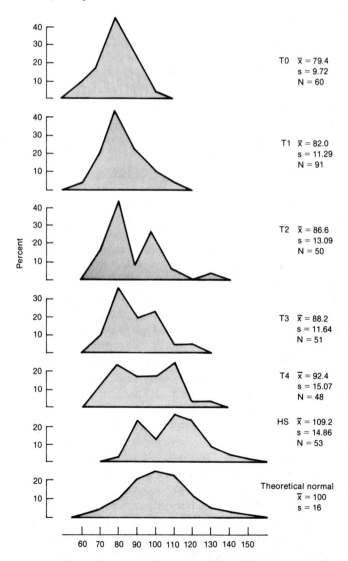

children increased in cognitive ability as a result of their one treatment period (although very little compared to the other groups) but also that they retained the increase through the first year of primary school.

An interesting and potentially important characteristic of the curves in Figure 3.3 is the apparent increasing bimodality of the distribution of the groups with increasing length of treatment, in addition to higher means and upward movement of both extremes. The relatively small sample sizes and the fact that these results were found only once make it hazardous to look upon them as definitive. However, the progression across groups is quite uniform and suggests that the issue of individual differential response to equivalent treatment should be studied more carefully.

SOCIAL SIGNIFICANCE OF GAINS

Group HS was included in the study for the purpose of establishing a baseline indicating what could be expected of children when conditions for growth and development were optimal. In this way the effectiveness of the treatment could be evaluated from a frame of reference of the social ideal. It can be seen in Table 3.4 that group HS increased in cognitive ability at a rate greater than the baseline group T1 during the 34 months before T1 entered treatment. This is equivalent to, and confirms, the previously reported relative decline in intelligence among disadvantaged children.[29, p. 258] Between the ages of 4 and 6 years, group HS children passed through a period of accelerated development that greatly increased the distance between them and all the treatment groups. The result, at age 77 months, was that group T4 arrived at a point approximately 58 percent of the distance between group HS and the untreated baseline group T1, group T3 arrived at 45 percent, and group T2 at 24 percent. Between 77 and 87 months, however, these differences appear to have diminished, even taking into account that group T1 entered treatment during this period. In order for these percentages to have been maintained, the baseline would have had to remain essentially unchanged. With respect to overall gains from 43 months to 87 months, the data show that reduction of the 1.5 standard deviation gap found at 43 months of age between group HS and the treated children required a duration and intensity of treatment at least equal to that of group T2; the group HS overall growth of 5.00 units of ability is less than that of all groups except T1.

As noted, group HS was not representative of the general population, but was a sample of children intentionally chosen from a subgroup above average in the society in characteristics favorable to general cognitive development. For the population under study, normative data do not exist; the "theoretical normal" distribution shown in Figure 3.3 represents the

U.S. standardization group of 1937.[30] As a consequence, the degree to which the treatments were effective in closing the gap between the disadvantaged children and what could be described as an acceptable level cannot be judged. It is conceivable that group HS children were developing at a rate superior to that of this hypothetical normal. If that was the case, the gains of the treated children could be viewed even more positively.

Recent studies of preschool programs have raised the question whether differences between standard intellectual performance and that encountered in disadvantaged children represent real deficits or whether they reflect cultural or ethnic uniquenesses. This is a particularly relevant issue where disadvantaged groups are ethnically and linguistically distinct from the dominant culture.[29, pp. 262-272; 31] The historical evolution of differences in intellectual ability found between groups throughout the world is doubtless multidimensional, with circumstances unique to each society or region, in which have entered religious, economic, ethnic, biological, and other factors in different epochs, and thus the simple dichotomy of culture uniqueness versus deprivation is only a first approximation to a sorely needed, thorough analysis of antecedents and correlates of the variations. Within the limits of the dichotomy, however, the evidence with regard to the children in our study suggests that the large differences in cognitive ability found between the reference group and the treated groups in 1971 should be considered as reflecting deficits rather than divergent ethnic identities. Spanish was the language spoken in all the homes, with the addition of a second language in some group HS families. All the children were born in the same city sharing the same communication media and popular culture and for the most part the same religion. Additionally, on tests designed to maximize the performance of the children from low-income families by the use of objects, words, and events typical in their neighborhoods (for example, a horse-drawn cart in the picture vocabulary test), the difference between them and group HS was still approximately 1.50 standard deviations at 43 months of age. Thus it is possible to conclude that the treated children's increases in cognitive ability are relevant to them in their immediate community as well as to the ideal represented by the high-status reference group. This will be more precisely assessed in future analyses of the relation of cognitive gains to achievement in primary school.

CONCLUSIONS

The results leave little doubt that environmental deprivation of a degree severe enough to produce chronic undernutrition manifested primarily by stunting strongly retards general cognitive development, and that the retardation is less amenable to modification with increasing age. The study shows that combined nutritional, health, and educational treatments between 3½ and 7 years of age can prevent large losses of potential cognitive ability, with significantly greater effect the earlier the treatments begin. As little as 9 months of treatment prior to primary school entry appears to produce significant increases in ability, although small compared to the gains of children receiving treatment lasting two, three, and four times as long. Continued study will be necessary to ascertain the long-range durability of the treatment effects, but the present data show that they persist at 8 years of age.

The increases in general cognitive ability produced by the multiform preschool interventions are socially significant in that they reduce the large intelligence gap between children from severely deprived environments and those from favored environments, although the extent to which any given amount of intervention might be beneficial to wider societal development is uncertain.[32] Extrapolated to the large number of children throughout the world who spend their first years in poverty and hunger, however, even the smallest increment resulting from one 9-month treatment period could constitute an important improvement in the pool of human capabilities available to a given society.

REFERENCES AND NOTES

1. D. B. Jelliffe, *Infant Nutrition in the Tropics and Subtropics* (World Health Organization, Geneva, 1968); C. D. Williams, in *Preschool Child Malnutrition* (National Academy of Sciences, Washington, D.C., 1966), pp. 3–8; N. S. Scrimshaw, in *ibid.*, pp. 63–73.

2. N. S. Scrimshaw and J. E. Gordon, Eds., *Malnutrition, Learning and Behavior* (MIT Press, Boston, 1968), especially the articles by J. Cravioto and E. R. De-Licardie, F. Monckeberg, and M. B. Stoch and P. M. Smythe; J. Cravioto, in *Preschool Child Malnutrition* (National Academy of Sciences, Washington, D.C., 1966), pp. 74–84; M. Winick and P. Rosso, *Pediatr. Res.* **3**, 181 (1969); L. M. Brockman and H. N. Ricciuti, *Dev. Psychol.* **4**, 312 (1971). As significant as the human studies was the animal research of R. Barnes, J. Cowley, and S. Franková, all of whom summarize their work in *Malnutrition, Learning and Behavior*.

3. A. Berg, *The Nutrition Factor* (Brookings Institution, Washington, D.C., 1973), p. 5.

4. In addition to the authors' own experience, that of pediatricians and nutrition specialists in Latin America, Africa, and Asia is highly uniform in this respect. In fact, a generally accepted rule in medical care of malnourished children is that improvement in psychological response is the first sign of recovery.

5. D. Kallen, Ed., *Nutrition, Development and Social Behavior*, DHEW Publication No. (NIH) 73-242 (National Institutes of Health, Washington, D.C.,

1973); S. L. Manocha, *Malnutrition and Retarded Human Development* (Thomas, Springfield, Ill., 1972), pp. 132–165.

6. J. Dobbing, in *Malnutrition, Learning and Behavior*, N. S. Scrimshaw and J. E. Gordon, Eds. (MIT Press, Boston, 1968), p. 181.

7. B. S. Bloom, *Stability and Change in Human Characteristics* (Wiley, New York, 1964); J. McV. Hunt, *Intelligence and Experience* (Ronald, New York, 1961); M. Deutsch *et al.*, *The Disadvantaged Child* (Basic Books, New York, 1967). As with nutrition studies, there was also a large amount of animal research on early experience, such as that of J. Denenberg and G. Karas [*Science* **130**, 629 (1959)] showing the vulnerability of the young organism and that early environmental effects could last into adulthood.

8. M. Pines, *Revolution in Learning* (Harper & Row, New York, 1966); R. O. Hess and R. M. Bear, Eds., *Early Education* (Aldine, Chicago; 1968).

9. The 1969–1970 debate over the effectiveness of early education can be found in M. S. Smith and J. S. Bissel, *Harv. Educ. Rev.* **40**, 51 (1970); V. G. Cicirelli, J. W. Evans, J. S. Schiller, *ibid.*, p. 105; D. T. Campbell and A. Erlebacher, in *Disadvantaged Child*, J. Hellmuth, Ed. (Brunner/Mazel, New York, 1970), vol. 3; *Environment, Heredity and Intelligence* (Harvard Educational Review, Cambridge, Mass., 1969); F. D. Horowitz and L. Y. Paden, in *Review of Child Development Research*, vol. 3, *Child Development and Social Policy*, B. M. Caldwell and H. N. Ricciuti, Eds. (Univ. of Chicago Press, Chicago, 1973), pp. 331–402; T. Kellaghan, *The Evaluation of a Preschool Programme for Disadvantaged Children* (Educational Research Centre, St. Patrick's College, Dublin, 1975), pp. 21–33; U. Bronfenbrenner, *Is Early Intervention Effective?*, DHEW Publication No. (OHD) 74-25 (Office of Human Development, Department of Health, Education, and Welfare, Washington, D.C., 1974).

10. S. Gray and R. Klaus, in *Intelligence: Some Recurring Issues*, L. E. Tyler, Ed. (Van Nostrand Reinhold, New York, 1969), pp. 187–206.

11. This study sprang from prior work attempting to clarify the relationship of moderate malnutrition to mental retardation, in which it became evident that malnutrition of first and second degree might be only one of many correlated environmental factors found in poverty contributing to deficit in cognitive performance. We selected children for treatment with undernutrition as the first criterion not to imply that this was the major critical factor in cognitive development, but to be assured that we were dealing with children found typically in the extreme of poverty in the developing world, permitting generalization of our results to a population that is reasonably well-defined in pediatric practice universally. Figure 3.1 allows scientists anywhere to directly compare their population with ours on criteria that, in our experience, more reliably reflect the sum total of chronic environmental deprivation than any other measure available.

12. H. McKay, A. McKay, L. Sinisterra, in *Nutrition, Development and Social Behavior*, D. Kallen, Ed., DHEW Publ. No. (NIH) 73-242 (National Institutes of Health, Washington, D.C., 1973); S. Franková, in *Malnutrition, Learning and Behavior*, N. S. Scrimshaw and J. E. Gordon, Eds. (MIT Press, Cambridge, Mass., 1968). Franková, in addition to showing in her studies with rats that

malnutrition caused behavioral abnormalities, also was the first to suggest that the effects of malnutrition could be modified through stimulation.

13. *First Health and Nutrition Examination Survey, United States, 1971–72*, DHEW Publication No. (HRA) 75-1223 (Health Resources Administration, Department of Health, Education, and Welfare, Rockville, Md., 1975).

14. H. McKay, A. McKay, L. Sinisterra, *Stimulation of Cognitive and Social Competence in Preschool Age Children Affected by the Multiple Deprivations of Depressed Urban Environments* (Human Ecology Research Foundation, Cali, Colombia, 1970).

15. D. B. Jelliffe, *The Assessment of the Nutritional Status of the Community* (World Health Organization, Geneva, 1966), pp. 10–96.

16. In programs that assess community nutritional conditions around the world, standards widely used for normal growth of preschool age children have been those from the Harvard School of Public Health found in *Textbook of Pediatrics*, W. E. Nelson, V. C. Vaughan, R. J. McKay, Eds. (Saunders, Philadelphia, ed. 9, 1969), pp. 15–57. That these were appropriate for use with the children studied here is confirmed by data showing that the "normal" comparison children (group HS) were slightly above the median values of the standards at 3 years of age. Height for age, weight for age, and weight for height of all the study children were compared with this set of standards. The results, in turn, were the basis for the Fig. 3.1 data, including the "stunting" (indication of chronic, or past, undernutrition) and "wasting" (indication of acute, or present, malnutrition) classifications of J. C. Waterlow and R. Rutishauser [in *Early Malnutrition and Mental Development*, J. Cravioto, L. Hambreaus, B. Vahlquist, Eds. (Almqvist & Wiksell, Uppsala, Sweden, 1974), pp. 13–26]. The classification "stunted" included the children found in the range from 75 to 95 percent of height for age. The "wasting" classification included children falling between 75 and 90 percent of weight for height. The cutoff points of 95 percent height for age and the 90 percent weight for height were, respectively, 1.8 and 1.2 standard deviations (S.D.) below the means of group HS, while the selected children's means were 3 S.D. and 1 S.D. below group HS. The degree of malnutrition, in accordance with F. Gomez, R. Ramos-Galvan, S. Frenk, J. M. Cravioto, J. M. Chavez, and J. Vasquez [*J. Trop. Pediatr.* **2**, 77 (1956)] was calculated with weight for age less than 75 percent as "second degree" and 75 to 85 percent as "first degree." We are calling low normal a weight for age between 85 and 90 percent. The 75, 85, and 90 percent cutoff points were 2.6, 1.7, and 1.3 S.D. below the mean of group HS, respectively, while the selected children's mean was 2.3 S.D. below that of group HS children. Examination of combinations of both height and weight to assess nutritional status follows the recommendations of the World Health Organization expert committee on nutrition, found in *FAO/WHO Technical Report Series No. 477* (World Health Organization, Geneva, 1972), pp. 36–48 (Spanish language edition). In summary, from the point of view of both the mean values and the severity of deficit in the lower extreme of the distributions, it appears that the group of selected children, at 3 years of age, can be characterized as having had a history of chronic undernutrition rather than suffering from acute malnutrition at the time of initial examination.

17. The data analyses in this article use individuals as the randomization unit rather than sectors. To justify this, in view of the fact that random assignment of children was actually done by sectors, a nested analysis of variance was performed on psychological data at the last data point, at age 7, to examine the difference between mean-square for variation (MS) between sectors within treatment and MS between subjects within treatments within sectors. The resulting insignificant F-statistic (F = 1.432, d.f. 15,216) permits such analyses.

18. Food and Nutrition Board, National Research Council, *Recommended Dietary Allowances*, (National Academy of Sciences, Washington, D.C., 1968).

19. D. B. Weikart acted as a principal consultant on several aspects of the education program; D. B. Weikart, L. Rogers, C. Adcock, D. McClelland [*The Cognitively Oriented Curriculum* (Eric/National Association for the Education of Young Children, Washington, 1971)] provided some of the conceptual framework. The content of the educational curriculum included elements described in the works of C. S. Lavatelli, *Piaget's Theory Applied to an Early Childhood Curriculum* (Center for Media Development, Boston, 1970); S. Smilansky, *The Effects of Sociodramatic Play on Disadvantaged Preschool Children* (Wiley, New York, 1968); C. Bereiter and S. Englemann, *Teaching Disadvantaged Children in the Preschool* (Prentice-Hall, Englewood Cliffs, N.J., 1969); R. G. Stauffer, *The Language-Experience Approach to the Teaching of Reading* (Harper & Row, New York, 1970); R. Van Allen and C. Allen, *Language Experiences in Early Childhood* (Encyclopaedia Britannica Press, Chicago, 1969); S. Ashton-Warner, *Teacher* (Bantam, New York, 1963); R. C. Orem, *Montessori for the Disadvantaged Children in the Preschool* (Capricorn, New York, 1968); and M. Montessori, *The Discovery of the Child* (Ballantine, New York, 1967).

20. H. McKay, L. Sinisterra, A. McKay, H. Gomez, P. Lloreda, J. Korgi, A. Dow, in *Proceedings of the Tenth International Congress of Nutrition* (International Congress of Nutrition, Kyoto, 1975), chap. 7.

21. Although the "Scree" test of R. B. Cattell [*Multivar. Behav. Res.* **2**, 245 (1966)] conducted on the factor analyses at each measurement point clearly indicated a single factor model, there does exist the possibility of a change in factorial content that might have affected the differences between group HS children and the others at later measurement periods. New analysis procedures based upon a linear structural relationship such as suggested by K. G. Jöreskog and D. Sörbom [in *Research Report 76-1* (Univ. of Uppsala, Uppsala, Sweden, 1976)] could provide better definition of between-occasion factor composition, but the number of variables and occasions in this study still surpass the limits of software available.

22. G. Rasch, *Probabilistic Models for Some Intelligence and Attainment Tests* (Danmarks Paedagogiske Institut, Copenhagen, 1960); in *Proceedings of the Fourth Berkeley Symposium on Mathematical Statistics* (Univ. of California Press, Berkeley, 1961), vol. 4, pp. 321–33; *Br. J. Math. Stat. Psychol.* **19**, 49 (1966).

23. B. Wright and N. Panchapakesan, *Educ. Psychol. Meas.* **29**, 23 (1969); B. Wright and R. Mead, *CALFIT: Sample-Free Item Calibration with a Rasch Measurement Model* (Res. Memo. No. 18, Department of Education, Univ. of

Chicago, 1975). In using this method, analyses included four blocks of two adjacent measurement points (1 and 2, 2 and 3, 3 and 4, 4 and 5). All test items applied to all children that were common to the two proximate measurement points were included for analysis. Those items that did not fit the theoretical (Rasch) model were not included for further analysis at either measurement point, and what remained were exactly the same items at both points. Between measurement points 1 and 2 there were 126 common items included for analysis; between 2 and 3, 105 items; between 3 and 4, 82 items; and between 4 and 5, 79 items. In no case were there any perfect scores or zero scores.

24. Let M_W = total items after calibration at measurement occasion W; $C_{W, L + 1}$ = items common to both occasion W and occasion W + 1; $C_{W, L - 1}$ items common to both occasion W and occasion W − 1. Since $C_{W, L + 1}$ and $C_{W, L - 1}$ are subsets of M_W they estimate the same ability. However, a change in origin is necessary to equate the estimates because the computational program centers the scale in an arbitrary origin. Let $X_{W, L - 1}$ and $X_{W, L + 1}$ be the abilities estimated by using tests of length $C_{W, L - 1}$ and $C_{W, L + 1}$, respectively. Then:

$$X_{W, L - 1} = \beta 0 + \beta X_{W, L + 1} \tag{1}$$

Since the abilities estimated are assumed to be item-free, then the slope in the regression will be equal to 1, and $\beta 0$ is the factor by which one ability is shifted to equate with the other. $X_{W, L + 1}$ and $X_{W + 1, L + 1}$ are abilities estimated with one test at two different ocasions (note that $C_{W, L + 1} = C_{W + 1, L - 1}$); then by Eq. 1 it is seen that $X_{W, L - 1}$ and $X_{W + 1, L - 1}$ are measuring the same latent trait. Because the scales have different origins, $X_{W + 1, L - 1}$ is shifted by an amount $\beta 0$ to make them comparable.

25. It must be acknowledged here that with this method the interpretability of the data depends upon the comparability of units (ability scores) throughout the range of scores resulting from the Rasch analysis. Although difficult to prove, the argument for equal intervals in the data is strengthened by the fact that the increase in group means prior to treatment is essentially linear. Further discussion of this point may be found in H. Gomez, paper presented at the annual meeting of the American Educational Research Association, New York, 1977.

26. T. W. Anderson, in *Mathematical Methods in the Social Sciences*, K. J. Arrow, S. Karlin, P. Suppes, Eds. (Stanford Univ. Press, Stanford, Calif., 1960).

27. R. D. Bock, *Multivariate Statistical Methods in Behavioral Research* (McGraw-Hill, New York, 1975); in *Problems in Measuring Change*, C. W. Harris, Ed. (Univ. of Wisconsin Press, Madison, 1963), pp. 85–103.

28. Gain during treatment period is defined here as the mean value of a group at a measurement occasion minus the mean value of that group on the previous occasion. Thus the group T1 gains that form the baseline for this analysis are the following: treatment period 1 = .72; period 2 = 1.44; period 3 = 1.74.

29. C. Deutsch, in *Review of Child Development Research*, vol. 3, *Child Development and Social Policy*, B. M. Caldwell and H. N. Ricciuti, Eds. (Univ. of Chicago Press, Chicago, 1973).

30. L. M. Terman and M. A. Merrill, *Stanford-Binet Intelligence Scale, Form L-M* (Houghton, Mifflin, Boston, 1960), adapted for local use.

31. F. Horowitz and L. Paden, in *Review of Child Development Research*, B. M. Caldwell and H. N. Ricciuti, Eds. (Univ. of Chicago Press, Chicago, 1973), vol. 3, pp. 331–335; S. S. Baratz and J. C. Baratz, *Harv. Edu. Rev.* **40**, 29 (1970); C. B. Cazden, *Merrill-Palmer Q.* **12**, 185 (1966); *Curriculum in Early Childhood Education* (Bernard van Leer Foundation, The Hague, 1974).

32. Colombia has now begun to apply this concept of multiform, integrated attention to its preschool age children in a nationwide government program in both rural and urban areas. This is, among developing countries, a rarely encountered confluence of science and political decision, and the law creating this social action must be viewed as a very progressive one for Latin America. Careful documentation of the results of the program could give additional evidence of the social validity of the scientific findings presented in this article, and could demonstrate the potential value of such programs in the other regions of the world.

33. Adapted from a procedure described by H. G. Birch and A. Lefford, in *Brain Damage in Children: The Biological and Social Aspects*, H. G. Birch, Ed. (Williams & Wilkins, Baltimore, 1964). Only the visual-haptic modality was measured.

34. The measure was constructed locally using some of the items and format found in C. Bereiter and S. Englemann, *Teaching Disadvantaged Children in the Preschool* (Prentice-Hall, Englewood Cliffs, N.J., 1969), pp. 74–75.

35. This is a locally modified version of an experimental scale designed by the Growth and Development Unit of the Instituto de Nutricion de Centro América y Panamá, Guatemala.

36. G. Arthur, *A Point Scale of Performance* (Psychological Corp., New York, 1930). Verbal instructions were developed for the scale and the blocks were enlarged.

37. D. Wechsler, *WPPSI: Wechsler Preschool and Primary Scale of Intelligence* (Psychological Corp., New York, 1963).

38. At measurement points 3 and 4, this test is a combination of an adapted version of the arithmetic subscale of the WPPSI and items developed locally. At measurement point 5, the arithmetic test included locally constructed items and an adaptation of the subscale of the WISC-R.[39]

39. D. Wechsler, *WISC-R: Wechsler Intelligence Scale for Children-Revised* (Psychological Corp., New York, 1974).

40. At measurement points 3 and 4 the mazes test was taken from the WPPSI and at point 5 from the WISC-R.

41. Taken from 39. The information items in some instances were rewritten because the content was unfamiliar and the order had to be changed when pilot work demonstrated item difficulty levels at variance with the original scale.

42. At measurement point 4 the test came from the WPPSI, at point 5 from the WISC-R.

43. At measurement point 4 this was from *WISC: Wechsler Intelligence Scale for*

Children (Psychological Corp., New York, 1949); at point 5 the format used was that of the WISC-R.

44. At measurement point 4 this test was an adaptation from the similarities sub-scale of the WPPSI. At point 5 it was adapted from the WISC-R. Modifications had to be made similar to those described in 38.

45. B. Inhelder and J. Piaget, *The Early Growth of Logic in the Child* (Norton, New York, 1964), pp. 151–165. The development of a standardized format for application and scoring was done locally.

46. This research was supported by grants 700-0634 and 720-0418 of the Ford Foundation and grant 5R01HD07716-02 of the National Institute for Child Health and Human Development. Additional analyses were done under contract No. C-74-0115 of the National Institute of Education. Early financial support was also received from the Medical School of the Universidad del Valle in Cali and the former Council for Intersocietal Studies of Northwestern University, whose members, Lee Sechrest, Donald Campbell, and B. J. Chandler, have provided continual encouragement. Additional financial support from Colombian resources was provided by the Ministerio de Salud, the Ministerio de Educación, and the following private industries: Miles Laboratories de Colombia, Carvajal & Cia., Cementos del Valle, Cartón de Colombia, Colgate-Palmolive de Colombia, La Garantía, and Molinos Pampa Rita.

WHITE ENROLLMENT STABILITY AND SCHOOL DESEGREGATION: A TWO-LEVEL ANALYSIS

Micheal W. Giles

The relationship between school desegregation and white enrollment stability has recently been the subject of considerable scholarly debate. Coleman et al. (1975), in a well publicized study of large-school districts, concluded that school desegregation accelerated the exodus of white students from urban schools. The obvious policy implications of this research have stimulated several replications and critiques. Pettigrew and Green (1976) in the most detailed analysis of Coleman's research criticized the sample selection and offered alternative explanations of the results. Furthermore, by augmenting his sample with several large southern districts they concluded that, contrary to Coleman et al., desegregation was unrelated to white-enrollment declines. Farley (1975), Fitzgerald and Morgan (1977), and Rossell (1976), using slightly different techniques and samples from Pettigrew and Green, arrived at the same conclusion—desegregation was unrelated to white-enrollment decline.

While the weight of evidence indicates that declines in white-student enrollments are not an inevitable consequence of school desegregation, there is substantial evidence that school desegregation has resulted in white withdrawals in some districts. Munford (1973) and Clotfelter (1976) in separate analyses of Mississippi school districts, report large declines occurring in some districts subsequent to school desegregation. Giles (1977b) reports that in a random sample of 100 southern school districts, many experienced no change or even gains in white enrollment with desegregation, but many others experienced large white-enrollment declines. Lord (1975) found that the number of private schools in the Charlotte-Mecklenberg, North Carolina, area had almost doubled in the first four years of desegregation, and in some areas of the district as many as 25% of the white students were withdrawn from the public schools. Outside the South, Bosco and Robin (1974) report dramatic declines in white enrollments in the Pontiac, Michigan, public schools after desegregation. Thus, decline in white enrollment appears to be a potential but not an inevitable outcome of school desegregation. The problem confronting social scientists is to specify the conditions which influence white-enrollment stability and instability in desegregated schools.

This problem is of more than academic interest. The courts have consistently held that fear of white withdrawal is not sufficient grounds to justify a denial of constitutional right. For example, when the school district asserted in *Monroe v. Board of Commissioners* (391 U.S. 450 at 459) that white students would "flee the system altogether" if desegregation occurred, the Supreme Court reasserted the principle of *Brown* that ". . . the vitality of these constitutional principles cannot be allowed to yield simply because of disagreement with them." The courts, however, have not been oblivious to the problems of white withdrawals. The Supreme Court declared state legislation unconstitutional which authorized the City of Scotland Neck, North Carolina, to separate itself from the desegregating Halifax County School District (*U.S. v. Scotland Neck*, 407 U.S. 483). This decision was based in part upon the Court's belief that the legislation would create a "refuge for white students of the Halifax County School system." The courts also have shown a willingness to consider the problem of white withdrawals in designing remedies for segregation. For example, a California state court mandated that busing distances in San Diego be less than five miles for fear that longer distances would increase white withdrawals (*Los Angeles Times*, 3/10/77:3).

Sensitivity to the factors influencing white withdrawal and hence the long term stability of desegregation is of even greater importance in light of the U.S. Supreme Court's recent decision in *Pasadena* v. *Spangler* (427 U.S. 424 [1976]). In *Spangler* the Court held that a Federal District Court could not order a local school board to readjust its school enrollments on a yearly basis after racially neutral assignment plans had been adopted. In support of its decision the Court cited its previous statement in *Swann* v. *Charlotte-Mecklenburg* (402 U.S. 1 [1970:32]) that

> neither school authorities nor district courts are constitutionally required to make year by year adjustments of racial compositions of student bodies once the affirmative duty to desegregate has been accomplished and racial discrimination through official action is eliminated from the system.

Thus, the District Courts appear to be bound by their initial desegregation decisions and unable to adjust desegregation plans to react to either demographic trends or the reactions of affected parents. In light of the *Spangler* decision, it is of paramount importance that initial desegregation plans be designed to provide long-term stability in racial enrollments. This goal requires that judges and other desegregation planners know the conditions influencing white-enrollment stability in desegregated schools.

Among the most frequently discussed correlates of white withdrawal is the level of black concentration. Higher black concentrations are commonly assumed to result in greater white withdrawal. For example, in the Wilmington, Delaware, desegregation case (*Evans* v. *Buchanan*, 416 F. Supp. 328), the District Court justified the inclusion of the predominantly white Newark School District in the desegregation plan by asserting that ". . . the stability of any desegregation plan is enhanced by the inclusion . . . of higher white concentrations [355]." Often this relationship is perceived as nonlinear with a tipping or threshold point. Below the threshold, whites are thought to be relatively insensitive to the black concentration. Above the threshold, white withdrawal accelerates with the black ratio until the school becomes all black. This interpretation is clearly accepted in the Federal District Court's conclusion in *U.S.* v. *Board of School Commissioners* (332 F. Supp. 655) that "when the percent of black pupils . . . approaches 40 more or less the white exodus becomes accelerated and irreversible."

There is relatively consistent empirical evidence of a linkage between racial concentration and white withdrawal. There is little agreement, however, about the structure of this relationship. Clotfelter (1976), in a study of private-school enrollment increases after desegregation in 78 Mississippi counties, found no relationship to the level of black concentration in counties 25% or less black. In counties more than 25% black, private school enrollment increased with the level of black concentration and the increases accelerated in counties more than 55% black. Giles et al. (1975) found that the rate of white withdrawal from desegregated public schools in seven Florida school districts was significantly higher if the school was 30% or more black. The rate of withdrawal, however, did not appear to increase with higher black concentrations above the 30% threshold. In a study of 100 southern districts, Giles (1977b) found changes in white enrollment to be unrelated to the percent black enrollment in the district until the black ratio exceeded 30%. Above that point, white withdrawal increased with the black concentration. Unlike Clotfelter, Giles found this relationship to be linear above 30%. Munford (1973) in his study of 30 Mississippi districts reports findings consistent with those of Giles. Several studies have reported simple linear relationships between percent black and white withdrawal without a threshold (Farley, 1975; Coleman et al., 1975; Fitzgerald and Morgan, 1977; Lord and Catau, 1977; Stinchcombe et al., 1969). Indeed, in their study of Baltimore, Stinchcombe et al. (1969: 134) conclude that "there is no 'tipping point.' Or rather, the 'tipping point' is zero. . . . Once a school is desegregated . . . the proportion is likely to go up each year in a steady fashion. . . ."

In addition to the lack of consistency concerning the structure of the relationship between percent black and white withdrawal, previous studies have suffered several shortcomings. First, such studies have sometimes ignored the source of school desegregation (Coleman et al., 1975; Stinchcombe et al., 1969). School desegregation occurs as a result of governmental intervention and/or as a product of residential desegregation. When desegregation occurs through government intervention, desegregated schools may be created without disturbing existing patterns of segregated housing. Children are simply transported out of their segregated neighborhoods and placed in desegregated schools. The white parent in this situation is confronted with a single racial stimulus, the percent black in the school. In contrast, when school desegregation results from neighborhood racial succession, the white parent is confronted with at least two racial stimuli, the percent black in the school and the percent black in the neighborhood. These are clearly two different decisional situations for parents and should be different experimental settings for the researcher.

A second limitation of much of the research purporting to deal with white flight is that it focuses solely on the school district as the unit of analysis. Rossell (1976), Farley (1975), Fitzgerald and Morgan (1977), Pettigrew and Green (1976), Coleman et al. (1975) and Munford (1973) all take as their dependent variable decreases in the total white enrollment in school districts. A logical linkage between percent black and white withdrawals, however, is at the level of the individual school. Parents do not reject school districts, they reject schools (Pettigrew and Green, 1976). Furthermore, for designing desegregation plans, knowledge at the individual school level is of particular practical importance. The few studies which have focused on the school level have invariably concentrated on only one district or a very few districts (Wegmann, 1975; Giles et al., 1975; Stinchcombe et al., 1969; Giles, 1977a; Lord and Catau, 1977).

The use of the district as the unit of analysis also has precluded the analysis of some potentially important linkages—most notably the relationship between the percent black in the school, the previous racial status of the school and white withdrawal. A common assumption is that whites will not attend previously black schools. White opposition is thought to arise from the stigma of poor educational quality attached to these schools and their location in predominantly black areas. Indeed, desegregation has often meant the closing of black schools, although conditions other than fear of white withdrawals have been cited in justification.

It is conceivable that the previous racial status of the school may not only directly affect white withdrawal, but also affect the relationship between the racial concentration in the school and white withdrawal. For example, white withdrawal might be unrelated to percent black enrollment in previously white schools but strongly related to it in previously black schools.

Adopting the individual school as the unit of analysis also allows the effect of variations in school-district racial balance on the relationship between school racial balance and withdrawal to be examined. The concentration of blacks in an area consistently has been shown to influence racial climates (Blalock, 1967). We would expect, therefore, that parents with children enrolled in a school 40% black might react quite differently depending upon whether the overall racial balance in the district was 10% black or 60% black. Thus, the findings by Giles et al. (1975) that the rate of rejection of desegregated schools increased dramatically when white children were moved from schools less than 30% black to schools more than 30% black may reflect the racial balances in the districts they studied (18% to 33%). It is conceivable that if the racial balances had been in the 40 to 50% black range, the threshold for rejection might have moved upward.

The present study reexamines the linkage between percent black enrollment and white withdrawal at both the school and school-district levels. Only districts and schools desegregating under government enforcement are examined. Two questions are addressed at both levels of analysis: (1) Does the rate of white withdrawal vary with the percent black enrollment? (2) If present, is that relationship linear? Three additional questions are examined at the school level: (3) Does the racial status of a school prior to desegregation affect the rate of white withdrawal? (4) Does the percent black in the district influence the rate of white withdrawal from the schools? (5) Does the relationship between the school's racial enrollment and the rate of white withdrawal vary by the racial status of the school before desegregation or by the percent black in the district?

DATA

The analysis focuses on a sample of school districts and their included schools. Eligibility for inclusion in the district sample pool was contingent on four factors. First, only districts included in the Department of Health, Education, and Welfare's racial and ethnic surveys of the public schools in 1967, 1968, 1970, 1972 and 1974 were eligible to be sampled. These suveys provide the student enrollment by race in every school in over 8,000 school districts each surveyed year. Second, the school district must have experienced either court ordered or HEW-enforced school desegregation within the 1968 through 1970 time period. Limiting the analysis to districts experiencing government induced desegregation minimizes the confounding effects of residential desegregation.[1] Furthermore, focus on those districts desegregating in 1968, 1969 or 1970 allows for information on the racial balances in the schools for at least one point in time prior to desegregation, 1967, and for at least two points in the postdesegregation period, 1972 and 1974. Third, since virtually all government induced desegregation between 1968 and 1970 occurred in the South, the study was confined to that region. Fourth, only school districts located in metropolitan areas were eligible for inclusion in the sample. Residential choice and mobility are greater in urban than in rural settings. We would expect, therefore, that white-enrollment stability would be more of a problem in the former than in the latter.

The sample was drawn by first constructing a list of all school districts located in southern SMSAs as defined in the 1970 census. Second, all districts for which data could not be found in the 1967 through 1974 HEW surveys were excluded from the list. Third, the Office of Civil Rights (OCR) of the Department of Health, Education, and Welfare assembled a list of the timing and mode of desegregation for over 1,400 southern school districts. Using this information, we deleted districts not reported as desegregating under court order or HEW plans in either 1968, 1969 or 1970 from the sample pool. One hundred school districts were then sampled from the pool. The 50 largest school districts were included automatically in the sample. An additional 50 were drawn by stratified random sampling to obtain variation in the district racial balance.

Accurate determination of the timing of desegregation in each district is essential to the study design. If the OCR date for desegregation in a district is incorrect, changes in racial balances arising from implementation of the desegregation plan will be confused with other sources of enrollment instability. To assure the accuracy of the date of desegregation, we contacted each of the 100 selected school districts by telephone and questioned them concerning the timing of desegregation. This information was then compared with the OCR date for desegregation and with the pattern of enrollment stability by race in the district. Desegregation should be accompanied by alteration in the racial balances in the schools of a district. In particular, we would expect to see evidence of blacks attending previously all-white schools and whites attending previously all-black schools. For 60 of the sampled school districts, information from all three sources indicated the same date for desegregation. For the remaining 40 there was disagreement among the information sources. For 17 of these 40, two of the three sources agreed on the desegregation date. In most cases, this involved the enrollment data supporting either the local school authorities' or the Office of Civil Rights's estimate of the date of desegregation. When agreement between two sources could be obtained, the date was accepted as the correct one for desegregation. In most cases, this involved a change of one year (e.g., the OCR said a district desegregated in 1968 but the district and the school enrollment data indicated that the change occurred in 1969). Conversations with the school officials suggest that these differences may have arisen from the OCR reporting the first year of a two-year desegregation plan as the year of desegregation or the year of its adoption rather than the year of its implementation. As a result of these changes 15 districts were found to be outside the 1968–70 time frame for the study. These districts along with the 18 districts for which all three sources differed over the timing of desegregation are excluded from the study. The resulting sample consisted of six districts that desegregated in 1968, 24 that desegregated in 1969, and 36 that desegregated in 1970. For simplicity, only the analysis for districts and schools desegregating in 1969 or 1970 are presented below.*

The 60 districts included in the analysis averaged about 24,000 students. The smallest district enrolled slightly less than 1,000 students and the largest district enrolled about 240,000. The districts averaged approximately 30% black in enrollment. This relatively high average reflects the sampling stratification which assigned a higher probability of inclusion to school districts with large black concentrations. Fourteen of these districts desegregated under HEW enforcement and the remainder under court order.

Data on enrollment by race in each school in the sampled districts were drawn from the HEW surveys for 1967, 1968, 1970, 1972, and 1974. Ap-

---

*For a list of districts see the Appendix on pages 165–166.

proximately 2,000 schools were included in these districts. Those schools for which enrollment data could not be identified for every surveyed year were omitted from the analysis. This resulted in a sample of approximately 1,600 schools. The loss of 400 schools is consistent with HEW's estimate of 10 to 15% error in the assignment of school identification codes on a year to year basis.

The dependent variable in the study is the rate of white enrollment change. This is operationalized as the percent change in white enrollments between two surveyed years:

$$\frac{W_t - W_{t-2}}{W_{t-2}},$$

where W_t = the white enrollment in a surveyed year, W_{t-2} = the white enrollment two years before W_t. If white enrollments decrease this index will assume a negative value and if white enrollments increase the index will become positive. If no change in white enrollments occurs, the index will be zero.

Four measures on the dependent variable are available for each school district—the percentage change in white enrollment between 1967 and 1968 ($[DWE_{1968} - DWE_{1967}]/DWE_{1967}$), between 1968 and 1970 ($[DWE_{1970} - DWE_{1968}]/DWE_{1968}$), between 1970 and 1972 ($[DWE_{1972} - DWE_{1970}]/DWE_{1970}$), and between 1972 and 1974 ($[DWE_{1974} - DWE_{1972}]/DWE_{1972}$). The first measure provides an estimate of white enrollment stability just prior to desegregation. The second measure provides a comparison of white enrollments before and after desegregation. The third and fourth measure white enrollment stability for time periods after desegregation.

At the school level only two measures on the dependent variable are available—the percentage change in white enrollment between 1970 and 1972 ($[SWE_{1972} - SWE_{1970}]/SWE_{1970}$) and between 1972 and 1974 ($[SWE_{1974} - SWE_{1972}]/SWE_{1972}$). White withdrawals from schools also may occur with the onset of desegregation and result in higher black enrollments than expected by the desegregation plan. An examination of white refusals to attend desegregated schools in the first instance necessitates a comparison between the expected black/white enrollments and the actual black/white enrollments in each desegregated school (Giles, 1977a). For example, if a district desegregated in the fall of 1970, the white enrollment projected for each school under the desegregation plan would be compared to the number of whites actually enrolled in that school in 1970. Reliance on HEW school census data limits the present study to consideration of white enrollment changes after the implementation of desegregation has occurred in a district. Thus, the phenomena of white withdrawal with the onset of desegregation is not considered at the school level in this study. However, it would seem reasonable to expect that the factors which influence white enrollment stability in desegregated schools also would influence, in similar ways, white decisions to attend or not to attend newly desegregated schools.

In schools with low white enrollment even small changes in the number of white students result in high percentage changes. For example, if a school has ten white students enrolled at t_1 and five white students enrolled at t_2, the percent white enrollment change is $-.50$ $([5-10]/10)$. In contrast, a school with 100 whites enrolled at t_1 must lose 50 whites by t_2 to have a comparable percent white enrollment change. To compensate for this problem, we excluded all schools enrolling fewer than 50 white students from the school level analysis.[2] This does not eliminate the problem, but substantially reduces its magnitude.

The black concentration in the schools and districts is measured straightforwardly as the percent black enrollment in each. The previous status of the schools is measured by their percent black enrollment in 1967. Some of the schools in the sample districts desegregated prior to 1968 probably as a result of modest redistricting or "freedom of choice" desegregation plans. However, the overwhelming majority of the schools were either predominantly white (less than 20% black) or predominantly black (more than 90% black). For analysis purposes, previous racial status is coded as two dummy variables. The first is coded one if a school was integrated in 1967 and zero otherwise. The second is coded one if a school was predominantly black in 1967 and zero otherwise.[3]

ANALYSIS

The relationships between percent white enrollment change and the independent variables are examined by means of regression analysis. In this analysis the percent white enrollment change between two surveyed years is regressed on the value of the independent variables in the first year of the comparison. For example, the percent black school enrollment in 1970 is used to predict percent white enrollment change between 1970 and 1972, and percent black school enrollment in 1972 is used to predict percent white enrollment change between 1972 and 1974. Analyses are conducted separately at the district and school levels.

District-Level Analysis

Previous studies have reached varying results with regard to the linkage between desegregation and white withdrawal. The white enrollment patterns in the districts studied appear to support such a linkage. On average white enrollments in these districts were stable prior to desegregation but decreased subsequent to the implementation of desegregation (Table 3.6). However, only two of these declines are statistically significant, and all are substantively trivial in magnitude. Furthermore, the districts varied considerably around these means. In the 1968–70 time period, for example, one district increased its white enrollment by 15% while another declined by 37%. This variability supports the conclusion that white withdrawals are not an inevitable result of school desegregation.

The extent to which variation in white enrollment changes among the districts is related to their percent black enrollment is examined in Table 3.7.[4] The 1967–68 period precedes desegregation in these districts. In Table 3.6 we saw that on average little change in white enrollment occurred during this time period. In Table 3.7 it appears that those changes that did occur were unrelated to the black concentration in these districts (see eq. 2.1 in Table 3.7). The percentage change in white enrollment between 1968 and 1970 provides a before and after desegregation comparison. The black concentration in the districts is strongly related to the percent white enrollment change in this time period.[5] Approximately half the variation in percent white enrollment change is explained by the percent black enrollment. As expected, the effect of percent black is negative with higher black concentrations resulting in declines in white enrollment. The pattern set in the 1968–70 time period continues in the 1970–72 time period. The relationship between percent black enrollment and white withdrawal appears somewhat diminished in the 1970–72 period but remains statistically significant. In the 1972–74 time period white enrollment declines continue to be significantly associated with percent black enrollment, but the regression coefficient and the variance explained by percent black enrollment are much smaller than in either the 1968–70 or 1970–72 time periods.

Clotfelter (1976), Munford (1973) and Giles (1977b) found nonlinear relationships between percent black and white withdrawal. Specifically, they found that whites were insensitive to racial concentrations of less than 25 (Clotfelter, 1976) to 35% (Giles, 1977b) black. A common procedure for

TABLE 3.6
District Level Mean Percent White Enrollment
Change by Time Period

Time Period	Mean
1967–68	.003
1968–70	−.030*
1970–72	−.039**
1972–74	−.013

*Significant at .05.
**Significant at .01.

TABLE 3.7
Unstandardized Regression Coefficients for
Percent Black and Percent Black Squared
on District Percent White Enrollment
Change by Time Period

Time Period	Intercept	% Black	(% Black)²	R²
1967–68				
eq. 2.1	.0175	−.0462		.00
2.2	−.0020	+.0974	−.2005	.01
1968–70				
eq. 2.3	.0962	−.3977**		.48
2.4	.0348	+.0535	−.6241*	.52
1970–72				
eq. 2.5	.0741	−.3464**		.37
2.6	.0348	+.3565	−.9258**	.49
1972–74				
eq. 2.7	.0318	−.1341*		.08
2.8	.0298	−.1211	−.0158	.08

*Significant at .05.
**Significant at .01.

testing the linearity of a relationship between a dependent and an independent variable in a regression equation is to share the independent variable, add it to the equation and test its significance. The results of this analysis for the relationship between percent black district enrollment and percent white enrollment change are presented in equations 2.2, 2.4, 2.6 and 2.8. In both the 1968–70 and 1970–72 time periods percent black enrollment squared is significant, indicating the presence of a nonlinear relationship.[6] The regression lines fitted by these equations are presented in Figure 3.4 for the 1968–70 period and Figure 3.5 for 1970–72. The relationships revealed in Figures 3.4 and 3.5 closely resemble the findings of Clotfelter (1976), Munford (1973) and Giles (1977b). Among districts less than approximately 30% black, differences in the percent black enrollment are not consistently related to differences in the percent white enrollment change in either time period. Indeed, for over 90% of these districts the change in white enrollment fell within a range of ±10% from zero. In contrast, among districts above 30% black, the rate of white withdrawal increases exponentially with higher percent black enrollments.

While the equations for the two time periods differ somewhat, the estimated percent white enrollment changes in the two time periods are virtually identical. For example, a school district with a 75% black enrollment in 1968 is predicted to lose approximately 28% of its white students be-

tween 1968 and 1970. Similarly, a district that is 75% black in 1970 is predicted to lose approximately 28% of its white enrollments between 1970
and 1972. Of course, a district that is 75% black in 1968 would be approximately 80% black in 1970, having lost 28% of its white enrollment and assuming no increase in its black enrollment. Given an 80% black enrollment, a 33% decline in white enrollments between 1970 and 1972 is
projected. In total such a district is predicted to lose more than half of its
white enrollment between 1968 and 1972.

The pattern of accelerating losses between 1968 and 1972 conforms to
the expectations of the tipping model. However, the tipping model would
predict this pattern to continue until the districts became all black. This
does not occur. In the 1972–74 time period percent black enrollment
squared is not significant (eq. 2.8), indicating that the relationship between
percent black and the rate of white withdrawal is linear in this time period
(eq. 2.7). Consistent with the findings for 1968–70 and 1970–72, equation
2.7 predicts that higher black enrollments will yield higher rates of white
withdrawal only among districts more than approximately 25 to 30%
black.[7] Among these districts, however, the estimated percent white enroll-

Figure 3.4. Estimated district percent white enrollment change between 1968 and
1970.

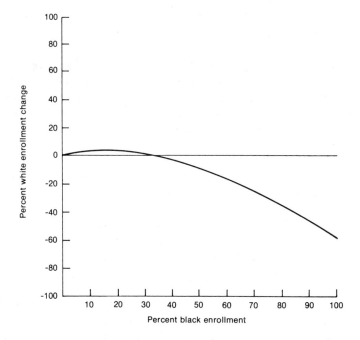

Percent white enrollment change

Percent black enrollment

Figure 3.5. Estimated district percent white enrollment change between 1970 and 1972.

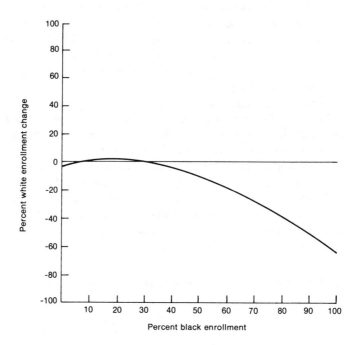

ment decline is far smaller than in the previous time periods. For example, a district that is 75% black in 1972 is predicted to lose only about 7% of its white enrollment between 1972 and 1974. Thus, rather than acceler- ated, the rate of white withdrawal is actually diminished between 1972 and 1974. Apparently, most parents who were sensitive to the black concentra- tion in their district and who could afford to, withdrew their children ei- ther with the onset of desegregation or in the first year or two after its im- plementation. While some districts continue to experience declines in white enrollments during the 1972–74 time period, these declines result largely from factors other than the level of black concentration.

Pettigrew and Green (1976) found that losses in black enrollment were also associated with higher percent black enrollments among their dis- tricts. They suggest that percent black is a surrogate variable for several unfavorable characteristics of a district which result in both white and black enrollment declines. Such an interpretation is not supported by the present data. Percent black enrollment is not significantly related to changes in black enrollment among the study districts.

In summary among the sampled districts percent white enrollment decline is associated with percent black enrollment in three of the four time periods examined. The exception is the 1967–68 time period which precedes widescale desegregation in these districts. In the 1968–70 and 1970–72 time periods percent change in white enrollment was relatively minor and unassociated with the level of black concentration among districts with enrollments less than 30% black. Among districts more than 30% black, the rate of white withdrawal increased exponentially with increases in the percent black enrollment. Higher black concentrations also resulted in greater percent white withdrawal between 1972 and 1974 in districts more than 30% black, but the relationship was linear not exponential, and the predicted declines were far less than in the 1968–72 time period. This result suggests that the effect of percent black on white withdrawal diminishes over time, contrary to the expectations of the tipping model.

The value of these findings for policy purposes depends on their generalizability beyond the districts included in the study sample. To assess the generalizability of the findings at the district level, we used equation 2.2 to estimate the percent white enrollment changes between 1968 and 1970 in an independently drawn random sample of 100 southern school districts which desegregated in 1969 or 1970.[8] This sample differed from the study sample in several ways. The districts were smaller, averaging approximately 6,500 in enrollment, more densely black, averaging approximately 40% black, and were rural as well as urban in location. Despite these differences, for approximately 65% of the districts the actual percentage change in white enrollment fell within $\pm.10$ of the estimates. This constitutes a 35% improvement in prediction over estimates based simply on the mean percent white enrollment change in our study districts.[9] Thus, the results of the present study provide at least rough guidance about what to expect in terms of white withdrawals at the district level when desegregation occurs.

School-Level Analysis

The relationships between changes in school enrollment and the independent variables are shown in Table 3.8. In both the 1970–72 and 1972–74 time periods, percent black enrollment is significantly and negatively linked to white enrollment stability (eqs. 3.1 and 3.6). Schools with high black enrollments at the beginning of each comparison period experience larger declines in white enrollments over the two year periods than do schools with low black enrollments. To test the linearity of these relationships, we squared the percent black enrollment in each school and added it to the regression equations. The results of this procedure are presented in equations 3.2 and 3.7. For both time periods percent black enrollment

TABLE 3.8
Unstandardized Regression Coefficients for Percent
White Enrollment on School Percent Black Enrollment,
District Percent Black Enrollment and Previous Status
of the School for Schools in Districts Desegregating
in 1969 or 1970 (n = 1,368)

	Inter-cept	School % Black	(School % Black)^2	District % Black	Previous Status BLACK	Previous Status INTE-GRATED	R^2
1970–72							
Equation 3.1	−.085	−.067*					.01
Equation 3.2	−.112	+.319**	−.555**				.02
Equation 3.3	−.025			−.266**			.03
Equation 3.4	−.097				.040	−.142**	.02
Equation 3.5	−.053	.417**	−.657**	−.268**	.093**	−.111**	.07
1972–74							
Equation 3.6	−.044	−.202**					.03
Equation 3.7	−.088	.345**	−.737**				.08
Equation 3.8	.008			−.341**			.04
Equation 3.9	−.079				−.070	−.103	.01
Equation 3.10	−.031	.410**	−.739**	−.253**	.016	−.028	.10

*Significant at .05.
**Significant at .01.

squared is statistically significant, indicating that the relationship between percent black school enrollment and white enrollment change is nonlinear. The shape of these relationships is presented in Figures 3.6 and 3.7.

For the 1970–72 time period equation 3.2 predicts that up to about 30% black, higher black concentrations actually are associated with smaller losses in white enrollment. Above 30% black, the rate of white withdrawal increases exponentially with higher black enrollments. A similar pattern appears for the 1972–74 time period although the downward slope appears to commence between 20 and 30% black. The relationship between percent black and percent white enrollment change also appears to be slightly stronger in the 1972–74 period. A school that is 75% black in 1970 is projected to lose approximately 18.5% of its white enrollments between 1970 and 1972, whereas a school that is 75% black in 1972 is estimated to lose 24% of its white enrollments between 1972 and 1974. Over the four year period a school that is 75% black in 1970 is projected on average to lose approximately 40% of its white students. While the relationship is significant in both time periods, only a small percentage of the variance in white enrollment change is explained by the percent black en-

Figure 3.6. Estimated school percent white enrollment change between 1970 and 1972.

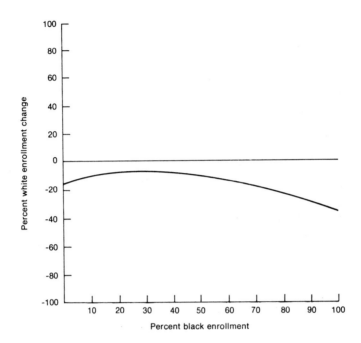

rollment. Thus, the fit of the data to the projections portrayed in Figures 3.6 and 3.7 is imprecise and, indeed, some high percent, black-enrollment schools may experience little decline in white enrollment.

The relationship between percent black enrollment and percent white enrollment change at the school level differs only slightly in the 1970–72 and 1972–74 time periods. In contrast, at the district level the relationship between percent black enrollment and percent white enrollment change was found to be diminished in the 1972–74 period. This difference in results suggests that white withdrawals may continue in response to higher percent black school enrollments even as the effect of percent black enrollment on white withdrawals at the district level subsides.

The relationship between the percent black enrollment in the district and percent change in white school enrollment is shown in equation 3.3 for the 1970–72 period and equation 3.8 for the 1972–74 period. In both time periods percent black in the district is significantly and negatively related to white enrollment change. The magnitude of the effect, however, is not

Figure 3.7. Estimated school percent white enrollment change between 1972 and 1974.

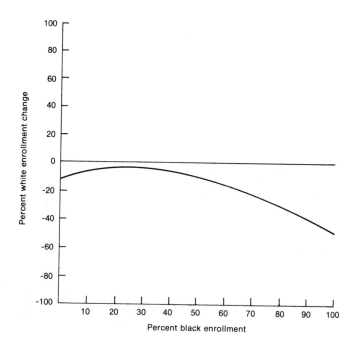

great. In both time periods a 10% higher black enrollment in the district yields, on average, about a 2.5% greater decline in white enrollment once the effects of the other independent variables are taken into account (eqs. 3.5 and 3.10). As might be expected, percent black school enrollment and percent black district enrollment are positively correlated ($r = .38$ for 1970–72 and $r = .40$ for 1972–74). The apparent effect of higher percent black school enrollments on white enrollment stability might simply reflect the greater likelihood of such schools being located in higher percent black districts (or vice versa). However, this is not the case. In equations 3.5 and 3.10 the effect of each independent variable is shown net of the effect of all other independent variables. Both the percent black enrollment in the school and in the district remain significant despite these controls. Petti-grew and Green (1976) assert that parents reject schools not school dis-tricts. These results indicate that, to the contrary, the rate of white with-drawal is influenced by the level of black concentration in both the school and the school districts. Regardless of their percent black enrollments, schools in high percent black districts lose more white students than do schools in low percent black districts and, regardless of the percent black enrollment in the district, high percent black schools lose more white students than do low percent black schools.

The effect of the previous racial status of the school on white enrollment stability is shown in equations 3.4 and 3.9. The pattern is erratic. In the 1970–72 period, schools that were integrated prior to 1968 experienced significantly greater white withdrawals than did schools that were previously white. On average, the losses were 14% greater before (eq. 3.4) and 11% greater after (eq. 3.5) controlling for the effects of the school and district percent black enrollments. In contrast, previously black schools actually gained white students between 1970 and 1972. It must be assumed that efforts to desegregate black schools lingered on in the 1970–72 time period and that the increases in white enrollments in these schools result from the reassignment of white students. In the 1972–74 time period the effects of previous status disappear. Neither previously integrated nor previously black schools differ significantly from the previously white schools in percent white enrollment changes in this period, once the effects of the percent black enrollments in the school and the district are controlled (eq. 3.10).[10]

Does the relationship between the percent black enrollment in the school and white enrollment change vary by the black concentration in the district and/or the previous racial status of the school? To address this question, we constructed interaction terms by multiplying the squared percent black school enrollment by each of the remaining independent variables. The resulting three terms were added to equations 3.5 and 3.10. For the 1970–72 time period none of these terms was statistically significant. This result suggests that the effect of the percent black enrollment in a school on white withdrawal was the same during this period regardless of the previous status of the school or whether the district was high or low in black concentration. In the 1972–74 period, one interaction term proved to be significant, percent black in the school by percent black in district. The sign of the coefficient was positive, indicating that white withdrawal from high percent black schools located in high percent black districts would be less than predicted by the simple additive model (eq. 3.10). Close analysis suggests that this effect arises from a nonlinear relationship between percent white enrollment change and district percent black enrollment.[11] Approximately a dozen schools located in districts more than 70% black in 1972 lost sizeable numbers of whites in the 1970–72 period but then became relatively stable in the 1972–74 period. With these schools removed, the interaction effect between percent black enrollment in the school and percent black enrollment in the district is no longer statistically significant.

In summary, among the schools examined the percent black enrollment is negatively related to percent white enrollment between 1970 and 1974.

This relationship is nonlinear. Among schools less than 20 to 30% black, increasing black enrollment bears little relationship to percent white enrollment change. Among schools more than 20 to 30% black, increases in percent black enrollment yield increasingly larger percentage declines in white enrollment. With the exception of schools in a few districts with high percent black enrollment, which appear to have stabilized their white enrollment in the 1972–74 period, the relationship between percent black school enrollment and percent white school enrollment change does not vary by the percent black in the district or the previous status of the school.

The relationship between the previous racial status of the school and white withdrawal is erratic. Schools integrated prior to desegregation appear to experience white withdrawal in the 1970–72 time period while previously black schools experienced gains. The latter appear to result from continued desegregation efforts. By the 1972–74 time period, previous status is unrelated to enrollment change.

Percent black at the district level also is negatively related to changes in white enrollment at the school level. Schools located in high percent black districts experience greater percentage declines in white enrollment than do schools in low percent black districts. As previously noted, a departure from this pattern appears among high percent black districts in the 1972–74 time period. The relationship between percent black district enrollment and percent white enrollment change at the school level differs somewhat from the findings at the district level. At the district level, the relationship between percent black enrollment and percent white enrollment change was nonlinear in the 1970–72 period, but at the school level the effect appears to be linear for the same time period. Results at the district and school levels may differ for at least two reasons. First, the school-level analysis is sensitive to enrollment shifts among the schools in a district as well as to movement to private schools and to other school districts. The district-level analysis only focuses on enrollment shifts to private schools and other school districts. Second, not all the schools in the sampled districts are included in the analysis. Schools for which data could not be found for each surveyed year between 1967 and 1974 were deleted from the study. These two factors may combine to produce slightly different results at the school and district levels. For example, high percent black districts may have closed schools as a result of declining white enrollments. The losses experienced by the closed schools would not appear in the school-level analysis. Furthermore, declines in white enrollments in other schools would be offset by the additional whites transferred from the closed schools. Under such circumstances the school-level analysis would show smaller white enrollment declines than would the district-level analysis.

The results of the school-level and district-level analyses also differ in the amount of variance explained. None of the variables taken either individually or in combination explains more than 10% of the variance in percent white enrollment change at the school level. This difference is not totally unexpected. In general disaggregated data will yield lower explained variance even when relationships are the same. Nevertheless, the low explained variance indicates that changes in white enrollments at the school level are largely a result of factors other than those included in the present study.

The policy significance of this low explained variance is dramatically illustrated when an attempt is made to generalize the findings beyond the present sample. Using equation 3.5, we computed estimates of the percent white enrollment change between 1972 and 1974 for approximately 600 schools in 11 districts desegregating in 1971 and 1972.[12] For approximately 50% of the schools the actual percent white enrollment change fell within $\pm.10$ of the estimates. However, approximately the same level of accuracy was achieved by simply predicting for each school the mean percent white enrollment change as occurred in the study schools. The projections in Figures 3.6 and 3.7, thus, provide little guidance for estimating changes in school enrollments. On the other hand, a separate analysis of the relationship between percent white enrollment change and percent black among these 600 schools found that relationship to be curvilinear with the rate of white withdrawal increasing exponentially above 30% black. The consistency of these results cannot be ignored.

DISCUSSION

Recent studies have produced conflicting evidence on the relationship between school desegregation and white enrollment declines. Some studies have found desegregation to be unrelated to changes in white enrollment, while others have clearly linked school desegregation to white enrollment declines. Therefore the appropriate query is probably not whether school desegregation leads to white withdrawal, but rather, what factors influence white enrollment stability and instability in desegregated schools.

The results of the present analysis indicate that, at least at the district level, percent black enrollment is one such factor. Districts less than roughly 30% black experienced only moderate white enrollment instability, which was unrelated to the level of black concentration. Among districts above 30% in black enrollment, the rate of white withdrawal increased exponentially with increases in percent black enrollment. These results suggest that, on average, school districts with less than roughly 30% black enrollment can be desegregated without experiencing drastic declines in white enrollment. For districts with enrollments more than 30% black, the policy implications of the study vary with the black enrollment. Among districts only slightly over 30%, the rate of white withdrawal is predicted to be small and should constitute little hindrance to desegregation. On the other hand, majority black districts are predicted to experience significant rates of white withdrawal. In such districts the results support the need for multiple district desegregation plans. By combining high percent black districts with surrounding low percent black districts, the overall black concentration can be reduced and the problem of white withdrawal reduced correspondingly. Failing the adoption of multiple district plans or other successful compensatory strategies, desegregation of districts with high percent black enrollments is predicted to be costly in terms of white withdrawals.

The relationship between percent black enrollment and white withdrawals at the school level is less clear. Percent black enrollment was found to be significantly related to white enrollment stability. The relationship was curvilinear and resembled closely in form the results at the district level. Despite the consistency of these findings, only a small percentage of the variance in white enrollment at the school level was explained by the percent black enrollment. Stated in practical terms, the actual percent white enrollment changes varied considerably around the estimates based on the percent black enrollment. Does this mean that percent black enrollment can be ignored in desegregation planning? We think not. Given the consistency of the results, a prudent policymaker would be wise to avoid majority black schools when possible.

Three limitations of the present study should be kept in mind by researchers and policymakers alike. First, at the school level the study focuses on stability after desegregation has occurred. If parents refuse to allow their children to attend previously black schools or schools planned to have high racial balances in the initial year of desegregation, then the effect of these variables is overlooked in the present study. Giles (1977b) finds just such a pattern for previously black schools in one southern metropolitan school district. Previously black schools experienced significantly lower white enrollments than planned in the first year of desegregation, but the enrollments were stable at that lower level in the second and third years of implementation. Given this limitation, policymakers would be premature to assume from these findings that parents are insensitive to the racial status of a school or its black concentrations.

Second, the districts examined in the present analysis experienced government induced desegregation. The predictions, therefore, would be modified for districts where residential desegregation is occurring or where whites are leaving for other reasons (e.g., general trends toward suburbanization). Third, the research has focused on southern districts and schools and in the strictest statistical terms is only generalizable to that region. Until sufficient desegregation occurs outside the South to provide a basis for research, however, reliance on the experience of the South would appear the only alternative to speculation.

NOTES

1. The effects of residential desegregation are not eliminated by focusing on districts experiencing government induced desegregation.
2. Preliminary analysis also was conducted for schools with white enrollment greater than or equal to 100. The results were comparable to the analysis for schools with white enrollments greater than or equal to 50. A few schools with erratic enrollment patterns also were deleted.
3. With both variables included in a regression equation the first contrasts percent white enrollment change in previously black and previously white schools and the second contrasts percent white enrollment change in integrated and previously white schools.
4. The regression analysis was conducted with three outlying districts removed: Conroe, Montgomery; Jasper, Walker; and Crawfordsville, Crittenden. The first two districts had relatively low black enrollments (8 to 15%) and experienced large increases in black enrollment betwen 1968 and 1970. Indeed, white enrollment in the Jasper school district increased by 40% between 1968 and 1970. In contrast, Crawfordsville school district was approximately 80% black and lost about 66% of its white enrollment between 1968 and 1970. These gains and losses are consistent with a relationship between percent black and white enrollment decline. However, the values for these districts departed to such a degree from the other districts that a more accurate picture of that relationship was provided by deleting them from the analysis.
5. Since both the dependent variable, percent white enrollment change, and the independent variable, percent black enrollment, contain the term total white enrollment, the presence of a relationship between the two variables might be a mathematical result of this common term. To examine this possibility the regression results at both the district and the school levels were controlled for total white enrollment. The results of the analysis were not altered by these controls. Thus, the relationships found between percent black and percent white enrollment change do not appear to be artifacts of the way in which the variables are defined.
6. If the deleted districts are included (see fn. 5), the quadratic term is nonsignificant for the percent change in white enrollment between 1970 and 1972. This is largely due to the effect of the Crawfordsville school district. As a result of a decline of approximately 66% in white enrollment between 1968 and 1970, only 61 whites were enrolled in the districts in 1970. An additional 26 white students were added between 1970 and 1972. This constitutes a 43% increase in white enrollment for a district over 90% black in 1970.
7. Equation 2.7 predicts that a district 24% black will lose .04% (+.0218 —

[.1341*.24]) white enrollment between 1972 and 1974. Below 24%, equation 2.7 predicts smaller percent white gains with increases in percent black enrollment.

8. These districts are the same as those analyzed by Giles (1977b).
9. Estimating that white enrollment in the supplemental district would equal the mean white enrollment in the study districts $\pm.10$ yields 54 errors. Estimates based on equation 2.2 $\pm.10$ produced 35 errors. This amounts to a 35% reduction in errors $(54-35)/54=.35$.
10. If the previous status variables are deleted from equations 3.5 and 3.10, the regression coefficients for the remaining variables are virtually unchanged.
11. Tests of the linearity of the relationship between all the independent variables and percent white enrollment decline were conducted as a preliminary step in the analysis. The nonlinearity of the relationship between school percent white enrollment change and district percent black was discovered in this preliminary analysis.
12. These 11 districts were inadvertently included in the original sample and data on their school enrollments were collected prior to discovery of the fact that they fell outside the study time frame.

REFERENCES

Blalock, Herbert M. 1967   Toward a Theory of Minority-Group Relations. New York: Wiley.

Bosco, James and Stanley Robin   1974   "White flight from court ordered busing?" Urban Education 9:87-98.

Clotfelter, Charles T.   1976   "School desegregation, 'tipping' and private school enrollment." Journal of Human Resources 11:28-49.

Coleman, James, Sarah D. Kelley and John Moore   1975   Trends in School Segregation, 1968–1973. Washington, D.C.: Urban Institute.

Farley, Reynolds   1975   "School integration and white flight." Pp. 1–20 in Gary Orfield (ed.), Symposium on School Desegregation and White Flight. Washington, D.C.: Center for National Policy Review, Catholic Law School.

Fitzgerald, Michael and David R. Morgan   1977   "Assessing the consequences of public policy: school desegregation and white flight in urban America." Paper presented to the annual meeting of the Mid-West Political Science Association, Chicago.

Giles, Micheal W.   1977a   "Racial stability and urban school desegregation." Urban Affairs Quarterly 12:499-510.
    1977b   "School desegregation and white withdrawal: a test of the tipping-point model." Mimeo. Department of Political Science, Florida Atlantic University.

Giles, Micheal W., Everett F. Cataldo and Douglas S. Gatlin   1975   "White flight and percent black: the tipping point re-examined." Social Science Quarterly 56:85-92.

Lord, Dennis   1975   "School busing and white abandonment of public schools." Southern Geographer 15:81-92.

Lord, Dennis and John Catau   1977   "School desegregation policy and intra-school district migration." Social Science Quarterly 57:784-96.

Munford, Luther   1973   "White flight from desegregation in Mississippi." Integrated Education 11:12-26.

Pettigrew, Thomas F. and Robert Green   1976   "School desegregation in large cities: a critique of the Coleman 'white flight' thesis." Harvard Education Review 46:1-53.

Rossell, Christine   1976   "School desegregation and white flight." Political Science Quarterly 90:675-98.

Stinchcombe, Arthur, Mary McDill and Dollie Walker   1969   "Is there a racial tipping point in changing schools?" Journal of Social Issues 25:127-36.

Wegmann, Robert G.   1975   "Neighborhoods and schools in racial transition." Growth and Change 6:3-8.

APPENDIX
Districts Included in the Study by State and County

State	District	County
Alabama	Athens	Limestone
	Attalla	Etonah
	Baldwin	Baldwin
	Bessemer	Jefferson
	Birmingham	Jefferson
	Gadsden	Etowah
	Jasper	Walker
	Limestone	Limestone
	Montgomery	Montgomery
	Phenix	Russell
	Russell	Russell
	Walker	Walker
Arkansas	Altheiner	Jefferson
	Crawfordsville	Crittenden
	Dollarway	Jefferson
	Earle	Crittenden
	Texarkana	Miller
	Turrell	Crittenden
Florida	Alachua	Alachua
	Dade	Dade
	Escambia	Escambia
	Leon	Leon
	Orange	Orange
Georgia	Dougherty	Dougherty
	Fulton	Fulton
	Walker	Walker

APPENDIX (*continued*)
Districts Included in the Study by State and County

State	District	County
Louisiana	Bossier	Bossier
	Caddo	Caddo
	Calcasieu	Calcasieu
	Lafayette	Lafayette
	St. Bernard	St. Bernard
	St. Tammany	St. Tammany
Mississippi	Rankin	Rankin
North Carolina	Ashboro City	Randolph
	Cumberland	Cumberland
	Durham City	Durham
	Durham	Durham
	Guilford	Guilford
	Orange	Orange
	Wake	Wake
South Carolina	Berkeley	Berkeley
	Charleston	Charleston
	Pickens	Pickens
Texas	Chapel Hill	Smith
	Cleveland	Liberty
	Conroe	Montgomery
	Houston	Harris
	Lamar	Fort Bend
	Liberty	Liberty
	Lubbock	Lubbock
	Mart	McLennan
	Port Arthor	Jefferson
	Richardson	Dallas
	San Angelo	Tom Green
	South Park	Jefferson
	Wilmer Hutchins	Dallas
Virginia	Amherst	Amherst
	Campbell	Campbell
	Dinwiddie	Dinwiddie
	Henrico	Henrico

Chapter 4

OCCUPATIONAL AND INCOME EQUALITY

Occupational attainment and economic advancement are the key indicators of mobility in a society's stratification structure. Indeed, the Civil Rights Act of 1964, the Economic Opportunity Act of 1964, and the creation of the Equal Employment Opportunity Commission (EEOC) have all been policy attempts to equalize opportunities.

Title VII of the Civil Rights Act made it unlawful for any firm or union employing more than twenty-five persons to discriminate. In 1972 Congress amended Title VII to expand the EEOC's authority to include state and local government employees as well as unions and businesses employing more than fifteen persons. This amendment permits the EEOC to handle problems affecting job equality throughout the entire employment system. Furthermore, Title VI of the Civil Rights Act provides for termination of federal funds from state and local programs administered in a discriminatory fashion.

The idea that substantive equality or equality of results is not, in the short run, necessarily achieved through the equalization of opportunities has led to a policy emphasis on positive action, which is generally referred to as "affirmative action." In 1965 President Lyndon Johnson issued Executive Order 11246, which required all federal contractors to take affirmative action in hiring minorities. Since then, the policy has been extended to include all private contractors, subcontractors, and unions dealing with the federal government. The overriding objective in all affirmative action programs is to increase employment for minorities and women.

In the process of implementing affirmative action, however, the policy intent of equal opportunity has become increasingly complex, controversial, and ambiguous. The present disputes over equalizing opportunities for minorities and women have resulted because some of the methods employed appear to many persons to be incongruent with some basic American values. Essentially, the policy dilemma is whether the government should discriminate in order to end discrimination by applying racial-preference programs, and whether affirmative action is consistent with the right of all persons to equal protection under the law as guaranteed by the Fourteenth Amendment. Inherent in this dilemma is the contradiction between a policy emphasis on process and an emphasis on result. One side argues that fair process defines and guarantees fair results, as well as affirms the value of individual equality of opportunity. The opposing side argues that if the result shows great disparity from group proportionality (in income, occupation, and education), that, in itself, testifies for discrimination and unfairness: Group proportional equality of results defines and guarantees fair process and equality of opportunity.

In the first article, David H. Rosenbloom evaluates the affirmative-action policy in federal personnel administration. The study examines the evolution of the program in terms of its goals and criteria for success, its implementation and its impact on black and female employment. Significantly, Rosenbloom shows that the mode of implementation, that is, the process evaluation, was such that there was little reason to expect that the program would bring a widespread change in the composition of federal personnel.

The second article, the McCrone and Hardy study, examines the overall impact of civil rights policies on the achievement of racial economic equality. As the authors point out, the cardinal problem in such an evaluation is to separate the effects of general economic conditions, for example, economic growth and employment, from the impact of the civil rights policies. Using a time-series regression analysis, the authors estimate the separate effects of cyclical economic conditions, and assess the overall and within-regions effects of civil rights policies on economic equality. The evaluation's major finding is that civil rights policies since 1964 have decreased the gap between black and white incomes, but that this is confined to the South.

THE FEDERAL
AFFIRMATIVE-ACTION POLICY

David H. Rosenbloom

On May 11, 1971, the United States Civil Service Commission (CSC) issued a memorandum allowing federal agencies to establish goals and timetables for the hiring of members of minority groups by their organizations.[1] The memo marked the first time in its thirty-year history that the
federal equal-employment opportunity (EEO) program had officially devi-
ated from an explicit policy of strict nondiscrimination and "color blind-
ness." Their previous policy had prohibited special or differentiated treatment of individuals based on their race.[2] Throughout the remainder of the
1970s, the new policy, generally referred to as "affirmative action" and
eventually widely utilized in American society, was the focal point of
much political controversy and public debate.[3] Yet, despite the widespread
concern with affirmative action, little effort has been made to evaluate its
effectiveness as public policy.[4] The present study addresses itself to this
task in a limited area by asking the straightforward question, "Has affirmative action in federal personnel administration worked?" As the evaluation proceeds, the reader will become aware that evaluation research is
fraught with difficulties and pitfalls. Hence, the study not only treats an
important area of public policy, but also serves to illustrate some of the
problems involved in evaluating public programs.

POLICY FRAMEWORK

At the outset it is important to place the federal affirmative-action program in its wider policy context. Demands for a "race conscious" public
policy developed during the late 1960s, when the removal of discriminatory barriers against blacks by the Civil Rights Act of 1964 and the Voting
Rights Act of 1965 did not lead to rapid change in their socioeconomic
and political condition. Dissatisfaction with earlier civil rights policy crys-
tallized in the black power movement, which rejected the goal of equal opportunity and sought substantive equality itself, whether through "repara-

tions" or policies such as affirmative action.[5] The federal government first endorsed race-conscious hiring of members of minority groups in the Philadelphia Plan of 1967, which applied to construction firms holding federal contracts in that city. In the realm of federal employment, it had long been held that there should be extensive employment of minority-group members and women because: (1) the government should set a positive example for the rest of the society; (2) if equal treatment did not occur in the federal government, it was doubtful that policies promoting it elsewhere could work; and (3) greater minority employment in the federal bureaucracy would make the government more representative of minorities politically and more effective in dealing with them.[6] Eventually, these concerns prompted the adoption of affirmative action in the federal government, although not without considerable resistance.

In order to comprehend the adoption and specific content of the federal affirmative-action policy, it is necessary to understand the character of the chief policymaker, the CSC.[7] The latter agency administered the EEO program from 1965 through 1978. It was also the federal government's central personnel agency from the adoption of the Civil Service Act of 1883 until its abolition by the Civil Service Reform Act of 1978. Throughout its existence the CSC has been primarily concerned with the creation and effective implementation of the federal merit system. The fundamental premise of that system has been that federal employment should be based on open, competitive examinations administered so as to select the best qualified employees.[8] Consequently, from a philosophical perspective, there was little conflict between the agency's predominant mission and its implementation of the principle of nondiscrimination within the framework of the EEO program. Indeed, nondiscrimination could even enhance the competitiveness of federal hiring procedures. In practice, however, conflict over merit achievement and nondiscriminatory principles has been manifested in some civil service examinations, which have a harsh racial impact in that they disproportionately exclude members of minority groups.[9] For this reason and others, including a lack of vigorous enforcement, by 1971 it appeared that the policy of nondiscrimination was having an inadequate impact on changing the social composition of the federal service.[10] This perception presented the CSC with a serious dilemma.

By the late 1960s, critics of the CSC's implementation of the federal EEO program had begun to advocate transferring that function to the Equal Employment Opportunity Commission (EEOC), which had jurisdiction over private employment practices at the time. The transfer did not occur until 1979, largely as a result of the CSC's opposition to it. In addition, as noted earlier, many persons advocated the adoption of an affirmative-action policy for federal employment. Although the CSC resisted both these approaches, it eventually came to see the latter as the lesser of two evils, primarily because the former—transferring the EEO program to the EEOC—would make the CSC somewhat subordinate to that agency.[11]

Despite the CSC's decision to authorize the use of affirmative action in federal personnel administration, the agency remained philosophically opposed to that policy, and, consequently, sought to qualify it in several important respects. The root of the conflict, from the CSC's perspective, was that merit demanded the employment of the best qualified, regardless of social characteristics, whereas affirmative action suggested that employment should be based on social characteristics rather than on other qualifications alone. To the extent that the latter approach prevailed, the merit system would be compromised, and the CSC would have to sacrifice a substantial share of its institutional values. Thus, in order to protect its meritist values, the CSC tried to subordinate affirmative-action policy to them.

First, affirmative action was to be confined to situations in which a federal agency had failed to hire substantial proportions of members of minority groups who were: (1) in possession of the requisite employment skills and (2) within the organization's normal recruitment area. Moreover, agencies' use of affirmative action was limited by openings within their ranks—new positions or openings could not be created solely for the sake of hiring members of minority groups. In the words of the official policy:

> Employment goals and timetables should be established in problem areas where progress is recognized as necessary and where such goals and timetables will contribute to progress, i.e., in those organizations and localities and in those occupations and grade levels where minority employment is not what should reasonably be expected in view of the potential supply of qualified members of minority groups in the work force and in the recruiting area and available opportunities within the organization. The skills composition of the minority-group population in the recruiting area used by the organization and the occupational nature of the jobs in the organization must be considered.[12]

To the extent that this policy directive was strictly applied, it is evident that the scope of affirmative action would necessarily be relatively narrow.

A second limitation on the application of affirmative action lay in the CSC's definition of a "minority-group member." For the most part this term has been used to include blacks, Hispanics (Spanish-surnamed persons), American Indians, and Orientals. Eskimos and Aleuts have also sometimes been considered within the ambit of federal affirmative action. On the other hand white ethnics other than Hispanics and religious minorities have been excluded from the affirmative-action process, despite the claims by some that they are substantially disadvantaged and culturally deprived.[13] Originally, women were not explicitly included in affirmative-action directives, but by 1973, CSC regulations clearly brought them within its scope.[14] The decision to apply affirmative action to some groups but not to others has been largely political and based on the groups' visibility in American society.

Another limitation imposed on affirmative action policy was that employment goals were conceived of as "targets" rather than as "quotas":

> A "goal" is a realistic objective which an agency endeavors to achieve on a timely basis within the context of the merit system of employment. A "quota," on the other hand, would restrict employment or development opportunities to members of particular groups by establishing a required number or proportionate representation which agency managers are obligated to attain without regard to merit-system requirements. "Quotas" are incompatible with merit principles.[15]

Considering goals as targets may help to protect the merit system, but it also means that there is no requirement that they be attained, which, in turn, suggests that program enforcement could be problematic and that under these conditions, affirmative action could emerge as a paper program.

A fourth limitation on the utility of the affirmative-action policy was that "agency action plans and instructions involving goals and timetables must state that all actions to achieve goals must be in full compliance with merit-system requirements."[16] Thus, affirmative-action policy was created as an overlay on merit procedures. In practice this severely reduces its efficacy because, in general, the federal merit system requires that applicants for federal positions be competitively examined for employment skills, and that any given appointment be made from among the top three ranking eligibles.[17] Therefore, the applicability of goals and timetables was largely limited to situations in which (1) qualified women or minorities within the agency's recruiting area were disproportionately excluded from employment by that organization, and (2) members of minority groups or women were found within the relatively small number of individuals who were able to obtain top-level eligibility rankings. To complicate matters, federal veteran preference regulations required that veterans, who are disproportionately white and overwhelmingly male,[18] be favored in such rankings.

Based on the foregoing restrictions on the application of federal affirmative action, the policy's impact on the composition of the federal workforce was necessarily limited. Before this proposition can be empirically tested, however, it is necessary to examine further the policy's objectives.

POLICY OBJECTIVES

The objectives of the federal affirmative-action program, as created and implemented by the CSC, have been ambiguous. While the CSC's immediate goal was only to forestall the transfer of the EEO program to the

EEOC, which was successfully achieved, affirmative-action policy has consistently been hampered by a duality of purpose. On the one hand an objective of affirmative action has been to create a "representative bureaucracy," that is, a federal executive branch whose social composition reflects that of the nation generally. The CSC articulated this objective as follows:

> We believe that to the extent practicable organizations of the Federal Government should, in their employment mix, broadly reflect, racially and otherwise, the varied characteristics of our population. This is a desirable goal to achieve within the context of employment on the basis of merit.[19]

On the other hand the purpose of affirmative action has sometimes been seen by the CSC, and often by others, as increasing the *number* of minority-group members and women employed in the federal government. Although these two purposes can be in harmony, depending on the social composition of any given agency, they can also militate against each other. Thus, the composition of some agencies, such as the EEOC, severely overrepresents members of minority groups, based upon their proportion in the society as a whole, while that of others, including the Department of Health, Education, and Welfare, overrepresents women in this sense. If the representational principle were to be followed, it might require using affirmative action for white males in such agencies, which is clearly contrary to policy directives, law, and the Constitution. It would also prohibit the establishment of goals and timetables for social groups that are already overrepresented, a restriction that has not been vigorously enforced. For instance, in 1974, the Department of Agriculture's Packers and Stockyards Administration set a goal of 100 percent female hiring for clerical positions.[20]

The duality of purpose behind the affirmative-action program makes evaluation difficult. One could evaluate the impact of affirmative action on the social representativeness of the federal bureaucracy. Equally important, though, is an evaluation of its impact on the social composition of the federal work force. The present analysis considers both these elements by concentrating on the latter approach and then assessing the impact of the observed changes on the bureaucracy's representativeness. First, however, it is necessary to engage in a process evaluation to assess better the probability that any changes observed stem from the operation of the policy itself, rather than from extraneous factors. It is necessary to examine whether the affirmative-action policy was implemented, and how, before attributing any changes in the social composition of the federal work force to it.

PROCESS EVALUATION

David Nachmias wrote: "Process evaluation is concerned with the extent to which a particular policy or program is implemented according to its stated guidelines."[21] To some extent, however, a process evaluation of federal affirmative-action policy is frustrated by the decentralized nature of program implementation.

The Equal Employment Opportunity Act of 1972 requires that "all personnel actions affecting employees or applicants for employment [in the federal government, with few exceptions] . . . shall be made free from any discrimination based on race, color, religion, sex, or national origin."[22] The act augmented the CSC's authority to enforce this requirement, which is similar to earlier ones appearing in the Civil Rights Act of 1964 and various executive orders, and to oversee the administration of EEO in the federal service generally. Specifically, the CSC was made responsible for an annual review and approval of federal agencies' national and regional EEO action plans.

In implementing this provision, the CSC's Office of Federal Equal Employment Opportunity (OFEEO), which was the CSC's major policymaking and monitoring body in the EEO realm, required that each agency action plan include a statement concerning the appropriateness of the goals and timetables approach for its own particular personnel situation. There was no requirement, however, that affirmative action actually be utilized. The OFEEO only reviewed national-level action plans, though, thereby leaving regional plans to be reviewed by the CSC's regional offices. Since fewer than 10 percent of all federal employees are employed in their agencies' headquarters, this meant that the plans concerning the vast bulk of federal positions were not monitored or evaluated by the OFEEO.

The decentralized nature of reviewing action plans was exacerbated by four additional factors: (1) the line of communication between the OFEEO and the CSC's regional offices was attenuated, running upward from the regions to the CSC's Deputy Executive Director, then to its Executive Director, then downward to the Assistant Executive Director, and finally to the Director of Federal EEO; (2) the CSC's regional offices made little effort to coordinate affirmative-action policy among themselves; (3) although regional action plans were supposed to follow the format and content of the agency's national plans, affirmative-action goals were to "be set at the lowest practicable level in the agency to assure that they [were] reasonable in terms of their relationship to hiring needs and the skills available in the recruiting area,"[23] thus assuring a great deal of flexibility; and (4) the links between agency headquarters and their regional and installation levels concerning affirmative action were often tenuous or even nonexistent. Indeed, it was not unusual for agency offices of EEO located at the headquarters level to be unaware of the goals and timetables set at the various field offices. Nor did the OFEEO have knowledge of affirmative action as it applied to 90 percent of the federal work force.

The CSC also required that agencies file a progress report along with their action plans so that the nonachievement or nonimplementation of affirmative action goals could be ascertained and investigated. For the most part, however, this was not done in a systematic fashion. In any event reporting followed the decentralized framework described earlier.

The decentralized nature of formulating and implementing affirmative-action goals and timetables followed the general pattern of the CSC's organization of the EEO program. The separation of the chief policymaking body from administrative matters inhibited evaluation of the operation of affirmative action and may have reduced the controversy associated with it. To an extent the CSC was able to reap gains from the symbolic aspects of affirmative action without severely threatening traditional merit-oriented personnel administration through its implementation. Agencies desiring to pursue affirmative action vigorously were largely free to do so, subject only to periodic inspection by the CSC, as, for the most part, were those choosing to ignore it. Neither Congress, the Executive Office of the President, the media, nor other interested parties were readily able to assess the operation of federal affirmative action. While this administrative framework may have served the CSC's political and organizational needs well, there was no reason to suspect that it promoted the effective use of affirmative action.

A full process evaluation of the federal affirmative action program was precluded by the decentralized nature of its implementation. While it was possible to determine whether agencies were establishing goals and timetables, and if so, to ascertain their content, it was impossible to find out whether goals were being achieved, ignored, or were serving to motivate behavior in any systematic fashion. The stark reality of the matter was that no one knew what happened to goals and timetables after they were established. This fact was uncovered through interviews with directors of EEO or their staffs in the departments of Agriculture; Health, Education, and Welfare; Housing and Urban Development; and Interior, as well as in the sizeable independent Veterans Administration and the General Services Administration. Extensive interviews were also held in the CSC's OFEEO.[24]

Being unable to determine whether goals and timetables were achieved, the evaluation had to be restricted to an investigation of their establishment. Information concerning the setting of affirmative-action goals and timetables was available through interviews and by obtaining the action plans of twenty-two agencies for calendar or fiscal 1973 and/or 1974.[25] Although the format and scope of these plans varied widely, their content can be described as follows:

Government Printing Office (1973): Four percent increase in the number of women and members of minority groups in supervisory and "uprate" positions in the production department.

EEOC (1974): Thirty percent of all new appointments over GS–9 level should be women; 5 percent of all new appointees should be Orientals and 5 percent should be American Indians.

General Services Administration (1974): Thirty-six percent of all hirees should be members of minority groups, 30 percent should be women; 54 percent of all those promoted should be minority-group members, and 44 percent should be women.

Army (1974): Increase the number of women in GS 13–15 by 0.5 percent of the total population in those grades; add 5 to 10 percent minorities and women to ranks GS 16–18; 25 percent of all senior-level placements should go to women, and 25 percent should go to members of minority groups.

Navy (1974): The employment of minority-group members in all subunits should be equal to at least 75 percent of the percent that is the minority in the recruiting area.

Interior (1974): Nationwide goal of 12 percent minority in the agency's workforce by 1977 (excluding Indians in the Bureau of Indian Affairs); add 50 women to GS–13 positions.

Transportation (1974): Action plan endorsed the use of goals, and in a separate action, the Secretary prescribed goals of increasing minority and female employment in the agency by 2.5 percent of the organization's work force.

Air Force (1973): Increase minority representation in the work force by 1 percent; increase the number of women and members of minority groups in grades GS 13–15 by 0.5 percent of the total number of positions in those grades; do the same at levels GS 16–18.

Agriculture (1974): The average hiring goals established by the bureaus that set goals for the following categories of positions were: professional hirees, 12 percent minority, 14 percent female; administrative hirees, 14 percent minority, 30 percent female; support position hirees, 17 percent minority; clerical hires, 28 percent minority, 77 percent female; lower-level technician hirees, 30 percent minority, 44 percent female.

NASA (1974): Increase minority employment by 6.1 percent of total agency employment; appoint 80 women and 80 minorities to professional positions.

Other agencies, including the departments of the Treasury; Labor; Commerce; Justice; Housing and Urban Development; and Health, Education, and Welfare endorsed the strategy of goals and timetables, but established no national goals and did not make available or possess centralized information concerning goals actually set by their regional and field installations. The same was true for the General Accounting Office, the CSC, the

Veterans Administration, the Small Business Administration, and the Post Office.

What conclusions can be drawn from this process evaluation? First, as one might expect, given the decentralized framework of the affirmative-action program, where used at all, goals and timetables tended to be set in a conservative fashion. Indeed, CSC guidelines anticipated this:

> Employment goals and target dates should be reasonable and flexible indicators for management action. If goals and timetables are realistic, they will probably be met. . . . Where they are not met, the reasons for this should be assessed by agency management to see if the goals or target dates for their achievement should be adjusted, or if additional . . . actions are needed, including the further commitment of resources to agency recruitment and upward mobility efforts.[26]

Clearly, from the perspectives of bureaucratic politics, the easiest approach for agency management was to set goals that were modest enough to be achieved without much difficulty. This was especially true to the extent that management was more interested in its own agency's mission than in EEO, something that almost all EEO officials maintain is virtually a universal condition. Still, setting modest goals was preferable to ignoring affirmative action entirely, which could have aroused attention in the OFEEO, Congress, or elsewhere.

Thus, it is not surprising that in agencies such as the Department of Transportation and the Air Force, the goals set were almost minuscule compared to the social underrepresentation of minorities and women in some of the grades to which they applied. The same was true of the Army's goal at the GS 13–15 level. The Department of the Interior's goal of 12 percent minority representation in its nationwide work force by 1977 left it, from a social standpoint, underrepresentative of minorities and did little to abate minority concentration in the agency's lowest grades. The Navy's nationwide goal for minority employment had the same effect. The goals set by several bureaus in the Department of Agriculture did little beyond reinforcing a concentration of members of minority groups and women in low-level positions. Finally, the goals set by NASA and the Government Printing Office were modest when viewed against the extent of minority and female underutilization in these agencies.

In a contrary vein a process evaluation of federal affirmative action indicates that some agencies did use goals and timetables in a vigorous fashion. Thus, the EEOC, as might be expected by virtue of its mission, established goals that were designed to increase substantially the number of women in its upper-level positions and Orientals and American Indians throughout its structure. Similarly, the affirmative-action goals set by some Department of Agriculture bureaus for professional and administrative positions were aimed at fostering significant change. Depending upon the number of positions actually available, the Army's goal of allotting 25 percent of all senior-level placements to minority-group members and women might also have comported with this pattern.

Based upon this process evaluation, it is reasonable to expect that an impact evaluation of the federal affirmative-action program will indicate that the availability of goals and timetables as an administrative technique for personnel change did not dramatically alter the composition of the federal work force, but rather, may have contributed to a limited expansion of minority and female employment.

IMPACT EVALUATION

According to Nachmias, "Impact evaluation is concerned with examining the extent to which a policy causes a change in the intended direction. It calls for delineation of operationally defined policy goals, specification of criteria of success, and measurement of progress toward the goals."[27] As noted earlier, the objectives of the affirmative-action program can be operationalized in two distinct but related ways. Here, the impact of affirmative action on the proportions of federal employees who are women or blacks will be considered first. The analysis will be limited to these two groups, rather than including all minorities, because the combined EEO-affirmative-action program has tended to concentrate resources upon them. Women and blacks also constitute the two largest groups at whom affirmative-action efforts are aimed. Proportions rather than actual numbers will be used to compensate for reductions and accretions in the number of positions at various levels of the federal service. In addition, the nature of available data requires that the analysis be limited to the general-schedule (GS) component of the federal work force. This contains roughly half of all federal civilian employees and includes most white-collar professional, administrative, technical, and support personnel. Moreover, in order to assess better the impact of affirmative action, this component of the federal work force will be considered by grade groupings. A second step in the evaluation will involve an assessment of the social representativeness of the general-schedule work force. Success will be specified as greater progress toward these objectives after the adoption of the affirmative-action policy rather than in the years immediately preceeding it. This brings a second aspect of the impact evaluation to the fore.

The evaluation design used here is commonly referred to as preprogram-postprogram design. Its ". . . obvious advantage . . . is that the program's target variable is compared with itself: a target variable is measured before implementation of the program (O_1); after implementation the same target variable is measured again (O_2). The difference scores are examined to assess the causal impact of the program (X)."[28] On the other hand such a design has a drawback in that ". . . changes in the target variables might have been produced by other events, not necessarily because of the policy."[29] While this possibility cannot be fully eliminated, it can be diminished by reducing the time between preprogram and postprogram measurements. Such a reduction in time frame can exacerbate the problem of the "regression artifact," however, which, in essence, is the possibility that either the preprogram period, postprogram period, or both are atypical in having witnessed extreme activity or inactivity that varies substantially from normal amounts of change. For example, if an evaluation of affirmative-action policy were limited to a single preprogram and postprogram year, it would run the risk that change during those years was abnormal. Hence, while reducing the time frame tends to guard against the impact of factors other than the policy change itself, it also includes the risk of analyzing atypical data.

In this analysis an effort will be made to guard against the effects of extraneous events and regression artifacts by limiting the time frame to the years between 1967 and 1976 inclusively, and by roughly comparing changes in the proportion of all general schedule workers who are women or blacks with changes in the employment patterns of these two groups in the private sector. Since the policy change under evaluation occurred in 1971, the choice of years will also be well balanced in terms of preprogram and postprogram assessments. Finally, 1976 is a reasonable cutoff point because it avoids the possibility that the impact evaluation of the affirmative-action program would be contaminated by any of numerous policy and organizational initiatives launched by the Carter administration, including reorganization of the EEO program, civil service reform, and the President's pronounced emphasis on appointing minorities and women to top political posts in the federal bureaucracy.

Blacks

Table 4.1 presents black federal employment in various general schedule groupings from 1967 to 1976. It is evident that some proportional increase in black employment has occurred. Thus, in grades GS 1–4, the proportion of the federal work force that is black increased slightly from 20.5 percent in 1967 to 21.1 percent in 1976. In grades GS 5–8 there was a more substantial increase from 11.6 percent to 17.4 percent over the same time period. In grades GS 9–11 the increase was from 4.3 percent to 8.4 percent,

TABLE 4.1

**Changes in Percentages of Blacks in Federal Employment,
By General Schedule Grade Groupings, 1967–1976***

GS Grade Group	*A* 1967	*B* 1971	*C* 1967–1971	*D* 1972	*E* 1976	*F* 1972–1976
1–4	20.5	21.8	1.3	22.0	21.1	−0.9
5–8	11.6	14.8	3.2	15.5	17.4	1.9
9–11	4.3	5.7	1.4	6.2	8.4	2.2
12–18	1.8	2.8	1.0	3.1	4.4	1.3

*Data are for November. The year 1971 is treated as preprogram because, despite its announcement in May 1971, the implementation of affirmative-action policy could not have affected black employment until 1972.
Source: U.S. Civil Service Commission, *Study of Minority Group Employment in the Federal Government* (Washington: Government Printing Office, 1969–1976).

and in grades GS 12–18 the percentage of blacks grew from 1.8 to 4.4 during the time period under consideration. During these years blacks comprised roughly 9 percent of the private-sector work force and comparable growth there was not evident.[30] Hence, there is strong evidence that the combined EEO–affirmative-action program has worked in the intended direction, although the question of its magnitude remains open to debate. But how much of this change can be attributed to affirmative action alone?

A better perspective on the impact of affirmative action policy is afforded by comparing the amount of change that occurred in the preprogram and postprogram periods. This provides an indication of the extent to which the availability of goals and timetables as a means for fostering change has, in fact, strengthened the preexisting EEO program. Such a comparison can be accomplished by contrasting columns C and F in Table 4.1. In so doing, it can be observed that to the extent that affirmative action is affecting the proportion of blacks in the federal service, it is having its greatest impact in the GS 9–11 group, where change in the postprogram period has been most pronounced. However, this change is nevertheless not substantially greater than that which occurred at the same levels during the preprogram period. In grades GS 1–8, change during the pre-affirmative action program was greater, and at the GS 12–18 levels, change was only slightly greater after the adoption of the affirmative-action policy.

These findings suggest that although the overall EEO program has fostered appreciable change, affirmative-action (goals and timetables) policy has not had a substantial and intended impact on the employment of blacks in the general schedule component of the federal bureaucracy. To a considerable extent, the reasons for this were explained in the process evaluation. However, at least one contaminating factor that may have suppressed the efficacy of affirmative action was extant: The number of positions in the general schedule was increasing substantially more rapidly during the preprogram period than after the adoption of affirmative action.[31] This undoubtedly made changing the social composition of the work force somewhat easier during the period in which EEO operated in the absence of goals and timetables. Nevertheless, it is clear that affirmative-action policy did not work well within the federal personnel environment that existed from 1972 to 1976, at least in the case of blacks.

Women

Evaluation of the impact of affirmative action upon the federal employment of women suggests that the policy of using goals and timetables may be somewhat more efficacious in their case, especially at midlevels of the general schedule, than in the case of blacks. Before addressing the data, however, a few historical observations are in order. In contrast to nondiscriminatory policy with regard to race and ethnicity, which was adopted in 1941, nondiscrimination based on gender was not fully mandated until the passage of the Civil Rights Act of 1964. In 1967 the Federal Women's Program was incorporated into the general EEO program for the first time. As noted earlier, when the CSC issued its policy directive authorizing affirmative action, it may not have anticipated that goals and timetables would be applicable to women, and it was not until 1973 that this was fully endorsed by commission regulations. Subsequently, though, official policy made no significant distinction between women and minorities in this regard.

Table 4.2 presents the federal employment of women in various general schedule groupings for selected years. The preprogram period used here had to be confined to 1969 and 1970 because data for earlier years and 1971 are not comparable with 1972 and subsequent data as a result of inconsistencies in treatment of the postal and other pay systems.[32] Thus, although the limited length of the preprogram must serve to reduce confi-

TABLE 4.2
Changes in the Percentages of Women in Federal Employment,
By General Schedule Grade Groupings, 1969–1976

GS Grade Group	1969	1970	1969–1970	1972	1976	1972–1976
1–6	73.1	72.3	−0.8	70.8	72.1	1.3
7–12	25.6	20.8	−4.8	21.1	28.1	7.0
13 and above	2.0	3.6	1.6	4.0	5.5	1.5

Source: U.S. Bureau of the Census, *Statistical Abstract of the United States, 1978*, p. 282, Table 461.

dence in the evaluation, it cannot be avoided. The postprogram period runs from 1972 to 1976. While the earlier year predates specific authorization to apply affirmative action to women, the original policy directive was not necessarily interpreted by all agencies as precluding the setting of goals and timetables for them. Again, 1976 is a desirable cutoff year because it avoids the potential contaminating effects of the presidential transition of 1977. The grade groupings reported follow the format used by the *United States Statistical Abstract.*

Table 4.2 indicates that the employment of women as a proportion of all general-schedule workers changed differentially during the 1969–1976 period. Thus, they declined slightly from 73.1 percent of the GS 1–6 work force in 1969 to 72.1 percent in 1976. On the other hand the proportion of positions held by women at the GS 7-12 and GS 13 and above levels increased during the same period by 2.5 percent and 3.5 percent, respectively. On balance, then, the EEO–affirmative-action program was associated with limited change in the intended direction, especially if one views the heavy concentration of women in low level jobs as a breach of equitable treatment. The extent to which these changes were associated with the existence of affirmative action alone remains to be considered.

Unlike Table 4.1, Table 4.2 indicates that change during the postprogram period was substantially greater in the intended direction in the middle levels of the general schedule than was the case in the preprogram years. Thus, whereas the employment proportion of women declined by 4.8 percent during the preprogram period, it increased by 7 percent after the adoption of the affirmative-action policy. At the same time, however, it appears that affirmative action did not contribute to the growth in the employment of women at the GS 13 and higher levels, as their proportional increase in those ranks was slightly lower in the postprogram period than in the preprogram years. The evidence pertaining to grades GS 1–6 is equivocal: While affirmative action may have contributed to a limited proportional increase in the employment of women, they also became more disproportionately heavily concentrated in low-level positions during the postprogram period.

These findings raise the question of why affirmative action appears to have been somewhat more efficacious with regard to women than with blacks. Part of the answer may lie in the fact that during the affirmative-action period, the employment of women in the private nonagricultural sector increased steadily from 29.3 percent of all workers to 30.9 percent.[33] Hence, the growing employment of women in the federal government was part of a more general trend in the society as a whole. Still, that trend does not seem strong enough to account for all the change in the employment of women at the middle levels of the general schedule. An additional factor may be that the underutilization of women has been based more upon discriminatory attitudes and practices than upon their economic and cultural distinctiveness. To the extent that this is the case, traditional, merit-oriented federal personnel administration is less likely to discriminate against them in a systematic fashion. Consequently, affirmative action as an overlay on those traditional practices may be a more viable policy with regard to women than to blacks and other minorities who, as a group, have suffered greater economic and cultural deprivations.

REPRESENTATIVE BUREAUCRACY

In view of the findings concerning the impact of affirmative action on the proportion of blacks and women employed in the federal government, it is unnecessary to devote much space to a discussion of the policy's contribution to the achievement of a socially representative bureaucracy. Clearly, as the information in Tables 4.1 and 4.2 indicates, in comparison to their numbers in the general work force, blacks and women are overrepresented in the lower grades and are severely underrepresented at the higher levels of the federal bureaucracy. Although affirmative action has contributed to better representation of these groups in some ranks, it has done so only marginally with regard to blacks, and it has not contributed forcefully to the employment of women where they are most underrepresented. Moreover, the evidence indicates that affirmative action has not been responsible for a substantial diminution of the overrepresentation of women and blacks in the lower ranks. Consequently, it can be concluded that to the extent that the purpose of affirmative action is to create a representative bureaucracy, it served this end only in a limited fashion with regard to women and blacks during the 1967–1976 period.

CONCLUSION

It is clear from this analysis that although the use of affirmative action in the federal government has had some impact, it has not dramatically changed the overall employment patterns of blacks and women, who constitute the two major groups toward whom the program is aimed. This, of course, is not to suggest that the policy is useless, but rather, to call attention to the fact that affirmative action alone, as constituted between 1972 and 1976, was less than wholly adequate in satisfying the nonsymbolic objectives of its supporters. Thus, as the process evaluation presented here indicates, the mode of implementation of affirmative action was such that there was little reason to expect that the policy would contribute to widespread change. In this sense the policy and its implementation may have been satisfactory from the point of view of the CSC, but not from the perspectives of those hoping for rapid and substantial change in the social composition of the federal work force. Better implementation may be forthcoming now that the EEO–affirmative-action program has been transferred to the EEOC. At a minimum this would require more centralized reporting on goals and timetables and better monitoring of efforts to fulfill them.

This evaluation of federal affirmative action points in another direction as well. It is evident that a better understanding of the factors that contribute to minority and female employment is necessary. Affirmative action, as policy, tends to deal with the symptoms of a social, economic, and political condition, but it fails to address causes. Rather, it seeks change by affording differential and benevolent treatment to members of groups that have been victimized by invidious discrimination in the past. Certainly, its efficacy could be enhanced by an understanding of the situations in which affirmative action is most likely to succeed or fail. For instance further examination of the application of affirmative action to women in midlevel, general schedule grades is clearly appropriate. Relatedly, research has indicated that agencies' missions may be important in terms of EEO and affirmative action.[34] What is unknown about affirmative action points toward the realization that social engineering is difficult and fraught with unanticipated consequences. Relatively simple solutions to complex problems are not the rule.

Finally, this analysis contains several lessons for the student of policy evaluation. It is evident that adequate data are not always available. Process evaluation can be frustrated by program decentralization. Even such straightforward questions as "When was a policy first implemented?" may elude precise answer. In addition even the most controversial programs may have minimal and ambiguous impacts on the problems to which they are addressed. Moreover, when change occurs, it is not always possible to attribute it to the policy itself. And in the end whatever the methodological, conceptual, and technical adequacy of an evaluation of public policy, the researcher must be prepared for the possibility that it will become the center of political controversy.[35]

NOTES

1. Robert Hampton, Chairman, U.S. Civil Service Commission, "Memorandum for Heads of Departments and Agencies" (May 11, 1971). Hereafter referred to as "May Memo."
2. On earlier developments of relevance to equal opportunity in federal employment, see David H. Rosenbloom, *Federal Equal Employment Opportunity*

(New York: Praeger, 1977) and Samuel Krislov, *The Negro in Federal Employment* (Minneapolis: University of Minnesota Press, 1967).

3. See *Board of Regents v. Bakke,* 46 Law Week 4896 (June 28, 1978) for a convenient recapitulation of arguments concerning affirmative action.

4. Related discussions concerning the impact of the Equal Employment Opportunity Act of 1972 can be found in W. H. Rose and T. P. Chia, "The Impact of the Equal Employment Opportunity Act of 1972 on Black Employment in the Federal Service," *Public Administration Review,* 38 (May/June 1978), 245-251; and James F. Guyot, "Arithmetic and Inference in Ethnic Analysis," Communication, *Public Administration Review,* 39 (March/April 1979), 194-197. See also Rose's response to Guyot, ibid., pp. 197-198. The controversy between Rose and Guyot illustrates the dangers of engaging in an impact evaluation in the absence of a process evaluation. Put simply, although the EEO act strengthened the CSC somewhat, it did not substantially change the nature of the EEO program, which was previously based on executive orders. Consequently, there was little reason to anticipate that the act would have a considerable impact on federal employment patterns.

5. See Stokley Carmichael and Charles V. Hamilton, *Black Power* (New York: Vintage Books, 1967), and Herbert J. Storing, ed., *What Country Have I?* (New York: St. Martin's Press, 1970), for comprehensive statements.

6. S. Krislov, *The Negro* and *Representative Bureaucracy* (Englewood Cliffs: Prentice-Hall, 1967 and 1974).

7. See Rosenbloom, *Federal EEO,* chaps. 4 and 5 for a more comprehensive discussion.

8. On the civil service reform of 1883, see David H. Rosenbloom, *Federal Service and the Constitution* (Ithaca: Cornell University Press, 1971), chap. 3; and Paul P. Van Riper, *History of the United States Civil Service* (Evanston: Row, Peterson, 1958).

9. See *Douglas v. Hampton,* 512 F2d 976 (1975), and more generally, David H. Rosenbloom and Carole C. Obuchowski, "Public Personnel Examinations and the Constitution," *Public Administration Review,* 37 (January/February 1977), 9-18.

10. From the perspectives of evaluation research, it is interesting to note that little empirical analysis was done on the matter, and virtually no one had a clear notion of what constituted adequate progress.

11. The author was able to ascertain this as a participant-observer in the CSC's EEO program at the time.

12. "May Memo."

13. See S. J. LaGumina and F. J. Cavaioli, *The Ethnic Dimension in American Society* (Boston: Holbrook, 1974) for a review of ethnicity in American life.

14. Federal Personnel Manual System Letter, 713-22, "EEO Plans," Appendix I, No. 9 (October 4, 1973).

15. "May Memo."

16. Ibid.

17. This practice is referred to as the "rule of three" and dates back to the nineteenth century. Although there are exceptions to its application, especially in

the top third of the federal bureaucracy, the rule of three remains standard operating procedure.

18. Alan K. Campbell, "Civil Service Reform: A New Commitment," *Public Administration Review,* 38 (March/April 1978), 102.

19. Letter of CSC Chairman Hampton to R. Kelley, Assistant Secretary of Defense, August 6, 1970. The letter was widely circulated among federal personnel officials.

20. U.S. Department of Agriculture, Equal Employment Opportunity Plan, 1974. When the author mentioned this goal to the Director of the Federal Women's Program, she replied, "Did they really do *that?*"

21. David Nachmias, *Public Policy Evaluation: Approaches and Methods* (New York: St. Martin's Press, 1979), p. 5.

22. 86 Stat. 103 (March 24, 1972).

23. Federal Personnel Manual System Letter, 713-22 (2g), October 1973.

24. Interviews took place in July 1974.

25. The agencies were the departments of State; Treasury; Justice; Commerce; Labor; Interior; Housing and Urban Development; Transportation; Health, Education, and Welfare; Agriculture; Army; Navy; and Air Force; and the General Services Administration, EEOC, Government Printing Office, Post Office, General Accounting Office, CSC, Veterans Administration, NASA, and the Small Business Administration. Together, these agencies employed more than 90 percent of the federal civilian work force.

26. Federal Personnel Manual System Letter, 713-22, Appendix I, No. 11 (October 4, 1973).

27. Nachmias, *Public Policy Evaluation,* p. 5.

28. Ibid., p. 49.

29. Ibid.

30. Guyot, "Arithmetic and Inference in Ethnic Analysis," Figure 2, p. 196.

31. U.S. Bureau of the Census, *Statistical Abstract of the United States,* 1978, p. 282.

32. See ibid., 1977, Table 448, p. 272, for an explanation. To complicate matters, it is not readily apparent how inconsistencies in the CSC's reporting of data can be explained. See U.S. Civil Service Commission, *Study of Employment of Women in the Federal Government* (Washington: Government Printing Office, 1973), see pp. 10 and 21 for an example.

33. See U.S. Bureau of the Census, *Statistical Abstract of the United States,* 1970-1977. The figures are for selected industries including manufacturing, mining, construction, transportation, public utilities, retail trade, finance, insurance, real estate, and services.

34. See Peter N. Grabosky and David H. Rosenbloom, "Racial and Ethnic Integration in the Federal Service," *Social Science Quarterly,* 56 (June 1975), 71-84.

35. Carol Weiss, "The Politicization of Evaluation Research," pp. 310-322 in *Cases in Public Policy-Making,* James Anderson, ed. (New York: Praeger, 1976).

CIVIL RIGHTS POLICIES AND THE ACHIEVEMENT OF RACIAL ECONOMIC EQUALITY, 1948–1975

Donald J. McCrone
Richard J. Hardy

Determining the effects, as well as the sources, of public policies is a fundamental task for economists and political scientists. Political scientists, until recently, were somewhat lax in fulfilling this role. As one political scientist noted, "Evaluation of policy is one of the least explored functional activities in the policy process" (Jones, 1970, p. 107). The marked shift during the 1960s in public policy regarding civil rights provides a realistic and significant opportunity to expand this activity and to assess the efficacy and limits of governmental action.

Civil rights policies are justified by appeals to several related, but frequently competing, values such as freedom, justice, and equality. The predominant value underlying these policies, however, is that of equality—racial equality (Dye, 1971). Racial equality was defined initially, in terms of equality of opportunity, but the emphasis has shifted toward the achievement of equality of condition. This shift is particularly salient regarding current federal policies committed to improving the economic status of black Americans (Masters, 1975). Unfortunately, commitments do not ensure results (Pressman and Wildavsky, 1973; Moynihan, 1969).

One crucial measure of the effects of these policies, if any, on the relative economic condition of blacks is changes in the black/white median income ratio among males.[1] While the black/white income ratio among males represents only one index of economic equality, it is perhaps the simplest and clearest single measure of status differences between the races (Franklin and Resnick, 1973). Family income ratios are suspect because of changes in family composition over time, while the female income ratio is contaminated by discrimination against females generally.

Today, social scientists agree generally that an ever-increasing income ratio is the sine qua non for attaining comprehensive racial equality, but disagree as to whether upturns in the ratio are due to shifts in governmental policy or cyclical changes in the economy (Freeman, 1973; Tobin, 1965). The purpose of this article is to assess the limits and efficacy of governmental action to date by determining whether civil rights policies since 1964 have systematically decreased the gap between black and white male incomes, both nationally and regionally. By employing time-series regression analysis, an examination will be made of the cyclical and secular changes in the income ratio, before and after the Civil Rights Act of 1964, in the hope of shedding new light on this issue.

CIVIL RIGHTS POLICIES SINCE 1964

We hypothesize that governmental policies concerning civil rights since 1964 have had a significant effect upon improving the relative income of black males. Several compelling reasons exist for this belief. First, the Civil Rights Act of 1964 signified, for the first time since Reconstruction, a strong and positive commitment by the federal government to the achievement of racial equality. The Civil Rights Act of 1957 was very limited in scope and the state antidiscrimination laws existing prior to 1964 were limited in their application and confined to non-Southern states where discrimination was less prevalent.[2] Thus, the 1964 Civil Rights Act broadened and deepened the federal commitment and extended this commitment to regions of the country—notably the South—where discrimination and income inequality were greatest (Gwartney, 1970a).

Title VII of the Civil Rights Act of 1964 made it unlawful for any firm or union employing more than twenty-five persons to discriminate. This covered initially an estimated 75 percent of the national labor force (U.S. Commission on Civil Rights, 1973). The Equal Employment Opportunity Commission (EEOC) was established under this act to secure compliance. Although Title VII did not grant the EEOC cease and desist powers, it did confer upon it the authority to investigate and negotiate complaints of discrimination. During its first seven years, the EEOC investigated nearly 80,000 of the more than 110,000 complaints of employment discrimination filed. In 1974 alone, the EEOC handled 62,099 cases of racial discrimination (Equal Employment Opportunity Commission, 1975). Furthermore, the Attorney General was empowered to bring suit or intervene in private litigation where a "pattern or practice" of discrimination was involved. In 1972, Congress amended Title VII to permit the EEOC direct access to federal district courts, and expanded the EEOC's authority to include state and local governmental employees as well as all businesses and unions employing over fifteen workers. This amendment allows the EEOC to handle systematic problems affecting job equality throughout an entire employment operation, rather than relying on individual complaints (EEOC, 1975). While the effectiveness of the EEOC has frequently been a source of debate, most experts agree that Title VII has expanded greatly the role of the federal government in the area of civil rights (Bullock, 1975; Glazer, 1975; Perlo, 1975; Adams, 1973).

Second, the courts have interpreted civil rights legislation in ways likely to spur demand for black workers. The litigation record in Title VII cases has been remarkably successful (Rosenthal, 1973). Courts have placed great weight on statistical evidence as to the number of black employees in various job categories, and have permitted class action lawsuits through a liberal interpretation of Rule 23 of the Federal Rules of Civil Procedure.[3] Perhaps more importantly, courts have helped check many subtle devices used by ingenious employers to circumvent Title VII. In a landmark case, *Griggs v. Duke Power Co.*, the court ruled that educational and psychological tests which bar more blacks than whites are invalid. In addition, courts have forbidden such practices as word-of-mouth job recruiting solely among white communities in *Parham v. Southwestern Bell Telephone Co.*, seniority systems which lock blacks into low paying jobs in *U.S. v. Local 189, United Papermakers and Paperworkers*, and the unjustified use of arrest records which tend to disqualify more blacks than whites in *Gregory v. Litton Systems, Inc.* Rulings such as these have no doubt prompted aggrieved minorities to seek judicial remedies while serving notice that arrant discrimination will no longer be tolerated.

Finally, the Civil Rights Act of 1964 engendered a series of policy enactments which carried the federal government into areas previously considered part of the state or private realm. Title VI provides for the termination of federal funds from any state or local program administered in a discriminatory manner. Since 1964, myriad manpower and affirmative action programs have expanded greatly. For example, Executive Order 11246, issued by President Johnson in 1965, requires all federal contractors to take "affirmative action" in the hiring of minorities. Unlike previous executive orders which were narrowly applied and often short-lived, E. O. 11246 extended affirmative action to all private contractors, subcontractors, and unions dealing with the federal government.[4] Federal officials estimated that in 1969, over 21 million persons, or approximately one-third of the labor force, were employed either directly or indirectly by the federal government (U.S. Commission on Civil Rights, 1970). In sum, there is ample justification for believing that governmental policies, ceteris paribus, should affect the median income ratio.

CHANGES IN THE BLACK/WHITE INCOME RATIO: AN OVERVIEW

Perhaps the first serious attempt to assess the vagaries of the black/white income ratio in the postwar period was that by Batchelder (1964). Batchelder's investigation of census data led him to conclude that the relative income status of black males had declined in all regions in the decade of the 1950s. He hypothesized that any future increase in the income standing of blacks during the 1960s would be a function of either a return to high levels of aggregate economic demand or civil rights action. A subsequent research note reported that the increased ratio of black to white incomes for the years 1963 and 1964 seemed to be a function of an improved economy (Fein, 1966).

In 1970, a research note of particular importance was proffered by Rasmussen. By using regression analysis to separate the cyclical effects from the secular trend, Rasmussen introduced a model which suggested that changes in the relative income of nonwhite males between 1948 and 1964 was a function of aggregate demand. The model is given by the following equation:

$$Y_t = 57 + 0.984 \ (\% \ \Delta GNP_t) - 2.7 \ (\% \ U_{t-1}) + 0.323 \ (T) \qquad (1)$$
$$ (0.250) (0.8) (0.150)$$
$$R^2 = .57$$

Where Y_t = nonwhite/white male income ratio by year
$\% \Delta GNP_t$ = the yearly percentage change in the real
Gross National Product (1958 $)
$\% U_{t-1}$ = the level of aggregate unemployment lagged one year
T = a time trend by year

(Figures in parenthesis under coefficients are standard errors of those coefficients.)

The regression coefficients reveal that the cyclical conditions of economic growth and unemployment had strong effects on the income ratio. When times are good, the income ratio increases. When times are bad, the income ratio declines. Despite a modest and barely statistically significant time trend toward greater equality, Rasmussen concluded that, because of an increasingly tight labor market, the ratio reflected cyclical changes rather than a secular trend.

The principal test of Batchelder's contention came, however, from Masters' praiseworthy time-series analysis (1975). Building upon Rasmussen's seminal regression model, Masters sought to determine the relative effects of cyclical changes and policy change (Civil Rights Act of 1964) on the income ratio. Masters formulated the following model:

$$Y_t = a \ (\% \ \Delta GNP_t) + b \ (\% \ U_{t-1}) \qquad (2)$$
$$+ \ c \ (T_1) + d \ (T_2) + e \ (D) + u_t$$

Where Y_t = the nonwhite/white male median income ratio year
                by year
$\% \ \Delta GNP_t$ = yearly percentage change in the real
                Gross National Product (1958 $)
$\% \ U_{t-1}$ = the level of aggregate unemployment lagged one year
T_1 = a time trend prior to 1964
T_2 = a time trend from 1964
D = a dummy variable for pre- and post-1964
U = error term

Applying this model to annual data for the period from 1948 through 1971, Masters obtained the following results:

$$Y_t = 56.5 + 0.56 \ (\% \ \Delta GNP_t) - 1.53 \ (\% \ U_{t-1}) + \qquad (3)$$
$$(0.23) \qquad\qquad (0.69)$$
$$0.05 \ (T_1) + 1.12 \ (T_2) + \ 0.77 \ (D)$$
$$(0.15) \qquad (0.33) \qquad (2.00)$$
$$\bar{R}^2 = .73 \qquad\qquad\qquad D.W. = 2.3$$

The cyclical conditions are still clearly operative, but Masters focuses our attention on the trend coefficients. Masters concluded that the thrust of the civil rights policies produced a definite upward secular trend in the income ratio, because the coefficient for T_2 (post-1964 trend) is statistically significant and significantly greater than the coefficient for T_1 (pre-1964 trend) and because the coefficient for D (pre- and post-1964) is positive. Hence, Masters corroborates the traditional liberal position of Allport (1954) and Myrdal (1944), who held that a precipitous event such as the policy shift symbolized by the 1964 Civil Rights Act would give impetus to a steady and continuous improvement in the relative position of blacks over time.

Masters' analysis is not definitive, however, for as he notes there are two contrasting views that offer compelling arguments which must be considered. The first is the radical view professed by Baran and Sweezy (1966), and Sherman (1972). While not gainsaying the initial impact of civil rights policies, this school believes that in the long run, the apparent economic gains for blacks will be eroded under the impact of recessions. As long as economic conditions are generally improving, the policies may work to a marginal extent, but the principle of last hired and first fired will eventually reassert itself. The radical view, then, expects the coefficient for T_2 to recede toward that of T_1 when economic conditions decline sharply.

The second major alternative to the liberal view of the effectiveness of civil rights policies is that of the conservatives, who, like Friedman (1962), claim that such policies are not only anathema to individual freedom, but will be effective only in the South. The policies are aimed specifically at the South (especially in the early stages) and, therefore, will have little effect upon the income status of blacks outside the South. If this view is correct, then, the coefficient for T_2 is different from T_1 only because of changes in the South.

MASTERS' MODEL RECONSIDERED

The genius of Masters' model lies in its utility for empirically assessing civil rights policies and the achievement of economic equality as well as determining the validity of the three aforementioned theoretical approaches. There are, however, several weaknesses in the model. One weakness is the untenable choice of 1964 as the dividing point. As justification, Masters asserts that ". . . the legislation is likely to affect both specific employer practices and general attitudes as soon as it is passed rather than just when it becomes legally effective." This explanation seems rather unconvincing due primarily to the difficulty in defining "general attitudes" or determining their intensity and span. If one desires to assess the impact of the 1964 act and subsequent legislation, it seems the more appropriate dividing point is 1965—when the law takes effect.

A second major weakness in Masters' work is that, though he rejects the radical view, his conclusions are based upon sharply limited variance in his two cyclical variables. The poorest showing in the GNP growth rate was −0.65 percent in 1970 and the highest unemployment rate was 5.7 percent in 1964. Thus, the secular trend claimed by Masters may be premature, if not spuriously dependent on generally good economic conditions. The true test of the radical position occurs after 1971 when a major recession produces a decline in the GNP of 2.86 percent and a record annual unemployment rate of 8.5 percent. Additional research, therefore, would reveal if the secular increase in the black/white income ratio is maintained even in the face of these substantial cyclical changes.

A final important weakness in Masters' work is his failure to evaluate adequately the impact of the civil rights policy changes by region. Instead of carrying forward his time-series analysis by examining the available annual data by region from 1953, he eschews the issue by changing the level of analysis to a static dichotomous comparison of Standard Metropolitan Statistical Areas in 1959 and 1969. To test the hypothesis that the impact of civil rights legislation would be confined mainly to the South, Masters calculated the black/white income ratios for those SMSAs which maintained a black population in excess of 200,000 based on the 1960 and 1970 census. While not denying that the greatest overall increase in the ratio occurred in the South, he found that the ratio increased somewhat in those Northern SMSAs which met his criteria. Masters concluded that regional differences diminished once the data are thus disaggregated. The fact remains that a two-point comparison (1960 and 1970) does not allow for the determination of secular trends nor control for annual cyclical changes. Further research, using regional time-series data, for the available period (1953–74), would disclose if the national increase in the relative income of black males is due to an across-the-board increase or substantial increments in particular segments of the country. Further analysis is warranted.

THE MODEL

The first two weaknesses in Masters' work are remedied readily. First, the equation is modified so that 1965 becomes the dividing point in the two time trends and dummy variable, instead of 1964. Second, the equation is updated through 1975 (see Note on Sources for all data used in this study) to obtain greater variance in the cyclical variables, thereby affording a better opportunity to test the radical claim. The new data and revised model yield the following estimates:

$$\text{National } Y_t = 59.35 + 0.84 \ (\%\Delta GNP_t) - 2.68 \ (\%U_{t-1}) \qquad (4)$$

$$\begin{array}{cccc} (1948\text{--}75) & (0.17) & (0.55) \end{array}$$

$$+ \ 0.29 \ (T_1) + 1.66 \ (T_2) + 0.34 \ (D)$$

$$\begin{array}{ccc} (0.12) & (0.23) & (1.48) \end{array}$$

$$\begin{array}{lll} R = .94 & R^2 = .88 & F = 33.13 \\ \overline{R} = .93 & \overline{R}^2 = .86 & D.W. = 2.2 \end{array}$$

These results provide striking support for Masters' original conclusions, but with enhanced clarity. First, the adjusted multiple coefficient of determination ($\overline{R}^2$) for our equation of .86 is better than Masters' original equation and indicates excellent fit. Second, the regression coefficients for the cyclical conditions of economic growth and rate of unemployment are sharper and more statistically significant. Third, the regression coefficients for the two time trends are also sharper and more statistically significant. Only the originally statistically insignificant regression coefficient for the dummy variable (D) declines and remains insignificant.

Our primary concern, however, is with the estimates for the two secular trends. Unlike Masters, but like Batchelder, we find a small, but statistically significant trend (0.29/year) for 1948–1964. Over this sixteen-year period, then, the gap between black and white incomes declined by about 4.5 percent. This is a glacial rate of change, at best. The coefficient for the secular trend since 1965 (1.66/year) is nearly six times as great as the earlier secular trend. This difference in slopes between T_2 and T_1 is significant at the .01 level, indicating a real change in trend. With these results, we can estimate the impact of the Civil Rights Act of 1964 and the policies it stimulated for the 1965–1975 period. We obtain this estimate by adding the coefficient of the dummy variable (D) to the difference between the coefficients of the two time trends (T_2-T_1) for an eleven-year period. The estimated effect through 1975 is:

$$\%\Delta Y_t = D + 11\,(T_2 - T_1) \qquad (5)$$
$$= .34 + 11\,(1.66 - .24)$$
$$= 15.41$$

If the above estimate is correct, the black/white median income ratio among males rose by over 15 percent as a result of the policy shift. The gap between black and white incomes declined as a function of policy action.

Before we become too complacent about the capacity of current civil rights policies to achieve racial economic equality, we must be clear on several points. First, the fact remains that by 1975 black median income was only 59.18 percent that of white median income. Second, a rate of change of 1.66 percent/year may strike many as little better than glacial movement. After all, at that rate of change, parity of income would not be achieved by civil rights policies until the end of this century. Third, an increase in unemployment of only 0.62 percent or a decrease in the gross national product of 1.98 percent erases any yearly gain achieved through civil rights policies. We can illustrate this process, and incidentally provide an opportunity for a true test of the predictive power of this model, by forecasting the black/white income ratio for 1976 and 1977 (Pindyck and Rubinfeld, 1976, pp. 156–158, 177–181). We can use actual and projected information on the $\%\,\Delta$GNP and $\%\,U_{t-1}$ for these years to estimate the

Predictions

1976 $Y_t = 59.35 + .84\,(6.2) - 2.68\,(8.5) + \qquad (6)$
$.29\,(0) + 1.66\,(12) + .34\,(1)$
$= 62.04$

1977 $Y_t = 59.35 + .84\,(4.3) - 2.68\,(7.7) + \qquad (7)$
$.29\,(0) + 1.66\,(13) + .34\,(1)$
$= 64.24$

continued effects of the current recession (Economic Outlook, U.S.A., 1976a #1 and 1976b #2).

In 1974, the income ratio stood at 63.4. The continuing impact of the recession is to *reduce* that ratio for 1975 and 1976. Only if the expected economic recovery generates substantial growth in the Gross National Product in 1977 and creates a significant reduction in the rate of unemployment will the ratio surpass the 1974 level. In other words, we cannot anticipate a *real* decline in the gap between black and white incomes until 1977, at the earliest. We should remember, however, that without the secular trend generated since 1965, the result of the current recession would have been roughly twice as severe.

Finally, like Masters, we have been assuming to this point that we can talk legitimately of a *national* secular trend. How warranted is this assumption?

THE REGIONAL IMPACT
OF CIVIL RIGHTS POLICIES, 1953–1974

The analysis of regional variations over time in the black/white income ratio is essential for two reasons. First, a number of studies suggest that increases in the income ratio nationally reflect the migration of blacks from the South to the less discriminatory and higher income regions of the country. Glenn (1963), for example, computed an index of regional migration and income for the period from 1940 to 1960 and concluded that "the rather pronounced improvement in the relative status of nonwhite males as a whole was mainly a function of the movement of nonwhites from the South to other regions." A similar conclusion was reached by Gwartney (1970) who noted that nearly all of the relative gains for nonwhites from 1937 to 1967 were eliminated once migration was controlled. Our two national secular trends (T_1 and T_2) could be based, then, on regional migration. Even the difference between the two trends could be accounted for by changing patterns of migration. If migration were relatively uncommon before 1965 and relatively common after 1965, the sharper trend in T_2 could be accounted for by differential rates of migration.

The evidence on regional migration contradicts, directly, this interpretation. Regional migration was *more* common before 1965, than after. The percentage of nonwhite population residing in the South declined by 8 percent during the 1950s, 5.6 percent between 1960 and 1964, but only 1.4 percent between 1964 and 1968 (Gwartney, 1970). Moreover, since that time, migration of nonwhites from the South has been only minimal. We are not arguing that regional mirgation does not account for any of the

South
$$Y_t = 53.68 + 1.15\,(\%\Delta\mathrm{GNP}_t) - 4.29\,(\%U_{t-1}) \qquad (8)$$
$$ (0.24) \phantom{(\%\Delta\mathrm{GNP}_t) -} (0.82)$$
$$+ 0.76\,(T_1) + 1.97\,(T_2) + 2.61\,(D)$$
$$ (0.24) (0.22) (0.37)$$

R = .96	R^2 = .92	F = 38.9
$\overline{R}$ = .95	R^2 = .91	D.W. = 1.92

North
East
$$Y_t = 81.14 + 0.28\,(\%\Delta\mathrm{GNP}_t) - 1.95\,(\%U_{t-1}) \qquad (9)$$
$$ (0.35) \phantom{(\%\Delta\mathrm{GNP}_t) -} (1.22)$$
$$+ 0.14\,(T_1) + 0.24\,(T_2) - 0.24\,(D)$$
$$ (0.36) (0.33) (0.54)$$

R = .54	R^2 = .29	F = 1.3
$\overline{R}$ = .35	$\overline{R^2}$ = .12	D.W. = 1.71

longterm secular trend. In fact, Gwartney's (1970) estimate that migration accounted for about 5 percent of the increases in the national income ratio in the 1950s and early 1960s is very compatible with our estimate of the secular trend before 1965. What regional migration cannot account for is the sharp rise in the trend after 1965. In fact, it can account for less of the trend after 1965 than before 1965.

Regional analysis is essential, also, because we expect the impact of civil rights policies since 1965 to be greater on racial income inequality in the South than in other regions. The South may be expected to show a greater decline in inequality for two related reasons. First, the primary focus of civil rights policies, especially in the earlier years, was on the reduction of overt, purposeful racial discrimination. Since racial income inequality is a function of both purposeful discrimination, and what may be termed structural discrimination based on such long-term factors as educational and occupational inequality, the region with the greatest reliance on purposeful discrimination will experience the greatest policy effect. We need not assume that only the South was engaged in purposeful discrimination to accept the notion that such discrimination was greater in the South than the North. Second, the implementation of civil rights policies was more immediate and vigorous in the South. In 1970, for example, the EEOC was particularly active in the South where two-thirds of the employer-union-agency charges were investigated (Equal Opportunity Commission, 1970).

A simple comparison of mean values of the black/white median income ratio before and after 1965 by region in Table 4.3 supports our expectation. The South stands out sharply in two regards. First, the income ratio for the South was about 30 percent below that of the other three regions before 1965. Second, the South shows a far greater jump in the income ratio after 1965 than do the other three regions. Applying our regression model to the annual data by region compels the same conclusion.

North
Central
$$Y_t = 76.70 + 0.31\ (\%\Delta\text{GNP}_t) + 0.11\ (\%U_{t-1}) \qquad (10)$$
$$ (0.45) \qquad\qquad (1.56)$$
$$- 0.38\ (T_1) + 0.48\ (T_2) - 0.06\ (D)$$
$$(0.46) \qquad (0.42) \qquad (0.69)$$

$$R = .61 \qquad R^2 = .37 \qquad F = 1.9$$
$$\overline{R} = .48 \qquad \overline{R^2} = .23 \qquad \text{D.W.} = 1.99$$

West
$$Y_t = 69.33 + 0.93\ (\%\Delta\text{GNP}_t) - 1.53\ (\%U_{t-1}) \qquad (11)$$
$$ (0.60) \qquad\qquad (2.09)$$
$$+ 1.15\ (T_1) + 1.12\ (T_2) + 1.62\ (D)$$
$$(0.62) \qquad (0.56) \qquad (0.93)$$

$$R = .60 \qquad R^2 = .36 \qquad F = 1.8$$
$$\overline{R} = .46 \qquad \overline{R^2} = .21 \qquad \text{D.W.} = 2.09$$

These regional regression equations indicate clearly that the national increase in the relative incomes of black males is *not* due to across-the-board increases as our national equation assumes, but is due to a marked increase in one region of the country—the South. In fact, we have no real confidence that secular improvements exist at all outside the South. Of the four regional equations, only that for the South is statistically significant, has generally reliable regression coefficients, or indicates a dramatic change in the secular trend after 1965. The equation for the South not only accounts for 92 percent of the variance in the Southern income ratio; the coefficient for T_2 (1.97) is nearly three times that of T_1 (.76) and the coefficient for D is strong and positive (2.61).

The presence of such a strong trend toward income equality after 1965 in the South cannot be explained away by reference to economic and social changes in the South. While the South has experienced rapid industrialization and urbanization in the post-World War II period, there is no evidence that these processes were accelerated sharply at or about 1965. The marked *change* in trend, then, cannot be accounted for by these processes.

The maximum effect of the policy shift in 1965 on the income ratio in the South may be estimated as before in equation (5).

TABLE 4.3
Mean Black/White Income Ratios
Before and After 1965, by Region

Region	Pre–1965	Post–1965	% Change
South	40.8	52.1	+11.3
West	71.7	74.4	+2.7
Northeast	73.6	73.6	0.0
Northcentral	75.9	80.3	+4.4

$$\%\Delta Y_t = D + 10\,(T_2 - T_1) \tag{12}$$
$$= 2.61 + 10\,(1.97 - .76)$$
$$= 15.7$$

The gap between black and white male incomes has declined, according to this estimate, by about 15.7 percent under the impact of civil rights policies since 1965.

As before, we can attempt to forecast the black/white income ratio for males in the South during the two years following available data, thereby testing our model and assessing the import of the current recession.

Predictions (South)

1975 $Y_t = 53.68 + 1.15\,(-2.94) - 4.29\,(5.6)$ (13)
        $+ .76\,(0) + 1.97\,(11) + 2.61\,(1)$
        $= 50.56$

1976 $Y_t = 53.68 + 1.15\,(5.86) - 4.29\,(8.5)$
        $+ .76\,(0) + 1.97\,(12) + 2.61\,(1)$
        $= 50.20$

Since the rate in the South stood at 53.9 in 1974, both 1975 and 1976 are forecast to be substantially below that level. The impact of unemployment on the ratio in the South is particularly disastrous.

The results for the other three regions (Northeast, North Central, West) are equally striking. The racial income ratio seems to wax and wane between about 70 and 80 percent, while averaging about 75 percent. Despite some tantalizing individual regression coefficients, some of which approach statistical significance, our overall conclusion must be that there is little evidence that either cyclical or policy conditions have much systematic effect on the racial income ratio outside the South.

Patterns of regional migration cannot account for these differential results. The income ratio outside the South may have been held down, especially in the earlier years, by migration from the South. Recent migrants would tend to enter the labor force at the bottom. This continuous process would hold down the median income of blacks, even if long-term black residents were making some advances in income.

As we saw above, however, net migration from the South has waned sharply since 1965. If migration were the factor that accounted for our null findings in the early period, the trend since 1965 should have been enhanced significantly. It was not. The lack of a secular trend since 1965 cannot be accounted for by regional migration.

These regional results are dismaying for at least two reasons. First, current civil rights policies are limited in their effect to the South. This is no mean achievement, for roughly half the black population of the U.S. resides in the South and the gap between black and white incomes was far greater in the South than in the non-South. Advances in economic equality in the South, therefore, make a substantial improvement in the economic conditions of blacks in the U.S. Nevertheless, the problem of racial economic inequality is a national one and little is being achieved outside the South.

A second dismaying feature of these regional results is their implications for economic equality even in the South. The South is making significant strides toward racial economic equality, but what happens when the South approaches the 75 percent income ratio outside the South? Is that the upper limit of income equality in the U.S. in the foreseeable future? Are the structural conditions of education, residence, occupation and so on in the U.S. likely to generate such an upper limit?

CONCLUSION

The achievement of racial economic equality in the U.S. is dependent on two major policy elements. First, the federal government must pursue anti-cyclical fiscal and monetary policies to ensure maximum economic growth and minimum unemployment. These cyclical conditions have more to do with immediate changes in the income ratio than anything else. Reducing unemployment to less than 5 percent and maintaining real economic growth of 3-4 percent would make a marked improvement in the relative condition of blacks.

Second, civil rights policies must be expanded and intensified if a substantial impact is to be made on racial economic inequality outside the South. Current policies seem to be effective only in the South and may have an upper limit of effectiveness at a ratio of 75 percent.

We believe the results of this research are important for policymakers, social scientists, and citizens who are concerned with the efficacy of governmental action to achieve racial economic equality. Federal policies of the 1970s will be of prime importance for the achievement of racial equality. Determining the ultimate limits and effects of these policies will be a matter for future investigation, but the results of our current research are clear. Greater effort must be expended on enacting and enforcing civil rights policies if further strides toward economic equality are to be made throughout the nation.

NOTES

1. Specifically, this ratio is the nonwhite median income divided by the white median income as recorded annually for males 14 years and over. A 100 percent ratio indicates perfect income equality. Since blacks comprise over 90 percent of the nonwhite population, the two terms are used interchangeably throughout this paper. The median income ratio is reported rather than the mean because it best reflects economic status of the populations and is the only statistic consistently reported by the federal government.
2. States which possessed laws prohibiting discrimination based on race prior to 1964 include: California, Colorado, Connecticut, Delaware, Illinois, Indiana, Kansas, Massachusetts, Michigan, Minnesota, Missouri, Nevada, New Jersey, New York, Ohio, Oregon, Pennsylvania, Rhode Island, Vermont, Washington, and Wisconsin. Source: *The Book of States*, 1970–71, Council of State Governments, Lexington, Ky.
3. For example, *Brown v. Gaston County Dyeing Machine Co.*, 457 F. 2nd 1377 (4th Cir. 1972); *Parham v. Southwestern Bell Telephone Co.*, 433 F. 2nd 421 (8th Cir. 1970); *United States v. Bethlehem Steel*, 446 F. 2nd 652 (2nd Cir. 1971).
4. The first such Executive Order (E.O. 8802) was issued by Franklin Roosevelt in 1941, and was confined mainly to the defense industry. In 1963, President Kennedy issued Executive Order 11114 which forbade racial discrimination in all federally financed construction projects. This order, however, was much more limited in scope than E.O. 11246.

NOTE ON SOURCES

Black/White Male Income Ratio: U.S., Department of Commerce, Bureau of the Census, *Current Population Reports*, Washington, D.C.: U.S. Government Printing Office, 1948–1974. Series P-60, "Money Income of Families and Persons in the U.S."

% Change in Real GNP: U.S., Department of Commerce, Bureau of Economic Analysis, *Long Term Economic Growth: 1860–1970*, Washington, D.C.: U.S. Government Printing Office, 1973. Series A2, pp. 182–3. Also U.S., Department of Commerce, Bureau of the Census, *U.S. Statistical Abstract: 1975*, "GNP in Current and Constant Dollars," No. 616, p. 381. The unit of analysis was Real Gross National Product measured in billions of 1958 dollars.

U_{t-1}: *Long Term Economic Growth, Ibid.*, Series B2, p. 212–3. Also *U.S. Statistical Abstract: 1975, Ibid.*, "Employment Statistics of the population by Sex and Race, 1950–75," No. 558, p. 343.

Black/White Male Income Ratio by Region: U.S., Department of Commerce, Bureau of the Census, *Current Population Reports*, Series P-60, "Region and Race—Persons 14 Years Old and Over by Total Money Income (1953–1974) by Sex," The Census Bureau regions are: Northeast: Maine, N.H., Vt., Mass., R.I.,

Conn., N.Y., N.J., and Pa.; North Central: Ohio, Ind., Mich., Ill., Wis., Minn.,
Iowa, Mo., Kans., Nebr., S.D., N.D.; South: Del., Md., D.C., W. Va., Va., N.C.,
S.C., Ga., Fla., Ala., Miss., Tenn., Ky., Ark., La., Texas, Okla.; West: all other.
Note: 1953 was the first year regional income data was reported by the govern-
ment.

REFERENCES

Adams, Arvil V. 1973. Evaluating the success of the EEOC compliance process.
Monthly Labor Review, 96 (May 1973): 26–29.
Allport, Gordon W. 1954. *The nature of prejudice.* Reading, Massachusetts: Ad-
dison-Wesley.
Baran, Paul A. and Paul M. Sweezy. 1966. *Monopoly capital.* New York: Monthly
Review Press.
Batchelder, Alan B. 1964. Decline in the relative income of Negro men. *Quarterly
Journal of Economics*, 78 (November 1964): 525–548.
Bullock, Charles S., III. 1975. Expanding black economic rights. In Harrell R.
Rogers, Jr., ed., *Racism and inequality: The policy alternatives.* San Francisco:
Freeman and Co., pp. 75–124.
Dye, Thomas R. 1971. *The politics of equality.* New York: Bobbs-Merrill.
Economic Outlook, U.S.A. 1976a. Vol. 3, #1 (Winter, 1976): p. 5.
Economic Outlook, U.S.A. 1976b. Vol. 3, #2 (Spring, 1976): p. 24.
Equal Employment Opportunity Commission. 1975. *9th annual report.* Washing-
ton, D.C.: U.S. Government Printing Office.
Fein, Rashi. 1966. Relative income of Negro men: Some recent data. *Quarterly
Journal of Economics*, 80 (May 1966): 80.
Franklin, Raymond S. and Solomon Resnik. 1973. *The political economy of racism.*
New York: Holt, Rinehart and Winston.
Freeman, Richard B. 1973. Changes in the labor market for black Americans.
Brookings Papers on Economic Activity, No. 1 (January 1973): 67–120.
Friedman, Milton. 1962. *Capitalism and freedom.* Chicago: University of Chicago
Press.
Glazer, Nathan. 1975. *Affirmative discrimination: Ethnic inequality and public
policy.* New York: Basic Books.
Glenn, N. D. 1963. Some changes in the relative status of American nonwhites,
1940 to 1960. *Phylon*, 24 (Summer 1963): 109–122.
Gwartney, James. 1970a. Discrimination and income differentials. *American Eco-
nomic Review*, 60 (June 1970): 398–408.
———. 1970b. Changes in the nonwhite/white income ratio, 1939–67. *The American Economic Review*, 60 (December 1970): 872–83.
Jones, Charles O. 1970. *An introduction to the study of public policy.* Belmont, California: Duxbury Press.
Masters, Stanley H. 1975. *Black-White income differentials: Empirical studies and
policy implications.* New York: Academic Press.

Moynihan, Daniel P. 1969. *Maximum feasible misunderstanding: Community action in the war on poverty.* New York: Free Press.

Myrdal, Gunnar. 1944. *An American dilemma: The negro problem and modern democracy.* New York: Harper and Row.

Perlo, Victor. 1975. *The economics of racism U.S.A.: Roots of black inequality.* New York: International Publishers.

Pindyck, Robert S. and Daniel L. Rubinfeld. 1976. *Econometric models and economic forecasts.* New York: McGraw-Hill. pp. 156–58; 177–81.

Pressman, Jeffrey L. and Aaron Wildavsky. 1973. *Implementation.* Berkeley: University of California Press.

Rasmussen, David R. 1970. A note on the relative income of nonwhite men, 1948–1964. *Quarterly Journal of Economics,* 84 (February 1970): 168–172.

Rosenthal, Albert J. 1973. Employment discrimination and the law. *Annals of the American Academy of Political and Social Sciences,* 407 (May 1973): 91–101.

Sherman, Howard. 1972. *Radical political economy.* New York: Basic Books.

Tobin, James. 1965. On improving the economic status of the negro. *Daedalus,* 94 (Fall 1965): 878–98.

U.S. Commission on Civil Rights. 1970. *Federal civil rights enforcement effort.* Washington, D.C.: U.S. Government Printing Office.

———. 1973. *Federal civil rights enforcement effort.* Washington, D.C.: U.S. Government Printing Office.

Chapter 5

HOUSING AND COMMUNITY DEVELOPMENT

Historically, the provision of adequate housing has been an activity of the private sector, although the housing market has always depended on government economic policies and the enforcement of agreements regarding property rights. Prior to the New Deal government involvement in the area of housing was to a large extent regulatory. It prohibited slums and required tenement owners to upgrade their properties. When they have evolved, such regulatory policies have most often been local in scope.

Direct federal involvement dates from the 1930s, when the National Housing Act of 1934 and the United States Housing Act of 1937 were enacted. Under the National Housing Act the Federal Housing Administration (FHA) was established. FHA insures lenders against loss should borrowers default on home-mortgage payments. Under FHA financing mortgages can cover up to 97 percent of appraisal value in new and existing housing, and for veterans mortgages can cover 100 percent of the appraised value. Under this program which is the cornerstone of federal housing policy, the largest number of loans have been issued on moderately priced houses. The emphasis on home ownership by the working- and middle-class families enhanced suburbanization, even though this was not its intended objective.

The Housing Act of 1937, and the many amendments and revisions enacted since its passage, was designed to meet the problem of inadequate housing. At the outset the act provided for loans to assist in slum clearance and the building of low rental housing. The act established a federal housing agency, the Housing Assistance Administration, to provide low rent public housing for the poor who could not afford adequate housing on the private market. The act also established the principle that local communities would decide for themselves whether or not to develop public housing programs and that they would determine where facilities would be located and who would live in them.

In 1968 the National Commission on Urban Problems made four major observations concerning housing policies since the 1930s[1]:

1. Direct government involvement in the housing sector has been increasing since the 1930s, but there has not been any direct or massive intervention to alter the supply and quality of housing. The emphasis has been on the provision of incentives to private enterprise.
2. Housing policies have had unanticipated consequences. These have adversely affected residents in particular urban areas.
3. Decisions on public housing and urban-renewal programs have not been based on systematic evaluations.
4. The government was urged to measure its housing programs against some estimates of national housing needs, rather than against past levels of performance.

In the Housing and Urban Development Act of 1968, Congress reaffirmed the earlier policy goal of "a decent home and a suitable environment for every American family," while acknowledging that the goal had not been fully realized. The 1968 Act declared that nearly every American could be provided a decent home and a suitable living environment "within the next decade by the construction and the rehabilitation of twenty-six million housing units, six million of these for low and moderate income families." This bill, and the appropriations made by Congress, placed housing on the nation's priority list. Yet, not only were the 1968 targets elusive, but the act fell short of describing the nation's actual needs.

In 1974 Congress enacted the Housing and Community Development Act as an amendment to the Housing Act of 1937. As it affects the provision of housing for the poor, this legislation differs from earlier housing acts in several ways. First, it takes the federal government out of the construction phase of publicly assisted housing because no funds were authorized by this act for building public-housing facilities. The law also provides a system of rent supplements to those eligible for participation. Finally, the act modified earlier rent subsidy programs by providing more flexibility of income eligibility and broader rental limits for federally subsidized units.

In the first article in this chapter, Anthony Downs evaluates the overall effectiveness of federal housing policies in the 1960s and the early 1970s. Since policymakers did not develop any clear, accurate, and widely accepted conceptual framework of how housing markets and urban development work, evaluations in this area must rely, in Downs' words, on "arbitrary distinctions, heroic assumptions, and controversial judgments." Accordingly, the author divides housing policies into four types—indirect influences, direct financial influences, direct housing subsidies, and community-related programs—and assesses their relative effectiveness in achieving ten presumed objectives. The evaluation is theoretical-analytical, serving more as a starting point for future research rather than providing conclusive findings. Yet, such an approach is extremely needed in policy areas lacking conceptual and theoretical foundations.

In the second article Frank Porell focuses specifically on housing programs aimed at low-income households. After discussing the complexities of identifying and measuring the goals and criteria of success, the author critically examines the various housing programs from three perspectives: process evaluation, economic analysis, and cost-benefit analysis.

NOTE

1. Report of the National Commission on Urban Problems, *Building the American City* (Washington, D.C.: Government Printing Office, 1968).

THE SUCCESSES AND FAILURES OF FEDERAL HOUSING POLICY

Anthony Downs

To assess the effectiveness of federal housing-related policies in the 1960s and early 1970s, it is necessary to make some arbitrary distinctions, heroic assumptions, and controversial judgments. The first arbitrary distinction is to divide all federal housing-related policies into the following four categories:

1) *Indirect influences:* Actions influencing *housing production* through monetary, fiscal, and credit policies aimed primarily at maintaining prosperity or fighting inflation.

2) *Direct financial influences:* Actions aimed at affecting the *total supply* of housing through credit and institutional arrangements rather than direct financial aid. An example is the creation of the Federal Home Loan Mortgage Corporation to help establish an effective secondary market in mortgages.

3) *Direct housing subsidies:* Actions aimed at increasing the supply of housing directly available to low-income households. Examples are the Section 235 and 236 programs.

4) *Community-related programs:* Actions that affect the structure of urban areas and therefore impact housing markets and the neighborhood conditions incorporated in the everyday meaning of the term "housing." Examples are the Interstate Highway Program, urban renewal, and the Model Cities Program.

The second arbitrary distinction consists of dividing the time under consideration into three periods: (1) low-priority period (1960 through 1965); (2) reassessment period (1966 through 1968); (3) high-production period (1968 through 1972, and perhaps longer).

Evaluating policies requires comparing their results with the objectives they were intended to achieve. Congress adopted in 1949 a national housing goal of "providing a decent home and a suitable living environment for every American family," and in 1968 Congress linked that goal to a production target of 26 million additional housing units from 1968 through

1978, 6 million for occupancy by low-income and moderate-income households. Since that basic goal conceals many ambiguities, I will make the heroic assumption—derived from Congressional legislation, Administration statements, and my observation of federal behavior—that federal housing-related policies were designed to achieve the following major objectives:

1. *High-level housing production*—encouraging private construction of enough new housing units to serve needs created by rising total population, rising incomes, demolition, and migration.
2. *Adequate housing finance*—providing a sufficient flow of mortgage and other funds to finance the production described above.
3. *Reduced housing costs*—reducing the cost of housing occupancy (including costs of construction, land, financing, and operation) so that more households can afford decent units.
4. *Overall economic stabilization*—causing countercyclical changes in total housing production to help stabilize the overall economy.
5. *Stabilization of housing production*—insulating the home-building industry from large-scale fluctuations associated with the general business cycle. (This objective is diametrically opposed to the preceding one.)
6. *Attraction of private capital*—designing incentives to encourage private capital to finance most housing production, including that for low-income and moderate-income households.
7. *Housing assistance to low-income and moderate-income households*—enabling such households living in substandard quality units to occupy decent units, and financially aiding such households who now pay inordinately high fractions of their incomes to occupy decent units.
8. *Increased home ownership.*
9. *Improved inner-city conditions*—helping large cities to upgrade deteriorating older neighborhoods and to prevent further decay in aging "gray areas."
10. *Creation of good new neighborhoods*—helping private developers and local government create desirable new neighborhoods in subdivisions and new communities.

Many other secondary objectives were also served by housing-related policies, but I have limited this enumeration to only the primary ones. The objectives listed above are not entirely consistent with each other. Overall economic stabilization, in particular, often conflicts with almost all the others, since it requires sharp reductions in housing production during upswings in the rest of the economy.

THE "TRICKLE-DOWN" PROCESS

To evaluate housing-related policies, it is necessary to understand the "trickle-down" or "filtering" process that dominates American urban development. All newly built U.S. urban housing (except mobile homes, which are not allowed in most parts of metropolitan areas) must meet the relatively high standards of size and quality set in local building codes and zoning regulations. The cost of meeting those standards is quite high. Consequently, less than half of all U.S. households can afford to occupy newly built housing without either receiving a direct subsidy or spending over 25 percent of their incomes on housing. Hence, only households in the upper half of the income distribution normally live in brand-new housing.

This pervasive exclusion of low-income and moderate-income households from brand-new units has profound impacts upon our housing markets—and upon American society in general. Throughout the world, new urban housing is mainly constructed on vacant land around the edges of already built-up neighborhoods. Therefore, all urban areas normally expand outwards. Most of the newest housing is always on the outer edge; most of the oldest housing is in the center; and moderately-aged housing lies in between.

Outside the U.S., households of all income levels may be found at any given distance from the center of urbanization. Both poor and rich live in older housing near the center—the poor in deteriorated units, the rich in units they have maintained or rehabilitated. Similarly, both poor and rich live in brand-new housing on the urban periphery—the poor in low-quality shacks they have built themselves, and the rich in new units constructed to high-quality standards. Middle-income groups concentrate in the rings between the center and the outer edge, occupying "used" housing that is still of good quality.

In the United States, it is illegal both to build brand-new low-quality housing units and to allow older units to deteriorate into low-quality status. But the laws against these two types of substandard housing are not enforced to the same degree. Laws against *new* low-quality units are rigorously enforced in all urban areas. Therefore, only households in the upper half of the income distribution can afford to live in much of the urban periphery where new growth is concentrated. But laws against *older* low-quality housing are only moderately enforced in most older neighborhoods. They are almost totally ignored in areas where the most deteriorated units are found. This is not an evil conspiracy between local officials and landlords. Rather, it is a necessary recognition of the inability of many very poor housholds to pay for high-quality housing. No such recognition, however, is extended to the poor in newly built areas. There, local officials zealously exclude the poor by enforcing high-quality housing standards to the letter.

This process creates a major spatial separation of households by income group in U.S. urban areas. The most affluent urban housholds reside mainly around the suburban periphery; the poorest urban households are concentrated in the oldest inventory near the center (sometimes in older suburbs, too); and middle-income groups live in between. Moreover, each neighborhood goes through a typical life cycle. When it is first built, the brand-new housing units there are occupied by relatively affluent households. Then, as these housing units age slightly, the most affluent households move on to still newer areas farther out. Other households move in who are somewhat lower in the *relative* income distribution, but still have good incomes. This "trickle-down" process continues as these housing units age. But they still provide excellent shelter as long as their occupants maintain them well.

Eventually, however, the income groups who move in are too poor to maintain these units—especially since maintenance costs have by then risen, and lending institutions are reluctant to risk funds in improving them. Then the housing deteriorates markedly and the neighborhood becomes a "slum." This life cycle normally takes from forty to sixty years. (Some older neighborhoods never experience it because they are so well located that wealthy households remain and maintain the property in good condition.)

For the predominant majority of households in U.S. metropolitan areas, this "trickle-down" process works very well. It furnishes good-quality housing in neighborhoods free from the vexing problems of extreme poverty, since nearly all very poor people (except some elderly residents) are excluded. But for the poorest urban households, especially poor minority-group members, this process is a social disaster. It compels thousands of the poorest households to concentrate together in the worst-quality housing located in older neighborhoods near the urban center. This causes a "critical mass" effect that multiplies the impact of many problems associated with poverty. Such neighborhoods become dominated by high crime rates, vandalism, unemployment, drug addiction, broken homes, gang warfare, and other conditions almost universally regarded by Americans as undesirable. Most households with high enough incomes to have a choice of living somewhere else move out. So do many employers and retailers anxious to escape such conditions. This withdrawal of those with economic and other resources further weakens the neighborhood and removes many possible checks to the negative forces described above. Only a minority of the people living in these areas of concentrated poverty engage in destructive behavior; so the real victims are the non-destructive majority of poor residents there. They are prevented from moving out by the exclusionary barriers erected in most middle-income and upper-income neighborhoods. Thus, they must bear the social costs of providing the fine-quality neighborhoods enjoyed by the upper two thirds of the income distribution.

Yet prosperous households have strong arguments against opening up their neighborhoods to unrestricted entry by low-income households. They have observed the destructive environments in concentrated poverty areas, and they do not want such conditions where they live. They have no way of screening low-income households entering their areas to keep out destructive ones while admitting the non-destructive majority; so they prefer to keep *all* poor households out. This attitude is reinforced by their experience that nearly all non-poor households stop moving into a neighborhood whenever many poor people enter. As normal housing turnover proceeds, the area inevitably becomes mainly poor, because only other poor households are willing to move in. This causes a temporary decline in property values that threatens the major investment residents have made in their homes. Thus, many powerful forces pressure middle-income and upper-income households to persist in exclusionary behavior—in spite of its unjust consequences for the nondestructive majority of low-income households "trapped" in concentrated poverty areas.

This explanation may seem far removed from evaluating federal housing-related policies, but understanding the "trickle-down" process is crucial for comprehending how those policies actually worked. In fact, the failure of federal officials to develop such an understanding caused them to be surprised by the many unexpected consequences of their actions, as will be explained later in the article.

OTHER KEY BACKGROUND FACTORS

Before examining federal housing-related policies and actions, it is necessary to describe several additional background factors. First, there was an acute housing shortage during and right after World War II. But from 1950 onwards, the number of housing units built each year exceeded the number of new households formed, gradually easing the shortage. (Table 5.1 shows housing starts from 1950 through 1972.) *An approximate balance was attained between total supply and total demand in most urban housing markets by 1960.* True, several million urban households were still in substandard or overcrowded units. But most urban households that could afford decent housing were living in such housing by 1960, except in racially segregated areas.

Second, until the late 1960s, *housing production had a natural tendency to move in a countercyclical pattern in relation to general economic activity.* Most buyers of new or existing homes borrow large fractions of the total cost and finance it over long time periods. Hence, the amount they must pay each month is strongly affected by the interest rate. When interest rates rise, therefore, many households who could formerly afford to buy new housing can no longer do so. Conversely, when rates fall, many more households can afford to buy homes. Developers of rental apartments also

TABLE 5.1
Annual Housing Starts by Type, 1950–1972[1]

Year	Conventionally Constructed Housing Starts[2]	Mobile Homes	Total Housing Starts
1950	1,951,648	63,100	2,014,748
1951	1,491,207	67,300	1,558,507
1952	1,504,520	83,000	1,587,520
1953	1,438,372	76,900	1,515,272
1954	1,550,445	76,000	1,626,445
1955	1,645,715	111,900	1,757,615
1956	1,345,739	104,800	1,450,539
1957	1,221,647	107,600	1,329,247
1958	1,375,588	100,400	1,475,988
1959	1,528,836	120,500	1,649,336
1960	1,272,137	103,700	1,375,837
1961	1,365,000	90,200	1,455,200
1962	1,492,400	118,000	1,610,400
1963	1,642,000	150,840	1,792,840
1964	1,561,000	191,320	1,752,320
1965	1,509,600	216,000	1,725,600
1966	1,195,900	217,000	1,412,900
1967	1,321,817	240,000	1,561,817
1968	1,545,500	318,000	1,863,500
1969	1,499,920	413,000	1,912,920
1970	1,466,759	401,000	1,867,759
1971	2,084,500	496,570	2,581,070
1972	2,378,500	575,900	2,954,400

[1]*Source:* U.S. Department of Housing and Urban Development, Division of Research and Statistics; and Mobile Home Manufacturers Association.
[2]Conventionally *constructed* housing starts can be financed with either VA- and FHA-insured mortgages or *conventional mortgages.*

borrow heavily and are therefore similarly affected. But short-term borrowers of money for other purposes—such as consumer loans or business investment in plants and equipment—are less sensitive to changes in interest rates. When the economy moves from a recession into general prosperity, there is rising competition for funds, and interest rates of all types go up. Because a slight rise in mortgage interest rates cuts down the number of borrowers sharply, lenders shift their funds into nonhousing channels where they can get higher rates without losing volume. Housing starts therefore decline because of inability to finance mortgage loans. When a general recession occurs, other demands for funds slack off, and more money becomes available for mortgage loans. Mortgage rates drop and terms (length of loan and amount of down-payment required) improve, so housing production rises.

Third, *the single most dynamic force in the housing markets of most large metropolitan areas in the 1960s was the rapid growth of the black and Spanish-speaking populations in central cities.* The resulting "massive" transitions of whole neighborhoods from mainly white to mainly non-white occupancy did not reduce housing segregation, but it greatly improved the amount and quality of housing available to minority-group members. Moreover, it generated large-scale movement of white households into outlying suburbs.

THE LOW-PRIORITY PERIOD: 1960–1965

In the early 1960s, housing was not regarded as a high-priority item of domestic concern by Congress or the executive branch. The general goal of providing "a decent home and a suitable living environment for every American family" had been stated in 1949, but no specific production targets had been adopted by Congress. Federal housing policy was vested in the Housing and Home Finance Agency (HHFA), which did not enjoy departmental status. Major housing-related policies and actions in this period can be summarized under five principal headings.

1) *Total housing production was still viewed by federal economic policymakers as a countercyclical force useful in stabilizing the economy as a whole.* Hence, the monetary and fiscal conditions dominating housing production were oriented toward nonhousing objectives, with their impact upon housing treated as a residual rather than a controlling or central factor.

2) *The preferential tax and mortgage insurance treatment provided to home owners continued to stimulate ownership as a preferred form of tenure during this period, although apartment construction began rising toward the middle of the decade.* Home owners who occupy their own dwellings can deduct their mortgage interest and local property taxes from their federally taxable incomes. This tax saving provides a hidden housing subsidy that accrues mainly to households in the upper half of the income distribution. Even in the early 1960s, this hidden subsidy to the relatively affluent was far larger than all direct subsidies to poorer households combined. Moreover, mortgage insurance provided by the Federal Housing Administration made home ownership possible for more and more Americans. By 1960, 61.9 percent of all occupied housing units were owner-occupied, as compared to 55.0 percent in 1950, and 43.6 percent in 1940. Home ownership held its own in the 1960s but did not expand much. This resulted from the

rise in multifamily units (mainly rental units) to around 33 percent of total starts in the mid-1960s and 40 percent in the early 1970s.

3) *Federally financed highway construction and urban renewal programs were designed in part to bolster central-city economies, but they actually stimulated rapid population growth and job expansion in the suburbs.* Urban expressways were supposed to help downtown centers maintain dominance over their surrounding areas. Urban renewal was intended to remove blight and to promote economically self-sustaining redevelopment. These programs succeeded in aiding many downtowns—as evidenced by the surge of major downtown investments in private office buildings and public facilities in the late 1960s. But such programs also produced the following unforeseen "side effects" that heavily counteracted their positive achievements:

> Thousands of small industries and retail businesses displaced by highways and urban renewal simply went out of business, and even more displaced industries and retail operations moved to newer, larger, and more efficient suburban sites.
>
> Hundreds of thousands of low-income households displaced by urban renewal and highway clearance shifted into older housing in nearby once-stable neighborhoods. Hence, blight was often just moved rather than eliminated.
>
> Radial and circumferential expressways made outlying locations more convenient than congested near-in locations; so many warehouse and distribution facilities moved away from central-city sites.
>
> Commuting between relatively distant suburban homes and downtown or other in-city jobs became much easier; so millions of households shifted from central-city housing into growing suburban subdivisions.
>
> Since the worst urban blight was in concentrated poverty areas, urban renewal efforts focused upon removing blight-created vacant sites in such areas. But most firms and households with enough money to support self-sustaining redevelopment would not locate there, because those sites were still surrounded by concentrated poverty.
>
> Highway routes and urban renewal projects were often deliberately located in poor, minority-group neighborhoods to force relocation of groups regarded as undesirable by the local power structure. This tactic created unfair hardships for those displaced, and merely shifted minority-group occupancy to other nearby neighborhoods.

Why did the private interests, federal officials, and Congressmen who designed these programs fail to anticipate such consequences? First, very few of them understood the nature of urban areas or the dynamics of the "trickle-down" process. Second, each major federally funded policy was initiated for rather narrowly conceived reasons by a specialized group with no responsibility for coping with its broader consequences. For example, highway engineers and the automobile industry promoted giant urban expressways in order to move traffic and increase road capacity, but they had little comprehension of, or concern for, the likely impacts upon the local tax base or the fabric of urban life. Third, there was no effective way to coordinate all these specialized programs at the local level, since no one local government had overall responsibility for an entire metropolitan area. These three factors resulted in a complete inability to orchestrate specialized federal programs into a unified theme—or even to achieve minimal coordination among them.

4) *Production of directly subsidized housing for low-income and moderate-income households was kept at very low levels during this period by small-scale Congressional appropriations and local resistance to such housing.* From 1960 through 1965, only 283,610 directly-subsidized housing units for low-income and moderate-income households were started. That was 3.2 percent of all conventionally constructed housing built during this low-priority period. Rising black occupancy of large high-rise public housing projects in big cities was generating increased local resistance to construction of any public housing except that occupied by the elderly. After the 221 (d) (3) program was passed, some subsidized units for moderate-income households were created. However, federal officials responsible for promoting subsidized housing tended to measure their performance against past low levels of such output, rather than against any quantified concept of "national needs."

5) *In spite of low production of subsidized units directly available to the poor, housing conditions in most urban areas improved for all income groups because total production, less demolitions, exceeded net household formation.* Hence, the "trickle-down" process had some positive effects. From 1960 to 1965, the number of U.S. households rose by 4.452 million, according to Census Bureau estimates. But total housing starts (including mobile homes) equalled 8.161 million units. Subtraction of 600,000 demolitions per year yields a net increase of 5.161 million units—or 709,000 more than the increase in households during that period. This "surplus" should be reduced somewhat to allow for needs generated by migration. Nevertheless, subsequent data have shown that housing quality was improving in most urban areas from 1960 through 1965.

THE REASSESSMENT PERIOD: 1966–1968

A number of dramatic events from 1965 to 1968 caused a nationwide reassessment of the low priority the federal government had been placing upon meeting housing needs. Most striking were the civil disorders that occurred in over 150 cities from 1965 through early 1968. In the summer of 1967, President Lyndon Johnson appointed a National Advisory Commission on Civil Disorders to investigate the causes of and possible remedies for these disturbances. By March 1968, the Commission had produced a report setting forth its major findings. It recommended massive expansion of the production of directly subsidized units for low-income and moderate-income households to 600,000 units in the next year, and 6 million units in the next five years.

A second crucial event was the severe "credit crunch" in housing mortgage markets in 1966. In 1965, just as the economy was recovering from its slight slump in 1963, rapid escalation of the Vietnam conflict required large federal outlays. Combined with ongoing prosperity, as well as spending on the space program and Great Society programs, this caused an extraordinary expansion in overall economic activity. By 1966, the Federal Reserve Board decided to sharply curtail the growth of the money supply to reduce inflationary pressures. This produced a sudden jump in interest rates, which in turn resulted in a startling reduction in available mortgage funds. Non-subsidized conventional housing starts dropped 22.3 percent from 1.446 million in 1965 to 1.124 million in 1966—the lowest level since before 1950. In Southern California, the nation's largest housing market, total starts plunged to one third of the all-time record level attained in 1963, and the local building industry was decimated. Leaders in both home building and savings and loan associations began lobbying to insulate mortgage credit more completely from cyclical changes in general credit availability. This led to the creation of non-budgetary agencies capable of borrowing funds in the nation's bond markets to support mortgages when cyclically tied sources of funds dried up. Moreover, a new form of security backed by mortgages was developed, but in a form more attractive to pension funds and other large-scale investors. Consequently, mortgage markets became considerably more insulated from the general business cycle than they had been in the past—though by no means fully insulated.

A further stimulus to the reassessment of housing priorities came from two reports by federally appointed commissions. The National Commission on Urban Problems, headed by former Senator Paul H. Douglas, was appointed by President Johnson in 1967 in response to a 1965 Congressional directive. The Commission held public hearings in many cities, commissioned dozens of fact finding studies, and presented a final report entitled *Building the American City* in late 1968. This report urged the federal government to measure its housing programs against some estimate of "national housing needs," rather than against past levels of performance. The Commission also recommended that 2.0 to 2.25 million housing starts be undertaken every year, including at least 500,000 units for low-income and moderate-income households other than the elderly. The second commission was the President's Committee on Urban Housing, a group of prestigious citizens headed by industrialist Edgar F. Kaiser. Appointed by

President Johnson in June 1967, it focused on methods of making housing available to American households at lower cost than in the past. The Committee's final report, *A Decent Home*, recommended that Congress adopt a ten-year production goal of 26 million additional housing units, including at least six million for lower-income families. Still another major event contributing to the reassessment of housing priorities was the elevation of the former Housing and Home Finance Agency to Cabinet status in 1965 as the new Department of Housing and Urban Development.

The culmination of all these events was passage of the Housing and Urban Development Act of 1968. This landmark bill set an official housing production target of 26 million additional new and rehabilitated units to be built from 1968 through 1978, including six million units available to low-income and moderate-income households. Toward this end, it created two new, generously funded housing-subsidy programs for moderate-income households that combined an interest subsidy, depreciation tax shelter, and some features of a housing allowance. These were the Section 236 program for rental housing, and the Section 235 program for ownership housing. Also included among the Act's provisions were the creation of secondary mortgage market instruments to help insulate mortgage credit from the business cycle; liberalization of credit terms on market-rate mortgage loan insurance for households in high-risk areas, or with relatively poor credit, or making very small down-payments; expanded funding for public housing, and an emphasis on creating scattered-site, low-rise units to avoid excessive poverty concentration; guaranteeing of privately issued bonds to finance new communities; and changes in the urban renewal program emphasizing shorter-range, more comprehensive actions and requiring more housing for low-income and moderate-income households on renewal sites.

This bill, plus the major appropriations for it passed by Congress, signaled a dramatic rise in the status of housing and housing-related problems on the nation's priority list. Combined with the Model Cities Act passed earlier, the Housing and Urban Development Act of 1968 created a whole arsenal of housing and community development tools that—in theory—were capable of responding effectively to many of the physical and social problems plaguing urban areas.

THE HIGH-PRODUCTION PERIOD: 1968–1973

Before the Democratic Administration responsible for the Housing and Urban Development Act of 1968 could carry it out, it was replaced by a new Republican Administration in 1969. As a result, there was an almost total turnover of top-level personnel in HUD, the Bureau of the Budget, and the White House. But even if the Democrats had stayed in power, a major turnover would probably have occurred in accordance with the "Law of Inescapable Discontinuity": *High-level federal personnel change so fast that almost no major federal program is ever initially conceived of, drafted into legislation, shepherded through Congress, and then carried out by the same officials.* Therefore, no program is ever perceived in the same way by those who put it into effect as by those who invented it.

Another important determinant of the behavior of federal officials is the "Law of Compulsive Innovation": *Newly installed administrators have a strong desire to reject what their predecessors have started, and to emphasize programs they create themselves so they can claim full credit for whatever success results.* Consequently, they tend to ignore the lessons their predecessors have learned from experience. It was difficult, however, for the incoming Republicans to start over completely, since the massive Housing and Urban Development Act of 1968 had just been passed and funded. So HUD's new managers expressed their originality by emphasizing housing production and technology as the keys to urban problems, and de-emphasizing other facets of urban development. Unfortunately, as Secretary Romney soon discovered, this partial approach to solving urban problems ignored the perplexing social difficulties that had become visible in the reassessment period.

A corollary of the "Law of Compulsive Innovation" had an even more drastic impact upon HUD's behavior: *Whenever one party replaces the other in the executive branch, the newcomers have a compulsive desire to reorganize nearly every agency.* Since all human organizations are imperfect, and large bureaucracies are especially subject to inertia and malfunction, it is always easy to justify reorganization as "required" to improve performance. HUD and FHA were subjected to several overlapping reorganizations that involved both reshuffling functions in Washington and creating a whole new decentralized layer of regional offices. The internal confusion generated by these reorganizations had a devastating impact upon HUD's capabilities.

The new team at HUD charged off in pursuit of technical improvements in housing production by launching Operation Breakthrough. This was to be a three-phased movement encouraging more mass-production of housing in factories to meet large aggregated markets, thereby achieving economies of scale that would reduce housing costs. The first phase was to design new ways to build housing industrially; the second phase was to demonstrate those new methods by constructing such housing on a number of prototype sites; and the third phase was to serve large-scale markets with those systems that appeared most successful.

Meanwhile, however, a series of other developments stimulated the most massive housing production in American history. The Nixon Administration's response to inflation in 1968 and 1969 was to induce a nationwide recession through flattened federal spending and tight monetary policy. Hence builders had difficulty obtaining adequate mortgage credit in 1970 for conventionally-financed units. But Section 235 and Section 236 financing was available, so thousands of builders shifted to the new direct-subsidy program. Non-directly subsidized housing starts fell from 1.382 million in 1968 to 1.036 million in 1970—the lowest total since before 1950. But subsidized starts shot upward from 163,360 in 1968 (the record high before the new programs were available) to over 430,000 in both 1970 and 1971. Thus in 1971 the number of directly-subsidized housing units started was *nine times* as great as the annual average in the low-priority period.

At the same time, the number of non-child-oriented households was rising rapidly in the late 1960s, and many wanted to find relatively inexpensive housing even if it did not meet the high-quality standards required of conventionally-built new units. Therefore, consumer acceptance of mobile homes escalated dramatically. From 1955 through 1961, around 100,000 mobile home units were shipped annually. But from 1962 onwards, annual shipments rose steadily, reaching over 500,000 units by 1972. In fact, since 1969, one out of every five new housing units created in the United States each year has been a mobile home.

Moreover, in 1971 there occurred the usual huge movement of financial resources into housing right after the low point in a general recession as savings flows into savings and loan associations reached all-time highs. This traditional surge of mortgage credit was augmented by the flight of investment funds from the stock market. Although the stock market recovered sharply from its 1969–70 downslide during 1971 and 1972, by 1973 it was well below its 1965 and 1966 levels. In the past, major controllers of many investment funds had always avoided real estate as too risky and specialized. But now they compared this long-term stagnation in stock values with the steady and seemingly endless rise in land values and real property prices during the same period, and consequently, pension funds, bank trust departments, and large corporations began to put billions into real estate from 1970 through 1973. Moreover, dozens of real estate investment trusts (REITs) issued stock in equity markets and used the billions so raised to invest in real estate. The result was a flood of credit into real estate markets unprecedented in both size and duration. This flood was responsible for the sudden escalation of non-subsidized conventionally-built housing starts from the post-War low of 1.035 million units in 1970 to 2.028 million in 1972—almost a doubling in two years. Millions of 95-percent loans greatly expanded the market for housing ownership, helping to support these enormous production levels without any great rise in vacancies. By 1972, rising prosperity offered another such support as the economy moved into a traditional upswing. But real estate credit did not soon decline as in past upswings.

The consequence of these various developments was a rise in total housing starts to a plateau of about 1.9 million units annually from 1968 through 1970—a total exceeding any previous annual production level except the 2.0 million units in 1950. Then, in 1971 and 1972, housing starts shot up to 2.6 million and 3.0 million units respectively.

THE DARK SIDE OF HIGH PRODUCTION

The massive levels of housing production generated a number of major consequences wholly unexpected by the federal government, and quite disruptive to its housing policies:

1) The ability of the supposedly obsolete housing industry to produce 3.0 million units in a single year—including 2.4 million "stick-built" units (i.e., not factory-built like mobile homes)—proved that industrialized housing was not necessary to reach the nation's housing goals, as Operation Breakthrough had supposed. Operation Breakthrough did persuade many states to adopt statewide building codes for industrialized housing, but it failed to produce housing units at lower cost than traditional methods or to aggregate markets that were large enough to absorb truly mass-produced factory housing.

2) HUD and the Congress had assumed the nation had a housing *shortage* when they established the 10-year goal of 26 million additional units in 1968. They failed to recognize that many of the worst-quality units to be replaced were in rural areas—but most new housing production was in urban areas. Hence, the total number of housing units available in many large metropolitan areas shot up well above the number of households there. This accelerated the entire "trickle-down" process. Millions of white households moved out of central cities to new suburban units, and black and Spanish-speaking households moved out of the worst housing into the units thus made available. *The stunning success of HUD's efforts to increase total housing production—actually produced largely by factors beyond HUD's control—thus generated the unexpected and undesirable result of rising abandonment and vacancy in the concentrated poverty "ghettos" of many large cities.*

3) The new direct-subsidy programs shifted the initiative in creating housing for low-income and moderate-income households to private builders rather than government bureaucrats. These programs also funded large numbers of such units and created strong tax-shelter incentives for private investment in them. As a result, HUD's new area offices were swamped

with applications to create and purchase new and rehabilitated subsidized units, and high-level officials pressured the area offices to speed up processing. This occurred in the midst of the personnel disruptions caused by HUD's reorganizations, and thus led to a breakdown in HUD's administrative controls in many areas. Thousands of poor households were bilked by unscrupulous speculators. A few outright corrupt practices by FHA officials were uncovered in some cities, and the resulting scandals shocked Secretary Romney and FHA leaders into denouncing their own programs.

4) HUD began experiencing the high costs of emphasizing housing production without paying much attention to neighborhood conditions. Many poor families bought housing units at full market interest rates under programs that allowed tiny down-payments or accepted poor credit risks. The majority of such purchases successfully enabled low-income households to benefit from home ownership for the first time, but a significant number resulted in defaults and HUD repossessions. These defaults were concentrated in big-city poverty areas at the bottom of the "trickle-down" process. The number of units across the nation repossessed by FHA rose from its normal level of about 50,000 at any one time to over 200,000 by 1973. HUD officials regarded this not as a costly if unavoidable result of rapid escalation of housing aid to the poor, but as a "disaster."

5) The high annual cost of directly subsidizing large numbers of new housing units over the lifetimes of their mortgages began to dawn on HUD officials (although it had always been readily calculable). This cost might escalate to $7.5 billion per year by 1978 if all six million subsidized units are built by that time. True, $5.7 billion per year was already being spent in 1971 on *indirect* subsidies through home owner deductions of mortgage interest and property taxes. But those subsidies mainly to the affluent did not appear in the federal budget, so Administration officials ignored them in calculating costs.

6) Other difficulties began appearing in the direct-subsidy programs. Where many subsidized new units were clustered together—as in many public housing projects—the "flooding" of the neighborhood with low-income and moderate-income households often led to general deterioration in the surrounding area. Some subsidized units were of poor-quality construction; many were occupied by households who were not "truly poor," such as young married graduate students with temporarily low incomes. Furthermore, the rising number of directly-subsidized units placed in middle-income suburbs began to alarm the Administration's political constituents. Finally, many middle-income households began complaining when they saw poorer households living nearby in better units than they enjoyed themselves, thanks to subsidies they were helping to pay for.

These developments led the Administration to declare a moratorium on further approvals of directly-subsidized units after January 1973—both to cut costs and to reassess alternative subsidy policies. HUD also stopped all federal community development programs (urban renewal, sewer and water facility construction, open space support, Model Cities, and public facility construction) for one year. It proposed that Congress shift future funding for them into a special revenue-sharing fund to be distributed directly to cities and states in accordance with a fixed formula. This proposal amounted to abdication of any specific responsibility for these activities by the federal government. Apparently, the Administration thought that categorical aid programs had failed to improve urban conditions, or it wanted to pass the political "hot potato" of making decisions concerning these touchy matters to someone else, or both.

EVALUATING FEDERAL
HOUSING-RELATED POLICIES: 1960–1972

Because both federal housing-related policies and their objectives are so complex, there is no simple way to evaluate those policies. As a means of assessing them, I have prepared the *evaluation matrix* which appears in Table 5.2. It presents my evaluations of the relative effectiveness of all four types of housing-related policies (shown in the first four columns of the matrix) in achieving all 10 primary objectives (shown in the rows). The matrix also contains a fifth column that shows my opinion concerning the *overall effectiveness* of *all* federal policies in achieving each objective. In each of the 50 cells of this matrix, policy effectiveness is "scored" on a five-position scale: very effective (+ +), moderately effective (+), moderately ineffective (–), very ineffective (– –), and not relevant (NR). These ratings represent my subjective judgments, based upon the points set forth throughout this paper.

I have assessed the performance of both *Indirect Influences* and *Community-Related Programs* (columns I and II) over all three time periods (that is, from 1960 through 1972). I believe these policies were applied throughout all three periods to about the same degree of intensity in relation to their maximum potential. In contrast, I have assessed the performance of both *Direct Financial Influences* and *Direct Housing Subsidies* (columns III and IV) only during the high-production period—that is, from 1968 through 1972. I believe these policies were not applied with sufficient intensity during the two earlier periods to provide a fair test of their effectiveness. A second qualification is that the entire evaluation matrix applies only to the effectiveness of these policies in metropolitan areas. Most federal housing-related policies have not been aimed at rural areas and

TABLE 5.2
Evaluation Matrix: Types of Federal Housing-Related Policies

Objectives	I Indirect Influences[1]	II Community Related Programs[1]	III Direct Financial Influences[2]	IV Direct Housing Subsidies[2]	V All Types Considered Together
1) High-Level Housing Production	+ +	NR	+ +	+	+ +
2) Adequate Housing Finance	+ +	NR	+ +	+	+ +
3) Reduced Housing Costs	− −	NR	− −	− −	− −
4) Overall Economic Stabilization	+ +	NR	−	−	+
5) Stabilization of Housing Production	−	NR	+ +	−	−
6) Attraction of Private Capital	+ +	+	+ +	+ +	+ +
7) Housing Assistance to Low- and Moderate-Income Households	− −	− −	−	+	+
8) Encouraging Home Ownership	+	−	+ +	+	+
9) Improved Inner City Conditions	− −	−		−	− −
10) Creation of Good New Neighborhoods	+ +	+	+ +	+	+ +

[1]Assessed for period 1960–1972
[2]Assessed only for period 1968–1972

small cities; hence, they have been very ineffective in those places. This summary evaluation indicates that, in my opinion, federal *urban* housing-related policies of all types considered together were:

Very Effective in generating high-level housing production, providing adequate housing finance, attracting private capital into housing, and creating good-quality new neighborhoods.

Moderately Effective in promoting overall economic stabilization, providing housing assistance for low-income and moderate-income households, and encouraging home ownership.

Moderately Ineffective in stabilizing housing production.

Very Ineffective in reducing housing costs and improving conditions in deteriorating inner-city neighborhoods.

ADDITIONAL CONCLUSIONS

Some additional conclusions can be drawn from this analysis, and from other data not included here. First, neither the executive branch nor Congress has developed any clear, accurate, widely accepted conceptual "model" of how housing markets and the dynamics of urban development really work. This lack has resulted in the adoption of federal policies that generated theoretically foreseeable—but in fact unforeseen—adverse consequences. I believe the description of the "trickle-down" process presented in this article provides a basis for such a model.

Second, the level of total housing production crucially affects nearly all aspects of federal housing-related policy. When really high-level production is attained (as from 1968 through 1972), metropolitan area housing markets "loosen" as net additions to supply exceed the additional demand generated by population increases and rising incomes. Most of the newly built units are located in suburban areas, and their availability tends to draw middle-income and upper-income households out of older and less desirable central-city and near-in suburban neighborhoods. This allows all income groups—including the poorest—to improve their housing, because it increases the housing choices available to them. But it may also result in abandonment of the worst-quality units, a spreading of concentrated poverty into adjacent neighborhoods, and falling property values in older areas. Hence it can be fiscally and socially damaging to central-city governments. Conversely, when total housing production remains moderately low, as it did in the early 1960s, metropolitan area housing markets tend to "tighten"; and when total production falls drastically—as it did in the 1940s—acute housing shortages may develop. Such conditions generate rising rents and home values (unless they are constrained by rent and price controls). These conditions aid central-city governments fiscally, but reduce the housing choices available to all income groups, especially the poorest.

Third, although high-level housing production aids low-income households through the "trickle-down" process, their housing conditions are improved to a much greater extent when large numbers of good-quality units (either new or existing) are made available to them through direct housing subsidies—as was done from 1968 through 1972. Consequently, providing adequate housing aid to such households requires a high level of direct federal housing subsidies, as well as high-level total housing production.

Fourth, housing production in the United States is much more strongly affected by indirect financial influences—especially federal monetary policies—than by federal policies aimed specifically at housing. Hence the federal government's key housing policies are still determined more by its attempts to influence the general level of prosperity than by its attempts to affect housing in particular. Moreover, improving housing conditions clearly has a lower national priority than maintaining general prosperity. The "natural" countercyclical forces in housing markets make the deliberate varying of housing production levels a relatively easy and effective way to help maintain general prosperity. Since (1) the vast majority of Americans are already well-housed, (2) the poor as a group receive much greater benefits from high-level prosperity than from federal attempts to improve their housing, and (3) the housing industry exhibits amazing flexibility of output (though with some serious internal costs), at least some subordination of housing improvement to the maintenance of general prosperity seems reasonable.

Fifth, the most serious urban housing problems involve many factors other than physical dwelling units, including income poverty that prevents millions of households from being able to pay for decent housing; high-quality local housing standards that exclude the poor from living in more prosperous areas; destructive personal behavior patterns exhibited by a small percentage of the residents in concentrated poverty areas that make their neighborhoods undesirable places in which to live; and middle-class withdrawal that takes place in and near concentrated poverty areas. Experience proves that attempts to combat the most serious urban housing problems are certain to fail unless they respond effectively to these factors, as well as to needs for physical dwelling units.

However, governments at all levels (federal, state, and local) almost never adopt policies that adequately respond to all the relevant factors. Instead, they tend to make partial, selective policy responses focused mainly upon physical production or construction, rather than social factors, because the former are both more visible and much easier to control than the latter. Governments are not likely to take actions that would upset the basic institutional structures supporting the entire "trickle-down" process, or the established behavior patterns involved in that process. The "trickle-down" process depends institutionally upon fragmented local government jurisdictions, plus spatial separation of lower-income households (especially those containing minority-group members) from middle- and upper-income households. Hence federal policies rarely challenge these established arrangements—at least not intentionally. Another class of policies that governments usually avoid are those requiring considerable time between inputs (which cost money) and outputs (which generate political support); the timing of recurrent elections gives most political leaders short-run perspectives. These biases make federal policies far less effective in dealing with the needs of low-income households in areas of concentrated poverty than in dealing with the needs of middle-income and upper-income households on the urban periphery.

Finally, despite the intractability of urban "housing problems," a major change in federal housing-related policies in the mid-1960s greatly increased their effectiveness in dealing with those problems. Instead of continuing to measure the performance of federal housing-related policies solely in relation to what they had achieved in the past, the federal government reassessed its priorities and began measuring that performance against a quantified conception of "national needs." Moreover, that conception was based upon the almost utopian goal of completely eradicating substandard housing in the United States in a single decade. This radical shift of perspective was accompanied by a sharp escalation in the resources devoted to housing production, and outputs of both total housing units and directly-subsidized units shot up so high that many unexpected adverse consequences began to appear. This led to the current pause in direct federal subsidies (and probably a slowdown in total production), which may be accompanied by another reassessment and a new perspective.

LOOKING TOWARD THE FUTURE

As was noted earlier, housing problems are closely interrelated with poverty, business cycles, the nation's financial structure, inner-city decay and crime, and many other social issues. Therefore, it is almost impossible to answer the question of what future federal housing-related policies should be without going into the nation's entire range of social and economic policies. The best I can do here is discuss what I believe federal policy ought to be toward certain key housing variables.

Total Housing Production

To meet the needs of future population growth plus replacement of deteriorated dwellings, annual total production of new units over the next decade ought to average much more than in the 1960s—say, about 2.6 million units including mobile homes. (It is inescapable and probably desirable, however, that housing production fluctuate countercyclically to at least some degree; thus this high average level would not be attained in every year.) Because most new units will be built in the suburbs, such high-level production could run into two serious problems. First, it will stimulate continued withdrawal of middle-class households from central cities. This will cause spreading abandonment and neighborhood decay unless we devise new methods of managing older neighborhoods and fund significant urban renewal efforts there. Second, rapid extension of suburban development is already generating tremendous resistance in the form of a burgeoning "antigrowth movement" all across the nation. Activists in this movement range from ecologists rightly worried about environmental damage to selfish suburbanites trying to evade their share of metropolitan costs and to exclude the poor. Because of their combined efforts, future urban growth will be accompanied by stricter public controls and regulations aimed at upgrading the quality of urban development. This is clearly desirable, but it will probably raise development costs and may make sustaining high-level production difficult.

Community Development and Land-Use Planning

Instead of wastefully "throwing federal money" at tough domestic problems like these, the Nixon Administration proposes to throw federal money at state and local governments and let them worry about such problems. This "hot potato" policy involves minimum federal guidelines and therefore only a small chance of achieving any national objectives across the country. It will, however, probably result in special statewide or regional regulation of proposed land development with large-area impacts—big shopping centers, airports, power plants, expressways, and environmentally fragile sites like beaches or wetlands. It would be desirable for the federal government at least to sponsor the formation of some model standards for setting ground rules within which private developers must operate and passing judgment on their proposed projects. But to achieve any national goals like forming well-planned, economically integrated "new cities," it will also be necessary either to maintain federal categorical subsidy programs, or to sneak tougher federal guidelines back into revenue sharing.

Providing Housing for Low-Income and Moderate-Income Households

The Nixon Administration has proposed permanently cutting back the annual level of newly-constructed subsidized units for low-income and moderate-income households. Instead, it would eventually assist such households through a nationwide housing allowance. Undoubtedly, we need to supplement the incomes of the poor through improved income maintenance and job creation programs even more than we need to improve their housing. Since a housing allowance is mainly a form of general income maintenance, it is sensible to adopt one as long as Congress will not adequately fund direct income maintenance. Moreover, providing aid to such households on the demand side (by *either* direct income maintenance or a housing allowance) would stimulate their greater use of the existing inventory of older housing, which is more efficient than building new units for them. Yet we also need to construct significant numbers of new units for such households. This would (a) expand the supply available to them and thereby avoid the inflationary effects of just increasing demand (as happened with Medicare); (b) allow some economic integration in new-growth areas where 50 million more Americans will reside in the next 25 years, but where there is no existing inventory; and (c) create certain types of units not provided by private builders (such as large ones for big families). Thus, *both* demand-side and supply-side subsidies—funded at significant levels—are required to meet the housing needs of low-income and moderate-income households.

Combatting Inner-City Decay

The greatest *urban* housing deficiencies are in the decaying environments of inner-city "crisis ghettos" and nearby areas. Paradoxically, I believe the intractable social problems of these areas cannot be resolved without creating many subsidized housing opportunities for poorer households in suburban and other non-poverty neighborhoods. In the long run, reducing the poverty concentrations produced by the "trickle-down" process is essential to either upgrading existing inner-city populations or redeveloping their neighborhoods with "balanced mixtures" of households from all income groups. And such reduced concentration of the poor can occur only through their voluntary dispersal into housing scattered outside inner-city areas. Middle-class resistance to such a dispersal strategy is so powerful, however, that few politicians dare to confront it. In the absence of any significant start toward dispersal (which had begun on a small scale through the Section 235 and 236 programs stopped by the moratorium), the best federal policies toward such areas would include: improved income maintenance and job opportunities, rather than direct physical investment in housing; reform of the criminal justice system to produce at least a minimal degree of security in these areas; experimental testing of new methods of centrally managing entire inner-city neighborhoods to combat abandonment and decay; and requiring that a certain fraction of special revenue sharing funds be used to cope with inner-city problems.

Financing Future Housing

Two big factors in financing the recent high level of housing production have been the big shift of institutional investors into real estate from the stagnant stock market, and the requirement that savings and loan associations must invest most of their assets in mortgages. If the recent dual devaluation of the dollar stimulates a boom in U.S. manufacturing and agriculture, and thereby creates a rising stock market, institutional funds may not flow into housing so strongly. Also, if some financial reformers have their way, savings and loan associations will be freed from ties to mortgages in return for giving up rate ceilings on the interest they and banks can pay to depositors. These developments could prevent a return of the easy mortgage money conditions that stimulated record housing production from 1971 up to the tight-money period in late 1973. In that case, either future consumers would have to pay higher fractions of their incomes for housing, or production totals would remain at 1960s levels, causing possible market shortage conditions in many areas. Ironically, the best way to insure good financing for housing is to keep the U.S. economy in a near-recession condition—or at least to keep the stock market from rising. What federal policy should be in this thorny matter is hard to discern, since every alternative produces serious negative results. But in any case, considering these potential financing difficulties, the rising costs to builders of wages, material and land, and the increasing environmentalist resistance to suburban growth, the chances are great that in the future housing will absorb a higher percentage of the average consumer's income than it does today.

Clearly, diagnosing the past is easier than prescribing for the future with confidence. Yet housing is not a pressing concern for most Americans because they are better housed than ever before. Hence it is not likely that future federal policies will place a very high priority on removing the ever-diminishing—but still large—complex of social conditions erroneously known as America's "housing problem."

THE EVALUATION OF FEDERAL LOW-INCOME HOUSING POLICY AND PROGRAMS

Frank W. Porell

In terms of both expenditures and multiplicity of programs, federal involvement affecting the housing consumption of low-income households is not a small endeavor.[1] In light of this commitment and the finite limits of societal resources, the need for rational evaluation of programs and policies should be obvious. The purpose of this paper is to present a critical overview of efforts of evaluating low-income housing programs and policies. An exhaustive survey is beyond the scope of this paper; rather, certain representative works will be critically assessed from methodological and substantive bases.

A casual inspection of the housing literature immediately suggests the relative sparsity of efforts directed at evaluating low-income housing programs and policies. Also until recently, few works have incorporated much rigor in these evaluation efforts. The paucity of rigorous efforts may be attributable to a variety of factors such as diffused and ambiguous goals, output-measurement problems, or the difficulty of identifying causal linkages between program inputs and outputs. In order to assess the success or failure of housing program/policy evaluation, it is essential that problems attributable to limitations of evaluation methodologies or tools be distinguished from more general problems stemming from the limits of our substantive understanding of housing markets. This paper will attempt to clarify what critical problems/issues must be addressed to advance the state of evaluation of low-income housing programs.

The first section will address questions concerning the impact of low-income housing programs from a general viewpoint. The second section will shift toward program-level assessments from process, economic, and benefit-cost evaluation perspectives. The frontiers of low-income housing policy evaluation is discussed in the third section via an overview of the ongoing HUD-sponsored, housing-allowance experiments. The last section contains a brief synthesis and overall assessment of progress and remaining issues/problems in evaluating low income housing programs.

THE AGGREGATE IMPACT OF LOW-INCOME HOUSING POLICY: A MACRO-PERSPECTIVE

Since the primary objectives of low-income housing policy are generally related to providing adequate quality housing to low-income groups, the aggregate impact of government policy could conceivably be gauged by the incremental decline in occupancy of inadequate housing attributable to housing programs. Although the concept is straightforward in principle, its empirical application to housing policy is not so clear. Nearly all works addressing the historical and/or contemporary development of United States housing policy devote some discussion to longitudinal trends in the quality of the physical stock and to housing production trends. The usual data presented (Tables 5.3 and 5.4) might suggest significant improvement in the lowest quality physical stock concurrent with substantial increases in subsidized housing production in recent years. Although few persons would overtly argue that causal linkages exist between these trends, the casual reader may easily be left with such an impression and others concern-

TABLE 5.3
Housing Standards Measures, 1940–1970

Standard	1940	1950	1960	1970
Percent of units lacking some or all plumbing facilities	45.2	35.4	16.8	6.5
Percent of units dilapidated or needing major repairs	17.8	9.8	6.9	4.6*
Percent of units substandard (dilapidated or lacking plumbing facilities)	49.2	36.9	18.2	9.0
Percent of units with 1.51 or more persons per room	9.0	6.2	3.6	2.0
Percent of renter households paying greater than 25% of income on housing	NA	NA	35.0	39.0

NA = not available
*Since the 1970 Census did not include estimates of dilapidated units, this figure was estimated from a sample of fifteen cities by the Bureau of the Census.
Sources: U.S. Department of Commerce, Bureau of the Census, (i) *Census of Housing,* (ii) *Current Population Survey.*

TABLE 5.4
Annual Housing Starts by Type, 1960–1972

Year	Conventionally Constructed Starts	Subsidized Starts	HUD Subsidized Starts	Subsidized Starts as Percent of Total Starts
1960	1,272,137	32,400	28,800	2.3
1961	1,365,000	36,162	30,341	3.8
1962	1,492,400	38,896	27,242	2.7
1963	1,642,000	47,625	33,897	3.0
1964	1,561,000	55,094	43,515	3.6
1965	1,509,600	63,686	48,176	4.3
1966	1,195,900	70,941	48,484	6.1
1967	1,321,817	91,370	64,869	7.1
1968	1,545,500	165,218	137,355	11.0
1969	1,499,920	199,933	167,813	13.6
1970	1,466,759	429,797	372,013	30.0
1971	2,084,500	430,052	355,414	21.0
1972	2,378,500	340,257	247,819	14.4

Source: U.S. Department of Housing and Urban Development, Division of Research and Statistics.

ing the impacts of low-income housing policies and programs. The purpose of this section is to clarify how much we really know about housing program/policy impacts by identifying the key issues related to those elements.

The definition and measurement of housing quality is an essential factor to be reckoned with in assessing the impact of housing policy, since the national housing goal presumably has been the provision of a "decent home and suitable living environment" for all. Not only does the goal itself reek with ambiguities which impede quantitative measurement of progress, but, coincidentally, certain unique features of housing exacerbate the difficulty of obtaining reliable and unambiguous measures of quality. When housing is properly viewed as a multidimensional bundle of dwelling, neighborhood environment, and public service attributes, the inseparability of locational environment, public service, and structural attributes causes immediate difficulties in the cardinal measurement of quality of intangible attributes (whose value is dictated by household demand preferences), and the weighting and aggregation over individual attributes to get an overall quality measure. Even more tangible structural quality measures, e.g., size and material composition, succumb to aggregation and attribute weighting issues. Evidence of the ambiguity of structural quality measures is found in the proliferation of varied building and housing codes nationally (National Commission on Urban Problems, 1968) and the continual change and eventual abandonment of structural quality measures by the U.S. Bureau of the Census (Baer, 1972).

The ambiguities present in attempts of quantifying housing quality deem that almost any measure of progress toward national housing goals be quite tenuous. In practice housing analysts have either resorted to crude but available housing standards data compiled by the U.S. Bureau of the Census (Table 5.3),[2] or they have focused sole attention on the means of reaching goals as reflected in production trends (Table 5.4) or in similar input measures (Weicher, 1977). The latter means approach ignores relationships between means and ends by an implicit acceptance of the efficacy of the filtering or "trickle-down" process of housing markets as a means of providing adequate housing to low-income groups via residential turnover. Not only do the vagaries of the "trickle-down" concept lead one to question the means approach to assessment of progress,[3] but also comparison of program alternatives for improving the housing consumption of lower income households is problematic, if not impossible, unless housing services outputs are explicitly considered. In a discussion of Planning-Programming-Budgeting Systems (PPBS), Schultze (1969) mildly ridicules the hypothetical situation of a highway program with the objective of "building highways" and program output measured as "miles of concrete laid." Yet, in many ways this is precisely the manner in which national housing goals and outputs have been viewed under the 26-million-unit production goal of the Housing Act of 1968.

The question of the aggregate impact of national housing policy can only be truly assessed by comparing what *would* have happened in the *absence* of governmental activity to what has actually occurred. Casual inspection of trends in Tables 5.3 and 5.4 alone tells us very little about impact of policy. Since housing demand should be functionally related to income, and since incomes in general rose faster than housing prices over previous decades, one might expect that housing conditions would have improved without government intervention simply due to general economic growth. Likewise, it would not be unreasonable to expect that part of the response of the supply sector to demand shifts would be increased housing production. Although one must resort to statistical methods indirectly to infer governmental impact since "what would have happened" is obviously unobservable, it may be useful to outline some theoretical expectations concerning impacts of production- and demand-oriented programs before mentioning the few empirical efforts aimed at addressing policy impacts.

In general theoretical expectations about the relative effectiveness of production-oriented versus demand-oriented strategies for increasing the housing consumption of low-income households rests upon the long-run elasticity of the supply of housing attainable by low-income groups. In an informal sense the elasticity of supply reflects how responsive the housing supply sector is to changes in price. The supply of housing services may expand by either adding units to the standing stock or by upgrading, downgrading, or conversion of the standing stock on the part of sellers of housing. Since most new construction is high priced, the supply elasticity in low-rent sectors would largely reflect the degree to which sellers of housing respond to increases and decreases in demand by upgrading or downgrading their housing.[4] An inelastic or elastic supply of housing would suggest a less than, greater than, or equal proportionate response on the part of the supply sector to changes in prices. Figure 5.1 graphically illustrates

Figure 5.1. Demand and production strategies: effects on aggregate housing consumption. Source: This figure has been adapted from Solomon (1974).

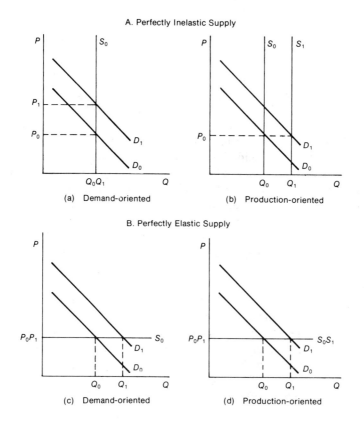

the extremes of perfectly inelastic and elastic supply conditions upon pro-
duction- and demand-oriented strategies. Graphs A(a) and A(b) of Figure
5.1 correspond to situations of perfectly inelastic supply. In Graph A(a) let
us consider a demand-oriented strategy, such as a rent-voucher program,
whose aim is to increase the effective purchasing power of households to
expand housing consumption, but which does not directly affect the supply
side of the market. The effect of such a program would be to increase housing demand and thus shift the demand curve upward to the right. Since no
supply expansion of housing services would occur via the activities of sellers of housing, households with greater purchasing power would simply
bid up prices of the existing stock. The target efficiency, or ratio of benefits
received by intended households to total benefits, of such a program would
be virtually nil or negative under these conditions. In Graph A(b) consider
a production-oriented strategy such as public housing which not only increases the effective demand of households via subsidy but also directly increases the supply of housing services by adding to the existing stock. Under perfectly inelastic supply conditions, the logic of construction-oriented
public housing programs is clear. However, let us consider Graphs B(c)
and B(d), where supply is assumed to be perfectly elastic. The general
housing consumption levels of the production-oriented strategy and subsidy would be virtually the same as that of the demand-oriented strategy under these conditions. The latter subsidy strategy would not involve construction subsidies of any sort, but the supply of housing services would be
expanded via the activities of sellers of housing. Further, a production-oriented strategy without subsidy, i.e., no shift in demand curve, would have
virtually no impact on housing consumption. Public housing would, in essence, simply replace units that would have otherwise been built or rehabilitated. Although one would expect the supply elasticity of low-rent
housing to be less than perfect due to such things as claimed high costs of
conversion and institutional barriers, litle consensus exists on how elastic
the supply sector actually is. Muth's findings (1960) indicate a quite elastic
long-run supply schedule as evidenced by a 90 percent adjustment of the
housing stock to increased housing demand within six years. On the other
hand de Leeuw and Ekanem (1971) suggest that the long-run supply elasticity for rental housing falls in the range of 0.3 to 0.7, and Ozanne and
Struyk (1978) suggest a lower bound of 0.3 from the standing stock. The
issue is important and has considerable implications toward a variety of
topics in housing research.[5] While it is beyond the scope of this paper to directly address the supply-elasticity issue, the simple examples presented in
Figure 5.1 serve to illustrate the difficulty of interpreting either aggregate
inputs (production levels) or aggregate outputs (housing conditions) without a careful understanding of the underlying mechanisms of the housing

market. Under different long-term supply-elasticity conditions, the "with and without" approach to impact measurement can lead to different conclusions.

On an empirical level there has been a paucity of works addressing the aggregate impact of low-income housing policy upon housing markets. Swan (1976), in essence, asked if the subsidized starts in Table 5.4 added to the total volume of housing starts or if starts in the nonsubsidized private sector have merely been replaced by subsidized production. His empirical results suggested that any incremental effects of production subsidies on actual housing starts have been minor. Increased competition for financing, due to the increased demand for new subsidized units, caused mortgage-interest rates to rise, which, in turn, reduced the demand for nonsubsidized units. Davis, Eastman, and Hua (1974) sought to identify the empirical determinants of the shrinkage of low-quality dwellings (as measured by the first two standards in Table 5.3)[6] in United States central cities over the period 1960–1970. Their empirical results suggested that low-cost, new construction had relatively little impact on the reduction in low-quality units because other demand factors, such as the rate of change of poor households, tend to swamp the effects of supply factors.

Although the results of these studies do not represent sufficient evidence to indicate housing program failures, they serve to illustrate the hidden complexities in aggregate trends, e.g., in Tables 5.3 and 5.4, and the difficulties in ascertaining anything meaningful about the effectiveness of housing programs and policies from such a broad perspective. In fact it would be safe to partially support the closing statement of Weicher (1977) regarding progress toward the national goal of a decent home for all families by 1980. Although it is not clear whether we will know if that goal is ever to be met—due to its ambiguity—given the rate of progress in the social sciences, a well-developed body of analysis of housing is unlikely to emerge for some time. Thus Weicher (1977) may be correct in his assertion that even if the goal is met, we are most likely to be ignorant of how we got there.

LOW-INCOME HOUSING POLICY: PROGRAM-LEVEL ASSESSMENTS

In the previous section the complexities of identifying and measuring the aggregate impact of federal housing policy were noted. In light of the ambiguities present in aggregate perspectives, attention is often focused in a more piecemeal fashion at particular programs. The purpose of this section is to provide a brief overview of several of the general approaches taken to evaluate the effectiveness of housing programs aimed at improving the housing consumption of low-income households. In general housing program evaluation has proceeded in three major directions: process-oriented evaluation, economic analysis of programs, and benefit-cost analysis. The state of the art of these approaches also will be critically reviewed.

An Overview of Housing Programs: General Impressions of Successes and Failures

For the sake of simplicity, the bulk of major governmental programs aimed at low-income households may be categorized as shown in Figure 5.2. The general objective of all programs has been to provide adequate housing to low-income households at rents or prices below market levels. The major differences among the programs is whether units are governmentally or privately produced, and whether target groups are homeowners or renters.[7] For example the major difference between the public-housing program and the rent-supplement program is that units in the latter program are privately produced and financed (although FHA insured), whereas units in the former program are developed, owned, and administered by local housing authorities. The Section 235 rental program differs from the rent-supplement program in that the latter program primarily provides an interest subsidy, i.e., the difference between the market interest rate and 1 percent, to mortgagers and developers. Although all the programs in Figure 5.2 involve subsidies to households of some sort by placing maximum rent-to-income ratios, all are production oriented, that is, they "increase" the supply of adequate low-income housing.

Figure 5.2. Categorization of major housing-subsidy programs.

			Target Subsidy Group	
			Renter	Owner
Producer	Government		Public Housing	
	Private	Subsidized	Section 236 Turnkey Public Housing	Section 235
		Non-subsidized	Section 221(d) (3) Rent Supplement Section 23 Leasing	

While general impressions about the impacts and the efficacy of governmental low-income housing programs vary, one can safely conclude that more negative than positive attributes of these programs have been emphasized in the literature. Kristoff (1972) noted that complaints about the detrimental aspects of these programs have covered a spectrum of issues. Critics often state that the programs have led to the building of the wrong type of housing in the wrong places, and that the programs have benefited the wrong people at great expense to the government. Others argue that government-subsidized housing lacks proper amenities, is demeaning to occupants, and has been built in unmarketable, deteriorated central-city areas, thereby promoting racial and social segregation. Many critics feel that the programs have not benefited the truly poor, whose incomes are insufficient to pay the necessary rents or mortgages, which, in turn, lead to mortgage defaults, foreclosures, and rent delinquencies. Finally, others maintain that the programs have enriched builders, developers, and real-estate dealers because of overpriced and shoddy construction. In essence, the major complainants suggest that the government's low-income housing programs have not fared well on counts of vertical and horizontal efficiency. Vertical efficiency—sometimes called target efficiency—measures the proportion of benefits that reach intended beneficiaries. Similarly, contentions that few of the poor have actually benefited suggest little horizontal efficiency, or that a low proportion of the target population is actually served. Let us examine the type of evaluation efforts that have been the sources of these general impressions.

Process Evaluations

The earliest and most prevalent evaluations of housing programs of necessity focused upon public housing; these include the works of Fisher (1959), Stone (1973), Friedman (1967), and Freedman (1969). A representative work focusing on privately produced, but government subsidized, housing programs is the work of Downs (1973). These efforts may be best classified as process evaluations. Broad in scope, these works typically address numerous aspects of the programs, ranging from the political processes involved in the program development to the implementation processes and operations of the program. In general the evaluations proceed by attempting to clarify the goals of the various programs and to identify how political, legal, and administrative factors facilitated or impeded progress toward the goals. Clarification and statement of the objectives or goals of the programs is the initial problem faced in these efforts. While the vagaries of national housing goals already noted may be sufficient to illustrate this, a few additional comments serve as further illustration. Downs (1973) listed seven primary and six secondary objectives of federal housing subsidy programs derived from statutes set forth by the Committee on Banking and Currency, U.S. House of Representatives (1971). These goals are shown in Table 5.5. Aside from the fact that these goals were presumably restated about thirty-four years after the inception of public housing in the United States, experts have often noted that the ambiguity, multidimensionality, and possible incompatibility of the "refined" goals on Table 5.6 make effective analysis, criticism, and evaluation of current housing programs difficult, if not impossible.[8] A more dramatic example of conflicting goals was cited by Meehan (1977) regarding the Pruit–Igoe housing development in St. Louis.[9] If one takes the objective of stimulating local economies via increased activity in the housing industry literally, Meehan (1977) noted that the Pruit–Igoe development should then be counted among the great successes of federal housing policy, rather than among the more prominent failures. Because of their great development cost, short duration, and costly liquidation, Meehan (1977) sarcastically argued that they contributed a greater stimulus to the local economy in the short run than any other development in the city's history. Although few persons would seriously argue that Pruit–Igoe was a dramatic success on this basis, the development serves to present some critical problems in

TABLE 5.5
Primary and Secondary Goals of U.S. Housing Policy

Primary Goals
- To provide housing assistance to low-income households now living in substandard units to occupy decent units, and aid households now paying inordinately high fractions of their incomes to live in decent units.
- To provide housing assistance to moderate-income households.
- To provide housing assistance to specific groups such as the elderly.
- To encourage home ownership among households regardless of income.
- To stimulate the economy by increased activity in housing industry.
- To increase the total available supply of decent quality units.
- To improve the quality of deteriorated neighborhoods.

Secondary Goals
- To provide housing assistance to colleges.
- To stabilize the annual output of the housing industry at a high level.
- To encourage housing innovations that improve design, reduce cost, etc.
- To create employment, entrepreneurship, and training opportunities among residents of low-income areas.
- To encourage maximum feasible participation of private enterprise in meeting housing needs.
- To achieve greater spatial dispersion of low- and moderate-income housing outside of concentrated poverty areas.

Source: Committee on Banking and Currency, U.S. House of Representatives (1971).

evaluating housing programs from a process perspective. Although multi-dimensionality of goals is not unique to housing, its effects greatly exacerbate the difficulties of attaining objective evaluation of housing programs.

Two related issues arise because of the multidimensionality of goals. One issue is the difficulty of obtaining objective measures of success toward meeting any particular goal. Although most studies of this sort do not explicitly rank programs, the few efforts to do so, such as that of Downs (1973), have involved subjective rankings. First, evaluating how much better one program is in meeting a goal than another is generally impossible. This, however, should not be construed as a reason to rely on senseless quantitative measurement. Given the development and production emphases of programs, progress has tended to be measured in terms of inputs such as dollars spent, units produced, or units demolished, rather than in the output provision of housing services. Second, the multiple nature of the goals introduces questions of separability among goals and programs and the weighting of various goals. Not only is any particular program likely to affect multiple goals, but the goals themselves may exhibit varying degrees of separability. Improving the quality of deteriorated neighborhoods should increase the supply of decent quality units, yet whether increasing the supply of decent quality units simultaneously improves the quality of deteriorated neighborhoods is less obvious. The weighting of goals is a crucial element, since there is generally no common denominator, such as dollars, from which to compare successes toward meeting various goals. How do we compare the merits of a program that provides some minimal housing assistance to a vast number of households against a program that provides substantial assistance via the production approach to a lesser number of households. In either case households should benefit. Yet the worth or value of the benefits distribution cannot readily be compared.[10] The problem of multiple goals and their weighting can generally be addressed only in an ad hoc manner. Either the analyst assigns possible weighting schemes (Downs, 1973; Solomon, 1974) and further assesses the sensitivity of results to various schemes, or, and this is more likely, the analyst passes the buck to a decisionmaker. Given this unenviable task, the decisionmaker is likely to be given a table similar to Table 5.6, which is adapted from Downs (1973). Given the limits of human comprehension, even understanding the totality of the table, let alone ascribing meaningful weights in order to draw meaningful conclusions, is an admirable feat.

Lest this critique be construed as overly harsh, these comments should clearly be placed in their proper perspective. To overlook the significant contributions of process-type evaluations of governmental housing programs would be myopic. These evaluations have imparted an invaluable

TABLE 5.6
Effectiveness of Housing Subsidy Programs
in Meeting 14 National Goals

Objectives	Section 236 New Construction	Public Housing	Section 221d(3) New Construction	Section 23 Leasing
1. Assisting low-income households by improving units	ME	VE	VE	VE
2. Assisting low-income households by raising incomes	VI	VI	VE	VE
3. Assisting moderate-income households by improving units	VE	VI	VI	VI
4. Assisting moderate-income households by raising incomes	VI	VI	VI	VI
5. Assisting special groups in need	VE	VE	VE	VE
6. Encouraging home ownership	VI	VI	VI	VI
7. Stimulating the economy	VE	ME	VI	VI
8. Increasing total supply of decent units	VE	VE	ME	ME
9. Improving deteriorated neighborhoods	VE	VE	VE	VE
10. Stabilizing housing industry output	ME	VI	VI	VI
11. Encouraging innovations	VI	VI	VI	VI
12. Creating economic opportunity in poverty areas	ME	VE	VI	VI
13. Encouraging private resource participation	VE	VI	ME	ME
14. Achieving spatial dispersion	VE	VI	VI	VE

Code: VE = very effective; ME = moderately effective; VI = very ineffective
Source: This table was adapted from Downs (1973), pp. 38–39. The purpose of illustration is solely to exhibit the difficulty of interpretation rather than to comment on the quality of the work.

understanding of the general nature and operations of programs. Nevertheless, the limits of these policy-evaluation tools should be recognized if we are to begin to answer the difficult questions relating to what federal housing policy should be.

Economic Analyses of Programs

The economic analysis of government low-income housing programs has taken two primary directions: Efforts have been addressed toward analyzing the economic incentives of housing programs and their implications for program costs, and economists have invoked fundamental microeconomic principles to assess the efficiency of alternative housing programs in maximizing societal benefits.

The efforts of Welfeld (1973) and Muth (1975) address the economic incentives of programs. Typically, these works apply informal economic reasoning to the structural elements of programs, either inductively or deductively explain the implications, and derive rough estimates of the financial implications. For example Muth (1975) considers the economic implications of federal subsidization of capital costs on the costs of public-housing programs. In the production of public housing, the various inputs into the production process, such as land, structural elements, operation, and maintenance, are, as with most other goods and services, to some degree substitutable.[11] In other words inputs may be traded off to produce similar output levels. The relative prices of the inputs and the technologies of the process jointly determine the efficient combination of inputs used. In light of the current energy situation, the potential trade-offs between capital expenditures and annual maintenance expenditures can be illustrated by considering the trade-off between the initial home insulation costs and the annual heating costs. More or better insulation materials at the time of construction is more costly initially, but it should reduce the annual expenditure for heating. Relative prices come into play when one weighs rising fuel costs against the cost of insulation materials. The greater economic incentive is to insulate a home more intensively, or alternately, to invest in a greater fixed capital cost in order to reduce future heating expenses.

As long as producers face the correct market prices for inputs, the economic incentives should lead to efficient input combinations. Muth (1975) argued that as a result of federal capital subsidies, local housing authorities faced an "effective price" of capital significantly below that faced by private developers and, thus, they inefficiently overutilized capital in public housing. Although local housing authorities could, in a sense, purchase a dollar's worth of annual capital expenditure for five cents, the annual cost to society was still one dollar. Given this financial incentive to substitute capital for current maintenance expenditures, Muth maintained that a chronic complaint that public housing was poorly maintained should surprise no one. To do otherwise would not be rational under the incentives imposed. He further estimated that if the rental payments of public housing tenants were directly subsidized without any distortion of relative capital and maintenance input prices, six housing units could have been provided for the true resource cost paid for five under the program.[12]

In many respects the typical economic analysis of housing programs is conceptually similar to the process-type evaluations described earlier. In fact one could plausibly argue that there is little difference other than disciplinary approach. While the latter economic analysis seeks to identify inefficiencies in resource allocation due to program structure, the former process studies impart information about administrative, organizational structure and broader social impacts. Both approaches are somewhat piecemeal in the sense that particular attributes of the programs are generally appraised individually. Any overall appraisal falls subject to the multiplicity and inseparability of program effects that were mentioned earlier. Thus, assessment of the overall relative merits of different programs is still left somewhat murky.

The second type of economic analysis of housing programs addresses the relative efficiency of housing program types in improving the general welfare of program recipients via conventional welfare economics. A general conclusion drawn from these analyses is that a rent-voucher program, where the effective price of housing is reduced and the household chooses the desired level of housing consumption at a reduced price, is more efficient than a public-housing program where households face an all-or-nothing housing choice at reduced prices. And an unrestricted income subsidy, where the effective price of housing is left unchanged and the household freely allocates the subsidy, is even more efficient in improving the welfare of recipients than a rent-voucher program. A typical demonstration of this is found in DeSalvo (1971), Bish (1969), Prescott (1974), Aaron and von Furstenberg (1971), Smolensky (1968), among others, and the following discussion draws freely from these works.[13]

To aid the noneconomist in understanding the economic arguments presented here, it is useful to review briefly some basic concepts. In general a competitive housing market is assumed, so that supply is responsive to demand and households are not restricted by artificial barriers restricting housing consumption.[14] Our attention will be focused on the housing consumption decision of the individual household. It is assumed that households are rational in the sense that they attempt to maximize their overall utility, or satisfaction, derived from consumption of housing and all other goods and services, subject to an income or budget constraint. For simplicity all goods and services are divided into two types: housing services and all other goods and services. Quantities of these services will be denoted as H and X, respectively. Three basic concepts are necessary to understand the following analysis: utility indifference curves, budget constraints, and conditions for budget-constrained, utility maximization.

Figure 5.3 illustrates the utility indifference curves for two levels of utility or satisfaction. For a given level of satisfaction or utility, an indifference curve such as U_0 would represent all combinations of H and X for which, on the basis of preference patterns, the household would be indifferent. Thus in Figure 5.3 a household would be equally satisfied in consuming h_0 units of housing service and x_0 units of all other goods and services or h_1 units of H and x_1 units of X.[15] Higher indifference curves represent higher levels of satisfaction under the premise that more is better than less. Thus, a household at point c is better off than one at point a since it can consume more housing, H, at c than at a with no reduction in X.

Figure 5.4 illustrates the resource or budget constraint of a household and how relative price or income changes shift the budget line. As a resource constraint, the budget line A–A^1 denotes all feasible combinations of

Figure 5.3. Utility indifference curves.

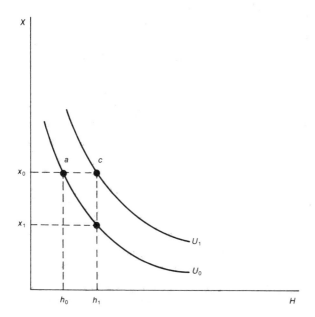

Figure 5.4. Household budget lines.

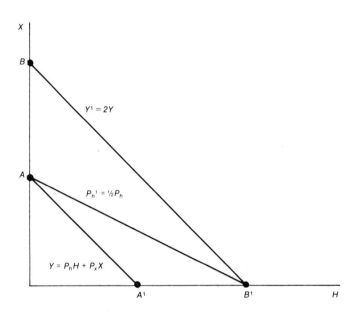

H and X a household could purchase at prices P_h and P_x, respectively, with a total income Y. From the equation of the budget line

$$Y = P_x X + P_h H$$

the intercepts denote the maximum amount of units of H or X that could be purchased by devoting all income to one or the other. If income is increased from Y to Y^1, where $Y^1 = 2Y$ the curve $B–B^1$ remains parallel to $A–A^1$, but it is shifted outward due to increased purchasing power. On the other hand, if the unit price of housing is halved, as in

$$(P_h^1 = \tfrac{1}{2} P_h)$$

without an increase in Y, the slope of the budget line is flattened as in $A–B^1$ to reflect the increased purchasing power due to the price decline.

Finally, in Figure 5.5 the utility indifference curves $U(H,X)$ and the income constraints are combined to illustrate the optimal allocation of Y to H and X, given the preferences for H and X encompassed in $U(H,X)$ and their relative prices, P_h and P_x. Since the household is constrained to the budget line $A–A^1$, it can reach the level of satisfaction U_0 at the two points b and c on its budget constraint. However, these points are not optimal. The household can reach a higher indifference curve than U_0 at c (and thus be better off), by reducing its consumption of H and increasing its consumption of X. In fact the rational household would continue to do so until it reaches point d. At the point of tangency between the highest utility curve U_1 and the budget constraint, the household maximizes its satisfaction and is best off.

Having illustrated these three fundamental concepts, it is fairly straightforward to analyze the relative efficiency of public-housing, rent-voucher, and general-income subsidies in improving household welfare. In order to introduce some realism into the discussion, some of the numerical estimates of Muth (1975) and Olsen (1968) are incorporated. In a sense these figures correspond to the average public-housing tenant in the mid-1960s. Olsen (1968) suggested that at this time the typical public housing tenant paid a rental of $47 per month, or one-fifth of an average income of $235 per month. Bish (1969) cited data of the Department of Housing and Urban Development that suggests that households of the lowest income dec-

Figure 5.5. Individual household utility maximization.

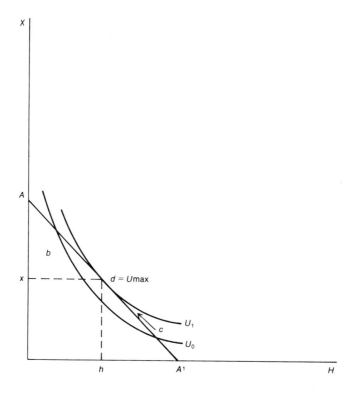

ile spent an average of 22 percent of their income on housing. For simplicity the prices of H and X (or P_h and P_x) are assumed to be $1 per unit initially. Thus, the average household could hypothetically purchase 235 units of H or X if only one or the other was purchased. The initial private housing situation is depicted at point a in Figure 5.6.

Two points must be noted to introduce public housing correctly into the analysis. First, DeSalvo (1971) rightfully contended that public housing consumption is virtually an all-or-nothing choice on the part of households. Muth (1975) estimated that the equivalent private-market rent of public housing units was about $177 per month. Thus, in terms of a dollar unit price, 177 housing-service units were offered to tenants via public housing. Second, the effective unit price of housing was reduced to below market levels to public housing tenants via rent subsidies. Since the average household paid $47 in rentals for 177 units of housing services, the effective unit price faced by residents was about 27 cents. Given the choice

Figure 5.6. Household consumption in private market, public housing, and rent voucher plan.

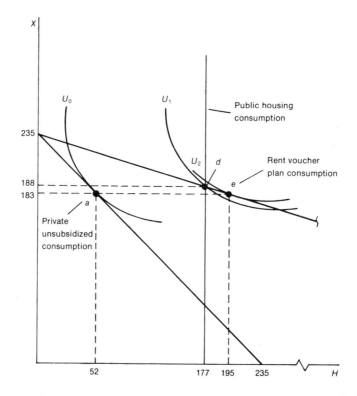

of occupying public housing, an eligible household faced the dichotomous choice of its current housing consumption of 52 service units at market price or the 177 service units offered by public housing at a monthly rental of $47. Under the flatter, reduced price budget line in Figure 5.6, the public-housing tenant would be "forced" to consume at point d. Under these conditions the public-housing tenant is definitely better off at d than a. There the tenant reaches a higher satisfaction level U_1 by consuming 125 more units of housing and 5 more units of other goods and services. This supports Muth's contention that the excessive waiting lists for public housing in the 1960s suggested it was a preferred alternative despite all of the critical writings about squalid living conditions.[16]

The relative efficiency of a rent voucher program can also be depicted in Figure 5.6 by assuming that the voucher recipient is allowed free choice of housing at an effectively reduced unit price rather than at the predetermined public housing offering. Assuming that voucher recipients would face the same 27-cent unit price of housing, the rational household should simply maximize its utility subject to the flatter budget line. By assuming a particular functional form for the household's utility function, $U(H,X)$, the optimal consumption levels of H and X may be analytically solved for. Using a Cobb-Douglas utility function and a rent-income ratio of .22, the free choice, rent-voucher housing consumption is increased to 195 units at point e of Figure 5.6.[17] The household is better off at point e over d since it reaches a higher utility level, U_2. The household would voluntarily consume less of other goods and services than before since the "bargain" unit price of housing had stimulated a trade-off of X for more H. In other words the household was institutionally constrained by public-housing regulations, e.g., units assigned on some type of family-size basis, from consuming its desired housing-consumption level at these reduced prices.[18] The relative efficiency of a voucher scheme is evident when one considers the amount of governmental subsidy required for the household to voluntarily choose to consume 177 units of housing at a reduced unit price. The idea is to treat 177 units of housing as the minimum amount the government would deem adequate for low-income households to consume. By raising the unit price of housing from 27 cents to 29.2 cents, the rational household would outlay about $52 per month for 177 units of H under a rent-voucher plan. The government subsidy would be reduced from $130 to $125 per month. Although the household would be somewhat worse off since it would reduce its consumption of X from 188 to 183.3 units, the efficiency is clear since the public-housing tenant would purchase an additional $4.70 worth of goods and services at a $5 cost to the government.[19]

The relative efficiency of a cash-grant income subsidy versus a rent-voucher subsidy is easily assessed by comparing the amount of direct subsidy required to allow the household to reach the same satisfaction level under both programs.[20] The rent voucher scheme in Figure 5.6 is restated in Figure 5.7 to illustrate this comparison. Using the same numbers and assumptions stated earlier, at a subsidized price of 27 cents, the household would choose point *e*. Similarly, a household facing existing market prices would voluntarily consume at point *f* in Figure 5.6, given an unrestricted income subsidy of $125 per month. Substitution of a cash grant for the price subsidy for *H* leads the household to reduce its housing consumption drastically to 79 units by trading off *H* for *X*. The government subsidy cost under the rent-voucher scheme is $143 monthly, if the household consumes at point *e* in Figure 5.7. Although the household is equally satisfied at *e* or *f* by nature of the indifference curve, the cash grant is obviously a more efficient mechanism for increasing overall household welfare.

Despite the obvious allocation efficiency of cash grants in maximizing the welfare of recipients, DeSalvo (1971) noted two reasons that society may opt instead to provide subsidized housing of some variety. One reason

Figure 5.7. Household consumption in rent voucher and income subsidy plans.

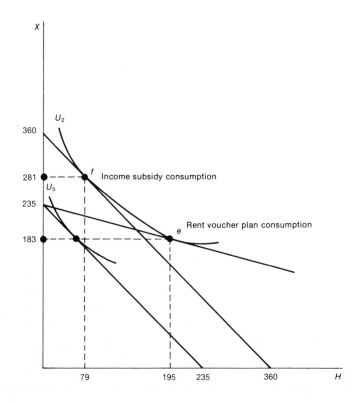

is that providers of the benefits may raise their own satisfaction level by knowing that recipients occupy standard housing. Recipients of cash grants may not choose to do so. Second, housing programs may produce spillover benefits to nonrecipients such as those persons associated with elimination of slums and blight. With this latter point in mind, in the next section we shall examine the benefit-cost analysis of housing programs in greater detail.

Benefit-Cost Analyses of Housing Programs

The purpose of benefit-cost analysis is to address a fundamental question beyond the scope of the evaluation methods discussed thus far. The prior methods are useful in comparing the relative efficacy of alternative programs, but are inadequate in assessing whether any program is justifiable at all from an efficiency standpoint. Unless the benefits to society derived from the program exceed the societal costs associated with it, the alternative of doing nothing may be superior in society's view.

Although low-income housing programs are largely income-transfer programs in the sense that a rent subsidy that allows households to purchase housing at below market rents is essentially a transfer payment from other households via taxes and does not involve use of scarce resources per se, the concept and measurement of spillover benefits to nontenants is crucial to their economic justification. For the most part benefit-cost analyses of housing programs (see DeSalvo, 1974; Murray, 1975; Olsen and Prescott, 1969; Bish, 1969; Prescott, 1974; Sumka and Stegman, 1978; and Solomon, 1974)[21] rest on the individual welfare analysis of households described in the previous section to obtain measures of individual tenant benefits. DeSalvo (1971) emphatically argued that the tenant subsidy, or the difference between the market rent of units and what the tenant actually pays, overstates the magnitude of net tenant benefits so that housing programs can only be economically justified on the basis of external spillover benefits. To see this let us consider the situations described earlier and introduce the element of resource costs into the picture.

The true resource costs of housing programs of this sort are the value of resources necessary to provide the required level of housing services. This resource cost could presumably be estimated from careful examination of development, production, and operating costs. Yet, this cumbersome approach is rarely pursued. Generally, costs are roughly approximated on the basis of average data and applied to particular studies (see Sumka and Stegman, 1978, and Solomon, 1974). The critical reliance on nontenant benefits for justification is most apparent by considering that if public housing were provided as efficiently as privately produced housing, the resource cost-per-unit would be reflected directly in the market-rent level.[22] Using the market-rent level as the lower-bound resource cost, it becomes clear that gross private tenant benefits must exceed or equal market rents if programs are to be economically justified on this basis alone.

The market value of the typical public-housing unit in the mid-1960s of about $177 per month was noted earlier. Tenants paid $47 per month rental outlay, and presumably, they valued the housing service by at least that amount or they would not have participated in the program. A tenant subsidy of $130 per month overstates the benefits of the rent subsidy since it has already been shown in Figure 5.6 that a $125 per-month, direct-income subsidy would allow the household to reach a satisfaction level, U_2, that is higher than that attainable via public housing. The proper estimate of net tenant benefits, or the consumer surplus value of the income subsidy, is the amount of income that would have to be given to the tenant to be as well off as in public housing. Using the same assumptions and figures noted in the previous section, this income subsidy would amount to about $92 per month.[23] Thus, the gross private-tenant benefit would total about $139 per month under the conditions stated earlier. Since the private market rent of units was $177 per month, the minimum amount of nontenant spillover benefits to justify the program would be on the order of $38 per month per dwelling, if the units were produced as efficiently as their equivalents in the private sector.

The foregoing analysis suggests that the onus of justifying housing subsidy programs clearly falls into the measurement of external spillover benefits, or consumption externalities and information problems associated with the merited aspects of housing.[24] It is commonly believed the consumption of adequate housing confers benefits on others than those consuming it, or that positive spillovers exist. Some persons argue that upgrading substandard housing raises surrounding property values of nonrecipients since poor quality housing may impose diseconomies upon higher valued properties in the form of capital losses from decreased property values (Davis and Whinston, 1961). Others have suggested that relationships exist between poor housing and crime, delinquency, and disease propensity, all of which affect other persons substantially. The empirical questions concerning these effects are far from resolution. There is ample empirical evidence that good housing creates monetary spillover benefits to other nearby housing, but the spatial extent of this spillover is thought to be small. Evidence of spillovers capitalized into nearby property values from government-housing programs has been mixed. Nourse (1963) found no evidence that public-housing projects in St. Louis increased the value of surrounding properties. DeSalvo (1974), on the other hand, found some indication of upgrading in neighborhoods surrounding the Mitchell-Lama

projects in New York City, but was unable to express these spillover benefits in monetary terms. Overall, one could conclude that the empirical evidence thus far is scanty and inconsistent. There is also ample evidence that
poor housing is associated with poor health, social maladjustment, and
crime propensity. Both the causality of the relationships, and thus, the extent to which good housing reduces crime, ill health, and other social ills
has long been scrutinized and debated. Rothenberg (1976), Kasl (1976),
Sanoff and Burgwyn (1976), and Glazer (1967) all discuss these critical issues in some detail. As Kasl (1976) and Weicher (1976) aptly state, it is
easy to show that rich people living in high-quality housing are less prone
to commit crimes or to contract certain diseases. It is difficult to show that
housing has a causal effect apart from characteristics of the occupants under study. This evidence, or lack of it, should not be construed to suggest
that improved housing does not generate positive spillover benefits. It is
fair to say that no conclusions can be made on this issue.

The implications of this discussion on the program-level evaluation of
federal housing policy are somewhat double-edged. It is apparent that the
voluminous research has increased our understanding of what has gone
wrong in past housing programs in terms of their political, administrative,
economic, and program-implementation aspects. On the other hand, it
may be fair to say that more evidence exists on what we do not know than
on what we do know about government low-income housing programs.
Whether one opts for the half-full or half-empty characterization of progress, one must recognize that since the moratorium on government housing programs in the early 1970s,[25] the Department of Housing and Urban
Development has made serious efforts toward reexamining the directions
of federal housing policy. The strongest evidence of this is probably the
large-scale housing allowance experiments being conducted to examine the
demand-and-supply effects of demand/consumption-oriented programs.

FRONTIERS OF U.S. LOW-INCOME
HOUSING POLICY

The frontier and future direction of U.S. low-income housing policy (see
Bendick and Zais, 1978) may well be reflected in the ongoing Experimental Housing Allowance Program (EHAP) initiated in 1972 by the Department of Housing and Urban Development. In terms of dollars expended, it
is probably the largest social experiment ever conducted. The experiment
is actually composed of three separate experiments, each focusing on different aspects of housing-allowance systems. The Housing Allowance Demand Experiment (HADE) primarily addresses questions of how low-in-

come households respond to different housing allowance formulas and varied restrictions on their use. The Housing Allowance Supply Experiment (HASE) is designed to address the measurement of market supply response to full-scale programs, as well as community attitudes toward the programs. Finally, the Administrative Agency Experiment seeks to identify various institutional channels for delivering the allowance and various program management and operation alternatives. This section will briefly review some preliminary findings from the HADE and HASE experiments. No effort is made to describe program details or to critique the methodologies or experimental designs of the experiment.

The basic objective of the HADE, which is conducted primarily in Pittsburgh and Phoenix, is to test the extent to which the expected effects of direct cash-housing assistance actually occur in practice. From the earlier welfare analysis of housing-subsidy strategies, the reader is familiar with the general expectations of providing low-income households with assistance in varying degrees. To the extent that inadequate housing consumption is attributable to a lack of purchasing power, the logical conclusions of these analyses suggest that housing-allowance recipients increase their housing consumption. The real question is the degree of increase. Bendick and Zais (1978) reported preliminary results suggesting that recipients do not spend large amounts of their additional purchasing power on housing. The subsidy-induced housing expenditures did vary expectedly with respect to whether the subsidy was earmarked for housing or unrestricted. In Pittsburgh and Phoenix recipients of earmarked subsidies increased their rental outlays by about 10 percent. About $13 of the $50 average monthly subsidy in Pittsburgh and $26 of the average monthly subsidy of $80 in Phoenix were allocated to increased rental outlays. Rental outlays did not increase upon reception of unearmarked subsidies in Pittsburgh, and they increased by only $15 monthly in Phoenix. A most interesting implication of these results is the implied low-income elasticities of demand in the range of .19 to .40, when common consensus has suggested it falls around .75.[26] While the full implications of the unresponsiveness of household rent outlays cannot yet be assessed, the experimental situations may generate further insight into this question.

The critical question addressed in the HASE experiment is whether increased housing expenditures by allowance recipients enabled the consumption of better housing services or whether they simply bid up market rents due to an inelastic supply. The importance of the responsiveness of supply, e.g., upgrading and increased maintenance expenditures, upon the efficacy of demand/consumption-oriented programs was discussed earlier. A second question of importance is whether the portability of allowances tied to households rather than to dwelling units can allow positive changes in the economic, social, and racial patterns of neighborhood populations.

The ten-year experiment has been in operation for more than two years in Brown County, Wisconsin (Green Bay), and St. Joseph County, Indiana (South Bend). Again, Bendick and Zais (1978) reported some interesting two year results. The allowance experiments thus far have not generated major repairs, new construction, or general neighborhood upgrading. About one dwelling unit in three has been repaired as a consequence of inspections for occupancy by allowance recipients, with the median cash outlay being about \$10.[27] On a more promising level, however, preliminary data suggest that housing allowances may have a favorable impact on the maintenance of units. Reinspection of units for EHAP eligibility have shown significant reductions in failure rates since the inception of the program. It seems that the prospect of future reinspection may generate minor upkeep-maintenance outlays. Finally, the work of Barnett (1979) suggested that contrary to most gloomy forecasts of sharp short-run rent increases due to the infusion of greater demand and an inelastic supply, pure price effects of increased rents due to the experiment account for no more than a 10 percent increase in expenditure. Thus, the preliminary results of the HASE experiment have been both promising and discouraging.

Overall, the successes or failures of the Housing Allowance Experiments cannot yet be readily evaluated. Some might argue that the experiments have been a costly means of verifying things that are already known, or that, at least, should have been known. Yet preliminary results suggest that things do not always happen exactly as textbook theories suggest. Are the differences due to the limited duration of the experiments, which, in turn, lead households to adjust their expected behavior? Are the results generalizable to a full-scale national program? All of these questions will linger on for some time, but the new approach to housing-policy evaluation is refreshing in light of past experiences in housing-policy formulation at national levels.

SYNTHESIS AND OVERALL ASSESSMENT

Several factors clearly stand out during an overview of past efforts. One is our limited knowledge of the operation and functioning of housing markets. The complexities of the market have impeded significant progress toward understanding the impact that federal housing policy has had on the current housing situation. By moving from an overall perspective to a program-level assessment, one does not bypass the problems that arise from ignorance. The process and economic analyses of government low-income housing programs, despite their piecemeal nature, have provided considerable insight into the operations of past programs. Much has been gained by knowing what went wrong with earlier and current programs, but very little is known about what is the right thing to do now. Economic analysis has produced theoretical rationales for the relative efficiency of various programs in improving the welfare of low-income households. Yet the crucial question of whether any program is justifiable from an economic efficiency standpoint is empirically unanswerable at this time. Economic justification hinges upon the empirical verification of societal spillover benefits conferred on households other than program recipients, and here, the complexities of the housing market has caused answers to remain elusive.

To reaffirm an earlier point, the successes and failures of housing programs and policy evaluations are most likely a mixed bag. Given the vagueness of national housing goals, one might conclude that progress has been made in spite of the difficulties faced. The probable future directions of program and policy evaluation in housing seem promising as evidenced by the housing-allowance experiments. Although one would hardly believe that such social experiments will solve America's housing problems, the evidence thus far suggests that much needed insight into the workings of the housing market will be gained, and that future housing policy may someday escape from the burden of the current ignorance.

NOTES

1. The author is grateful to Joseph DeSalvo for his comments on an earlier draft of this paper. All responsibility for remaining errors lies with the author.
2. Housing standards in Table 5.1 are normative judgments of housing needs independent of household-demand preferences. See Baer (1972) for a discussion of their evolutionary development in the United States.
3. Despite the wide recognition of the filtering process in the housing literature, there is little consensus toward defining it, let alone measuring it. See Grigsby (1963) and Davies (1978) for reviews of the literature.
4. More formally, the price elasticity of supply is defined as the percentage change in quantity supplied due to a 1 percent change in price. Since the standing stock is virtually fixed over substantial time periods, and sellers of housing cannot instantaneously adapt their units to demand shifts, it is important to stress the focus on long-run supply.
5. Although the assumption of a perfectly elastic supply is popular in housing research, many researchers have strongly argued against it and the subsequent possibility of long-run equilibrium in housing markets. See Ingram, et al. (1972), Kain and Quigley (1975), Straszheim (1975), Whitehead and Odling-Smee (1975), and Kirwan and Ball (1977).
6. The incompatibility of the 1960 and the 1970 Census definitions of substandard housing preclude definitive estimates of this decline; however, Census figures suggest the reduction falls in the range of 40–60 percent.

7. See Welfeld (1973) and Downs (1973) for brief summaries of more detailed characteristics of the programs.

8. Another example of the ambiguity of federal housing policy is evidenced by the numerous papers invited by HUD (1976) for purposes of reexamining the rationale for government intervention in housing.

9. See Rainwater (1967) for a discussion of the Pruit–Igoe project and its problems.

10. In economics this issue amounts to the problem of interpersonal utility comparisons.

11. Here the term "production" is being used in the general sense of the provision of housing services over time, rather than the construction of the physical unit. Hence, operation and maintenance expenditures are included as inputs.

12. This estimate was derived under the assumptions that (1) capital was foregone elsewhere in the economy when shifted to public housing, (2) some limited degree of substitutability exists between capital and current costs, (3) public housing is produced as efficiently as private housing, and (4) public housing differs from private housing only because of differences in capital costs.

13. This efficiency issue is not unique to housing. In fact, standard microeconomics texts generally address it.

14. Thee is little consensus on how competitive local housing markets really are. Olsen (1969) provided a theory and some empirically testable implications. Kain and Quigley (1975), among others, argued that significant imperfections exist.

15. The shape of the curve suggests that as a household consumes more of H relative to X, the marginal value of an additional unit falls, since it must forego units of X (to remain at the same satisfaction level), and X then becomes relatively scarce.

16. See Salisbury (1958), Rainwater (1970), and Friedman (1967).

17. Use of the Cobb-Douglas function (discussed in any standard microeconomics text) implicitly assumes unitary price and income elasticities. In other words the effective increase in purchasing power due to rent vouchers is proportionately distributed among H and X. See DeSalvo (1971) for further detail on how point e is computed.

18. Under different initial conditions and different functional forms for $U(H,X)$, the optimal rent-voucher plan consumption of H could fall short of, or equal to, the 177 units provided under public housing. In the former case public housing would lead households to overconsume housing. There is some confusion as to which occurrence is most likely. Unless more complex utility functions than the Cobb-Douglas are used, public-housing overconsumption relative to rent-voucher plans would require that households increase their expenditures on housing after public housing occupancy. Bish (1969) argued that the most prevalent case is that households reduce housing expenditures by public housing. The latter case is consistent with the example above.

19. The 29.2 cent unit price is solved for by inserting $H = 177$ into the optimal expenditure equation derived from constrained utility maximization problem, treating the unit price as variable. The government subsidy is simply found by

multiplying $H = 177$ by the price subsidy, or the difference between the dollar market price and the reduced price.

20. This is formally called the Hicksian "price equivalent variation" of consumer surplus. See Hicks (1956).

21. Actually, most of these works (Murray, 1975; Olsen and Prescott, 1969; and Bish, 1969) primarily address the measurement and/or distribution of tenant benefits rather than costs and benefits. All generally have started from the same methodological perspective.

22. Most analysts (Muth, 1975; Welfeld, 1970; and Smolensky, 1968) would argue that public housing is not produced as efficiently as its private-sector counterparts.

23. This is considerably higher than the $71 per month estimate of Muth (1975). This is the result of different utility functions and assumed income elasticities of housing. See DeSalvo (1971) for how the solution is arrived at. Also, it should be noted that aggregation of this net benefit over units requires that the aggregate program not affect the relative costs of housing and other goods in the economy, and that all participants value a dollar of benefits equally.

24. One accepted rationale for government intervention in private markets is that consumption of certain goods, e.g., housing and education are so meritorious that they should be publicly subsidized or provided. A general discussion of merit goods may be found in Steiner (1969). DeSalvo (1976) discusses the theoretical aspects of housing as a merit good.

25. The moratorium imposed by President Richard Nixon in 1973, in essence, suspended the operation of all principal subsidized (production-oriented) housing programs while all federal efforts in the housing field were reassessed. The National Housing Policy Review was a central component of the reassessment. The general recommendations of this review supported demand-oriented housing policy rather than supply/production-oriented policy. The exposition in this section has attempted to clarify the economic logic behind the shift in policy direction.

26. The term "income elasticity of demand" expresses the effects of marginal change in income, i.e., a 1 percent change, upon housing expenditures. See de Leeuw (1971) and Mayo (1978) for reviews of studies.

27. In general allowances were tied to requirements that households occupy certain minimum-quality housing. Preliminary results suggest that program participation varies inversely with the stringency of standards.

REFERENCES

Aaron, Henry J., and G. M. von Furstenberg. "The Inefficiency of Transfers in Kind: The Case of Housing Assistance." *Western Economic Journal*, 9 (1971), 184–191.

Baer, William C. "The Evolution of Housing Indicators and Housing Standards." *Public Policy*, 24 (1972), 361–393.

Barnett, C. Lance. "Expected and Actual Effects of Housing Allowances on Housing Prices." *Paper P-6184.* Santa Monica: Rand Corporation, 1979.

Bendick, Marc, and J. P. Zais. "Incomes and Housing: Lessons from Experiments with Housing Allowances." *Paper 249-9.* Washington, D.C.: Urban Institute, 1978.

Bish, R. L. "Public Housing: The Magnitude and Distribution of Direct Benefits and Effects on Housing Consumption." *Journal of Regional Science,* 9 (1969), 425-438.

Committee on Banking and Currency. U.S. House of Representatives. *Basic Laws and Authorities on Housing and Urban Development.* Washington, D.C.: U.S. Government Printing Office, 1971.

Davis, G. W. "Theoretical Approaches to Filtering in the Urban Housing Market." *Urban Housing Markets: Recent Directions in Research and Policy,* edited by L. S. Bourne and J. R. Hitchcock. Toronto: University of Toronto Press, 1978, pp. 139-163.

Davis, O. A., and A. Whinston. "The Economics of Urban Renewal." *Law and Contemporary Problems,* 26 (1961), 163-177.

Davis, Otto A., Eastman, C. M., and C. Hua. "The Shrinkage in the Stock of Low-Quality Housing in the Central City: An Empirical Study of the U.S. Experience." *Urban Studies,* 2 (1974), 13-26.

de Leeuw, Frank. *Operating Costs in Public Housing: A Financial Crisis.* Washington, D.C.: Urban Institute, 1969.

———. "The Demand for Housing: A Review of Cross-Section Evidence." *Review of Economics and Statistics,* 53, February 1971, 1-10.

de Leeuw, Frank, and N. F. Ekanem. "The Supply of Rental Housing." *American Economic Review,* 61 (December 1971), 806-817.

DeSalvo, Joseph S. "A Methodology for Evaluating Housing Programs." *Journal of Regional Science,* 11 (1971), 184-191.

———. "Neighborhood Upgrading Effects of Middle-Income Housing Projects in New York City." *Journal of Urban Economics,* 1 (1974), 269-277.

———. "Benefits and Costs of New York City's Middle Income Housing Program." *Journal of Political Economy,* 83 (August 1975), 791-805.

———. "A Rationale for Government Intervention in Housing: Housing as a 'Merit Good.' " *Housing in the Seventies: Working Papers,* 1. Washington, D.C.: U.S. Government Printing Office, pp. 286-304.

Downs, Anthony. *Federal Housing Subsidies: How Are They Working?* Lexington, Mass.: Lexington Books, 1973.

———. "The Successes and Failures of Federal Housing Policy." *The Public Interest,* 34 (1974), 124-145.

Fisher, Robert M. *Twenty Years of Public Housing.* New York: Harper and Brothers, 1959.

Freedman, Leonard. *Public Housing: The Politics of Poverty.* New York: Holt Rinehart, & Winston, 1969.

Friedman, Lawrence. *The Government and Slum Housing.* Chicago: Rand McNally, 1967.

Glazer, Nathan. "The Effects of Poor Housing." *Journal of Marriage and the Family*, 29 (1967), 140–145.

Grigsby, William G. *Housing Markets and Public Policy*. Philadelphia: University of Pennsylvania Press, 1963.

Hicks, J. R. *A Revision of Demand Theory*. Oxford, England: Clarendon Press, 1956.

Ingram, G. K., et al. *The Detroit Prototype of the NBER Urban Simulation Model*. New York: Columbia University Press, 1972.

Kain, J. F., and J. M. Quigley. *Housing Markets and Racial Discrimination: A Microeconomic Analysis*. New York: National Bureau of Economic Research, 1975.

Kasl, S. V. "Effects of Housing on Mental and Physical Health." *Housing in the Seventies: Working Papers*, 1. Washington, D.C.: U.S. Government Printing Office, 1976.

Kirwan, R. M., and M. J. Ball. "Accessibility and Supply Constraints in the Urban Housing Market." *Urban Studies*, 13 (1977), 11–25.

Kristoff, Frank S. "Federal Housing Policies: Subsidized Production, Filtration, and Objectives: Part I." *Land Economics,* 48 (1972), 309–320.

———. "Federal Housing Policies: Subsidized Production, Filtration, and Objectives: Part II." *Land Economics,* 49 (1973), 163–175.

Lowry, Ira S. "The Housing Assistance Supply Experiment: An Overview," *Paper P-5567.* Santa Monica: Rand Corporation, 1976.

Mayo, Stephen K. "Theory and Estimation in the Economics of Housing Demand." Paper presented at meeting of American Economic Association, 1978.

Meehan, Eugene J. "The Rise and Fall of Public Housing: Condemnation without Trial." In *A Decent Home and Environment*, edited by D. Phares. Cambridge, Mass.: Ballinger, 1977, pp. 3–42.

Murray, Michael P. "The Distribution of Tenant Benefits in Public Housing." *Econometrica*, 43 (1975), 771–788.

Muth, Richard F. "The Demand for Non-Farm Housing." In *The Demand for Durable Goods*, edited by A. C. Harberger. Chicago: University of Chicago Press, 1960, pp. 24–96.

———. *Cities and Housing*. Chicago: University of Chicago Press, 1969.

———. "Public Housing: An Economic Evaluation." In *Perspectives on Housing and Urban Renewal*, edited by I. Welfeld et al. New York: Praeger.

National Commission on Urban Problems. *Building the American City*. Washington, D.C.: U.S. Government Printing Office, 1968.

Nourse, Hugh. "The Effect of Public Housing on Property Values in St. Louis." *Land Economics*, 39 (1963), 433–441.

Olsen, E. O. "A Welfare Economic Evaluation of Public Housing." Ph.D. Dissertation, Rice University, 1968.

———. "A Competitive Theory of the Housing Market." *American Economic Review*, 59 (September 1969), 612–622.

Olsen, E. O., and J. R. Prescott. "An Analysis of Tenant Benefits of Government Housing Programs with Illustrative Calculations from Public Housing," *Paper P-4129.* Santa Monica: Rand Corporation, 1969.

Ozanne, L., and R. J. Struyk. "The Price Elasticity of Supply of Housing Services." In *Urban Housing Markets: Recent Direction in Research and Policy*, edited by L. S. Bourne and J. R. Hitchcock. Toronto: University of Toronto Press, 1978, pp. 109–138.

Prescott, J. C. "Rental Formation in Federally Supported Public Housing." *Land Economics*, 43 (1967), pp. 341–345.

———. *Economic Aspects of Public Housing*. Beverly Hills, Calif.: Sage, 1974.

Rainwater, L. *Behind Ghetto Walls*. Chicago: Aldine, 1970.

Rothenberg, Jerome. "A Rationale for Government Intervention in Housing: The Externalities Generated by Good Housing." *Housing in the Seventies: Working Papers*, 1. Washington, D.C.: U.S. Government Printing Office, 1976, pp. 251–266.

Salisbury, Harrison. *The Shook-Up Generation*. New York: Harper, 1958.

Sanoff, H., and H. K. Burgwyn. "Improved Housing and Health State: A Focus on Rural Housing." *Housing in the Seventies: Working Papers*, 1. Washington, D.C.: U.S. Government Printing Office, 1976, pp. 512–530.

Schultze, C. L. "Why Benefit-Cost Analysis." In *Program Budgeting and Benefit-Cost Analysis*, edited by H. H. Hinrichs and G. M. Taylor. Pacific Palisades, Calif.: Goodyear, 1969.

Smolensky, E. "Public Housing or Income Supplement: The Economics of Housing for the Poor." *Journal of the American Institute of Planners*, 34 (1968), pp. 94–101.

Solomon, A. P. "Housing and Public Policy Analysis." In *Housing Urban America*, edited by J. Pynoos et al. Chicago: Aldine, 1973.

———. *Housing the Urban Poor: A Critical Analysis of Federal Housing Policy*. Cambridge, Mass.: MIT Press, 1974.

Steiner, Peter O. "The Public Sector and the Public Interest." In *Public Expenditures and Policy Analysis*, edited by R. H. Haveman and J. Margolis. Chicago: Markham, 1969, pp. 21–58.

Stone, Michael E. "Federal Housing Policy: A Political-Economic Analysis." In *Housing Urban America*, edited by J. Pynoos et al. Aldine: N.Y., pp. 423–433.

Straszheim, Mahlon. *An Econometric Analysis of the Urban Housing Market*. New York: National Bureau of Economic Research, 1975.

Sumka, Howard J., and M. A. Stegman. "An Economic Analysis of Public Housing in Small Cities." *Journal of Regional Science*, 18 (1978), 395–410.

Swan, Craig. "Housing Subsidies and Housing Starts." *Housing in the Seventies: Working Papers*, 2. Washington, D.C.: U.S. Government Printing Office, 1976.

U.S. Department of Housing and Urban Development. *Housing in the Seventies: National Housing Policy Review*. Washington, D.C.: U.S. Government Printing Office, 1976.

Weicher, John C. "The Rationale for Government Intervention in Housing: An Overview." *Housing in the Seventies: Working Papers*, 1. Washington, D.C.: U.S. Government Printing Office, 1976, pp. 181–191.

———. "A Decent Home: An Assessment of Progress Toward the National Housing Goal and Policies to Achieve It." In *A Decent Home and Environment*, edited by D. Phares. Cambridge, Mass.: Ballinger, 1977, pp. 137–155.

Welfeld, Irving. "Toward a New Federal Housing Policy." *The Public Interest*, 19 (1970), 31–43.

————. *America's Housing Problem: An Approach to Its Solution*. Washington, D.C.: American Enterprise Institute for Public Policy Research, 1973.

White, H. C. "Multipliers, Vacancy Chains, and Filtering in Housing." *Journal of the American Institute of Planners*, 37 (1971), 88–94.

Whitehead, C. M. E., and J. C. Odling-Smee. "Long Run Equilibrium in Urban Housing—A Note." *Urban Studies*, 12 (1975), 315–318.

Chapter 6

LAW ENFORCEMENT AND CRIMINAL JUSTICE

Crime—its costs and the fears it generates—constitute a major problem in American society. Crime rates have risen rapidly in the last two decades, and Americans have become increasingly frightened of becoming crime victims. Crime, in fact, limits the freedom of many individuals: Businesses fail under the weight of thefts; families move out of high-crime neighborhoods; parks and public gatherings are avoided; and millions live in fear and distrust of their fellow citizens.

Traditionally, the execution of crime control policy had been pursued through the state and local governments. Crime became a national issue in the 1964 presidential election, and a nationwide "War on Crime" was launched early in 1965 by President Lyndon Johnson, who called on everyone to "not only reduce but banish crime."

The first major piece of legislation to move the federal government into local law enforcement was the Law Assistance Act of 1965, which authorized the U.S. Attorney General to carry out studies, to "collect, evaluate, publish, and disseminate information," and to make direct grants to states and local communities for purposes of educating and training personnel involved in the criminal justice system. At the same time Johnson established the Commission on Law Enforcement and Administration of Justice. In its report, *The Challenge of Crime in a*

Free Society, the commission made a series of recommendations on how to reduce crime. The report began: "There is much crime in America, more than is ever reported, far more than is ever solved, far too much for the health of the Nation." The commission found the criminal justice system to be antiquated, often invisible, and lacking in resources. They pointed a finger at poor police training and unqualified local judges. According to the report, an effective federal program to fight crime would include state and local planning, education and training of criminal justice personnel, advisory services for criminal justice organizations, a national system of information coordination, model projects, and provisions for technological development and research.

In the Crime Control and Safe Streets Act of 1968, Congress created the Law Enforcement Assistance Administration (LEAA) within the Department of Justice to channel federal grants-in-aid to the states for use in upgrading state and local law-enforcement programs. Most of these funds were to be used by the states as they saw fit in improving state and local law enforcement. LEAA budgets rose rapidly, starting at $63 million in 1968 and leveling off at about $800 million each year in the mid-1970s. The Crime Control Act of 1973 reestablished the roles of state and local government in crime-related issues. A Congressional report stated: "Crime is essentially a local problem that must be dealt with by state and local governments to be controlled effectively."[1] At the same time the act required local governments with populations of 250,000 or more to submit comprehensive plans to the states when they sought funds. In this way Congress mandated both "planning" and "comprehensiveness" into the activities of state and local criminal justice systems.

Government programs have been aimed at three components of the criminal justice system—the police, the courts and the corrections agencies. In general police departments suffer from shortages of manpower, poorly trained personnel and inefficient organization and administration. In 1973 the National Advisory Commission on Criminal Justice Standards and Goals took the position that a truly professional police force required college-trained workers who had specialized in various areas of policing such as patrol, department specialties, and administration. The Commission also saw the development of an appropriate police education program as a major task facing educators, police, and other criminal justice administrators.[2]

Operating inefficiencies throughout the court system have created major problems in the criminal justice system. Court dockets are overloaded, which results in delayed and diminished justice. There is a great disparity in the quality of justice from the lower to the higher courts. As the President's Commission on Law Enforcement and the Administration of Justice pointed out:

> No program of crime prevention will be effective without a massive over-haul of the lower criminal courts. The many persons who encounter these courts each year can hardly fail to interpret that experience as an expression of indifference to their situations and to the ideals of fairness, equality, and rehabilitation professed in theory, yet frequently denied in practice.[3]

Observations that the chances of former convicts to make success-ful transitions to normal life are slim, and that those chances decrease the longer that a person is imprisoned, led to the development of many programs devoted to the rehabilitation of offenders. Goal statements of such programs usually include the following: (1) establishment of programs of treatment, counseling, and training within correctional in-stitutions as well as in low-security community facilities, to impart skills needed in the community and the work habits necessary to maintain employment; (2) replacement or modification of inadequate correction-al institutions into facilities of more appropriate size, design, and loca-tion for their rehabilitative purpose; (3) revision of qualification of stan-dards and inservice training programs to upgrade the status and performance of custodial officers; and (4) establishment and mainte-nance of low-security community facilities located and programmed for effective collaboration with employers of educational facilities.

The article by Yong Hyo Cho examines the extent to which control and service policies have an impact in reducing serious crimes and suppressing the upward trends of crime rates in the nation's fifty larg-est cities. Using twenty-eight policy measures and crime data reported by the Federal Bureau of Investigation, Cho employs structural equa-tions to determine that service policies such as education, antipoverty program expenditures, and low-rent public housing affect crime rates more often than do control policies such as expenditures for police protection, expenditures for courts, and expenditures for corrections.

In the second article, Palumbo and Sharp develop a model of pro-cess evaluation based on panel interviews and apply it to a community corrections program in Kansas. The authors stress the importance of process evaluation and show that the community corrections program involves varying and, to a certain extent, incompatible goal perspec-tives. They also show that the decentralized nature of the program provides ample opportunity for the implementation process to produce unintended consequences.

The Nagel and Neef article centers on the impact of jury size on the probability that an average defendant will be convicted. The authors base their evaluation on deductive modeling; they take the position that the deductive approach enables estimates of the effects of policy changes before the changes are adopted, thereby reducing the risk of failure. The deductive approach is also useful in cases where meaningful direct empirical data are unavailable.[4]

NOTES

1. U.S. Congress, Conference Report, 93rd Congressional Conference, 1st Session, House Report No. 93–401, July 1973, p. 1.
2. National Advisory Commission on Criminal Justice Standards and Goals, *Police* (Washington, D.C.: 1937), p. 378.
3. President's Commission on Law Enforcement at the Administration of Justice, *Task Force Report: The Courts* (Washington, D.C.: Government Printing Office, 1967).
4. For a comprehensive discussion of deductive modeling in the context of policy evaluation, see Stuart S. Nagel, *Decision Theory and the Legal Process* (Lexington Mass.: Heath, 1979) and Stuart S. Nagel and Marian Neef, *The Legal Process: Modeling the System* (Beverly Hills, Calif.: Sage Publications, 1977).

A MULTIPLE REGRESSION MODEL FOR THE MEASUREMENT OF THE PUBLIC POLICY IMPACT ON BIG CITY CRIME

Yong Hyo Cho

ANALYSIS OF POLICY IMPACT

Comparative policy analysis has been one of the most active areas of political science research in the past several years. Conceptual models have been advanced and refined. Public policy outcomes are measured (most often by the level of expenditures for various functions and by the level of revenues from various sources), variables influential in determining the policy outcomes are identified, and the policy variance among the different government jurisdictions is systematically explained.[1]

Only a few studies have attempted to examine whether the differences in the policy level produce different results in policy impact. Sharkansky related the expenditure policies to the service outcomes, such as relationship of expenditure level for highway function to highway safety, expenditure level for education to test scores, and expenditure level for natural resources to the frequency of recreational use of natural resources for hunting and fishing, etc.[2] State legislative apportionment as a policy outcome has been analyzed in several studies to measure its impact on the spending and taxing behavior of the states.[3]

The purpose of this paper is to make a systematic inquiry into the public policy impact on crime-deterrence in the nation's major cities. The central question raised here is this: When the policy level is higher, does the crime rate or the crime rate change become measurably lower? As a way of answering this question, we examine the strength and direction of statistical relationships between selected measures of public policy and selected measures of crime rate and crime rate change. For this analysis, we use the 48 largest U.S. cities plus Akron, Ohio as our sample.[4] These cities are selected as our sample not because they represent the cross-section of the nation's cities, but because comparable data necessary for our analysis are more often available for those large cities. The statistical technique used for this operation is the multiple regression technique. The analytical methods will be more fully elaborated later.

In response to the rising crime rates in our cities, policy attention at all levels of government has been, and still is, focused on *control policies*. The control policies refer to those policies for law enforcement and criminal justice that directly affect governmental capacity to handle criminal acts and criminals. *Social service policies* are usually excluded from consideration for a development of comprehensive crime policy strategy. The social service policies refer to those policies that provide amenities and opportunities essential for the enhancement of the quality of urban life. They may contribute to the weakening of crime-inducive influences in the community and may be expected to be a deterrence to crime. Therefore, both control and service policy measures are included in the present study for the evaluation of their crime-deterring impact.

We often hear the complaint that social scientists are deprived of experimenting with public policy for the evaluation of its implications and for the formulation of the policy attuned to the reality. Policy experimentation is politically unpopular and unsupported, for it is costly, time-consuming, and most of all politically risky.[5] However, we argue here that experimentation in the sense that controlled and designed trial prior to formal adoption and implementation of the policy is not always indispensable for policy formulation or policy evaluation. The reason is that every public policy can be viewed as experimental, for public policies are always open to revisions through whatever feedback there may be available.

It is true that the evaluation of the existing policies will not tell us what new policies, unrelated to those policies in effect, are needed. But this evaluation will show us what modifications in the existing policies are needed to strengthen those policies in such a way as to produce the desired impact. This evaluation, when adequately performed, will satisfy most of the evaluation need for policy formulation. Policy formulation seldom involves a new policy which is unrelated to the existing policies, but policy formulation is usually a matter of modifying the ongoing policies. The findings of some recent studies, that incrementalism is characteristic of policymaking at all levels of government, provide empirical evidence. For example, budget policymaking is most likely to follow the pattern of budget policy in the preceding budget year.[6]

Some earlier studies have explored the relationships of some control policies to crime rates. A number of sociologists have studied what legal sanction does to crime-deterrence.[7] Their findings tend to support the contention that punishment in a way serves as a deterrent. They found that certainty of punishment is inversely correlated with various crime rates, while severity of punishment is inversely correlated with homicide rate only. Ira Sharkansky examined the relationships between per capita expenditure for police protection and crime rates and found positive correlations. He interpreted this finding as an indication that money is spent where the problem is.[8]

THE MODEL FOR ANALYSIS

The framework of analysis that underlies our model used here for the measurement of the policy impact on urban crime is approached from a comparative and macroanalytic perspective. The model contains three principal components: (1) the crime rates and crime rate trends; (2) the measures of public policy; and (3) indicators of the ecological environment.

As schematically illustrated in Figure 6.1, the interaction of the forces in the ecological environment is conceived to be the primary influence in the determination of the occurrence of crime. We disregarded in our model other possible influences, such as psychological and moral influences, for example, not because they are important, but because they are more suitable for a micro-analytic concern.

Figure 6.1. A model for the analysis of policy impact on city crimes.

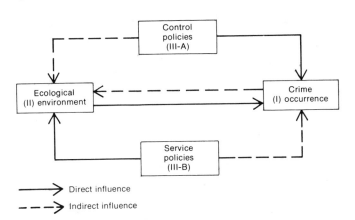

Public policies are conceived to be an intervention device in the process of criminal behavior at two separate points to suppress criminal tendency. Control policies are conceived to intervene primarily in the end process of criminal behavior to prevent crime, to arrest, to punish, or to rehabilitate criminals. We want to test whether the differences in the level of control policies make a difference in the rates of crime occurrence or in the trends of crime occurrence. Service policies are conceived to intervene in the interaction process of the ecological forces of the environment. The service policy intervention is conceived to weaken the crime-inducive influence in the ecological environment by improving the environmental quality and life opportunity for self-fulfillment. We test here if there is any evidence that the differences in the level of service policies make a difference in the rates of crime occurrence and in the trends of crime occurrence.

Studies of ecological correlates of crime variance within a city or among the cities indicate that various ecological variables are significantly correlated with crime rates. The findings of these studies are instructive for the purpose of the present study. First, some ecological variables such as racial composition (percent Negro), ethnic composition (percent foreign born), personal income levels, level of educational attainment, crowdedness of housing, etc., are found to be significantly correlated with one or more measures of crime rates. Second, more importantly, these findings indicate that "the criminogenic forces" are not alike for all types of crimes.[9] The findings in the ecological correlates of crime make it clear that an undistorted assessment of policy impact on crime requires a systematic control for ecological variables which are significantly correlated with crime rates or crime rate trends.

The Regression Model

Our analysis here is performed in two stages. First, we identify and select the ecological variables which are significantly correlated with crime measures. Since the ecological variables correlated with different crime measures are not alike, we selected the important ecological variables for each of the crime variables separately. Second, we assessed the impact of each of the control and service policy measures on the variance of crime rates or crime trends after controlling for the selected ecological variables. For both of these operations, we used stepwise multiple regression analysis.[10]

The regression model used for the identification and selection of the influential ecological variables is:

$$Yc_1 = A + b_1X_1 + \ldots + b_nX_n + e_1 \tag{1}$$

Where Yc_1 represents the estimated (or computed) value of crime rate or crime trend; A represents constant; X_1 through X_n represent the ecological variables regressed against the crime variable; b_1 through b_n represent the regression slopes for the ecological variables X_1 through X_n; and e_1 represents the error term. Through the stepwise regression procedure, the most significant ecological variable (X_1) is first picked and regressed against the crime variable (Y) and then X_2, X_3, etc. in the order of the strength of the variables. This process creates as many regression equations as there are ecological variables strong enough to be picked and included in the regressions. Of these, the one equation in which all of the ecological variables in the regression are significant simultaneously is identified and the ecological variables included in the regression are selected as the major criminogenic variables for the control purpose.[11]

We insist here that every control variable must have a statistically significant bearing on the dependent variable. This is the point where the way we use the regression procedure differs from the way the regression technique is usually employed for statistical tests in other studies. Unless the control variables are statistically significant, the statistical controls are (though provided to make it possible to measure the relationship of the test variable to the dependent variable more accurately) most unlikely to improve accuracy in the measurement of the relationship.[12] The reason is simply that controlling "wrong" variables is more likely to produce a statistical artifact than eliciting a substantive truth.

The regression model for the assessment of the policy impact while controlling for the criminogenic variables is identical with that used for the selection of the criminogenic variables. However, the regression model in this case includes only those significant criminogenic variables and one policy variable whose impact is assessed. This regression model is expressed as follows:

$$Y_{c2} = A + b_1X_1 + \ldots + b_nX_n + b_{pi}X_{pi} + e_2 \qquad (2)$$

Where X_{pi} represents the policy variable tested

The regression model used here is an additive model, not a multiplicative (or interactive) model, for two reasons. First, our effort is not merely to create the best fitting equation, but to test the impact of policy variables on crime variance based on a rigid significance test. Second, because of this rigid selection criterion of the variables for inclusion in the regressions, the variables (whether they be crime, policy, or ecological ones) included in the regressions are expected to have a high degree of linearity in their interrelationships.[13]

In the following, we describe the variables comprising the three components of our model: (1) dependent variables, crime rates, and crime rate trends; (2) test variables, control and service policies; and (3) possible control variables, the ecological variables.

Crime Rates and Crime Rate Trends (Dependent Variables)

The crime data are derived from the 1970 and 1965 issues of the *Uniform Crime Report* of the Federal Bureau of Investigation. We only include the seven categories of serious crimes in our analysis—homicide, forcible rape, robbery, aggravated assault, burglary, larceny, and auto theft. Two minor alterations are made to the original data: exclusion of negligent manslaughter from homicide and exclusion of the cases involving less than $50 from larceny.

The decision to use the FBI crime data is not without the knowledge that the reliability and accuracy of these data have been questioned for good reasons. First, the FBI statistics are considered to report offenses substantially below the rate uncovered by surveys. Second, the comparability of the data among different cities is questionable, for the classification and reporting systems of criminal offenses do vary among the city police departments. It is often the case that an offense reported as assault at one place is reported as something less serious elsewhere.[14]

In spite of these alleged shortcomings, the FBI data are used here, for they are still the single source of cross-sectional data and thus the most economic way of obtaining such data.

The crime rates are measured in terms of the number of offenses in each category per 100,000 population. There are, of course, other ways to construct crime rates such as "victim-specific index." Instead of computing crime rates in relation to total population, for example, burglary rates may be computed in relation to the number of opportunities to be burglarized, such as the number of commercial establishments or the number of homes, etc. Similarly, auto theft rates may be computed in relation to the number of registered cars in the community.[15] We did not follow this procedure not because it is undesirable, but because of the difficulty in obtaining the data necessary to estimate the chances to be victimized. The crime rate trends are measured by computing the 1970 crime rate as a percent of the 1965 crime rate for each category of crime.

Policy Variables (Test Variables)

Twenty-eight policy variables are selected, twenty-one control policies and seven social service policies. These policy measures are classified into eight categories, six for control policies and two for service policies, according to the dominant characteristics of the policy substances.

Control Policies

A. Financing Policies
   1. Per capita expenditures for police protection, 1969–70
   2. Per capita expenditures for courts, 1969–70
   3. Per capita expenditures for correction, 1969–70
   4. Per capita expenditures for all criminal justice functions, 1969–70

B. Professionalism
   5. Patrolman's salary-entrance, 1970
   6. Patrolman's salary-maximum, 1970
   7. Monthly pay per full-time prison employee, March, 1970

C. Manpower
   8. Police department employees per 100,000 population, 1970
   9. Sworn police officers per 100,000 population, 1970
   10. Correctional employees per 100,000 population, 1970
   11. Number of prison employees (full-time equivalent) per 100 inmates (employee-inmate ratio), March 1970

D. Facilities and Equipment
   12. Total motor vehicles used by police department per 100,000 population, 1970
   13. Police cars per 100,000 population, 1970
   14. Police motorcycles and scooters per 100,000 population, 1970
   15. Prison crowdedness (number of inmates as a percent of the capacity of the prison), 1970
   16. Prison facilities—index of comprehensiveness, 1970

E. Injustice of the Justice System Due to Operational Delay or Bias
   17. Percent inmates not arraigned plus arraigned and awaiting trial, 1970

F. Centralism-Decentralism of State-Local Criminal Justice System
   18. Local percent of state-local expenditures for total criminal justice operations, 1968–69
   19. Local percent of state-local expenditures for police protection, 1968–69
   20. Local percent of state-local expenditures for courts, 1968–69
   21. Local percent of state-local expenditures for correctional activities, 1968–69[16]

Service Policies

G. Service for Opportunity
   22. Per capita anti-poverty program expenditures by Office of Economic Opportunity (OEO), Standard Metropolitan Statistical Areas (SMSA), 1968–69
   23. Per capita county and city (CAC) expenditures (SMSA), 1968–69
   24. Per capita expenditures for local public schools, 1969–70
   25. Number of pupils per teacher, 1970

H. Service for Environment
   26. Number of low-rent public housing units per 1,000 occupied housing units, 1970
   27. Per capita expenditures of sanitation other than sewage, 1969–70
   28. Per capita expenditures for parks and recreation, 1969–70[17]

Some of the policy variables present rather complex measurement problems. Since the local government system governing a city area varies from place to place, the criminal justice system operating within each city area also varies. This governmental system variation must be taken into consideration when local criminal justice policies in a municipal area are to be measured on a comparable basis for cross-sectional comparison. For example, in New York City all local functions for police, court, and correction are the responsibility of the city government. In contrast, in the city of Akron, the municipal police maintains an exclusive jurisdiction within the municipal boundaries, but local judicial functions and correctional functions are a shared responsibility between the county and municipal governments. This problem is resolved by allocating the city-share of the county-provided services for courts and correction based on the city-county proportion of population.[18]

Ecological Variables (Possible Control Variables)

Nineteen ecological variables are included in our analysis to seek out statistically significant criminogenic variables for the control purpose. The nineteen variables represent demographic characteristics (population size and density, population composition, and population shift), housing conditions, living standards and consumerism, and physical structure of the community. Some important variables are not included here, for the 1970 U.S. census results are at this time not yet fully available. Some of them are education level, occupational characteristics, industrial structure, personal income, divorce and separation, and employment status, etc. Some of our included variables are different from those used in earlier studies attempting to obtain the ecological correlates of city crime rates. They are: (1) population shift variables; (2) a measure of consumerism, per capita retail sales (what we really wanted to use for this measure was consumer loans outstanding per capita, but we failed to locate the data); and (3) variables describing the physical make-up of the community by ascertaining the percent assessed valuation of single-family house, multiple dwelling, and commercial and industrial properties.

The specific variables are shown under appropriate categories.

I. Demographic Variables
A. Size and Density
    1. Total population in thousands, 1970
    2. Population density (population per square mile), 1970
B. Population Composition
    3. Percent population nonwhite, 1970
    4. Percent population under age 18, 1970
    5. Percent families headed by female with own children under age 18, 1970
    6. Percent primary male individuals of total population, 1970
C. Population Shift
    7. Percent change in total population, 1960–70
    8. Percent change in white population, 1960–70
    9. Percent change in nonwhite population, 1960–70

II. Housing Variables
    10. Percent housing owner-occupied, 1970
    11. Percent housing crowded (more than one person per room), 1970
    12. Percent housing substandard (lacking some or all plumbing), 1970

III. Income and Living Standards
    13. Per capita personal income (SMSA), 1968
    14. Median value of owner-occupied housing, 1970
    15. Median monthly rent, 1970
    16. Per capita retail sales (proxy of consumerism), 1967

IV. Physical Structure of the Community
    17. Percent assessed value of single-family houses, 1967
    18. Percent assessed value of multi-dwellings, 1970
    19. Percent assessed value of commercial and industrial property, 1967[19]

FINDINGS

The highlights of our findings are presented in Tables 6.1 through 6.10. None of the policy measures showed a significant relationship to the four indices of crime rate trends: aggravated assault, burglary, larceny, and auto theft. The regression results for these crime variables are not reported here.

Each table shows four statistics which define the relationships of selected policy variables to a crime rate or crime rate trend variable after controlling for the selected criminogenic variables. The four statistics are simple r, partial r, F value, and the percent of the variance in the crime variable accounted for by the policy measure (R^2 change). Statistical relations reported between crime rate and criminogenic variables include simple r, F value and the percent of the variance in the crime variable accounted for by all the criminogenic variables together (R^2). Partial correlation coefficient is not computed for the criminogenic variables and R^2 change for them is not reported in the tables.

Homicide

Table 6.1 reports the relationships of those significant public policy measures and criminogenic variables to willful homicide rate. It has been known that homicide is mostly committed by persons who know the victim in a private setting. For this reason, control of homicide through public policy is considered ineffective. However, our results shown in Table 6.1 indicate that six policy measures are significantly correlated with homicide rate, four control and two service policy measures.

All four control policy variables represent prison policies. When the local prisons are overcrowded and the judicial system is overburdened or unfair, as evidenced by a large proportion of the local prison inmates not being arraigned or not yet tried, the homicide rate in the city tends to be higher. On the contrary, when prison employees are more professional and employee-inmate ratio is higher, the homicide rate tends to be lower. These relationships, however, do not necessarily lead us to conclude that overcrowded prisons and pretrial incarceration would result in more homicide, while professionalism and generous staffing of prison employees would reduce homicide rate. Rather, the prisons may be overcrowded and judicial proceedings may be overburdened because there are too numerous crimes including homicide. The community can pay its prison employees better and keep the employee-inmate ratio high because crime rate including homicide is low in the community.[20] Granted that the causal relationships cannot be resolved, however, the findings are informative in that po-

TABLE 6.1
Relationships Between Willful Homocide and
Public Policy Controlling Major Criminogenic
Variables in the 49 Large U.S. Cities, 1970

Criminogenic Variables Controlled	r	Partial	F Value	R² Change
% Families Headed by Female	0.649	N.C.	3.91	N.I.
% Nonwhite	0.632	N.C.	13.04	N.I.
% Commercial and Industrial Property	0.509	N.C.	3.65	N.I.
Monthly Rent	−0.163	N.C.	5.96	N.I.
Retail Sales	0.227	N.C.	8.52	N.I.
$R = 0.817$				
$R^2 = 0.667$				
Control Policy				
Prison Crowdedness	0.269	0.430	8.83	0.062
% Inmates Not Arraigned or Awaiting Trial	0.273	0.221	2.01	0.016
Monthly Pay for Prison Employees	−0.064	−0.299	3.83	0.030
Employee-Inmate Ratio	−0.159	−0.284	3.42	0.027
Service Policies				
Low-Rent Public Housing	0.429	−0.393	7.14	0.052
Exp. for Parks and Recreation	−0.109	−0.362	5.90	0.044

N.C. = Not Computed
N.I. = Not Included

lice policies are not related to homicide, but correctional policies are. This simply confirms the fact we already know, that the police and law enforcement are not likely to prevent homicide.

The two service policies are inversely correlated with homicide rate. When policy support for urban life environment is strong, such as for more low-rent public housing and more parks and recreation services, the homicide rate tends to be lower.

Forcible Rape

As Table 6.2 shows, only two policy variables are significantly correlated with forcible rape: patrolman's salary at entrance and the level of municipal expenditure for sanitation other than sewage. When patrolmen's entrance salary is higher and sanitation expenditure is greater, the forcible rape rate tends to be lower. It is evident that public policies are generally unrelated to this crime.

TABLE 6.2
Relationships Between Forcible Rape and
Public Policy Controlling Major Criminogenic
Variables in the 49 Large U.S. Cities, 1970

Criminogenic Variables Controlled	r	Partial	F Value	R^2 Change
% Male	0.402	N.C.	12.18	N.I.
% Families Headed by Female	0.380	N.C.	2.32	N.I.
% Population Under 18	−0.148	N.C.	5.40	N.I.
$ Monthly Rent	0.086	N.C.	2.74	N.I.
$R = 0.599$				
$R^2 = 0.359$				
Direct Control Policies				
Patrolman's Salary-Entrance	0.113	−0.230	2.23	0.034
Social Service Policies				
Per Capita Exp. for Sanitation	−0.069	−0.235	2.34	0.036

N.C. = Not Computed
N.I. = Not Included

Robbery

Many policy variables, particularly control policies, are significantly related to robbery as Table 6.3 shows. Expenditure policies for police, court, correction, and all criminal justice operations are positively correlated with the robbery rate. Two measures of police manpower policy and the measure of local decentralism of state-local court expenditure are also positively correlated with robbery. When more funds are used for criminal justice functions and more manpower is available to the city police, the robbery rate tends to be higher. It makes no sense to think that more expenditures for criminal justice operations and more police manpower tend to contribute to more robbery in the community. This finding may indicate the pattern of policy response to the rising crime rate in the community. What is not apparent, but detectable, is this: When robbery rate, along with other crime, goes up, the public pressure for more police protection and tougher criminal justice operations ensues. Policy decisions responding to public pressure of this nature increase expenditures and expand manpower for law enforcement and criminal justice, but reduction in robbery rate does not follow.[21]

Two service policies are significantly related to the robbery rate: CAC expenditure positively and low-rent public housing inversely. Although public housing in general, and low-rent public housing in particular, are

TABLE 6.3
Relationships Between Robbery and Public Policy
Controlling Major Criminogenic Variables
in the 49 Large U.S. Cities, 1970

Criminogenic Variables Controlled	r	Partial	F Value	R² Change
% Families Headed by Female	0.636	N.C.	4.63	N.I.
Population Density	0.604	N.C.	11.80	N.I.
% Nonwhite Population	0.595	N.C.	4.52	N.I.
P.C. Income	0.316	N.C.	3.14	N.I.
$R = 0.796$				
$R^2 = 0.633$				
Control Policies				
P.C. Exp. for Police	0.757	0.312	4.32	0.036
P.C. Exp. for Court	0.622	0.374	6.50	0.051
P.C. Exp. for Correct.	0.598	0.281	3.43	0.029
P.C. Exp. for Total Criminal Justice	0.759	0.359	5.90	0.047
Police Employees Per 100,000 Population	0.739	0.330	4.87	0.040
Sworn Police Per 100,000 Population	0.727	0.333	4.99	0.041
Local % State-Local Court Exp.	0.176	0.264	3.00	0.026
Service Policies				
P.C. Exp. by CAC	0.306	0.249	2.63	0.023
Low-Rent Public Housing	0.278	−0.311	4.28	0.035

N.C. = Not Computed
N.I. = Not Included

often criticized and degraded for being less than suitable for human habitation and for being a breeding ground of crime, the presence of more low-rent public housing in the community is strongly correlated with lower homicide rate and lower robbery rate. Residents in public housing may find that life there is more normal and stable than the learned critics view it from outside.[22]

Aggravated Assault

Table 6.4 shows that two control policies and three service policies are significantly related to aggravated assault. Local decentralism of police expenditure tends to be closely associated with lower rate of aggravated assault in the community.[23] When local prisons are overcrowded, however, the rate of aggravated assault tends to be higher.

The OEO expenditure does not seem to help cut crimes. Rather, a higher level of OEO expenditure is associated with a higher rate of assault. It

TABLE 6.4
Relationships Between Aggravated Assault and
Public Policy Controlling Major Criminogenic
Variables in the 49 Large U.S. Cities, 1970

Criminogenic Variables Controlled	r	Partial	F Value	R² Change
% Families Headed by Female	0.489	N.C.	8.75	N.I.
% Housing Crowded	0.372	N.C.	5.35	N.I.
% Population Under 18	−0.123	N.C.	2.78	N.I.
$R = 0.582$				
$R^2 = 0.338$				
Control Policy				
Local % State-Local Exp. for Police	−0.092	−0.283	3.58	0.053
Prison Crowdedness	0.284	0.266	3.12	0.047
Service Policy				
P.C. Exp. by OEO	0.374	0.281	3.54	0.053
P.C. Exp. for Parks and Recreation	−0.066	−0.266	3.12	0.047
P.C. Exp. for Local Schools	0.230	0.249	2.72	0.041

N.C. = Not Computed
N.I. = Not Included

TABLE 6.5
Relationships Between Burglary and Public Policy
Controlling Major Criminogenic Variables
in the 49 Large U.S. Cities, 1970

Criminogenic Variables Controlled	r	Partial	F Value	R² Change
% Male	0.477	N.C.	11.98	N.I.
% Nonwhite	0.405	N.C.	7.79	N.I.
$R = 0.589$				
$R^2 = 0.346$				
Control Policy				
Local % State-Local Exp. for Police	0.071	−0.217	2.05	0.030
Prison Facilities	0.066	−0.264	3.16	0.046
Service Policy				
P.C. Exp. by CAC	0.363	0.238	2.52	0.037
P.C. Exp. for Sanitation	0.070	−0.239	2.55	0.037
P.C. Exp. for Parks and Recreation	0.026	−0.235	2.45	0.036

N.C. = Not Computed
N.I. = Not Included

may be that the distribution of OEO funds are more favorable to those cities where crime problems are more serious along with other urban problems. A higher spending for recreation is associated with a lower rate of aggravated assault. More expenditure for local schools is, curiously enough, significantly associated with a higher assault rate.

Burglary

When the local percentage of state-local expenditure for police is high and local prison facilities are more comprehensive, burglary rate in the community tends to be lower (see Table 6.5). A higher level of expenditures for sanitation and recreation is strongly correlated with a lower rate of burglary, but CAC expenditure is positively correlated with burglary as in the case of robbery and aggravated assault.

Larceny

Public policies as represented in this study are totally unrelated with larceny except for the expenditure level for parks and recreation. As shown in Table 6.6, only per capita expenditure for parks and recreation shows a significant inverse correlation with larceny.

TABLE 6.6
Relationships Between Larceny and Public Policy
Controlling Major Criminogenic Variables
in the 49 Large U.S. Cities, 1970

Criminogenic Variables Controlled	r	Partial	F Value	R^2 Change
% Population Under 18	−0.429	N.C.	11.70	N.I.
% Single Family Housing Value Assessed	0.031	N.C.	11.77	N.I.
% Owner-Occupancy	−0.216	N.C.	5.25	N.I.
% Comm. and Indust. Property Assessed	−0.002	N.C.	2.81	N.I.
Median Value of Owner-Occupied Housing	0.214	N.C.	2.10	N.I.
$R = 0.618$				
$R^2 = 0.381$				
Control Policy	— — —	— — —	— — —	— — —
Service Policy				
P.C. Exp. for Parks and Recreation	0.080	−0.328	4.70	0.067

N.C. = Not Computed
N.I. = Not Included

TABLE 6.7
Relationships Between Auto Theft and Public Policy
Controlling Major Criminogenic Variables
in the 49 Large U.S. Cities, 1970

Criminogenic Variables Controlled	r	Partial	F Value	R^2 Change
% Commercial and Industrial Property	0.635	N.C.	15.31	N.I.
% Male	0.453	N.C.	7.53	N.I.
% Families Headed by Female	0.465	N.C.	2.76	N.I.
$R = 0.727$				
$R^2 = 0.528$				
Control Policy				
Monthly Pay for Prison Employees	0.146	−0.363	6.22	0.062
Service Policy				
P.C. Exp. by CAC	0.287	0.257	2.90	0.031
P.C. Exp. for Parks and Recreation	−0.124	−0.322	4.74	0.049
P.C. Exp. for Schools	0.007	−0.232	2.34	0.025

N.C. = Not Computed
N.I. = Not Included

TABLE 6.8
Relationships Between the Percent Change in Willful
Homicide Rate from 1965 to 1970 and Public Policy
Controlling Major Criminogenic Variables
in the 49 Large U.S. Cities

Criminogenic Variables Controlled	r	Partial	F Value	R^2 Change
Commercial and Industrial Property, 1967	0.466	N.C.	3.778	N.I.
Change in White Population, 1960–70	−0.455	N.C.	2.884	N.I.
Retail Sales, 1967	0.311	N.C.	2.256	N.I.
$R = 0.563$				
$R^2 = 0.317$				
Control Policy	---	---	---	---
Service Policy				
Low Rent Public Housing	0.097	−0.285	3.628	0.056
Per Capita Expenditure for Sanitation	0.371	0.242	2.557	0.040

N.C. = Not Computed
N.I. = Not Included

Auto Theft

Only one control policy variable, professionalism measure of prison employees, reveals an inverse relation to auto theft, implying that auto theft is less frequent when the prison employees are better paid (see Table 6.7). Of the service policies, when expenditures for parks and recreation and for schools are kept high, auto theft is low. But the CAC expenditure is positively associated with auto theft as the OEO and CAC expenditures are with other crimes such as burglary, assault, and robbery.

TABLE 6.9
Relationships Between the Percent Change in Forcible
Rape Rate from 1965 to 1970 and Public Policy
Controlling Major Criminogenic Variables
in the 49 Large U.S. Cities

Criminogenic Variables Controlled	r	Partial	F Value	R² Change
Rent, 1970	0.474	N.C.	15.869	N.I.
Median Value of Owner-Occupied Housing, 1970	−0.066	N.C.	9.862	N.I.
P.C. Income (SMSA), 1968	−0.072	N.C.	5.676	N.I.
% Male, 1970	0.285	N.C.	7.731	N.I.
P.C. Retail Sales, 1967	−0.158	N.C.	7.363	N.I.
$R = 0.706$				
$R^2 = 0.498$				
Control Policy				
P.C. Exp. for Police, 1969–70	−0.007	−0.370	6.198	0.069
P.C. Exp. for Court, 1969–70	−0.010	−0.318	4.388	0.051
P.C. Exp. for Correction, 1969–70	0.009	−0.361	5.840	0.065
P.C. Exp. for All Criminal Justice Functions, 1969–70	0.006	−0.402	7.528	0.081
Police Dept. Emp., 1970	0.064	−0.388	6.901	0.075
Sworn Police Officers, 1970	0.029	−0.367	6.077	0.068
% Local, State-Local Exp. for all Criminal Justice Exp., 1968–69	0.010	−0.267	2.993	0.036
% Local, State-Local Exp., 1968–69	−0.364	−0.297	3.765	0.044
% Local, State-Local Correction Exp., 1968–69	−0.049	−0.352	5.514	0.062
Prison Crowdedness	0.131	−0.316	4.335	0.050
Service Policy				
P.C. Exp. for Schools, 1969–70	−0.391	−0.345	5.277	0.060

N.C. = Not Computed
N.I. = Not Included

Crime Rate Trend

The policy and ecological variables employed in the present study seem to be generally incapable of accounting for the variance in the crime rate trends. As shown in Tables 6.8, 6.9, and 6.10, the statistical evidence revealed by this analysis generally suggests that there is rather limited policy impact on the crime rate trends as such. Only two service policy measures are significantly correlated with homicide rate change, while ten control policy variables and a service policy measure are significantly correlated with rape rate trend. Only one service policy measure is inversely and significantly correlated with robbery rate trend. Neither ecological variables nor policy variables are systematically related to other measures of crime rate trends.

Moreover, some impact detectable does not lend itself to sensible interpretation. For example, low rent public housing is inversely related to homicide rate change, while sanitation expenditure is related positively to the same variable. In such a case, the findings tend to add confusion instead of providing a meaningful explanation.

SUMMARY AND CONCLUSION

Table 6.11 shows all of the policy variables that are significantly correlated with one or more crime variables while holding appropriate control variables constant. Sixteen of the twenty-one control policy variables (76.2 per-

TABLE 6.10
Relationships Between the Percent Change in Robbery
Rate from 1965 to 1970 and Public Policy
Controlling Major Criminogenic Variables
in the 49 Large U.S. Cities

Criminogenic Variables Controlled	r	Partial	F Value	R² Change
Population, 1970	0.468	N.C.	12.498	N.I.
% Non-White, 1970	0.199	N.C.	6.087	N.I.
$R = 0.562$				
$R^2 = 0.316$				
Control Policy	---	---	---	---
Service Policy				
P.C. Exp. for Sanitation, 1969–70	0.538	0.337	5.372	0.078

N.C. = Not Computed
N.I. = Not Included

TABLE 6.11
Relationships Between Policy Variables and Crime Variables: A Summary

Control Policy	Crime Rates							Crime Rate Trends			
	HOMICIDE	FORCIBLE RAPE	ROBBERY	AGGRA. ASSAULT	BURGLARY	LARCENY	AUTO THEFT	HOMICIDE	FORCIBLE RAPE	ROBBERY	Total
Exp. for Police			+						—		2
Exp. for Court			+						—		2
Exp. for Correct.			+						—		2
Exp. for All Justice			+				—				2
Patrolman's Salary-Ent.		—									1
Pay for Prison Employees	—						—				2
Police Dept. Employees			+						—		2
Sworn Officers			+						—		2
Employee-Inmate Ratio	—										1
Prison Crowdedness	+			+					—		3
Prison Facilities					—						1

TABLE 6.11 (continued)

Control Policy	Crime Rates							Crime Rate Trends			
	HOMICIDE	FORCIBLE RAPE	ROBBERY	AGGRA. ASSAULT	BURGLARY	LARCENY	AUTO THEFT	HOMICIDE	FORCIBLE RAPE	ROBBERY	Total
Pre-Trial Inmate	+										1
Local %, All Justice Exp.									−		1
Local %, Police Exp.				−	−						2
Local %, Court Exp.			+						−		2
Local %, Correct. Exp.									−		1
Service Policies											
OEO. Exp.				+							1
CAC. Exp.				+	+		+				3
Exp. for Schools			−				−		−		3
Low-Rent Public Housing	−		−					−			3
Exp. for Sanitat.	−	−						+		−	4
Exp. for Parks & Rec.	−			−	−	−	−				5
Total	6	2	9	5	5	1	5	2	10	1	46

+ = A positive relation (partial r)
− = An inverse relation (partial r)

283

cent) and six of the seven service policy measures (85.7 percent) are significantly correlated with one or more crime variables. This finding does indicate that service policies affect crime rates more often than control policies. It is also evident that policy impact is more clearly discernible in crime rates than in crime rate trends.

The relationships of the policy measures to the crime rate variance are not always consistent and sensible. In general, when policy levels are high for services for environment and for professionalism of criminal justice employees, prison manpower, prison facilities, judicial procedures, and localization of criminal justice financing, the occurrence of various crimes tends to be significantly less frequent. On the other hand, when the policy levels are high as measured by expenditures for various criminal justice functions, police manpower, and services for opportunities, the crime rates tend to be correspondingly high.

These findings support a conclusion that a high level of correctional policies and environmental service policies is most likely to be a significant deterrent. Better financing for criminal justice systems, more police manpower, and more opportunity services, however, are not likely to deter crimes. What implications does this conclusion offer for an ordering of public policy priorities for a more effective crime deterrence? The answer is: (1) improve correctional policies including manpower, professionalism, facilities, and procedures; and (2) improve service policies for the enhancement of environmental quality. After all, the often-heard argument that the inhumane punishment-oriented correctional system must be revamped to reduce recidivism and to cut crimes evidently points to the right track to follow as a step toward an effective crime control policy, the deterrence of crime.

NOTES

1. The works representing comparative policy analysis are too numerous to list all of them here. To cite just a few, see Alan K. Campbell and Seymour Sacks, *Metropolitan America: Fiscal Patterns and Governmental Systems* (New York: The Free Press, 1967); Thomas R. Dye, *Politics, Economics, and the Public* (Chicago: Rand McNally, 1966); and Ira Sharkansky, *The Politics of Taxing and Spending* (Indianapolis: The Bobbs-Merrill Co., 1969).
2. Ira Sharkansky, *ibid.*, chap. 6.
3. Thomas R. Dye, "Malapportionment and Public Policy in the States," *Journal of Politics*, 27 (August, 1965) and his *Politics, Economics, and the Public*; Alan Pulsipher and James Weatherby, "Malapportionment, Party Competition, and the Functional Distribution of Government Expenditures," *American Political Science Review*, 62 (December, 1968), 1207–1219; and H. George Frederick-

son and Yong Hyo Cho, "Legislative Apportionment and Fiscal Policy in the American States," a paper delivered at the Annual Meeting of the American Political Science Association, September, 1970, Los Angeles, California.

4. Akron is included in our sample, for Akron is one of the major cities in the northeastern Ohio region which is the project area of the parental study of which this paper is a part.

5. For a discussion on the difficulty in policy experimentation, see Lee Bawden and William Harrar, "The Use of Experimentation in Policy Formulation and Evaluation," a paper presented at the 1972 National Conference of the American Society for Public Administration, Statler-Hilton Hotel, New York City, March 21–25, 1972.

6. For federal experiences, see Aaron Wildavsky, *The Politics of the Budgetary Process* (Boston: Little, Brown, 1964); for state-local experiences, Ira Sharkansky, *The Politics of Taxing and Spending* (Indianapolis: The Bobbs-Merrill Co., 1969), chap. V; and for municipal experiences, John P. Crecine, "A Simulation of Municipal Budgeting: The Impact of Problem Environment," in Ira Sharkansky (ed.) *Policy Analysis in Political Science* (Chicago: Markham Publishing Co., 1970); and his *Government Problem Solving: A Computer Simulation of Municipal Budgeting* (Chicago: Rand McNally, 1968). Most of all, Charles E. Lindblom made perhaps the greatest contribution to the development of the theory of incremental policymaking. See his, "The Science of Muddling Through," *Public Administration Review* (Spring, 1959), pp. 79–88; and "Decision-Making in Taxation and Expenditure," in *Public Finance: Needs, Resources and Utilization* (Princeton: National Bureau of Economic Research, 1961), pp. 295–336.

7. See, for example, Frank D. Bean and Robert G. Cushing, "Criminal Homicide, Punishment, and Deterrence: Methodological and Substantive Reconsideration," *Social Science Quarterly* (November, 1971), pp. 277–289; Charles R. Tittle, "Crime Rates and Legal Sanction," *Social Problems*, 16 (Spring, 1969), pp. 409–423; and Louis N. Gray and J. David Martin, "Punishment and Deterrence: Another Analysis of Gibbs' Data," *Social Science Quarterly*, 50 (September, 1969), pp. 389–395; Jack P. Gibbs, "Crime, Punishment, and Deterrence," *Social Science Quarterly*, 48 (March, 1968).

8. "Government Expenditures and Public Services in the American States," *American Political Science Review* (December, 1967), pp. 1066–1077.

9. See, for example, Calvin F. Schmid, "Urban Crime Areas: Part I," *American Sociological Review*, 25 (August, 1960), 527–542; Calvin F. Schmid, "Urban Crime Areas: Part II," *American Sociological Review*, 25 (October, 1960), 655–678; Roland J. Chilton, "Continuity in Delinquency Area Research: A Comparison of Studies for Baltimore, Detroit, and Indianapolis," *American Sociological Review*, 29 (February, 1964), 71–83; Judith A. Wilks, "Ecological Correlates of Crime and Delinquency," in the President's Commission on Law Enforcement and Administration of Justice, Task Force Report: *Crime and Its Impact—An Assessment* (Washington: U.S. Government Printing Office, 1967); Karl Schuessler and Gerald Slatin, "Sources of Variation in U.S. City Crime, 1950 and 1960," *Journal of Research in Crime and Delinquency*, 1 (July, 1964), 127–148; Karl Schuessler, "Components of Variation in City

Crime Rates," *Social Problems*, **9** (Spring, 1962); and Richard Quinney, "Structural Characteristics, Population Areas, and Crime Rates in the United States," *The Journal of Criminal Law, Criminology, and Police Science*, **57** (1966), 45–52.

10. The computer program used for this operation is "Stepwise Multiple Regression Analysis," *SPSS*, Version of March 13, 1971.

11. Every one of the criminogenic variables selected for each crime variable is simultaneously significant at 0.05 level based on the *F* value of the variable and the degree of freedom of the regression equation. Some ecological variables so selected are common for more than one crime measure, while some others are unique for a particular crime variable. The ecological variables selected and controlled as criminogenic variables for each crime variable are shown in the tabular presentation of the findings, but they are not discussed in this paper.

12. Some statistically insignificant independent variables are often retained in a regression as control variables on the ground that these variables are conceptually relevant. Even though they are considered to have a conceptual relevancy in an a priori logic, when statistical or empirical evidence does not back it up, their conceptual relevancy remains yet to be proved. For some studies controlling statistically insignificant variables for statistical tests, see Thomas R. Dye, *Politics, Economics, and the Public* (Chicago: Rand McNally, 1966); Ira Sharkansky, "Regionalism, Economic Status, and the Public Policies of American States," *Social Science Quarterly* (June, 1968), pp. 9–26; and Kent P. Schwirian and Anthony J. Lagreca, "An Ecological Analysis of Urban Mortality Rates," *Social Science Quarterly* (December, 1971), pp. 575–587.

13. For a discussion on the performance of additive and multiplicative models in regression analysis, see Walter Dean Burnham and John Sprague, "Additive and Multiplicative Models of the Voting Universe: The Case of Pennsylvania: 1960–1968," *American Political Science Review*, **64** (June, 1970), 471–490; Frank D. Bean and Robert G. Cushing, *op. cit.*; and Hubert M. Blalock, *Social Statistics* (New York: McGraw-Hill, 1960), p. 313.

14. See, for example, Marvin E. Wolfgang, "Urban Crime," in James Q. Wilson (ed.), *Metropolitan Enigma* (Garden City: Doubleday & Company, Inc., 1970), pp. 270–311; Sophia M. Robinson, "A Critical View of the Uniform Crime Reports," *Michigan Law Review*, **64** (April, 1966), 1031–1054; and especially, the President's Commission on Law Enforcement and Administration of Justice, *The Challenge of Crime in a Free Society* (Washington: U.S. Government Printing Office, 1967), pp. 20–22.

15. See Wolfgang, *ibid.*, p. 294.

16. The data sources for control policy variables are as follows: The four variables of financing policies are derived from the Bureau of the Census, *City Government Finances in 1969–70*. Variables 5, 6, 8, 9, 12, 13, and 14 are derived from International City Management Association, *The Municipal Yearbook*, 1971. Variables 7, 11, 15, 16, and 17 are derived from the unpublished data furnished by Law Enforcement Assistance Administration which was gathered by the 1970 local jail census. Variable 10 was derived from Bureau of the Census, *Local Government Employment in Selected Metropolitan Areas and Large Counties: 1970*. Variables 18, 19, 20, and 21 are derived from Law Enforcement

Assistance Administration and Bureau of the Census, *Expenditure and Employment Data for the Criminal Justice System, 1968–1969.*

17. Variables 22 and 23 are derived from Bureau of the Census, *Statistical Abstract,* 1970. Variables 27 and 28 are derived from Bureau of the Census, *City Government Finances in 1969–70.* Variable 24 is derived from Bureau of the Census, *Local Government Finances in Selected Metropolitan Areas and Large Counties: 1969–70.* Variable 25 is derived from HEW, *Education Directory: Public School Systems, 1969–1970* and Bureau of the Census, *Local Government Employment in Selected Metropolitan Areas and Large Counties: 1970.* Variable 26 is derived from HUD, *Local Authorities Participating in Low-Rent Housing Programs as of December 31, 1970.*

18. For example, to compute total local correctional expenditures per capita for the city of Akron, we first computed the city expenditure for correction per capita. Then we computed the county expenditure for correction per capita, using the total population in the county including the city population. Assuming that city use of the county-provided services for correction is equal to other residents elsewhere within the county, the two per capita expenditure figures for correction are combined to develop total local expenditures for correction in the city of Akron or whichever government it is that provides the service. Similar procedures have been followed wherever multiple government units provide a given service in the city area included in our sample.

19. The data sources for ecological variables are as follows: Variable 13 is derived from *Statistical Abstract, 1970.* Variable 16 is derived from Bureau of the Census, Census of Business: 1967, *Retail Trade Area Statistics, Parts I, II and III* (Washington: U.S. Government Printing Office, 1970). Variables 17, 18, and 19 are derived from Bureau of the Census, Census of Government: 1967, *Taxable Property Values* (Washington: U.S. Government Printing Office, 1968). All the other variables are derived from Bureau of the Census, Census of Population: 1970, *General Population Characteristics,* Final Report PC(1)-B (Washington: U.S. Government Printing Office, 1971) and *1970 Census of Population and Housing,* Final Report PHC(2)-2.

20. Bean and Cushing faced a similar dilemma in their interpretation of the relationship of the certainty index of punishment to lower crime rate. See *op.cit.*

21. For example, more expenditures for police and increased police manpower in particular do not necessarily improve police protection, as Dr. Savas illustrates with the experience of the New York City police. See E. S. Savas, "Municipal Monopoly," *Harper's Magazine* (December, 1971), pp. 55–60.

22. Robert Coles' works on various groups of American poor in rural as well as urban areas shed a new light on the life of these economically and socially disadvantaged groups including, perhaps, those living in public housing. See the cover story of *Time,* February 14, 1972.

23. This finding contradicts the general contention that a centralized law enforcement system such as state control or regionalization of law enforcement systems will be more effective in crime control. See, for example, June Romine and Daniel L. Skoler, "Local Government Financing and Law Enforcement," *The American County* (May, 1971), pp. 17–43; and Dae Hong Chang, "Police Reorganization a Deterrent to Crime," *Police,* 12 (April, 1968), 73–79.

PROCESS VERSUS IMPACT EVALUATION OF COMMUNITY CORRECTIONS

Dennis Palumbo
Elaine Sharp

In 1977, with the passage of its Community Correction Act, Kansas joined a handful of states and counties that have committed themselves to a policy of community corrections. The essence of community corrections is that incarceration of offenders in state penal institutions should be minimized, and that, except for those committing certain violent crimes, i.e., rape and murder, supervision and rehabilitative efforts at the community level are preferable. The decentralized community corrections approach is, in part, a response to the rising costs of incarceration in prisons, but perhaps more so, it is based on the failure of existing penal institutions to rehabilitate offenders. Community corrections, therefore, is an important new turn in corrections policy.

How can we determine whether or not community corrections are successful? The typical response to this question is to conduct an impact-evaluation study of existing community corrections programs to see whether they are achieving their goals. Yet, because process evaluation looks at how the policy is being implemented instead of just looking at its impact, it is a more effective way to evaluate community corrections. It is this method that we use in this paper. A model of implementation is needed in order to do a process evaluation, and such a model is presented in this paper. Finally, the model is applied to community corrections in Kansas as a means of indicating the ways in which survey data collected during the initial stage of implementation are a crucial part of process evaluation.

PROCESS AND IMPACT EVALUATION

Two distinct types of evaluation are usually recognized by evaluation researchers: (1) process and (2) impact evaluation. David Nachmias wrote that process evaluation "is concerned with the extent to which a particular policy or program is implemented according to its stated guidelines" while impact evaluation "is concerned with examining the extent to which a policy causes a change in the intended direction."[1] In the most concise terms, impact evaluation is the study of the extent to which goals have been achieved, whereas process evaluation is the study of how a program has been implemented.

Two major difficulties with impact evaluation suggest that it should not be done in the absence of process evaluation. First is the question of how to conduct an impact evaluation for a policy that has vague or conflicting program goals. Impact evaluation ". . . calls for delineation of operationally defined policy goals, specification of criteria of success, and measurement of progress toward the goals."[2] But many programs have vague goals, and, at times, they may have several general and even contradictory goals. For example the Kansas Community Corrections Act states that two of its goals are to "protect society" and also to "promote economy in the delivery of correctional services."[3] In addition to the fact that protecting society is a vague goal, these two goals may be in conflict because it may be impossible to protect society and, at the same time, promote economy. If so, has the policy failed? And which of these two goals should be given priority in an evaluation? Process evaluation helps answer these questions because, when we follow the process of implementation, we can see the specific meanings that are given to these goals as the policy is implemented.

Second, there is the problem of interpreting impact-evaluation results. An impact evaluation that shows that the stated goals have not been achieved does not tell us whether the failure is due to a flaw in the theory underlying the policy or to poor implementation. Only through process evaluation can the latter be determined. Impact evaluation can show whether a program has succeeded or failed, but it is not designed to show why a program has failed, or whether the program has succeeded only because program goals were modified during implementation.

Process evaluation is particularly useful as an alternative form of evaluation when the objective is to describe how a program is being implemented. It also can be used with impact evaluation. In fact we contend that an impact evaluation should not be conducted without an accompanying process evaluation. Impact evaluation is static analysis, analogous to a snapshot taken at one instant in time. It represents the situation at that instant, but if the picture is taken at a time when things are changing, then it gives a false idea of what is happening or what the final impact will be. Process evaluation, on the other hand, is dynamic analysis; it enables researchers to follow changes as they occur and to identify the point at which a policy becomes institutionalized and changes cease. At this time an impact analysis should be conducted, because only then can the final impact be measured.

Thomas Smith wrote: "Governmental policies are designed to induce change in society. By the implementation of governmental policies, old patterns of interaction and institutions are abolished or modified and new patterns of action and institutions are created."[4] Process evaluation is the study of the development and institutionalization of these new patterns of interaction. By focusing on change and on the context of program implementation, process evaluation can show why a program has or has not achieved certain goals, and why and how the goals come to be defined and redefined during their implementation.

Impact evaluations have been done with respect to community-corrections programs in several states.[5] These studies focus on the extent to which recidivism is reduced, public safety maintained, and costs controlled. Some evaluations have found that recidivism and costs are lower for offenders sent to community-corrections programs as compared to those sent to prisons, while others have found the opposite. Without a process evaluation it is impossible to determine why the results are so disparate.

MODEL FOR PROCESS EVALUATION— CONCEPTUALIZING THE IMPLEMENTATION PROCESS

While there is a model for impact evaluation—that is, the impact-effectiveness model that is based on experimental design,[6]—there is no comparable model for process evaluation. Mostly, this is because process evaluation requires a theory of the implementation process. In order to tell if what happens during a particular implementation is good or bad, one needs to know what is supposed to occur. But no theory of implementation exists for community-corrections programs,[7] although some research has produced building blocks that make it possible to develop a model of policy implementation that can, in turn, be used to guide a process evaluation of community corrections. These blocks are used to develop the model of the implementation process that follows.

The heart of the approach to process evaluation is the notion that implementation is a continuation of the change process that is initiated at the policy-formulation stage. Pressman and Wildavsky defined implementation as "a process of interaction between the setting of goals and the actions geared to achieving them."[8] Similarly, Berman emphasized that implementation involves a mutual adaptation between a program and the organizational setting for implementation.[9] Neither of these definitions say that policy goals invariably will be or *should* be implemented according to the way they were initially conceived. Both definitions indicate that goals generally are adapted or changed during the implementation of a policy. The appropriate question, then, to ask about implementation is: How much change can be expected to occur during implementation? There will be changes in the goals, changes in the implementing agency, and, if the policy is successful, changes in the target group at which the policy is aimed. Thus, in community corrections, for example, one would expect that the goal of protecting society will change during implementation to a more specific and concrete goal. This is called the goal-clarification process. Clarification occurs as the implementing agency fits the policy into its standard operating routines, as negotiation takes place among the various agencies involved in implementation, and in response to pressures put on the implementing agency by various elite groups, including community notables, legislators, and other active groups.

Of course, not all of the changes that occur are positive or move in the direction intended by the policy; otherwise, there would have been many more successful public policies than there have been. Negative changes do occur, including the substitution of goals that are contrary to those originally intended by the policy, a complete breakdown in the implementation process, or inept or inadequate implementation. This is called the goal-dissolution process. For example this might occur in community corrections if no one adopted the program and the state rejected the policy. Gross et al describe an example of this when they write about how an educational agreement originally endorsed heartily by teachers and administrators slowly dissolved until the teachers came to oppose the policy.[10] Pressman and Wildavsky also describe how disagreement over the Economic Development Act (EDA) program in Oakland (California) came to the surface during implementation, thereby making the sustenance of the goals originally conceived by planners impossible.[11]

Implementation involves change and, therefore, the purpose of process evaluation is to determine how much change occurs and to study the conditions that produce goal clarification and goal dissolution. Three groups of factors are related to the change process during implementation: policy, organizational, and political characteristics.

Policy Characteristics

The first two characteristics of policy are the specificity of policy goals and the extent or scale of change intended. Policies that are vague and general as opposed to being specific and policies that are designed to accomplish large-scale as opposed to small-scale change have a greater likelihood of ending in goal dissolution rather than in goal clarification. Two outcomes are likely for such goals: agreement on goals may dissolve so that no impact at all occurs, or more likely, goals will be considerably changed in the implementation process so that something quite different than was originally intended is actually achieved. But whether the change that occurs is positive (clarification) or negative (dissolution) depends upon the organizational and political characteristics of the policy setting, which are discussed in greater detail later.

A third important characteristic of policy is its complexity. Pressman and Wildavsky note that in their study of the implementation of an EDA program in Oakland, a number of implementation problems were due to the complexity of the policy involved.[12] Where a large number of implementing agencies were involved, where administration involved multiple decision points, each of which was contingent on a prior decision, and where the policy design requires joint action among agencies that may not have developed institutionalized patterns of cooperation, the dissolution of goals is a more likely outcome than clarification. Pressman and Wildavsky saw complexity as leading to dissolution, and hence, to implementation failure, but it is also possible that other characteristics of the implementation setting will interact with policy complexity and produce goal clarification rather than dissolution. For example, in the implementation of community corrections in Des Moines, turf battles between agencies at the beginning were overcome, and collaboration among the various agencies developed.[13] Greater complexity does suggest a greater likelihood of goal dissolution, but mutual adaptation is also a possibility.

A fourth policy characteristic is whether policies are optional or mandatory.[14] A mandatory policy is automatically applicable to all cases within the defined scope, whereas choice determines applicability for an optional policy. The mandatory-optional distinction becomes particularly interesting when the process evaluation of intergovernmental policies is considered. Some intergovernmental policies, such as the Federal Water Pollution Control Act, are required by law, and in such situations, process evaluation should focus upon the mechanisms for compliance that are part of the policy package. In these cases the extent and type of goal adaptation becomes a function of the character and effectiveness of the compliance methods used. Many intergovernmental policies are optional; often a policy is formulated at one level of government, but in order for implementation to occur, other units of government must choose to participate. In these cases, process evaluation should focus upon the adoption process and the incentives that are used rather than on the compliance mechanisms.[15] Community corrections involves the latter type of change.

Characteristics of the Implementing Agency

Four policy characteristics which may be expected to have an impact upon the extent and character of goal change in the implementation process have been identified—clarity, scope, complexity, and whether the policy is mandatory or optional. Characteristics of the implementing organizations are also crucial to what happens during implementation. Nimmer noted that reform must conform to the normal behavior within a system, and that there is, therefore, no universally applicable reform package that can be designed for all agencies under all conditions. He wrote that "identical reforms implemented in two or more courts often have dissimilar impacts."[16] This is due, to a great extent, to differences in characteristics of the implementing organizations. Among the factors that are important are an organization's leadership, resources, constituency, and organizational experience. If the leadership understands and is committed to a policy goal, if the organization has a constituency which perceives benefits it will receive from the policy, if adequate resources are available, and if the structure of the organization is such as to maximize compliance by all personnel with the leadership's policy commitments, then goal change during implementation is minimized, and there is little chance that a dissolution will occur.

The organizational setting for implementation, however, should be viewed as involving groups with varying self-interests, commitments, and resources. The organizational context for implementation, wrote Bunker, may usefully be thought of as a series of leverage points.[17] He suggests that actors in an implementing organization vary in terms of their agreement with the policy, their power resources, and the salience of the policy issue to them. The organizational context for implementation may be seen as a three-dimensional space, and "each of the actors potentially involved with the implementation at issue may be located at some point in this three-dimensional space."[18] The implementation process is viewed as the series of strategies by which individuals can be moved toward positions in this space that facilitate implementation of the policy. For example one individual may be high in political power and agree with the policy goal, but the policy goal may not be very salient to him or her. A successful implementation strategy would aim at increasing the salience of the policy issue for that person.

Our theory of implementation suggests that process evaluation must focus upon the perspectives of various actors at various levels of influence within the implementing organization, and upon the strategies and incentives that have the potential for moving them to positions favorable to positive, rather than negative, goal change. To do this may require getting the person or group's agreement to a policy goal, increasing the salience of the goal to them, or increasing the power resources required to carry out the goal.

Implicit in the foregoing discussion is the notion that the congruence of the policy with institutionalized patterns of interest in the organization may be expected to condition the implementation process. The self-interests of those responsible for implementing the policy are crucial for successful adoption. Robert Yin argued that in public bureaucracies, innovations are more likely to be adopted if they appeal to the self-interest of the organization, which usually consists of "its growth, increase in hierarchical status, or likelihood of survival."[19] Yin distinguished between two innovative processes: a rational, problem-solving process, which is likely to result when the external environment yields a demand for improved performance, and a bureaucratic process, which is dependent upon the perceived survival needs of the organization. Policy formulated on the basis of a rational, problem-solving approach, which pays little attention to the survival needs of implementing agencies, is more likely to lead to dissolution of goals. On the other hand policy that is congruent with organizational self-interests is more likely to be implemented with less change.

Characteristics of the Political Setting

The political setting in which the implementing organization operates also influences the way a policy is implemented. Research on innovations and policy implementation suggests that the crucial political variables include the character of elite support for the policy and the extent to which target groups are mobilized to support the policy. Van Horn and Van Meter, for example, wrote:

> Where the problems to be remedied by a program are severe and private citizens and interest groups are mobilized in support of a program, it is more likely that implementors will accept the policy's goals and objectives. Officials are compelled to accede to program standards by political demands within their jurisdictions.[20]

In contrast they note that the political environment can provide a resource for actors opposed to implementation, particularly with respect to intergovernmental policy:

> The impact of federal enforcement activities may be mitigated when state and local implementors are opposed to certain aspects of the program and can enlist the support of organizational superiors or their congressional delegations.[21]

The importance of political setting on policy innovation is also noted by Yin who, in his analysis of 140 case studies of technological innovation, found that those that are supported by a mayor or chief executive are more likely to be incorporated into an organization's regular bureaucratic routine than those that do not have such support.[22]

PROCESS EVALUATION AND THE
KANSAS COMMUNITY CORRECTIONS ACT

How does this model of the implementation process relate to an evaluation of community corrections? As noted earlier, the essence of community corrections, in Kansas and elsewhere, is the idea that incarceration of offenders in isolated state penal institutions should be minimized. It is based on the premise that rehabilitation will be much more successful if it is conducted with the participation of the community to which the offender is supposed to adapt. The community-corrections approach incorporates a host of corrections policy initiatives, such as the expanded use of probation and parole, supervised work-release programs, and rehabilitative counseling efforts. But the community-corrections program incorporates this variety of corrections policies in a special way. Like many of the urban programs of the 1960s, community corrections is first and foremost a decentralization program. It is structured to allow communities to develop their own unique approaches to the handling of offenders. This is particularly evident in the Kansas Community Corrections Act, which provides the structure and financial incentives for counties to adopt a community-corrections program, but does not mandate participation in the program or even specify the correctional methods that communities should use.

Specifically, the Kansas Act authorizes the state's Secretary of Corrections to make grants to counties for the development, implementation, operation, and improvement of community-correctional services. In order to qualify for grants, counties must create a corrections advisory board composed of a sheriff, chief of police, county district attorney, district court judge, education professional, representative appointed by the state's Secretary of Social and Rehabilitation Services, three members appointed by county commissioners, and three members appointed by cities in the county or in a set of cooperating counties. Participating counties must develop a comprehensive plan, which must be approved by the Secretary of Corrections. All counties with a population over 30,000 are eligible for the program. Smaller counties may enter the program either through multicounty cooperative arrangements or through special authorization by the Secretary of Corrections.

Upon approval of the comprehensive plan, the county (or multicounty unit) qualifies for receipt of a grant, the amount of which is based upon a formula derived from per-capita income, per-capita taxable valuation, crimes per-one-thousand population, and percent of county population between five and twenty-nine years of age. Each county receiving grants is charged for the per diem costs for persons from the county who are committed to the Secretary of Corrections for confinement except for those convicted of certain classes of felonies. These costs, and the costs of any other correctional services the county wishes to purchase by contract from the state, are deducted from the county's grant, with the stipulation that the amount charged to a county may not exceed the amount of the grant for which it is eligible.

A number of variables are related to how the act will be implemented once it is adopted by a county. First, there is the clarity and scope of the policy. As we said above, the Kansas legislation has vague and general goals, and it involves large-scale change. In addition the program is open-ended with respect to the intermediate goals required to achieve the goals stated in the act. The specific rehabilitative methods and corrections innovations are expected to emerge from a county's comprehensive planning process; they are not stipulated in the act. The act is structured to promote goal clarification at the county level; hence, considerable change in goals during implementation, in addition to variations from county to county, are to be expected.

That the Kansas community corrections effort is a complex policy innovation is indicated by the fact that only one county made much progress toward implementing the program in the first year after the bill was passed. To be adopted, community corrections requires a large degree of interagency cooperation among courts, attorneys, probation and parole officers, social service agencies, volunteer groups, law-enforcement officials, state and local elected officials, and business and community leaders. A particular individual or group of individuals must also make a special effort to get the program started.

The policy is complex not only in the number of groups involved, but in the fact that joint action is required among them. Implementation of community corrections by any one county requires, at a minimum, the following: (1) that a community-corrections county advisory committee be set up and agree on a comprehensive plan; (2) that the plan be approved by the Secretary of Corrections; (3) that judges act in accord with the spirit of the plan; (4) that social-service agencies be available to provide the required services; (5) that law-enforcement officers do not try to sabotage the program; (6) that citizens in the communities not object to having offenders located within the county; (7) that business firms provide jobs for offenders; (8) that probation and parole officers work with the county units that provide social and rehabilitation services; (9) that sufficient physical facilities be made available to house offenders; and (10) that the state department of corrections personnel cooperate with county officials. Because of these requirements, a strong possibility exists that there will be a dissolution of agreement on goals at the outset, and that the act will not be successfully implemented.

This study of the implementation of Community Corrections in Kansas relied upon several methods of collecting data. First, the authors became involved in helping to get the community-corrections program implemented, thus acting in the dual role of being a part of the implementation process while simultaneously attempting to understand it. This participation gives us first-hand access and knowledge about the implementation process that is akin to, but not identical with, participant observation. Second, survey research over time was used as a means of seeing how perceptions of goals change and how various implementation difficulties serve either to overcome or to slow down the implementation process. Most implementation studies are fielded retrospectively so they determine why a program has failed after it has been judged a failure, or, at best, when the process of implementation has already been under way for some time. Such surveys are less likely to show the process of goal change, which is crucial to understanding the implementation process.[23] Time-series data of the kind collected for this study provides base-line data against which changes in goal perspectives, interagency cooperation, and perceptions of implementation difficulties or effective strategies can be measured.

The authors' participation as change agents began six months after the Kansas Community Corrections Act became law. They sponsored a Community Corrections Conference in collaboration with the State Department of Corrections in November 1978. About 250 individuals attended this conference, including social and rehabilitation service workers, police officers, prosecuting attorneys, Department of Corrections personnel, judges, and interested community leaders. The conference was held before any county decided to adopt the program and before the Department of Corrections issued its guidelines for participating counties, thus providing an opportunity for potential participants to receive information about the legislation and to discuss guidelines for preparing comprehensive plans and possible implementation problems.

The initial expectations and goal perceptions of the individuals who attended this conference are important for understanding how community corrections is implemented, because these individuals constitute a large part of the community and state notables who will be involved in implementing the program (for example, the conference's keynote speaker subsequently became the Secretary of Corrections for the state when its new governor was elected). A questionnaire was administered to all conference participants. Follow-up questionnaires were planned for the first two years of implementation, several of which were administered at regional conferences held in fall 1979. The questionnaires were designed to show the dynamics of changes in goals.

The questionnaire data collected at the November 1978 conference revealed a number of potential implementation difficulties. For example there was a great diversity of opinion about what the principal goal of the legislation should be. This is reflected in the data in Table 6.12.

A majority of the participants saw community involvement as the major goal of the act, but a substantial proportion of respondents said that rehabilitation and adjustment of offenders was the major goal. Others saw the act primarily as a way to reduce recidivism or to ensure humane treatment of offenders. When asked which goal the legislature principally had in mind, 44 percent of the participants selected reduced costs of incarceration. Thus, there was considerable discrepancy between what various participants involved in implementing the act saw as the major goal and what they believed the legislature wanted. This disparity in perceptions about the goals of the act indicated that the process of goal clarification had already begun.

Did such changes in goal perceptions constitute a positive rather than negative adaptation of the goals of community corrections? Although there was no mention of promoting community involvement in the legislation itself, it seemed clear that this would have been in line with the philosophy underlying community corrections. The promotion of community involvement would be considered goal clarification rather than goal dissolution, although those who originally opposed the policy might not have agreed with this view.

TABLE 6.12
Responses to the Question "Which of the Following
Do You Believe to Be the One Major Goal
of the Community Corrections Act?"

	%	n
Good method to rehabilitate offenders/ best way to help offenders adjust	24	37
Promote total community involvement in corrections/encourage participation of widest array of groups	54	83
Reduce recidivism	9	14
Provide humane treatment of offenders	4	6
	100	140

TABLE 6.13
Perceptions of Effectiveness of Community Corrections
with Regard to Administrative Simplicity

Not at all effective	1	12%	(18)
	2	33%	(51)
	3	22%	(34)
	4	23%	(36)
	5	9%	(14)
Very effective	6	1%	(1)

Survey data showed that potential implementors perceived community corrections as a complex policy. Table 6.13 shows responses to the question, "How would you rate the community-corrections act in regard to administrative simplicity?"

Many respondents rated community corrections as not at all or close to not at all effective with regard to administrative simplicity. What are the implications of this perception of policy complexity? Pressman and Wildavsky, in their implementation study, found that implementation failed partly because program complexity was not adequately appreciated in advance. Commitment to policy goals dissolved as numerous, unforeseen delays and difficulties were unexpectedly encountered. This suggests that if potential implementors are cognizant of the complexity of a policy and the administrative difficulties that will be entailed, two implementation paths may result—either the policy will not be adopted at all because it is viewed as an administrative nightmare or the commitment to adopt the policy will be accompanied by considerable attention to the development of coordinating mechanisms and other means of adapting to the demands of a complex policy.

With respect to the implementation of the Kansas community-corrections program, it is too early to determine whether potential implementors will develop coordinating mechanisms to overcome the implementation difficulties of this complex policy. Table 6.14 does provide some indication of the extent to which the complexity of the program will affect its implementation. Respondents were asked whether they thought community corrections would be instituted in their county in the next two years. Table 6.14 shows the cross-tabulation of those responses with responses to the complexity item in Table 6.13.

Respondents who believed the community corrections was relatively simple administratively were most likely to report that community corrections would be instituted in their county within the next two years; respondents who perceived that community corrections was administratively complex were much less sanguine about the likelihood of community cor-

TABLE 6.14
Perceived Likelihood of Adoption and Perceptions
of Community Corrections Complexity

		Rating of Effectiveness of Community Corrections in Regard to Administrative Simplicity			
		NOT AT ALL			VERY EFFECTIVE
		1 and 2	3	4	5 and 6
Will community corrections be instituted in your	Yes	68%	67%	79%	89%
county in two years?	No	32%	33%	21%	11%
	No	(50)	(30)	(28)	(9)

rections being instituted in their county. In short perceptions of administrative complexity did appear to be linked with expectations of the success or failure to adopt the program. The fact that no counties had completed the adoption process a year after the act was passed is an indication of the complexity of the program.

Survey data also sheds some light on the organizational and political context that conditioned the implementation process. Respondents were asked where in their county opposition to community corrections was most likely to come from, and they were asked to list in order of importance the three agencies they believed would be most important in making the implementation of community corrections successful. The first question tapped policy support versus opposition; the second question tapped the power and resources dimension. Table 6.15 shows that those perceived as being opposed to the policy (the community at large and elected officials) were not likely to be perceived as being necessary to the success of community corrections.

Similarly, those likely to be viewed as having the power to make or break the policy (courts and attorneys) are seen as least opposed to community corrections. With exception of the elected officials category, which was chosen second most frequently for importance in making community corrections work and second most often with respect to likelihood of opposition, Table 6.15 shows that the organizational and political climate for implementation was favorable. Those who opposed the program were the least important to successful implementation.

As noted earlier, a favorable organizational context for implementation requires that a policy appeal to the self-interests of those who must implement it. Is this the case in community corrections? Can this appeal be evaluated? To a certain extent the self-interests of bureaucrats were a matter to

TABLE 6.15
Perceived Sources of Opposition to Community Corrections
and Perceptions of Agencies Most Important to
Success of Community Corrections

	Policy Opposition First Ranking on: Where Is Opposition to Community Corrections Most Likely to Come from?		Power/Resources First Ranking on: Groups You Believe Will Be Most Important in Making Community Corrections Work.	
	%	N	%	N
Community/community groups	43%	(53)	5%	(7)
Elected officials	25%	(30)	16%	(22)
Law enforcement officers	22%	(27)	9%	(12)
Courts and attorneys	7%	(9)	40%	(55)
Service agencies	2%	(2)	11%	(15)
Probation vs. parole	1%	(1)	6%	(8)
Department of corrections	0%	(0)	14%	(20)

be discovered through extensive interviewing and theoretical deductions. As Table 6.16 indicates, rehabilitation-service professionals were most supportive of community corrections. This is to be expected, because the policy enhanced their role in corrections. The policy is based on the rehabilitative-services model that is most congenial to the helping professions from which most rehabilitation-service workers come. Table 6.16 also shows that Department of Corrections workers were about as likely as were rehabilitation service workers to support community corrections, whereas professionals associated with the court system were not as likely as corrections personnel were to support community corrections, and those associated

TABLE 6.16
Support for Community Corrections, by
Organizational/Professional Affiliation

	Organizational/Professional Affiliation			
To What Extent Do You Favor or Support the Concept of Community?	MUNICIPAL POLICE/ SHERIFFS	DEPARTMENT OF CORRECTIONS	JUDGES/ DISTRICT ATTORNEYS	REHABILI- TATION SERVICES
Corrections: Strongly favor	36%	71%	30%	75%
Favor somewhat	45%	26%	60%	25%
Somewhat disfavor	18%	3%	10%	0%
N=	(22)	(38)	(10)	(12)

with law enforcement were least likely to favor community corrections. This is consistent with the common understanding of the self-interests of these professionals. Law-enforcement officials generally believe, for example, that community corrections makes their work more difficult. Furthermore, the program is inconsistent with their ideological approaches to offenders. Police officers perceive that they will be rewarded for "making a good pinch," not for helping to monitor offenders or referring them to appropriate counseling services. Similarly, the diversionary aspects of community corrections are contradictory to the interests of judges and district attorneys who seek to maximize their control over offenders.

CONCLUSIONS

Process evaluation is a study of change over time; consequently, a complete process evaluation requires time-series data. The material reported here is only the first part of a process evaluation of community corrections in Kansas. The evaluation will continue, probably for at least two more years, as implementation proceeds. The evaluation will monitor changes in goal perceptions and changes in the perceptions of various self-interested groups. It will also identify the strategies for cooperation and the specific interorganizational conflicts that arise during implementation.

In this paper we have proposed a model of the implementation process. That model, which explicitly defines implementation as a continuation of the change process, identifies three categories of factors that affect implementation and serve to set the agenda for process evaluation.

Using data collected during the initial stage of implementation, ways were indicated in which the factors identified in the conceptual model could be applied to community corrections. The data permitted the isolation of some likely implementation problems and also provided tentative predictions about future happenings. For example it was shown that the community-corrections program involved varying and, to some extent, incongruous goal perspectives. The decentralized, optional character of the policy implies that community corrections is likely to be implemented in different ways in different counties, and there is also ample opportunity for the implementation process to yield results different from what legislators may have intended.

Furthermore, community corrections is a complex policy, and it is perceived as such by most potential implementors. This suggests the need for advance preparation of cooperative networks. It also leads to the prediction that counties which already have well-developed systems of social services and which have begun the work of coordinating social-service agencies with corrections efforts will be among the first to adopt community corrections and the most likely to institutionalize community corrections with a minimum of negative change.

Finally, at some point in the process, it may be possible to consider the impact that the community-corrections policy had in Kansas. The model of implementation suggests that although the implementation process involves continuous change with regard to the goals of policy, at some point the policy will become institutionalized. When it is, the innovation may be regarded as established practice, and relatively little change should be expected after this occurs. The process-evaluation approach enables us to determine when institutionalization occurs, and thus permits an accurate impact evaluation. We plan to follow the implementation of community corrections in Kansas up to this final point.

NOTES

1. David Nachmias, *Public Policy Evaluation: Approaches and Methods* (New York: St. Martin's, 1979), p. 5.
2. Ibid., p. 5.
3. Kansas House Bill No. 3112, Section 2.
4. Thomas B. Smith, "The Policy Implementation Process," *Policy Sciences*, 4, (1973), 200.
5. David Boorkman; Ernest J. Fazio, Jr.; Noel Day; and David Welnstein, *An Exemplary Project; Community-Based Corrections in Des Moines* (Washington, D.C., U.S. Department of Justice, National Institute of Law Enforcement and Criminal Justice, November 1976). H. P. White, *Community Treatment Centers: Evaluation Report* (Oklahoma City, Oklahoma: Oklahoma Crime Commission, no date). Kenneth F. Schoen, "The Community Corrections Act," *Crime and Delinquency* (October 1978), pp. 458–464. Robert Rosenblum and Debra Whitcomb, *An Exemplary Project: Montgomery County Work Release/Pre-Release Project* (Washington, D.C., National Institute of Law Enforcement of Criminal Justice, June 1978).
6. Tom R. Houston, "The Behavioral Sciences Impact-Effectiveness Model," in *Evaluating Social Programs*, Peter Rossi and Walter Williams, eds. (New York: Seminar, 1972), pp. 51–65.
7. Paul Berman, "The Study of Macro- and Micro-Implementation," *Public Policy* (Spring 1978), 157–184.
8. Jeffrey Pressman and Aaron Wildavsky, *Implementation* (Berkeley, Calif.: University of California Press, 1973), p. XV.
9. Berman, *Study*, p. 172.
10. Neal Gross, Joseph B. Giacquinta, and Marilyn Bernstein, *Implementing Organizational Innovations, A Sociological Analysis of Planned Educational Change* (New York: Basic, 1971).
11. Pressman and Wildavsky, *Implementation*.
12. Pressman and Wildavsky, *Implementation*, 87–124.

13. David Boorkman, *et al.*, *An Exemplary Project.*
14. Raymond Nimmer, *The Nature of System Change* (Chicago: American Bar Association, 1978).
15. Berman, *Study*, p. 169.
16. Nimmer, *System Change*, p. 181.
17. Douglas Bunker, "Policy Sciences Perspectives on Implementation Process," *Policy Sciences* 3 (1972), 75–80.
18. Bunker, "Political Sciences Perspectives," p. 76.
19. Robert Yin, "Production Efficiency Versus Bureaucratic Self-Interest: Two Innovative Processes," *Policy Sciences*, 8 (1977), 381–399.
20. Carl Van Horn and Donald Van Meter, "The Implementation of Intergovernmental Policy," in *Public Policymaking in a Federal System*, Charles O. Jones and Robert D. Thomas, eds. (Beverly Hills, Calif.: Sage, 1976), p. 56.
21. Ibid., p. 57.
22. Yin, "Production Efficiency," p. 396.
23. For an example of an implementation study that uses time-series data on implementation perspective, see Sarah Liebschutz, "General Revenue Sharing as a Political Resource for Local Officials," in Charles O. Jones and Robert D. Thomas, *Public Policymaking in a Federal System,* pp. 103–128. Liebschutz interviewed local officials and gathered archival data for the period immediately prior to the Local Fiscal Assistance Act of 1972, and she continued her observations during the first four entitlement periods of the act.

THE IMPACT OF JURY SIZE ON THE PROBABILITY OF CONVICTION

Stuart Nagel
Marian Neef

Since *Florida v. Williams*,[1] there has been considerable debate in the law review and social science literature concerning the impact of switching from a twelve-person jury to a six-person jury on the probability of an average defendant being convicted.[2] That debate may be quite relevant to the question of what is the optimum jury size since those who advocate twelve-person juries often express a concern that six-person juries will be substantially more likely to convict the average defendant and thus the innocent defendant as well. On the other hand, those who advocate six-person juries often express a concern that twelve-person juries will be substantially less likely to convict the average defendant and thus the guilty defendant as well.

The framework for analysis being utilized in this article is that of indirect deductive modeling because meaningful direct empirical data is not available for comparing twelve-person juries with six-person juries as will be described. Deductive modeling involves drawing a conclusion about the effect of switching from a twelve-person jury to a six-person jury from (1) certain known facts about twelve-person juries and by (2) reasoning from analogy to certain simple mathematical models that deal with independent probabilities and statistical averaging. Even if meaningful direct empirical data were available, deductive modeling has the advantage of being able to determine the effects of legal policy changes before the changes are adopted, thereby avoiding possible accompanying damage and the bureaucratic difficulties of restoring the status quo.

EMPIRICAL COMPARISONS BETWEEN
TWELVE AND SIX-PERSON JURIES

At first glance, one might think an appropriate way to determine the relation between jury size and conviction probability would be simply to compare the conviction rates in a state that uses twelve-person juries with a state that uses six-person juries. That approach is likely to be meaningless, however, because any differences we find in the conviction rates may be determined by differences in the characteristics of the law, the people or the cases in the two states rather than to differences in their jury sizes. For example, it is impossible to draw any meaningful conclusion from comparing the conviction rate in Illinois where twelve-person juries are used with the conviction rate in Oregon where six-person juries are used since there is no way to hold constant the differences in their criminal laws, their jurors and their case facts. The problem of controlling for those conviction-related variables (which seem to be more important than jury size) is not sufficiently lessened by comparing all twelve-person jury states with all six-person jury states, since the six-person jury states may be the ones that were more conviction-prone to begin with rather than be a random sample from within the fifty states.

As an alternative, one might suggest making before-and-after comparisons in a single state in order to control better for those kinds of characteristics which do not generally change so much over a short period of time. If the conviction rate before was 64% with twelve-person juries, the conviction rate after with six-person juries might be substantially lower rather than higher, although most defense attorneys would predict a higher conviction rate with six-person juries. The conviction rate, however, might actually rise because by their predicting a higher conviction rate with six-person juries, defense attorneys might therefore be more likely to plea bargain more of their clients under the new system and then bring only their especially pro-defense cases before the new six-person juries. In other words, if defense attorneys themselves really believe six-person juries are more likely to convict, this belief could cause a change in their plea bargaining behavior and thus a change in the type of cases they are willing to take to a jury trial. Under such circumstances, the nature of the new cases (not the change in the jury size) would cause the drop in the conviction rate, and there would be no accurate way to separate out those two potentially causal influences in such a before-and-after study.

As another alternative, one might suggest working with experimental juries all of whom would hear exactly the same case. Half of the juries would be six-person juries, and half would be twelve-person juries. Any differences between the two sets of juries could not be explained by saying they were hearing different cases or operating under different legal rules. People would also be randomly assigned to the two sets of juries so that the randomization process would tend to eliminate the explanation that people on the twelve-person juries were different people than those on the six-person juries. This experimental analysis, however, has the big defect that it in effect involves a sample of only one case. Whatever differences or non-differences are found may be peculiar to that one case being very pro-prosecution, pro-defense, pro-divisive or simply unrealistic, and the results may thus not be generalizable.

Theoretically, the one-case problem could be overcome by video-taping fifty criminal cases and playing the fifty video tapes to fifty randomly selected twelve-person juries and then fifty randomly selected six-person juries. The cost of doing so might, however, be prohibitive, and a sample of much less than fifty would not be large enough to generalize from. The cost would be especially prohibitive if each criminal case had to be acted out like a movie in view of the fact that video-taping of actual criminal cases is prohibited in almost all states. The cost might also be prohibitive if substantial sums of money have to be paid to people in order to get a representative sample of the population to cooperate. Even a sample of fifty or more video tapes would be meaningless if the twelve-person juries did not convict 64% of the time since that is the conviction percentage with real twelve-person juries.

DEDUCTIVE COMPARISONS BETWEEN
TWELVE AND SIX-PERSON JURIES

One remaining alternative is to try to determine the effects of different jury sizes by deducing conclusions from certain known facts and reasonable assumptions. One known fact is that the average twelve-person jury convicts 64% of the time according to the University of Chicago jury research conducted by Harry Kalven and Hans Zeisel. That data was gathered from a nationwide sample of thousands of juries and is still the best analysis of jury conviction rates, as indicated by its frequent citation in the recent jury size literature. Also known from that research is that the average juror votes to convict 68% of the time.[3] If jury voting were like flipping twelve independent coins, then we would expect the average juror to vote to convict 96% of the time. This is so since each coin would have to be unbalanced in the direction of coming up heads or conviction 96% of the time in order to average twelve heads on twelve flips 64% of the time. In other words, only .96 (rather than any other number) multiplied by itself twelve times equals .64. On the other hand, jury voting may be like bowling where all the pins tend to fall together if the evidence ball is well placed, or else none or less than all tend to fall if the evidence ball in effect goes in the gutter or away from the strike zone. If the bowling analogy applies, then we would expect each pin to have about a .64 propensity or 64% chance of falling over out of every 100 balls thrown at the pins.[4]

Since we know the average juror has a .68 propensity to vote to convict, this in effect informs us that jury voting is much closer to the bowling analogy (.64 propensity) than the coin-flipping analogy (.96 propensity), since the actual .68 figure is closer to .64 than to .96, although somewhere in between those two model figures. We can determine where in between by simply thinking of the .68 as representing a weighted average between the bowling .64 and the coin-flipping .96. If the bowling .64 is given a weight of 1.00, then the coin-flipping .96 must be given a weight of .13 for the .68 to be a weighted average in the formula .68 = [(1.00) (.64) + (.13) (.96)] / (1.00) + .13). This weight of .13 for the coin-flipping approach or model when the bowling approach has a weight of 1.00 will be useful to us in determining the probability of an average defendant being convicted with juries smaller than twelve.

For example, with a representative jury of six persons, the bowling approach says the probability of a conviction is still .64 because either all the pins fall over 64% of the time, or less than all of the pins fall over the other 36% of the time. The coin-flipping approach, however, says that with a jury of six persons the probability of a conviction drops to .78 which is the same as the .96 propensity multiplied by itself six times rather than twelve times. Thus, if the bowling approach yields a probability of .64 and receives a weight of 1.00, and the coin-flipping approach yields a probability of .78 and receives a weight of .13, then the combined probability of a conviction with a six-person jury would be .66, which is the same as [.64 + (.13) (.78)] / 1.13. This means that when moving from a twelve-person to a six-person jury, the probability of a conviction of the average defendant is likely to rise only two percentage points from 64% to 66% if all other relevant things are held constant besides jury size and the conviction probability.

The same simple but meaningful analysis can be applied to analyzing the effect of reducing the fraction required to convict from unanimity to 10/12 as was allowed in *Apodaca v. Oregon*.[5] The bowling approach says that with a 10/12 rule, the probability of a conviction is still .64 because the pins are doing whatever happens to the average pin. If the average pin falls over, then all the pins fall over. If the average pin does not fall over, then all the pins do not fall over although they do not necessarily all stand up. The coin-flipping approach says that with a 10/12 rule, the probability of a conviction becomes .99 since the probability of exactly twelve out of twelve heads or conviction votes is .64 (with coins that individually have a .96 probability of coming up heads), and the probability of exactly eleven out of twelve heads is .29 with such a set of coins, and the probability of exactly eleven out of twelve heads is .29 with such a set of coins, and the probability of exactly ten out of twelve heads is .06. Thus, the probability of at least ten out of twelve heads or conviction votes is .99 which is the same as .64 + .29 + .06. Therefore, if the bowling approach yields a probability of .64 and receives a weight of 1.00, and the coin-flipping approach yields a probability of .99 and receives a weight of .13, then the combined probability of a conviction under a 10/12 rule would be .68, which is the same as [.64 + (.13) (.99)] / 1.13. This means that when moving from a 12/12 rule to a 10/12 rule, the probability of a conviction of the average defendant is likely to rise four percentage points from 64% to 68% if all other things are held constant such as the type of cases and the nature of the jurors.

This deductive analysis involved in determining the impact of jury size on conviction is summarized in Table 6.17. The initial premises relate to the fact that an average twelve-person jury convicts 64% of the time, and an average juror on a twelve-person jury votes to convict 67.7% of the time. The intermediate premises deal with what percent of the time we would expect an average juror to convict if jury decision-making followed the independent probability model (i.e., 96.4% of the time) or the averaging model (i.e., 64.0% of the time). The initial and intermediate premises lead to the intermediate conclusion that jury decision-making is 13% in conformity with the independent probability model, and 87% in conformi-

TABLE 6.17
The Impact of Jury Size on the Probability of Conviction

I. Basic Symbols

PAC = probability of an average defendant before an average *jury* being convicted (empirically equals .64 for a twelve-person jury shown to two decimal places).

pac = probability of an average defendant receiving from an average *juror* a vote for conviction (empirically equals .677 for a juror shown to three decimal places).

II. Implications of the Coin-Flipping Analogy (Independent Probability Model).

$PAC = (pac)^{NJ}$.

.64 = $(pac)^{12}$, which deductively means the coin-flipping pac is .964.

III. Implications of the Bowling Analogy (Averaging Model)

PAC = pac.

.64 = pac, which deductively means the bowling pac is .640.

IV. Weighting and Combining the Two Analogies

Actual
pac = [weight (coin-flipping pac) + (bowling pac)] / (weight + 1)

.677 = [weight (.964) + (.640)] / (weight + 1), which deductively means the relative weight of the coin flipping analogy to the bowling analogy is .13.

V. Applying the Above to a Six-Person Jury

PAC = [weight (coin-flipping PAC) + (bowling PAC)] / (weight + 1)

PAC = $[.13 (.964)^6 + (.64)]$ / 1.13, which deductively means PAC with a six-person jury is .66.

VI. Applying the Above to a Decision Rule Allowing Two of Twelve Dissenters for a Conviction

PAC = [weight (coin-flipping PAC) + (bowling PAC) / (weight + 1)

PAC = [.13 (.99) + (.64)] / 1.13, which deductively means PAC with a 10/12 rule is .68.

ty with the averaging model. Those premises and the intermediate conclusion deductively lead to a finding that a six-person jury deciding unanimously would convict 66% of the time, and that a twelve-person jury allowing for two dissenters would convict 68% of the time.

SIGNIFICANCE AND EXTENSIONS OF THE ANALYSIS

Therefore, adopting a 10/12 rule has more impact on increasing the probability of convicting an average defendant than adopting a 6/6 rule or a six-person unanimous jury system. One might, however, say that neither change has much impact on conviction probabilities since they only increase those probabilities by two and four percentage points respectively. On the other hand, one might say that an increase from .64 to .68 represents over a 6% increase since .04 divided by .64 equals .0625. A 6% increase in the conviction probability could mean a substantial and undesirable increase in the number of truly innocent defendants being convicted, although we do not know how many innocent defendants go to a jury verdict out of the total number of jury verdicts. A 6% increase in the conviction probability could also mean a substantial and desirable decrease in the number of truly guilty defendants who are not convicted although we likewise do not know how many guilty defendants go to a jury verdict out of the total number of jury verdicts.

The same simple but meaningful analysis presented above can be applied to analyzing the effect of changing the jury size or the fraction required to convict on (1) the number of errors likely to be made with regard to convicting the innocent or (2) the number of errors likely to be made with regard to not convicting the guilty. Such an extension of the analysis requires that one be willing to make certain tentative assumptions about (1) the presence of innocent and guilty defendants in the jury decision-making process, (2) how much higher than .64 the probability is for convicting a truly guilty defendant, and (3) how much lower than .64 the probability is of convicting a truly innocent defendant. That extension could enable one to obtain insights with regard to arriving at an optimum jury size that will minimize the sum of both of the above-mentioned errors, where those errors are either weighted equally or with more weight to avoiding an error of convicting an innocent defendant.[6]

This same kind of simple deductive analysis from known facts to deduced conclusions can be applied to analyzing many other aspects of the judicial process where complete data is not available on the effects of certain judicial process changes. The data may not be available because the change has not yet occurred anywhere, or because the change has occurred but other things may have changed simultaneously which obscure the causal relationships.[7] An example of a judicial process change to which analogous deductive approaches might be meaningfully applied includes the impact of flat or nondiscretionary sentencing on plea bargaining even though no state has yet adopted such a sentencing system.[8] An example of a judicial process change which has been adopted in some states is gubernatorial appointment rather than election of judges. Judicial selection studies that involve comparisons across states or comparisons before and after a change in the selection method are largely unable to control for other relevant causal characteristics that may also differentiate the states or the time periods. Thus, a partially deductive approach may also be relevant to an analysis of the impact of judicial selection methods.[9] As with the impact of jury size, a combination of basic data and reasonable deductions may often produce useful insights for analyzing the impacts of judicial process changes.

In closing, it might be helpful to list the criteria of a good deductive model in order to facilitate extensions of this jury size analysis to other situations. There are at least eight such criteria. First, in random order, the premises about reality should be empirically validated or at least be consistent with related empirical knowledge. Second, premises about normative goals should be reasonably related to the goals that potential policymakers are likely to have, or at least the goals should be explicitly stated. Third, the conclusions that are derived should follow from the premises by logical deduction without requiring additional information. Fourth, the deductive model should serve a causal or prescriptive purpose, or some other useful purpose. Fifth, the model should indicate how its conclusions would change as a result of changes in its empirical and normative premises. Sixth, the model should have broadness in time, geography, and abstractness, but still be applicable to concrete situations. Seventh, the model should be simple and understandable, but still capture the essence of an important complex phenomenon. Eighth, the model should be revised in light of whatever empirical data is subsequently gathered relevant to either the premises or the conclusions.[10]

NOTES

1. *Williams* v. *Florida*, 399 U.S. 78 (1970). In *Colgrove* v. *Battin*, 413 U.S. 149 (1973), the Supreme Court held that a jury of six persons satisfies the seventh amendment guarantee of trial by jury in civil cases.
2. Richard Lempert, "Uncovering 'Nondiscernible' Differences: Empirical Research and the Jury-Size Cases," 73 *Michigan Law Review*, 644 (1975); Hans

Zeisel, ". . . And Then There Were None: The Diminution of the Federal Jury," 38 *University of Chicago Law Review* 710 (1971); Institute of Judicial Administration, *A Comparison of Six- and Twelve-Member Civil Juries in New Jersey Superior and County Courts* (1973); David Walbert, "The Effect of Jury Size on the Probability of Conviction: An Evaluation of *Williams* v. *Florida*," 22 *Case Western Law Review* 529 (1971); Alice Padawer-Singer and Allen Barton, "Interim Report: Experimental Study of Decision-Making in the 12- versus 6-Man Jury under Unanimous versus Nonunanimous Decisions" (Columbia Bureau of Applied Social Research, 1975); James Davis, et al., "The Decision Processes of 6- and 12-Person Mock Juries Assigned Unanimous and $\frac{2}{3}$ Majority Rules," *Journal of Personality and Social Psychology* (1975); and Edward Beiser and Rene Varrin, "Six-Member Juries in the Federal Courts," 58 *Judicature* 425 (1975).

3. The 64% conviction rate for twelve-person juries is given in Harry Kalven and Hans Zeisel, *The American Jury* (Boston: Little, Brown, 1966) at p. 56. The 68% pro-convictions voting rate for individual jurors is based on knowing in an averge sample of 100 cases how many cases would involve unanimous convictions, unanimous acquittals, and hung juries. The breakdown of the votes for hung juries is given in ibid., p. 160. According to the data, an average sample of 100 cases would involve 812 conviction votes out of 1,200 total votes for an average juror voting to convict 68% of the time.

4. For further detail on the deductive model presented here for determining the impact of jury size on conviction probability, see S. Nagel and M. Neef, "Deductive Modeling to Determine an Optimum Jury Size and Fraction Required to Convict," 1975 *Washington University Law Quarterly* 933–978 (1976).

5. *Apodaca* v. *Oregon*, 406 U.S. 404 (1972). On the same day in the case of *Johnson* v. *Louisiana*, 406 U.S. 356 (1972), the Court allowed the states to be able to convict by a decision of nine out of twelve jurors.

6. For further detail on finding an optimum jury size, see the article cited in note 4 above.

7. S. Nagel and M. Neef, "Determining the Impact of Legal Policy Changes Before the Changes Occur," in John Gardiner (ed.), *Public Law and Public Policy* (New York: Praeger, 1977), pp. 90–106.

8. S. Nagel and M. Neef, "Plea Bargaining, Decision Theory, and Equilibrium Models," 51 *Indiana Law Journal* 987–1024 (1976) and 52 *Indiana Law Journal* 1–61 (1976), especially at pp. 45–46.

9. S. Nagel, *Comparing Elected and Appointed Judicial Systems* (Beverly Hills: Sage Publications, 1973), especially p. 7.

10. For further details on deductive modeling especially as applied to legal and other policy problems, see Martin Greenberger, *Models in the Policy Process* (New York: Russell Sage, 1977); David Greenberg, *Mathematical Criminology* (Chicago: University of Chicago Press, 1977); Saul Gass and Roger Sisson, *A Guide to Models in Governmental Planning and Operations* (Environmental Protection Agency, 1974); and S. Nagel (ed.), *Modeling the Criminal Justice System* (Beverly Hills: Sage Publications, 1977).

Chapter 7

HEALTH CARE

The United States has never had a comprehensive, integrated policy to meet the health-care needs of all Americans. The provision of medical care services has been largely private, although the government has played an increasing role in supporting medical expenditures. By the mid-1970s total health expenditures had risen to almost 9 percent of the gross national product, and the federal share of the total health bills stood at 30 percent, an expenditure that entailed over $34 billion. Federal funding of the hospital component of health expenditures has increased to the point where the government now pays more than 40 percent of the nation's hospital bills.

Two major government programs—Medicare and Medicaid—were enacted as part of the Social Security Amendments of 1965. Medicare is a federal program that provides uniform benefits to the aged, disabled persons covered by Social Security, and those with end-stage renal (kidney) disease. Medicare includes hospital insurance financed through social security taxes and a physician reimbursement program. Medicaid is funded by the states with federal aid, which accounts for 50 to 78 percent of the costs.

The role of government in medical care also extends beyond these two programs. By exempting from taxable income an employer's contributions for health insurance, the government encourages the purchase of more insurance. Similarly, the government permits tax exemptions for medical expenses over a specified percentage of an individual's income.

Although great improvements have been made in the health of the American population, there are still major problems in the medical-care system. Current public concern and congressional debate center on the mounting cost of health care, the adequacy of coverage under present health-benefits programs, the distribution of health-care resources and the access of the population to health-care services, and the quality of health care.

Health-care costs. In recent years the cost of health care has become a major problem of concern. By the mid-1970s public and private spending for health-care services, medical-facility construction, research, and other health expenditures had risen to more than $140 billion and almost 87 percent of the monies spent for health care were for personal health-care services. By early 1980s health-care spending will account for more than 10 percent of the nation's gross national product.[1]

Adequacy of coverage. Personal health-care costs are met through direct payments by patients and through health-benefits programs, such as private health insurance and government programs, the most significant of which are Medicare and Medicaid. With rising costs of health care, however, the adequacy of these protective programs is being questioned, and many experts now feel that a national health insurance program is needed to protect all persons. Although most of the aged have some health-insurance coverage, most aged persons also directly pay for about 30 percent of their health-care expenditures. For persons under age 65, most protective coverage focuses on hospital-related services and is provided by employment-related group health insurance. More than one-third of the population under age 65, however, is not covered for home and office visits with physicians, and about 38 million individuals are without health-insurance protection of any kind for hospital care. Furthermore, in the mid-1970s, private health-insurance companies paid just over 35 percent of the personal health-care expenditures for those insured and under 65.

Distribution and access. Health resources are unequally distributed. Not all Americans have access to high-quality or even adequate medical care. For example, physicians are located in disproportionately large numbers throughout the northeastern and western regions of the country. Maldistribution also exists in inner-city and rural areas within the states. Some 145 counties with populations over 500,000 have no full-time physician in patient care, and the number of physicians in inner-city areas has been steadily declining for several years. In addition, specialization has accelerated so much that the number of physicians in general practice has reached a historic low of 20 percent.

Closely related to the costs of health care, the adequacy of coverage, and the maldistribution of resources is the problem of access to health care. The ability to pay for health care, the availability of health providers in highly populated areas, and the public's attitudes regarding health care have determined patterns of access, and these are unequally distributed.

Quality of health care. The evaluation of quality health care has not yet become an intrinsic part of health-care delivery, although quality-evaluation activities, in particular, within individual hospitals have been progressing, and these evaluations will continue to spread to other sections of health care.

The first article in this chapter examines the impact of Medicaid on access to medical care and utilization patterns in New York City. Based on five panels of home interviews, three before and two after Medicaid, Olendzki reports that the old and very sick (those eligible for Old Age Assistance and Aid to Disabled) actually received less care under Medicaid than before it, despite being seven years older than younger and less ill persons who used Medicaid. Olendzki suggests that the quality of care is affected by the patient's health status and by attitudes on entry to care, the suitability of the delivering institution, the application of treatment, and the outcomes of application.

The Marmor et al. article uses a quasi-experimental time-series design to analyze the Canadian experience with national health insurance, and estimates the impact of proposed national health-insurance plans in the United States. This is especially instructive given the current debate over national health insurance and the controversy over the extent to which the various proposed plans and bills will be able to meet the problems of the health-care system.

The Greer and Greer article centers on the complex problems of mental health and patterns of governance of Community Mental Health Centers (CMHC). The authors use analytic induction to evaluate the representational component of the CMHC legislation.

NOTE

1. For this and the following statistics, see Jack Ebeler et al., *National Health Insurance* (Congressional Research Service, Washington, D.C.: Government Printing Office, 1977).

MEDICAID BENEFITS MAINLY
THE YOUNGER AND LESS SICK

Margaret C. Olendzki

This report is part of a larger study of the impact of Medicaid on former welfare clients in New York City.* As the analysis has proceeded, it has become necessary to look with a larger and larger magnifying glass for the effects of Medicaid on the study population, for its impact was just not readily apparent to the naked eye. Finally, we were able to discover a group that had apparently benefited from Medicaid in terms of increased access to care and a larger volume of service: the parents in the AFDC Families. But this seems to have been at the expense of—or, to put it more neutrally, balanced by—the aged and sicker members of this welfare population, who actually received less medical care after Medicaid than before it.

The limits on generalizing these findings must first be emphasized. The subjects of this study are not typical of all intended beneficiaries of Medicaid. In the pre-Medicaid study period which constitutes the baseline of our study, they were on welfare all or part of the time, and so had access to free care under the welfare medical care system of the early 1960's. And they started out in a section of New York City—the east side of Manhattan—which is rather plentifully supplied with medical facilities. Nevertheless, the findings are believed to be of more than local significance. They do suggest taking a closer look at our stereotypes about the medical care situation of large sections of our urban poor.

METHOD

The study of the impact of Medicaid on former welfare clients was built on to a previous demonstration and research project, the Welfare Medical Care Project at the New York Hospital/Cornell Medical Center.[1] This

* Supported in part by Grant No. 380 from the Social and Rehabilitation Service and Social Security Administration.

parent study, carried out from 1960 to 1965, was an experiment in offering comprehensive care to welfare families under the auspices of one medical center. For one year, in 1961–62, all persons coming onto the public assistance rolls in the Yorkville Welfare District on the east side of Manhattan became the subjects of this coordinated care experiment. As they were accepted on welfare, they were allocated at random into a study group (60%) and a control group (the remaining 40%). Each welfare case in the study group received a letter inviting them and their families to receive all their needed medical care at the New York Hospital. The control group was left to seek care in the usual way from the places then serving the welfare population in the city. Three waves of home interviews—at intake to the study, one year later, and two years later—investigated health status, utilization patterns, attitudes to health and medical care, and satisfaction with services. The New York Hospital Project ended in mid-1965. There were 1,681 welfare cases, containing 4,189 persons, in the original study.

The impact of Medicaid study took advantage of the picture of indigent medical care pre-Medicaid that had incidentally been provided by the New York Hospital Project. The control group, which had not been "contaminated" by any medical care experiment, was of particular interest; but it was considered worthwhile to include the study group also in the follow-up. And so between 1967 and 1971, every effort was made to trace and reinterview the remainder of the 1,681-case panel of former welfare recipients.

According to welfare record studies made in 1961,[2] it was predicted that most of the panel would no longer be on welfare, or at least would only be using it sporadically. Such a marginally self-supporting segment of the population was felt to be most appropriate for a study of Medicaid, since nearly all would presumably be in need of help with their medical bills and would be poor enough to qualify for Medicaid. As it turned out, the proportion of those in our study population whom Medicaid maximally benefited shrank below original expectations. On the one hand, the dramatic rise in the welfare rolls in New York City and elsewhere changed the "natural history" of welfare dependency in this cohort of 1961 new admissions, so that far more of them than anticipated were found to be on welfare during the follow-up study. Since welfare recipients were entitled to free medical care before and after Medicaid, the latter did not make so much difference to them as to those off welfare. On the other hand, the drastic Medicaid cutbacks in New York State occurred at the height of the follow-up study, and considerably diminished the Medicaid-benefited from the other end of the economic spectrum by removing the higher income beneficiaries from the Medicaid rolls.

A fourth and fifth wave of home interviews was carried out in 1968–69 and in 1969–70: since intake to the original study was staggered over a one-year period in 1961–62, all later interview waves were similarly staggered. One in five respondents was found to be deceased by the final interview wave, but vigorous attempts to trace the rest resulted in interviewing in full 70 percent of those still living. Figure 7.1 shows the timing of the interviews and the number of respondents interviewed on each wave. The arrows pointing backward from the second through fifth interview waves indicate that respondents were asked on each occasion about the medical care they had obtained in the previous year. These two 2-year periods constitute the pre-Medicaid and post-Medicaid study periods discussed in this paper.

For simplicity's sake, and to avoid any bias resulting from differential losses on the various interview waves, this paper will deal only with the full follow-up group of 729 respondents who were interviewed on each of the five occasions. The respondent was usually the only adult in the welfare case, but if there was more than one adult, the respondent was chosen at random. The extent to which full follow-up respondents differ from the entire sample is described elsewhere.[3] Also the paper will limit the discus-

Figure 7.1. Timetable of the New York Hospital Project and impact of Medicaid studies.

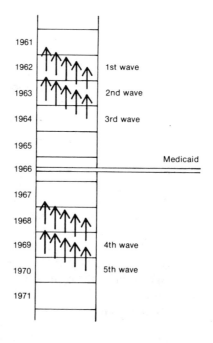

sion to ambulatory medical care, *i.e.*, physician visits as customarily defined.[4] Dental care, acute hospitalization, and institutionalization are dealt with elsewhere in the full report.

MEASUREMENTS

The architects of Medicaid expressed the hope that removing financial barriers to medical care would open up service to a hitherto unreached population, that it would encourage people to take advantage of preventive measures, and to come earlier for treatment when sick. To see if these hopes were fulfilled in our study population, four specific questions will be asked regarding the impact of Medicaid:

1. Did it improve access to care?
2. Did it increase volume of care in general?
3. Did it change people's utilization patterns?
4. Did it change the distribution of care?

The corresponding measurements to be used are as follows: (a) the *percentage of people seeing a doctor* during a given period (either one year or two years); (b) the *mean number of doctor visits* per person made within that period; (c) the distribution of the group's *utilization patterns*—how many people were high, medium, or low utilizers and whether or not this changed over time; (d) the *characteristics of the people* in whom changes in the above measures are observed.

FINDINGS

Three out of four of these measures are used in Table 7.1, in a comparison of the two-year study period before Medicaid with the two-year period after Medicaid. Utilization statistics are usually presented within one-year periods, but for certain purposes a two-year span is more useful. In general, the longer the time studied, the more stable will be the picture of a person's utilization patterns. Over the short run, a brief but infrequent illness may cause erratic variations and make a person who rarely sees a doctor look like a high utilizer. Over a longer time, these peaks will flatten out and give a truer picture of a person's usual or average medical-care-seeking behavior.

Table 7.1 shows the distribution of respondents into utilizer groups—non, low, medium, high, very high. The cutting points between the last four groups have been set here in terms of the full follow-up group's own

TABLE 7.1

Percentage Distribution of Persons Who Were
Non-, Low, Medium, High or Very High
Utilizers, and Mean Number of Visits,
Two Years Pre-Medicaid and Two Years
Post-Medicaid, Full Follow-up
Group (N = 729)

Utilizer Group	Two Years Pre-Medicaid	Two Years Post-Medicaid
Nonutilizer (0 visits)	9.1	12.6
Low utilizer (1-5 visits)	24.1	25.1
Medium utilizer (6-12 visits)	20.8	25.4
High utilizer (13-25 visits)	23.6	18.4
Very high utilizer (26 + visits)	22.4	18.5
Total	100.0	100.0
Mean visits in two years	18.8	16.8

utilization experience in the baseline period. They constitute quartiles, as well as the data would permit, of those making doctor visits pre-Medicaid. Once set, the same cutting points are retained to permit comparisons over time and across subgroups. The table makes it apparent that there is little scope for Medicaid to increase access to care in this particular population. During the two-year period before Medicaid, 90.9 percent of the respondents saw a doctor at some time; only 9.1 percent did not. This proportion of nonutilizers did *not* fall after Medicaid: it actually rose a little, to 12.6 percent. The proportion of low utilizers remained more or less unchanged; and there was a general shift of some four or five percentage points away from the higher utilization groups.

One hypothesis entertained by the critics of Medicaid was that its fee-for-service structure might encourage very high utilization, perhaps especially in the private sector. There is no evidence for this in our data, either in Table 7.1 or in other more detailed breakdowns.[5] In the category of persons making a very large number of visits (26 or more for a two-year period), there is a decline rather than an increase after Medicaid. Mean visits per person interviewed also declined from 18.8 in two years before Medicaid to 16.8 in the comparable period after. The explanation for the decrease seems to be that the high level of utilization before Medicaid left little room for increase. These are reported doctor visits in Table 7.1, and the checking against hospital records that was carried out during the New

York Hospital Project suggests that they are exaggerated by about 10 percent. But even allowing for the exaggeration and for the fact that these are adults rather than a cross-section of all age groups, the use of medical services is extremely high compared to the national average.

The New York Hospital Project, in the pre-Medicaid study period, itself sought to improve access to care and increase needed services for the study group who received the invitation to the New York Hospital. The high baseline utilization level may be due, then, to the influence of the Project rather than being true for the welfare population in general. Table 7.2 sorts the matter out by presenting data separately for study and control groups. It shows that the New York Hospital Project did contribute considerably to the high use of medical services pre-Medicaid. If only the control group is compared from one period to the other, a leveling out rather than a decline in utilization occurs. A marginal increase—on the level of half a visit a year—occurs in the mean number of visits. But there is certainly no rise in the percentage of people getting into the medical care system: nonutilizers remain between 14 and 15 percent.

A year-by-year analysis is shown in Table 7.3. The percentage of nonutilizers in a one-year period (Table 7.3) is of course quite different from the percentage in two years (Table 7.2). For instance, 23.9 percent of the control group failed to see a doctor in 1962 and as many as 32.4 percent in

TABLE 7.2

**Percentage Distribution of Persons in the Five
Utilizer Groups, and Mean Visits, in the
Two Years Pre- and Post-Medicaid, by
NYHP Study versus Control Group
(Study Group = 457, Control Group = 272)**

	Two Years Pre-Medicaid		Two Years Post-Medicaid	
Utilizer Group	NYHP STUDY GROUP	CONTROL GROUP	NYHP STUDY GROUP	CONTROL GROUP
Nonutilizer (0 visits)	5.9	14.3	11.4	14.7
Low utilizer (1-5 visits)	21.9	27.9	25.2	25.0
Medium utilizer (6-12 visits)	21.7	19.5	26.3	23.9
High utilizer (13-25 visits)	24.3	22.4	17.9	19.1
Very high utilizer (26 + visits)	26.3	15.8	19.3	17.3
Total	100.1	99.9	100.1	100.0
Mean visits in two years	21.1	14.8	17.2	15.9

TABLE 7.3

Percentage Distribution of Persons in the Five Utilizer Groups, and Mean Visits, by Interview Wave, by NYHP Study versus Control Group

(Study Group = 457, Control Group = 272)

Utilizer Group*	1962 NYHP STUDY GROUP	1962 CONTROL GROUP	1963 STUDY GROUP	1963 CONTROL GROUP	1968 STUDY GROUP	1968 CONTROL GROUP	1969 STUDY GROUP	1969 CONTROL GROUP
Nonutilizer (0 visits)	15.1	23.9	17.3	32.4	22.3	23.5	26.5	30.9
Low utilizer (1-2 visits)	14.9	23.2	19.0	18.4	18.2	16.2	15.3	16.5
Medium utilizer (3-7 visits)	23.6	22.4	27.4	20.2	26.0	29.4	29.5	26.5
High utilizer (8-15 visits)	23.9	16.9	18.4	14.3	16.8	16.9	15.3	13.2
Very high utilizer (16 + visits)	22.5	13.6	17.9	14.7	16.6	14.0	14.2	12.9
Total	100.0	100.0	100.0	100.0	99.9	100.0	99.9	100.0
Mean visits in two years	11.7	7.5	9.4	7.2	8.5	8.6	8.7	7.2

*Note change of cutting points for utilizer groups to reflect quartiles for one year rather than two.

1963; yet only a hard core of 14.3 percent failed to see a doctor in either year.

Table 7.3 suggests that both the New York Hospital Project and Medicaid produced a temporary rather than a permanent effect on utilization patterns. The study group's highest utilization occurred in 1962,* the first year of the Project: the control group's in 1968.† A plausible explanation

TABLE 7.4

Percentage of Persons Seeing a Doctor, and Mean Visits per Person Interviewed, by Wave, by Welfare Medical Status

Welfare/Medical Status 1968 & 1969

WELFARE STATUS	MEDICAID COVERAGE	NUMBER OF CASES[a]	*Percent Seeing Doctor* 1962	1963	1968	1969	*Mean Visits* 1962	1963	1968	1969
On	On	(414)	81.9	77.1	80.2	79.0	11.2	9.9	9.5	9.8
On and off } Off	On	(57)	87.7	78.9	80.7	64.9	8.6	7.1	9.9	7.1
On and off } Off	On and off	(197)	82.7	78.7	75.1	61.9	9.5	7.2	7.0	6.1
Off	Off	(44)	68.1	66.0	55.3	66.0	6.5	4.1	4.8	3.6

[a]Omits 14 cases with undetermined welfare status and Medicaid coverage.

* This shorthand will be used to denote the one-year period covered by the questions on the second wave interview. For each case, depending on the date of entry into the original study, it occurred some time between July 1, 1961 and June 30, 1963, *i.e.*, mainly in 1962 (Fig. 7.1).
† Similarly, between July 1, 1967 and June 30, 1969.

for the control group's decline in utilization from 1968 to 1969 is that it was caused by the Medicaid cutbacks. This, however, was not the case. Table 7.4 examines the relationship between welfare status and Medicaid coverage in the later study period, on the one hand, and utilization levels year-by-year on the other. Those who throughout 1968 and 1969 were on welfare (and hence automatically on Medicaid) tend to be the highest utilizers. Those few people on neither welfare nor Medicaid tend to be the lowest. But the utilization decline from 1968 to 1969 is not limited to those cut off Medicaid; it occurs just as much in those who remained covered by Medicaid but not welfare.

So far we have dealt with the full follow-up group as a whole, or with its randomly allocated breakdown into Project study and control groups. Let

TABLE 7.5
Percentage of Persons Seeing a Doctor, by Interview
Wave, by Selected Characteristics

	Number of Cases	1962	1963	1968	1969
All Cases	(729)	81.6	77.1	77.2	72.4
Sex:					
Male	(173)	81.5	74.6	68.2	63.6
Female	(556)	81.7	77.9	80.1	75.2
Birth year:					
Before 1900	(100)	83.0	84.0	68.0	66.0
1900-09	(93)	92.5	84.9	77.4	73.1
1910-19	(104)	82.7	75.0	82.7	76.9
1920-29	(158)	82.9	76.0	82.3	70.9
1930-39	(204)	76.0	73.5	73.0	74.5
1940-59	(70)	77.1	72.9	82.9	71.4
Ethnic group:					
White	(240)	80.8	77.5	75.4	66.2
PR	(374)	80.5	75.1	77.5	77.5
Black	(108)	87.0	82.4	80.6	69.4
Education:					
< 6 grades	(236)	82.6	78.4	77.1	72.0
6-8 "	(204)	83.3	78.4	77.4	78.9
9-11 "	(184)	79.3	74.5	78.8	69.0
12+ "	(102)	79.4	75.5	73.5	66.7
Welfare group at intake:					
Aged	(82)	82.9	86.6	67.1	66.2
Disabled	(98)	89.8	82.7	81.6	74.5
Single unemployed	(97)	80.6	79.6	76.5	69.1
1-parent family	(338)	81.1	74.5	76.9	73.7
2-parent family	(114)	76.1	70.8	82.3	71.7

us turn now, in the next three tables, to some of the demographic sub-groupings within this population.

Table 7.5 shows the percentage seeing a doctor each year, and Table 7.6 the mean number of reported doctor visits per person interviewed. Those that show a decrease in utilization after Medicaid are men; the older age groups, with an especially marked decrease in the percentage seeing a doctor each year; those who came on welfare at the beginning of the study in the Old Age Assistance and Medical Aid to the Aged categories; and to a lesser extent those originally on Aid to the Disabled, and the single unemployed on Home Relief; to some extent, all ethnic groups other than Puerto Rican.

Those that show an increase in utilization, on the other hand, are wom-

TABLE 7.6
Mean Visits per Person Interviewed, by Interview Wave, by Selected Characteristics

	Number of Cases	1962	1963	1968	1969
All Cases	(729)	10.2	8.6	8.6	8.2
Sex:					
Male	(173)	11.1	8.8	7.2	6.0
Female	(556)	9.9	8.5	9.0	8.8
Birth year:					
Before 1900	(100)	11.1	10.1	7.1	8.5
1900-09	(93)	13.8	12.0	11.7	8.7
1910-19	(104)	13.8	11.5	8.3	7.0
1920-29	(158)	10.6	8.7	10.5	11.5
1930-39	(204)	6.7	6.0	7.0	6.2
1940-59	(70)	7.9	4.6	7.2	6.7
Ethnic group:					
White	(240)	11.6	9.1	8.2	7.4
PR	(374)	9.0	7.3	8.8	9.0
Black	(108)	10.7	11.0	8.8	7.1
Education:					
< 6 grades	(236)	10.1	9.3	8.4	8.8
6-8 "	(204)	12.1	10.2	9.2	9.3
9-11 "	(184)	8.1	6.3	7.4	5.9
12+ "	(102)	10.1	7.5	9.7	8.1
Welfare group at intake:					
Aged	(82)	10.4	10.6	7.3	8.9
Disabled	(98)	15.9	12.4	10.6	7.6
Single unemployed	(97)	13.9	11.9	7.6	7.4
1-parent family	(338)	8.5	6.9	8.7	8.1
2-parent family	(114)	6.8	5.7	8.2	9.0

TABLE 7.7
Utilization Turnover Group from Two Years
Pre-Medicaid to Two Years Post-Medicaid,
by Welfare Grouping at Intake

| Utilization Turnover Group | Welfare Grouping at Intake | | | | | |
	AGED	DISABLED	UN-EMPLOYED	1-PARENT FAMILY	2-PARENT FAMILY	TOTAL
Low-low	15.8	10.2	15.5	19.2	24.6	18.0
Low-medium	8.5	2.0	9.3	13.9	14.0	11.1
Low-high	2.4	5.1	2.1	3.3	8.8	4.1
Medium-low	13.4	10.2	12.4	12.1	13.2	12.2
Medium-medium	11.0	15.3	11.3	17.2	11.4	14.5
Medium-high	8.5	3.1	6.2	7.4	6.1	6.6
High-low	14.6	11.2	14.4	3.6	5.3	7.5
High-medium	15.9	17.3	11.3	10.9	5.3	11.5
High-high	9.8	25.5	17.5	12.4	11.4	14.4
Total	99.9	99.9	100.0	100.0	100.1	99.9
Number of cases	(82)	(98)	(97)	(338)	(114)	(729)
Increased	19.4	10.2	17.6	24.6	28.9	21.8
Same	36.6	51.0	44.3	48.8	47.4	46.9
Decreased	43.9	38.7	38.1	26.6	23.8	31.2

en; the middle and younger age groups, especially the youngest; those originally on Aid to Dependent Children (mothers with children) and still more the two-parent families originally on Temporary Aid to Dependent Children or Home Relief; Puerto Ricans. There is no consistent relationship with educational level, but some suggestion that the better educated tended to increase their utilization after Medicaid.

The tables so far report aggregates for each group or subgroup without regard to how individuals changed over time. Table 7.7 examines the turnover from Time 1 (before Medicaid) to Time 2 (after Medicaid). To make it simpler, we return to the two-year periods as units of analysis, and combine respondents into three rather than five utilizer groups: low (which includes zero), medium, and high. Again, the cutting points are set so as to obtain groups that at Time 1 are of approximately equal size.

Slightly less than half of the respondents, or about 47 percent, remained in the same broad utilization group before and after Medicaid: 18.0 percent low-low, 14.5 percent medium-medium, and 14.5 percent high-high. As the previous tables have led us to expect, more people moved down a utilization group—from high to medium or low, or from medium to low—than moved up. Those that moved down to lower utilization groups were the aged, the disabled, and the single unemployed, in that order. The one-parent family heads moved up somewhat. But the greatest movement up the utilization group scale was in the two-parent families.

DISCUSSION

As people age, they tend to use more medical care. Disabilities, especially those severe enough to merit support on public assistance in the Aid to the Disabled category, tend to progress and presumably require increasing medical attention. How is it, then, that with the passage of six to eight years between study periods, the aged and disabled received *less* care after Medicaid than before?

The answer has already been suggested. They were receiving so much medical care before Medicaid, there was little room for increase. The New York Hospital Project certainly increased utilization over the regular welfare medical care system that obtained in New York City in the early sixties; but even in the control group whose members reflected the existing system unaffected by any experiment, utilization rates were not low.

Table 7.8 supplies additional evidence that under the welfare medical care system before Medicaid at least the sick got treatment. The table shows the conditions that, in response to a check list, the respondent said he had at intake in 1961–62; and when questioned two years later, he said they had persisted into or through that two year interim. (Conditions the respondent had at intake, but not during the subsequent two years, are not tabulated here.) The table shows, for each condition, the number of persons who reported seeing a doctor at some time during the two years *specifically for that condition.* The proportion for which a doctor was consulted was high: four out of five for all conditions and even more (88%) for the most life-threatening conditions.*

CONCLUSION

In conclusion, one must again stress that these findings are by no means generalizable across the board. Medicaid undoubtedly reached new target populations, and increased much needed services to very sick people in other parts of the country, where the services previously available to the poor were much more scanty than in New York City. On the other hand, the findings reported here are believed to be of more than local interest. There are other parts of New York City, and other urban ghettoes, similar to the one in our study, where the planners, providers, community leaders, and others speak as if there were a great "unreached" target population out there to whom we must bring new services. Our data suggest that one at least consider the possibility that access to care, and total volume of medical services, are not necessarily major problems in such areas. Quality

* As defined by the agreement of two consultant physicians.

TABLE 7.8
Conditions Reported at Intake and Persisting
into or through the Pre-Medicaid Study Period,
and Whether or Not Doctor Was Consulted,Total
Sample Interviewed on Third Wave, N = 1,200

Condition	Saw Doctor in Past Two Years	No Doctor in Past Two Years	Total
Arthritis	152	31	183
Varicose veins	104	46	150
*Hypertension	94	15	109
Sinus trouble	78	31	109
*Heart trouble	94	8	102
Allergies	70	22	92
Asthma	56	12	68
Hemorrhoids	38	21	59
Anemia	32	7	39
*Kidney, bladder disease	28	5	33
*Arteriosclerosis	26	3	29
*Diabetes	25	3	28
Hernia	20	5	25
Stomach ulcers	19	5	24
Lung trouble (excl. tb)	17	3	20
Thyroid	8	4	12
Tuberculosis	7	2	9
Epilepsy	9	0	9
Parasites	1	7	8
Rheumatic fever	7	0	7
Tumor	6	0	6
*Liver disease	3	2	5
Gallstones	3	1	4
*Stroke	3	0	3
*Cancer	2	0	2
Syphilis	1	0	1
Total	903	233	1,136

Percent of all conditions for which a doctor was seen 79.5
Percent of especially life-threatening conditions (asterisked) for which a doctor was seen 88.4

*As defined by the agreement of two consultant physicians.

of care, effectiveness, coordination, and follow-through—the deficiencies of our system lie equally in these aspects of health care delivery.

Although intended primarily as a study of the impact of Medicaid, the investigation of the last five years continues to be also an examination of the long-term effects of the New York Hospital Project. Comparisons between the two types of medical care experiments are unavoidable. The Project represented a special medical care program with what would now be called "outreach"—the letter of invitation to the New York Hospital; Medicaid represents a mere removal of financial barriers to care. Both had measurable impact, but along the variables we have so far examined, both here and in previous reports,[2] the effect of the Project was greater than that of Medicaid. This suggests that there are considerable limitations to the extent to which money alone will cure the health care ills of the urban poor.

REFERENCES

1. Goodrich, Charles H., Olendzki, Margaret C., and Reader, George G.: Welfare Medical Care: an Experiment. Cambridge, Harvard University Press, 1970.
2. Olendzki, Margaret C., Goodrich, Charles H., and Reader, G. G.: The significance of welfare status in the care of indigent patients. A.J.P.H. 53, 10:1676, 1963.
3. Olendzki, Margaret C.: The Impact of Medicaid on Former Welfare Clients. Final report to the Social Rehabilitation Service and the Social Security Administration, Grant No. 380.
4. See Interviewing Methods in the Health Interview Survey, Vital and Health Statistics, Series 2, Number 48, USDHEW, HSMHA, p. 60.
5. Goodrich, Olendzki, and Reader, *ibid.*; Olendzki, Margaret C., Grann, R. P., and Goodrich, Charles H.: The impact of medicaid on private care for the urban poor. Med. Care 10, 3:201, 1972.

NATIONAL HEALTH INSURANCE: SOME LESSONS FROM THE CANADIAN EXPERIENCE

Theodore R. Marmor
Wayne L. Hoffman
Thomas C. Heagy

INTRODUCTION

Concern about problems of medical care and issues of national health insurance are salient features of contemporary American politics. Within the larger public there is a broadly diffused sense of unease about the costs of illness and the reliability of access to medical services.[1] In the arena of national politics there has been visible attention to the details of competing national health insurance proposals and some searching for realistic appraisals of the effects of alternative interventions on problems of cost, quality and access. This is clearly an atmosphere in which informed understanding of other national experiences with governmental health insurance could aid policy discussion and choice.

Canada's experience, in particular, holds potentially important lessons for American decisionmaking. Canada's encounter with the effects of a national health insurance program, which predates, but is closely akin to some current American proposals, offers a natural experiment that deserves careful examination. Our purpose is to use the Canadian experience as a model predicting both the *impact* on the medical care system of the enactment of national health insurance and the *reactions* of national policymakers and the general public to these changes.

The case for American scrutiny of Canadian national health insurance experience rests on at least two propositions. First of all, the health care concerns of the two societies are strikingly similar. Worry about the increased proportion of national resources going to medical care is widespread, and some uncertainty about the marginal benefits of increased expenditures is visible among the public officials of both countries. Beyond resource costs, there is common concern about equal access financially, geographically and socially. Among a relatively small but vocal group in each country there is substantial interest in questions of quality and organization of care, and ferment about regulating medical care providers. Finally, after many years of similar focus on expansion of medical care facilities and personnel, there are parallel Canadian and American efforts to reduce, particularly, the use of expensive hospital services and to resist any increase in the number of hospital beds, and, to a lesser extent, physicians and some other medical care resources.

Our second proposition is that Canada, quite simply stated, is enough like the United States to make the effects of Canadian health insurance policies rather like a large natural experiment. The industrial countries of the West share, of course, a great number of medical policy concerns, but major political, social, economic, or cultural differences raise questions about whether the United States would have similar experiences with similar public policy intervention.[2] These differences are far less marked with Canada. Our particular two-nation research design would be termed a "most similar systems" approach in the more technical social science literature on cross-national comparisons.[3] This paradigm requires that the nations compared share a broad array of factors which might be causally related to the narrower features of central analytic concern. This is the case for our comparison. Canada has extensive decentralization of authority with a tradition of dispute over federal power analogous, though by no means identical, to controversies over American federalism. The structure of the health industry and the history of voluntary health insurance in Canada and the United States are strikingly similar. American and Canadian hospitals are largely "voluntary" and not government-owned, and physicians in both are still paid under a largely fee-for-service system. The two countries adjusted similarly to the growth of health insurance, which was primarily private at first, but in the postwar period increasingly public in character.[4]

Two major differences between the American and Canadian experiences are often put forward against using Canada as a "most similar system." These are the greater independence of the Canadian provincial governments, and the different route followed by Canada to national health insurance. The major implication of the greater *independence*, both constitutionally and politically, of the Canadian provincial governments is that to the extent United States policymakers build in a greater role for the states, *ceteris paribus*, the more the problems of cost control and national standards for the national government will imitate the Canadian experience.

American planners, however, possess a policy option denied to the Canadian planners by constitutional stricture—the option of a centralized federal system. In the American context, the extent of state involvement is a matter for public choice.

Turning to the second major Canadian–American difference, observers recall that Canada's first big step toward national insurance came via the hospital sector in 1958, followed a decade later by full-scale coverage of physician services. In contrast, the United States' advance on the road to national health insurance has been an incremental extension of coverage to additional segments of the population, first the aged, then the poor, and perhaps finally the full citizenry. The implication of this difference for political characterizations of the welfare state debate in the two countries may be great, but the limitation it places on the likely consequences of a national health plan seems small. The routes to full coverage have been different, but, once arriving at the same point, the concerns and policy options that result from that public commitment are likely to bear a strong resemblance. In summary, the number of shared similarities makes Canadian experience with health policy instruments a valuable source of conditional predictions for the United States.

This paper addresses the implications of Canadian national health insurance experience for problems of rising cost and unequal access to medical care. Canadian policies have been several years ahead of the United States in attempting some measures for the control of costs and the fairer distribution of medical care. Our analysis shows that the United States health policies, though lagging, have been remarkably similar in outcome. The power of the comparison is enhanced by the fact that American outcomes matched the *predictions that could have been made on our knowledge of Canadian experience alone.* We can predict the consequences of policy choice not only in terms of the key indicators of health care inflation, utilization, access and distribution, but also with respect to the likely concerns such first-stage effects will generate among politicians and administrators. Such policy analysis may make the appraisal of similar instrumentalities in American proposals more realistic and informed than usual.

It is perhaps appropriate here to mention a serious difficulty in transplanting Canadian experience into the current American debate over national health insurance. Canada does not constitute a laboratory for the full range of health insurance programs. Without extensive coinsurance or deductibles, Canada does not allow us a test of such a national scheme in practice, though her reluctance to employ such policies may be relevant to the discussion. Further, the reputed advantages of prepaid group practice cannot be tested from Canadian experience, nor can the way be seen for using national health insurance as a prod for the expansion of that delivery mode. Group practice, quite simply, has been too small a part of Canada's experience for exportation of lessons. It should thus be emphasized that the Canadian experience bears most directly on those American proposals that closely resemble it.

HISTORICAL BACKGROUND OF CANADIAN NATIONAL HEALTH INSURANCE[5]

Fundamental to an understanding of health care legislation in Canada is the fact that the constitutional division of powers between the provinces and the federal government puts health care (with a few minor exceptions) squarely in the jurisdiction of the provinces. This jurisdictional factor has had a fundamental effect on the form, and, to a lesser extent, the content of all of the legislation leading up to and including National Health Insurance.

The National Health Grant Program, beginning in 1948, provided the financial basis for a nationwide program of hospital expansion. Unlike the similar program in the United States (under the Hill-Burton Act), this expansion of hospital facilities was specifically intended to prepare the way for national hospital insurance which was subsequently enacted in 1957, and implemented beginning in 1958; the last province, Quebec, joined in 1961. A program for insurance covering physician and related services was enacted in 1966 (the Medical Care Act) with the various provinces joining between 1968 and 1971.

Both programs (hospital and physician service insurance) provide for government subsidy (averaging 50%) of programs set up and administered by the provinces, provided the programs meet certain standards of universality, coverage, and administration. Although joining is optional for each province, the financial incentives for doing so proved to be irresistible and every province participates in both programs. The percentage of subsidy by the federal government varies for different provinces. It is higher for provinces that spend less per capita on covered medical services, the highest subsidy being about 80%.

The provinces are permitted (with considerable limitations) to utilize point of services charges to raise revenue or discourage unnecessary utilization, but these have been unpopular, and only three provinces (Alberta, British Columbia, and the Northwest Territories) currently use them. For most Canadians, national health insurance contains no deductible and no copayment up to the federally mandated standards. To go beyond the standards of the public program (especially the ward accommodation standard for hospitalization), many Canadians purchase supplementary coverage insurance.

INFLATION AND COST CONTROL POLICY

Broadly speaking, the striking fact about cross-national cost comparisons between Canada and the United States are the parallel experiences. The trends of prices, utilization, and expenditures are similar and the proportion of national resources spent on health is almost identical[6] (see Figures 7.2 and 7.3). By the late 1960s there was a sense of inflationary crisis in both countries and a common worry about ways to contain that inflation.[7] For simplicity, we will discuss Canadian cost experience with hospitals separately from physicians' services. (While it is convenient to treat these

Figure 7.2. Expenditures on personal health care in the United States and Canada, 1953–1971 (as a percentage of personal income). Sources: United States—Reinhardt and Branson, "Preliminary Tabulation of Selected Comparative Statistics on the Canadian and U.S. Health Care Systems," (August 1974) mimeograph. Canada—Robert G. Evans, "Beyond the Medical Marketplace: Expenditures, Utilization and Pricing of Insured Health in Canada," Table 3, p. 140, in Spyros Andreopoulos, ed., *National Health Insurance: Can We Learn from Canada?* (New York: John Wiley and Sons, 1975).

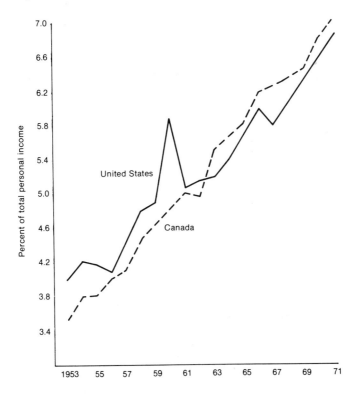

separately, it must be kept in mind that physicians have a major role in the determination of hospital expenditures.)

Hospitals

What are the implications of the growth of Canadian hospital expenditures and governmental efforts to restrain it? It should be noted that Canada and the United States proceeded in the postwar period from somewhat different starting points as to number and costs of beds; they have experienced very similar trends. Canada still remains more generously supplied

Figure 7.3. Comparison of trends in hospital sector in the United States and Canada, 1961–1971. Sources: Unadjusted Data—Reinhardt and Branson, "Preliminary Tabulation of Selected Comparative Statistics on the Canadian and U.S. Health Care Systems," (August 1974) mimeograph. U.S. Price Deflector (Consumer Price Index)—Bureau of Labor Statistics, *Monthly Labor Review* (various issues). Canada Price Deflator (Consumer Price Index)—Statistics Canada, *Canada's Yearbook*.

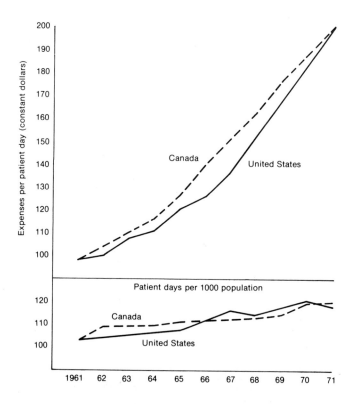

with hospital beds per capita and has higher rates of hospital admissions, patient days of care and expenditures per capita[8] (see Figure 7.4).

American interpreters of Canada must understand that national hospital insurance, in and of itself, does not seem to have caused rapidly increased use of hospitals in Canada. But it did bring more rapid increases in expenditures for hospital services.[9] Most of the postwar increases in hospital expenditures in both America and Canada are accounted for by growth in expenses per patient day, not increased per capita utilization. From 1953 to 1971, Canadian hospital expenditures per capita (in constant dollars) increased 259% while hospital patient days per capita only increased 29%.[10] Thus, increased utilization accounted for only a small part of the total increase in expenditures. The most important part of the increase in real expenditures on hospitalization can be attributed to the increase in the rela-

Figure 7.4. Hospital utilization—Canada and the United States, 1960–1971. Source: Reinhardt and Branson, "Preliminary Tabulation of Selected Comparative Statistics on the Canadian and U.S. Health Care Systems," (August 1974) mimeograph.

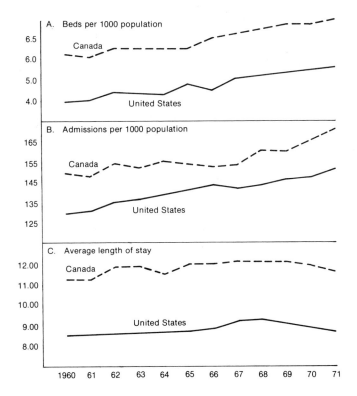

tive wages of hospital workers. Evans estimates that from 1953 to 1971, the average wage of hospital workers increased 68% more than the average wage of all industrial workers.[11]

R. G. Evans' interpretation[12] suggests that hospital admission is not very sensitive to price; i.e., reduction in point-of-service costs of care did not lead to a large increase in utilization. Based on his view, it follows that co-payment mechanisms designed to reduce costs by directing incentives at patients will have little effect on utilization, will redistribute costs to the ill, and, in hospitals, will not restrain increasing costs.[13] This interpretation of Canadian hospital inflation, for purposes of American discussion, raises doubts about the value of cost-sharing provisions in a number of current national health insurance proposals.

The fact that Canadian hospital cost increases were dramatic in the late 1960s, on the other hand, has serious implications for proposed methods of restraining hospital expenditures in the United States, such as detailed budget review, incentive reimbursement schemes with global (as opposed to line) budgeting and direct bed control. Canada has employed detailed budget review for more than a decade, and while it is apparently a good instrument for detecting fraud, it has not been judged a successful expenditure restraint and has been partially replaced in some provinces with global budgets and special incentives.[14] Indeed, it appears fair to conclude that Canadian officials have accepted a bed supply strategy of hospital expenditure control. The cutting off of national grants for hospital construction in 1969 parallels the interest in the United States in controlling hospital inflation by reducing the number of hospital beds or at least halting any increase in them. Both the use of supply controls and the concern for better incentive reimbursement schemes can thus be understood as responses to the failure of detailed review as a major cost-control measure.

Faced with the inability of budget review to limit cost escalation, Canadian officials experimented in the late 1960s with incentive reimbursement approaches to hospitals. The governmental task forces on the costs of medical care made much of the increases in efficiency which were thought to be available to the hospital sector. But according to two Canadian analysts,[15] incentives to better management as a technique of overall cost containment does not seem as powerful a policy variable as making hospital beds more scarce. This interpretation ought to be viewed in light of the faith so many American economists have in devising a reimbursement method which would make the hospital sector largely self-regulating.

The Canadian experience suggests that there are serious limitations to reportedly sensible reimbursement schemes, a caveat that could be of great import. Some American policy commentators firmly believe that "reimbursement patterns must be changed so that hospitals are no longer guar-

anteed that revenues will equal costs regardless of their productivity."
They hold out the hope for an

> ... incentive reimbursement system ... advocated to promote hospital effi-
> ciency and rationalize capital expenditures. Hospitals would be reimbursed
> on a case basis, taking account of the case mix of the hospital and its teaching
> program; the system would be based on a formula that assured the hospital of
> average efficiency recovery of operating and capital costs. Deficits would
> force inefficient hospitals to improve their management, change the nature of
> their operations, or shut down.[16]

Our Canadian interpreters provide evidence that such a system, however
appealing theoretically, is very hard to implement. A number of actual
conditions weaken the operation of a self-regulating reimbursement
scheme: for political reasons, poorly managed hospitals are rarely allowed
to fail; capital funds are supplied separately from operating budgets; case
mix adjustments are not well worked out; and hospital managers do not
seek "profits" as strongly as increased services and thereby larger budgets.
Whatever the reason, the Canadian turn toward supply constraints[17] rather
than relying on fine-tuned management incentives is revealing.

National health insurance in the United States has been presented by
some as the remedy to cost inflation and by others as a source of even
greater inflation.[18] But, in the debate over the causes and character of and
appropriate remedies for hospital inflation, a common thread has been the
belief that hospitals are used inappropriately and that savings are possible
by the more sensible use of these very expensive health items. This may be
thought of as the "hospital substitute" theory: the view that insurance programs should have very broad benefits so as to discourage the use of expensive benefits like hospitalization for pecuniary rather than medical reasons. This rests in turn on the view that excessive hospitalization does take
place, and that alternatives—whether nursing homes or outpatient clin-
ics—would save money. Yet, according to Evans, "unless new facilities are
balanced by withdrawal of the old, total costs rise." He cites Alberta's experience as evidence that well-developed out-of-hospital convalescent systems do not necessarily reduce hospital costs per capita and explains why
"reimbursing agencies [may] fear ... that attempts at partial efficiency
[hospital substitution] may raise overall health costs."[19] In the United
States, Martin Feldstein found that extended care facilities raise the cost
per hospital *episode*. What is saved in lower acute care stays is lost in longer extended care stays.[20]

Even if increased nursing homes were matched by decreased hospital
beds, it is not clear that any savings would be realized. The lower average
costs per patient day of nursing homes compared to hospitals does not im-

ply that it costs hospitals more than nursing homes to provide convalescent care. In fact, we would expect hospitals to be able to provide lower cost convalescent care than nursing homes because of economies of scale associated with having convalescent beds and acute beds in the same institution.

One can see, without understanding the full complexity of medical economics, why some infer that limiting the supply of beds is more effective in reducing unwarranted hospitalization than a hospital substitute strategy promoted by more comprehensive benefits to deal with the problem of unwarranted hospitalization. But the diagnosis that Canada has had "too many general hospital beds" which cost them a "great deal of money" must acknowledge the equally striking fact that, according to the then-Deputy Minister of Health and Welfare, "once a modern hospital is built, it is politically very difficult to close."[21]

Making hospital beds scarcer is a cost-control strategy with strong advocates in the United States. For the short term, at least, it appears that such crude policies are likely to be more effective than subtle management measures of theoretical force for which one cannot find large-scale instances of successful use and impact. Many Canadian interpreters judge detailed budget review a time-consuming, conflictual, and relatively inefficient means of restraining hospital expenditure increases. The continuing appeal of global budgeting is that as an anti-inflation measure, it does no worse than detailed budgeting; as a device for disbursement of funds, it is less conflictual to administer. The failure of both the line-by-line and the global budget technique to control Canadian inflation provides a demonstration lesson for the United States. Short of direct government control over wages, there appear to be few policy alternatives to bed control that have much chance of success in controlling health expenditures in the hospital sector.

Physicians

There are at least three important topics in the American health care debate for which Canadian experience with medical insurance is strikingly relevant: complaints about the fees and incomes of physicians; the impact of their practices on the total costs of health care; and the controversy over different strategies to redistribute physician services by location and by specialty. The complaint in the United States is that we have too few doctors in the places or specialties of greatest need and that not only are fees and incomes quite high, but physicians also contribute to the escalation of health care costs in a number of indirect ways. One strategy that has been advanced in the United States—and is embodied in the fee schedule provisions of several national health insurance bills—is detailed specification of fees and peer review of the appropriateness of the pattern of care as well as of the appropriateness of the price per unit service. What can we learn from reported Canadian experience on the likely implications of such a strategy?

The comparative data on change in the ratio of the Physicians' Fee Index to the Consumer Price Index, presented in Figure 7.5, shows that at about the time of the introduction of medical insurance, Canadian physicians' fees started a sharp decline relative to the other prices. Figure 7.6 illustrates, for the same time period, the corresponding movement in the net income (in constant dollars) of Canadian and United States physicians. The contrast of fixed fees control with continued growth of real incomes suggests that explicit fee schedules, as currently understood and imple-

Figure 7.5. Ratio of physician fees index to the consumer price index in the United States and Canada, 1957–1972 (1957 = 100). Source: Reinhardt and Branson, "Preliminary Tabulation of Selected Comparative Statistics on the Canadian and U.S. Health Care Systems," (August 1974) mimeograph.

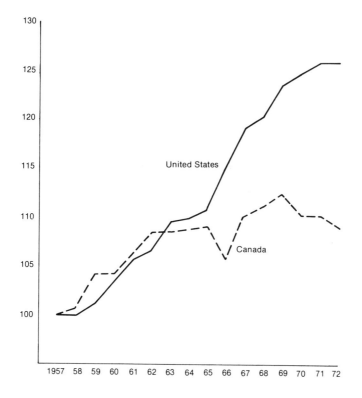

mented, will not restrain physician incomes nearly as much as the policy's most ardent backers have suggested.

This does not imply that open-ended fee reimbursement systems are superior or even acceptable. Rather, it points out that sufficient attention was not paid to the mechanisms by which average net physician incomes would rise markedly under Canada's Medicare program. Planners there sought to implement physician reimbursement at 85% or 90% of established fee schedules. They largely succeeded, but percentage reimbursement, predicated on the basis of a published fee schedule rather than on an estimate of actual average fees received before national health insurance,

Figure 7.6. Ratio of physician net income to consumer price index in the United States and Canada, 1959–1971 (1959 = 100). Source: United States—Unadjusted Data, *Statistical Abstract of the United States*, U.S. Department of Commerce, Bureau of the Census (various issues). Price Deflator (Consumer Price Index)— *Monthly Labor Review*, Bureau of Labor Statistics (various issues). Canada—Unadjusted Data, Evans, in Spyros Andreopoulos, ed., *National Health Insurance* (New York: John Wiley and Sons, 1975), p. 70. Price Deflator (Consumer Price Index)—Statistics Canada, *Canada's Yearbook*, 1972.

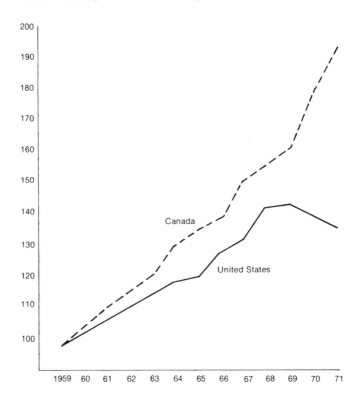

TABLE 7.9
The Effect of National Health Insurance on Net
Physician Earnings. [Divided by the Consumer Price
Index] Percentage Change over Two-Year Periods

Province	First Full Year of Province's Participation in a Program Covering Physician Services	Period Ending with First Full Year of Province's Participation	Immediately Previous Period
Saskatchewan	1963*	32.5% (1961–63)	2.7% (1959–61)
British Columbia	1969	5.3 (1967–69)	16.5 (1965–67)
Newfoundland	1970	26.2 (1968–70)	21.4 (1966–68)
Nova Scotia	1970	34.4 (1968–70)	21.1 (1966–68)
Ontario	1970	12.5 (1968–70)	17.0 (1966–68)
Manitoba	1970	37.1 (1968–70)	12.3 (1966–68)
Alberta	1970	10.6 (1968–70)	26.5 (1966–68)
Quebec	1971	42.1 (1969–71)	8.2 (1967–69)
Prince Edward Island	1971	60.5 (1969–71)	1.0 (1967–69)
New Brunswick	1971	26.6 (1969–71)	10.6 (1967–69)
Average		28.8%	13.7%

Source: Nominal Data, Spyros Andreopoulos, ed., *National Health Insurance: Can We Learn from Canada?* (New York: John Wiley and Sons, 1975), p. 70.
Price Deflator (Consumer Price Index), Statistics Canada, *Canada's Yearbook*, 1972.
*Saskatchewan adopted a provincial health insurance prior to National Health Insurance.

provided the mechanism by which large-scale increases in physician earnings were produced. According to R. G. Evans, "the single most prominent influence of health insurance in Canada has been to increase the earnings of health providers."[22] This is somewhat obscured in Figure 7.6 because of the various dates different provinces entered the Medicare (physicians' services) program. By standardizing the provinces on the dates they entered the program, Table 7.9 shows how large the impact of National Health Insurance really was on physician income. The average increase in net physician income (deflated by the Canadian Consumer Price Index) was more than twice as great during the transition to National Health Insurance as the increase in the immediately previous period. Studies in Quebec show absolutely no increase in the number of physician visits per capita after Medicare.[23] While comparable data is not available for other provinces, there is no reason to expect substantial differences. Thus it does not appear that the increase in physician income can be attributed to increased workloads.

The American discussion of fee-for-service reimbursement under national health insurance should clearly indicate the indirect mechanisms by which net physician earnings are likely to rise. There are at least two of importance. The first and simplest is the reduction of bad debts under national health insurance. The financial impact of bad debt reduction varies with the proportion of bad debts and expenses that physicians face. The main point, however, is that the introduction of the debt-reduction mechanism will cause incomes to rise without an increase in workload, because of both the elimination of the bad debt losses and the reduction of expenses associated with debt collection.

The second mechanism by which physician incomes may rise is closely akin to the first. Physicians have traditionally varied their fees somewhat in relation to income and insurance coverage. Under conditions of national health insurance they try to establish their highest rates as "customary" even though those rates are not necessarily the average fee received or even the most frequently asked fee. If national health insurance reimburses at the highest rate, net earnings will increase and, just as with bad debt reduction, will not show up as official fee increases.

What is at issue is the appropriate standard for fee-for-service remuneration under national health insurance. It seems clear that average fees received should be the appropriate standard and not so-called customary charges. But that standard requires detailed information on the actual fees of physicians broken down by specialty and region. Such information is not currently available in the United States.

Further, we should anticipate from Canadian experience that physician incomes will be a contentious public issue, not simply between the profession and the government but involving considerable public clamor. Disputes over physician incomes in British Columbia, Ontario, and Quebec (among others) have been among the most conspicuous of the postenactment politics of national health insurance. All American discussants are prepared for controversy concerning the level of fees in a national health insurance program, the question of direct or assignment billing and the variation in fees by education or location. But few have extensively considered how fees should be adjusted when a government program removes bad debts and "reduced" fees completely. Canadian experience highlights this issue, which American policymakers should consider as payment methods and levels are debated.

A related remuneration issue involves professional review of the patterns of service. "Peer review" is already a heated issue among American physicians. The Canadian concern about patterns of costly service which do not show up in extra billing, but in extra servicing, is parallel. One apparent lesson drawn from Canada is that a claims review procedure works well for the egregious cases of excessive and inappropriate claims but that the fee-for-service system's tendency toward increased units of care and altering the mix of procedures is very hard to control. It is worth noting at this point a paradox regarding the insistence on fee-for-service payment in societies like Canada and the United States and the increased threats to professional independence which the governmental review of such a payment method entails. Brian Abel-Smith suggests that

. . . world experience has shown, as the United States experience is also beginning to show, the paradox underlying attempts to preserve the free and independent practice of medicine. At first sight, fee-for-service payment enables private free-market medicine to be readily combined with health insurance. In practice, it is not long before interference with medical practice becomes much greater than occurs or needs to occur when physicians are salaried employees in government service. Physicians are made answerable for each of their acts. Because there are incentives for abuse, restrictive and punitive safeguards are established to prevent abuse from occurring. Sometimes the punishment falls on the physicians, but sometimes it falls on the patient.[24]

Whatever world experience has shown about the problems of fee-for-service payment, Canadian experience suggests for America this mode of payment will predominate in the post-national health-insurance world. Indeed, the problems of making fee-for-service regulation appropriate without its being excessively punitive should occupy the attention of planners more than imagining general shifts from present fee-for-service methods to other forms like capitation and salary.[25] Concern for wholesale transformation may drive out discussion of marginal improvements in the present dominant method of payment, or of ways to adjust national health insurance to other less traditional remuneration methods.

For some American health care discussants, increasing the supply of physicians is a strategy for improving both the distribution of physicians and for restraining through competition doctors' fees. That strategy appears, from Canadian experience, to lack promise on either count. And, to the extent physicians determine the use of other medical care services, it presents additional inflationary problems. The common sense view that increasing the supply of physicians will improve either the distribution or the price greatly is challenged now by a number of Canadian commentators, and the national government publicly expresses concern that a "saturation point for certain specialties is very close or has been reached in a number of provinces."[26] While there appears to be some improvement in supplying physicians to under-doctored areas, dramatic increases in physician numbers apparently do not restrain fees through competition. Given the nature of medical care which inhibits patients from questioning the price or quantity of services provided, and the existence of widespread private insurance, the ability of competition to limit physician income was weak even before the start of national health insurance. It may well be that the role of "national health insurance [in Canada has] been to relax further any market constraints on how physicians manipulate utilization to generate income."[27]

British Columbia, as Evans points out, is typically near the top in the levels of fees and near bottom in average physician incomes, which is related to its being the province with the largest number of doctors per capita. Increasing physician supply apparently is a weak and expensive instrumentality for coping with the problems of cost increases and the maldistribution of physician manpower.

While one suggestion for controlling costs is increasing the supply of doctors prior to implementing national health insurance, another prominent suggestion is that patient financial participation—through either deductibles or coinsurance—will introduce a needed and efficacious degree of cost-consciousness. Canadian analysts take a much less enthusiastic view of significant patient copayment. Where modest copayment was tried under Canadian Medicare—in Saskatchewan during 1968 to 1971—its effect on expenditures is unknown. But its impact on utilization was disproportionately felt by the poor and the old.[28] Moreover, there is little evidence in Canada that copayment reduced the "least medically necessary" care, and hence, there are distributional grounds for questioning this policy instrument. Finally, some commentators hold that the patient, once in the medical system, is dependent on the physician's judgments about further care and consequently that patient copayment is mistargeted away from the doctor, the "gatekeeper," to further medical services. What copayment does do, as Evans has pointedly written, "is reduce program costs by transferring them back to the ill rather than forward to taxpayers," and to reduce disproportionately patient-initiated physician contacts compared to physician-initiated ones. In Canada, he judges, this is "politically highly unpopular, and consequently co-payments as a means of cost-control appears . . . a dead issue."[29]

Copayment is most clearly not a "dead" issue in the United States; indeed, all of the current major proposals rely on family copayment for the great bulk of current average family health expenditures. Two considerations shape the United States discussion differently from Canada's. One is the effort to make copayment more equitable by varying the amounts with family income, thus trying to reduce the disproportional burden which fixed dollar copayments represent for the poor. The difficulty here is that the likely supplementation of national health insurance proposals of either the 1974 Nixon or Kennedy–Mills type would reduce the out-of-pocket expenditures of the middle and upper income groups buying supplementary insurance.[30] The major effect of copayment under those plans would be to reduce government program costs. In addition, it is certain that the supplementation by private insurance, with the resulting distribution of actual cost-sharing, would be sharply different from that of the formal proposals. The second American consideration is the search for ways to limit substantially the federal program costs of national health insurance, one means of which is the substantial patient cost-sharing just noted. In the political discussions of 1974, considerable efforts have been made to show limited amounts of "new" federal expenditures, even if such arrangements represent misleading labelling of required non-governmental expenditures as "private."[31] On the other hand, paying for the total United States personal health care bill through governmental budgets does have an impact on the opportunities for other governmental initiatives. The current Canadian emphasis on holding down medical expenditure increases illustrates the perception that governmental opportunities for other programs are severely constrained by the increasing share of the public budget devoted to health insurance.

ACCESS TO CARE

What are the implications for the United States of Canadian findings about the impact of national health insurance on access to medical care services? What does national health insurance mean for the utilization of medical care services generally? What, further, does the Canadian experience teach us about the distributional consequences of national health insurance on access by income class? These questions are important in the current American national health insurance debate. There is the hope that lowering financial barriers will distribute access to care much more fairly than our present arrangements and help reduce the striking inequalities in the probabilities that similar medical problems will receive equal medical attention by race, income, location, age, and connection with physicians. Both projections must be carefully considered because the Canadian experience offers mixed results.

First, on the basis of Canada's experience, we should expect relatively modest changes in the overall utilization of medical care services. In both the hospital and physican sectors changes in use were relatively modest in the wake of national insurance.[32] The fears of run-away utilization resulting from "cheap" care thus appear unrealistic and ignore the impact of pre-existent health insurance, the barriers to care which financing will not change, and the rationing which doctors will impose. This is an issue where the findings of the natural experiment—Canada—conflict with projections of sharply increased use (or crowded offices) based on estimates of the elasticity of demand for medical care in the United States.[33] Canadian findings, while discomforting about rising expenditures, are certainly less alarming on the issue of overall increases in actual or attempted utilization.

One's judgment of the impact of Canadian national health insurance on the distribution of access depends very much on initial expectations. Reported evidence suggests that national health insurance reallocated access to some extent from "rich" to "poor." This is true in the Beck study of Saskatchewan. Measuring access by the proportion of nonusers of medical care services by income class, the findings were that nonuse by the lowest income class declines substantially and nonuse by other income classes remains stable. The Enterline et al. study in Quebec shows not only an increase in the use of physician care by income groups under $5,000, but a decline in physician visits for income groups above $9,000. Table 7.10 provides the summary of the redistributive effect reported by Enterline and his colleagues.[34] But the evidence is not that such redistribution took place everywhere nor that national health insurance eradicated differences in access by income class. Disparities in access remain. Observers emphasize that the problem of access remains only partially solved in the wake of national health insurance. As Castonguay suggests in his emphasis on the problems remaining, "achieving access to care is not strictly a financial problem; physical and psycho-social barriers are also of significant importance."[35]

We should note, however, the direction of redistribution in favor of the less advantaged. A recent critique of American Medicare by Karen Davis argues that equal entitlement to program benefits has unequal results with greater benefits for the higher income aged and that income-conditioned programs like Medicaid partially redress the balance. Because American

TABLE 7.10
Redistributive Effects of Medicare Measured by
Average Annual Visits to a Physician by Income
Group Before and After Medicare, 1969–72
(In Montreal Metro Area)

Income in Dollars	Average Number of Visits	Percent Change in Visits
$0–3,000	7.8	+18
$3,000–5,000	6.0	+9
$5,000–9,000	4.7	No change
$9,000–15,000	4.9	−4
$15,000 and over	4.8	−9
All income groups	5.0	No change

Source: Modified from Castonguay, Table 4, p. 117, in Spyros Andreopoulos, ed., *National Health Insurance: Can We Learn from Canada?* (New York: John Wiley and Sons, 1975).

Medicare has significant cost-sharing, we should approach this interpretation with caution. It may well be that America's better-off aged are less deterred by cost-sharing, use more expensive services, and are much more likely to buy supplementary insurance. If that is the case, and if Medicaid reduces those out-of-pocket expenditures for the poorest, one should expect that the poorest and the richest would use disproportionately large shares of the Medicare budget.[36] The Canadian case suggests that where out-of-pocket costs are almost zero, equal benefits are associated with increasing access for the disadvantaged.

There seems agreement that removing financial barriers through national health insurance is insufficient for producing equal access to care. One should distinguish between equal use by income class, region, and sex from equal access measured by the likelihood of identical medical responses to similar health conditions. Canada has not, it appears, achieved equality on the first count; in contrast, there is evidence in the United States that the poor (under $3,000/year) see doctors as much as or more often than their Canadian compatriots. But the probability that a given symptom will stimulate care varies markedly with socioeconomic characteristics. What Canada suggests is that national health insurance contributes to greater equalization of access, but that it neither solves the problem nor eradicates concern for further amelioration. We should note the increases in availability of medical care personnel where financial incapacity was a problem before national health insurance; LeClair reports that in Newfoundland, the supply of medical practitioners in relation to population increased between 20% and 30% in the first three years of the Medicare program.[37]

The issue of access highlights an interesting difference in the focus of current American and Canadian discussions of medical care. Canadian commentators now sharply distinguish between access to good health and access to medical care services. The 1974 pamphlet *A New Perspective on the Health of Canadians*[38] illustrates the distinction and emphasizes that Canadians cannot expect substantial improvements in their health status through medical care. Though this argument is made in the United States, it is often employed to discourage national health insurance itself. Yet it makes an enormous difference whether one highlights the non-medical care determinants of health status before or after the introduction of national insurance. The arguments for national health insurance concern the access to and consequences of medical services use as much as—if not more so than—the means to healthiness. Canadians take for granted now that illness no longer is associated with fears of destitution; they hardly mention that one of the most central impacts of national health insurance was the improved access to protection against financial catastrophe. Once that is accomplished and it is recognized that access is dependent upon variables other than income, it may well be that American leaders will also focus on trying to influence environmental factors as the "key to better national health and reduced rate of increases in health costs."

CONCLUSION

The primary purpose of Canadian hospitalization and physician insurance was to eliminate financial barriers to health care. In this it succeeded. But it also produced results which were not the product of conscious decisions by the Canadian government, but were essentially unexpected side-effects of the particular programmatic forms of national health insurance adopted. The most important of these, and one that is greatly concerning Canadians, is increased inflation in the health sector. Perhaps the most important lesson from the Canadian experience is that national health insurance will feed the fires of medical inflation unless the system has very strong anti-inflationary mechanisms built into it. By providing for administration by the provinces and heavy subsidy by the federal government, no single agency in the Canadian system has both the means and the incentive to control inflation. Because of the federal subsidy, the provinces lack sufficient incentive; because of provincial administration, the federal government lacks the authority. It should be cause for concern that some of the more prominent United States proposals for national health insurance are similar to the Canadian system in failing to provide a single level of government with both the means and the incentive to control the inflationary effects of a national health insurance program.[39] And it is instructive that the federal government in Canada recently proposed a new system under which 100% of the marginal cost of medical services under the program would be borne by the provinces.[40]

NOTES

1. The nature and magnitude of this public worry has been analyzed by Ronald Andersen et al., "The Public's View of the Crisis in Medical Care: An Impetus for Changing Delivery Systems?" *Economic and Business Bulletin*, Vol. 24, No. 1 (Fall 1971), pp. 44–52.
2. There is evidence, in fact, that a variety of health care concerns—rising costs, interest in rationalization, worry about efficacy and patient satisfaction—are evident throughout Western Europe and North America irrespective of the details of medical care's public financing modes. See Anne R. Somers, "The Rationalization of Health Services: A Universal Priority," *Inquiry*, Vol. 8 (1971), pp. 48–60.

    The enumeration of health care concerns is extraordinarily extensive in both Canada and the United States. Note particularly, however, the interest in similar Canadian health insurance concerns and experience by the U.S. Congress' Committee on Ways and Means in its review of issues of national health insurance: "The material on Canada is in considerably more detail than that presented for other nations since the Canadian experience seems more relevant to U.S. policy." Committee on Ways and Means, *National Health Insurance Resource Book* (Washington, D.C.: Government Printing Office, 1974), p. 111.

3. A concise discussion of comparative research design useful for cross-national policy study, including the "most similar system" and "most different system" approach, is found in Adam Przeworski and Henry Teune, *The Logic of Comparative Social Inquiry* (New York: John Wiley and Sons, 1970).

4. There is a large literature on Canada's movement toward national health insurance. Among the more helpful brief interpretations, see Malcolm G. Taylor, "The Canadian Health Insurance Program," *Public Administration Review*, Vol. 33, No. 1 (Jan./Feb. 1973), pp. 31–39; J. E. F. Hastings, "Federal-Provincial Insurance for Hospital and Physicians' Care in Canada," *International Journal of Health Services*, Vol. 1, No. 4 (Nov. 1971), pp. 398–414. For fuller treatment, the basic source is the *Report of the Royal Commission on Health Services* (Hall Commission; Ottawa: The Queen's Printer, 1964) and supporting studies. For the physician sector more generally, see B. R. Blishen, *Doctors and Doctrines: The Ideology of Medical Care in Canada* (Toronto: University of Toronto Press, 1969).

   For similar information on the U.S. from a comparative perspective see Odin Anderson, *Health Care: Can There Be Equity? The United States, Sweden, and England* (New York: John Wiley and Sons, 1972), and T. R. Marmor, *The Politics of Medicare* (Chicago: Aldine, 1973).

5. The information in this section came from Maurice LeClair, "The Canadian Health Care System," in Spyros Andreopoulos, ed., *National Health Insurance: Can We Learn from Canada?* (New York: John Wiley and Sons, 1975), pp. 11–42. This is a collection of papers by participants in the Sun Valley Health Forum on National Health Insurance.

6. See, for example, *National Health Expenditures in Canada, 1960–71 with Comparative Data for the United States*, Health Program Branch, Ottawa (Oct. 1973), and the documentation presented by Stuart Altman in "Health Care Spending in the U.S. and Canada," in Andreopoulos, op. cit. For the proportion of national resources expended in health, see Altman, pp. 193–94.

7. The Canadian alarm was fully expressed in the *Task Force Reports on the Cost of Health Services in Canada* (Ottawa: The Queen's Printer, 1970), 3 vols. Concern about the rate of inflation in the health care field was plain as well in the Economic Council of Canada's Seventh Annual Review, *Patterns of Growth* (Sept. 1970). The parallel American preoccupation with rising medical care costs was perhaps best evidenced by the production in the first Nixon Administration of a "white paper" on health which catalogued familiar diagnoses of the ills of the industry.

   These same concerns were apparent in the hearings on national health insurance before the Ways and Means Committee in Oct./Nov. 1971; 93rd Congress, 2nd Session, 11 volumes (Washington, D.C.: Government Printing Office, 1971).

8. See for the period 1966–72, Maurice LeClair, "The Canadian Health Care System," in Andreopoulos, op. cit., Table 3; for the earlier period, see Andersen and Hull, "Hospital Utilization and Cost Trends in Canada and the United States," *Medical Care*, Vol. 7, No. 6 (Nov./Dec. 1969), special supplement, Table 5, p. 13; compare Altman in Andreopoulos, op. cit., p. 198, and Table 5. Canada has been and continues to be a heavier spender in the hospital sector.

9. This information is consistent with that of Andersen and Hull, op. cit., and R. G. Evans' chapter, "Beyond the Medical Marketplace: Expenditure, Utilization and Pricing of Insured Health Care in Canada," in Andreopoulos, op. cit.

10. The nominal data is from R. G. Evans, ibid., pp. 138–142. The price deflator is the Canadian Consumer Price Index from: Statistics Canada, *Canada's Yearbook* (1972).

11. R. G. Evans, ibid., p. 146.

12. R. G. Evans to R. A. Berman, letter, July 2, 1974, on the subject of major issues to be highlighted for Sun Valley conference on Canada's experience with national health insurance.

13. The inability of increased copayment mechanisms to restrain costs arises only partly because hospital utilization is relatively insensitive to price. Equally important is the fact that the patient's copayment represents only a very small part of his total cost of hospitalization, which includes not only the direct cost of hospital services, but also physicians' fees, foregone earnings, and general inconvenience.

14. For a discussion of the reliance on detailed, line-item budget review as the mechanism of budgetary control during the first decade of Canada's national hospital insurance, see Evans, and LeClair, in Andreopoulos, op. cit., pp. 151–155 and 57–58, respectively. For the arguments justifying less detailed budget review, see Claude Castonguay, "The Quebec Experience: Effects on Accessibility," in Andreopolous, op. cit., pp. 106–107, including an explanation of global budgeting.

15. Compare the comments of R. G. Evans, and M. LeClair, in ibid., pp. 151–155 and 64–65, respectively.

16. Judy and Lester Lave, *The Hospital Construction Act: An Evaluation of the Hill-Burton Program, 1948–1973* (Washington: The American Enterprise Institute for Public Policy Research, 1974), p. 3.

17. For discussion of this policy change, see Robin Badgley et al., *The Canadian Experience with Universal Health Insurance*. Third annual report, Department of Behavioral Science, University of Toronto (August 1974), p. 135 f (unpublished).

18. See Theodore R. Marmor, Donald A. Wittman, and Thomas C. Heagy, "Politics, Public Policy, and Medical Inflation," in Michael Zubkoff, ed., *Health: A Victim or Cause of Inflation* (New York: Millbank Memorial Fund, 1975).

19. Evans, in Andreopoulos, op. cit., p. 154.

20. Martin Feldstein, "An Econometric Model of the Medicare System," *Quarterly Journal of Economics*, Vol. 85, No. 1 (Feb. 1971).

21. M. LeClair, in Andreopoulos, op. cit., p. 15.

22. Evans, in ibid., p. 133.

23. Castonguay, in ibid., p. 116.

24. Brian Abel-Smith, "Value for Money in Health Services," *Social Security Bulletin*, Vol. 37, No. 7 (July 1974), p. 22.

25. For evidence on the practically invariant relationship between dominant methods of physician remuneration before and after the enactment of universal government health programs among western industrial democracies, see William Glaser, *Paying the Doctor: Systems of Remuneration and Their Effects* (Baltimore: Johns Hopkins Press, 1970), and Marmor and Thomas, "The Politics of Paying Physicians . . . ," *International Journal of Health Services*, Vol. 1, No. 1 (1971), pp. 71–78. The actual working-out of these common constraints in the Canadian case is mentioned in all of the papers in Andreopoulos, op. cit.

26. LeClair, in Andreopoulos, op. cit., p. 76. The "super-saturation-spillover" approach is criticized in John R. Evans, "Health Manpower Problems: The Canadian Experience," prepared for the Institute of Medicine, Washington, D.C., 1974, p. 15.

27. R. G. Evans, in Andreopoulos, op. cit., p. 162.

28. Discussed in LeClair, in ibid., pp. 48–49 and Table 7, based on R. G. Beck, "The Demand for Physician Services in Saskatchewan," unpublished Ph.D. thesis, University of Alberta, 1971. The major conclusion of Beck's study is "that co-payment provisions reduce the use of physician services by the poor by an estimated 18 per cent. The impact upon the poor, it was observed, is considerably greater than the reduction of service experienced by the entire population, which has been estimated at 6 to 7 percent."

29. Evans letter to Berman, July 2, 1974; also see LeClair, ibid., p. 79, for discussion of the physician as the "gatekeeper" of medical care expenditures.

30. This prediction is based on the experience under the Medicare program and the substantial incentives to buy health insurance in the current tax laws. For a discussion of these incentives and the magnitude of their impact see Mitchell and Vogel, "Health and Taxes: An Assessment of the Medical Prediction," *Southern Economic Journal* (Apr. 1975).

31. This issue is clearly defined by Karen Davis in the chapter on "National Health Insurance," in Blechman, Gramlich, and Hartman, *Setting National Priorities: The 1975 Budget* (Washington, D.C.: The Brookings Institution, 1974). See, also, T. R. Marmor, "The Comprehensive Health Insurance Plan," *Challenge* (Nov./Dec. 1974), pp. 44–45.

32. For the hospital sector, see Evans, in Andreopoulos, op. cit., Table 4, p. 142, and the report that "hospital utilization rates rose steadily from 1953 to 1971 at about 1.4 percent per year increase in patient days per 1000 population and about 1.3 percent per year in admissions" and that the main increase in these rates came in the period before national health insurance, pp. 3–4 of discussion of issues paper. See LeClair, Table 5, discussed at p. 88, on changes in per capita physician use, all "consistent with the view" that government medical insurance did not generate a surge of patient-initiated demand.

33. See, for instance, Newhouse, Phelps, and Schwartz, "Policy Options and the Impact of National Health Insurance," *New England Journal of Medicine*, Vol. 290, No. 24 (June 13, 1974), pp. 1345–1359.

34. R. G. Beck, "Economic Class and Access to Physician Services Under Medical

Care Insurance," *International Journal of Health Services*, Vol. 3, No. 3 (1973), pp. 341–355; P. E. Enterline et al., "The Distribution of Medical Care Services Before and After 'Free' Care—The Quebec Experience," *New England Journal of Medicine*, Vol. 289, No. 22 (Nov. 28, 1973); R. F. Badgley et al., "The Impact of Medicare in Wheatville, Saskatchewan, 1960–65," *Canadian Journal of Public Health*, Vol. 58, No. 3 (Mar. 1967).

35. Castonguay, in Andreopoulos, op. cit., p. 100.
36. See Karen Davis, op. cit., pp. 214–217.
37. LeClair, in Andreopoulos, op. cit., p. 75.
38. Marc Lalonde, *A New Perspective on the Health of Canadians*, Government of Canada, Ottawa, Apr. 1974.
39. See the discussion of unbalanced political interests in Marmor, Wittman and Heagy, "Politics, Public Policy, and Medical Inflation," op. cit.
40. LeClair, in Andreopoulos, op. cit., p. 81. For the view that such concentrated financing (or, more unlikely, almost complete patient financing of medical care) is a necessary condition for curbing medical inflation, see Marmor, Wittman, and Heagy, ibid.

GOVERNANCE BY CITIZENS' BOARDS: THE CASE OF COMMUNITY MENTAL HEALTH CENTERS

Scott Greer
Ann Lennarson Greer

In 1963 the first Community Mental Health Center (CMHC) Act was signed into law. According to Foley (1977:40), "The mandate of the CMHC Act was to deliver readily accessible treatment and preventive services and to assure continuity of quality care without regard to a patient's ability to pay." By 1978 over five hundred federally funded Community Mental Health Centers were in operation. Created by President John F. Kennedy shortly before his death, greatly strengthened by President Lyndon Johnson, and suffering continual assault from President Richard Nixon and Gerald Ford, the centers managed to survive into the Carter administration.

The "grand design" saw the entire country divided into service or "catchment" areas of manageable and economic size, within which CMHCs would provide mental health treatment to persons in their own community. Meanwhile, the state mental health hospitals would be phased out as increasingly effective chemotherapy permitted ill persons to be freed of their restraints. The treatment would be comprehensive, that is, it would range from prevention to care and cure. The eventual aim was to normalize mental illness so it would be viewed as an illness comparable to any other, and therefore, to increase and improve the use of mental health services. The rural "insane asylums" run by the states would eventually be abandoned or converted to other uses. The National Institute of Mental Health (NIMH) was made responsible for awarding CMHC grants and monitoring CMHC performance. The basic staffing grant was to decline on a formula basis over several years until none was needed.

Federal funding of mental-health services through CMHC grants changed a system which had previously been almost entirely the duty of the states. Under the new act, funding for mental services was to be shared by the states, the local governments, and the federal government. Criteria for CMHC grants defined type and range of services to be offered—initially, there would be five; later, twelve. Although provisions of the act have been altered by a series of amendments and a revision of the act in 1975, "The ultimate control of the CMHC program remains with NIMH, not with the states" (Foley, 1977:41).

Within the general requirements of NIMH funded programs, the control of each CMHC is vested in a community citizen's board:

> The first CMHC legislation left these boards' functions and responsibilities undefined and accountability was not fixed. But the 1975 legislation required these boards to be composed, where practical, of residents of a catchment area, with one-half the board drawn from non-health care providers. Each board is to meet at least once a month, establish general center policy, approve the center's annual budget, and appoint the center director (Foley, 1977:42–43).

The board is also required to reflect the population of the catchment area with respect to age, sex, class, and ethnicity.

THE EVALUATION STUDY

In 1977 a research group at the Urban Research Center of the University of Wisconsin–Milwaukee was funded to study the role of these citizens' boards in the governance of CMHCs.* We did not expect to find much ex-

* NIMH Award R12 MH28448.

isting literature on these governing boards; after all, they had only been mandated for three years. We were taken aback by the paucity of data and theory on control boards in general and for control boards of not-for-profit private corporations in particular. They are important and rapidly growing devices; Peter Drucker (1978) has called the latter a "third sector" between the public and the private in our society.

We had no universal parameters to speak of, and, given the state of our ignorance, a national sample seemed premature. Therefore, we decided to study boards which were exceptionally successful, knowing we could waste a great deal of time and money on ghost governments and shadow boards. The null hypothesis was, in fact, "staff domination of the board," a common proposition in the study of organizations. We saw the study of successful boards as a step to developing theoretical propositions and efficient, economical indicators that would allow us to test propositions concerning important aspects of boards.

The research was done in two stages. First, a detailed mail questionnaire was sent to the executive director and board president of every CMHC that (1) was or had been funded by NIMH and (2) had been in existence for at least three years. While the response rate was 77 percent of the centers (at least one questionnaire was returned), in only 50 percent of the cases did both officials return questionnaires. From this data some facts stood out. A large proportion of the boards, including most of the boards in California, New York, Kansas, and Georgia, were not formally recognized as governing bodies; they were "advisory boards." Control remained where it had always been—in hospital boards and county boards. From the limited sample it was also clear that by one measure of success, i.e., demographic representation, most boards were failures, with weak representation by the poor, women, and ethnic minorities. Based on the mail questionnaire and the recommendations of NIMH regional offices and the National Council of Community Mental Health Centers, fourteen seemingly successful boards were selected for more in-depth study. In these cases both director and board president thought the board was a good one, and that it was effective in a wide array of causes. Each board reflected the demographic composition of the catchment area. Finally, the boards constituted a fifty-fifty mixture of poverty and nonpoverty areas, and they were scattered among the ten administrative regions of DHEW. A senior researcher visited each candidate center and conducted interviews with the director and the president of the board. Wherever practical, he or she also attended board and/or committee meetings.

A team of three interviewers, including two senior-grade staff members, was sent to each center. During a week in residence, around thirty-five relevant persons, including presidents and other board members, directors and other staff members, psychiatrists and psychologists in private practice, and other institutional actors whose work related closely to the center's (welfare officials, judges, and hospital administrators) were interviewed. At the crudest level researchers found one or two measures that validated their assumption of "success": the median tenure of the executive directors in the chosen centers (twelve years) was five times the median tenure for the directors responding to the mail questionnaire overall.

ABOUT CMHCS

Even with the small sample of centers studied intensively, it becomes clear that there is no set pattern for CMHCs. Federal requirements for (1) decentralized control by local boards and (2) required diversity (twelve services*) allow great leeway to local imagination and circumstances. CMHCs vary by catchment-area population, by local definitions of mental health and illness, by funding and relations with various levels of government, by management philosophy, and by mental health philosophy. In structure they range from centers entirely housed in one place to those with a campus or even scattered "satellites" throughout one community to those which are essentially consortia of specialized service centers. Equally diverse are their self-definitions. Some centers are committed to the medical model, concerning themselves with the chronically ill discharged from state mental hospitals, as was intended in the original act. Others interpret the twelve services required after 1975 so broadly that they offer help for rape victims, marriage counseling, obesity control, and pregnancy prevention. Those adhering to the medical-model position accuse the centers with the broadly defined purpose of neglecting the real problem—the chronically ill or those in hazard of serious illness such as schizophrenia. They see this as an evasion, a middle-class strategy to normalize mental illness by servicing needs that could and should be serviced elsewhere. Those adhering to the broader definition are more concerned with prevention, and they consider centers focused on very sick people as little more than the conventional state hospitals in new forms. So vague is the definition of mental health, and so varied is its interpretation by the centers that the centers appear to have nothing in common other than the taking of federal funds and the successful effort to abide by the law with respect to board composition. Yet, this is to be expected when one considers their history.

Few CMHCs were planned as entities; instead, they grew like a farm-

---

* The twelve services are: inpatient; outpatient; partial hospitalization; emergency; consultation and education; children's services; alcoholism treatment; drug addiction treatment; screening residents for the courts; keeping track of patients discharged; prevention and publicity, and program evaluation.

house to which one room after another is added. Furthermore, they grew rapidly, often starting, for example, with a small child-guidance center through which they obtained a CMHC grant that enabled them to expand to five services, then twelve, and often more. They are further differentiated by their ongoing efforts to prepare for "graduation," or loss of federal funds. With so much required by the act, the twelve services are not equally emphasized; some are so central as to set the character of the whole CMHC, while others are given scant attention. In view of the open-ended objectives of mental health services and with scarce resources, it is perhaps inevitable that the profiles of center services will reflect the concerns of the executive director and the boards. This is affected—some would say, distorted—by methods of funding from state and local governments and other buyers of mental health services. With the end of federal support, this is apt to become an even more powerful influence. In its annual report one CMHC featured a chart showing the public and private agencies which had an impact on the center through funding and/or regulations; there were seventeen. Each, in some degree, got what it paid for.

SUCCESS, TENSIONS, AND CHOICES

At this stage of analysis, one can make only tentative statements about successful boards. There are, for one thing, many kinds of success, and furthermore, one kind may be bought at the expense of another. A state funding formula may allow centers the luxury of financial security, but at the price of built-in incentives that ensure mediocrity. Conversely, centers with little state support may thrive under the shadow of possible bankruptcy, while board and staff cooperate in search of new markets and services valuable enough to compete in the marketplace. In this analysis centers are approached as organizations facing choices, whether consciously or not, between two or more courses of action, all of which they need but cannot equally afford. Tensions include those generated around three foci: definition of mission, board composition and function, and board-staff relations.

Definition of Mission

Some ambiguity is produced by multiple missions. Three stand out: A center is charged with the cure of the curable, the care of the chronic, and the prevention of mental illness leading to hospitalization. Ideally, as seen from Capitol Hill, a good center would be one that did all three well. In the real world, where CMHCs are located, this doesn't happen. Discussing the questions of care for the chronics with one director, he thought it over a moment, then said that it could be done for the catchment area, but it "would cost $2 million a year" (over two-thirds of the center's entire budget).

The emphasis a center chooses has an impact on the population with which it does its major business. If the center is concerned with the cure of incipient chronic schizophrenia, for example, it will deal with many persons suffering from severe disorientation, who are, perhaps, in pain or perhaps a danger to themselves or to others. Further, they will be persons who do not have the resources to find private care; thus, they are apt to be poor and often from an ethnic minority. If a center emphasizes care of the chronic, it will be filled with damaged human beings who look and act strangely but are partially able to care for themselves. If, however, a center concentrates on prevention and research, the target population will be schoolteachers (educating them as to what they should be sensitive to in students' behavior), children, married couples with difficulties, parents and children with difficulties, and the like. Prevention brings in more attractive people than does care and safer people than does cure.

There is some indication that the direction a center chooses will be influenced by the guild in charge and modified by board preferences. In this view psychiatrists are interested in curing the most seriously ill who can be cured; psychologists and social workers are interested in prevention; recreational therapists are concerned for the care of the chronically ill. The ordinary citizen representative on the board is usually most enthusiastic about prevention, especially preventive services to children. A usually small but significant number are on the board because they are or have been in trouble, or they have family members who are seriously ill: They tend to be concerned with the less attractive cases—the seriously ill and the chronics.

Board Composition and Function

There are three classes of board members: those representing local government, those representing constituent agencies of a consortium, and those representing the community. Representatives of local governments are either elected or appointed by elected bodies. While they have the advantage of legitimacy, they are often uninformed about mental health and uninterested in the subject, which is rarely of much political importance. Members representing constituent agencies of a consortium-type CMHC are a means of keeping agencies interested in the turf and program of their service but are less interested in the CMHC's overall goals. Thus, they create a centrifugal force on the board. Government appointees also are said to be poor attenders.

Boards with a majority of members from the community-at-large were the focus of this study. These citizens are typically selected because they are interested in the treatment of mental illness and in the CMHC as a community asset. They dominate the private, not-for-profit corporations. Their roles vary, in part, according to why they are on the board. Their interest may derive from expertise. One center had a board that included a top management consultant, a former cabinet member, and an attorney who had access to powerful officials ranging from the Senate to the State House (and who wrote the state mental health law). It may also derive from "old family" or civic status. Finally, a board member may derive legitimacy because he represents the population; in one New England CMHC the catchment area included forty-six inhabited towns; at the last annual town meeting, forty-three towns voted to support the center with local tax monies. It is a very poor part of a poor state, but the center board included members from most of the towns, and had spokespersons in others.

The act does specify demographic fidelity to the population, but says nothing beyond this. Even so, there are recurring tensions between these requirements and who will serve as board members.

Board-Staff Tensions

A major tension between board and staff is the question of control. There are boards where the director dominates, either through charisma and old friendship ties or through organizational manipulation (such as seeing that there is no contact between staff and board members, and no board members on the premises of the center except for board meetings). This promotes dull meetings, a lack of creativity, and few board-initiated proposals.

A more common situation is dominance by the director plus a small inner circle of articulate and concerned board members. A small board with high status and highly skilled members seems to be optimal for the "partnership" model so often evoked.

Then there is the board-dominated center. This kind of center seems to be vulnerable to governance by a single person or a small clique, and tension between the professional values of the staff and the values of the board is ubiquitous. Such situations may be rooted in the participatory democracy of the 1960s; in any event, such centers are likely to be marked by rapid turnover of directors.

Finally, in cases of stalemate or simple lack of concern on the part of board and director, staff domination may occur. When there is no strong policy center, the mental health professionals do what all professionals tend to do—what they like to do and what they think is important. The sense of overall priority is lost, and it is likely that costs will get out of hand. We did not visit such a center, although we were told this had been true at one site prior to the present director's incumbency; and we heard stories of such staff domination in several regions. A few examples seem to have great impact on the thinking of other directors and more knowledgeable board members.

Apart from the issue of control, there are other tensions surrounding the question of board responsibility. Is the board accountable to the democratic ideal, or is it accountable to health goals? If the latter, then do you need more than a board of health experts? If the former, is there a danger of losing the goal—better mental health services—in the vagaries of the democratic process, which range from selection to board process to policymaking. On the other hand, experts may be insensitive to community desires.

The board may see itself as a watchdog, but a watchdog for whom? At one extreme it is a watchdog for the constituents whom it represents. But who are these constituents? Does a black lay preacher speak for blacks, for poor people, or for the African Methodist Episcopal Church? Another form of watchdog mentality is carried over intact by members from corporate boards in the private sector. Much is made of the legal accountability of the board for finances, personnel policy, and so on. But this is misplaced in a private, nonprofit corporation. For one thing there is no bottom line, showing that resources spent have resulted in profits. Some liken the role of a CMHC to that of a defense contractor who is the sole provider of important weaponry—but the contractor is still in business for profit—as Lockheed discovered—and the corporate directors still look to profit, if not to a share of the market, as a measuring rod for the performance of management. In the absence of a profit line, the board of the CMHC tends to fall back on cost-per-unit-of-service, which is all very well, but it obscures the more important question: Is a service worth doing at any price? Does society profit from the service?

Another tension is that between the policymaking role of the board and mangement by the executive director. All pay lip service to the strict separation of policy and management; few heed it consistently. But since the board is not made up of mental health professionals, how can it develop the tools for summarizing performance, measuring cost against benefit, and judging the success of a program against the alternative uses of the same resources? Boards with heavy representation from the business sector are most likely to undertake policy evaluations, monitor management (though not necessarily by personal inspection), and initiate new policy for old services, or even new services. Such boards are demographically representative only in very unusual communities.

DATA BASE AND METHOD OF ANALYSIS

The initial list of field-site interviewees was compiled in collaboration with the center director and board president at our separate interviews with them. It was expanded as others suggested persons able to offer a perspective on the role played by the center and the center board in the community.

This strategy, necessitated by the need to use with optimum effect the limited time at the field sites, is one particularly susceptible to the charge that we would hear what particular individuals wanted us to hear. While this is to some extent unavoidable, pains were taken to get a balanced view. Directors, board presidents, and others helped in this regard. They were asked to select persons based on a check list.* In addition we specifically asked our local advisors to provide the names of the center's major critics as well as its fans and its lukewarm friends. We interviewed recent arrivals to board membership as well as long-time members, minority representatives, and departed board members. Beyond this a snowballing effect allowed us to move from these interviewees to others suggested when critical or unexpected themes gained importance. We feel our best defense against the danger that our data might contain damaging bias was our strategy of sending one or two senior field associates to each site to interview personally and to have them accompanied only by advanced graduate students, who were also involved intellectually with the substance and the methodology of the investigation.

Because this was a qualitative investigation, we deliberately kept our research strategy flexible in order to accommodate new ideas and data needs. Interviewees were encouraged to volunteer examples to illustrate their remarks or to give substance to their opinions. Apparent contradictions were pursued. In most cases, all the persons on the check list were interviewed, as well as others suggested as particularly being relevant to understanding the role of this board in this center in this community. We encountered great cooperation from all concerned.

The interviews usually lasted about one-and-one-half hours. With directors interview time often totaled six or eight hours. We kept notes during the interviews, recording what was said in detail, and, to the extent possible, verbatim.

---

* This check list included: CMHC board members, former board chairpersons, mental health professionals (affiliated with the center and elsewhere), mayors, county supervisors, assemblymen, aldermen/precinct captains, health officers/commissioners, former CMHC board/committee members, officers of Mental Health Association, heads of hospital or county board, officers of Mental Retardation Association, police/judges, school officials, teachers, church leaders, hotline personnel, welfare department personnel, United Fund personnel, public-health nurses, center volunteers, newspaper reporters, state health officials, correctional institution officials, social-service agency personnel, rehabilitation agency personnel, Health Systems Agency staff.

Method of Analysis

The method used, analytic induction, is a technique developed and refined by social scientists beginning in the 1950s (Robinson, 1950; Turner, 1953; Barton and Lazarsfeld, 1969a, 1969b; Becker, 1958; Glaser, 1965) to collect, analyze, and present in scientifically sound propositions findings from data that are collected in unstructured or semistructured formats. It is a dynamic technique attuned to the possibilities of conceptual emergence (new ideas, new relationships, third variables inherent in qualitative data), yet it also provides rigor to the analysis and presentation of findings—attention is paid to classification, magnitude, deviation, and proportion. It differs from an analysis based on the observations of shrewd observers whose accounts, while rich in ideas and anecdotes, do not presume to the status of science. The researcher using analytic induction maintains a rigorous interplay between data and conceptual formulation. He or she continually poses theoretical interpretations for data that are collected. Each proposition in a theoretical model is checked for validity against carefully recorded interviews. Specifically, each remark that is related to a proposition is noted for its tendency to support or disconfirm the proposition. When the fit is not perfect, as in the deviant case, propositions are altered or eliminated according to the implications of the data. Analytic induction requires that propositions not be put forth until they are congruent with all data. In any written presentation of data, each unexplained exception to a proposition is scrupulously reported. The process of fitting generalizations to data continues until no data in the interview or field notes are unexplained, or, if unexplained, unreported. Thus no deviant cases remain hidden in the data. Confidence in propositions hinges not on probabilities of occurrence, as it may when a random sample is involved, but on the lack of exceptions.

Example of the Analytic Process

An example of this process will illustrate for the reader unfamiliar with the techniques of analytic induction the way in which (1) the consistency of response is used to establish internal validity of propositions and (2) how theory is complicated and refined through a continual interaction of concepts and propositions with the data. Suppose that we believe that the data will support the proposition that minority-group board members differentiated themselves from majority members in their expression of concern for minority-group use of their centers. We know, however, that this may be a reflection of our own biases. Therefore, we pose a general proposition to be examined: Minority-group board members, irrespective of social class, give emphasis in their thinking to minority-group problems; this is not true for majority-group board members.

Coded interviews from 150 board members confirm that all minority-group board members interviewed mentioned minority-group utilization of the center as a problem. Sometimes it was raised as a problem of inadequate center publicity in the minority community, sometimes as the lack of bilingual staff, sometimes as a problem involving other cultural barriers, sometimes as a lack of programs attuned to specific minority-group problems, but minority-group board members always identified center problems with serving a minority community.

We look for more subtlety in the interviews: How often were these problems mentioned first by minority-group board members? How often did the issue arise only late in a long list of problems? How often was it only in response to a specific probe from the interviewer? How much time did the interviewee spend discussing these problems relative to others discussed?

For the moment let us consider the second part of the proposition. Do white board members fail to express concern with minority-group problems? Sorting through the coded data, we find that twenty-seven white board members in a group of one hundred did mention minority utilization. Who are these people? We examine the data in search of an encompassing category. Are they all at one or two centers, where some unusual situation has produced this heightened awareness—perhaps a newspaper series or a picketing of the center by militant members of a minority group? Did these white board members quote a minority-group member of their board as the source of their knowledge of these problems, suggesting a learning process? Or are these mentioners of minority-group problems people who mentioned so many problems that virtually no issue was excluded?

Imagine for the moment that we find that white board members who mention minority issues serve in disproportionate numbers on racially diverse boards, but that the relationship is not perfect. Returning to the data, we find that where white members do not express minority concerns, it is on boards where minority-group members have attended board meetings infrequently. This form of analysis will ultimately lead to confirmation of certain propositions. The combination of these propositions with others similarly generated will be the basis for generating a complex, grounded theory, the generalizability of which may then be tested by a probability sample.

Already noted is the fact that the NIMH requirement that governing boards be demographically representative has been generally ignored or honored only by token representation, an implementation problem also noted for other major health and welfare programs (Rosenblatt, 1978). The mail questionnaire speaks to this failure by showing a negative relationship between representation and (1) the director's happiness with the board and (2) the director's length of tenure. The qualitative data allows careful examination of cases where an effort was made in good-faith to achieve representation.

What are the trade-offs involved in recruiting a board that is representative of the population to be served? For one thing such representation must also include actors important to the center's major public sectors and professionals competent at handling the relevant issues. The alternatives are (1) a large proportion of silent board members, (2) rubber-stamp boards created by directors who use techniques of insulation, (3) disruption and even destruction of the center as an operating unit, or (4) noncompliance with the federal law.

ONE SUCCESSFUL CASE: ESPANIOLA COUNTY CMHC

The following case study illuminates some of the choices and tensions attending success at one level—that of obtaining a representative governing board for the CMHC.

Espaniola County is a county in the Southeast with a population of approximately 240,000. About half the people live in a small metropolitan area, including and surrounding a city of 60,000. The remainder of the population is rural. The county is 80 percent white, as is the city (70 percent). The family median income is low ($6,219), and nearly 20 percent of the total population and over 45 percent of the black population have incomes below the federal poverty level.

The dominant government unit, the county, is run on a commission system. The political climate of the county is consistently described as conservative ("Any chance they get, they all troop out and vote for George Wallace."). Respondents consistently indicated a preference for local over federal control, though with considerable sophistication. One board member, an economically influential person, indicated that he saw little role for the federal government as a direct actor, "except in redistribution of income." Many interviewees indicated a strong preference for private over public enterprise. The government of the county and the city seem to be openly dominated by economically influential persons who believe that what's good for business is good for the community. These Southern cities combine the Old South (hierarchy and *noblesse oblige*) and the New South (admiration for those who promote economic progress). Thus, another board member said:

> The important families go way back. My family goes back to 1820, before we were a state. Con, who will be the next president, his family came here after the Civil War, as a matter of fact; the business was founded in 1887.

Note that the old families are not necessarily very old, but that the two he mentioned were both very successful in business.

It is the belief of all but one interviewee that mental health services are stigmatized by the community generally. Widespread stigma is compounded by the general view of the center as a "welfare operation," which it is, though its client population is not much poorer or blacker than the general population. Thus, the average residents of Espaniola County have their choice between accepting the stigma or going without help.

Mental health services were late in coming to the county:

> When [Memorial] Hospital opened in October 1951, two rooms for psychiatric patients were made available on the medical floor. In October 1952 the first civilian neuropsychiatrist began practice as a member of a group of other physicians. The local climate was not overly receptive. He was required to obtain the chief nurses' permission before his patients could be admitted and give assurance that they would not disturb the other patients.
>
> Two years later the Child Guidance Clinic was established through efforts of parents, Junior Woman's Club, School Board and County Commissioners. When pressured to assume responsibility for indigent adult psychiatric patients who had no other source of care, the staff of some six professionals set up a pilot program.... Without compensation they conducted a weekly night clinic from 1957 to 1959. It met a growing need. The staff recommended that the Clinic become the Espaniola County Guidance Clinic, open to all age groups; the board of directors concurred....
>
> About the time the County Guidance Clinic outgrew quarters at the health department building, the Congress passed the Community Mental Health Center Act.*

The center is housed in a white stucco building with an orange roof. It is in the midst of a neighborhood of small, ramshackle, wood-frame houses. It is racially integrated, although there are probably more blacks than whites, as judged from driving around and noticing who is on the streets. Several buildings are part of the CMHC, housing spin-off programs as well as the original Child Development Center. These are adjacent to Memorial Hospital, a large and prosperous institution. Some blocks away is Community Hospital, another affiliated institution. Unlike Memorial, it has a poverty-ridden look to it and is much smaller. (It later turned out that the "hard cases" were segregated, which, in effect, meant that the latter hospital accepted most of the blacks; Memorial, the whites.)

The CMHC itself also appears somewhat shabby. Corridors are narrow; people look harassed. The entrance lobby is small, and the receptionist and

---

* From a journal article.

cashier are located behind a glass enclosure. Behind it, however, is a large waiting room with clients, who suffer all kinds of problems, and their relatives, mostly waiting silently. Occasionally, a seriously disturbed person creates an uproar. The director's office is back in a corner reached through narrow corridors. His secretary has a space outside his office. The whole place seems overcrowded and not particularly clean.

The center prides itself on providing the full range of services required by NIMH, plus others of its own choosing. It also takes pride in a recent accreditation by the Joint Commission on Accreditation of Hospitals. Its budget is large, approximately $5 million annually, and in 1976–1977 it treated 10,348 clients. Clients are crudely classified into the Adult and Adolescent Counseling Program (4,511), Alcohol Counseling Program (2,581), Child Development Program (2,121), or the Drug Abuse Program (1,135). In addition to these programs, some 5,000 staff hours went into consultation and education. Seventy-two percent of costs went for salaries and wages.

The monies to run the center almost all come from public sources. The federal government pays thirty-seven percent, the state thirty-two percent, the county and city nineteen percent (about two-thirds of the 19 percent is county funding, according to our interviewees). Fees pay only 9 percent, and miscellaneous sources supply the remaining 3 percent. In short this is a private, not-for-profit corporation, 88 percent of whose income is generated by taxes.

Voluntarism

The center is and has been from its origin an expression of middle-class voluntarism. It was founded by volunteers as a Child Guidance Center, and at least half of the influential board members were founders. All of these are clearly from the civic and economic elite. The center began with citizens volunteering for what they considered a public purpose. They were not just any citizens; they were energetic, concerned members of the community power structure. This group has always seen the CMHC as theirs; they are the delegates of the larger community. A staff member said: "I think our board is a benevolent board. They want to include everyone, but they are narrow in terms of the community they've been exposed to." They have never accepted any notion that basic policy for the center as an organization could be delegated to the professional staff. The general program is determined by the sources of funding and the requirements of NIMH. But, as the most influential board member said: "It's a concept well expressed in the federal legislation. Mental health services are best delivered on the local level by organizations locally controlled."

From 1968 the CMHC's operations and budget expanded with remarkable speed to remarkable size. As an ex-board member said:

> The reason I declined to serve another term was simply that the operation had gotten so large that one was a member of a board spending millions of dollars of the public's money, and I didn't feel I had time to keep in touch, to be involved enough in that kind of operation to be competent. I really wondered if things wouldn't get out of hand, and they'd come back to me and say: "Look, you were a director, why did you let it happen?" The budget during my three years' involvement went from $150,000 a year to over $3 million a year.

The Mission

There is general acceptance of the twelve mandated services, but considerable disagreement over emphasis. The board president says, "The CMHC provides the most cost effective and efficient way of dealing with problems coming under the general area of mental health." The director of the center says:

> We care for the chronically ill; we have 400 people who are. It depends upon your resources. If we had a smaller budget, that's probably what we would do. What we do is a function of existing resources and the expectation of funding sources.
>
> CMHCs can't deal effectively with the (discharged) state hospital people. Funds aren't there for halfway houses. But that is why Congress appropriated the money in the first place, to phase out the state institutions. Also court decisions around the right to treatment were a great impetus. . . . The next likely thing which may have an effect may come in the area of the right of an individual to the most appropriate treatment in the least restrictive setting. It involves, of course, a tremendous expectation of CMHCs or some other creature. Tremendous money is needed. Currently, there are pennies allocated. In our area alone, we figure it would require a million or a million-and-a-half dollars more. It hasn't been done, I think, because the money hasn't been tied to it.

Another staff member succinctly said: "Sure, you may know where the needs are, but you go where the funds are. If there's money for children and not for adolescents, children get the service."

When asked what services they would want dropped in the event of mandatory retrenchment, most board members who could conceive of such an eventuality mentioned consultation and education, a service which yields no revenue and usually accounts for a miniscule portion of the budget. Prevention was also mentioned. Members questioned how it could be demonstrated that one had prevented mental illness? One businessman who has headed the board thinks that retrenchment should first include getting more labor out of the staff and, second, getting rid of the elderly and the exhospital patients. Another person thought the thing to do was to increase "sales," i.e., get more clients, which brings to mind the comment of another staff member:

> At the center, we still don't have a good public-relations program. Partly, that's because we don't know how we want to present ourselves. There are clear differences of opinion. Some people think we should be a business with social-service aspects. Others think we should be a social-service agency with business aspects. Or we could be a McDonald's of social service—mental health services for the poor people, not the services you get on the tenth floor, with plush carpeting, but a place that delivers a reasonably good product in a pleasant environment for a reasonable price. With McDonald's, everybody knows them and their product and is pretty well satisfied.

Thus, there is considerable uncertainty about the range of services to be supplied and emphasis on each. There is also uncertainty about the status of the center—is it public or private? A community physician, who is part-time staff with the center, summarizes the situation:

> One thing that bothers me about treatment over there is that it's directed to the social or cultural rather than the medical. At the beginning, the law was really trying to take care of the indigent medically ill, but in the '60s we trained a lot of social workers, sociologists, and the like. Now they have got to have jobs. They are not trained to take care of the mentally ill. They are trained to handle social problems, people who are old, lonesome, unhappy.
>
> I am definitely not opposed to the CMHC movement. What I am opposed to is . . . the director says we are a free-standing enterprise. We're in competition with everybody. Really, that's taxpayers' money. They should be servicing poor people, not serving paying patients for fees.

Board Composition and Function

The board is a self-perpetuating oligarchy, with new members suggested at random, interviewed and screened by staff and/or board members, and approved by the existing board. In size the board has increased from the original five-member group of the Child Development Center to its present thirty-nine members. Of these, twenty-one are governing members; the remainder act in an advisory capacity. This arrangement has several advantages: First, various interests may be represented for the governing board's benefit without dispersing control; second, since the advisory board has a one-year term, as contrasted with a three-year term for the governing board, it is a less onerous duty to take on; third, those on the advisory board may become educated to board ways and in the process be considered as candidates for the governing board.

A quorum consists of the majority of the governing board, and is the official voting procedure, but in practice, voice vote by *all* board members is the rule. Should there ever be a serious division, only governing board members could vote. This has never occurred.

Of the thirty-seven members, twelve are women; eight are blacks; thirty-four are between the ages of twenty-five and sixty-five. Three have Ph.D.s or M.D.s, and five are mental-health-service workers. There is representation from the Medical Association, the Junior Women, the State Mental Health System, and the Clergyman's Association. The board defines itself as being representative of the community. Among its greatest virtues, it feels, are the members' willingness to work. We saw and heard nothing to refute these two suppositions.

The board has strong clerical and professional support. One staff member works half-time on board matters, and each committee of the board is assigned to senior staff members. While only the director sits regularly at the board meetings, staff that might be useful for given issues attend the meetings during the time when that issue is discussed. On the whole the distinction between board and staff is emphasized sharply, yet the board committees have considerable interaction with the staff.

The size of the board obviously could facilitate an approach to demographic representation; however, the reason given for its size by the president was different:

> The primary purpose of enlarging it was to develop a standing committee system so that all business would go through initial committees having five–fourteen people prior to ever getting to the board. The feeling was we were creating five miniboards. These are Personnel, Finance, Research and Evaluation, Planning, and Liaison. Each committee has seven to eight members and a staff person. Business passes from these to the Executive Committee.

The Executive Committee consists of the chairman of these committees, plus officers of the board and a member-at-large. In general the full board approves the actions of the Executive Committee. As the director remarked, "You've read on majority rule vs. consensus boards. We have a consensus board."

Nevertheless, the board does conform in general to the demographic distribution required by NIMH. It is, at the same time, a board laden with experts. This is no accident. When NIMH regulations requiring demographic reflection of the catchment-area population were instituted, the center set out to comply. The demographic make-up of the catchment area was compared with the make-up of the board (Table 7.11), and the search was on for individuals who had the requisite attributes. There was also concern that some new members have the requisite skills to staff the committees (financial, legal, community liaison, and so on), some standing in the community (old family, wealth, influence), and hold government office. Then, too, they must be willing to work hard and take the job seriously.

TABLE 7.11
Board of Directors Demographics

	Catchment Area (Percent)		Current Board (20 Members)		Projected Board (21 Members)		Need (Number)
			NUMBER	PERCENT	NUMBER	PERCENT	
Sex							
Male	49.8		14	70	10	48	−4
Female	50.2		6	30	11	52	+5
Age		Ad-					
Under 25	(52)	justed	(0)	(0)	(11)	(52)	(+11)
18-25	11	21	0	0	4	19	+4
26-39	18	28	7	35	6	29	−1
40-54	16	27	10	50	6	29	−4
55 up	14	24	3	15	5	24	+2
Race							
White	79.4		17	85	17	81	0
Non-white	20.6		3	15	4	19	+1
Employment							
Civilian	69		16	80	14	67	−2
Government	31		2	10	5	24	+3
Unemployed	7		2	10	2	9	0
Residence							
Espaniola	54.8		19	95	12	57	−7
Outside Espaniola	44.8		0	0	9	43	+9
Outside C.A.			1	5	0	0	−1

Note: Percentages for under 18 redistributed into other categories.

Thus, a matrix was created, with demographic attributes as one dimension and skills the other. A staff member worked full-time at the job of finding prospects, and the president of the board spent most of his lunch hours and evenings interviewing people:

> The first step was to interview the entire board in respect to the kinds of attributes that were needed on the board—this included the active board members and, of course, the relevant staff of the center. They then went to major service clubs, went to industry personnel offices; we went to all sorts of organizations that have boards. They rounded up approximately five hundred names. These were then broken down by the dimensions in which NIMH wanted compliance. These would be age, race, sex; and then what turned out to be very difficult was to find able people outside the city, in the county, who were willing to drive in and back—which in some cases was sixty miles.
>
> Well, OK, now you've got these people identified and a recommendation for them is filled out by the staff who interviewed the relevant referees and, if you get repeaters, you probably have a strong candidate. It then goes to the appropriate board committee, and a staff member interviews the candidate, saying, "I am updating prospective board member lists," and so, sort of indirectly, without committing yourself to somebody, you get their cooperation and you interview their employers, their associates, and so forth. Then the community-liaison-committee chairperson talks to the board president and to other people who might know the candidate and, finally, he interviews the

candidate, or someone who knows the candidate interviews him. Finally, the formal decision goes from the liaison committee to the executive committee.

The president who presided over the development of the recruitment system told us:

> I think that was my biggest accomplishment. An awful lot of time and effort went into getting a broadly responsible set of people, broadly representative, with the skills to make it work. . . . It is easy to get black postmen. However, what we want is to get decision makers in the black community. . . . We run the gauntlet from federal judges to janitors, from enormously wealthy people to people who probably are under the poverty line.

The most underrepresented segment of the population, however, is the last category. The poor who will and can participate in such a gathering are rare. Young people are underrepresented for similar reasons. When asked about the gender imbalance, we were told that the women who had social standing of their own were rare in Espaniola County.

Board and Staff

At the time we studied the center, the key relationship was that between director and board president. They conferred at least weekly. (Staff estimates of time invested by the board came to about four hours for ordinary members each month and twenty hours or more for officers.) When asked which was most important, the general agreement was that the director was ("You can get by for a year with a weak president, but a weak director, or one who doesn't believe in the board, can be a disaster."). Within the board power is concentrated in the hands of the Executive Committee. As one critical staff member said:

> It's the power structure. Executive Committee is the power structure. Very often they feed the data and opinions to the other committees to get what they want from them (and they are in a position to do this). And they give the others the data that will lead them to a specific conclusion. And the other committees see that this is what the power structure wants, and that inclines them to come out with the right decision. The trouble with powerful committees is that they take power from somewhere else.

The Executive Committee includes most of the members reputed to be most influential, and its recommendations are very rarely turned down by the full board. It also tends to include past presidents who know the center's business and history and persons with parliamentary skills. In the words of one member, "What it takes is a strong director and two or three determined board members."

The board tends to define itself as analogous to the board of any private corporation; this allows hardbitten capitalists to use public monies with a clear conscience. An ex-president stated:

> We're willing to compete—to compete with private psychiatrists, private consulting psychologists. Our center *is* a private facility. We do sell on the market, though our markets may be governments. The Department of Defense is a good parallel.

The rationalization of using public monies for a privately governed enterprise in Espaniola County leads to a management orientation. The same person said, "Our management techniques are mostly imposed on the staff by the board. The staff, they're very, very able, but they are inexperienced." As a justification for this supervision, which can be seen as meddling, or the confusion that results over management policy, someone stated:

> The director is as gifted an individual as I have ever met; but I don't consider him an Espaniolan, with the stake that I have. I've noticed the staff's willingness to take risks that I would not take, because I won't want it to explode in my face. I intend to live here the rest of my life. They can go to Colorado or Vermont and get another job.

Senior staff express clearly their ambivalence toward the continual surveillance and criticism from the board, yet they feel the board has a right and perhaps a duty to be critical, and that the center operates better for it.

This definition of the board's status, rights, and responsibilities is curiously hybrid. Its origins were probably in the boards of charitable organizations, where people influential in getting money, together with experts who ran the organizations, had a legitimate right to decide on how to spend it. But when one is operating with a budget in which eighty-eight cents of every dollar come from some branch of government, legitimacy is problematic. A voluntary organization, self-selected and self-perpetuating, is running a private not-for-profit corporation which dispenses over $5 million a year in the same way. It sees itself as top management, as well as policymaker, for the center.

What does the board do for the center? In response to our mail questionnaire, the director indicated that the board had had considerable success in these directions: selecting and evaluating the director (the first could be self-serving, the second could not); allocating the budget; setting policies; developing affiliation with other organizations; informing the community about the center; upgrading facilities; monitoring performances; adding needed services and obtaining support, general and financial. One leading board member said:

> We have a volunteer effort from our board which persuades the County Commission to make their contribution. Local government dollars are indis-

pensable (for matching funds), and without a committed board it would be hard to come by. The first president was extremely generous with his time, with his attention, and with his contacts. And he even loaned the center money, loaned them his credit. He set a standard that was important.

One member of the five-person County Commission is on the center's board. The director said, "He doesn't participate much in meetings, but I've got to have him. He gets us our money."

Of the advantages and disadvantages of citizen boards, the current president stated:

The advantages are: First, without the board, forget getting enough money to run the center. Second, we get input we might not otherwise get, that is, another type of board might not get the same input. Third, there is a better reception in the community. I have heard comments that people aren't as suspicious because we have so many blacks, so many women . . . and are a nonprofit corporation.

As for the disadvantages: First, running the center is a very complex process. It is very difficult for the average citizen to comprehend the business point of view, the professional point of view. They could, but with the time they are willing to give, no. Most of us have no understanding of the professional side, no means to evaluate what's going on there. Second, it is a tremendous burden on the staff to try to keep boards as informed as possible. They have the task of educating us so that we can make good decisions. That takes a lot of time.

As for the board's competence, a senior staff person had this to say:

They know an amazing lot. . . . I believe in control/counter control. I believe that it's necessary to maintain quality. Making us public increases the probability of quality services. If we didn't have a board and had to make public our operations, we wouldn't be so concerned with cost-benefit outcomes. That's the difference between private practice and public: The first will answer only to themselves; the public practice is answerable to and for many more people.

There is little evidence that the board ever interferes in the actual therapeutic and care operations of the center. Even a disgruntled staff member did not indicate this. In fact, he underlined the point made by the president about the board's professional ignorance:

It's almost comical when I go before them with something about drug abuse. They don't know what I'm talking about. I could tell them the right treatment is to have drug patients play leapfrog. I'm being facetious, but they don't know what's going on in our services.

Obviously, there must be a fund of trust among the director, senior staff, and, through them, the one hundred fifty employees of the center.

IMPLEMENTATION WITH MANY MASTERS

The public purpose of establishing representative citizens' boards to govern CMHCs, as with Health Service Agencies and other nonprofit corporations serving public interest, was to ensure that the values of all segments of the population were honored in decision-making processes. Implementing such a purpose is difficult. The statute itself is vague (no selection mechanism is stipulated), and the regulations tend to be mechanical. This leaves great leeway for the officials responsible for implementation at regional, state, and center level to "interpret" in the light of local conditions. Nor is it at all certain that individuals chosen by social attributes represent a consensus or even the median position of blacks, women, and poor people. The public purpose may be served, but only with a heroic effort by staff and board of each CMHC.

Yet the representation and ability of the citizens' boards depends upon the fairness and integrity of a large number of public enterprises. As Klarman (1977:34) said, "The merits of the staff cannot alone produce the necessary sensitivity and responsiveness. . . . the role of the lay board of directors is central." Rosenblatt (1978:264), after considering all the difficulties in demographic representation, came to this conclusion:

> Finally, it is important to remember that the value of consumer participation and agency explanation does not lie solely in the opportunity to secure a different outcome. What Professor Tribe has termed "the right to be heard from, and the right to be told why . . . express the elementary idea that to be a *person*, rather than a *thing*, is at least to be *consulted* about what is done with one." Expressed in political terms, this root concept of human dignity highlights the need for a reconstruction of the democratic process, in which consultation over fundamental human needs is not made meaningless by a labyrinthine bureaucracy. By offering unorganized interests the *right* to participate in programs for their own benefit, the traditions of structural due process also help to encourage its exercise and thereby help to strengthen democratic capacity.

The concept of representation of the unorganized is almost a logical contradiction. Klarman (1977:34) stated the problems:

> How should board members be selected? What should board members know in order to discharge their obligations to the community, as well as to pass on the technical merits of the work done by staff? What steps should they take to implement their recommendations? These are difficult questions to answer because they have received so little study to date.

And, perhaps in response to these complex problems, as well as to the jealousy of such august interests as hospital boards and county boards, the tide of participatory democracy in the form of federally mandated citizens' boards seems to be receding. President Carter's Mental Health Proposal of 1979 not only fails to mention citizens' boards, but would subordinate to other entities, or discontinue support for, the CMHCs themselves (Mental Health Reports, 1979).

The Role of Case Studies and Analytic Induction in Evaluation Research

Legislation, particularly at the federal level, creates programs with many, and often antagonistic, constituencies in mind. Only infrequently, if ever, is legislation in such amorphous areas as mental health, health, or social welfare, built on known ways of achieving or measuring goals. Legislation is a blend of contradictions and unknowns, which asks more that problems be engaged than that outcomes be achieved. Discretion to interpret and to implement passes to administrative bureaucracies and local delivery units. What, then, is the role of evaluation? In the case portrayed here, we took it to require, first, a determination of the interpretations which have, in fact, defined the program, and second, the circumstances which have circumscribed the interpretations. It can be determined that demographically representative boards have not been achieved. But knowing this is not to know much, for the demographic board was not an objective, but rather, was a mechanism created to interpret and make meaningful the "intent" of the legislation. Evaluation, then, must incorporate examination of what resulted. What was gained in the eyes of those involved; what was lost? What did it cost? Is the mechanism a difficult but meaningful one or a hopeless mistake?

Intensive case study employing systematic analytic induction is the only way to evaluate such phenomena. It is guided by theory thought relevant to the problem and research grounded in data that can provide the basis for defining units, measuring and testing variables, and finally, analyzing outcomes of programs which are complex, and which require, if their evaluation is to be meaningful, appropriately complicated theory.

REFERENCES

Barton, A. H., and Lazarsfeld, P. F., 1969a. Some Functions of Qualitative Analysis in Social Research. In *Issues in Participant Observation*, ed. G. J. McCall and J. L. Simmons, pp. 239–245. Reading, Mass.: Addison-Wesley.

———. 1969b. Qualitative Support of Theory. In *Issues in Participant Observation*, pp. 163–196.

Becker, H. S., 1958. Problems of Inference and Proof in Participant Observation. *American Sociological Review* 23: 652–660.

Drucker, Peter F., 1978. Managing the "Third Sector," *The Wall Street Journal,* October 3, 1978.

Foley, Henry A., 1975. *Community Mental Health Legislation.* Lexington, Mass.: Lexington Books.

———, 1977. Community Mental Health Programming. In *Regionalization and Health Policy,* ed. Eli Ginsberg, pp. 37–47. Washington, D.C.: U.S. Government Printing Office.

Glaser, B. G., 1965. The Constant Comparative Method of Qualitative Analysis, *Social Problems* 12: 436–445.

Klarman, Herbert E., 1977. Planning for Facilities. In *Regionalization and Health Policy.* Washington, D.C.: U.S. Government Printing Office, pp. 25–36.

Mental Health Reports, 1979. Vol. 3, Number 10, May 1.

Robinson, W. S., 1950. The Logical Structure of Analytic Induction. *American Sociological Review,* 16: 812–818.

Rosenblatt, Rand E., 1978. Health Care Reform and Administrative Law: A Structural Approach, *The Yale Law Journal,* Vol. 88, Number 2, pp. 243–336.

Turner, R. H., 1953. "The Quest for Universals in Sociological Research." *American Sociological Review,* 18: 604–611.

Chapter 8

ENERGY AND TRANSPORTATION

The diagnosis of the United States energy crisis is rather straightforward: While demand for energy has been increasing, supplies of oil and natural gas have been diminishing. In the 1950s and the 1960s the real price of energy fell about 30 percent, and until the sharp escalation of world oil prices in 1973–1974, United States consumption of energy increased at an average annual rate of 3.5 percent. The availability of cheap energy contributed to the production of capital goods, such as cars, factory equipment, and homes, that use energy inefficiently. But the present scarcity of energy supplies, coupled with higher prices, threatens not only the nation's economic performance but also many aspects of the American way of life.

The government has attempted to develop three major energy objectives: to reduce dependence on imported oil and reduce vulnerability to supply interruptions; to keep imports sufficiently low to weather the period when world oil production approaches its capacity limitations; and, in the long run, to develop renewable sources of energy. To these ends the National Energy Plan has emphasized a commitment to conservation and fuel efficiency. The underlying logic of this policy commitment is that by reducing the need for energy in transportation, industry, and housing, the dependency on foreign oil and domestic production will drastically decline. In fact it has been estimated that the country's wasted energy is substantially greater than the total amount of oil imports. At the same time, by reducing the need for additional domestic energy production, two other objectives could be ac-

376

complished. The supply of capital for economic growth could increase, and the environment could be better protected.

Most public programs in the area of energy enacted in the last decade or so, as well as pending legislation, take a conservation ethic as their guiding principle. The 55 mile-per-hour speed limit passed by Congress in 1974; the 1975 legislation requiring that the average mileage of new cars be 20 miles per gallon by 1980 and 27.5 miles per gallon by 1985; the appropriations that have been made on public transit systems; and the various voluntary tax credit plans for homeowners and businesses who improve energy efficiency are all conservation programs.

Although intuitively appealing, the conservation ethic involves changing the values, attitudes, and habits of a large segment of the public, and such a major change is not easy. Furthermore, the extent to which the present conservation measures could save energy, and whether they represent the most efficient policy option for achieving the conservation goals, are serious questions that call for systematic analyses. The crisis mentality has fostered decisions based on the argument that anything that saves energy, no matter what its dollar cost, is good and should be advocated and funded. For example the belief that public transportation always saves energy has recently been challenged. Charles Lave pointed out that the new generation of transit systems appears to waste energy: "The amount of energy *invested* (author's emphasis) in constructing BART (the Bay Area Rapid Transit) is so large, and the operation-energy savings so small, that BART will require 535 years to break even on its investment, much less save energy."[1] Similarily, there are serious reservations as to whether the lowered speed limit is the only or the best policy for achieving the goals of conservation.[2]

The first article in this chapter, by Pietro S. Nivola, focuses on energy policy by analyzing the new natural gas regulatory legislation passed in 1978. Nivola reviews the history of federal gas-price controls and evaluates the recent reforms intended to alleviate shortages and improve the regulatory structure. A central theme of the article is that government policies have enhanced the energy crisis, especially in the field of natural gas, which is the nation's single largest domestically produced fuel, and that a major problem with these policies concerns their implementability.

The second article evaluates the national lowered speed limit. Clotfelter and Hahn present a theoretical rationale for the establishment of a speed limit to meet fuel-saving goals, and then calculate the benefits and the economic costs of the policy. Although the authors find that

the benefits outweigh the costs, they suggest that speed limit is neither the only nor the most effective policy for achieving the goals of
conservation.

The third article evaluates the BART experiment. Webber reviews
the initial objectives for the BART system, their modifications, and the
system's failures to meet its objectives. Failure, however, does not
necessarily lead to search for other policy options. As Webber points
out, ideology and public relations have played a significant role in all
the stages of the BART experiment.

1. Charles A. Lave, "Transportation and Energy: Some Current Myths," *Policy Analysis* (Summer 1978), 303.
2. Charles T. Clotfelter and John C. Hahn, "Assessing the National 55 m.p.h.
   Speed Limit," this chapter.

ENERGY POLICY: THE NATURAL GAS POLICY ACT OF 1978

Pietro S. Nivola

In late May 1978 when House and Senate conferees finally forged a compromise that became the basis of the new Natural Gas Policy Act
(NGPA), the event was acclaimed historic by many. Agreement had been
reached on the centerpiece of President Jimmy Carter's original energy
program. Energy Secretary James R. Schlesinger proclaimed "the end of
the Thirty Years' War" over gas price controls.[1] A *New York Times* edito-
rial spoke of "the end of an era" and "the beginning of a serious national
energy policy."[2] As debate over the natural-gas conference report dragged
on through the summer and into the fall, however, these sorts of pro-
nouncements seemed increasingly difficult to understand. Not only did
Congress remain bitterly split over the basic aims of the proposal (indeed,

just before its final roll call, the House passed by a mere one-vote margin, 207–206, a key procedural motion on which the fate of the entire gas bill seemed to hang[3]) but many observers began to suspect that the struggle to adopt NGPA would soon be matched, if not eclipsed, by the ordeal of carrying it out.

NATURAL GAS REGULATION

The difficulties that have bedeviled federal regulation of natural gas for the past quarter-century are now widely acknowledged and familiar to most persons. The background bears repeating, however, so that one can determine which of the old inadequacies the new law clears up.

The Supreme Court's *Phillips* decision in 1954 directed the Federal Power Commission (FPC) to control prices of gas sold by independent producers to interstate pipelines.[4] The commission thereby acquired a regulatory task that has posed fundamental problems of feasibility, fairness, and efficiency. In accordance with established utility-type regulatory practice, the commission was obligated to base wellhead prices on a "just and reasonable" rate of return—often an imponderable, given conditions of varying risk—and on historical production costs, which can be inappropriate as guides to costs in future production, or may be mostly undiscernable, since much natural gas is produced jointly with oil, and the costs of this so-called "associated" or "casinghead" gas cannot be readily separated from those of crude oil. To better modulate these determinations according to the circumstances of individual firms, the FPC initially sought to make rates on a company-by-company basis. But with tens of thousands of producers involved, this quickly became impossible. Within one year of the *Phillips* case, 11,000 rate schedules awaited adjudication.[5] By 1959 the estimate was that it would have taken until the year 2043 to get through the commission's existing caseload.[6]

So, in 1960, the commission, again under some pressure from the Supreme Court, was forced to scrap the case-by-case approach in favor of an area-rate system.[7] Instead of deciding the rates that each producer would be permitted to charge, the new scheme was to impose a maximum price for gas, based on the average cost of production in each of the nation's producing regions. The innovation partially reduced the FPC's administrative burden, since once price ceilings were set for each region, the commission now had to consider in detail only those interstate contracts that were above the ceiling. In some other respects, though, the new method proved worse than the old. The earlier attempt to handle producers one by one, though ultimately impractical, at least seemed to result in more responsive price treatment. (In fact, in spite of the backlog, or perhaps because of it, wellhead prices between 1954–1959 somehow managed to double.[8]) Under the area-rate process, on the other hand, new contract prices for gas going to interstate pipelines were effectively frozen through most of the 1960s.[9]

The area-rate proceedings added another twist: the concept of "vintaging." In roughest terms a distinction was now drawn between newly produced gas and gas that was already flowing. Lower ceilings were set for the latter on the theory that, given general increases in demand or greater willingness of consumers to pay higher prices, limits had to be imposed on the economic rents, or windfall profits, that accrued to producers selling already-discovered gas with capital investments that were long since paid back.[10] New gas, on the other hand, was made eligible for higher ceilings to promote exploration and expand supply. The virtue of vintaging was that it prevented a potentially huge, and not necessarily productive, income transfer from consumers to suppliers, which is not to say that the concept raised no other issues of equity.[11] Existing pipelines with contracts to purchase large volumes of old gas had an advantage over newer pipelines that had to contract for the more expensive new gas. Similarly, customers of pipelines with higher percentages of new gas paid more for their purchases than did customers served by pipelines with old gas. The FPC now had to adduce not just the "right" prices for different types of gas, but also suitable definitions of "old" and "new." If new gas prices applied primarily to newly completed wells, an incentive could exist for producers to cap many "uneconomic" old wells—or at least, fail to recondition them for drilling into deeper reservoirs in the same field.[12] A potential danger of the multi-tiered price structure, therefore, was that it could deter intensive development of some existing fields, which were a prime source of new supplies.

Ironically, another side effect of the FPC policies during the 1960s was that instead of relieving noncompetitive conditions in the natural gas industry, economic concentration increased. Unable to risk drilling costs that might have exceeded the low ceilings of the period, large numbers of minor independents were forced to liquidate or merge with larger, more established companies.[13] The other major consequence of the policies, most observers now agree, was that they induced sharp increases in gas consumption while discouraging exploration and development of fields where production costs were high. By the end of 1968 the American Gas Association (AGA) reported that domestic consumption was exceeding additions to reserves. The developing shortages, arriving at a time when control of the FPC was shifting to a Republican administration, prompted an almost frenetic series of regulatory adjustments, climaxed by a decision to replace the various area rates with a nationwide lid, which was successively lifted until prices for newly produced, or contracted, gas sold in interstate commerce had more than tripled.

Despite the remedy the FPC was unable to avert the drastic gas curtailments that struck the Northeast and Midwest during the mid-1970s, causing widespread economic dislocation; additional demand for replacement fuels, including expensive imports; and other maladies.[14] Some argued that the stimulus was too little too late, that prices of gas produced and sold within the same state (so-called intrastate gas, over which the FPC lacked jurisdiction) remained significantly higher than the regulated gas sold across state lines (interstate gas), thus encouraging producers to avoid dedicating supplies to the latter. Others contended that the rapid progression of higher prices granted between 1969 and 1976 simply tempted producers to withhold output in anticipation of still higher rates, if not eventual decontrol,[15] and that the price disparity between markets would diminish with signs of an impending glut in the intrastate sector.[16] What few would dispute is that the course of natural gas policy had become singularly unpredictable. Presidents Richard Nixon, Gerald Ford, and Jimmy Carter had all recommended fundamental revisions of the pricing arrangements. Once again deregulation measures were being agitated in Congress. Meanwhile, prices were being raised and regulatory requirements sporadically relaxed (or changed), but this was all done at FPC discretion—and no producer could be sure that the commission—or the courts—might not later reverse the trend. Producers had experienced a history of regulatory ambivalence. In the southern Louisiana rate proceedings of 1968, for instance, prices were rolled back and the industry was ordered to refund hundreds of millions of dollars. Another, more recent rollback occurred in 1976, when the FPC changed its mind about the proper price for 1973–1974 vintage gas. The courts, too, have kept producers guessing. For example an attempt by the FPC to exempt small producers from price controls was overturned by the federal Court of Appeals for the District of Columbia. When the commission sought to relieve gas shortages by authorizing 180-day emergency sales above extant ceilings, the same court in 1975 suspended the ruling, although later the Court's stay was vacated by the Supreme Court. Arguably, much of the failure of gas regulation in recent years—most notably, the belated and still tenuous supply response to numerous price increases[17]—might be understood in these terms: Producers simply did not know what the government would do next. Thus, almost all the recent legislative proposals dealing with natural gas—including the original gas provisions of the Carter Administration's National Energy Plan, several substitutes initiated in Congress, and the Natural Gas Policy Act of 1978, which grew out of all of them—were concerned with providing more specific incentives to producers, safeguards for consumers, and meeting other goals such as greater equity for all parties and more administrative ease. More generally, they were concerned with clarifying the rules of the game and giving them a final statutory basis.

THE NEW REGIME

The new legislation breaks with past policies inasmuch as it eventually will release newly discovered gas from price controls. A cursory glance might leave the impression that the quantity of gas affected will be small since the definition of new gas is restrictive. The volume actually will be substantial because, although new gas itself is not defined as generously as some would like, NGPA erects other categories of gas that are technically not labeled new but which qualify for similar interim-pricing provisions and eventual deregulation. Specifically, gas designated new is gas produced from (1) new Outer Continental Shelf leases; (2) onshore reservoirs from which natural gas was not produced in commercial quantities prior to April 20, 1977; and (3) new onshore wells that are two-and-a-half miles or more from the nearest existing well or at least one thousand feet deeper than the deepest completion location of all existing wells within a two-and-a-half-mile radius.[18] Such gas receives an initial price about 18 percent higher than the maximum price under pre-NGPA law. This price will rise roughly 10 percent each year until deregulation.[19] What appears more noteworthy is that production under a second classification—namely, gas from new onshore-production wells—which comprises most newly spudded wells drilled short of the distance and depth requirements for new gas in old reservoirs, is governed by terms not very much different from those of the latter: Its base price is comparable to that of new gas, although it will escalate at a somewhat lower rate in the future, and it is also to be freed from controls ultimately. The bill also creates another category of gas, the so-called high-cost genre, which will receive even more favorable treatment. Methane gas from coal seams and gas derived from geopressurized brine, Devonian shale, or new wells 15,000 feet deep will all be deregulated within one year of the bill's enactment. According to a source at the AGA, the deep-well provision alone encompasses over 30 percent of all known gas.[20] It is fatuous, therefore, to insist, as some industry hardliners and conservative Republicans did during the congressional debate, that the act does not seriously contemplate significant price deregulation.

The real question about the 1978 gas act is not whether its intent is to deregulate, but rather, how deregulation will occur. To begin with, the process will be a lengthy one for all items except high-cost gas. New gas and a portion of new onshore production gas will be decontrolled but in

1985, but much new onshore production (from wells shallower than 5,000 feet) will not be decontrolled before 1987. Until then the question of whether the government established rates are correct remains. Indeed, for the immediate future, this old dilemma takes on an added dimension as the new law brings the intrastate market under federal controls for the first time.

It may well be that a long transition period is necessary to absorb what would otherwise be a sudden shock to consumers and the economy as controls are lifted. On the other hand NGPA's transitional rates for most newly produced gas, though decidedly higher than past rates, have not started out much above the price levels that probably would have prevailed even if NGPA had never become law. This is not just because the act has clamped a lid on intrastate prices. Through 1977–1978, the Federal Energy Regulatory Commission (or FERC, as the old FPC is now called) postponed a decision on a new interstate price ceiling, pending congressional resolution of the natural-gas issue. During the summer of 1978 there was a rumor to the effect that FERC was prepared to reset the limit on interstate prices for post-1977 vintage gas to somewhere between $2 and $2.60 per thousand cubic feet (Mcf) if Congress rejected the compromise bill.[21] The maximum price for new gas under the compromise was put at $2.09, as of January 1979.[22] And while it is true that prices in the act are scheduled to rise significantly each year until decontrol, industry representatives point out that gas producers have experienced tremendous cost increases in recent years.[23] Since the stipulated escalation formula for new gas is based not on rates of inflation in the industry but on the GNP deflator plus about 4 percent, the permissible new gas rates between now and 1985 still may fail to keep pace with rising production costs, as well as with the equivalent cost of oil.[24] If one were comparing the interim price paths of the Natural Gas Policy Act with FPC policies of the 1960s, the law's provisions would loom indisputably as models of regulatory flexibility, but in light of more recent decisions by the commission (which, between 1970 and 1976, effectively permitted average prices to climb 400 percent[25]), it is by no means obvious that the new regime represents a sharp departure from the status quo ante, at least so far as immediate price incentives to producers are concerned.[26]

From a producer's vantage point, relative certainty with respect to the higher price levels through 1985, which additional FERC pricing opinions would have lacked, is a recognizable gain. Whereas FERC's prospective rulings would have been vulnerable, as always, to years of litigation and unforseeable changes in the composition of the commission, the new price schedules are mostly subject only to a lesser peril—congressional amendments. Yet, in the context of the act's protracted phase-out of controls, the added certainty about prices during the changeover may do less than is commonly anticipated to spur production from conventional fields prior to 1985, either because many producers may wait to see deregulation to believe it, so to speak, or because they may reasonably expect even greater profitability after the trigger date. This danger was stressed, albeit in different ways, by liberal and conservative critics of the legislation. For example during floor action on September 11, 1978, Senator Clifford P. Hansen (R., Wyo.) said:

> Nor is the prospect of "deregulation" beyond 1985 likely to add much incentive. For drillers now, 1985 is a long way off. As it comes closer, it will be more and more tempting to wait until after 1985 to drill, to see whether it actually comes off. The bill only guarantees deregulation for the first 6 months of 1985. . . . [After this six-month trial period, the bill would permit the President or Congress to reimpose controls for eighteen months.][27]

Senator William Proxmire (D., Wisconsin) that same morning said:

> I cannot think of any investment one can make which is guaranteed to go up 3 or 4 percent more than inflation. If there is one, I am sure a great deal of money would go into it. So why would any rational natural gas producer respond to this bill by making supplies available when he can keep them in the ground? Obviously, the ground is a much better bank than he could find in a bank or he could find in any stock-market investment or any real-estate investment that one could count on.[28]

It is also conceivable that some of the prescribed rates may turn out to be too high from time to time. In the months preceding the passage of NGPA, when market forces were more or less determining prices in the unregulated intrastate sector, there were indications that recent contract prices were slipping to levels at or below the base levels proposed in the gas bill. Granted, this was probably a short-term adjustment to work off a temporary surplus, but it also suggested that under comparatively free market conditions, gas prices could move fluidly down as well as up. Although in principle the same should apply when high maximum rates are locked in by statute, there may be some tendency in such a market for ceilings to become floors. If the government-sanctioned rates act as guideposts—that is, if buyers and sellers begin looking to the ceilings as suitable indicators of what the traffic will bear, especially when the market's signals are volatile or unclear—the net effect, at least in some periods, could be to induce higher prices than might otherwise occur.[29] Whatever the case, the point is that no one can say for sure exactly what the new price structure will do— and if it turns out to be another mistake, it could again be one of long duration.

These vicissitudes, however, do not constitute distinctive defects in the legislation, for they could apply to practically any proposal in which deregulation were slowly phased in. A more basic weakness would seem to involve the subtleties of deciding which gas gets what price in concrete situations. The problem arises because of the act's cumbersome taxonomy of gases. The conference committee that drafted NGPA chose to modify the traditional, vintage-based concept of new gas by adding criteria aimed at stimulating new discoveries, rather than mere in-fill drilling into existing reservoirs (what Senator Ernest F. Hollings [D., S.C.,] once described as the producers' penchant for "putting another straw into the old soda . . . and calling it new gas"[30]). In already productive reservoirs, therefore, depth and spacing standards for new-gas wells were specified to distinguish these installations from other, presumably less exploratory drilling. The notion might seem ingenious, but in practice, it may often leave a producer wondering which of several different rates, and even decontrol dates, his product will receive until such time as the appropriate authorities determine definitively the location at which his drill-bit found gas. To illustrate, suppose a new well is placed into an old reservoir and inside the two-and-a-half mile perimeter of an existing well. Suppose also that the marker well—and, in fact, none of the other old wells within the perimeter—is deeper than four thousand feet. If the new well were to probe at least a thousand feet further than the deepest old well, its output could earn new gas prices with deregulation in 1985. But if the same well shaft were to stop short of that magic depth, no matter how tantalizingly close, the gas drawn through it would presumably come under a different pricing formula, namely, that of shallow new onshore production, which would not be deregulated until 1987.

The mechanism for settling the specific cases is one that Congress often employs when confronting sensitive issues of eligibility: decisions are mostly left to the states. Given the nuances of assigning particular prices to individual wells, a large measure of administrative decentralization is unavoidable. The pivotal role of the states, however, portends several likely implications. One is that the authorities in most producing states will tend to favor higher prices rather than lower ones, and quick deregulation rather than slow where there is any question.[31] (Such a course of action, after all, would boost royalty payments and revenues from severance taxes.) The second is that certain producing states—California and New Mexico, for example—might respond somewhat differently, thereby creating some noticeable variations in the classification of gas.[32] A third is that the national contest between consumer and producer groups will be carried to numerous state capitals, perhaps more forcefully than ever before. And finally, the amount of litigation may ultimately intensify, if interested parties start going to the courts over variability in state determinations and the constrained federal review of them mandated in the act. At a minimum these developments would not dispel some of the uncertainties that many persons believe have hindered vigorous exploration for new natural gas in recent years. Opponents of gas deregulation have consistently maintained that deregulation will mean high prices with no assurance of yielding major new supplies. Partisans are sometimes given to imagining that decontrol will usher in a sudden millenium in gas production. A somewhat more cautious optimist might ask whether the new gas law, complicating the experiment as it does, might create or aggravate conditions that will prove the skeptics right. That outcome, in turn, could provoke a reimposition of controls shortly after their termination.

REGULATING DEREGULATION

This brings us to the most troublesome feature of the recent legislation; administratively, it appears to create about as much regulatory complexity as it takes away, at least for the time being and maybe for longer. One commonly overlooked reason is that a section of the act reopens the formidable question of how to allocate gas supplies in the event of shortfalls. It took years of trial and error—not to mention court challenges—for the FPC to arrive at a workable curtailments policy. Now it would seem that significant parts of the system are to be revamped, beginning with revised priority schedules, that is, lists of precisely who should or should not get certain amounts of gas.

A second drawback is that the act actually codifies a multitude of categories of gas—seventeen to be exact. Stripper wells, offshore wells, and wells on state owned land all get their own pricing and regulatory specifications. Over ten thousand gas wells are drilled each year in the United States. The prospect of having to classify each one of them—especially when many may fall between categories or belong to more than one—seems bewildering. The number of individual cases that the FERC will be asked to review could make the process become perfunctory and require a huge bureaucracy. This is not to imply that under a continuation of the old regulatory structure matters would all have been that much simpler. (Contrary to an assumption seemingly held by some of the act's adversaries, there would not necessarily have been fewer gas categories operative in the years ahead, for example).[33] Still, for a bill intended in part to consolidate and streamline the patchwork of regulations that had evolved over the years, NGPA's level of complexity in many respects seems comparable to that of the disease that the bill was supposed to cure.

At least one part of the law indubitably adds complications that did not exist earlier. A major concern of the legislators was to shield residential consumers from the brunt of higher gas prices. To do this, the framers of the act deemed it necessary to continue regulation for some time not only of all sales of gas from the wellhead, but also, of most purchases of it by end-users. The instrument chosen to achieve this goal is an elaborate form of incremental pricing, designed to ensure that industrial users will pay the increased costs of gas disproportionately.[34] A lot of controversy over this scheme focused on its underlying logic or efficacy. Opponents charged that affected industries would simply pass their disproportionate gas costs onto consumers in the form of higher product prices, thereby vitiating much of the consumer protection the plan envisages. Some critics also argue that industrial gas users will react by converting to oil, diminishing industrial gas use, and potentially saddling residential consumers with rates even higher than would obtain absent incremental pricing.[35] Defenders of the policy, on the other hand, advance a sophisticated rationale, which if correct, discounts these potential dysfunctions.[36] They believe that by overcharging industrial users, not only will conservation be encouraged where it can make the biggest difference, but great pressure will be exerted on pipelines to shop for the lowest prices. Large industrial users, unlike residential consumers, are in a position to influence a pipeline's bids by threatening to shorten or discontinue high-volume, year-round contracts. As for the pipelines, without this countervailing force, they might bid up producer prices indiscriminately. (With pipeline rates still regulated, pipeline companies will continue to maximize their revenues by increasing the throughput. The fear exists that vigorous competition to purchase available supplies could inflate wellhead prices inordinately once limits on the latter are lifted.) Yet clearly, if one accepts this reasoning, incremental pricing can serve as an indirect restraint on prices at the wellhead, which is undoubtedly why proponents insisted upon it once they conceded to the gradual elimination of direct field-price controls.

But such issues aside, consider the practical aspects of implementation. In particular, how is NGPA's particular version of incremental pricing supposed to work? Pipelines and distribution companies selling expensive gas will be required to subsidize residential consumers by levying a surcharge on sales to industrial users. Moreover, the process by which the surcharges and the subsidies are calculated and implemented involves several steps, as even the following simplified illustration demonstrates. Suppose that a pipeline is marketing high-priced gas through local distributors. This new gas was acquired for $1.75 per-million-British-thermal-units (MMBtu). The pipeline will be required to maintain an incremental pricing account based on the portion of the pipeline's acquisition cost of gas that exceeds a certain threshold—in this case, FERCs just and reasonable cost-based rate of $1.48 per MMBtu. Imagine, too, that during a specified time span, residential consumers purchase 125 million units of the gas and industrial customers buy 250 million units. The total volume sold is then multiplied by the difference between the wellhead purchase price and the designated threshold: 375 million units × $0.27 = $101.25 million. Now, further assume that with markups by the pipeline and the distributors, the gas in question retails for $2.25 per MMBtu, while the price of alternative fuel (such as a No. 2 fuel oil) in the region is $2.50 per MMBtu. To determine the share of the incremental pricing cost account to be billed to the industrial users, the pipeline, first, subtracts from the alternative fuel cost the retail, or "burner-tip," price of the gas ($2.50 − $2.25), and then multiplies this difference by the volume of industrial consumption ($0.25 × 250 million units), thus obtaining the sum of incremental costs ($62.5 million) to be distributed among the industrial facilities.[37] Although the remainder of the account (that is, the $38.75 million left after $62.5 million is deducted from $101.25 million) is then rolled back into the rates charged all customers, the net effect of the industrial passthrough in this example is to give residential buyers a $0.50 credit per MMBtu of new gas consumed (since $62.5 million ÷ 125 million units = $0.50).

From even this highly schematic description, it is obvious that pipelines and distributors will acquire an accounting task which, if not unmanageable, will nonetheless entail considerable costs. After all most pipelines will be filled with more than one type of gas, and distribution companies will have to segregate them for record-keeping purposes, since not all will require incremental pricing. To complicate matters, the legislation actually prescribes not one but several different formulas, depending on the category of gas to be incrementally priced. (Thus, new and new-onshore production gas require accounts computed on a base of $1.48 per MMBtu, while gas from stripper wells, for example, qualifies for a threshold pegged to a higher rate, and high-cost gas falls under still another arrangement.) Moreover, to calculate the industrial surcharges in each case, one must figure out the applicable alternative fuel costs for specific classes of industrial facilities in appropriate regions. Nonarbitrary designations will be hard to make. Additionally, there is the question of exactly when the surcharges are to be passed through, since, presumably, distributors and pipelines must first wait to see how much gas the industrial and residential users have actually used. The act says only that there is a "calendar period involved," at the end of which the volumes delivered would be measured and the passthroughs computed. It may not be easy to arrive at suitable accounting intervals that will neither subject end-user rates to significant short-term fluctuations nor keep industrial users in the dark for months over the final rates payable for the gas that they have contracted to receive.

What represents a burden for the gas industry's transmission companies and industrial buyers could become an administrative quagmire for FERC and the state public-utility commissions, whose job will be to supervise the system and guard against abuses. To enforce this mode of incremental pricing, one wonders whether the authorities might not find themselves having to monitor countless transactions, not only those between pipelines and local distributors, but also those between pipelines or distributors and end-users.[38] All this is in addition to a more basic problem which is that of deciding precisely whom to price incrementally. At first surcharges will be billed only to large industrial boiler-fuel users, but in a second phase, the law calls for an extension of the system (subject to congressional confirmation) to include a group of medium-sized facilities and industries that burn gas in process (textile mills, glass factories, and petrochemical plants, for instance). FERC is charged with setting up the two-stage application, specifying exemptions, and even ruling selectively as to the termination of incremental pricing.[39] Needless to say, the entire operation could be beset by appeals and law suits. Furthermore, the amount of detailed data the agency will need to formulate workable rules is awesome. Much of the information (the data for many agricultural uses and small boiler-fuel users, for instance) is not readily available. FERC must collect it, and make sense of it, all within eighteen months of enactment. These barriers are not insurmountable. FERC officials have repeatedly indicated that the task of carrying through the incremental pricing plan will be difficult but feasible. Most interstate pipelines evidently feel the same way (the AGA, which represents these interests, supported NGPA). Moreover, the designers of the plan argued, not unpersuasively, that if incremental pricing is to be imposed at all, its present formulation, however knotty, is the only effective one. Still, one must question whether a compromise that trades the distant—and, some would say, all the more dubious—benefits of deregulation for additional immediate reams of red tape is a bold stride toward an orderly energy policy.

All this leads to a final sobering thought about the Natural Gas Policy Act, namely, that its regulatory impact is likely to be more onerous for small companies than for large ones. This is not, however, because the NGPA deliberately favors "big oil." (On the contrary, several parts of the act appear to serve the interests of minor independents—low-volume stripper wells, as an example, are handled quite generously—while other key sections seem unmistakably disadvantageous to the industry's giants. Gas from newly discovered reservoirs on the Outer Continental Shelf will remain under price controls if the drilling occurs in areas that were leased before April 20, 1977. For several of the major oil companies, whose activity centers increasingly on the Outer Continental Shelf, this means that deregulation will not cover most of their current offshore drilling opportunities.) Rather, it is chiefly because survival in an environment of intricate government regulations demands not just clever management but also a large financial cushion and, equally crucially, an internal bureaucracy. In other words the successful firms are likely to be those resourceful enough to cope with the complex paperwork, informational costs, and court cases associated with the government's regulations. The successful firms may also tend to be the ones equipped with armies of lawyers and accountants poised to pore over the detailed requirements in search of the inevitable loopholes and gray areas where leverage could be applied at the administrative or guidance levels. The problem is not new. Government regulation has taken its toll of minor firms for years. But in the case of natural gas, a central concern has been to counteract the oligopolistic tendencies of the industry. This, after all, was one of the main justifications for price control in the first place. Inasmuch as the new legislation increases bureaucratic encumbrances, it may perpetuate—indeed, even exacerbate—the tendency of earlier gas regulation to accomplish the inverse of what it intended.

CONCLUSION: WHERE THINGS STAND

Since 1974 Congress on at least six different occasions has tried to reform the regulation of natural gas. The latest attempt began with a special sense of urgency, but then lapsed into eighteen months of ponderous legislative negotiations. Why these interminable deliberations led in the end to a bill so problematical is too long and complex a story to be told here. A close look at the facts, I suspect, would discredit the usual explanations—those which summon up grand conspiracies by the oil-gas lobby, blame the current Administration for lack of leadership, or lament the regional preoccupations of legislators in the midst of a national crisis. More elucidating are the sharp ideological cleavages on energy issues in Congress and the near impossibility of legislating a comprehensive energy program, given the nature and persistence of these cleavages.

During the ninety-fifth Congress, any new regulatory scheme for oil or natural gas that was capable of threading its way through Capitol Hill had to recognize the competing claims of two evenly divided camps. These were the legislators who finally lacked confidence in the free-market solution to the problem of gas and oil scarcity, as opposed to those whose faith in the market often seemed limitless and naive. Even the most coherent, well-conceived policies can often run awry when they move from the drawing boards to be put into effect.[40] Yet, policies that must patch together fundamentally divergent principles, as was the case from the outset with the recent natural-gas compromise, virtually guarantee that the mechanics of implementation will be complex—and sometimes excruciatingly so. The

Natural Gas Policy Act of 1978 was probably all that could be expected, given the political climate in Congress. That is regrettable. Even more regrettable are any illusions that an elegant energy policy has been consummated, when one considers all the time and effort spent. What has really emerged is a modest improvement—and one whose toughest tests undoubtedly lie ahead.

NOTES

1. *The New York Times* (May 25, 1978).
2. Ibid.
3. The decisive vote in the House of Representatives came October 13, 1978, on a motion to keep the controversial gas-pricing conference report in a package with other more popular parts of the overall energy bill. By forcing an up or down vote on the energy package as a whole, rather than permitting separate roll calls on each of its parts, the prospects of passage were greatly improved. If a separate roll call had been held on the gas section alone, that part of the energy legislation might well have been doomed.
4. *Phillips Petroleum Co.* v. *Wisconsin*, 374 U.S. 672 (1954). Actually, FPC regulation of natural gas began under the Natural Gas Act of 1938, but it was not until the *Phillips* case that the act was interpreted to authorize FPC regulation of "arm's length" sales by producers to interstate pipelines.
5. Robert B. Helms, *Natural Gas Regulation: An Evaluation of FPC Price Controls* (Washington, D.C.: American Enterprise Institute for Public Policy Research, 1974), p. 19.
6. Paul W. MacAvoy and Robert S. Pindyck, *Price Controls and the Natural Gas Shortage* (Washington, D.C.: American Enterprise Institute for Public Policy Research, 1975), p. 12.
7. In *Atlantic Refining Co.* v. *Public Service Commission*, 360 U.S. 378 (1959), otherwise known as the CATCO case, the Supreme Court ruled that the FPC wellhead price-regulation procedures were inadequate.
8. Richard B. Mancke, *The Failure of U.S. Energy Policy* (New York: Columbia University Press, 1974), p. 111.
9. An illuminating analysis of this period is found in the MacAvoy and Pindyck, *Price Controls*, pp. 13–16. According to MacAvoy and Pindyck, the FPC had imposed a temporary freeze on prices, pending completion of the various area-rate proceedings at which permanent ceilings were to be determined. But the proceedings went on for years. (The Permian Basin hearings, for example, were first announced in December 1960; a final FPC opinion was not handed down until August 1965; and Supreme Court approval of the opinion did not come until three years later.) Not only did the delay subject producers to seemingly endless uncertainty regarding the price levels that would ultimately emerge, but when the permanent ceilings were finally set, they were inevitably founded on regional cost data derived from the long interim period of fixed

prices. Since producing companies had taken on mostly those drilling projects with costs low enough to be profitable under the freeze in that period, the FPC's eventual price ceilings reflected depressed cost estimates. Thus, real prices in the mid-1960s were held at levels comparable to those prevailing in the late 1950s.

10. Helms, *Natural Gas Regulation*, p. 23. For further discussion of the rationale underlying this arrangement, see Stephen Breyer and Paul W. MacAvoy, "The Natural Gas Shortage and Regulation of Natural Gas Producers," *Harvard Law Review*, 86 (April 1973), pp. 949–985, passim; Clark A. Hawkins, "Structure of the Natural Gas-Producing Industry," in *Regulation of the Natural Gas Producing Industry*, Keith C. Brown, ed., (Washington, D.C.: Resources for the Future, 1972), pp. 161–162.

11. On this point see Edward J. Mitchell, *U. S. Energy Policy: A Primer* (Washington, D.C.: American Enterprise Institute for Public Policy Research, 1974), p. 56.

12. Patricia E. Starrett, *The Natural Gas Shortage and the Congress* (Washington, D.C.: American Enterprise Institute for Public Policy Research, 1974), pp. 34–35.

13. U.S. Senate, Committee on Commerce, *Hearings, Consumer Energy Act of 1974, April 22–23, 1974* (Washington, D.C.: U.S. Government Printing Office, 1974), p. 1561.

14. Gas curtailments during winter 1977 caused 8,900 plant shutdowns and periods of unemployment for some 549,000 workers in the East and Midwest. *Congressional Quarterly Almanac* (1977), p. 648. Meanwhile, estimates indicated that the shortages were costing consumers billions of dollars each year through increased use of alternate fuels (No. 2 fuel oil, liquified and synthetic natural gas, etc.) and higher unit costs due to unused pipelines.

15. See, for example, the position of Lee C. White, a former FPC commissioner, in U.S. Senate, Committee on Commerce, *Hearings, Consumer Energy Act of 1974* (Washington, D.C.: U.S. Government Printing Office, 1974), Appendix, p. 2050.

16. Beginning in spring 1978, there were reports of downward pressure on intrastate gas prices in *Business Week* (May 29, 1978), p. 29 and *Congressional Quarterly Weekly Report* (September 16, 1978), p. 2454. Some knowledgeable observers have contended that exact parity between intrastate and interstate rates is unnecessary to move supplies from the former into the latter. These observers argue that under the old dual market system, the interstate sector was able to attract supplies even at prices somewhat below prevailing intrastate rates, because certificated interstate dedications were assured an uninterrupted, long-term market. Thus, according to these sources, all that was needed was for the price levels in the two sectors to approximate each other roughly.

17. Net domestic production of natural gas peaked in 1973 at 22.6 trillion cubic feet (Tcf). Output declined until 1977, when net gas production stabilized at 19.5 Tcf. The 11,000 gas wells completed in 1977 were a record, and additions to proven reserves that year were at their highest level since 1970 when Alaskan reserves were added. What these data do not convey is the fact that the

great majority of wells completed were developmental rather than exploratory, and that reserves discovered per-foot-drilled have declined steadily since 1971. See: U.S. Senate, Committee on Energy and Natural Resources, *Natural Gas Pricing Proposals: A Comparative Analysis* (Washington, D.C.: U.S. Government Printing Office, 1977), pp. 11, 13. Thus, overall proven reserves of natural gas in the United States declined for the tenth straight year in 1977. American Gas Association, *Gas Facts, 1977 Data* (Arlington, Vir.: American Gas Association, 1978), p. 1.

18. U.S. Senate, "Joint Explanatory Statement of the Committee on Commerce," *Natural Gas Conference Report* (August 18, 1978), p. 78. Note: Gas from an existing well can also qualify as new gas if the depth of the well was increased after February 18, 1977, by at least one thousand feet more than the deepest "completion location" of all existing wells within a two-and-a-half-mile radius.

19. The pre-NGPA interstate ceiling price was $1.48 per thousand cubic feet (Mcf). The initial ceiling price of new gas under NGPA was set at $1.75 per Mcf beginning April 20, 1977. Since NGPA's starting price was then adjusted monthly, by the time the act was signed into law, the ceiling stood at $2.07. It is misleading to infer, however, that NGPA thus signified an actual new-gas price increase of 40 percent over the old baseline ($1.48), since, under the old law, the latter would also have been adjusted upward by November 1978.

20. "Conference Report on Natural Gas," *Environmental Study Conference Senate Floor Brief,* 1 (July 31, 1978), p. 5.

21. *Congressional Record,* 124 (September 18, 1978), p. S15296.

22. Federal Energy Regulatory Commission, "New Ceiling Prices for U.S. Natural Gas," reported in *The Oil and Gas Journal* (November 20, 1978), p. 57.

23. Between 1967–1976 the average cost-per-gas-well-drilled increased 91.8 percent. The average cost-per-foot-drilled rose 116 percent. *Congressional Record,* 124 (September 27, 1978), p. S 16243. During Senate hearings in June 1977, a spokesman for Mobil Oil noted that using 1975–1976 cost data, even the FPC's own costing model would have indicated that the industrywide unit cost of new gas already averaged about $2.30 per Mcf. U.S. Senate, Committee on Energy and Natural Resources, *Hearings, Natural Gas Pricing Proposals of President Carter's Energy Program, June 13–14, 17, 1977* (Washington, D.C.: U.S. Government Printing Office, 1977), p. 355. According to recent Department of Commerce estimates, the cost of drilling machinery and equipment rose 15 percent over the year beginning October 1977. Reportedly, many industry managers agree that increases in costs will stay well ahead of the general rate of inflation, perhaps by as much as 20 to 30 percent. Randy Sumpter, "U.S. Producers Caught in Cost/Price Squeeze," *The Oil and Gas Journal* (December 4, 1978), p. 27.

24. Adam Clymer, "Uncertain Gas Outlook," *The New York Times* (May 26, 1978), p. D3.

25. *Congressional Record,* 124 (September 19, 1978), p. S 15413.

26. To be sure, one can speculate over whether NGPA's base prices encompass a much larger amount of newly produced gas than would otherwise have been covered by a new FERC national area-rate determination if NGPA had never

passed. The answer would depend on the specifics of the hypothetical FERC opinion and on its timing, since the new rate would have applied only to new contracts entered into after the decision.

27. *Congressional Record*, 124 (September 11, 1978), p. S 14880.
28. Ibid., p. S 14885.
29. This may have been what Senator Lowell P. Weicker, Jr. (Republican, Connecticut), among others, was suggesting in repeated criticism of the gas compromise. During a speech on the Senate floor, September 12, 1978, Weicker noted:

> [T]here should always be the prospect of prices going down. Under this bill there is no such prospect. Do not forget that a free market involves that possibility, whereas under this so-called "deregulation" bill, the price always goes up every year.

See also *Congressional Record*, 124 (September 12, 1978) p. S 14960.
30. *Congressional Quarterly Almanac* (1975), p. 258.
31. Despite the great effort in NGPA to define new and other categories of gas rigorously, the states will undoubtedly enjoy some discretion in applying these standards. A principal reason is that the definitions rely on concepts that are themselves hazy. The depth and distance requirements for new gas in old onshore reservoirs, for example, are measured in terms of "completion locations." What are these? The law defines a completion location as "any subsurface location from which natural gas is being or has been produced in commercial quantities." U.S. Senate, *Natural Gas Conference Report* (August 18, 1978), "Sec. 2. Definitions," p. 3. That there is room for interpretation here seems obvious. See U.S. Senate, Committee on Energy and Natural Resources, *Hearings, June 13–14, 17, 1977,* pp. 439, 588–589.
32. It is interesting to note that on a key gas-deregulation measure before the House on August 3, 1977, the California delegation split 16–27, with the majority voting against decontrol. In 1977 New Mexico became the first state to adopt price controls on gas produced and sold within the state. A ceiling of $1.44 per Mcf was imposed on all pre-1975 production.
33. As of 1977, there were at least five different vintages of gas operative under the various FTC opinions of recent years. Under the pre-NGPA system, additional vintaging by FERC would undoubtedly have created still more categories between 1978 and 1985. Furthermore, some of the gas categories in the Natural Gas Policy Act simply incorporate categories already established. In their fight to block enactment of the new law, some critics have depicted the status quo as vastly preferable in its simplicity to what was contemplated by the new legislation. This was misleading.
34. Several different forms of incremental pricing were considered by Congress. The gas conference committee, however, finally settled on the present version. Although more intricate than some other alternatives, it is presumably designed to prevent local distribution companies from rolling in high-priced gas with cheaper gas and ultimately charging all customers an average price. It does this via an involved accounting procedure that forces pipelines and dis-

tributors to pass through a savings to residential customers and higher charges for low-priority users at the retail level. For this reason the particular mechanism embodied in the legislation is sometimes referred to as incremental pricing "to the burner-tip." Some important details of the incremental pricing procedure have yet to be made final by the supervising agency, FERC.

35. Industrial gas use performs an important load-balancing function during emergencies and curtailments. The large industrial users are typically the first to be curtailed, so as to ensure gas supplies for residential use. Loss of industrial loads due to permanent conversions of alternate fuels could force distribution utilities to enlarge storage, pipeline, and other facilities, at considerable capital cost, in order to maintain unimpaired gas flows to residential consumers during shortfalls. Additionally, under state utility regulation, industrial uses often bear a portion of the fixed charges of the distribution utility. Reductions in industrial gas usage would terminate these rate-cutting credits, and hence, shift to residential users those portions of fixed charges previously assigned to industrial accounts. Federal Energy Regulatory Commission, "Comments of United Distribution Companies Pursuant to the Notice of Informal Public Conference and Inquiry Dated January 12, 1979," Washington, D.C.: FERC document, Docket No. RM 79–14, p. 11.

36. Some of the underlying premises were suggested in an explanatory statement issued by the House-Senate conferees accompanying the initial draft of the natural-gas conference report. See U.S. House of Representatives, Committee on Interstate and Foreign Commerce, "Joint Explanatory Statement of the Committee on Conference; Economic Analysis of [the Natural Gas] Conference Agreement" (July 31, 1978), pp. A5–A6.

37. In the simple illustration set out here, it is assumed that all industrial users are subject to incremental pricing. In reality only a subset will be, as there are provisions for statutory and discretionary exemptions from low-priority-use categories.

38. The difficulty of ensuring compliance with the welter of federal oil-gas price regulations of recent years is now being underscored by the growing DOE investigation of widespread violations of oil-price controls. (Richard Halloran, "U.S. Says 7 Concerns Billed $1.7 Billion Over Oil-Price Limit," *The New York Times*, May 3, 1979, pp. 1, D11.) Whatever else the Natural Gas Policy Act may achieve, it is not likely to simplify DOE's or FERC's enormous enforcement problems.

39. For instance the passthroughs to incrementally priced users generally terminate when the costs of gas to these users reaches the Btu-equivalent price of alternate fuel (for the most part, No. 2 fuel oil). But FERC is given discretion in certain cases to allow the cutoff to be set as low as the Btu-equivalency for No. 6 fuel oil, when this is deemed necessary to prevent industrial users from converting to alternative fuels and thereby shifting the cost burden of gas back onto high-priority, or residential, consumers. U.S. Senate, "Joint Explanatory Statement of the Committee on Conference," *Natural Gas Conference Report* (August 18, 1978), pp. 99–100

40. See Jeffrey L. Pressman and Aaron Wildavsky, *Implementation* (Berkeley,

Calif.: University of California 1973), ch. 3; David Nachmias, *Public Policy Evaluation* (New York: St. Martin's 1979), pp. 2–5; Eugene Bardach, *The Implementation Game: What Happens After a Bill Becomes a Law* (Cambridge, Mass.; MIT Press, 1977), pp. 3–6; Herbert Kaufman, *Red Tape: Its Origins, Uses, and Abuses* (Washington, D.C.: Brookings Institution, 1977), ch. 2.

ASSESSING THE NATIONAL 55 M.P.H. SPEED LIMIT

Charles T. Clotfelter
John C. Hahn

INTRODUCTION

One of the U.S.A.'s most tangible responses to the Arab oil embargo and subsequent higher oil prices was the 55 m.p.h. speed limit passed by Congress on January 2, 1974. Although compliance has been by no means universal, the law resulted in a dramatic decrease in average driving speeds on highways. Between 1973 and 1974, the proportion of vehicles exceeding 65 m.p.h. fell from 50 to 9% on rural interstates and from 16 to 2% on urban interstates. The average speed on those highways dropped from 65.0 to 57.6 and from 57.0 to 53.1 m.p.h., respectively. Spurred by the increasing use of citizen band radios and an apparent decline in the law's popularity, speeds have begun to inch back up, but not to any large degree. In 1975, average speeds held steady on rural interstates and increased to 54.7 m.p.h. on urban interstates.[1] The extent to which this decrease in average speed is a result of the new speed limit is unclear, but there is every reason to believe that most of it is due to the speed limit and not due to higher gasoline prices. While higher prices have probably been responsible for a decrease in the number and length of trips taken, they have made little difference in the personal costs of driving at different speeds. In the absence of evidence to the contrary, we therefore assume in this paper that the reduction in speeds between 1973 and 1974 is due wholly to the adoption and partial enforcement of the new speed limit. However, alternative assumptions as to the extent of speed reductions due to the speed limit would make little qualitative difference in the conclusions.[2]

The reduced highway speeds resulting from the speed limit produce clear benefits for the nation. Supporters of the law emphasize the fuel savings possible from reduced driving speeds as a major benefit of the law. More recently, advocates have pointed to declines in highway fatalities as another important benefit. On the other hand, the reduced speeds may also impose sizeable costs by increasing the time which must be spent on the road for a given trip. The loud protests by independent truckers indicate only a part of this time cost. In terms of additional productive or otherwise valuable time spent on highways, this could represent a substantial economic cost. Given the social importance of the twin goals of saving fuel and reducing highway fatalities as well as the potential importance of the economic cost of increased travel time, it is useful to address the question of whether the new speed limit can be justified in terms of broad concepts of economic efficiency. To answer this question requires consideration of the general case for govenment regulations of driving speeds as well as an empirical evaluation of the costs and benefits of this particular speed limit.

The section of this paper analyzes the decision-making of the individual driver and evaluates in normative terms the justification for government intervention. The third section presents a rough calculation of the costs and benefits of the 55 m.p.h. speed limit, using available data concerning driver behavior and the law's effectiveness. The final section concludes the analysis with a brief consideration of alternative policies.

DRIVING DECISIONS AND THE SPEED LIMIT

Since a change in the speed limit is a policy directed at changing the behavior of individual motorists, it is essential to begin by considering a model of individual driving choices. The major choices facing an individual motorist involve the frequency and length of trips, the route to take, the time of day or week to travel, the occupancy rate of the vehicle, and the driving speed. A national speed limit is likely to affect primarily two of these choices: how much to drive and how fast to drive. A decrease in the speed limit can be expected to result in substitution to other modes of transportation for some trips and in the complete elimination of other trips. This substitution creates problems in measuring both the costs and benefits of the new speed limit, a point to which we will return in the next section.

The second and more crucial choice for motorists concerns the decision about how fast to travel, given that a trip will be made. Drivers may be seen as having a demand for travel speed while driving, as indicated by a representative motorist's demand curve D in Figure 8.1. The curve slopes down to the right because the marginal benefit in terms of value of time saved decreases with each increment in speed. The area under any segment of the demand curve gives a rough approximation of the driver's gross willingness to pay for an increase in his rate of travel speed.

The private costs borne by drivers are represented by the marginal cost curve MC_0. Included in MC_0 are the costs of gasoline, other operating costs, and the certainty equivalent value of possible death or injury to driver and passengers.[3] Since engine efficiency decreases at higher speeds, the total cost of fuel consumption per miles rises with speed. Whether the marginal cost of increments in speed rises or falls is uncertain, however. For simplicity, the marginal cost curves in Figure 8.1 have been drawn ap-

Figure 8.1. Determination of average driving speeds.

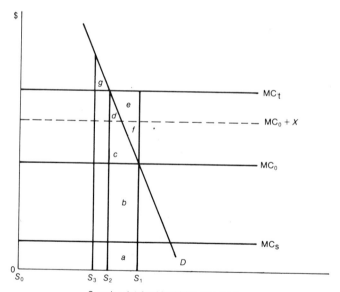

Speed maintained in driving one mile (m.p.h.)

D = motorist's demand for travel speed

MC_s = expected external marginal costs, in terms of probability of death, or injury to others

MC_0 = operator's own marginal cost, in terms of operating costs and probability of death or injury to driver and passengers

X = excess of social marginal cost of fuel over market price of fuel

$MC_t = MC_s + MC_0 + X$

proximately horizontal, although the essential points of the analysis would be the same in the other cases as well. The probability of death or injury also tends to increase with speed.[4] If left to decide his own speed, the motorist will drive at an average speed S_1, the point at which marginal benefit just equals private marginal cost.

Because there are costs that drivers do not take into account, however, S_1 is not the socially optimal speed. The driver's individual calculus ignores two components of social cost. First, one motorist's presence on the road increases the probability of death or injury for other motorists as well as the probability of property damage. The marginal social cost of the increased probability of such deaths, injuries, and damage is represented by MS. By ignoring these costs, the individual drives at a faster speed than is socially optimal. This external cost alone may be sufficient justification for public establishment of a speed limit.[5]

A second component of social cost is ignored by the individual motorist if for some reason the market price of gasoline differs from the social marginal cost (or shadow price) of gasoline. In the case of the United States, the social marginal cost of fuel has recently been considerably higher than prevailing market prices, owing to a government policy of controlling the price of domestic oil. Whether or not there is any social cost in being dependent on foreign oil per se, the social marginal cost should at least be reckoned on the basis of this more costly foreign oil.

The socially optimal speed is that at which the social marginal cost of increasing the speed of travel is equal to social marginal benefit. If private benefits equal social benefit, that is, if the social value of a traveler's time equals the private value, the efficient speed is S_2, a speed that is lower than that which would be chosen by individuals acting alone. The social cost of allowing motorists to increase their speeds from S_2 to S_1 would be the extra social cost not compensated by additional benefit, or the triangle formed by areas e and f. By the same token, this would be the social benefit of reducing travel speed from S_1 to S_2. This reasoning constitutes the justification for, first, imposing a speed limit and, second, decreasing the speed limit in response to an increase in the social cost of driving. However, it is quite possible that the new speed limit may not be set at the optimal speed. If the speed were reduced from S_1 to S_3, for example, net benefits would be represented by areas e and f, less area g, the latter area being the net social cost of reducing the speed from S_2 to S_3. If the speed were initially S_2, and then were reduced to S_3, there would be a clear social loss, represented by area g. Clearly, a given reduction in the speed limit may or may not be desirable.

While it is impossible to relate, a priori, actual driving speeds to speeds shown in the figure—because to do so would require knowledge of the "true" optimal driving speed—this graphical analysis is useful in identifying the components of any cost-benefit analysis of the new national speed limit. For example, assuming that the reduction implied by a national speed limit is from S_1 to S_2, what would be the costs and benefits? For one individual traveling one mile, the cost would clearly be the reduction in the area under the demand curve, areas a, b, c and d. This is essentially the value of the increased travel time necessitated by the slower travel speed.

There would be three major benefits of the new speed limit. The probability of death or injury to pedestrians and to other motorists and the probability of property damage would be reduced, thus reducing the expected external cost of driving. The area under MS_s (a) represents this benefit. Second, the probability of death or injury to driver and drivers would likewise decline, as would the private operating cost per mile. This benefit is represented by the area under the private MC_0 curve (a plus b). Finally, since the social cost of fuel exceeds the private cost, the fuel savings yields an additional social benefit of c plus f. The sum of these various benefits— or reduced social costs—is the entire area under the social marginal cost curve: areas a through f. If this area exceeds the corresponding area under the demand curve, as it does in the example of moving from speeds S_1 to S_2, the change results in a net social benefit.

In sum, because the social cost of driving exceeds the private cost, motorists acting individually will drive too fast. It is therefore possible to justify in principle a number of corrective policies on efficiency grounds. One such policy is a speed limit. Whether the actual reduction to 55 m.p.h. is in fact justified, however, is a question which invites empirical investigation in the form of cost-benefit analysis. In the following section we turn to the issues that would be involved in such an investigation. The question of alternative policies which might also be justified is taken up in the final section.

MEASURING THE COSTS AND BENEFITS: SOME ROUGH ESTIMATES

In this section we present a suggestive outline for an economic analysis of the 55 m.p.h. speed limit. While it is by no means intended as a full cost-benefit analysis of the law, the analysis below attempts to provide rough estimates for the major costs and benefits, using readily available data. Specifically, we attempt to estimate actual costs and benefits resulting from the implementation of the national 55 m.p.h. speed limit between 1973 and 1974. This contrasts with an evaluation of the *potential* costs and benefits that could be obtained if drivers were to obey the new speed limit universally. The latter approach, taken by Castle, is of limited practical importance and is furthermore incorrect to the extent that it ignores any additional enforcement costs necessary to insure compliance.[6]

Evaluating actual rather than hypothetical changes raises at least three problems. First, as noted above, the increase in the cost of gasoline which did in fact accompany the imposition of the speed limit leaves open the possibility that some of the decrease in driving speeds may be the result of the higher prices rather than the speed limit. As noted above, this is unlikely and in this paper it is assumed that all of the decrease is due to the speed limit. Second, the changes in the speed limit and in the price of fuel were accompanied by a reduction in traffic. This reduction calls for a modification in the valuation of lost time that would not be considered in the evaluation of a hypothetical slow-down of all trips. This problem is discussed below in the section on costs. A third difficulty produced by evaluating actual changes in behavior lies in allocating that portion of reduced fatalities, injuries and incidents of property damage actually due to the decreased speed. Fortunately, independent estimates are available for this purpose in the important case of fatalities.

COSTS

Time Cost

The major cost of this national speed limit is clearly the value of the additional time spent in driving at new, slower speeds. For simplicity, if the law affected only the speed at which motorists drive—and not their decisions to drive, stay at home, or take other forms of transportation—the time cost of the law would be simply the number of additional hours spent driving multiplied by the average value of time. Indeed, this assumption of no change in driving behavior underlies Castle's hypothetical valuation of time cost due to a decrease in driving speed from 70 to 55 m.p.h. In fact, motorists did cut back their driving from 1973 to 1974, and it is reasonable to believe that this was due not only to the increased price of gasoline but also to the increased time cost of driving. Consumers in effect avoided part of the impact of the increased driving times by substituting other modes of travel and even other activities (including staying at home more often) for driving. Since individuals made them voluntarily, such substitutions would be expected to involve not more, and probably less, cost than the driving which would have been done. To calculate increased driving time using the beginning year mileage would therefore overstate the social cost of the speed limit. On the other hand, to calculate the increased driving time using the second year mileage would clearly understate the cost because the fact that motorists were forced into previously undesirable behavior would be ignored.

This problem of valuation is an example of the venerable index number problem, and occurs because households have changed their behavior over time in response to changes in relative costs and benefits, thus avoiding some of the costs.[7] In such a case, no unambiguous calculation can be made. It is possible only to suggest bounds for the correct value. For the present application, an upper bound estimate of the time lost due to the new speed limit in 1974 takes the number of vehicle-miles traveled in 1973 as a basis for calculation. Where VM represents vehicle-miles, S is average speed, and R is the average occupancy rate per vehicle, the number of hours lost on a given class of highways is:

$$H = ((VM_{73}/S_{74} - (VM_{73}/S_{73}))R. \tag{1}$$

Where this expression is applied to each of three major highway classifications, shown in the Appendix, the number of hours lost is some 1.87 billion. Replacing the 1973 occupancy rate and number of vehicle-miles by the 1974 values yields the lower bound estimate of 1.72 billion hours. It is useful to note that even these two estimates do not necessarily establish the boundaries for the "true" number of hours lost. Each estimate is itself subject to error, due to any errors in measurement or to the possible existence of other factors affecting speeds or miles traveled.

The average value of commuting time has been the subject of considerable study, but estimates of the value of travel time of long-distance motorists or commercial drivers are more difficult to obtain. In order to obtain a reasonable average value to travel time for all motorists, we use two alternative values for the ratio of the value of travel time to the wage rate of those in the labor force: 42% from Lave's empirical analysis, and 33% from Dewees' evaluation of the literature on this question.[8] In 1974, the average wage was approximately $5.05 an hour for all members of the labor force.[9] We assume the same value for other adults not in the labor force in order to take account of the value of their non-market production.[10] Given the alternative estimates of the ratio of the value of travel time to the wage, the implied average values of time are $1.68 and $2.12 per hour. For convenience, other drivers and riders are also assumed to have the same value of time as members of the labor force; however, this is probably an overstatement for this relatively small group. Applying this first figure to the lower bound estimate of hours lost yields a lower bound estimate of increased time of $2.89 billion. Applying the higher value of time to the alternative estimate of time yields an upper bound figure of $3.96 billion. Since the time cost is by far the most important cost of the new speed limit, it is important to emphasize the caveats that apply to these figures. First, the estimates of the value of travel time employed above are based on studies of commuters. To the extent that vacation and other long-distance travelers may have lower values of time, the values used may provide overestimates. Second, the opportunity cost of increased transport time for commercial vehicles is not adequately reflected in these values of time. The costs of additional travel time for these vehicles is likely to be more, rather than less, than the values used in the calculations. These considerations imply that a complete analysis of the time costs of the speed limit should involve separate calculations by class of motorist and vehicle.

Compliance and Enforcement Costs

Motorists have hardly welcomed the new speed limit with open arms. In order to attain even the levels of compliance that have been reached, certain costs have had to be incurred. New signs had to be made, information on the law had to be disseminated, and some additional enforcement measures had to be undertaken. The measurement of enforcement costs is problematical. On the one hand, casual observation suggests that patrol activity has increased in order to enforce the lower speeds. However, it has apparently been impossible or undesirable in general to hire new personnel to enforce the new speed limits. The increased patrol activity can thus come only at the expense of other police functions. Another cost that is potentially easier to measure is the modification of speed limit signs. One indication of this cost is the amount that states requested from federal highways funds for this purpose. Twenty-five states filed reports on these expenditures, amounting to a total of $707,302. This is surely an underestimate in that only half the states reported. Apparently states would be reimbursed for these expenses under general highway financing if they did not apply under this specific category.[11] Nevertheless, if all states spent on per capita basis what these states reported, the total would be about $1.23 million. If these modifications had, say, three year lives, then the yearly cost of modification would be $0.41 million. Given the weak incentives for state reporting, this must be considered a low estimate. Finally, the federal government has engaged in an advertising campaign to encourage compliance with the speed limit. The Transportation Department has spent some part of its total of $2 million advertising and public information budget on this project, and there have no doubt been further costs due to time and space donated by media for related public service messages.[12] There are, however, no data on these costs. We therefore make the modest assumption that the yearly cost of this campaign is 10% of this budget, or $200,000, plus an equal amount for donated media time and space. This gives a total for compliance costs of $0.8 million, with police enforcement costs left unmeasured.

Benefits

Gasoline Saved

Because the gasoline economy of engines generally improves as speeds are decreased over the range from 70 to 55 m.p.h., the reduction in average speeds produced by the new speed limit has resulted in a sizeable gasoline savings. For the average automobile, the miles per gallon ratio rises from 13.3 m.p.g. at 70 m.p.h. to 14.9 at 60 m.p.h. to 16.9 at 50 m.p.h.[13] Given this technical information and the data given in the Appendix for vehicle-miles traveled and average speeds, it is possible to estimate the number of gallons saved due to the decrease in average driving speeds. As in the calculation of time costs, it is possible only to give upper and lower bound estimates for the amount of gasoline saved, one estimate based on each year's vehicle-miles traveled. Using vehicle-miles for 1973 yields the upper bound estimate of the number of gallons saved (G):

$$G = (VM_{73}/MPG_{73}) - (VM_{73}/MPG_{74}), \qquad (2)$$

where MPG is the average miles per gallon for vehicles on a given class of highways.[14] The actual calculations shown in the Appendix yield an upper bound estimate of 3.50 billion gallons and a lower bound of 3.39 billion gallons saved in 1974. Again, possible measurement errors imply that neither estimate should be taken as precise bounds on the "true" value.

Determining the proper valuation of this fuel saving is a more difficult task. In 1974, the average retail price of gasoline was 52.8 cents per gallon, implying a savings of about $1.8 billion.[15] However, this market price failed to reflect the social cost of gasoline due to the government's price control of "old" domestic oil and to the entitlements program. Intended to equalize the cost of crude oil to refiners after the escalation of the price of foreign oil, the entitlements program effectively guaranteed that the proportion of cheap "old" oil would be the same for all refiners.[16] Thus, the average cost of oil going into refineries was a weighted average of expensive foreign and new oil on the one hand, and cheaper old oil on the other. Because increases in national oil consumption would have to come from the expensive foreign sources, however, the social marginal cost of crude oil was the foreign price, not this weighted average. Likewise, the social marginal cost for gasoline would be, in effect, the market price that would prevail if all gasoline were refined entirely from imported oil or, equivalently, the market price that would prevail in the absence of price controls and entitlements. In other words, the value of resources used up when a gallon of gasoline was consumed was not the artificially low price paid by consumers, but rather the value of goods and services foregone in this country as a result of using one gallon of gasoline made from foreign oil.

In order to arrive at a rough approximation of this price, we assumed that the actual wholesale price of gasoline is a weighted average of two hypothetical wholesale prices: that of gasoline refined from domestic oil ($pd*$) and that of gasoline refined from foreign oil ($pf*$). Where h is the ratio of the domestic price of oil to the average foreign price and j is the proportion of the nation's oil supply that is foreign, the wholesale market price per gallon (P) is assumed to be:

$$P = jP_f^* + (1 - j)P_d^*. \tag{3}$$

If the ratio of hypothetical gasoline prices (P_d^*/P_f^*) is the same as the ratio of crude oil prices (h), then the market price is

$$P = jP_f^* + (1 - j)hP_f^*. \tag{3'}$$

The hypothetical wholesale price of foreign gasoline is then

$$P^* = P/(j + (1 - j)h). \tag{4}$$

Adding the actual 1974 retail markup per gallon yields the hypothetical retail price of foreign gasoline, which, as we argue above, is a better measure of the social marginal cost of gasoline than is the actual retail price.

In 1974 imported crude oil constituted 28.4% of the crude oil going to refineries in the U.S., not counting stock used. Thus j was equal to 0.284. The average price at which regular gasoline was purchased by full-service retail outlets (P) was 43.1¢ and the average selling price was 52.8¢ for an average markup of 9.7¢.[17] The ratio of average domestic crude oil prices at the wellhead to average imported oil prices in 1974 was 0.573.[18] Substituting these values into equation (4) yields an estimate of the wholesale price of gasoline refined from foreign crude oil of 62.1¢ per gallon. Adding the actual markup of 9.7¢ per gallon yields a retail price of 71.8¢ and adjusted fuel savings figures for 1974 of $2.43 billion as a lower bound and $2.52 billion as an upper bound, some 36% higher than the figures based on actual selling prices. It is worth noting that another form of substitution—the increasing use of self-service stations—probably makes this estimate, with its assumption of a constant markup, a slight overstatement. But given the time costs to purchasers and the slight savings obtainable in most locations, this does not seem to be an important source of error.

Fatalities Averted
A second major benefit of the 55 m.p.h. speed limit—one that seems to have been almost an afterthought by policymakers—is the reduction in highway fatalities that has resulted. Fatalities fell from 55,087 in 1973 to

46,049 in 1974, a decrease of 16.4%.[19] Besides the change in the speed limit, several other factors are responsible for this decrease, including the overall reduction in travel, the reduction in average occupancy, increased use of seat belts, and a shift toward daytime driving. Clearly, it is necessary to separate the effect of the speed limit from these other, largely related, effects. Examining changes in fatalities in two separate 4-month periods between 1973 and 1974, the National Safety Council estimated that the reduction in travel speed accounted for 46 to 59% of the total reduction in fatalities.[20] Applying these proportions to the total reduction in fatalities yields estimates of 4,157 and 5,332 as the number of fatalities averted due to the new speed limit.

The social cost of a fatality includes the loss of earnings, the pain and suffering caused, and the loss of home and family duties performed. Despite the metaphysical nature of the problem, economists have devised ways of arriving at empirical estimates of the value of life. A study by the Transportation Department estimated the total social cost of a traffic fatality at about $200,000 in 1972, or about $240,000 in 1974 dollars.[21] This figure agrees quite closely with an estimate by Thaler and Rosen of about $200,000 in 1967 dollars, using quite different methodology.[22] In the present context, it is probably more appropriate to interpret such estimates as implying a value of about $240,000 for a 1% increase in the probability of death for one hundred drivers than to take this money figure to summarize "the value" of a life. In the aggregate, however, both interpretations imply multiplying $240,000 by the number of fatalities averted by the new speed limit, yielding alternative estimates for this benefit of $997.7 million and $1,279.7 million.

Injuries Averted

Nonfatal injuries also declined between 1973 and 1974, from 2,835,683 to 2,653,057.[23] There has however been no analysis of the portion of that decline which is attributable to the new speed limit. In the absence of such information, we assume as two estimates the proportions used in connection with fatalities above, 46 and 59%. These estimates yield injury reductions of 84,008 and 107,749 between 1973 and 1974. Among injuries, three levels of severity can be distinguished: permanent total disability, permanent partial disability and permanent disfigurement, and no permanent injury. In 1971 the proportions of traffic injuries accounted for by each was 0.2, 6.5 and 93.3%, respectively; the average cost in 1971 of each was estimated by the National Highway Traffic Safety Administration to be $260,300, $67,100, and $2,465, respectively.[24] This distribution yields an average cost of $8,745 in 1974 dollars, per injury. Applying this figure to the two estimates of injuries averted yields estimates of the social benefit of injury reduction of $734.6 million and $942.3 million.

Reduced Property Damage

The reduction in speeds was accompanied by a reduction in property damage as well as injuries and fatalities. Between 1973 and 1974 the number of incidents involving property damage fell from 25.8 million to 23.1 million.[25] There is, however, no data to indicate the effect of the new speed limit on this reduction. Lacking such data, we made the alternative assumptions that 50% and that 25% of this reduction was the result of the new speed limit. These rough calculations yield estimates of 1.30 and 0.65 million as the number of incidents of property damage averted due to the implementations of the 55 m.p.h. speed limit. Applying an estimate of $300 average cost per incident of property damage in 1972—$363 in 1974—yields an upper bound estimate of cost savings due to the lower speeds of $471.9 million and a lower bound estimate of $236.0 million.[26]

Summing Up

Table 8.1 summarizes the estimates of benefits and costs. Separate totals of all upper bound and lower bound estimates are presented in order to suggest limits on the reasonable values of each. Total costs range from $2.89 billion to $3.96 billion. Total benefits are uniformly higher, at $4.40 billion and $5.21 billion. On the basis of these total figures, even modest estimates of the benefits of the 55 m.p.h. speed limit exceed the upper bound estimate of costs. Given these rough figures, therefore, the law can be judged to have results which are on balance beneficial.

Several qualifications are very much in order, however. In general, the quantitative estimates of costs and benefits are subject to error of an uncertain magnitude. To some extent we have attempted to allow for this error

TABLE 8.1
Total Costs and Benefits of the 55 m.p.h. Speed Limit,
1974 ($ Millions)

	Upper Bound Estimates	Lower Bound Estimates
Costs		
Time cost	3,969.0	2,892.1
Compliance and enforcement	0.8	0.8
	3,969.8	2,892.9
Benefits		
Gasoline saved	2,515.1	2,434.8
Fatalities averted	1,279.7	997.7
Injuries	942.3	734.6
Reduced property damage	471.9	236.0
	5,208.4	4,403.1

by presenting alternative estimates of most magnitudes. However, there remains little available empirical basis for some of the calculations. Two specific assumptions for which there is empirical support are also worth noting. First, the most important single number in the analysis is probably the value of traveler's time. Derivation of the average wage for members of the labor force is straightforward, but there is disagreement concerning the ratio of the value of travel time to the wage. Thus two alternative estimates are used. One difficulty lies in determining the opportunity cost for the time of adults not in the labor force and children. The procedure used in the present study assumes that the value of time is the same for all drivers and riders, that is, the same for members of the labor force. This of course overstates the average value of time and thus tends to put the cost estimates on the high side. That problem aside, it is clear that the assumed ratio of the value of travel time to the wage rate is a most important parameter in the analysis. Both the values of 42% and 33% yield cost estimates less than the calculated benefits. In order for costs to equal benefits, that ratio would have to reach 51% in the lower bound case and 55% in the upper bound case. Both of these values lie outside the range of values usually found.

A second important set of assumptions involves the relationship between speed and average gasoline consumption. The figures used, which are published by the Federal Highway Administration, relate to actual average consumption rates by automobiles at different speeds. The Environmental Protection Agency publishes a different set of consumption rates based on steady cruise speed which seem to be less realistic. The use of the latter figures would yield considerably less fuel savings, although the reduction would not be sufficient to cause either estimate of total benefits to be exceeded by the corresponding value of costs.[27]

CONCLUSION

The two most important goals of the 55 m.p.h. speed limit appear to be fuel savings and increased highway safety. The present paper presents, first, a theoretical justification for the establishment of a speed limit in order to meet these goals and, second, an empirical analysis of the specific speed limit instituted in the United States in 1974. While based on rough calculations, the empirical analysis indicates that the benefits of the program outweigh the economic costs. This is certainly not to say, however, that this speed limit is the only or the best policy for achieving the goals of conservation and highway safety. Indeed, a speed limit appears to be a second— or third—best policy for achieving both safety and conservation goals. It is quite possible that other policies, aimed directly at these goals, would be more effective. Alternative policies could also eliminate the present inequity of penalizing, in terms of time costs, drivers of efficient compacts and gas guzzlers alike.

Several possible policies could be used to replace or, more likely, complement a national speed limit. For example, gasoline prices—and thus the cost of driving—could be raised by taxing gasoline or by the elimination of the entitlements program. Both have been proposed by the Carter administration, the latter through an end to entitlements and a crude oil equalization tax. Income effects would be offset by comparable reductions in personal taxes. Similar effects could be achieved by the taxation of automobiles on the basis of rated fuel consumption. This also has been proposed in the Carter energy package.[28] The effectiveness of this policy would depend on the increased inducement to keep old big cars and on the effect of increased efficiency on total driving. Policies aimed directly at reducing highway fatalities would include requiring seat belts to be worn by all oc-

APPENDIX
Calculation of Time Costs and Energy Savings

A. Increased Travel Time	1973	1974
Vehicle miles (VM) (millions)		
Rural main[a]	462,979[b]	446,212[c]
Rural secondary	105,639[b]	103,147[c]
Urban interstate	128,342[b]	127,673[c]
Average speed (S)[d]		
Rural main	60.3	55.3
Rural secondary	52.6	49.5
Urban interstate	57.0	53.1
Average occupancy rate (R)	1.9	1.8
	Lower Bound	*Upper Bound*
Number of hours lost[e] (thousands)	(Using 1974 VM,R)	(Using 1973 VM,R)
Rural main	1,204,318	1,318,993
Rural secondary	221,055	238,973
Urban interstate	296,119	314,216
Total	1,721,492	1,872,182

B. Fuel Economy and Gasoline Saved	Average m.p.g.[f]		Gasoline Saved (Millions of Gallons)[g]	
	1973	1974	LOWER BOUND	UPPER BOUND
Rural main	14.4	15.8	2,774.0	2,878.3
Rural secondary	16.4	17.0	222.5	227.9
Urban interstate	15.5	16.3	394.6	396.7
Total dollar value at 71.8¢ per gallon ($millions)			2,434.8	2,515.1

[a] Includes rural interstate and rural primary.
[b] U.S. Department of Transportation, Federal Administration, *Highway Statistics 1973*, pp. 75–76.
[c] U.S. Department of Transportation, Fed. Highway Administration, *News*, Dec. 30, 1975.
[d] U.S. Department of Transportation, Office of Public Affairs, *Fact Sheet*, "The National 55 m.p.h. Speed Limit," May 14, 1976, p. 7.
[e] From equation (1).
[f] Derived from Alexander French, "Highway Planning and the Energy Crisis," U.S. Department of Transportation, Federal Highway Administration, May 1973, figure 24.
[g] From equation (2).

cupants of automobiles or requiring air bags to be installed in new cars.[29] Mandatory seat belt laws have been used in Australia, France and Canada, and there is evidence to suggest that fatalities have been reduced as a result.[30] Both policies would entail economic costs, but these costs may be well below the present time costs involved in the speed limit. A gasoline tax would also tend to reduce accidents and fatalities by reducing average driving speeds, although the amount of such reduction would be quite small. The optimal tax is one which would make the driver's private marginal cost of traveling at a higher speed equal to the social marginal cost of driving faster. Each of the policies discussed here would of course have distributional consequences which to some extent could be modified, if necessary, through the income tax and related transfers.

NOTES

1. U.S. Department of Transportation, Office of Public Affairs, *Fact Sheet*, May 14, 1976, p. 7.
2. As is discussed below, effects of the change in average driving speeds dominate the empirical measures of costs and benefits. Only the relatively unimportant compliance and enforcement costs are not a function of speed. If only three-fourths of the reduction were due to the speed limit, both costs and benefits would therefore be reduced by virtually the same proportions.
3. As distinct from the expected cost of death or injury, the certainty equivalent is the sure cost such that the motorist would be indifferent between that cost and the unlikely but uncertain prospect of death or injury on the road.
4. For the individual driver, the probability of death or injury also tends to increase at speeds which diverge from the average speed on the highway, as does the probability of inflicting harm on other motorists. For this reason, the individual's driving speed is partly a function of the speed of others, and vice versa.
5. Government intervention is justified provided that the costs associated with administering such intervention do not outweigh the inefficiency costs caused by the externality. The analysis might also justify a tax which varied with driving speed, although the administrative costs of levying such a tax would certainly be prohibitive.
6. Gilbert H. Castle, "The 55 MPH Speed Limit: A Cost/Benefit Analysis," *Traffic Engineering* (January 1976), 11–14.
7. Zeckhauser and Fisher present a general discussion of such "averting behavior," the valuation problems which are implied by such behavior. See Richard Zeckhauser and Anthony Fisher, "Averting Behavior and External Diseconomies," Kennedy School of Government Discussion Paper 41D, April 1976.
8. Charles A. Lave, "The Demand for Urban Mass Transportation," *Review of Economics and Statistics* 52 (August 1970), 320–323; Donald N. Dewees,

"Travel Cost, Transit, and Control of Urban Motoring," *Public Policy* 24 (Winter 1976), 61.

9. Total wages and salaries, other labor income and proprietors' income in 1974 was $895.6 billion. The labor force was about 93.2 million, and the average weekly working week in non-agricultural private establishments was 36.6 hours. U.S. Department of Commerce, Bureau of Economic Analysis, *Survey of Current Business*, July 1975, p. 13; U.S. Bureau of the Census, *Statistical Abstract of the United States 1975*, pp. 343, 353.

10. The difficulties of measuring the value of time, and leisure time in particular, are well known. For example, it is possible to argue that the use of the average wage understates the value of time of adults not in the labor market simply because they have chosen to remain out of the labor force at that wage. On the other hand, those not in the labor force may well be less productive on average and thus have a lower social opportunity cost.

11. U.S. Department of Transportation, Federal Highway Administration, "Federal-Aid Highway Funds Obligated for Speed Limit Sign Modifications, January 2, 1974 to Date," May 1976.

12. Charles T. Clotfelter, "The Scope of Public Advertising," in David G. Tuerck (ed.), *The Political Economy of Advertising* (Washington: American Enterprise Institute for Public Policy Research, 1978), Table 2.

13. U.S. Department of Transportation, Federal Highway Administration, "Highway and the Petroleum Problem—4 Reports," FHWA Bulletin, October 2, 1975, p. 24.

14. Average fuel economy rates are interpolated, using average vehicle speed and average fuel economy at each speed interval. However, since the rate of improvement in fuel economy is not constant over all speeds, the actual rate of consumption depends on the distribution of speeds and thus this estimate is at best an approximation.

15. Federal Energy Administration, *Monthly Energy Review*, May 1976, p. 54.

16. Federal Energy Administration, *Annual Report 1975/1976* (Washington, D.C.: Government Printing Office, 1977), pp. 44–45.

17. Federal Energy Administration, *Monthly Energy Review*, May 1976, pp. 6, 54.

18. Federal Energy Administration, *Monthly Energy Review*, February 1976, p. 57.

19. U.S. Department of Transportation, Federal Highway Administration, *Fatal and Injury Accident Rates*, 1974, p. 26.

20. National Safety Council, Statistics Division, "Factors Contributing to the Reduction of Motor Vehicle Traffic Fatalities," October 1974 and March 1975, Chicago, Illinois. Reduction in speed accounted for 11 of the 24% decrease between the January–April periods and 10 of the 17% decrease in the May–August periods.

21. U.S. Department of Transportation, National Highway Traffic Safety Administration, *Societal Costs of Motor Vehicle Accidents*, Preliminary Report, April 1972, p. 4.

22. Richard Thaler and Sherwin Rosen, "The Value of Saving a Life; Evidence from the Labor Market," University of Rochester Discussion Paper, 1973.

23. U.S. Department of Transportation, Federal Highway Administration, *Fatal and Injury Accident Rates*, 1974, p. 38.

24. U.S. Department of Transportation, National Highway Traffic Safety Administration, *Societal Costs of Motor Vehicle Accidents*, Preliminary Report, April 1972, p. 4.
25. National Safety Council, *Accident Facts*, 1974 and 1975.
26. *Societal Costs of Motor Vehicle Accidents*, p. 12.
27. These fuel efficiency rates are 22.5 m.p.g. at 40 m.p.h., 21.5 at 50, 19.5 at 60, and 17.3 at 70. U.S. Environmental Protection Agency, *A Report on Automotive Fuel Economy*, 1974, p. 10. These yield the alternative table:

	Average m.p.g.		Gasoline Saved (Million Gallons)	
	1973	1974	LOWER BOUND	UPPER BOUND
Rural main	19.4	20.4	1127.5	1169.9
Rural secondary	21.0	21.6	136.5	139.7
Urban interstate	20.1	20.9	243.1	244.3
Total			1507.1	1563.9
Dollar value at 71.8¢ per gallon ($millions)			1082.1	1122.9
Total benefits would then be $3.1 billion to $3.8 billion.				

28. U.S. Executive Office of the President, *The National Energy Plan* (Washington, D.C.: Government Printing Office, 1977), pp. 36, 51.
29. Another possibility would be simply to make drivers strictly liable for injuries caused by their driving.
30. National Safety Council, *Accident Facts*, 1975, p. 52.

THE BART EXPERIENCE— WHAT HAVE WE LEARNED?

Melvin M. Webber

The Bay Area Rapid Transit system (BART) has many characteristics of a huge social experiment—in vivo, as it were. Key element in a bold scheme to structure the future of the San Francisco region, BART was to stem the much-feared decline of the older metropolitan centers, while helping to give coherent order to the exploding suburbs. By offering a superior alternative to the automobile, BART was to make for congestion-free commuting. If successful, it would provide a model for rationalizing transportation and metropolitan development elsewhere.

It was experimental only in the sense that nothing quite like it had ever been tried before. Nowhere in America had a regional rail system been built in contemporary times, and nowhere in the world had such a rail system been built in an auto-based metropolitan area. Although novelty inevitably implied risk, BART was nevertheless promoted with the high confidence, if not certainty, that governmental projects seem to require. Its developers saw it as a sure bet.

They could not have chosen a better test site. The auto-ownership rate in the Bay Area is one of the world's highest, and auto-using habits are firmly entrenched, fostered by an early full-freeway system. The metropolitan region is built around a traditional European-type center with a large concentration of office employment and related service employment. Outside the small but high-density central city, which is set at the tip of the peninsula, the metropolitan settlement is organized in low-density suburban patterns, all of which were built around automobile transport. For test purposes, the Bay Area is further advantaged by having its urbanized areas topographically molded into narrow strips that parallel San Francisco Bay and follow the narrow valleys—a configuration superbly suited to the geometry of railroad lines, which also makes for long travel distances that, in turn, cry out for high-speed modes of transport. (The average Bay Area commuter lives 15.8 miles from his job; by comparison, Los Angeles commuters are only 8.9 miles away, Chicago commuters 6.6 miles, Philadelphia commuters 4.4 miles). What better place, then, to test whether a technologically superior system could stem the decline of traditional public transit and at the same time compete with the automobile as the dominant commuter mode and shaper of metropolitan growth? If it didn't work here, the odds of its working in less suited areas would surely be low.

Following some protracted and perhaps inevitable construction and debugging delays, BART began carrying passengers in September 1972. In response, a massive effort has been launched to monitor its effects. The BART Impact Program is carefully watching a wide array of potential consequences, under the sponsorship of the Department of Transportation and the Department of Housing and Urban Development, with the local Metropolitan Transportation Commission in the key resarch and management roles. The aim is to learn what might be germane to other metropolitan areas and to derive some lessons from the Bay Area experience that might inform federal policy. Meanwhile, however, several other metropolitan areas have already developed transit schemes that resemble BART, without waiting for the findings of the Bay Area studies. Federal subsidies have already been allocated to Washington, Atlanta, and Miami; and several other cities are under consideration.

It will of course be some time before definitive results of the BART evaluation are in, but enough impact research has now been done to permit an early appraisal of how well BART is accomplishing the objectives that motivated its construction. In turn, enough has been done to permit some judgments concerning the wisdom of building BART-like systems elsewhere. As we shall see, BART's score is pretty low, implying that prospects for other cities are dim.

INITIAL OBJECTIVES

The original plans for the BART system were formulated in the mid-1950's. At that time Americans perceived the major urban policy issues to be decentralization, "urban sprawl," and the decline of the central cities, particularly of their central business districts. Federal government activities were focused upon urban-renewal programs aimed at bringing middle-class suburbanites back and rejuvenating what was dolefully mourned as the "dying heart of the city." Some prophets were predicting an impending demise of metropolitan centers, as the automobile opened opportunities for free movement in all directions and combined with rising incomes to allow average families spacious suburban houses in spacious settings.

These prospects were greeted with exaggerated gloom in San Francisco. Surely, no other American city is as proud and narcissistic—no civic leaders elsewhere so obsessed by their sense of responsibility for protecting and nurturing their priceless charge. The idea that San Francisco might go the way of Newark or St. Louis was utterly abhorrent. And so it was, as the San Francisco Chamber of Commerce proudly reported in a multi-page advertisement in *Fortune*, that the civic leaders of San Francisco and their neighboring kin initiated a major effort to keep the Bay Area from going the way that cities of lesser breed were headed. The campaign was masterful in both conception and execution.

San Francisco had long been the major business and financial capital of the Western states, but it had been challenged since World War II by Los Angeles and, in the mid-1950's, was barely holding its own against explosive growth in Southern California. Probably as fundamental a motivation as any behind BART was the desire to keep "The City" as attractive to corporate headquarters, financial institutions, and upper-middle-class residents as it traditionally had been. Of course, those with personal economic interests in the central district were especially keen to promote BART. It would be simplistic, however, to ascribe their promotional fervor to their private considerations alone. Imbued with civic pride and the spirit of community enterprise, none doubted that he was involved in a happy symbiotic crusade in which everyone would be a winner.

The Golden Gateway redevelopment project was one response to the doom-sayers. Launched in 1955, it has by now successfully converted a decayed produce-market district into a spanking new cluster of high-rise office buildings, luxury residences, elaborate hotels, restaurants, and the like. Delayed for years by lawsuits, the Yerba Buena redevelopment project, the sister enterprise aimed at remodeling a 19th-century district lined with residential hotels, warehouses, and a skid row, may soon finally convert the "South of Market" street district from a low-class neighborhood to a prestige address. Between them, the two redevelopment efforts may total up to 10 million square feet of high-rise office space. More than that, they have contributed immensely to the prosperity of the San Francisco central district and to its competitive posture.

So huge an expansion in floor space and commensurate office employment obviously demanded a comparable expansion in transport capacity. BART was to provide a major increase in accessibility, supplemented by extension of the freeway system and improvements in downtown parking.

But BART was intended to do far more than bring commuters into San Francisco; it was conceived from the start as a regional system that would foster the growth of the entire Bay Area. With trains stopping on average at only 2.5-mile intervals, each station would be highly accessible, with a competitive advantage over other locations in the rivalry for apartment houses and for offices and other commercial establishments. The designers expected stations in suburban centers to attract major concentrations of offices and retail shops, while outlying stations would become surrounded by high-density housing and shopping facilities, serving commuters to the regional centers.

Simultaneously, the designers intended BART to supply the essential accessibility that would convert downtown Oakland into a major regional center. The junction of BART's four lines in the middle of Oakland's business district would indeed make that the most accessible point along BART's 71-mile route. Oakland has responded by launching its own downtown redevelopment project, which is now turning a marginal shopping area into a modern-looking business complex.

The civic leaders who promoted BART chose a rail system over additional highway improvements because they feared that the prophets of intolerable congestion might be right. The prospect that more population and more automobiles would overload the capacities of road systems seemed plausible enough to commend a system that simultaneously had a high capacity yet was conservative in its space demands. And besides, since San Francisco was a world center along with Paris, London, and New York, didn't it deserve a subway system comparable to others in its league?

DESIGN CONSIDERATIONS

The design criteria were thus clear: The new system had to be (1) capable of bringing increasing numbers of peak-hour commuters from near their suburban homes to within a few minutes' walk of their downtown offices, (2) attractive enough to travelers to be more than competitive with the automobile, and (3) financially viable.

The planners' response was to design a modern, electrified suburban railroad. Believing that buses could not attain the speed necessary to make them attractive to commuters, they rejected the alternative of using them as rapid-transit vehicles. Instead, they modeled their system after the New Haven and Long Island railroads, giving it much better downtown distribution with several subway stations under the main streets of San Francisco and Oakland.[1]

BART is misnamed as a "rapid transit" system. It is a hybrid among rail transportation systems, combining features of interurban electric lines, central-city subway lines, and current suburban railway lines, with the design elegance of modern aircraft and the control instrumentation of early spacecraft. As a hybrid it represents a compromise among desirable qualities of the several transport types. Unlike the interurban electric railways it cannot run in non-stop from outlying suburbs, and unlike New York subways it can offer no express service, because each station along the route is a mandatory stop. Unlike the subways of Paris, Tokyo, or London, which are interconnected networks of lines, BART offers one route in each compass direction and hence only limited distribution across the urbanized area it serves.

Because of its misnomer and because it fits none of our stereotypes, BART has been befuddling its critics, who seem unable to categorize it tidily. The important fact is that BART was designed to meet the rather specific purposes enumerated above, and those purposes happen not to be the ones by which some critics have judged it, reflecting social concerns that were not widely shared when BART was designed. For example, it was never intended to serve the kinds of short-distance trips that local buses, trolley cars, and center-city subways serve. It was not designed to carry low-income persons from central-city homes to suburban factories, even though BART officials belatedly voiced such claims.

Rightly or wrongly, BART was designed to transport peak-hour commuters from suburbs to central business districts. In turn, it was intended to generate the following effects:

reduce peak-hour highway traffic congestion
reduce time expended on commuter travel
foster central district growth

generate development of subcenters throughout its region

raise land values

accommodate suburbanization of residence and centralization of employment

reduce land area devoted to transportation facilities

The expectations of some enthusiasts have sometimes been rather extreme, viewing BART as a remedy for whatever snake oil fails to cure. In turn they have generated a wave of criticism in both the popular and professional media that has often been comparably extreme. Such expectations and criticism are unreasonable. BART represents a serious response to perceived problems in regional development, planned with the advice of some of the world's most accomplished engineers and designers. Because it is the first of its kind and is now being watched so closely by officials in other cities around the world, and because it is so terribly expensive, we must soberly check whether the outcomes its planners expected are being realized.

BART'S PATRONAGE

Prior to the 1962 bond election that authorized BART, the key informational document was the so-called *Composite Report*, published in May 1962.[2] Among the important expectations there were hopes (1) that BART would divert 48,000 workday autos from the streets and highways by 1974 and (2) that 258,500 daily passengers would be riding BART in 1975—157,400, or 61 percent, diverted from automobiles, 39 percent from existing transit systems.

Although 1975 has arrived and passed, it is not yet possible to submit those predictions to the definitive test, for BART was late in getting started, and thus has not yet developed a "seasoned" patronage. Moreover, the system has been so besieged by electronic and mechanical difficulties and rising costs that it is still not operating to design standards nor offering any weekend schedule. With these qualifications in mind, we can nevertheless compare the actual volumes being experienced with the predicted patronage.

The record of BART's average daily patronage is shown in Table 8.2, which also indicates the forecasted levels. Some of the shortfall must reflect the chronically unreliable schedules and the associated long waiting times at stations, owing to equipment failings. Some of the shortfall must also reflect sheer deficiencies in prediction; the forecasters had little prior experience to base projections upon, because there had never been a BART-like system in this kind of metropolitan area or the analytic tools for forecasting the demand for this new product.

TABLE 8.2
Forecast as Against Actual BART Patronage, June 1976

	Average Weekday Trips		
Route Segment	1961 FORECAST FOR 1975	1976 ACTUAL	ACTUAL AS PERCENT OF FORECAST
Transbay	77,850	53,880	69
East Bay	129,493	39,725	31
West Bay	51,153	37,765	74
Total	258,496	131,370	51

The Concord line into San Francisco is proving highly attractive, with peak-hour standees outnumbering seated passengers. When enough cars are available to provide seats for most riders, patronage will undoubtedly exceed current levels. Other lines are doing much less well, however, and the net effect is that *total patronage is running at about half of the initial expectations.* Instead of the 258,500 weekday passengers forecasted, only 131,400 were riding in June 1976. Peak-hour riders across the bay number 8,000, a little over one-fourth of the designed capacity of transbay trains— 28,800 seated passengers per hour.

There are several surprises in those figures, however. Although the *Composite Report* expected that 61 percent of riders would be diverted from private automobiles, in fact *only 35 percent formerly made the trip by car.* In response to a BART customer survey, about a fourth of the riders said they had not made the trip at all before BART began operating. However dramatic the apparent volume of newly generated travel may be, it actually represents only a small portion of new trips BART has triggered, for it has generated additional *auto* trips as well.

BART initially reduced the number of cars on the streets and highways by 14,000 (not 48,000, as forecast). In turn, in accordance with the Law of Traffic Congestion (which holds that traffic expands to fill the available highway space until just tolerable levels of congestion are reached), other people began driving their cars on trips they would not otherwise make. Perhaps they are suburban wives who now have the family car during working hours. Perhaps people are visiting friends, now that highways are less crowded. Whoever they are, the net effect is an increase in the amount of sheer mobility within BART's region by both road and rail.

BART has brought about a rise in total transbay travel by both auto and public transit. Between 1973 and 1975, the proportion of daily transit riders on the bridge rose from 17 percent to 22 percent. Buses used to carry all 17 percent; they are now down to 10 percent, while BART is serving 12 percent, a third of them in midday. During the peak hours, BART and buses split the transit passengers evenly, each carrying 50 percent of them.

Half of all BART's transbay passengers formerly rode the bus. In contrast, those using *local* buses seem not to find BART as attractive, probably because of the wide station spacing. Indeed, even during the two-month transit strike, only 10 percent of the East Bay bus riders used BART instead. Three-fourths of all BART passengers travel over seven miles; half of them travel over 12 miles; a fourth over 19 miles! Clearly, BART is serving the long-distance travelers, as intended; but it is carrying only half as many travelers as intended.

THE EFFECT ON HIGHWAY TRAFFIC

BART's effects on auto traffic are a great disappointment. Although it has indeed attracted some 44,000 trips per day that used to be made in private cars, that is far fewer than the 157,000 forecasted. At most, the overall change in the three counties served may be a small net reduction in auto-traffic volume since BART began; but the change might also be a small net increase. The available regional data make either conclusion plausible.

There was a clear short-run reduction in auto traffic just when BART's transbay service began in September 1974, but BART may have had little to do with it. The gasoline shortage had just cut into auto use, and at the same time gas prices were rising to 60 percent above their previous levels. Simultaneously, economic recession was increasing unemployment levels (up to 11 percent in the Bay Area), while inflation was compelling many families to cut their spending levels and perhaps their automobile use.

Under those circumstances, we would normally expect reduced highway traffic volumes and, consequently, reduced congestion. In fact, traffic counters on the several Bay Area bridges do record a reduction in auto travel throughout the region in the period 1974–1975. But the surprising fact is that the Bay Bridge, which parallels BART's transbay tube, experienced a smaller proportional reduction than any of the other bridges across San Francisco Bay. Auto travel on the bridge was sustained despite the inauguration of BART transbay service. Paradoxically, because so many commuters switched from buses to BART, the number of buses in the bridge traffic stream was reduced, thus creating more space for cars. Contrary to plan, even if only to that extent, BART has made it easier to commute by car.

It is clear that the enthusiastic expectations of dramatic reductions in auto volumes have not been realized. If BART is having any effects on overall vehicular traffic on the Bay Bridge, they are as yet so slight as to be undetectable, not exceeding two percent or about one year's normal growth in traffic.

Pretty much the same picture emerges at the Berkeley Hills tunnels, where BART patronage has been high. The start of BART service in May 1973 was associated with a levelling of auto traffic volumes. However, a few months later traffic volumes rose again. They are now higher than ever in the auto tunnel that parallels BART's tunnel, and congestion tie-ups occur just about as frequently as they ever did.

California's Department of Transportation has made a serious attempt to measure BART's effects on highway congestion. On a few routes roughly paralleling BART's lines, peak-hour travel times were found to be reduced sharply when BART service began, demonstrating that even a few cars taken off a full freeway can convert sluggish traffic movement into a free-flowing traffic stream. It appears that where freeways ran at capacity levels, BART is making for appreciable improvement in travel times. However, the marginal autos that spell the difference between congestion and free movement are so few in number (even a two percent reduction can be sufficient) that one cannot count on their continued diversion. On some tested routes, travel times have already crept up to pre-BART levels. On a few they were unchanged throughout the pre-BART and post-BART periods.

So the conclusions are unambiguous. (1) BART is serving large numbers of suburban commuters, as predicted. (2) People are traveling more, by both car and public transit, despite rising energy costs and undoubtedly as a direct result of the new travel capacity that BART has supplied. (3) Half of BART's transbay riders come from buses, which BART has replaced— at very high cost, as we shall see later on. (4) BART has not effected a significant change in automobile-use habits, so traffic volumes and road congestion are still at just about pre-BART levels, but will no doubt rise as auto use increases.

THE EFFECT ON METROPOLITAN DEVELOPMENT

During the 12-year period 1964–75, 35 high-rise office buildings were completed in San Francisco's central district, enclosing 18,500,000 square feet of floor space. During the next six years an additional 17 buildings are scheduled for completion, enclosing another 10,000,000 square feet. These are the structures that followed approval of BART's construction plan, each within an easy 10-minute walk of a BART subway station. Comprising 52 buildings and over 28 million square feet, they were the *cause cé-lèbre* in the citizens' revolt against the "Manhattanization" of San Francisco, the joy of The City's regency, and the conundrum confronting transit planners elsewhere, who now wonder whether rapid-rail transit in their towns will trigger similar explosions. Whatever one's urban-design preferences—whether one loves or detests The City's new look—the question remains, what was BART's role in all that?

It is not clear to what extent BART caused the office boom, and to what extent the expected concentration of offices caused BART. Plausible explanations are obvious for either theory. BART officials like to claim credit for the spectacular change in San Francisco's skyline; they say it is a direct result of improved commuter access from the metropolitan region. However, they also argued from the outset that BART was primarily needed because forecasts of impending downtown office employment raised the specter of the ultimate traffic jam. The rub is that those forecasts were based explicitly on the assumption that BART would be built. If that reasoning were carried full circle, it should then be inferred that, without BART, there would be fewer offices concentrated downtown, less concentration of traffic downtown, more decentralized patterns of office employment, and hence no need for a BART-type system. Needless to say, that circle of reasoning is usually not closed.

Large-scale office construction in other Western and Midwestern metropolitan centers suggsts that the building boom might have happened anyway, for many of them have had similar booms, although none except Chicago has had anything like BART in sight. During the 12 years following BART's successful bond election, San Francisco's high-rise office buildings were expanded by 4,200 square feet for every 1,000 people in the metropolitan region. By contrast, Houston, the automobile city *par excellence*, added 5,500 square feet per 1,000 population, Chicago 4,500, and Dallas 3,500.

The past couple of decades have marked America's transition to the post-industrial service economy. Growing proportions of all jobs are in management and related services, new occupations that are conducted in offices rather than in factories. San Francisco has always been a center for the service occupations, and high proportions of firms coming to Northern California have traditionally sought locations in The City. Accelerating expansion of service activities during the 1950's, 1960's, and 1970's coincided nicely with the civic determination to renovate the city center. New office space was quickly filled, encouraging others to invest in rentable space; and they in turn found other waiting tenants within the growing services sector eager to be in the center of things. In effect, optimistic prophecies of blossoming central business activity became self-fulfilling. The more buildings that touched the skyline and the greater the subway-construction mess along Market Street, the more that companies wanted to be in on the action; and more engendered still more. Once the old-fashioned boomtown spirit spread, it became self-generating, building on its own image, enticing still more firms in search of the prestigious addresses, proving once again that nothing succeeds like success.

Surely BART was part of the generating force, for it was a massive piece of the big construction set. But there are no categorical answers to the question about the size of BART's role in San Francisco's reconstruction. I am inclined to think that it would have happened anyway, but that BART nonetheless made its happening bigger and quicker.

Is the story likely to be repeated elsewhere? Probably only in those cities having a comparable attraction for headquarters offices and ancillary business services. However, as the experiences of Houston, Dallas, and Denver emphatically show, a BART-type rail system is not a necessary condition for a city building boom of this sort. Unquestionably, adequate transport services are essential, but effective transport comes in many other forms as well. Those other Western cities have been undergoing explosive central office-building expansion while relying on automobiles and buses. But for the promotional attraction of BART, San Francisco might have done as well with intelligent development of its own road transport system.

SUBURBAN SPUTTER

The initial plan for BART was also to generate growth at selected subcenters throughout the metropolitan region. In addition to the high average speed, that was the other rationale for widely spaced stations. The planners fully expected that increased accessibility at train stations would make the surrounding areas attractive to business firms and apartment dwellers, following the model of earlier commuter railroads in the East. In turn, clusters of offices, shops, and high-density housing around these stations would visibly restructure the region, stemming the drift toward low-density dispersion and urban sprawl.

It is now 14 years since the BART project was approved, and there is, as yet, little evidence to corroborate those forecasts and hopes. Most suburban stations stand in virtual isolation from urban-development activity in their subregions, seemingly ignored by all except commuters who park their cars in BART's extensive lots.

By being heavily subsidized and charging fares well under its actual costs, BART has appreciably reduced monetary commuting expenses for outlying suburbanites who work in the central cities. *Thus, rather than deterring suburban sprawl, BART may instead be encouraging it.* The unexpected popularity of its suburban Concord line clearly signals the response of suburbanites to the bargain rates being charged. We know of no explicit empirical evidence that BART is bringing about further suburban spread, but the parallel history of freeway-induced reductions in travel costs is unambiguous. Even though BART's land-use effects may not yet have been made manifest, the longer-run expectations should be clear. If BART is to influence the future course of suburban development at all, it seems as likely that it will be an agent in spreading suburban growth as in concentrating it.

Perhaps a basic flaw in the initial planning was the failure to take into account existing high-level (and virtually homogeneous) accessibility throughout the Bay Area. The ubiquitous network of streets, highways, and freeways, combined with extremely high auto availability, made for a context that scarcely resembled the 19th-century urban settings that earlier suburban railroads were fitted into. Bay Area residents move about within the metropolitan area with great freedom; they can go from virtually anywhere to anywhere else with only occasional delays, because the road network makes all points within the region highly accessible to all others.

When BART added additional accessibility on top of existing levels, it was proportionally only a small increment. Suburban and downtown stations are only slightly more accessible now than before BART was installed, scarcely enough to have significantly affected the location plans of many households and firms. If the rail line had been the major access route, things would have been different. But overall accessibility in this road-rich metropolitan region has not been appreciably modified, and so neither have urban development patterns.

Land use and transportation systems are highly interdependent. BART's failure to attract many riders may also be contributing to its failure to attract building investors in the areas of its stations. Moreover, seeking to reduce land-purchase costs while encouraging the park-and-ride habit, BART designers located stations at some distance from established suburban business centers and then surrounded them with parking lots. As a result, potential developers are compelled to build outside easy walking distance, and so most go to the established centers instead. It is almost as though the right-of-way agents who purchased property and the engineers who located the stations were either oblivious or opposed to the objective of fostering suburban clustering. It is also reasonable to believe that land-use effects take a long time to become manifest, especially in an auto-oriented society, and that we shall therefore have to wait another 10 years or so before we will know whether BART will affect development at all.

WHO RIDES AND WHO PAYS

Everyone expected from the outset that BART would have to be bought with solely local funds. There were no other options at the time, for BART's planning preceded by a decade federal government financial support for transit. Indeed, it may be that BART's favorable publicity may have so popularized rail transit that in some degree BART is responsible for the availability of federal subsidy funds today. But at the time it was being designed, the Bay Area was on its own.

The plan was to draw upon the traditional source for local capital improvements, general obligation bonds secured by a property tax. Those were the bonds approved in November 1962—at that time, the largest local bonding referendum ever, amounting to $792 million. The fund was to be sufficient to pay the full costs of all the capital plant except the transbay tube and the rolling stock. The tube was to be built with tolls collected from bridge users. Rolling stock and all operating expenses were to be paid from fares collected from BART users.

Subsequently, when capital costs began to exceed initial estimates, it became necessary to find other resources. Among those explored were supplements to auto-license fees, higher bridge tolls, and general highway-improvement funds. These were forcibly opposed by those who disliked a direct tax on motorists. In the end, the 1969 state legislature authorized a $150 million bond issue, financed by a one-half of one percent addition to the general sales tax within the three-county district that was to be served by BART.

These three sources of capital funds (property taxes, sales taxes, and bridge tolls) then still turned out to be insufficient, for there was not yet enough money to buy the cars. Fortunately, the federal transit grant program was initiated in time to permit BART to purchase its rolling stock (federal grants have by now amounted to $305 million), and a parallel state-aid program was initiated that now yields an annual subsidy (about $2.6 million this year).

The 1962 *Composite Report*, circulated prior to the public vote on the bonds, had presented a favorable estimate of operating revenues and costs for 1975–76. BART's own current financial reports now present a far more gloomy picture (see Table 8.3).

When it became apparent that fares would be insufficient to cover the costs of rolling stock and operations, the 1974 state legislature authorized,

TABLE 8.3
BART Operating Revenues and Expenses
(Fiscal Year 1975–76)

	Millions of Current Dollars	
	1962 COMPOSITE REPORT	ACTUAL (PRELIMINARY)
Gross fare and concession revenue	$24.5	$23.7
Operating expense	13.5	64.0
Net	$11.0 surplus	$40.3 deficit

as emergency aid against the impending operating deficit, a temporary extension of the one-half of one percent sales tax to be applied to the operating deficit. This yields about $28 million per year, enabling BART to continue operating until the latter part of 1976, by which time an extension or some other operating subsidy will be needed.

As of June 1976, the overall picture of BART expenditures and sources of funds looked like this:

TABLE 8.4
Sources of Funds for BART

	Millions of Current Dollars	Percent of Total
Capital funds		
General obligation bonds	$792	50
Sales tax revenue bonds	150	10
Toll bridge revenues (for transbay tube)	180	11
Federal grants	305	19
Miscellaneous revenues	159	10
Total	$1,586	100
Annual operating funds (1975–76 estimates)		
Fares and concession revenue	$23.7	37
Sales tax revenue (0.5 percent)	27.7	43
Property tax revenue (5¢ for operations)	5.0	8
State aid (0.25 percent sales tax)	2.6	4
Federal aid	.5	1
Borrowings against capital account	4.5	7
Total	$64.0	100

Over 60 percent of capital costs and about 55 percent of operating costs are being paid by all residents of the three-county district through taxes on property and retail sales, both inherently regressive modes of taxation. E. G. Hoachlander has estimated the incidences of BART's property and sales taxes and compared them with household incomes.[3] His findings indicate that both taxes fall proportionately far more heavily on households with low incomes than on wealthier ones.

In an effort to keep track of customers' characteristics and preferences, BART has been conducting a periodic survey of its riders. The last completed survey was made in May 1975, eight months after transbay service started and two-and-a-half years after East Bay trains began running. The riders' own reports on their incomes reveal that they are not a representative sample of the Bay Area population. They are drawn far more heavily from the upper sectors of the income distribution than from the lower, re-

Figure 8.2. Income Comparison of BART Taxpayers and BART Riders.

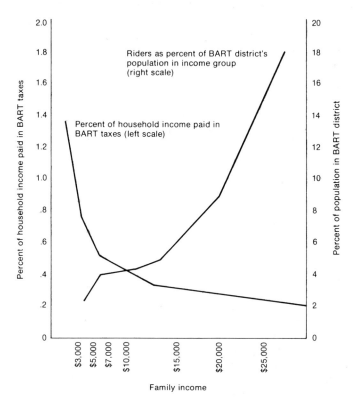

flecting, no doubt, the system's attractiveness to long-distance suburban commuters. Figure 8.2 compares the income distribution with the proportions of family incomes devoted to BART taxes. The ratio of these two curves is 40 to one: The percentage of income paid to provide tax support for each ride taken is 40 times greater for an individual in the lowest income group than for one in the highest income group. Clearly, the poor are paying and the rich are riding.

COMPARATIVE COSTS

Every trip calls for three kinds of expenditures. There are the dollar costs that auto owners and transit agencies pay for vehicles, fuel, roadways, drivers' salaries, interest charges, insurance, and so on. There are the time expenditures made by travelers, who seem to make sensitive assessments of the lengths of time they must spend riding vehicles, getting to and from vehicles, and especially transferring and waiting for the next vehicles to arrive. The third kinds of costs are external to the transportation systems: annoyances borne by neighbors who must suffer noise, pollution, congestion, and other nuisances that transportation systems and their patrons impose.

To compare the costs of alternative travel modes, one must tote up the monetary outlays, the time expenditures, and the social costs associated with each mode, preferably on standardized scales and in common coinage. This is obviously difficult to do, if only because each mode of travel provides somewhat different qualities of service and because some costs and some benefits are not directly traded in pecuniary terms. But it is not impossible to do.

A group of economists at Berkeley, led by Professors Theodore Keeler and Leonard Merewitz and Dr. Peter Fisher, recently completed a careful study aimed at comparing the full costs of standardized trips on BART, local buses, and private cars.[4] Their findings indicate that *the bus is consistently more cost-efficient than even a subcompact automobile, at virtually all levels of traffic density and at current averages of 1.5 persons per car.* No surprise there. But they also find that the bus is consistently cheaper than BART for comparable qualities of service, whichever set of technical assumptions is built into their estimating formulas. *Moreover, and to everyone's surprise, their findings show that a subcompact automobile is also cheaper than BART, except when travel densities approach 20,000 passengers per hour within a single traffic corridor.*

BART's maximum design capacity on the transbay and West Bay lines is 28,800 seated passengers per hour (72 passengers per car, 10-car trains spaced at 90-second intervals). So far BART has not approached that level of patronage. In Wolfgang Homburger's October 1975 survey, BART's maximum single-hour transbay load was 8,120 eastbound passengers at the height of the evening peak period. Instead of 28,800 passengers *per hour* in each direction, BART's transbay patronage was only *28,500 per day.*

Philip Viton has computed the full costs of carrying one passenger on a representative trip by BART, bus, and auto. He concluded that *even when BART achieves its full design efficiency, it will still run on all its lines at higher costs per passenger trip than buses, and its costs may continue to be more than those of an automobile even then.*

The estimates are based on assumptions most favorable to rapid transit. They assume a hypothetically optimized system in which schedules of buses and trains minimize riders' waiting time and agencies' operating costs. Estimates for automobiles include governmental costs of building, maintaining, and policing highways, individuals' total costs of buying and operating private cars, and the external costs of pollution. For each mode, a concerted effort has been made to account for all monetary and non-monetary costs borne by governments, travelers, and neighbors.

The dollar-equivalent costs are estimated against a set of variables related to interest rates on investments, value of travelers' time while riding, value of their time while getting to a train or bus, and the average lengths of trips. BART trip-cost estimates are highly sensitive to variations in interest rates, because of the large capital investment; and they compare best against bus and car when computed for long-distance trips. As we shall see, because very few Bay Area commuters live within an easy walk of a BART station, BART trip-cost estimates are particularly sensitive to assumptions about the value of the access time.

There is some disagreement among economists on the dollar values to be assigned to passengers' time, but all agree that some dollar equivalents must be included in estimating total costs. After all, BART did go to great expense to offer high speeds, presumably because its designers believed that passengers value their time, preferring a brief trip to an extended one. Similarly bus operators work for short headways and for on-schedule performance because they believe that passengers' dollar-clocks click fastest when they are waiting for a bus to come. (If those beliefs were in error, the appropriate response would be to slow down the trains and to delay the buses. Obviously those strategies would be absurd.) The consensus among students of "modal choice" is that average passengers clock their walking-and-waiting time about three times more heavily than their riding time.

In an effort to avoid any inferences of negative bias, the estimates presented here have been deliberately biased in favor of BART. Throughout, wherever the estimate equations permit a choice of values, we have selected the combination of permissible variations to show BART trip-costs at their lowest levels when compared with the bus and the car.

The comparisons in Table 8.5 present the full costs of carrying a hypothetical commuter 15.7 miles across the Bay from Orinda to San Francisco's Montgomery Street in the morning peak hour. We assume that he lives two miles from the BART station, which he reaches by a local feeder bus, and that he walks a quarter-mile from the Montgomery Street station to his office. Alternatively in our example, he could ride a bus from near his home to the Montgomery Street BART station, or he could drive his car and park in a public garage near his office.

Actual peak-hour volumes on the transbay routes for both bus and BART are only about 8,000 passengers per hour. At that volume, a bus ride costs $3.21 and a BART ride costs $6.77, with private cars in between. We have also computed estimates under less favorable, but nevertheless

TABLE 8.5
Full Costs of Peak-Hour Trip from Orinda
to Montgomery Street[1]

Number of Passengers in Peak Hour	Auto		Bus	BART Plus Feeder Bus
	STANDARD	SUBCOMPACT		
1,000	$4.49	$4.05	$8.51	$34.08
5,000	4.49	4.05	3.72	9.20
8,000[2]	4.49	4.05	3.21	6.77
10,000	4.49	4.05	2.99	5.99
20,000	4.49	4.05	2.59	4.26
30,000	4.49	4.05	2.44	3.64

[1]In 1972 dollars. These are low estimates, computed to be most favorable to BART. Costs to
   agency plus time costs to riders plus social costs to neighbors.
[2]Current peak volume on both bus and BART.

reasonable, assumptions concerning the value of commuters' time and the
rate of interest on capital invested. For that same ride from Orinda to
Montgomery Street at present peak-hour patronage, full costs would then
be $5.83 on the bus and $11.96 on BART.

When BART has been finally debugged and operates at full schedule
and full efficiency, with a fully seasoned patronage, it will surely be carrying more riders; and so both average and marginal costs will then fall. The
most favorable estimate for seasoned operation on that same commuter
trip from Orinda to Montgomery Street is unlikely to fall below $6.00,
however. (The less favorable, but still reasonable estimate is $10.00 for that
trip.) In contrast, the full cost of a nearly equivalent ride on a bus would be
between $3.00 and $5.00, and the cost of driving a standard sedan would
be between $4.50 and $7.50, all costs included. Under those circumstances,
BART is unlikely ever to replace other modes of travel, so long as travelers
are permitted free choice. Perhaps only under regulated market conditions,
imposing mandatory constraints on use of buses and cars, might BART
carry the volumes of passengers that were forecasted for it.

THE FINANCIAL PICTURE

All estimates above are economic costs—i.e., they reflect costs to the economy, representing the opportunity costs of using resources for these purposes rather than some others (Table 8.6).

Alternatively, we might examine accountant costs—i.e., the costs as
they might be seen by BART's internal bookkeepers. That picture is some-

TABLE 8.6
BART's Annual Expense and Patronage Account
(Fiscal Year 1975–76)

Item	Amount
Annualized capital costs	$ 82,400,000
Annual operating cost	64,000,000
Total cost for year	$146,400,000
Number of trips during year	32,700,000
Average cost per trip	$4.48

what different. Annualizing BART's total capital costs to find its annual "mortgage payments" at its favorable 4.14 percent interest rate, adding in its current operating costs, then dividing by annual passengers carried, the cost per trip comes to be about $4.48. With fares averaging around 72¢, the average subsidy then comes to about $3.76 per ride.

Two major factors are of interest here to officials in other cities. First, direct costs to the BART district are high because the system was financed largely from local sources. With federal subsidies now available, no other metropolitan area will finance a transit expansion on its own again. Second, BART's capital-intensive plant makes it inherently expensive. Subways and elevated, exclusive, grade-separated rights-of-way cost a lot, no matter how crudely or elegantly they are constructed. Besides, BART spent a great deal of money in pioneering research and development for new systems, the benefits of which will now accrue to other cities that build subsequently. But BART had one advantage over all other descendent systems. It was built with pre-inflation dollars. However exorbitant its costs may seem, they appear cheap relative to comparable systems under construction in Washington and Atlanta.

Rail-transit systems are inherently capital-intensive. When they are also burdened with very high labor costs, as BART is, operating expenses may become excessive. BART's operating costs are running at about 15.7¢ per passenger mile, while the local bus system is costing about 13.6¢. Despite the all-out effort to reduce manpower requirements by automating train operations and assigning only one attendant per train, BART now finds itself with a wage bill only slightly less than that of the local bus system— 10.5¢ per passenger mile compared to about 13.2¢ for the bus. In part because of a federal requirement that led to a costly union contract and in part because of the high-priced engineering and planning staff it maintains, BART has not yet shown how to cut the labor and operating costs that have been hurting public transit systems of late.

As a result, it has been in a virtually continuous financial crisis. Governments can continue to "throw more money at it," but the real solution is for BART to attract sufficient patronage at least to carry its operating costs, as planned. The question, then, is why haven't Bay Area travelers been flocking to this outstanding transportation system.

WHAT WENT WRONG?

BART was designed to be a superior way for Bay Area commuters to get to work. Its promoters believed that if only superb transit service were offered, commuters would gladly give up their private cars. Because commuters are not responding as expected, it is important that we understand why.

The clue may lie in the few, but key design decisions that were made in the early stages of BART planning and that then fixed the system's essential character. It now appears in retrospect that those design features preordained BART's failure to lure the motorist.

At the time BART's designs were being drawn, the postwar auto boom was a major factor in metropolitan growth, and freeways were accorded high priority. At the same time, public transit systems were falling into disrepair or being abandoned, and patronage was declining everywhere, projecting the prospect of a virtually all-auto transportation system. BART was seen as a lower-cost alternative to freeways and as a means for both reversing the trend and preserving the option of public transit. The design strategy was to top the automobile by producing a transit system that would incorporate and improve upon the automobile's most attractive features, thus making the transit system more than competitive.

The designers concluded that high speed, high comfort, high style, and downtown delivery were the attributes that matter most to motorists; and BART was then designed to outdo the car on those four counts. BART's management has delivered the system promised in its original specifications. Unfortunately, however, these may not be the features that will entice mass patronage.

The emphasis on high speed between stops and on comfort and overall aesthetic excellence quickly led to the decision to build a rail system, and that in turn led to a logically necessary network of decisions concerning equipment design, electronic control gear, roadbed standards, station qualities, and the like. As Randall Pozdena has insightfully noted, each of these decisions was simultaneously a decision to trade off other potentially desired qualities. Some of the more important sacrifices and compromises he identified are in Table 8.7.

Of course every design for a complex system must make these sorts of trade-offs, for it is seldom possible to enjoy all advantages simultaneously.

TABLE 8.7
Design Trade-offs and Compromises

Selected Qualities	Sacrificed or Compromised Qualities
1. High average speed between stations, therefore widely spaced stations.	1. Closely spaced stations, therefore ease of access to stations.
2. Mainline system serving major traffic corridors.	2. Network of transit lines serving sub-areas of the region. Ability to complete trip in a single vehicle without having to transfer to and from feeder system.
3. Batch-type transport mode: cars in trains carrying many passengers.	3. Flow-type transport mode: smaller vehicles carrying comparable numbers of passengers at shorter headways, with branching local distribution at origin and destination.
4. Fixed rail on exclusive grade-separated right-of-way.	4. Flexible routing in response to changing travel patterns. Economy of construction. Right-of-way usable by other vehicles. Disabled vehicles do not disrupt operation of entire line.
5. Limited number of access points into system, to encourage clustered urban development.	5. Compatibility with footloose trends and low-density settlement patterns.
6. Frequent service with stops at all stations.	6. Differentiated service with both "local" and "express" operations.
7. High aesthetic and comfort standards.	7. Economy of construction.
8. Regional long-haul design.	8. Local trip-making capability.

It is the tragedy of the BART story, however, that the chosen attributes compelled the sacrifice of features that were essential for attracting riders. Most important by far are the first four in the table. By choosing mainline rail, the designers created a system geometry that puts BART out of walking distance of most residents.

The designers seem to have been most concerned with the attractiveness of the BART system as seen by passengers after they arrive at the station.

Station decor is handsome; waiting time for trains was to have averaged a brief 45 seconds; 80-miles-per-hour speeds make for short elapsed time en route; and the station at the other end of the trip is also aesthetically pleasing. But outside BART's premises, the passengers are on their own. They must find their way to the station by bus, car, or foot, make the transfer, and then find their way at the other end after leaving the BART station. While they are BART's guests they are treated very well; outside the premises they are rather neglected.

Oddly enough, although the designers have always been explicit about the critical role of bus access to the system, the planning process was rather nonchalant about creating it. There was little effective planning for feeder-bus service until the period just preceding opening day, and it is still quite inadequate in the outlying suburbs.

MAKING THE WRONG CHOICES

During the past 15 years, at least a dozen major studies have investigated the ways travelers assess costs when deciding how they will make intra-metropolitan trips. With remarkably small variation among the cities examined, the studies all conclude that *the time spent inside vehicles is judged to be far less onerous than the time spent walking, waiting, and transferring, by a factor of up to 3 or 4 times. For commuters waiting on platforms, the factor may be as high as 10 times!*

BART designers were obviously unaware of these findings; the research was conducted after the key BART decisions were made. Indeed, their own understanding was just the opposite, as this key conclusion of the 1956 basic design report indicates:

> ... interurban rapid transit must be conceived as providing only *arterial* or *trunk-line* connections between the major urban concentrations of the region. ... We are convinced that the interurban traveler, facing the choice between using his private automobile or using mass transportation, will be influenced in his choice more by the speed and frequency of interurban transit service than by the distance he must travel in his own car or by local transit to reach the nearest rapid transit station.

Herein may lie a clue as to why their strategy erred. Their fixation on high speed meant that riders spend relatively short amounts of time in BART's vehicles, but this is the kind of time that travelers place a low cost upon. That fixation has also inevitably meant long access times, which travelers account as a high cost. The desire for high speed led to wide spacing between stations, and that, combined with the skeletal mainline-route pattern, compels most travelers to use some kind of feeder service getting from home to BART. The use of a feeder bus compounds the onus of waiting and transferring, and many potential BART patrons have therefore simply decided to ride the bus all the way through to their destinations, instead of making the transfer. Many others have simply decided to continue driving their cars. The reasons for both decisions should now be clear.

Buses and cars mixed into the traffic stream operate at slower speeds than 80-mile-per-hour trains, of course. However, trains must stop at each station every 2.5 miles or so. Meanwhile buses and cars on freeways usually move along nonstop until they reach the terminal or exit. The net effect is that *scheduled running times for some East Bay peak-hour express buses to San Francisco are just about the same as for BART trains.* Of course, whenever an accident or a breakdown clogs the freeway, traffic slows down or stops; but BART's frequent breakdowns almost even the score. Overall, where express bus service is available, the advantages of no-transfer rides and steady freeway movement make the bus competitive in route time.

The major competitive advantage of buses, however, derives from the savings they permit in access time. Buses have the capacity to thread into residential districts, collecting passengers near their homes. Automobiles do even better than that, parked in the owner's garage and available at his call. Whatever the cost of traffic congestion, access time is zero. However unpleasant the bus may be, access time is low. In these respects, the bus and the car are functional opposites of BART; they trade off high speeds en route in favor of easy access.

It seems that BART's mistake was made at the outset, when the wrong technology was chosen. Instead of lavishing primary attention on in-vehicle travel time and physical amenities, which called for a mainline rail system on an exclusive grade-separated right-of-way, the designers would have attracted more riders by adopting more automobile-like technology. A system that could pick up passengers within a short walk of their homes and deliver them, in the same vehicle, to within a short walk of their jobs would have been far more likely to entice them out of private cars. The success of both the new Golden Gate buses from Marin County to San Francisco and the express buses from the East Bay suggest that high-quality bus service can attract significant numbers of commuters.

It is the door-to-door, no-wait, no-transfer features of the automobile that, by eliminating access time, make private cars so attractive to commuters—not its top speed. BART offers just the opposite set of features to the commuting motorist, sacrificing just the ones he values most. This was a fundamental mistake. Given commuters' propensities to weight system access and waiting time so heavily and to place much less importance on in-vehicle time, it is scarcely any wonder that BART has not lured them away.

Moreover, the error is compounded by the high construction and operating costs compelled by the insistence upon high speed. That initial standard in turn determined much of the overall and detailed designs: a new and separated guideway, automatic controls, unconventionally wide-gauge rails, a highly stable roadbed, light-weight cars of unprecedented design, a highly specialized and high-priced work force, and so on. If its stations were more closely spaced, if its routes were more extensive, if it were not so difficult to get to it, BART's patronage would certainly be far higher. The paradox is that potential passengers are not using it because it is too rapid.

WAS IT WORTH IT?

Having spent $1.6 billion to avert the trend to the auto-highway system, BART is now serving a mere two percent of all trips made within the three-county district, and about five percent of peak-hour trips. Some 50,000 of its daily passengers have been diverted from inexpensive buses to expensive trains, 46,000 from private cars and car pools, and several thousand more from the latent pool of trips not previously made. The overall effect has been to leave highway congestion levels just about where they would have been anyway. BART may have been influential in propagating downtown building construction, but it has not yet had any visible effect on suburban development.

The most notable fact about BART is that it is extraordinarily costly. It has turned out to be far more expensive than anyone expected, and far more costly than is usually understood. High capital costs (about 150 percent of forecast) plus high operating costs (about 475 percent of forecast) are being compounded by low patronage (50 percent of forecast) to make for average costs per ride that are twice as high as the bus and 50 percent greater than a standard American car. With fares producing only about a third of the agency's out-of-pocket costs, riders are getting a greater transportation bargain than even bus and auto subsidies offer; and yet only half the expected numbers are riding. The comparative full costs of a typical transbay peak-hour commuter trip on BART are about $6.80, on a bus $3.25 and in a small car $4.00—computing all those estimates with variables that make BART appear most competitive. The total economic costs of even a large-sized American car are still lower than BART's for a transbay commuter trip—all-day parking charges, highway construction, pollution, and all other measurable costs included.

The 50,000 passengers BART has diverted from buses could be carried in brand-new luxury buses at a total capital investment of under $13 million. The BART system cost $1,600 million. The costs of buying a whole fleet of new buses sufficient to carry all BART's passengers projected to 1980 would be under $40 million, or about half of one year's worth of BART's annual mortgage payment alone. One is compelled to ask, was it worth it? Was it wise to have built so costly a system?

Rather than reverting to pre-auto technology, the designers might instead have sought a competitor to the automobile that, by incorporating similar service capabilities, might then be more likely to induce commuters to switch. Among currently available alternatives are express buses that collect passengers near their homes, or subscription buses that pick them up at their doors, then use urban freeways to speed them to job centers; jitneys and group taxis, the major transit modes in many parts of the world, which use automobiles as public transit vehicles, interlacing residential districts and delivering directly to employment places; and franchised van pools that operate as a quasi-bus and quasi-car pool, providing door-to-door service at both ends of commuters' trips, albeit with some rigidity in scheduling.

These are automobile-like modes that more nearly approximate the door-to-door, no-transfer, flexible-routing features of the private car than do 10-car trains on fixed mainline rails. Although they all surely lack the high technological glamour of BART-like systems, they can approximate BART's in-route speeds; they can greatly reduce system-access time; and furthermore, as Professor McFadden's surveys in the Bay Area indicate, where time and money costs are equal, most travelers seem not to be taken by the glamour of BART over the bus anyway. In any case, with the ratio of capital costs between BART and buses on the order of 40 to one, and with operating costs per passenger-mile essentially the same, it would seem that investment prudence is therefore on the side of the express bus.

Experience with express bus service is still rather sparse, however; and so we can have no assurance that the high levels of transit patronage that BART was aiming for are attainable with buses either. Although we do now know that express buses work, we do not know whether they work well enough. Much more experimentation with various sorts of auto-like and bus-like modes is called for, including experiments with pricing schemes that charge motorists and transit riders the full costs of travel.

There are surely many who still believe that BART will eventually make it—that only start-up problems, overly publicized equipment failures, and annoying delays dissuaded potential patrons. Given enough time, they believe, BART's trains will run on time and will then become the powerful magnets capable of attracting motorists at last. Given the uncertainties that bedevil this business, they might of course be right; only the test of time can tell. But even if BART were today carrying all 258,500 daily passengers originally projected for 1975, at present average fares it would be earning only $46,000,000 per year, or less than three-fourths of its *present* operating costs.

THE POWER OF PROMOTION

If BART has achieved any sort of unquestionable success, it is as a public relations enterprise. BART has projected a superb image from the start: a high-speed, futuristic transport mode that would transport commuters in luxurious comfort without economic pain. It became one of the more effective signs of the Bay Area's avant-garde spirit, the very symbol of Progress.

As a result, it may be that BART's most successful effects have been felt outside the Bay Area. Urbanists and civic officials throughout the world have become intimately familiar with its promises. Many, in turn, have been encouraged to propose various sorts of modern rail systems for their own cities, some of them aided by the same consultants who mothered BART through its Bay Area gestation. Despite its problems, BART has both popularized and legitimized modern rail transit, and that much-reproduced photograph of the BART lead car has become a heraldic symbol on rail-promotion banners everywhere.

Back home in the Bay Area, the picture is rather more gloomy. Half the expected riders have chosen the convenience of their private cars or the local bus that also runs them close to their jobs. Real estate developers seem to believe that auto access is more important for their potential customers or tenants, and so they have pretty much ignored the locational opportunities BART stations opened to them. People quietly pay property and sales taxes, unable to do anything much about the BART levies, whether they like them or not, whether they benefit from them or not. Governmental officials, caught with a large investment, outstanding bonds, and rapidly rising operating costs, keep priming BART with the hope that it will eventually run on its own. According to one careful student of BART's finances, they would find it more cost-effective to abandon the train service and convert the rights-of-way into exclusive bus lanes instead. It is unlikely that any public officials will find that politically acceptable, however, especially when BART is still so new. Besides, public officials seem to be constitutionally incapable of admitting error.

The whole affair again raises some persistent questions about the analytical and ideological bases underlying local political decisions, about the locus of accountability, and about governmental capacity for learning. From the beginning, BART's planners were handicapped, because the state of transport-choice theory was so inadequate that it was impossible to simulate accurately what would happen if BART were built. They did not even have adequate descriptive data showing how people choose among travel modes, especially travelers having choices among three such first-rate systems as are now offered in the Bay Area. It was therefore virtually impossible to forecast patronage or revenues with any precision. The science of transport planning has simply been inadequate to warrant the level of confidence that has accompanied this project. However cautious the disclaimers that were attached to the forecasts, once in print the numbers somehow became reified, then accepted as facts by political leaders, voters, and bond buyers. One wonders to what degree ideological leanings affected personal beliefs when the forecasts were inherently so uncertain.

BART is the manifestation of a wide array of ideologies that must have made it attractive to a wide array of publics. It symbolizes the frontiers of science and technology and, simultaneously, the nostalgic old railways of the elder statesman's youth. It is the rationally efficient means for reducing land consumption, and it simultaneously reflects the romantic desire to capture the ethos of Parisian urban life. It is seen as sound business by both merchants and city officials, and as the instrument of sound development policy by city planners. It is the darling of the anti-auto, anti-technology ideologues and also of the engineers who admire its technological sophistication. Many people believed in BART for many reasons. The mere failure to meet its objectives is not likely to shake such faith, particularly when the appraisal is made in merely pecuniary terms.

Many are wholly pleased with the BART system. It offers perhaps the smoothest and quietest ride in the world. The cars and stations are physically handsome and pleasant. Fares are low and travel speeds are high. Save for the initial equipment failures, it is almost exactly the physical system that was promised to the 1962 voters. For those who can use it conveniently, it is superb. For others, the very fact that it was built is itself an achievement, for BART was surely one of the more spectacular civic projects, and the transbay tube one of the more daring engineering feats of our time. From those special perspectives, BART has been an unqualified success.

But the question remains whether leaders in other metropolitan areas can learn from BART's experience that these perspectives are illusory. Having been built in a metropolitan area offering what are probably the best test conditions in the country, BART is not passing the most important of those tests. It is struggling with persistent fiscal crises, with no prospect of ever becoming the self-supporting system the voters were promised. The poor continue to pay and the rich to ride, with no visible prospect that this will change. Its patronage remains low despite low fares and rising gasoline prices, and that situation seems to be stable too. Save for the possible influence on downtown San Francisco and Oakland, it has had few detectable effects on urban development patterns, and its effects on traffic congestion are similarly undetectable. Clearly, BART has not earned a passing grade on the significant tests. One wonders, then, what underlies the professional confidence of transit consultants, and what sorts of politics and ideologies in local and federal governments continue to promote BART-like systems elsewhere.

BART has been heralded as pacesetter for transit systems throughout the world. The evidence so far suggests that it may also become the first of a series of multi-billion-dollar mistakes scattered from one end of the continent to the other.

But in the long run, say, in 50 years when the bonds will have been retired, when everyone will regard BART as just another built-in feature of the region, rather like Golden Gate Park, perhaps no one will question whether BART should have been either built or abandoned. It will then be regarded as a handy thing to have, a valuable facilitator of trips that would not otherwise be made by the elderly and the young, a blessing that enriches the quality of Bay Area life. And who will gainsay then the wisdom of having built a white elephant today?

NOTES

This article is the result of a collective effort by the following contributors: Seymour Adler, George Cluff, Kevin Fong, E. Gareth Hoachlander, Wolfgang S. Homburger, Leonard A. Merewitz, Mary Jo Porter, Randall J. Pozdena, David Reinke, and Philip A. Viton. The review was undertaken at the suggestion of Wilfred Owen. It was supported by the Institute of Transportation Studies at the University of California, Berkeley. Henry Bain has been our most perceptive critic.

1. The proposal was presented in Parsons, Brinckerhoff, Hall, and Macdonald, *Regional Rapid Transit*, Report to the San Francisco Bay Area Rapid Transit Commission (January 1956).

2. Parsons, Brinckerhoff, Tudor, Bechtel; Smith, Barney, and Company; Stone and Youngberg; and Van Beuren Stanbery; *The Composite Report, Bay Area Rapid Transit*, Reports submitted to the San Francisco Bay Area Rapid Transit District (May 1962).

3. E. Gareth Hoachlander, *Bay Area Rapid Transit: Who Pays and Who Benefits?* (Berkeley, University of California, Institute of Urban and Regional Development, 1976).

4. Theodore E. Keeler, Leonard A. Merewitz, and Peter M. J. Fisher, *The Full Costs of Urban Transport*, three volumes (1975); Randall J. Pozdena, *A Methodology for Selecting Urban Transportation Projects* (1975); and Philip A. Viton, *Notes on the Costs of Mass Transit in the Bay Area* (Berkeley, University of California, Institute of Urban and Regional Development, 1976).

5. Parsons, Brinckerhoff, Hall, and Macdonald, *op. cit.*, p. 38.

Chapter 9

EVALUATION
AND PUBLIC POLICY

A major purpose of evaluation research is to improve the quality of public decisions and the operations of public programs. Indeed, many of the evaluations included in this book were sponsored by government agencies with the tacit understanding that their findings would be incorporated in future decisions. Still, the record of research-evaluation utilization by policymakers is far from being impressive. In fact, most observers agree that evaluation research is underutilized. As a means of summarizing the book, this chapter centers on the problems and prospects of research utilization.

In the first article Aaron Wildavsky advances the thesis that evaluation is primarily an organization problem, and that the needs of organizations conflict with the very premises of evaluation, especially in situations in which the evaluation findings call for change. By considering how an organization devoting itself to evaluation might function, and how people within the organization would behave, the paper suggests that it will be difficult to "marry evaluation and organization." Notwithstanding the difficulties involved in such a marriage, Wildavsky suggests a number of ways to accommodate the tensions resulting from the necessity to evaluate organizations and their performance.

The second paper, by Nachmias and Henry, points out the problems involved in the conceptualization and measurement of research utilization, and discusses the methodological and political-bureaucratic barriers to effective utilization. Taking an ideal policy process as a point of reference, the article advances a number of propositions that explain underutilization, and suggests a number of methods that might enhance utilization, including a utilization plan in the evaluation study.

440

THE SELF-EVALUATING
ORGANIZATION

Aaron Wildavsky

Why don't organizations evaluate their own activities? Why do they not appear to manifest rudimentary self-awareness? How long can people work in organizations without discovering their objectives or determining the extent to which they have been carried out? I started out thinking it was bad for organizations not to evaluate, and I ended up wondering why they ever do it. Evaluation and organization, it turns out, are to some extent contradictory terms. Failing to understand that evaluation is sometimes incompatible with organization, we are tempted to believe in absurdities much in the manner of mindless bureaucrats who never wonder whether they are doing useful work. If we asked more intelligent questions instead, we would neither look so foolish nor be so surprised.

Who will evaluate and who will administer? How will power be divided among these functionaries? Which ones will bear the costs of change? Can evaluators create sufficient stability to carry on their own work in the midst of a turbulent environment? Can authority be allocated to evaluators and blame apportioned among administrators? How to convince administrators to collect information that might help others but can only harm them? How can support be obtained on behalf of recommendations that anger sponsors? Would the political problem be solved by creating a special organization—Evaluation Incorporated—devoted wholly to performing the analytic function? Could it obtain necessary support without abandoning its analytic mission? Can knowledge and power be joined?

EVALUATION

The ideal organization would be self-evaluating. It would continuously monitor its own activities so as to determine whether it was meeting its goals or even whether these goals should continue to prevail. When evaluation suggested that a change in goals or programs to achieve them was desirable, these proposals would be taken seriously by top decision makers. They would institute the necessary changes; they would have no vested interest in continuation of current activities. Instead they would steadily pursue new alternatives to better serve the latest desired outcomes.

The ideal member of the self-evaluating organization is best conceived as a person committed to certain modes of problem solving. He believes in clarifying goals, relating them to different mechanisms of achievement, creating models (sometimes quantitative) of the relationships between inputs and outputs, seeking the best available combination. His concern is not that the organization should survive or that any specific objective be enthroned or that any particular clientele be served. Evaluative man cares that interesting problems are selected and that maximum intelligence be applied toward their solution.

To evaluative man the organization doesn't matter unless it meets social needs. Procedures don't matter unless they facilitate the accomplishment of objectives encompassing these needs. Efficiency is beside the point if the objective being achieved at lowest cost is inappropriate. Getting political support doesn't mean that the programs devised to fulfill objectives are good; it just means they had more votes than the others. Both objectives and resources, says evaluative man, must be continuously modified to achieve the optimal response to social need.

Evaluation should not only lead to the discovery of better policy programs to accomplish existing objectives but to alteration of the objectives themselves. Analysis of the effectiveness of existing policies leads to consideration of alternatives that juxtapose means and ends embodied in alternative policies. The objectives as well as the means for attaining them may be deemed inappropriate. But men who have become socialized to accept certain objectives may be reluctant to change. Resistance to innovation then takes the form of preserving social objectives. The difficulties are magnified once we realize that objectives may be attached to the clientele—the poor, outdoor men, lumbermen—with whom organizational members identify. The objectives of the organization may have attracted them precisely because they see it as a means of service to people they value. They may view changes in objectives, therefore, as proposals for "selling out" the clients they wish to serve. In their eyes evaluation becomes an enemy of the people.

Evaluative man must learn to live with contradictions. He must reduce his commitments to the organizations in which he works, the programs he carries out, and the clientele he serves. Evaluators must become agents of change acting in favor of programs as yet unborn and clienteles that are unknown. Prepared to impose change on others, evaluators must have sufficient stability to carry out their own work. They must maintain their own organization while simultaneously preparing to abandon it. They must obtain the support of existing bureaucracies while pursuing antibureaucratic policies. They must combine political feasibility with analytical purity. Only a brave man would predict that these combinations of qualities can be found in one and the same person and organization.

Evaluation and organization may be contradictory terms. Organizational structure implies stability while the process of evaluation suggests change. Organization generates commitment while evaluation inculcates skepticism. Evaluation speaks to the relationship between action and objectives while organization relates its activities to programs and clientele. No one can say for certain that self-evaluating organizations can exist, let alone become the prevailing form of administration. We can learn a good deal about the production and use of evaluation in government, nonetheless, by considering the requirements of obtaining so extraordinary a state of affairs—a self-evaluating organization.

THE POLICY-ADMINISTRATION DICHOTOMY REVISITED

Organization requires the division of labor. Not everyone can do everything. Who, then, will carry out the evaluative activity and who will administer the programs for which the organization is responsible?

Practically every organization has a program staff, by whatever name called, that advises top officials about policy problems. They are small in numbers and conduct whatever formal evaluation goes on in the organization. They may exert considerable power in the organization through their persuasiveness and access to the top men, or they may be merely a benign growth that can be seen but has little effect on the body of the organization. Insofar as one is interested in furthering analytical activities, one must be concerned with strengthening them in regard to other elements. The idea of the self-evaluating organization, however, must mean more than this: a few men trying to force evaluation on an organization hundreds or thousands of times larger than they are. The spirit of the self-evaluating organization suggests that, in some meaningful way, the entire organization is infused with the evaluative ethic.

Immediately we are faced with the chain of command. How far down must the spirit of evaluation go in order to ensure the responsiveness of the organization as a whole? If all personnel are involved there would appear to be insuperable difficulties in finding messengers, mail clerks, and secretaries to meet the criteria. If we move up one step to those who deal with the public and carry out the more complex kind of activity, the numbers involved may still be staggering. These tens of thousands of people certainly do not have the qualifications necessary to conduct evaluative activities, and it would be idle to pretend that they would. The forest ranger and the national park officer may be splendid people, but they are not trained in evaluation and they are not likely to be. Yet evaluation activity appropriate to each level must be found if evaluation is to permeate the organization.

There has long been talk in the management circles of combining accountability with decentralization. Organizational subunits are given autonomy within circumscribed limits for which they are held strictly accountable to their hierarchical superiors. Central power is masked but it is still there. Dividing the task so that each subunit has genuine autonomy would mean giving them a share in central decisions affecting the entire organization. Decentralization is known to exist only to the extent that field units follow inconsistent and contradictory policies. One can expect the usual headquarters–field rivalries to develop—the one stressing appreciation of local problems and interests, the other fearing dissolution as the mere sum of its clashing units. Presumably the tension will be manifested in terms of rival analyses. The center should win out because of its greater expertise, but the local units will always be the specialists on their own problems. They will have to be put in their place. We are back, it seems, to hierarchy. How can the center get what it wants out of the periphery without over-formalizing their relationship?

One model, the internalized gyroscope, is recorded in Herbert Kaufman's classic on *The Forest Ranger*. By recruitment and training, the forest rangers are socialized into central values that they carry with them wherever they go and apply to specific circumstances. Central control is achieved without apparent effort or innumerable detailed instructions, because the rangers have internalized the major premises from which appropriate actions may generally be deduced. The problem of the self-evaluating organization is more difficult because it demands problem solving divorced from commitments to specific policies and organizational structures. The level of skill required is considerably higher and the locus of identification much more diffuse. The Israeli Army has had considerable success in inculcating problem-solving skills (rather than carrying out predetermined instructions) among its officers.[1] But their organizational identification is far more intense than can be expected elsewhere.

Suppose that most organizational personnel are too unskilled to permit them to engage in evaluation. Suppose it is too costly to move around hundreds of thousands of government officials who carry out most of the work of government. The next alternative is to make the entire central administration into an evaluative unit that directs the self-evaluating organization. Several real-world models are available. What used to be called the administration class in Great Britain illustrates one type of central direction. They move frequently among the great departments and seek (with the political ministers involved) to direct the activities of the vast bureaucracy around them. They are chosen for qualities of intellect that enable them to understand policy and for qualities of behavior that enable them to get along with their fellows. At the apex stands the Treasury, an organization with few operating commitments, whose task it is to monitor the activities of the bureaucracy and to introduce changes when necessary. Economic policy, which is the special preserve of the Treasury, is supposed to undergo rapid movement, and its personnel are used to changing tasks and objectives at short notice. Though divorced in a way from the organizations in which they share responsibility with the political ministers, top civil servants are also part of them by virtue of their direct administrative concerns. Complaints are increasingly heard that these men are too conservative in defense of departmental interests, too preoccupied with immediate matters, or too bound by organizational tradition to conduct serious evaluation. Hence, the Fulton Report claimed, they adapt too slowly, if at all, to changing circumstances. Tentative steps have been taken, therefore, to establish a Central Policy Review Staff to do policy analysis for the cabinet and to otherwise encourage evaluative activity.

Germany and Sweden have proceeded considerably further in the same direction. Departments in Sweden are relatively small groups of men concerned with policy questions, while administration is delegated to large public corporations set up for the purpose.[2] The state governments in Germany (the *Lander*) do over 90 percent of the administrative work, with the central government departments presumably engaged with larger questions of policy. The student of public administration in America will at once realize where he is at. The policy-administration dichotomy, so beloved of early American administrative theorists, which was thoroughly demolished, it seemed, in the decades of the '40's and '50's, has suddenly reappeared with new vitality.

The policy-administration dichotomy originated with Frank Goodnow and others in their effort to legitimate the rise of the civil service and with it the norm of neutral-competence in government. They sought to save good government from the evils of the spoils system by insulating it from partisan politics. Congress made policy, and the task of the administrative apparatus was to find the appropriate technical means to carry it out. Administrative actions were thought to be less general and more technical so that well-motivated administrators would be able to enact the will of the people as received from Congress or the President. Civil servants could then be chosen on the basis of their technical merits rather than their partisan or policy politics. An avalanche of criticism, begun in earnest by Paul Appleby's *Policy and Administration*, overwhelmed these arguments on every side. Observation of congressional statutes showed that they were often vague, ambiguous, and contradictory. There simply were not clear objectives to which the administrators could subordinate themselves. Observation of administrative behavior showed that conflicts over the policy to be adopted continued unabated in the bureaus and departments. Important decisions were made by administrators that vitally affected the lives of people. Choice abounded and administrators seized on it. Indeed, they were often themselves divided on how to interpret statutes or how generally to frame policies under them. Interest groups were observed to make strenuous efforts to get favorable administrative enactments. Moreover, sufficiently precise knowledge did not exist to determine the best way to carry out a general objective in many areas. Given the large areas of uncertainty and ignorance, the values and choices of administrators counted a great deal. Taken at this level there was not too much that could be said for maintaining the distinction between policy and administration. Nevertheless, nagging doubts remained.

Were politics and administration identical? If they were, then it was difficult to understand how we were able to talk about them separately. Or was politics simply a cover term for all the things that different organs of the government did? If politics and administration could be separated in some way, then a division of labor might be based on them. No doubt the legislative will, if there was one, could be undermined by a series of administrative enactments. But were not these administrative decisions of a smaller and less encompassing kind than those usually made by Congress? Were there not ways in which the enactments of Congress were (or could be) made more authoritative than the acts of administrators? Overwhelming administrative discretion did violence to democratic theory.

As the world moves into the 1970s, we will undoubtedly see significant efforts to rehabilitate the policy-administration dichotomy. The dissatisfactions of modern industrial life are being poured on the bureaucracy. It seems to grow larger daily while human satisfaction does not increase commensurately. It has become identified with red tape and resistance to change. Yet no one can quite imagine doing away with it in view of the ever-increasing demand for services. So politicians who feel that the bureaucracy has become a liability,[3] clientele who think they might be better served under other arrangements, taxpayers who resent the sheer costs, policy analysts who regard existing organizations as barriers to the application of intelligence, will join together in seeking ways to make bureaucracy more responsive. How better do this than by isolating its innovative functions from the mass of officialdom? Instead of preventing administration from being contaminated by politics, however, the purpose of the new dichotomy will be to insulate policy from the stultifying influences of the bureaucracy.

WHO WILL PAY THE COSTS OF CHANGE?

While most organizations evaluate some of their policies periodically, the self-evaluating organization would do so continuously. These evaluative activities would be inefficient, that is, they would cost more than they are worth, unless they led to change. Indeed the self-evaluating organization is purposefully set up to encourage change.

The self-evaluating organization will have to convince its own members to live with constant change. They may think they love constant upset when they first join the organization, but experience is likely to teach them otherwise. Man's appetite for rapid change is strictly limited. People cannot bear to have their cherished beliefs challenged or their lives altered on a continuing basis. The routines of yesterday are swept away, to be replaced by new ones. Anxiety is induced because they cannot get their bearings. They have trouble knowing exactly what they should be doing. The ensuing confusion may lead to inefficiencies in the form of hesitation or random behavior designed to cover as many bases as possible. Cynicism may grow as the wisdom of the day before yesterday gives way to new truth, which is, in turn, replaced by a still more radiant one. The leaders of the self-evaluating organization will have to counter this criticism.

Building support for policies within an organization requires internal selling. Leaders must convince the members of the organization that what they are doing is worthwhile. Within the self-evaluating organization the task may initially be more difficult than in more traditional bureaucracies. Its personnel are accustomed to question policy proposals and to demand persuasive arguments in their support. Once the initial campaign is proven successful, however, enthusiasm can be expected to reach a high pitch after all existing policies have been evaluated, new alternatives have been analyzed, and evidence has been induced in favor of a particular alternative. The danger here is overselling. Convinced that "science" is in their favor, persuaded that their paper calculations are in tune with the world, the evaluators believe a little too much in their own ideas. They are set up for more disappointment from those who expect less. How much greater the difficulty, then, when continuous evaluation suggests the need for another change in policy. Now two internal campaigns are necessary: the first involves unselling the old policy and the second involves selling the new one. All virtues become unsuspected vices and last year's goods are now seen to be hopelessly shoddy. Perpetual change has its costs.

Maintenance of higher rates of change depend critically on the ability of those who produce it to make others pay the associated costs. If the change makers are themselves forced to bear the brunt of their actions, they will predictably seek to stabilize their environment. That is the burden of virtually the entire sociological literature on organizations from Weber to Crozier. The needs of the members displace the goals of the organization. The public purposes that the organization was supposed to serve give way to its private acts. Its own hidden agendas dominate the organization.

Rather than succumb to the diseases of bureaucracy, the self-evaluating organization will be tempted to pass them on to others. The self-evaluating organization can split itself off into "evaluating" and "administering" parts, thus making lower levels pay the costs of change, or it can seek to impose them on other organizations in its environment. We shall deal first with difficulties encountered in trying to stabilize the evaluative top of the organization while the bottom is in a continuous state of flux.

Let us suppose that an organization separates its evaluative head from its administrative body. The people at the top do not have operating functions. They are, in administrative jargon, all staff rather than line. Their task is to appraise the consequences of existing policies, work out better alternatives, and have the new policies they recommend carried out by the administrative unit.

Who would bear the cost of change? One can imagine evaluators running around merrily suggesting changes to and fro without having to implement them. The anxiety would be absorbed by the administrators. They would have to be the ones to change gears and to smooth out the difficulties. But they will not stand still for this. Their belief about what is administratively feasible and organizationally attainable must be part of the policy that is adopted. So the administrators will bargain with the evaluators.

Administrators have significant resources to bring to this struggle. They deal with the public. They collect the basic information that is sent upward in one form or another. They can drag their feet, mobilize clientele, hold back information, or otherwise make cooperation difficult. The evaluators have their own advantages. They have greater authority to issue rules and regulations. They are experts in manipulating data and models to justify existing policies or denigrate them.

Held responsible for policy but prohibited from administering it directly, the evaluators have an incentive to seek antibureaucratic delivery systems. They will, for example, prefer an income to a service strategy.[4] The evaluators can be pretty certain that clients will receive checks mailed from the central computer, whereas they cannot be sure that the services they envisage will be delivered by hordes of bureaucrats in the manner they would like. Providing people with income to buy better living quarters has the great advantage of not requiring a corps of officials to supervise public housing. Evaluators do not have the field personnel to supervise innumerable small undertakings; they, therefore, will prefer large investment projects over smaller ones. They can also make better use of their small number of people on projects that are expensive and justify devotion of large amounts of analytical time. Contrarywise, administrators will emphasize far-flung operations providing services requiring large numbers of people that only they can perform. In a house of many mansions they will be the masters.

There are circumstances, of course, in which administrators and evaluators will reverse their normal roles. If the evaluators feel that there is not enough government employment, for example, they may seek labor-intensive operations. Should the administrators feel they are already overburdened, they may welcome policies that are easily centralized and directed by machines performing rote operations. The more likely tendency, however, is for administrators and evaluators to expand into each other's domain. Each one can reduce the bargaining powers of the other by taking unto himself some of his competitors' advantages. Thus the administrators may recruit their own policy analysts to compete with the evaluators who, in turn, will seek their own contacts within the administrative apparatus in order to ensure a steady and reliable flow of information. If this feuding goes far enough, the result will be two organizations acting in much the same way as the single one they replaced but with additional problems of coordination.

EVALUATION, INCORPORATED

It is but a short step from separating evaluation from administration to the idea of rival teams of evaluators. A rough equivalent of a competitive market can be introduced by allowing teams of evaluators to compete for direction of policy in a given area. The competition would take place in terms of price (we can accomplish a specified objective at a lower cost), quality (better policies for the same money), quantity (we can produce more at the same cost), maintenance (we can fix things when they go wrong), experience (we have a proven record), values (our policies will embody your preferences) and talent (when it comes down to it, you are buying our cleverness and we are superior). The team that won the competition would be placed in charge until it left to go elsewhere or another team challenged it. The government might raise its price to keep a talented team or it might lower it to get rid of an incompetent one. The incentives for evaluation would be enormous, restrained, of course, by ability to perform lest the evaluators go bankrupt when they run out of funds or lose business to competitors.

The first task of the new enterprise would be to establish its own form of organization. What organizational arrangements are necessary to make competition among evaluators feasible?

Evaluators must either be assured of employment somewhere or engage in other dispensible occupations from which they can be recruited at short notice. A handful of evaluators could always be recruited by ad hoc methods from wherever they are found. But teams of evaluators sufficient to direct major areas of policy would be difficult to assemble at short notice. They would all be doing different things instead of working together, which is part of the experience they need to be successful. Nor can they form a team unless they can all promise to be on the job at a certain time if their bid is successful, yet at the same time have other jobs to fall back on if they are turned down.

In the previous model, where the evaluators generate new policies and the administrators carry them out, these bureaucrats carried the major burden of uncertainty. Under the new model this imbalance is redressed because the evaluators have to worry about security of employment. Few people like to shift jobs all the time; even fewer like the idea of periodic unemployment alternating with the anxiety of bidding to get jobs and performing to keep them. Mechanisms will be found, we can be certain, to reduce their level of uncertainty to tolerable dimensions.

Evaluators may choose to work within existing administrative organizations, accepting a lower status, learning to live with disappointment, in return for job stability. This is one pattern that already exists. Evaluators may go to private industry and universities on the understanding they will be able to make occasional forays into government as part of a tiny group of advisors to leading officials. This is also done now. Both alternatives do away with the idea of competition; they merely graft a small element of evaluation onto existing organizations on a catch-as-catch-can basis.

In order to preserve evaluators who are in a position to compete for the direction of policy, it will be necessary for them to form stable organizations of their own. Like the existing firms of management consultants they resemble, these evaluators would bid on numerous projects; the difference would be that they would do the actual policy work as part of the public apparatus rather than making recommendations and then disappearing. Evaluation, Incorporated, as we shall call it, would contain numerous possible teams, some of whom would be working and others who would be preparing to go to work. The firm would have to demand considerable overhead to provide services for the evaluators, to draw up proposals, and to compensate those of its members who are (hopefully) temporarily out of work. Keeping Evaluation, Incorporated, solvent by maintaining a high level of employment will become a major organizational goal.

Evaluation, Incorporated, is an organization. It has managers who are concerned with survival. It has members who must be induced to remain. It has clients who must be served. So it will constitute itself a lobby for evaluation. When the demand for its services is high, it will be able to insist on the evaluative ethic; it will take its services to those who are prepared to appreciate (by paying for) them. But when demands are low, Evaluation, Incorporated, must trim its sails. It has a payroll to meet. Rather than leave a job when nonanalytical criteria prevail, it may have to swallow its pride and stay on. Its managers can easily convince themselves that survival is not only good for them but for society, which will benefit from the good they will be able to do in better times.

If their defects stem from their insecurities, the remedy will be apparent; increase the stability of evaluators by guaranteeing them tenure of employment. Too close identification with party or policy proved, in any event, to be a mixed blessing. They feasted while they were in favor and famished when they were out. Apparently they require civil service status, a government corporation, say, devoted to evaluation.

Perhaps the General Accounting Office (GAO), which is beginning to do analytic studies, will provide a model of an independent governmental organization devoted to evaluation. Since it has a steady source of income from its auditing work, so to speak, it can afford to form, break up, and recreate teams of evaluators. Its independence from the Executive Branch (the Accountant General is responsible to Congress and serves a 15-year term) might facilitate objective analysis. But the independence of GAO has been maintained because it eschews involvement in controversial matters. If the new General Evaluation Office (GEO) were to issue reports that increased conflict, there would undoubtedly be a strong impulse to bring it under regular political control. The old auditing function might be compromised because objectivity is difficult to maintain about a program one has sponsored, or because public disputes lower confidence in its operations. Opponents of its policy positions might begin to question its impartiality in determining the legality of government expenditures. Yet protection would be difficult to arrange because the new GEO did not have a political client.

By attending to the problems of an organization that supplies evaluation to others, we hope to illuminate the dilemmas of any organization that wishes to seriously engage in continuous analyses of its own activities.

Evaluation, which criticizes certain programs and proposes to replace them with others, is manifestly a political activity. If evaluation is not political in the sense of party partisanship, it is political in the sense of policy advocacy. Without a steady source of political support, without that essential manifestation of affection from somebody out there in society, it will suffer the fate of abandoned children: the self-evaluating organization is unlikely to prosper in an orphanage.

ADJUSTING TO THE ENVIRONMENT

The self-evaluating organization is one that uses its own analysis of its own programs in order to alter or abolish them. Its ability to make changes when its analysis suggests they are desirable is an essential part of its capacity to make self-evaluation a living reality. Yet the ability of any single organization to make self-generated changes is limited by the necessity of receiving support from its environment.

The leaders of a self-evaluating organization cannot afford to leave the results of their labors up to the fates. If their "batting average" goes way down, they will be in trouble. Members of the organization will lose faith in evaluation because it does not lead to changes in actual policy. Those who are attracted to the organization by the prospect of being powerful as well as analytical will leave to join more promising ventures, or old clients will become dissatisfied without new ones to take their place. As the true believers depart, personnel who are least motivated by the evaluative ethic will move into higher positions. Revitalization of the organization via the promotion and recruitment of professing evaluators will become impossible.

In order to avoid the deadly cycle—failure, hopelessness, abandonment—leaders of the self-evaluating organization must seek some proportion of success. They must select the organization's activities, not only with an eye toward their analytical justification, but with a view toward receiving essential support from their environment. Hence they become selective evaluators. They must prohibit the massive use of organizational resources in areas where they see little chance of success. They must seek out problems that are easy to solve and changes that are easy to make because they do not involve radical departures from the past. They must be prepared to hold back the results of evaluation when they believe the times are not propitious; they must be ready to seize the time for change whether or not the evaluations are fully prepared or wholly justified. Little by little, it seems, the behavior of the leaders will become similar to those of other organization officials who also seek to adapt to their environment.

The growing conservatism of the self-evaluating organization is bound to cause internal strains. There are certain to be disagreements about whether the organization is being too cautious. No one can say for sure whether the leaders have correctly appraised the opportunities in a rapidly shifting environment. If they try to do too much, they risk failure in the political world. If they try to do too little, they risk abandoning their own beliefs and losing the support of their most dedicated members. Maintaining a balance between efficacy and commitment is not easy.

Now the self-evaluating organization need not be a passive bystander negotiating its environment. It can seek to mobilize interests in favor of the programs it wishes to adopt. It can attempt to neutralize opposition. It can try to persuade its present clientele that they will be better off, or instill a wish to be served on behalf of new beneficiaries. One fears that its reputation among clientele groups may not be the best, however, because, as a self-evaluating organization, it must be prepared to abandon (or drastically modify) programs and with them the clientele they serve. The clients will know that theirs is only a marriage of convenience, that the self-evaluating organization is eager to consider more advantageous alliances, and that they must always be careful to measure their affection according to the exact degree of services rendered. The self-evaluating organization cannot expect to receive more love than it gives. In fact, it must receive less.

Evaluation can never be fully rewarded. There must, in the nature of things, be other considerations that prevail over evaluation, even where the powers that be would like to follow its dictates. The policies preferred by the self-evaluating organization are never the only ones being contemplated by the government, there are always multitudes of policies in being or about to be born. Some of these are bound to be inconsistent with following the dictates of evaluation. Consider the impact of fiscal policy upon analysis. Suppose the time has come for financial stringency; the government has decided that expenditures must be reduced. Proposals for increases may not be allowed no matter how good the justification. Reductions may be made whether indicated by analysis or not. Conversely, a political decision may be made to increase expenditure. The substantive merits of various policies have clearly been subordinated to their immediate financial implications.

Evaluation may be wielded as a weapon in the political wars. It may be used by one faction or party versus another. Of particular concern to the self-evaluating organization is a one-sided approach to evaluation that creates internal problems. It is not unusual, as was recently the case in Great Britain when the Conservative Party returned to office, for a government to view evaluation as a means of putting down the bureaucracy. A two-step decision rule may be followed: the recommendations of evaluation may be accepted when they lead to reduction and rejected when they suggest increases in expenditure. Before long the members of the organization become reluctant to provide information that will only be used in a biased way. The evaluative enterprise depends on common recognition that the activity is being carried out somehow in order to secure better policies, whatever these may be, and not in support of a predetermined position. If this understanding is violated, people down the line will refuse to cooperate. They will withhold their contribution by hiding information or by simply not volunteering to find it. The morale of the self-evaluating organization will be threatened because its members are being asked to pervert the essence of their calling.

It's the same the whole world over: the analytically virtuous are not necessarily rewarded nor are the wicked (who do not evaluate) punished. The leaders of the self-evaluating organization, therefore, must redouble their effort to obtain political help.

JOINING KNOWLEDGE WITH POWER

To consider the requirements necessary for a self-evaluating organization is to understand why they are rarely met. The self-evaluating organization, it turns out, would be susceptible to much the same kinds of anti-evaluative tendencies as are existing organizations. It, too, must stabilize its environment. It, too, must secure internal loyalty and outside support. Evaluation must, at best, remain but one element in administrative organizations. Yet no one can say today that it is overemphasized. Flights of fancy should not lead anyone to believe that inordinate attention to evaluation is an imminent possibility. We have simply come back to asking how a little more rather than a little less might become part of public organizations. How might analytic integrity be combined with political efficacy?

Evaluative man seeks knowledge, but he also seeks power. His desire to do good is joined with his will to act powerfully. One is no good without the other. A critical incentive for pursuing evaluation is that the results become governmental policy. There is little point in making prescriptions for public policy for one's own private amusement. Without knowledge it would be wrong to seek power. But without power it becomes more difficult to obtain knowledge. Why should anyone supply valuable information to someone who can neither help nor harm him? Access to information may be given only on condition that programmatic goals are altered. Evaluative man is well off when he can pyramid resources so that greater knowledge leads to enhanced power, which, in turn, increases his access to information. He is badly off when the pursuit of power leads to the sacrifice of evaluation. His own policy problem is how to do enough of both (and not too much of either) so that knowledge and power reinforce rather than undermine one another.

The political process generates a conflict of interest within the evaluative enterprise. The evaluators view analysis as a means of deciding on better policies and selling them to others. Clients (elected officials, group leaders, top administrators) view analysis as a means of better understanding the available choices so they can control them. Talk of "better policies," as if it did not matter who determined them, only clouds the issues.

The evaluative group within an organization would hope that it could show political men the worth of its activities. The politicians, in turn, hope to learn about the desirability of the programs that are being evaluated. But their idea of desirability manifestly includes the support which programs generate for them and the organizations of which they are a part. Hence evaluation must be geared to producing programs that connect the interests of political leaders to the outcomes of governmental actions; otherwise, they will reject evaluation and with it the men who do it.

A proposed policy is partly a determinant of its own success; the support it gathers or loses in clientele is fed back into its future prospects. By its impact on the future environment of the organization, the proposed policy affects the kinds of work the organization is able to do. Pure evaluative man, however single-minded his concentration on the intrinsic merits of programs, must also consider their interaction effects on his future ability to pursue his craft. Just as he would insist on including the impact of one element in a system on another in his policy analysis, so must he consider how his present recommendations affect future ones. A proper evaluation includes the impact of a policy on the organizations responsible for it.

Consider in this organizational context the much-discussed problem of diverse governmental programs that may contribute to the same ends without anyone being able to control them. There may be unnecessary redundancy, where some programs overlap, side by side with large areas of inattention to which no programs are directed. More services of one kind and less of another are provided than might be strictly warranted. Without evaluation no one can really say whether there are too many or too few programs or whether their contents are appropriate. But an evaluation that did all this would get nowhere unless it resulted in different institutional processes for handling the same set of problems.

Even on its own terms, then, evaluation should not remain apart from the organizations on which it is dependent for implementation. Organizational design and policy analysis are part of the same governmental process. If an organization wishes to reduce its identification with programs (and the clients who support them), for example, so that it can afford to examine different types of policy, it must adopt a political strategy geared to that end.

The self-evaluating organization would be well advised not to depend too much on a single type of clientele. Diversification is its strategy. The more diverse its services, the more varied its clientele, the less the self-evaluating organization has to depend on any one of them, the more able it is to shift the basis of its support. Diversity creates political flexibility.

Any organization that produces a single product, so to speak, that engages in a limited range of activities is unlikely to abandon them willingly.

Its survival, after all, is bound up in its program. If the program goes, the organization dies. One implication drawn from these considerations is that the traditional wisdom concerning governmental organization badly needs revision.[5] If the basic principle of organization is that similar programs should be grouped together, as is now believed to be the case, these organizations will refuse to change. On the contrary, agencies should be encouraged to differentiate their products and diversify their outputs. If they are not faced with declining demand for all their programs, they will be more willing to abandon or modify a single one. The more varied its programs, the less dependent the organization is on a single one, the greater its willingness to change.

No matter how good its internal analysis, or how persuasively an organization justifies its programs to itself, there is something unsatisfying about allowing it to judge its own case. The ability of organizations to please themselves must ultimately (at least in a democratic society) give way to judgment by outsiders. Critics of organizations must, therefore, recognize that their role is an essential one. Opposition is part and parcel of the evaluative process. The goal would be to secure a more intelligent and analytically sophisticated level of advocacy on all sides. Diverse analyses might become, as Harry Rowen has suggested, part of the mutual partisan adjustment through which creative use is made of conflicts among organized interests.

Competition, per se, however, need not lead to fundamental change. Organizations may go on the offensive by growing bigger instead of better, that is, by doing more of the same. The change in which they are interested is a change in magnitude. We are all familiar with the salesmanship involved in moving to new technologies or larger structures where internal dynamism and grandiose conceptions are mistaken for new ideas. Motion may be a protection against change.

Competition, if it is to lead to desirable consequences, must take place under appropriate rules specifying who can make what kind of transaction. No one would advocate unrestrained competition among economic units in the absence of a market that makes it socially advantageous for participants to pursue their private interests in expectation of mutual gain. Where parties are affected who are not directly represented in the market, for instance, the rules may be changed to accommodate a wider range of interests. Competition among rival policies and their proponents also takes place in an arena that specifies rules for exercising power in respect to particular decisions. Evaluators must, therefore, consider how their preferred criteria for decision will be affected by the rules for decision in political arenas within which they must operate.

We have, it appears, returned to politics. Unless building support for policies is an integral part of designing them, their proponents are setting themselves up for disappointment. To say that one will first think of a great idea and then worry about how it might be implemented is a formula for failure.[6] A good evaluation not only specifies desirable outcomes but suggests institutional mechanisms for achieving them.

If you don't know how to make an evaluation, it may be a problem for you but not for anyone else. If you do know how to evaluate, it becomes a problem for others. Evaluation is an organizational problem. While the occasional lone rider may be able to fire off an analysis now and then, he must eventually institutionalize his efforts if he is to produce a steady output. The overwhelming bulk of evaluation takes place within organizations. The rejection of evaluation is done largely by the organizations that ask for it. To create an organization that evelutes its own activities evidently requires an organizational response. If evaluation is not done at all, if it is done but not used, if used but twisted out of shape, the place to look first is not the technical apparatus but the organization.

Organization is first but not last. Always it is part of a larger society that conditions what it can do. Evaluation is also a social problem. So long as organizational opposition to evaluation is in the foreground, we are not likely to become aware of the social background. Should this initial resistance be overcome, and individual organizations get to like evaluation, however, it would still face multiple defenses thrown up by social forces.

EVALUATION AS TRUST

For the self-evaluating organization all knowledge must be contingent. Improvement is always possible, change for the better is always in view though not necessarily yet attained. It is the organization *par excellence* that seeks knowledge. The ways in which it seeks to obtain knowledge, therefore, uniquely defines its character.

The self-evaluating organization would be skeptical rather than committed. It would continuously be challenging its own assumptions. Not dogma but scientific doubt would be its distinguishing feature. It would seek new truth instead of defending old errors. Testing hypotheses would be its main work.

Like the model community of scholars, the self-evaluating organization would be open, truthful, and explicit. It would state its conclusions in public, show how they were determined, and give others the opportunity to refute them. The costs and benefits of alternative programs for various groups in society would be indicated as precisely as available knowledge would permit. Everything would be aboveboard. Nothing would be hidden.

Are there ways of securing the required information? Can the necessary knowledge be created? Will the truth make men free? Attempting to answer these profound queries would take me far beyond the confines of this exploratory article. But I would like to suggest by illustration that the answers to each of them depend critically on the existence of trust among social groups and within organizations. The acceptance of evaluation requires a community of men who share values.

An advantage of formal analysis, in which the self-evaluating organization specializes, is that it does not depend entirely on learning from experience. That can be done by ordinary organizations. By creating models abstracting relationships from the areas of the universe they wish to control, evaluators seek to substitute manipulation of their models for events in the world. By rejecting alternatives their models tell them will work out badly (or not as well as others), these analysts save scarce resources and protect the public against less worthy actions. Ultimately, however, there must be an appeal to the world of experience. No one, not even the evaluators themselves, are willing to try their theoretical notions on large populations without more tangible reasons to believe that the recommended alternatives prove efficacious.[7]

Since the defect of ordinary organizations is that they do not learn well from experience, the self-evaluating organization seeks to order that experience so that knowledge will be gained from it. The proof that a policy is good is that it works when it is tried. But not everything can be tried everywhere. Hence experiments lie at the heart of evaluation. They are essential for connecting alleged causes with desired effects in the context of limited resources.

The ability of the self-evaluating organization to perform its functions depends critically upon a climate of opinion that favors experimentation. If resources are severely constrained, for example, leading to reluctance to try new ventures, the self-evaluating organization cannot function as advertised. Should there exist strong feeling that everyone must be treated alike, to choose another instance, experimentation would be ruled out. Take the case of the "More Effective Schools" movement in New York City. The idea was to run an experiment to determine whether putting more resources into schools would improve the performance of deprived children. In order to qualify as a proper experiment, More Effective Schools had to be established in some places but not in others, so that there would be control groups. The demand for equality of treatment was so intense, however, that mass picketing took place at the school sites. Favored treatment for these schools was taken as *prima facie* evidence of discrimination. It became apparent that More Effective Schools would have to be tried everywhere or nowhere. Clearly the social requisites of experimentation would have to exist for self-evaluating organizations to be effective. Unless groups trust each other, they will neither allow experiments to be conducted nor accept the results.

Although ways of learning without experimentation may be found, no evaluation is possible without adequate information. But how much is enough? Hierarchies in organizations exist in order to reduce information. If the men at the top were to consider all the bits of data available in the far-flung reaches of the organization, they would be overwhelmed.

As information is weeded and compressed on its way through the hierarchy, however, important bits may be eliminated or distorted. One of the most frequently voiced criticisms of organizations is that the men at the top do not know what is going on. Information is being withheld from them or is inaccurate so that they make decisions on the basis of mistaken impressions. The desire to pass on only good news results in the elimination of information that might place the conveyer in a bad light. Top officials may, therefore, resort to such devices as securing overlapping sources of information or planting agents at lower levels. There are limits to these efforts, however, because the men at the top have only so much time to digest what they have been told. So they vacillate between fear of information loss and being unable to struggle out from under masses of data.

How might the self-evaluating organization deal with information bias? Organization members would have to be rewarded for passing on bad news. Those who are responsible for the flow of information must, at the least, not be punished for telling the truth. If they are also the ones in charge of administering the policy, it will not be possible to remove them for bad performance because once that is done their successors will be motivated to suppress such information. The top men must themselves be willing to accept the blame though they may not feel this is their responsibility and though their standing may be compromised. The very idea of a hierarchy may have to give way to shifting roles in which superior and subordinate positions are exchanged so that each member knows he will soon be in the other's position. The self-evaluating organization clearly requires an extraordinary degree of mutual trust.

The spread of self-evaluating organizations could enhance social trust by widening the area of agreement concerning the consequences of existing policies and the likely effects of change. Calculations concerning who benefited and to what degree would presumably aid in political cost-benefit analyses. The legitimacy of public institutions would be enhanced because they resulted from a more self-consciously analytical process that was increasingly recognized as such. Evaluation would be informative, meliorative, and stabilizing in the midst of change. It sounds idyllic.

More information, per se, need not lead to greater agreement, however, if the society is wracked by fundamental cleavages. As technology makes information more widely available, the need for interpretation will grow. Deluged by data, distrustful of others, citizens may actually grow apart as group leaders collect more information about how badly off they are compared to what they ought to be. The more citizens trust group leaders rather than governmental officials, the greater the chance their differences will be magnified rather than reconciled. The clarification of objectives may make it easier to see the social conflicts implicit in the distribution of income or cultural preferences concerning the environment or the differing styles of life attached to opposing views of the ideal society. Evaluation need not create agreement; evaluation may presuppose agreement.

NOTES

1. Dan Horowitz, "Flexible Responsiveness and Military Strategy: The Case of the Israeli Army," *Policy Sciences*, Vol. 1, No. 2 (Summer 1970), pp. 191–205.
2. Hans Thorelli, "Overall Planning and Management in Sweden," *International Social Science Bulletin*, Vol. VIII, No. 2 (1956).
3. The most dramatic and visible change can be found in the American presidency. Presidents have increasingly bureaucratized their operations. Within the Executive Office there now exist sizeable subunits, characterized by specialization and the division of labor, for dealing with the media of information and communication, Congress, foreign and domestic policy, and more. At the same time, Presidents seek the right to intervene at any level within the Executive Branch on a sporadic basis. The administrators are being prodded to change while the President stabilizes his environment. Thus we find President Nixon saying that he wants something done about that awful Bureau of Indian Affairs, as if it did not belong to him, or asking citizens to elect him again so he can save them from the compulsory busing fostered by his own bureaucracy. He wants to escape blame for bureaucratic errors but keep the credit for inspiring changes.
4. See Robert A. Levine, "Rethinking our Social Strategies," *The Public Interest*, No. 10 (Winter 1968).
5. William A. Niskanen, *Bureaucracy and Representative Government* (Chicago: Aldine-Atherton, 1971).
6. For further discussion along these lines see Jeffrey L. Pressman and Aaron Wildavsky, *Implementation: How Great Expectations in Washington Are Dashed in Oakland* (Berkeley: University of California Press, 1973).
7. An exception of a kind is found in the area of defense policy where the purpose of the analytical exercises is to avoid testing critical hypotheses. Once the hypotheses concerning a nuclear war are tested, the evaluators may not be around to revise their analyses. See Aaron Wildavsky, "Practical Consequences of the Theoretical Study of Defense Policy," *Public Administration Review*, Vol. XXV, No. 1 (March 1965), pp. 90–103.

THE UTILIZATION
OF EVALUATION RESEARCH:
PROBLEMS AND PROSPECTS

David Nachmias
Gary T. Henry

One of the principal purposes of policy-evaluation research is to aid policy-makers in developing public policy. Many evaluation studies are carried out with the expectation that their findings will be incorporated in the decision-making process. Indeed, the expectation of research utilization is explicit in the definition of evaluation research; it is research that retrieves systematic information about the cost and impact of policy outcomes for the purposes of altering or refining the policy to better accomplish its goals. Although the questions that guide evaluation research are often important in enhancing the understanding of sociopolitical phenomena and human behavior, the incentive to improve the public-policy process is a major factor accounting for the growth of the discipline.

Furthermore, research utilization is one social benefit that may help to defray the costs of research. A single effort at evaluation, the New Jersey Income-Maintenance Experiment, cost $8 million, involved 1,350 families, and lasted for a period of five years. Federal legislation now requires that 2 to 5 percent of the resources spent on public programs be used to support systematic evaluations. This allocation of increasingly scarce resources to evaluation research calls for an examination of the extent to which research findings are being utilized in improving the public-policy process. The utilization of evaluation has become an area of investigation that transcends the immediate concerns of evaluation research.

Research interest in utilization is quite recent. Little over a decade ago, the prevailing belief was that research questions concerning utilization were of secondary importance, because policymakers would obviously incorporate systematic-evaluation findings into the decision-making process. The policymakers' commitment to evaluation was manifested in appropriations for evaluation research and the creation of evaluation offices and positions within the various levels and branches of government. This led to the expectation that evaluation findings, once available, would become an integral component of public decision making. It is now evident that evaluation research is neither all-powerful nor all-weak, and that some evaluation findings help to shape policy decisions while others are ignored. Although it might be too early to assess the overall impact of evaluation research on policymaking, some tendencies and explanations begin to emerge; they are described in this article.

WHAT IS RESEARCH UTILIZATION?

At present there is neither a precise definition of the term "utilization" nor a consensus regarding the manner in which it can be researched. This should not be too surprising because the concept embodies the complex notion of influence, that is, the capacity to induce change in behavior. In other words, if policymakers make a decision based upon research findings that in the absence of research findings they would not have made, one could infer that the evaluation findings influenced that particular decision. From this perspective, utilization can only be inferred; it cannot be directly observed. Moreover, in practice, it is rarely possible to reconstruct the exact flow of information, interactions, and events that led policymakers to adopt a particular policy. Public policymaking is a complex, dynamic process involving situational, structural, and motivational components, as well as a multiplicity of participants that have overlapping but also divergent interests and values. For instance, even though the attentive public and policymakers share a broad agreement that something has to be done with respect to the energy crisis, President Jimmy Carter, Congress, the Federal Energy Regulatory Commission (FERC), and the various interest groups involved in this policy area disagree on what should be done and how to do it. The policies resulting in such cases are not only extremely difficult to evaluate, but the evaluation findings, no matter how conclusive, influence the behavior of only some policymakers. This, in turn, suggests that patterns of utilization have to be examined within the various levels of decision making, as well as along the entire policy process.

The difficulties involved in directly observing the utilization of evaluation research, coupled with the structural fragmentation of government and the multiplicity of actors in the policy process, have led to the development of indicators of utilization. Approximations rather than direct measures, these display certain inherent limitations. Nonetheless, the following five indicators, to a certain extent, tap important aspects of utilization.

Relations Between Evaluation Findings and Policy Outputs

This indicator is the most closely associated with the conceptualization of utilization from an influence perspective. All other things being equal, if, for example, the evaluation findings show that a particular program does not exert the intended impact on the target variable(s), and if, subsequently, policymakers discontinue the program or radically alter it, this could be interpreted as research utilization. In the real world, however, all things are usually unequal, and, as discussed in the following sections, evaluation findings are often inconclusive, and policy outputs are usually incremental, thus making attempts to assess the relations between the two a formidable task. But even in cases where the evaluation findings are conclusive and the policy outputs are nonincremental, explicit, and measurable, the demonstration of cause-and-effect relations calls for demanding theoretical and methodological considerations, as pointed out in the introductory overview of public policy evaluation.

Access to Policymakers

The concern of this indicator is whether evaluation findings reach the attention of the relevant policymakers. Indeed, policymakers may not be aware of the research findings, for there are structural and behavioral factors in the public decision-making process that serve as barriers to the free flow of information. In the legislative and executive branches, policymakers are increasingly dependent on the information supplied and filtered by the public bureaucracy. Over the years the discretion of this nonelective component of government has greatly increased, and in many cases access by policymakers has been determined exclusively by it.

Formal Institutionalization of Evaluation

This indicator of utilization refers to the extent to which evaluation activities are formally institutionalized and regularized in the various levels and branches of government. Underlying this indicator is the assumption that if evaluation becomes a routine organizational activity, it will systematically be channeled through the various decision points, thus increasing the potential for utilization.

In recent years government agencies have added evaluation to their other functions; they have established evaluation units and created new positions for evaluators. Within the executive branch, for example, the Office of Management and Budget (OMB) has redefined its mission to "initiate a multiagency cooperative effort to upgrade and strengthen the overall quality and relevance of evaluation carried out by the various federal agencies and to assure that evaluation results are utilized in arriving at major policy decisions."[1] Similarly, the Legislative Reorganization Act of 1970 was intended to make the General Accounting Office (GAO) a principal source of information for Congress about the impacts of public programs, their operation, and cost-effectiveness.[2] State and local governments followed a similar route of formal institutionalization.

Although formal institutionalization of evaluation activities may enhance utilization, it cannot be assumed that this institutionalization is divorced from ongoing organizational processes. These processes, in turn, intervene between institutionalization and effective utilization. For example, the proximity of the evaluation unit or the evaluator to the locus of policy-making, and the tendency of organizations to resist change are two important factors.[3]

Benefit-Cost

Essentially, this indicator calls for relating the costs of a particular evaluation to the benefits it could produce in the overall costs of the program, its implementation, and its effectiveness in accomplishing the program's goal(s). A marginal benefit is used as a criterion for utilization. As pointed out in the introduction, the major problem with such an indicator—and with cost-effectiveness evaluations in general—is that, in many cases, benefits are not amenable to measurement in monetary terms because they are not reflected in the marketplace. Furthermore, the formulation of an optimal rule that will demonstrate how to maximize utilization is not always possible.

Knowledge Building

The knowledge-building aspect of evaluation research is the least direct indicator of utilization. Evaluation research has contributed to methodological as well as to substantive issues; however, the impacts of such contributions are cumulative, and their assessment cannot be made instantaneously. Cumulative contributions may set an overall trend in a policy area rather than affect a particular policy decision. As Thomas Cook pointed out, "To evaluation researchers who value knowledge building, the slogan 'We are working for twenty years from now, and not today' is no idle slogan."[4] The knowledge-building indicator is mostly concerned with the progress of evaluation research as a scientific discipline that will, in the long run, influence public policy than it is with immediate applications of knowledge.

Although imperfect, these five indicators tap some important aspects of utilization. As utilization research advances, these indicators will be refined and validated, and others will be developed. At the same time the idea of influence will continue to underlie the process of concept formation.

Closely related to the conceptualization of utilization in terms of influence is the question concerning its antecedents: What accounts for systematic variations in patterns of utilization? Why do some research findings find expression in policy outputs while many others do not? Two distinct clusters of factors—methodological and political-bureaucratic—are suggested in the following sections to explain variations in utilization.

METHODOLOGICAL FACTORS

The methodology employed in an evaluation study is of cardinal importance for producing credible findings that can be utilized by policymakers. At present, however, there are neither standardized evaluation methods nor generally accepted professional norms governing evaluation as a professional activity. Indeed, this is characteristic of any new and rapidly developing scientific discipline. Methodologies are crystalized and norms are established as a discipline or a subdiscipline reaches a state of maturity. Yet, this lack of established methods and agreed-upon professional norms contributes to underutilization of evaluation. Various evaluative studies of the same programs produce different, noncomparable, and often contradictory findings, and evaluation results have not generally provided an accumulating, increasingly accurate body of evidence. As Buchanan and co-authors observed:

> A major reason why evaluation results have had limited effects on programs and decision making is that evaluation planners generally lack a framework that, first, would provide a set of standardized and compatible measures for the decision-making system, program activities, and the socioeconomic environment, and second, would permit specification of known and assumed relationships among these measures. As a result, evaluation findings have tended to be nonaccumulating, noncomparable, and characterized by low or unknown validity and reliability.[5]

There is no theory of evaluation per se, nor is there any one methodology that would be applicable to all public policies at all levels of operation. Instead, the general principles of scientific research in the social sciences guide evaluation researchers. A number of distinct problems make the application of these principles to evaluation research complex.

First, evaluation researchers do not participate in the formation of the policy or the program. The program itself, its goals, and the measure(s) for its success are usually given: "Program evaluation starts with a program—with an ongoing activity already shaped by forces and events which cannot be reshaped to suit the investigators' convenience. The [research] question comes second; the research design, third. Necessarily, the quality of the design suffers."[6] Furthermore, often neither the goals nor their criteria for success are well defined or made operational by the policymakers. Although approximations are attempted, room always exists for ambiguity and inconclusiveness. For example, the goals and the criteria for success of a compensatory educational program can be understood and researched differently by various evaluators: Educational motivation, educational aspirations, self-esteem, cognitive development, and social skills are all plausible goals that have been documented in educational research as enhancing educational achievement. But if the findings show, for example, gains in the program participants' self-esteem, the question of whether that is what the policymakers intended to accomplish remains unanswered. Even if all the aforementioned goals were to be accomplished by the program—in practice, a rather remote possibility—other interpretations of the program's intent could be articulated, e.g., educational attainment, affective development, physical fitness, and opening up opportunity structures. Indeed, the more abstract and vague the goals and their criteria for success, the greater will be the number and the variety of interpretations at the research and policymaking levels. Many of these interpretations will be noncomparable and probably contradictory. Consequently, the research findings will be noncomparable, nonaccumulating, and will have low utilization prospects.

Another major methodological problem is that many studies are conducted within the political-bureaucratic context. When this occurs, investigators have only a limited degree of discretion in deciding important issues, such as what variables to focus on, what research design to employ, what type and size sample to use, and how to manage the study. In some cases these and other methodological issues are determined by the sponsoring agency. As Carol Weiss pointed out:

> The new-style evaluation money, although larger in amount than ever before, comes ringed around with restrictions. Not only do government "RFPs" (requests for proposal, the specifications of the research to be done and its scheduling) specify many of the details of objectives, indicators, timing, analysis, and reporting which used to be thought of as the evaluator's bailiwick, but government agencies are requiring increasingly close surveillance during the course of the study.[7]

In other cases, these issues are resolved through negotiation and compromise, and in still others, through decisions made in the field, often in directions that impinge on the integrity of the research design and the validity and reliability of the measuring procedures. This, in turn, diminishes the chances for utilization.

The Case of Head Start

The Ohio University and Westinghouse Learning Corporation evaluation of Head Start is one relatively well-documented case that exemplifies the arguments made so far.[8] In late 1964, Head Start was initiated by the Office of Economic Opportunity (OEO) as a means of helping disadvantaged preschool children learn skills that would help them perform better in primary school. The program was widely supported, and by 1968 over 13,000 centers were established throughout the country with a budget of $323 million. In 1968 OEO issued a request for proposals for a nationwide impact evaluation of the program. As specified by the RFP, the research question was the extent to which Head Start was having an impact on the cognitive and affective skills of children who participated in the program. The RFP called for an ex-post-facto research design. From the OEO list of centers, 225 were screened, and 104 were earmarked for the evaluation. From these centers, 1,980 students who had attended Head Start and who were then in the first, second, and third grades were randomly selected. Comparison groups totaling 1,983 students who matched on such items as sex, race, and kindergarten attendance were drawn from the eligible population that had not attended the program. Standardized and newly constructed tests were used to measure cognitive and affective development. The evaluation findings were summarized by the contractors as follows:

> In sum, the Head Start children cannot be said to be *appreciably* different from their peers in the elementary grades who did not attend Head Start in most aspects of cognitive and affective development measured in this study, with the exception of the slight, but nonetheless significant, superiority of full-year Head Start children on certain measures of cognitive development.[9]

Although criticism over the methodological shortcomings of the proposed evaluation, e.g., the variables to be investigated, the ex-post-facto research design, the validity of the tests, were clearly articulated and raised by Head Start administrators *prior* to the decision to issue a RFP, the Office of Research, Plans, Programs and Evaluations (RPP&E), with the approval of Bertrand M. Harding, then Acting Director of OEO, activated the study. Not surprisingly, much of the controversy over the reported findings focused on methodological issues. It was charged that the evaluators did not analyze the impact of the programs on such objectives as health, nutrition, and community needs; that the study failed to assess variations among the various projects and sites; that the research design was inadequate; that the samples were not representative of the populations involved; that the measuring instruments lacked validity because they were not designed to test disadvantaged children, and that the study did not take into account the positive effects that Head Start children had on their nonparticipating classroom peers.

It is significant to note that these criticisms were anticipated prior to the execution of the study; political and bureaucratic pressures, however, on OEO outweighed the methodological considerations. The Head Start experience suggests that compromises in the rigor of the methodology (even when the sponsoring agency mandates or is willing to accept less rigor) make evaluation findings subject to criticism and hinder their utilization. (Faced with these inconclusive evaluation results and a politically supportive climate, Congress reacted by increasing Head Start's funds from $377 million in 1972 to $625 million in 1978; other public programs fare differently.)

The Time Factor

Time is yet another artifact of the public-policy process that complicates the application of scientific principles to evaluation research and hinders utilization. Rigor in methodology carries with it time requirements. In the case of Head Start, a methodologically superior, longitudinal investigation advocated by Head Start officials was rejected by OEO in favor of the one year of ex-post-facto study. A major reason for this decision was time: Congress pressured the agency to produce evaluative evidence within a fairly short time.

The time factor is a problem that cuts across major aspects of evaluation research. It represents an inherent and continuous conflict between methodological and political-bureaucratic needs. Although time should not be a constraint in scientific research, it is naive to suppose that scientists do not operate under time pressures. Furthermore, time may be a critical factor in evaluation research when the concern is utilization. For evaluation research to be useful to policymakers, it has to produce credible results before decisions are made, and in many cases at the very early stages of the policy cycle.

The case of the New Jersey Income Maintenance Experiments exemplifies these observations. The evaluations were commissioned by OEO in 1968. The purpose of the experiments was to determine the amount of work reduction that would result from the adoption of a negative-income-tax policy.[10] The experiments were designed to produce findings after five years of field observation. After less than a year of field work, a proposal for the nationwide implementation of a negative-income-tax policy—the Family Assistance Plan (FAP)—was put forward. This created a sense of urgency on the part of policymakers to obtain evidence from the experiments. Reacting to pressure from OEO officials, the investigators released preliminary results based on one year's work. Even though the findings indicated a slight increase in work effort by those receiving a negative income tax, Congress did not enact the proposal. Subsequent interviews with members of the relevant congressional committees elicited a common response: The tax experiments provided only tentative and inconclusive evidence.[11] Thus, when policymakers might have utilized sound evidence, the time requirements of the methodology precluded their doing so, and when the study provided the evidence on which a decision could reasonably be used, policymakers were no longer interested. The evaluator, as Walter Williams pointed out, "occupies a most ambiguous spot: on the one hand, a threat with potentially harmful results; on the other hand, a questionable commodity because he has no available results."[12]

THE POLITICAL-BUREAUCRATIC CONTEXT

The political-bureaucratic context within which evaluation research is performed not only presents problems in the application of a rigorous methodology, but also presents major obstacles for utilization. These obstacles are inherent in the structure of public policymaking bodies and the motivations of policymakers. Before discussing these impediments, it would be useful to outline the characteristics of an ideal policymaking process.

An Ideal Policymaking Process

Decisions in such a process would be informed by evaluative research concerning the impacts, implementation, and cost-effectiveness of public programs. Evaluation research would be an integral component of the decision-making process, and the actors in the process would demand and rely upon evaluation findings to guide their decisions. Such informed decisions would serve the public better than decisions made in the absence of or in disregard for evaluation.

A policy-decision process in which evaluation research would play such a role requires several essential characteristics. First, policy objectives must be known, clear, consistent, and agreed to by the actors in the process. Whenever possible, as Robert Haveman noted, "Trade-offs among these objectives would be known and decision makers would seek in all their decisions to equate the marginal benefit of achieving any one of the objectives with that of achieving any other."[13] Second, policymakers should have knowledge of the impacts, implementation, and cost-effectiveness aspects of public programs that is as valid, reliable, and complete as scientific research is capable of producing. Such knowledge must be open to scientific criticism and subject to further research. Third, once programs are activated, there should be a minimum of stability in their duration and in their substance in order to make sound evaluations possible and useful.[14] The fourth characteristic concerns the motivations that guide the behavior of public policymakers. An ideal motivational structure would be one in which the general public interest would serve as the criterion for making policy decisions. This criterion does not presuppose altruism: The self-interests of policymakers would be enhanced as a broader public interest is attained. Although the process of making the concept "public interest" (or "social welfare") operational is fraught with difficulties, it implies at the minimum that the impacts and the costs of public programs on all individuals or groups must be articulated and taken into account when making policy decisions.* A more demanding criterion is that "any sacrifice in one or more values which is required by a policy is more than compensated for by the attainment of other values."[15]

The Actual Policy Process

The actual policy process is at wide variance with the ideal model. Policy goals are multiple, vague, unstable, conflicting, and often cause disagreement among the participants in the process. Policymakers have at best incomplete knowledge on the effectiveness of programs, and this competes with a host of other considerations—including power motivation—that influence their behavior. The policymakers' motivational structure is not always compatible with the public interest. Consequently, the potential for utilization is impaired.

One way to account for the actual policy process is to focus on how participants in the process operate within the ongoing political system, because public policymaking in general, and utilization in particular, cannot be divorced from their contextual setting. Two attributes of the political system—fragmentation and biased pluralism—need consideration in this regard.

---

* It is beyond the scope of this article to address the issues involved in making "social welfare" operational as a criterion for public policy. See, for example, Barry Brian, *Political Argument*, London: Routledge & Kegan Paul, 1965; Virginia Held, *The Public Interest and Individual Interests*, New York: Basic Books, 1970; and Jerome Rothenberg, *The Measurement of Social Welfare*, Englewood Cliffs, N.J.: Prentice-Hall, 1961.

Fragmentation

Policymaking is a highly fragmented process. There are myriad sites of policymaking. Public policy is made by all branches of the national government and, increasingly, by the public bureaucracies.[16] The Executive branch, Congress, the Supreme Court, and the federal bureaucracy are all involved in the formulation, implementation, and evaluation of public policies. In addition, public policy is made at all levels of government—federal, state, and local—sometimes cooperatively, sometimes antagonistically, and sometimes independently of each other. Policymakers in all these governments are subject to varying environmental, social, and political pressures.

Fragmentation, traditionally advocated because it provides checks and balances that limit the power of any single decision-making body, is a serious obstacle to research utilization. Each decision-making unit defines the scope of a policy, its goals, its measures of success, and so on in accordance to its particular needs and assessments. Evaluation findings, in turn, have multiple audiences, each of which can interpret the findings differently, and each of which can, theoretically, veto all or part of a decision. Furthermore, because of sharp variations in the ways in which programs are made operational and then managed, the task of aggregating program findings across the various sites becomes formidable.

Biased Pluralism

The multiplicity of public decision-making bodies, coupled with the fragmentation of the overall policymaking process, is closely related to the conception of American politics as being pluralistic. Classic pluralists contend that the democratic political process can accurately express the benefits and costs of public decisions to all citizens through the continuing interactions of interest groups among themselves and with policymakers. Pluralism, in the words of William Connolly

> . . . portrays the system as a balance of power among overlapping economic, religious, ethnic, and geographical groupings. Each "group" has some voice in shaping socially binding decisions; each constrains and is constrained through the processes of mutual group adjustment; and all major groups share a broad system of beliefs and values, which encourages conflict to proceed within established channels and allows initial disagreements to dissolve into compromise solutions.[17]

Such a system, the argument goes, encourages coalition formation and vote trading. Stable patterns do not form, but are ever changing. Consequently, the ability of any one group to influence the government in its favor is limited. In the long run all groups obtain at least some of their goals. Furthermore, if all citizens participate in such groups, the interactions of countervailing groups will produce public policies that serve the general public interest rather than any single private interest.

Leaving aside the conceptual validity and the desirability of having a pluralist system, the reality is that pluralism has not worked to enhance the public interest. Some groups have a cumulative advantage over others in matters of public policy; many citizens are not members of any active interest group; groups are governed by oligarchies; and many societal concerns and interests are not articulated and registered because they are not regarded as legitimate or important by members of the oligarchies, and in turn, by policymakers. Policymakers are not motivated by the general public interest, but rather, by the demands of those groups which they identify with. As Theodore Lowi wrote:

> The most important difference between liberals and conservatives, Republicans and Democrats—however they define themselves—is to be found in the interest groups they identify with. Congressmen are guided in their votes, presidents in their programs, and administrators in their discretion, by whatever organized interests they have taken for themselves as the most legitimate; and that is the measure of legitimacy of demands.[18]

Disjointed Incrementalism

The context within which public policy is being made has led to a policymaking process that is at variance with the ideal process. David Braybrook and Charles Lindblom coined the term "disjointed incrementalism" to describe the actual policymaking process.[19] Essentially, they view public policy as a continuation of past policy activities subject only to incremental modifications. Policymakers do not regularly review the whole range of existing and proposed policies, identify explicit goals, systematically assess the benefits and costs of alternative policies in achieving goals, and then make decisions based on this information. Rather, disjointed incrementalism consists of the following attributes:

1. Policy choices are at the margin of the status quo.
2. Only a few policy alternatives are considered, and these alternatives are incremental changes in the status quo.
3. Only a few consequences are examined for any given policy.
4. Adjustments are made in the objectives of policy in order to conform to a given means of policy. They imply a reciprocal relationship between ends and means.

5. Problems are reconstructed in the course of policy deliberation.
6. Analysis and evaluation occur sequentially, with the result that policy consists of a long chain of amended choices.
7. Analysis and evaluation are oriented toward remedying a negatively perceived situation, rather than toward reaching a preconceived goal.
8. Analysis and evaluation are undertaken throughout the polity, and consequently, these activities are fragmented and disjointed.

These attributes of the actual policymaking process all present obstacles to the utilization of evaluation findings. If prior policy commitments serve as the basis for future policy decisions, negative evaluation findings will be discredited and resisted. If political expediency is valued more than scientific knowledge is, the potential for utilization is undermined a priori.

PROSPECTS FOR INCREASING UTILIZATION

The methodological and political-bureaucratic problems discussed so far raise the question of whether evaluation research in general, and utilization in particular, could be made to serve public policy more effectively. Indeed, it is unrealistic to expect that the ideal policy process would replace the actual policy process. Proposals for improvement, therefore, must take into account the feasibility for implementation. The following four observations reflect this concern.

1. Improvement in the Quality of Evaluation Research

As noted throughout this chapter, evaluation research is fraught with difficulties, and many evaluations fail to meet the standard scientific procedures. In fact, Ilene Bernstein and Howard Freeman found that of all the evaluation studies that received support from the federal government, fewer than 20 percent "consistently follow generally accepted procedures with respect to design, data collection, and data analysis."[20] Notwithstanding the problems inherent in the conduct of evaluation research, the perfection of its methodological and theoretical foundations would make research findings more useful to policymakers, but this could not be expected to result in instantaneous utilization in each and every case. Yet, the knowledge-building component of utilization would certainly be affected and, eventually, would be manifested in public policy. Furthermore, as evaluation research reaches the state of scientific maturity, it will become increasingly difficult to ignore the findings it will produce, as is the case with basic research.

2. Institutionalization

In spite of the impediments discussed in previous sections, changes designed to institutionalize evaluation and utilization more effectively have occurred throughout the government in recent years. The Congressional Budget Act of 1974 created two new committees in Congress, a new staff unit with analysis and evaluation responsibilities—the Congressional Budget Office—and a new budgetary process and appropriations process. These institutions could serve Congress much as the Office of Management and Budget serves the president. Similarly, in the explanation of Section 201(a) of the Legislative Reorganization Act of 1970, the House Committee on Rules stated that the intent of the act was that the Comptroller General "shall review and analyze program results which will assist Congress to determine whether those programs and activities are achieving the objectives of the law." In addition central evaluation offices have been established in the various federal, state, and local levels.

Given the political-bureaucratic context within which evaluation is carried out, such commitments to evaluation and research utilization cannot be expected to produce immediate and dramatic results. Institutionalization is a slow, time-consuming process that threatens the status quo and the status of the participants involved in the process. Yet, if the commitments to institutionalize evaluation and utilization persist and even intensify, and if the evaluations are scientifically sound, the prospects for utilization will be brighter in years to come.

3. Integration of Evaluation with Policy Making

Although analytically distinct, evaluation and policymaking should be more fully integrated in the public policymaking process. At present explicit links between evaluation activities and policymaking are lacking. Evaluators share oversimplified assumptions about the decision-making structure and process, and policymakers often do not explain objectives and needs for information. Although the links between evaluation and policymaking cannot be identical in all policymaking bodies, organizational adaptations could be made in congruence with the functions, needs, and ways of operations that characterize particular policymaking bodies. For example, the General Accounting Office has developed a model statute, suggesting to Congress how objectives might be explicated in relatively precise terms. Similarly, organizational adjustments are being made in federal agencies to structure the formal relations between evaluation and an agency's decision processes. In the absence of such a relationship, Buchanan et al. noted: "The same types of evaluation questions are raised year after year in different decision contexts . . . without any apparent contribution or resolution by the evaluation system."[21] If the evaluation findings are to penetrate decision-making bodies, evaluation has to become a formal, integral component of the decision-making process.

4. Inclusion of Utilization Plans in Evaluation Studies

By and large evaluation studies have not included utilization plans in reports of their findings. The responsibility for utilization has been assumed to rest exclusively in the hands of policymakers. But the latter need precisely this kind of information in order to act upon evaluation findings. In fact, utilization plans could be included in the evaluation proposal; this would help to clarify the possible policy implications of the findings. Such an approach has the advantage of closely relating evaluation and utilization research activities and of committing, to a certain extent, both evaluators and policymakers to a systematic consideration of prospects and strategies for utilization.

In sum, while the actual policy process both impedes utilization and creates serious methodological problems for evaluation research, some steps have been taken—and others could be taken—to improve the potential role of evaluation in public policy. Only time will tell, however, whether the potential of evaluation research will materialize and whether it will serve to reduce the gap between the ideal and the actual public policymaking process.

NOTES

1. Frank L. Lewis and Frank G. Zarb, "Federal Program Evaluation From the OMB Perspective," *Public Administration Review*, 34 (July–August 1974), 312.
2. See Keith E. Marvin and James L. Hendrick, "GAO Helps Congress Evaluate Programs," *Public Administration Review*, 34 (July–August 1974), 327–333.
3. Aaron Wildavsky maintains that organization and evaluation are, in fact, contradictory concepts. See "The Self-Evaluating Organization" in this volume.
4. Thomas D. Cook, "Utilization, Knowledge-Building, and Institutionalization: Three Criteria by Which Evaluation Research Can Be Evaluated," in *Evaluation Studies: Review Annual*, Thomas D. Cook et al., eds., vol. 3, Beverly Hills, Calif.: Sage, 1978, 20.
5. Garth Buchanan, Pamela Horst, and John Scanlon, "Improving Federal Evaluation Planning," *Evaluation*, 1:2 (1973), 87.
6. Harold Orlans, *Contracting for Knowledge* (Washington, D.C.: Jossey-Bass, 1973), p. 123.

7. Carol J. Weiss, "The Politicization of Evaluation Research," *Journal of Social Issues*, 26 (Autumn 1970), 59.
8. The following discussion draws from Walter Williams and John W. Evans, "The Politics of Evaluation: The Case of Head Start," *The Annals of the American Academy of Political and Social Sciences*, 385 (September 1969), 118–130; and Victor Cicarelli, *The Impact of Head Start: An Evaluation of the Effects of Head Start on Children's Cognitive and Affective Development*, vol. 1 (Bladensburg, Md.: Westinghouse Learning Corporation, 1969).
9. Victor Cicarelli, *Impact of Head Start*, p. 8.
10. David Kershaw, "A Negative Income Tax Experiment," and Albert Rees, "An Overview of the Labor-Supply Results," in this volume.
11. Margaret E. Boeckmann, "Policy Impacts of the New Jersey Income Maintenance Experiment," *Policy Sciences*, 7 (March 1976), 53.
12. Walter Williams, *Social Policy Research and Analysis* (New York: Elsevier, 1971), 100.
13. Robert H. Haveman, "Policy Analysis and Congress: An Economist's View," in *Public Expenditures and Policy Analysis*, Robert H. Haveman and Julius Margolis, eds. (Chicago: Rand McNally, 1977), 2nd ed., p. 580.
14. Aaron Wildavsky, *Speaking Truth to Power: The Art and Craft of Policy Analysis* (Boston, Mass.: Little, Brown, 1979), p. 219.
15. Thomas R. Dye, *Understanding Public Policy* (Englewood Cliffs, N.J.: Prentice-Hall, 1972), p. 27.
16. For a comprehensive discussion of the dominant role of the bureaucracy, see David Nachmias and David H. Rosenbloom, *Bureaucratic Government U.S.A.* (New York: St. Martin's, 1980).
17. William E. Connolly, "The Challenge to Pluralist Theory," in *The Bias of Pluralism*, William E. Connolly, ed. (New York: Atherton, 1969), p. 3.
18. Theodore J. Lowi, *The End of Literalism*, New York: Norton, 1969, p. 72.
19. David Braybrooke and Charles E. Lindblom, *A Strategy of Decision: Policy Evaluation as a Social Process* (New York: Free Press, 1963). The following discussion is derived from chapter 15.
20. Ilene N. Bernstein and Howard E. Freeman, *Academic and Entrepreneurial Research* (New York: Russell Sage Foundation, 1975).
21. Garth Buchanan, Pamela Horst, and John Scanlon, "Improving Federal Evaluation Planning," p. 90.

Acknowledgments (continued)

Stuart Nagel and Marian Neef, "The Impact of Jury Size on the Probability of Conviction." Reprinted from *The Justice System Journal*, vol. 2, no. 3 (Spring 1977), pp. 226–232, by permission of the Institute for Court Management.

Margaret Olendzki, "Medicaid Benefits Mainly the Younger and Less Sick." Reprinted from *Medical Care*, XII, 2 (February 1974), pp. 163–172, by permission of J. B. Lippincott Company.

Theodore R. Marmor, Wayne L. Hoffman, and Thomas C. Heagy, "National Health Insurance: Some Lessons from the Canadian Experience." Reprinted from *Policy Sciences*, 6 (1975), 447–466, by permission of Elsevier Scientific publishing Company.

Charles T. Clotfelter and John C. Hahn, "Assessing the National 55 m.p.h. Speed Limit." Reprinted from *Policy Sciences*, 9 (1978), 281–294, by permission of Elsevier Scientific Publishing Company.

Melvin M. Webber, "The BART Experience—What Have We Learned?" Reprinted with permission of the author from: *The Public Interest*, No. 45 (Fall 1976), pp. 79–108. © 1976 by National Affairs, Inc.

Aaron Wildavsky, "The Self-Evaluating Organization." Reprinted from *Public Administration Review* © 1972 by The American Society for Public Administration, 1225 Connecticut Avenue, N.W., Washington, D.C. All rights reserved.